TH. FILM
EXPERIENCE

THE FILM EXPERIENCE
AN INTRODUCTION

Timothy Corrigan

University of Pennsylvania

Patricia White

Swarthmore College

BEDFORD / ST. MARTIN'S   Boston   ◆   New York

For Bedford/St. Martin's

Developmental Editor: Mikola De Roo
Art Editor: Lisa Schlein
Senior Production Editor: Michael Weber
Senior Production Supervisor: Joe Ford
Marketing Manager: Richard Cadman
Art Director: Lucy Krikorian
Cover and Text Design: Wanda Kossak
Copyeditor: Wendy Polhemus-Annibell
Indexer: Maro Riofrancos
Photo Research: Alice Lundoff
Cover Photo: Photofest
Composition and Layout: DeNee Reiton Skipper
Printing and Binding: R. R. Donnelley & Sons Company

President: Joan E. Feinberg
Editorial Director: Denise B. Wydra
Publisher for History and Communication: Patricia Rossi
Director of Marketing: Karen Melton Soeltz
Director of Editing, Design, and Production: Marcia Cohen
Managing Editor: Erica T. Appel

Library of Congress Control Number: 2003107546

Manufactured in the United States of America.

9   8   7   6
f   e   d

For information, write: Bedford/St. Martin's, 75 Arlington Street, Boston, MA 02116   (617-399-4000)

ISBN-10: 0-312-25566-7
ISBN-13: 978-0-312-25566-4

Published and distributed outside North America by
PALGRAVE MACMILLAN
Houndmills, Basingstoke, Hampshire RG21 2XS and London
Companies and representatives throughout the world.
ISBN: 1-4039-3234-4
A catalog record for this book is available from the British Library.

Acknowledgments

Acknowledgments and copyrights appear at the back of the book on page 527, which constitutes an extension of the copyright page.

This book is dedicated to Kathleen and Lawrence Corrigan and Marian and Carr Ferguson, and to Max Schneider-White, who made his debut during its writing.

Preface

Experience is not what happens to you; it is what you do with what happens.

—Aldous Huxley

Watching movies is an experience that most of us have enjoyed for many years. We are all aware of the pleasures of the movies: of becoming captivated by the imaginary worlds brought to life on the screen, of observing our favorite stars, of delving into different film genres, and of watching certain moments and movements in film history. Yet these are usually scattered impressions that we rarely coordinate into a working knowledge of film and film form—a knowledge that would inevitably add to our enjoyment and understanding of the movies. Cultivating and encouraging that knowledge in a way that is accessible to beginning film students is the primary aim of this book. *The Film Experience: An Introduction* offers students a serious, comprehensive introduction to the art, industry, culture, and—above all—the experience of the movies, and it gives instructors enough scope and flexibility to use the book to complement a range of approaches to film and media studies.

The Film Experience maintains a unique double focus that distinguishes it from all other introductory film texts: it presents films both as works of art that employ formalist techniques and as richly layered cultural practices. By emphasizing both the formal and cultural elements of film, *The Film Experience* ensures that introductory students get the most complete picture possible of both the medium and the discipline. The careful attention to formalist concepts gives students an understanding of the institutions and practices that make films possible. Our distinctive focus on the surrounding cultural and theoretical influences on film production means as well that students gain a greater understanding of films not only as individual works but also as part of a broader film culture. Based on our own first-hand experiences as teachers, we believe this holistic approach will enable students to view films from multiple angles with a more perceptive eye. (And although *The Film Experience* was specifically designed for introductory film courses, this multidimensional approach also makes it suitable for other film courses, including film history, film genre, and film theory and methods courses.)

Our overall objective is not to tell students *what* to think about film but rather to show them *how* to think about film, presenting them with multiple lenses through which they can analyze movies. Toward this end, *The Film Experience* offers numerous features designed to engage beginning students, while providing them with the practical information they need to view films critically and analytically, to develop ideas and interpretations of their own, and to write about those ideas thoughtfully.

A Broad Spectrum of Detailed Examples and Illustrations

The Film Experience provides students with a complete spectrum of detailed definitions, examples, and illustrations that carefully explain cinematic techniques, the commercial forces of the film industry, and the shifting cultural frameworks through which we understand films. Careful and lucid discussions of mise-en-scène, cinematography, editing, and film sound are supported by a plenitude of illustrations and examples.

- **Scope and flexibility through a balanced survey of films from around the world**   Examples are drawn from an extraordinarily varied and globally extensive group of films. Using classic and contemporary films from Hollywood (*Citizen Kane, The Searchers, Vertigo, Do the Right Thing*), experimental and challenging films outside the mainstream (*Meshes of the Afternoon, Sunless, Daughters of the Dust, Orlando*), and international films (*The Battleship Potemkin, Rashomon, Breathless,* and *The Apple*), *The Film Experience* engages students through the movies they know and, at the same time, points them toward movies they should know and those they may wish to know. Through the range of its examples, the book promotes the diverse practices, audiences, and history that define the film experience today. Because films are not always released in the same year in which production is completed, the correct release year for certain films is debatable. Throughout this text, we have used the most widely agreed upon release dates for students' historical reference.

- **The most extensive art program in any film introduction**   Talking about the cinema requires the best possible images for reference. Consequently, the discussions of film techniques and organizations in *The Film Experience* are supported by the most extensive art program in any introductory film text. With more than 700 images, *The Film Experience* visually reinforces all the major techniques and concepts and the range of film traditions discussed in the text. In Chapter 3, on cinematography, an insert with more than forty full-color images illustrates the use of color.

  The vast majority of this book's images are actual film frames from digital sources, not publicity or production stills. (The latter are photographs taken during filming with a still camera, usually one that is placed in a position different from that of the motion-picture camera.) We have also selected the best available editions, and the aspect ratios of the original films are preserved unless such sources were unavailable. Our aim in these choices was to reproduce images that accurately reflect the films from which they are taken, giving students precise visual reference points for discussion and analysis.

- **Extensive coverage of the different major organizational structures used to make films**   Additional chapters on narrative cinema, documentary and experimental films, and movie genres offer sophisticated and precise examinations of those larger organizations and experiences of the movies.

Pedagogically Friendly Features That Teach Students the Language of Film Study

Offering far more than the list of definitions often found in other texts, *The Film Experience* teaches students film terminology through incisive discussions of particular films.

- **Clear explanations and definitions of fundamental film terms**
  Throughout the book, key terms appear in boldface, and an extensive end-of-book glossary is an easily accessible source for the vocabulary of film studies. From beginning to end, *The Film Experience* introduces this terminology in a way that brings the concepts and language of film studies to life, so that students' analyses of films, both in class discussions and in their written work, become more perceptive and intelligent.
- **"In Focus" sections that show key film concepts at work**   Three "In Focus" sections per chapter demonstrate how the film technique or concept introduced in that chapter informs and enriches particular films. A detailed analysis of *The Grand Illusion,* for example, illustrates framing and camera movement; an examination of editing in Buster Keaton's *The General* offers sharp insights into that film, while demonstrating specific editing strategies.
- **Handy film terminology reference card**   To assist students further, this two-color, two-sided laminated card lists major film terms and concepts students most frequently refer to when critically viewing films or while writing papers. Students can easily carry this card into the theater or the classroom. (To order this card packaged with your students' copies of *The Film Experience,* use ISBN 0-312-41917-1.)

More Writing Help than Any Other Text

The Film Experience gives introductory students practical, step-by-step guidance for analyzing films critically and shaping their ideas as they think and write about film.

- **Three "Viewing Cues" boxes in every chapter encourage critical viewing habits**   Keyed to the specific topics discussed in each section, these boxes offer students cues for film analysis that can be applied to any film shown in class. These practical checklists suggest questions for students to ask themselves when analyzing a particular element or technique.
- **A full chapter of practical advice for researching and writing about film**   *The Film Experience* offers more detailed instruction and more student writing examples (including an annotated sample student essay) than any film text. Chapter 12, "Writing a Film Essay," is a step-by-step guide to writing papers about film, including taking and organizing notes, choosing a topic, developing a thesis and argument, doing research, distinguishing between reviews and critical essays, and completing a polished essay.
- **A Book Companion site at <bedfordstmartins.com/filmexperience>**
  A free resource for all users of *The Film Experience,* this site includes links to other film resources, downloadable versions of all the "Viewing Cues," the unabridged glossary, quizzes, and other support material.

Comprehensive Examination of the Cultural and Historical Energy of Film Studies

As perhaps its most distinctive and innovative feature, *The Film Experience* examines and explains the cultural and historical contexts that make the movies so meaningful and so varied for viewers. Throughout the book, students are prompted to explore spectatorship—the relationships between viewers, viewing situations, and films—as a way of understanding a range of possible meanings, responses, and interpretive strategies.

- **Coverage of the commercial practices of the film industry** The first chapter, on distribution, promotion, and exhibition, immediately introduces students to the important commercial and industrial dimensions of films and shows how these cultural forces play key roles in the film experience.
- **Two full chapters on film history** These chapters expose students to the diverse range of historical models and perspectives that influence how we watch and evaluate movies. Chapter 9 examines the traditional method of talking about the dominant Hollywood history of the movies from 1895 to today. Chapter 10 introduces alternative and more inclusive approaches to film history, including global cinema from the pre–World War II period to today, African American film history, American women film history, and gay and lesbian film history.
- **"Cultural Spotlight" sections frame film within its broader social context** "Cultural Spotlight" sections in every chapter introduce students to specific, intriguing aspects of the film experience—such as the impact of digital technology on the cinema, the Japanese narrative tradition of the *benshi*, the history of film archives, and local film genres that emerge in different countries.

A Comprehensive, Accessible Introduction to Film Theory

Students are quick to recognize the complexities of film studies. Accordingly, *The Film Experience* also introduces readers to the widest variety of theoretical models, giving them a complete picture of both the medium and the discipline.

- **A full chapter on film theory** Chapter 11 presents students with the core schools and debates, including realism and formalism, Marxism, semiotics and structuralism, poststructuralism and feminism, cultural studies, film philosophy, and postmodernism and new media.
- **"Critical Voices" that showcase the work of notable film scholars** Balancing both contemporary and classical critical perspectives on film, these sections appear at the end of every chapter. They contain primary source excerpts that introduce students to the insights, methods, and styles of some of the field's most important scholars and writers, from classical film theorist Béla Balász to contemporary writer Carol Clover. Each excerpt is keyed to the subject of the chapter and allows students to experience some of the scholarly variety and energy that

have always played a large part in film culture. At the conclusion of each chapter, short bibliographies direct students to other writings and research.

Acknowledgments

A book of this scope has benefited from the help of many people. A host of reviewers, readers, and friends have contributed to this book: Patrice Petro, Lucy Fischer, Ivone Margulies, Jonathan Kahana, Amelie Hastie, David Cook, Vivian Sobchack, Michael Chaiken, William Van Wert, Meta Mazaj, Rob Gage, Hildy Tow, Carr and Marian Ferguson, Gustavus Stadler, Lisa Kennedy, Lisa Cohen, Anna McCarthy, and Mara Fortes.

Instructors throughout the country have reviewed the book and offered their advice, suggestions, and encouragement at various stages of the project's development: Nora M. Alter, University of Florida; Constantin Behler, University of Washington, Bothell; J. Dennis Bounds, Regent University (Virginia); Richard Breyer, Syracuse University; Lucy Fischer, University of Pittsburgh; Jeremy Butler, University of Alabama; Jill Craven, Millersville University; Robert Dassanowsky, University of Colorado, Colorado Springs; Eric Faden, Bucknell University; Stefan Fleischer; State University of New York, Buffalo; Brian M. Goss, University of Illinois at Urbana–Champaign; Mark Hall, California State University–Chico; Tom Isbell,University of Minnesota–Duluth; Christopher Jacobs, University of North Dakota; Jonathan Kahana, Bryn Mawr College; Joe Kickasola, Baylor University; Arthur Knight, College of William and Mary; Gina Marchetti, Ithaca College; Ivone Margulies, Hunter College, City University of New York; Joan McGettigan, Texas Christian University; Mark Meysenburg, Doane College (Nebraska); Charles Musser, Yale University; Mark Nornes, University of Michigan; Patrice Petro, University of Wisconsin-Milwaukee; Kimberly Radek, Illinois Valley Community College; Frank Scheide, University of Arkansas; Jeff Smith, Washington University (St. Louis); Vivian Sobchack, University of California, Los Angeles; Maureen Turim, University of Florida; Leslie Werden, University of North Dakota; Jennifer Wild, The University of Iowa; Sharon Willis, University of Rochester; and Sarah Witte, Eastern Oregon University.

Special thanks go to the following individuals and organizations for their assistance and expertise in acquiring photo stills: Anthology Film Archives; Robert Haller; Jessica Rosner at Kino International; Beth and Margaret at Narberth Video & Entertainment; the McCabe Library acquisitions and circulation staff and the Instructional Technology and Media Services staff at Swarthmore College; Rob Epstein and James Chan at Telling Pictures; TLA Video (especially Jon Krumbiegel and Gary Berenbroick); and Joseph Yransky. James Fiumara provided assistance in many ways, most notably in assembling the material for the glossary.

At Bedford/St. Martin's, we thank Tisha Rossi, sponsoring editor, for her belief in and support of this project from the outset. We are grateful to editor Michael Bagnulo for his guidance during the project's earlier stages and to editor Mika De Roo for her editorial acumen and commitment to moving the project from the manuscript stage to a final book. We are indebted to art editor Lisa Schlein and photo researcher Alice Lundoff for their extraordinary work acquiring every piece of art in this book; the art program was a tremendous undertaking, and the results are beautiful. The handsome page layouts were created by DeNee Reiton Skipper. We thank Carina Schoenberger, editorial assistant, for helping coordinate the numerous reviews and focus groups as well as other tasks, big and small; Erica Appel, managing editor, Michael Weber, senior project editor, and Joe Ford, senior production supervisor, for their diligent work on the book's production; and Lucy Krikorian, art director, for overseeing a beautiful design and cover. We also express thanks to new media editors Coleen O'Hanley and David Mogolov for their work on the companion Web site for *The Film Experience*.

We are especially thankful to our families, Marcia Ferguson and Cecilia, Graham, and Anna Corrigan, and Cynthia Schneider and Max Schneider-White. Finally, we are grateful for the emergence and growth of our writing partnership and for the rich experiences this collaborative effort has brought us. We hope this joint project will be the first of many together.

Timothy Corrigan
Patricia White

Brief Contents

Contents

4. Relating Images: Editing   110

5. Listening to the Cinema: Film Sound   166

PART II
ORGANIZATIONS: FROM STORIES TO GENRES   213

PART III
HISTORIES: HOLLYWOOD AND BEYOND 325

PART IV
REACTIONS: READING AND WRITING ABOUT FILM 417

THE FILM
EXPERIENCE

Introduction

Imagine two friends watching two movies together over the weekend. On a Friday evening in 1997, they go to a large-screen theater in town to see the re-release of George Lucas's intergalactic blockbuster *Star Wars* (1977). The following Sunday they rent a movie from their local video store, Mike Leigh's *Secrets and Lies* (1996), a modestly budgeted British film about an interracial family in London.

Star Wars features Hollywood stars and presents a wide array of heroes, villains, action, and special effects. Before seeing it, the couple had read about its re-release in widely circulated advertisements and reviews in newspapers, had seen the original version and the rest of the *Star Wars* trilogy on videotape several years earlier, and had no trouble finding this ballyhooed re-release at a theater in town since it was distributed to practically all corners of the world. For the first time, however, they see *Star Wars* on a large screen in a public theater, along with a large audience, many of whom are seeing the film for the second or third time. They watch in silence and only after they leave do they talk over favorite moments with friends who have also seen it. Although they agree that the special effects—after two decades of sophisticated advancements in computer technologies—seem pretty rudimentary, they enjoy the added computer-generated effects and find the climactic battle with the Death Star **[Figure 1]** more exciting than ever when seen on a big screen.

Secrets and Lies, on the other hand, is a very different kind of movie. It uses understated British actors and moves through complex social and psychological issues involving a white working-class mother, Cynthia, and her newly discovered black upper-middle-class daughter, Hortense. The two friends seek out *Secrets and Lies* because they had seen and liked Mike Leigh's earlier film, *Life Is Sweet* (1991), had read that *Secrets and Lies* had been nominated for an Oscar for best director, and consequently noticed it prominently displayed in the art film section of a local video store. They see *Secrets and Lies* on a television in one of their homes, often commenting on the action as they watch. Later, in order to answer some

Figure 1 *Star Wars* (1977). Watching a blockbuster—again.

Figure 2 *Secrets and Lies* (1996). Seeking out the unusual.

questions about the film, they look online for information about contemporary British cinema, its historical emphasis on social realism, and Leigh's unique way of directing actors. They are not quite sure why the movie ends the way it does—with the half-sisters talking about their newly discovered relationship and, after the revelation of so many secrets and lies, Cynthia contentedly remarking, "This is the life" **[Figure 2]**. Nonetheless, both viewers find the ending strangely moving. Indeed, their appreciation of that final scene grows when they learn that Leigh had allowed his actors to improvise lines and actions in this and other scenes.

Viewing and enjoying movies as diverse as these two films and watching them in such different ways is commonplace today. More kinds of movies are available to us in more types of venues than ever before, and different film cultures in the United States and around the world offer an expanding variety of ways of seeing, understanding, and enjoying movies. We can watch the short silent films of Charlie Chaplin on the DVD player of our laptop, see a televised release of *Lawrence of Arabia* (1962) on consecutive Sunday and Monday nights, and join lines of viewers to see a premiere of *The Lord of the Rings: The Two Towers* (2002) on a large screen in an old movie palace. Our responses to these films—how and why we like or dislike, understand or do not understand, these movies—are more than ever a product of the many diverse attitudes, backgrounds, and interests we, the viewers, bring to the movies.

The following chapters aim to introduce the movies by following these multifaceted personal and social experiences. From the very beginning we insist that viewers and viewing situations represent a dynamic plentitude of perspectives that need to be considered seriously and rigorously if those experiences are to be fully understood and appreciated. Chapter 1 is indicative of our overall approach; there, we examine how formal materials and our initial responses to them are prepared by the larger cultural and historical frameworks of promotion, distribution, and exhibition. In Part I, the first section of the book, we present fundamental materials about technical and aesthetic compositions and organizations of movies: about mise-en-scène, cinematography, editing, and sound. Later chapters introduce other specific dimensions of the film experience within the broader cultural dynamics of how we produce meanings and assign values to these films:

- how narrative movies, as well as documentary and experimental films, organize time and space or communicate ideas and emotional experiences
- how the patterns and structures of film genres allow us to engage specific historical and social rituals, while guiding our understanding of individual movies
- how different conceptions of film history can direct and shape our responses to a particular movie, depending on the kind of history we associate with it
- how reading film criticism and theory and writing film essays and papers are pragmatic extensions and intensifications of our normal interactions with the cinema

Throughout the book, we work to place in the foreground what distinguishes our approach: that formal, technical, and empirical matter—the core material of film practice—must be understood in the context of how we actively engage films; and, more specifically, how we make personal, cultural, and historical meanings through the dynamics of those engagements. Chapters 2 through 5 on film form, for example, bracket the presentation of various formal strategies about shot composition or narrative structure with key frameworks for how we encounter those forms: a discussion of the larger cultural history that always provides a background for our movie experiences and a discussion of how we inevitably make meanings and evaluations by recognizing certain values and traditions informing those forms, techniques, and structures.

In each chapter, we punctuate the discussion with a number of short pedagogical features meant to direct readers to the abundance of practices, ideas, and positions within the history of movie culture:

- The **Cultural Spotlight** sections briefly identify historical and cultural variations on the major issues discussed in the chapter, variations that have shaped and influenced how viewers watch movies today.
- The **In Focus** sections examine a particular film in detail, according to the terms and tools of the chapter.
- The **Critical Voices** features present a scholar's or professional's influential, and sometimes controversial, critical perspective on the chapter topic.
- The **Viewing Cues** checklists help readers engage with and take notes on any film (such as the one that students are watching that week in class), according to the critical perspectives and terms introduced in the chapter.
- *The Next Level: Additional Sources,* an annotated bibliography, directs readers to further readings on the chapter topics.

While recognizing the impossibility of reflecting fully the range of examples in our global film cultures, our selection of films attempts to move in two directions: to acknowledge how Hollywood films represent most people's experience of the movies and to indicate the many other kinds of movies, from other cultural perspectives, that are more and more enriching our film experiences today.

The goals of this book are threefold: to activate viewers by promoting imaginative explorations of the movies from many angles, to insist that these explorations must be intellectually focused and exact, and to urge and celebrate the diverse activity of producing meanings and ideas about films. As film experiences increasingly become the center of so many contemporary cultures, this book aims to acknowledge and promote the rich and multifaceted nature of film experiences today and, at the same time, to introduce viewers to the pleasures of thinking hard about how and where movies make such a difference in their lives.

Preparing Viewers and Views: Distribution, Promotion, and Exhibition

It's not an accident that all the movies of the summer are rides. *Adrenaline! Our rhythms are radically different. We're constantly accelerating the visual to keep the viewer in his seat.*

—Barry Levinson, director of *Diner* (1982) and *Liberty Heights* (1999)

KEY OBJECTIVES

What draws us to a film and accounts for our enjoyment or lack of enjoyment of it? This chapter examines how movies attract us both emotionally and intellectually and how film culture prepares viewers for different ways of seeing a film, even before we actually see it. The chapter also argues that where and when we see a movie can alter our experience of it, and, in turn, our enjoyment and understanding of the movie. We will look carefully at

■ how our experience of movies and our taste for certain films have both personal and public dimensions

■ how the mechanisms of film distribution determine what we see

■ how film promotion attempts to predispose us to see films in certain ways

■ how film exhibition, whether in cineplexes or on television, can structure our response to films in particular ways

From virtually all places and all times in cinema history, films have focused on moviegoers, their passions, and their often unpredictable activities. In Buster Keaton's *Sherlock Jr.* (1924), a bumbling projectionist walks into the movie he is watching, transformed into a Sherlock Holmes–like detective investigating the world of the film. In Chantal Akerman's *Meetings with Anna* (1978), a young woman filmmaker's search for an audience for her recent film becomes a complex and tangled voyage into herself and her society. Most recently, in Spike Lee's bitter comedy *Bamboozled* (2000), racist stereotypes of the past return to make audiences, bizarrely and disturbingly, still laugh today. In each of these instances and in so many others, viewers and their views become the heart of the drama that is the film experience.

Preceding this drama is, of course, film production, a large and complex process in which industry and art, technology and imagination, entwine. **Film production** describes those industrial stages—from the financing and scripting of a film to its final edit—that contribute to the construction of a finished movie, a process overseen by a **producer** who usually steers and monitors each step of the process. Film production and producers are not, however, usually part of most of our experiences of the movies, except as their accomplishments appear in the completed film before us. After the bankers, writers, technicians, stars, and directors have all finished the work to produce a film, in short, the producer invariably must release and subject that film to the emotions, evaluations, and ideas of audiences who will like or dislike it, be mesmerized or bored by it, understand or misunderstand it. Indeed, in Robert Altman's dark parody of one Hollywood executive in *The Player* (1992), the art of contemporary film production degenerates entirely into the ruthless (and dangerous) business of trying to identify, capture, and manipulate sometimes resistant viewers.

In the drama of views and viewers, movies are always both a private and public affair. Since the beginning of film history, the power of movies has derived in part from our personal and sometimes idiosyncratic responses to a movie and in part from the social and cultural contexts that surround our experience of that film. One individual may react enthusiastically, on a personal level, to Ang Lee's *Crouching Tiger, Hidden Dragon* (2000), breathlessly absorbed in the balletic fights and intrigued by the feminist implications of the powerful female warriors in the film **[Figure 1.1]**. Another viewer might dislike the same film intensely because, unlike the first viewer, he has long been a fan of Hong Kong martial arts films and finds this a watered-down, Americanized version of those films. These individual reactions to films invariably have, in turn, public and social dimensions to them. When *Crouching Tiger, Hidden Dragon* first appeared, many viewers were quickly predisposed to appreciate it because of reviews and word-of-mouth praise that followed the film's appearances at the Cannes and New York film festivals and, later, its Academy Award nominations and wins for cinematography and score. Even the social context in which this film was first seen may have shaped and influenced how it was perceived. Watched on a large screen, where the spectacular visual effects were especially powerful and where a cheering audience added to the energy of the film, *Crouching Tiger* became, for some, a sporting event in which viewers fed off the enthusiasm of the entire audience and the larger social situation.

Figure 1.1 *Crouching Tiger, Hidden Dragon* (2000). Feminist fighters or Americanized clichés?

At the intersection of these personal and public experiences, each of us has developed different **tastes**—cultural, emotional, intellectual, and social preferences or interests that create expectations and lead us to like or dislike particular movies or parts of movies. Some tastes vary little from person to person—most people preferring good individuals to bad ones and justice served to justice foiled. Yet many tastes are unique products of our individual experiences, determined by experiential circumstances or experiential histories. Our experiential circumstances are the material conditions that define our identity at a certain time and in a certain place, such as our age, our gender, our race, and the part of the country or world in which we live. Our experiential histories are the personal and social encounters through which we have developed our identities over time, such as our education, our relationships, our travels, and even the other films we have seen. A young

Figure 1.2 *Shrek* (1999). A film that appeals to the young, the hip, and the ironic.

Figure 1.3 *Saving Private Ryan* (1998). A taste for war films.

American woman might naturally be drawn to Hollywood films and, because of her age, especially those that feature ironic humor and hip soundtracks, such as *Repo Man* (1984) and *Shrek* (1999) **[Figure 1.2]**. In contrast, because of his experiential history, a World War II veteran might have a particular interest in and taste for films about that war, such as *Mrs. Miniver* (1942), *The Longest Day* (1962), and *Saving Private Ryan* (1998) **[Figure 1.3]**.

At the movies, our tastes and responses relate indirectly to two complementary viewing activities that continually interact when we watch a film: identification and cognition. Clearly, the movies we like are not only the ones we can identify with personally or fully understand, but the simultaneous activities of identification and cognition do provide a framework that often shapes our tastes. Commonly associated with our emotional responses, **identification** at the movies suggests a complex process by which we empathize with, project onto, or participate in a place, an action, or a character—either separately or as these elements interact. Viewers who have lived through adolescence will respond empathetically to the portrayal of the social electricity and physical awkwardness of teenage sexuality in *American Graffiti* (1973) **[Figure 1.4]** or *The Breakfast Club* (1985). Each of us may identify with different characters or with parts of various characters (such as the nerd Brian and the prom queen Claire in *The Breakfast Club*), but the success of a film often depends on eliciting specific identification with one or two of the main characters (such as Curt and Steve, the two boys about to leave for college in *American Graffiti*). Similarly, while watching *An American in Paris* (1951), one viewer may instantly participate in the carefree excitement of the opening scenes by identifying with the artistic Montmartre neighborhood and street life, where she had experienced so

Figure 1.4 *American Graffiti* (1973). Empathizing with adolescence.

Figure 1.5 *An American in Paris* (1951). At home in foreign neighborhoods.

many memorable days as a college student in Paris [Figure 1.5]; another viewer, who has never been to Paris, participates vicariously in that romantic setting because the film so effectively re-creates an atmosphere with which he can identify.

Notions of identification at the movies often describe an emotional dimension to our experience, suggesting how the fun of film, like dreams, relates to our basic urges, desires, and memories. The pleasures of the movies, though, are also part of more rational reactions learned through our experiences in life and at the movies. These learned responses can be described as forms of comprehension or **cognition,** the intellectual and social processes by which we develop the ability to understand, interpret, and reflect on different dimensions of the movies. Watching a movie, in short, is not only an emotional experience that involves the identifying processes of participation and empathy, but also a cognitive process that involves the intellectual activities of comparison and comprehension. We bring assumptions about a location or setting to most films, we expect events to change or progress in a certain way, and we measure characters against similar characters encountered elsewhere. Along with our emotional identification with the terrors or triumphs of certain characters, therefore, *Gladiator* (2000) also engages us through numerous cognitive responses. We recognize and distinguish this Rome through particular visual cues—the Coliseum and other Roman monuments—known perhaps from pictures and other movies. During battles and fights, we put into play certain learned expectations about how those fights will proceed and who will likely win, although these actions in *Gladiator* may surprise us with the extremity of their graphic violence. [Figure 1.6]. Because of other experiences, we arrive at the film with specific assumptions about Roman tyrants and heroes, and we appreciate and understand characters like the emperor Commodus or the gladiator Maximus, more or less, as they successfully balance our expectations with innovations.

What we like or dislike at the movies can, in this way, often be connected to what we understand as part of the evolving processes of identification and cognition. Even as we are drawn to and bond with places, actions, and characters in films, we must sometimes reconsider how those

Figure 1.6 *Gladiator* (2000). Expectations and surprises about gladiators.

ways of identifying have (or could be) developed and changed by our intellectual development. Indeed, this process of cognitive realignment and reconsideration, which occurs with most films, determines to a large degree our reaction to a movie. In *The Bridges of Madison County* (1995), for example, Clint Eastwood, known for playing physically tough and intimidating characters, plays a reflective and sensitive lover, Robert Kincaid **[Figure 1.7]**. In this case, viewers familiar with Eastwood's other roles must rethink the expectations that had attracted them to that star and his usual character-roles (perhaps even identifying with them). Now those viewers must assess how those expectations have been complicated to challenge their understanding of *The Bridges of Madison County*. Does this shift suggest that the film is about a human depth discovered within older masculinity or about the maturing of that

Figure 1.7 *The Bridges of Madison County* (1995). Clint Eastwood, in a role with a different sort of masculinity.

masculinity through the encounter with an equally strong woman (Meryl Streep as Francesca Johnson)? Whether we are able to engage in that process or whether we find the realignment convincing will frequently lay the foundation for our response to the movie.

 VIEWING CUES: Your Knowledge of Film

■ Before you watch the next film in your class, examine your tastes in movies by jotting down information about them (perhaps as a long journal entry). What kind of films do you enjoy? Why? What specifically about this film initially attracts you to it or discourages you from seeing it?

■ Try to account for your tastes in movies. How do your personal circumstances in life (such as your age or your gender) shape your tastes in movies? Describe how your tastes have changed over the years and what you believe accounts for those changes.

■ Most moviegoers today have more expertise and knowledge about films than they usually recognize. In a few paragraphs, describe yours. What are the strengths of your understanding of films? Certain genres? Visual techniques? Music? Characters?

■ Before you see your next film, write down your expectations of it. What are you anticipating? After you see the movie, consider how your expectations were met or changed through the experience of the film.

■ After seeing that movie, describe how you identified with certain places, actions, or characters.

■ Consider how your understanding of places, actions, and characters come into play in this film. Does the movie rely on easily understood actions and characters, and if so, what makes them so easily comprehensible? Or does the film make those features sometimes difficult to understand? How so? And how do you then make sense of them?

Distribution: What We Can See

If the film experience usually becomes both an act of identification and an act of cognition, central to those experiences is how movie culture prepares us for those activities even before we sit down in front of a theater screen or video monitor. Whether we recognize it or not, our tastes, avenues of identification, and cues for understanding a film frequently come in advance. Although our decisions about which films to see can seem and often are whimsical or casual, our choices and attitudes can also be influenced, directed, and (to some extent) controlled by central parts of movie culture and the movie industry. What we see, how we see it, and even what we are unable to see (since many films never find a distributor) are not innocent activities. Preparing movies is not just about selecting actors or finding locations before filming begins. It is also about preparing viewers for their experience of watching the films. With an emphasis on the U.S. distribution system, which often controls even foreign theaters, we will begin by detailing how we can be predisposed to identify and understand a film even before we see it: how viewers for and views of movies are prepared by the social and economic machinery that directs and shapes those personal views through distribution and, as we will see later, promotion and exhibition.

At the beginning of cinema history, from about 1895 to 1910, audiences flocked to machines like the Vitascope (bought and marketed by Thomas Edison) to see virtually any images move, whether the image depicted a couple kissing or a crowd walking across the Brooklyn Bridge. There they found and enjoyed a constant supply of short films, such as historical reenactments found in movies like the gruesome *Execution of Czolgosz* (1901) and the fantasies and fairy tales of films like *The "Teddy" Bears* (1907). Today, we flock to movies made available through different paths of distribution, such as theaters, video stores, and television listings. For most of us, our tastes for and knowledge of films begin with and rely first on these avenues of distribution.

Distributing Different Views

Distribution is the practice and means through which certain movies are sent to and placed in theaters and in video stores or on television and cable networks. A **distributor** is a company that acquires the rights to a movie from the filmmakers or producers (sometimes by contributing to the costs of producing that film) and that then makes that movie available to audiences by renting or selling it to theaters or other exhibition outlets. The availability of a film is, in part, the result of which films are produced by movie makers, but the inversion of that logic is central to the economics of mainstream movie culture: Hollywood and many other film cultures produce movies that they assume can be successfully distributed. Film history has accordingly been marked with regular battles and compromises between filmmakers and distributors (either in the shape of studios or more modern institutions for distribution) about what audiences are willing to watch and which films can be successfully distributed. Indeed, a more negative situation is also true: viewers never see many good films that are produced but not distributed.

Consider the following examples of how the prospects for distributing and exhibiting a film can influence and often determine the content and form of a movie, including decisions about its length. From around 1911 to 1915, D. W. Griffith and other filmmakers struggled to convince movie studios to allow them to expand the length of a movie from roughly fifteen minutes to ninety minutes. Although longer films gradually began to appear, most producers felt that it would be impossible to distribute longer movies because they believed audiences would not sit still for more than twenty minutes. Griffith persisted and continued to stretch the length of his films, insisting that new distribution and exhibition patterns would create and attract new audiences—those willing to accept more complex stories and to pay more for them. The commercial and financial success of his *The Birth of a Nation* (1915) **[Figure 1.8]**, a three-hour epic distributed as a major cultural event comparable to a theatrical or operatic experience, thus became a landmark event and major force in overturning one distribution formula, which offered a program of numerous short films, and establishing a new one, which concentrated on a single **feature film,** a longer movie that is the primary attraction for audiences (see p. 24). After 1915, most films would be distributed with 90- to 120-minute running times, rather than in their previous 10- to 20-minute lengths.

Since 1915, this pattern for distribution has proved quite durable. In 1924, Erich von Stroheim handed his studio a nine-hour adaptation of Frank Norris's *McTeague*, retitled as *Greed*. Appalled by the length, studio executives re-cut the film to about two hours, emaciating the story but allowing them to distribute it for a profit. In 1980, United Artists decided to reduce the length of Michael Cimino's massive epic *Heaven's Gate* (1980) **[Figure 1.9]** from over four hours to 149 minutes in order to come closer to the standard film length. After the catastrophic failure of its first release to movie theaters, much of the original version was eventually restored, because it could now be distributed through the more flexible viewing conditions of home video.

Our experience of what a movie looks like—its length, its choice of stars, its subject matter, and even its title—is partly determined by decisions made about distribution even before the film is made available to us. Because most movies are produced to be distributed in certain ways and to certain kinds of audiences, distribution patterns can, in an important sense, make or shape a movie and our expectations about it. Whether a movie is available everywhere for everyone at the same time, released during the Christmas holidays, or available only in specialty video stores, each brings expectations attached to these distribution patterns that a particular film fulfills or frustrates.

Figure 1.8 *The Birth of a Nation* (1915). An epic change in film distribution.

Figure 1.9 *Heaven's Gate* (1980). Re-cut, re-released, and eventually restored for successful distribution.

As one of its primary functions, distribution determines how many copies of a film are available and the number of locations at which the movie can be seen. A movie can thus be distributed for special **exclusive release,** premiering in only one or two locations initially. A particularly dramatic example of this strategy is the restored version of Abel Gance's classic *Napoléon* (1927), an epic tale of the life of the French emperor that periodically presents the action simultaneously on three screens. The original film premiered in April 1927 (although the film was not shown in its entirety until a month later to a private audience and was subsequently distributed in the United States as a single-screen presentation). In 1981, the exclusive release of the restored film was accompanied by an orchestra and it appeared in only one theater at a time. In this most recent incarnation, *Napoléon* toured the country showing in only a very selective group of cities and theaters so that seeing it became a privileged event. Although each film will use an exclusive release in its own way, we generally approach these films expecting an unusual or singular experience created by a daring subject matter (such as the history of a nation) or a remarkable technological or formal achievement (such as a three- or four-hour running time).

A film with a mass circulation of premieres, sometimes referred to as **saturation booking** or a **saturated release,** is screened in as many locations in the United States—and sometimes abroad—as possible. For a potential blockbuster such as Steven Spielberg's *Jurassic Park* (1993) **[Figure 1.10]**, the distributors immediately release the movie in a maximum number of locations and theaters to attract the largest possible audience before its novelty wears off. In these cases, distribution usually promises audiences a film that appeals to most tastes (offering perhaps breathtaking special effects rather than controversial topics) and is easy to understand (featuring uncomplicated plots and characters). A **wide release** may premiere at as many as two thousand screens, whereas a **limited release** may initially be distributed only to major cities—such as Quentin Tarantino's *Reservoir Dogs* (1992), which first appeared in only seventy-five theaters—and then expand its distribution, depending on the film's success. The expectations for films

Figure 1.10 *Jurassic Park* (1993). Saturation booking and breathtaking effects.

following a limited release pattern are generally less fixed: they will usually be recognized in terms of the previous work of the director or an actor but will offer a certain novelty or experimentation (such as a controversial subject or a strange plot twist) that will presumably be better appreciated the more the film is publicly debated and understood through the reviews and discussions that follow its initial release.

As part of these more general practices, the history of distribution has developed other strategies that can shape or respond to the interests and tastes of intended audiences. **Platforming** releases a film in gradually widening markets and theaters so that it slowly builds its reputation and momentum through reviews and word of mouth. With **block booking,** a common practice until 1948 and still practiced in some ways today, a studio/distributor pressures a movie theater to accept and show smaller, less expensive films in order to gain the opportunity to show more popular movies as well. For instance, a cineplex might need to book a film like *True Romance* (1993) for a number of weeks in order to show *Jurassic Park* during the same time period. Although block booking allows us to see films other than blockbusters, it also establishes a hierarchy of quality by which distributors identify for us—whether we are aware of it or not—which movies are considered the most important films to see.

Since the latter part of the twentieth century, movies have also been distributed with an eye toward reaching specific **target audiences,** viewers who producers feel are most likely to want to see a particular film. Producers and distributors aimed *Shaft* (1971), an action film with a black hero, at the African American audience by distributing it primarily in large urban areas. With *Trainspotting* (1995), a hip tale of young heroin users in Edinburgh, distributors positioned the film to draw the art-film and younger audiences in cities, some suburbs, and college and university towns. The *Nightmare on Elm Street* movies (1984–1989), a violent slasher series about the horrific Freddy Krueger, were aimed primarily at the male teenage audience found in the cineplexes and, later, through video stores.

The various distribution strategies all imply important issues about how movies should be viewed and understood. First, by controlling the scope of distribution, these strategies determine the quality and importance of an audience's interactions with a film. As a saturated release, *Godzilla* (1998) aimed for the swift gratification of an exciting one-time event with a focus on special effects and shocks. Platformed gradually through expanding audiences, *Driving Miss Daisy* (1989) benefited from growing conversations and more careful reflections on the relationship between an older white woman and her black chauffeur **[Figure 1.11]**. No distribution pattern produces a single set of expectations, nor does the distribution method determine the meaning of a film. Yet distribution methods can lead viewers, overtly or subtly, to look at a film in certain ways. We come to a saturated release perhaps prepared to focus on the performance of a star, on the relationship to a best-selling novel, or on the new use of computer technology. With a platformed release, ideas and opinions about the film are already in the air and any controversy or innovation associated with it is often part of our initial viewing.

Figure 1.11 *Driving Miss Daisy* (1989). Platforming a film through more careful responses.

Second, in targeting audiences, distribution can identify primary, intended responses to the film as well as secondary, deviant (or unexpected) responses to it. *Scream* (1996) **[Figure 1.12]** and *Scream 2* (1997) would probably offend or confuse most elderly audiences unfamiliar with teenage horror films, but the targeted teenage audiences come prepared knowing the formulas and clichés associated with this kind of movie and are likely to see these films as spoofs and parodies of contemporary slashers. One set of responses is not necessarily better or more correct than another, but recognizing the part played by distribution targeting does allow a viewer to think

Figure 1.12 *Scream* (1996). Targeting the audience for slasher films.

more precisely and productively about the many social and cultural dynamics of responding to a movie. At the very least, this awareness indicates how our identification with and comprehension of films are as much a product of our social and cultural place as they are a product of the film's matter and form.

Video and Television Distribution

In recent years, movie distribution has increasingly taken advantage of television and video as avenues for distribution. From cable channels to VCRs (and eventually to direct computer access), more and more movies are presented through **television distribution**—the selection and programming, at carefully determined times, of movies made both for theaters and exclusively for television. Normally, there is a lag time between a theatrical release in a cinema and a video or cable release, but some movies are distributed directly to video or cable, such as the two sequels to the film *From Dusk till Dawn* (1996). Whether a movie is released later for television or is made expressly for video and television, this type of distribution aims to reach the largest possible audience and to raise revenues. Part of the motive in these cases may also be to add to the profits of a former hit or to reach more people with its message, such as when *Schindler's List* (1993) was featured as a prime-time television movie years after its original theater release. The promise of television revenues can reduce the financial risk for producers and filmmakers and thus, in some situations, allow more experimentation. This was certainly the case with the BBC's daring production of Dennis Potter and Jon Amiel's eight-hour *The Singing Detective* (1986), an extraordinary cinematic/televisual combination of musical and mystery genres that twists tales of World War II, childhood trauma, and the skin disease of a detective writer **[Figure 1.13]**.

Television distribution has both positive and negative implications. In some cases, films on television must adjust their style and content to suit the formats of time and space: scenes might be cut to fit a time slot or, as with *Schindler's List*, the film may be shown on two different nights, thus potentially breaking the flow and temporal impact of a movie. The size of the image might also be changed so that a widescreen film image will fit the shape of the television monitor. In other cases, television and video distribution may expand the ways a movie can communicate with its audience and experiment with different visual forms. *The Singing Detective* uses the long length of a television series watched within the home as the appropriate format to explore and think about the passage of time, the difficulty of memory, and the many levels of reality and consciousness that get woven into our daily lives. Indeed, this question can be asked of virtually any film: What about it seems best suited for distribution in movie theaters or distribution on television? What about it seems least suited?

As with cinema and television distribution, **video distribution** and **DVD distribution** determine the availability of films on videotape or digital video discs (DVDs) for rental or purchase in stores. Since the selection in video rental stores is based on a market perspective on local audiences as well as the tastes of the individual proprietors, movies on video and DVD wind up being distributed to certain cities or neighborhoods and excluded from other locations. Asian American neighborhoods are likely to have more Asian films in their local video store than are other

Figure 1.13 *The Singing Detective* (1986). A movie made for television.

neighborhoods. Chain stores such as Blockbuster Video are likely to concentrate on suburban neighborhoods and offer numerous copies of popular mainstream movies and to exclude some with daring subject matter. Some independent video stores specialize in art films or old movie classics.

For viewers, there are two clear consequences to these patterns of video distribution. First, video distribution can control—perhaps more so than theatrical distribution—local responses, tastes, and expectations: as part of a community anchored by that video store, we see and learn to expect only certain kinds of movies when the store makes five or six copies of one blockbuster film available but only one

Figure 1.14 Local video store. Catering to a community of film viewers.

or none of a less popular film. In fact, the control of video outlets extends even to altering or censoring a film when, as is done at the Blockbuster outlets, they edit out scenes or lines of a movie they consider offensive to the local community. The second consequence highlights the sociological and cultural formations of film distribution. As a community outlet, distribution through video stores becomes part of the social fabric of a neighborhood: the movies made available in rental stores tend to reflect the community, and the community tends to see itself in the kinds of movies it regularly watches. Viewers are consumers, and video stores can become forums in which the interests of a community of viewers—in children's film, Latino cinema, or less violent movies, for instance—can determine which films are distributed [Figure 1.14].

Distribution Timing

Distribution timing—when a movie is released for public viewing in certain locations—is another prominent feature of distribution (and, as we will see later in the chapter, of exhibition). Adding significantly to our experience of movies, timing can take advantage of the social atmosphere, cultural connotations, or critical scrutiny associated with particular seasons and calendar periods. The summer season and the December holidays are the most important in the United States because audiences usually have more free time. Offering a temporary escape from hot weather, a summer release like *Speed* (1994) also matches the thrills of the film with rides at an amusement park [Figure 1.15]. Christmas movies like *Miracle on 34th Street* (1947) promise a

Figure 1.15 *Speed* (1994). Movies as summer amusements.

Figure 1.16 *Miracle on 34th Street* (1947). Seasonal goodwill.

celebration of goodwill and community **[Figure 1.16]**. The Memorial Day release of *Pearl Harbor* (2001) immediately attracts the sentiments and memories of Americans remembering World War II and other global conflicts.

Mistiming a film's release can prove to be a major problem, as was the case with *A Little Princess* (1995), whose release unfortunately coincided with the more aggressively distributed *Pocahontas* (1995). Both films aimed for the same target audience of families with children, but *Pocahontas* was able to take advantage of Disney's large distribution system and was put in so many theaters that *A Little Princess* was virtually lost to audiences. As one would expect, avoiding unwanted competition with a film can be a key part of a distributor's timing: distributors accelerated the timing of the opening of *The Matrix* (1999) **[Figure 1.17]** precisely to avoid competition with *Star Wars Episode I: The Phantom Menace* (1999).

Of the several other variations on the tactics of timing, movies sometimes follow a **first release** or first "run" with a **second release** or second "run"; the first describes a movie's original premiere, while the second refers to the redistribution of that film months or years later. After its first release in 1982, for example, *Blade Runner* made a notable reappearance in 1992 as a longer "director's cut." While the first release had only modest success, the second (supported by a surprisingly large audience discovered in the video rental market) appealed to an audience newly attuned to the visual and narrative complexity of the movie. Audiences wanted to see, think about, and see again oblique and obscure details in order to decide, for instance, whether Deckard was a replicant or a human **[Figure 1.18]**. With second releases, financial reward is no doubt a primary goal, and the trend to "reissue" films like *Return of the Jedi* in 1997 testifies to the success of this formula: reappearing in 2,111 theaters, *Return of the Jedi*'s reissue earned another $46 million. Re-releases of either classic or popular films can also create new points of view, predisposing viewers to certain kinds of responses. They can initiate an emotional nostalgia for past experiences associated with an old film or, in some instances, provoke a specific curiosity about fresh material added to the re-release or about new information a viewer has acquired about a feature of the film.

With a film that may have been unavailable to viewers during its first release or that simply may not have been popular, a re-release can lend it

Figure 1.17 *The Matrix* (1999). Timing a release to avoid competition.

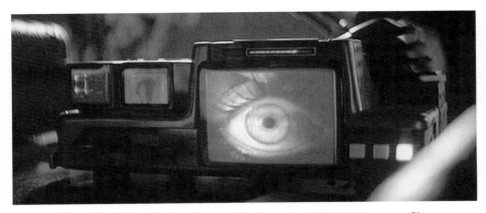

Figure 1.18 *Blade Runner* (1982, 1994). A second release as an invitation to re-see a film.

new life and reclaim viewers with new perspectives who approach the film through a process of rediscovery. When a small movie achieves unexpected popular or critical success, for example, it can then be redistributed with a much wider distribution circuit and to a more eager, sympathetic audience that is already prepared to like the movie. The initial distribution of Werner Herzog's *The Mystery of Kaspar Hauser* (1975) in Germany proved unsuccessful; after it garnered film festival prizes and was acclaimed overseas, the film was successfully redistributed in Germany. Similarly, television distribution can re-time the release of a movie to promote certain attitudes toward it. *It's a Wonderful Life* did not generate much of an audience when it was first released in 1946. Gradually (and especially after its copyright expired in 1975), network and cable television began to run the film regularly, and the film became a Christmas classic shown often and everywhere during that season **[Figure 1.19]**. In 1997, however, the television network NBC reclaimed the exclusive rights to the film in order to limit its television distribution to one showing each year and to try to make audiences see the movie as a special event.

Figure 1.19 *It's a Wonderful Life* (1946). Rediscovered through re-release.

The Repeat Viewer

As viewers, we are inevitably part of the distribution path of a film in ways that position us before that movie in different ways. Distributing a movie through one or more releases thus anticipates and capitalizes on an increasingly common variation in contemporary movie culture: the **repeat viewer** who returns during a first release to see the same movie more than one time. *Love Story* (1970), a tale of tragically doomed young love, was among the first modern movies to draw viewers back to the theater for multiple viewings, but films from Rudolph Valentino's *The Sheik* (1921) and *Gone with the Wind* (1939) to *Toy Story* (1995) and *The Sixth Sense* (1999) have each exploited this viewing pattern somewhat differently. Women return with women friends to share their adoration of Valentino; adults return with children to *Toy Story*, more interested in the inside jokes than the story; and fans of *The Sixth Sense* return to spot early clues that anticipate the surprise

Figure 1.20 *The Sixth Sense* (1999). Repeat viewing and new clues.

Figure 1.21 *The Sixth Sense* (1999). Seen again, the scene is not the same.

ending **[Figures 1.20 and 1.21]**. With repeat viewers like these, timing becomes more a function of the viewers' choices, not the distributor's. However, it also demonstrates the changing variety of experiences at the movies for the same individual: how a different time and place, different companions, and more knowledge about a movie can alter or enrich how a viewer comes prepared to see a film with different expectations and assumptions.

Whether as viewers of an exclusive Christmas release or as repeat viewers of an experimental film classic, the distribution path implicitly identifies us as a certain kind of audience (in terms of our age, gender, and other characteristics), as a viewer watching the movie in a certain place (in a theater or at home on a television), and as a moviegoer with certain habits (a midnight movie fan who regularly looks for the unusual film or the family that goes out during the holidays for inoffensive Hollywood fare). Thinking about a movie means considering carefully how it attempts to position us in a particular place and time because these positions can significantly influence much of how we understand movies.

 VIEWING CUES: Distribution

- Speculate—or do some research—on how the film you will watch next in class was originally distributed. What would this distribution strategy say about the kinds of responses the film was intended to elicit? Does knowing this strategy help you understand the film's aims better?

- How might the distribution of this film have been timed to emphasize certain responses? Would it have had a seasonal release? Why or why not?

- Try to identify the target audience of this film. How does that knowledge highlight certain themes of the movie? Is your group part of the target audience? Does the group's membership (or lack of it) affect its response?

- How might this movie have been distributed for video rental? In what kind of neighborhoods or stores? Why?

- Consider if and when this movie would have been shown on television. Why? How might its distribution on television have significantly changed the look or feel of the film?

- Would this movie have attracted repeat viewers? What elements or dimensions of this film suggest that the filmmakers would or would not have expected repeat viewings?

IN FOCUS

Distributing *Four Weddings and a Funeral* (1994)

Critically acclaimed and financially successful, *Four Weddings and a Funeral* achieved popularity as much because of its precisely developed distribution strategy as because of its clever plot and witty characters. Starring Hugh Grant, the film tells a relatively simple and witty tale: while he watches friends marry and start new lives together, this handsome young man seems incapable of maintaining a romantic relationship with a woman [Figure 1.22]. Eventually, of course, he discovers the right woman at one of those weddings. With little intrigue or shock to attract viewers, a film like this needs to court audiences carefully, providing them with information about the story and characters and drawing them slowly to its charms. For *Four Weddings and a Funeral*, distribution strategies would pave the way to those larger, informed, and more varied audiences.

To distribute this small and low-key British film, the U.S. distributor, Gramercy, chose to platform it through expanding markets. The film first opened in Los Angeles and New York, where the distributors felt confident about finding a cosmopolitan audience for a film that had the look and feel of an art film. Building on the preliminary success in those markets, the film next opened in single theaters in Chicago, Philadelphia, San Francisco, and numerous other large U.S. cities. In the third phase of this platformed release, Gramercy expanded its market nationally, circulating twelve hundred prints of the movie around the country. With each new stage of distribution, reviews and advertisements created a chain reaction of interest: good news from New York piqued the curiosity of viewers in Atlanta; praise from Pittsburgh about the understated humor drew crowds in Austin to a film that offered a look at relationships built not on special effects but on thought and affection. By the time the film reached this final phase of distribution, its reputation as an unusual but accessible movie had already prepared potentially suspicious viewers to see and enjoy it.

Figure 1.22 *Four Weddings and a Funeral* (1994). Distributing romance.

Like most smaller, independent films, *Four Weddings and a Funeral* intentionally avoided distribution during the summer and holiday seasons, when it would have had to compete with the release of blockbusters. Instead, it followed a successful premiere at the Sundance Film Festival with a release to just five theaters in early March. Over the next six weeks, its timing followed its successful platform release pattern, gradually increasing its appearance to nine hundred screens. In this case, distribution timing was less about creating a seasonal event defined by a specific release date (say, a Valentine's Day premiere) than about sustaining interest over a long period of time. Like the protagonist's own search for romance, the film's distribution aimed to develop the quality of the relationship over time rather than create a spectacular one-night stand [Figure 1.23].

The characters and story alone suggest the general target audience for the film: eighteen- to forty-year-olds. In fact, the marketing team was even more specific in assuming the film would attract—at least at first—young single

Figure 1.23 *Four Weddings and a Funeral* (1994). Developing the quality of the relationship.

people and primarily women who would respond to the wry British humor and to a romantic comedy about single life. Slightly older or married individuals would later be drawn to the film as, in the words of the distributor, "a non-Shakespearean *Much Ado About Nothing*." Beyond the theaters, the distribution of the film found, predictably, outlets on television and in video stores. Titillating but inoffensive, the episodic structure of *Four Weddings and a Funeral*, as it follows the main character though the five events of the title, already anticipates the commercial breaks of the U.S. television format that would equally accommodate its frothy humor. Nominated for Academy Awards for best picture and best original screenplay, it was distributed to video chains and specialty stores where it easily bridged the categories of European independent film and mainstream comedy.

Many kinds of audiences have seen and enjoyed *Four Weddings and a Funeral*. Viewers who saw the movie's premiere at the Sundance Film Festival no doubt had a different take on it than an audience who watched it months later in Minneapolis. Repeat viewers, who returned to see favorite scenes,

Figure 1.24 *Four Weddings and a Funeral* (1994). Addressing different audiences.

would experience and respond to the film in ways unlike those who saw its premiere. Indeed, an awareness of these distribution contexts suggests a variety of critical points about the film and how those distribution strategies can identify and draw out different responses to the movie. Younger viewers in Los Angeles who attend its first release may see it as a tongue-in-cheek fantasy about young love and the triumph of romance [Figure 1.24]. Older audiences who follow the critical responses to its different platforms might be more attuned to its slightly dark and serious themes about isolation and loss or to its specifically British dimensions, such as the witty and sophisticated play of dialogue. While the particular film always remains the same, distribution clearly inflects and directs our expectations by identifying viewers according to certain tastes, interests, and knowledge, and so prepares that audience to approach the film in certain ways. As *Four Weddings and a Funeral* demonstrates, the distribution of any film chooses its audiences and, in making those choices, distribution aims implicitly to identify viewers' knowledge, attitudes, and tastes. Grounded in that knowledge and those attitudes, viewers anticipate a movie: they come already prepared to identify with and understand a film in certain ways even before the first images move.

Marketing and Promotion: What We Want to See

Why and how we are attracted to the movies we see at particular places and times is a slightly different but equally important matter. Just as a film can be distributed in various ways, a movie can be marketed and promoted in different ways to shape and direct our interests in it. A film might be advertised in newspapers as the work of a great director, for example, or it might be described as a steamy love story and illustrated by way of a poster. Although these preliminary encounters with a film might seem marginally relevant to how we experience a film, promotional strategies, like distribution strategies, prepare us in important ways for how we will see and understand a film.

Promoting Our Interest

Marketing and promotion aim to generate and direct interest in a movie. Film **marketing** involves identifying an audience in order to bring a product (the movie) to the attention of buyers (viewers), so that they will come to consume (to watch) that product. Film **promotion** refers to the specific ways a movie can be made an object that an audience will want to see. No doubt the most common and potent component of the marketing and promotion of movies around the world is the **star system** (see pp. 54–55 and 461–63), which advertises a movie as the vehicle of one or more well-known actors (currently popular at that time and in that culture). Like other marketing and promotional practices, the star system aims to create, in advance, specific expectations that will draw an audience to a film. Quite often, these marketing and promotional expectations—that the film stars Whoopi Goldberg or is directed by British filmmaker Peter Greenaway, say—subsequently become the viewfinders through which an audience sees a movie.

A part of film culture since its early years, the mechanisms of marketing and promotion involve everything from newspaper and billboard advertisements to the previews shown before the main feature. The public appearances of stars on radio and television as well as the early screenings for newspaper critics, whose reviews coincide with the release of a film, are also forms of promotion. In addition, while movies have long been promoted through prizes and gifts [Figure 1.25], modern distributors are especially adept at marketing films through **tie-ins:** ancillary products such as tee-shirts, CD soundtracks, toys, and other gimmicks made available at stores and restaurants that advertise and promote a movie. *The Little Mermaid* (1989), for example, was anticipated with the replica toys of Ariel and the frequently performed song "Under the Sea."

A similar marketing blitz accompanied *Independence Day.* Given its carefully timed release on July 3, 1996, following weeks of advertisements in newspapers and on television, it would be difficult to analyze viewers' feelings about this film without taking into account the influence of these promotions. Defining the film as a science fiction thriller, the advertisements and reviews drew attention to its status as the film event of the summer, its suitability for children, and its technological wizardry.

Figure 1.25 Movie marquee. Promoting movies through prizes and gifts.

Figure 1.26 *Independence Day* (1996). Promoting racial harmony.

Figure 1.27 *Innocents of Paris* (1929). Marquee promoting the novelty of sound and song.

Figure 1.28 *Wag the Dog* (1997). White House scandals as a movie advertisement.

Promoted and released to coincide with the Fourth of July holiday, *Independence Day* ads emphasized its patriotic American themes. In that light, many posters, advertisements, and publicity stills presented actors Will Smith together with Bill Pullman or Jeff Goldblum, not only to promote those stars but also perhaps to draw attention to the racial harmony of the film and its appeal to African American and white audiences **[Figure 1.26]**. During the first month of its release, when U.S. scientists discovered a meteorite with fossils that suggested early life on Mars, promotion for the movie responded immediately with revised ads: "Last week, scientists found evidence of life on another planet. We're not going to say we told you so. . . ."

Typical of Hollywood, promotions and advertisements often emphasize the **"greater realism"** of movies, a strategy that promises audiences more accurate or more expansive reflections of the world and human experience. For *Dark Victory* (1939), a Bette Davis film about a socialite dying of a brain tumor, advertisements and press kits drew viewers' attention to the disturbing truth of a terminal illness, a reality that promotions claimed had never before been presented in movies. A related marketing strategy is to claim **"textual novelty"** in the film, drawing attention to new features such as technical innovations, a rising star, or the acclaimed book on which the film is based. With early sound films like *The Jazz Singer* (1927), *The Gold Diggers of Broadway* (1929), and *Innocents of Paris* (1929) **[Figure 1.27]**, marketing advertisements directed audiences toward the abundance and quality of the singing and talking that added a dramatic new dimension to cinematic realism. Today, promotions and advertisements can exploit new digital technologies, as when *Mask* (1994) touted everywhere the remarkable digital transformations of Jim Carrey's face and body, or they can take advantage of a timely political coincidence, as when *Wag the Dog* (1997) advertised its uncanny resemblance to a current sexual scandal in the Clinton White House **[Figure 1. 28]**.

Older films in current release and art films have less access to the mechanisms of promotion than do current mainstream films, and their promotion is not usually in the hands of film companies seeking huge financial profits. Even so, audiences for these films are led to some extent by what we will call **cultural promotion,** academic or artistic accounts that discuss and frequently value films as especially important in movie history or as aesthetic objects. A discussion of a movie in a film history book or even in a university film course could thus be seen as an act of "marketing," which makes clear that promotion is not just about urging viewers to see a film but is also about urging them to see it with a particular point of view. Although these more muted kinds of promotion are usually underpinned by intellectual rather than financial motives, they also deserve our consideration and analysis because they too shape our understanding of films. How does a specific film history text, for instance, prepare you to see a film such as *Bonnie and Clyde* (1967)? Some books promote it as a modern gangster film **[Figure 1.29]**. Others pitch it as an incisive reflection of the social history of the turbulent 1960s. Still other texts and essays may urge readers to see it because of its place in the opus of a major U.S. director, Arthur Penn. Even independent and classical movies require publicity: by promoting the artistic power and individuality of the director; by associating them with big-name film festivals in Venice, Toronto, and Cannes; or by calling attention, through advertising, to what distinguishes them from mainstream Hollywood films. In short, we do not experience any film with innocent eyes; consciously or not, we come prepared to see it in a certain way.

Figure 1.29 *Bonnie and Clyde* (1967). Gangster film or social commentary?

Advertising and Ratings

Advertising is a central form of promotion that uses television, billboards, film trailers or previews, print ads, and other forms of display to bring a film to the attention of a potential audience. Advertising can use the facts in and issues surrounding a movie in various ways. Advertising often emphasizes connections and differences with related or similar films or highlights the presence of a particularly popular actor or director: the poster for Charles Chaplin's *The Kid* (1921) **[Figure 1.30]** emphasizes the famous Chaplin, but unlike his well-known slapstick comedies, his serious demeanor in the poster suggests the serious themes of his first feature film, "a great Film he has been working on for a whole year." For different markets, *G.I. Jane* (1997) was promoted as a star vehicle for Demi Moore or as the latest film from Ridley Scott, the director of *Blade Runner*, *Alien* (1979), and *Thelma & Louise* (1991). It is conceivable that these two promotional tactics created different sets of expectations about the movie—one more attuned to tough female sexuality, the other to lavish sets and technological landscapes. As this example reveals, promotion tends not only to draw us to a movie but also to suggest what we will concentrate on as a way of understanding its achievement.

One of the most carefully crafted forms of promotional advertising is the **theatrical trailer,** which previews a few scenes from a film in theaters before the main feature film or, more commonly today, in

Figure 1.30 *The Kid* (1921). Poster advertising a new Chaplin.

Figure 1.31 *Eyes Wide Shut* (2000). Erotic trailer.

a television commercial. In just a few minutes, these trailers provide a compact series of reasons why a viewer *should* see that movie. A trailer for Stanley Kubrick's *Eyes Wide Shut* (2000) is indicative: typical of this kind of promotion, it moves quickly to separate large bold titles announcing the names of Tom Cruise, Nicole Kidman, and Kubrick, foregrounding the collaboration of a star marriage and a celebrated director of daring films. Then, against the refrain from Chris Isaak's soundtrack song "Baby Did a Bad Thing," a series of images condenses the progress of the film, including shots of Kidman undressing **[Figure 1.31]**, Cruise as Dr. Harford sauntering with two beautiful women, a passionate kiss shared by the two stars, two ominous-looking men at the gate of an estate (where the orgy would take place), and Cruise being enticed by a prostitute. Besides the provocative match of two star sex symbols with a controversial director, the trailer underlines the dark erotic mysteries of the film within an opulently decadent setting. It introduces intensely sexual characters and the alternately seedy and glamorous atmosphere of the film in a manner meant to draw fans of Cruise, Kidman, Kubrick, and dark erotic intrigue. That this promotion fails to communicate the stinging irony in the movie's eroticism may, interestingly, account for some of the disappointed reactions that followed its eager initial reception.

Trailers, posters, and newspaper advertisements select not only their images carefully but also their terminology in order to guide our perspective on a film even before we see it. Parodied brilliantly in *The Player* (1992), modern Hollywood can often promote a film with the language of **high concept,** a short phrase that attempts to sell the main marketing features of a movie through its stars, its genre, or some other easily identifiable connection **[Figure 1.32]**: in *The Player,* one film is described as "kind of a psychic political thriller with a heart"; other high-concept movies might be advertised as "Stanley Kubrick's exploration of pornography" or "In *Lara Croft: Tomb Raider* (2001), superstar Angelina Jolie brings the CD-ROM game to life." The rhetoric of movie advertising frequently descends into such silly clichés

Figure 1.32 *The Player* (1992). Producing high-concept films.

as "two thumbs up" or "action-packed, fun-filled adventure," yet promotional and marketing terms also use succinct descriptive terms to position a movie for particular expectations and responses. For example, the term *feature film*, originating in 1912 but becoming a key promotional strategy in the 1930s, describes a movie that is of a certain length (over seventy minutes), that is promoted as the main attraction or an **A picture** in a theater, and that promises high-quality stars and stories. Conversely, a **B picture** is a less expensive, less important movie that plays before the main attraction and indicates less visual and narrative sophistication. Just as today the term **blockbuster** prepares us for action, stars, and special effects, and **art film** suggests a slower, perhaps more visually and intellectually subtle movie, the terminology used to define and promote a movie can become a potent force in framing our expectations.

Rating systems, which provide viewers with guidelines for movies (usually based on violent or sexual content), are a similarly important form of advertising that can be used in marketing and promotion. Whether they are wanted or unwanted by viewers, ratings are fundamentally about trying to control the kind of audience that sees a film and, to a certain extent, about advertising the content of that film. In the United States, the current ratings system classifies movies as G (general audiences), PG (parental guidance suggested), PG-13 (parental guidance suggested and not recommended for audiences under thirteen years old), R (persons under age seventeen must be accompanied by an adult), and NC-17 (persons under age seventeen are not admitted). Most countries, as well as some religious organizations, have their own systems for rating films. Great Britain, for instance, uses these categories: U (universal), A (parental discretion), AA (persons under age fourteen are not admitted), and X (persons under age eighteen are not admitted). Interestingly, the age limit for X-rated films varies from country to country, the lowest being age fifteen in Sweden.

Figure 1.33 *Men in Black* (1997). Seeking a PG-13 rating.

A movie like *Free Willy* (1993), a tale of a child and a captured whale, depends on its G rating to draw large family audiences, whereas sexually explicit films like *Show Girls* (1995), rated NC-17, and Nagisa Oshima's *In the Realm of the Senses* (1976), not rated and confiscated when it first came to many countries, can use the notoriety of their ratings to attract curious adult viewers. When promotion casually or aggressively uses ratings, our way of looking at and thinking about the movie already begins to anticipate the film. For example, with an R rating, we might be made to anticipate a movie featuring a degree of sex and violence. A rating of G might promise happy endings and happy families. Recent movies, such as *Men in Black* (1997) **[Figure 1.33]**, have eagerly sought a PG-13 rating because that, ironically perhaps, attracts a younger audience of eight-, nine-, and ten-year-olds, who want movies with a touch of adult language and action.

Word of Mouth

Our experience at the movies is anticipated and directed in advance of our viewing of the film in less evident and less predictable ways as well. **Word of mouth,** the conversational exchange of opinions and information sometimes referred to as the "buzz" around a movie, may seem a somewhat insignificant or at least hazy area of promotion, yet it is an important social arena in which our likes and dislikes are formed and given direction by the social groups we move in. We know our friends like certain kinds of films, and we all tend to promote movies according to a **"sociology of taste"** whereby we judge and approve of movies according to the values of our particular age group, cultural background, or other social determinant. When marketing experts direct a movie at a target audience, they intend to promote that film through word of mouth, knowing viewers talk to each other and recommend films to people who share their values. Examine, for instance, how a group of friends might promote *Titanic* (1997) among themselves. Do they recommend it to one another because of the strength or attractiveness of the female character Rose, the breathtaking special effects

Figure 1.34 *Titanic* (1997). Promotion: word of mouth and a taste for the spectacular.

Figure 1.35 *Titanic* (1997). Promotion: a taste for class politics.

[Figure 1.34], or the confrontation between the rich and the poor **[Figure 1.35]**? What would each of these word-of-mouth promotions indicate about the social or personal values of the person promoting the movie and how he or she acts out of a sociology of taste?

Fan magazines have always extended word of mouth as a form of movie promotion and a sociology of taste. Popular since the 1920s, and sometimes called "fanzines," in recent years fan magazines have evolved into Internet discussion groups and **promotional Web sites.** Web sites, often set up by a film's distributor, have, in fact, become the most powerful contemporary form of the fanzine, allowing information about and enthusiasm for a movie to be efficiently exchanged and spread among potential viewers. Most famously, *The Blair Witch Project* (1999) Web site was established in advance of the film's release and used fake documents and clues to help generate word of mouth; the success of this strategy transformed this simple, low-budget horror film ($35,000) into a huge box-office hit ($15 million). In the spring of 2001, Steven Spielberg's *A.I.* and the new *Planet of the Apes* targeted e-mail accounts and set up Web-based games (in the case of *Planet of the Apes,* a global scavenger hunt called Project A.P.E.) that spread through chat rooms even before the films were released **[Figure 1.36]**. To encourage and develop individual interest in films, these fanzines and Web sites gather together readers and viewers who wish to read or chat about their ongoing interest in movies like the *Star Trek* films (1979–1994) or cult favorites like *Casablanca* (1942). Here, tastes about which movies to

Figure 1.36 *Planet of the Apes* (2001). Spreading the word on the Web.

like and dislike and about how to see them are both supported and promoted on a far more concrete social and commercial level. Information is offered or exchanged about specific movies, arguments are waged, and sometimes games or fictions are developed around the film. Magazines may provide information about the signature song of *Casablanca,* "As Time Goes By," and the actor who sings it, Dooley Wilson. Chat room participants may query each other about Mr. Spock's Vulcan history or fantasize about his personal life. Even before the release of *The Lord of the Rings: The Fellowship of the Ring* (2001), the filmmakers engaged fans of the Tolkien novel through e-mails and Web sites, trading information about the production for feedback on casting decisions and scene cuts. Here, the Internet promotes word

 VIEWING CUES: Promotion

■ Look at the advertisements that promote a particular film (perhaps the film you will watch next in class). What do the billboards, trailers, and newspaper advertisements communicate to you about this film? What do they emphasize? What new realities or innovations in film technique do they advertise? Has the film been packaged with high-concept or other terminology that pigeonholes the movie in a certain way?

■ What other strategies for promoting this movie have been used to shape and direct our understanding of it? Have you read something about this movie (in a book or magazine) that makes you think it is important in some cultural or historical way? Have you seen any Web sites for this movie? How do they highlight particular themes and reactions to the film?

■ Think about this film in terms of the rating assigned to it. Does its rating color your assumptions about the film, making you suspicious or curious in certain ways?

■ Has word-of-mouth promotion been an important vehicle for this film? How would you summarize the "buzz" that anticipated or surrounded the film? Can you analyze how it has prepared viewers with certain expectations?

■ After seeing the film, which of these promotional strategies seem most accurate? Most misleading? What about the film has been ignored or underplayed in any of these promotional strategies? For what possible reasons?

Promoting *The Crying Game* (1992)

Neil Jordan's *The Crying Game* is an ingenious example of various promotional maneuvers. A story about the sexual identity crisis of Fergus, a member of the Irish Republican Army (IRA), the film begins with the capture of Jody, a black British soldier. After witnessing Jody's violent, accidental death, Fergus flees to England, where he seeks out and falls in love with Dil, Jody's former lover **[Figure 1.37]**. Complicating this plot, Fergus does not realize, during the first part of their courtship, that Dil is a transvestite.

For both British and American audiences, the film was first promoted on the basis of its artistic novelty and integrity, which was associated primarily with Jordan's cultural reputation as a serious director of inventive British films, including *Mona Lisa* (1986). That *The Crying Game* was only moderately successful when first released in England can be attributed, in part, to the social context of its release: renewed IRA activity in England at the time may have made it difficult for British audiences to look past the subplot and concentrate on Jordan's artistic inventiveness or on the intriguing relationship between Fergus and Dil. The U.S. distributor, Miramax, also recognizing difficulties in distributing and promoting the film, was concerned about three traditional marketing taboos: race, political violence, and homosexuality. However, removed from the British-Irish political context, Miramax decided it could repackage the movie to promote it by drawing attention away from its political intrigue and focusing on the romantic and sexual "secret" of Dil's masculinity. The film broke box-office records in the United States for a British production. The promotional schemes in Britain and the United States resulted in significantly different ways of seeing and understanding the same movie.

At the center of its promotional history, *The Crying Game* required two different advertising approaches, one for the British release and another for

Figure 1.37 *The Crying Game* (1992). The IRA and sexual identity.

the U.S. release. The differences between these campaigns crystallize in the advertising posters used for the two promotions. In the British poster [Figure 1.38], a large facial portrait of Stephen Rea as Fergus holding a smoking gun centers the image, surrounded by smaller images of the faces of Jaye Davidson as Dil and Miranda Richardson as the femme fatale Jude. Numerous lines of print promote the film as "From the Director of *Mona Lisa*," "Neil Jordan's Best Work to Date," and "More Surprises Than any Film Since *Psycho*." The American poster features only the image of Miranda Richardson, with a smoking gun, set against a black backdrop [Figure 1.39]. The print is equally spare: "Sex. Murder. Betrayal." and, under the film's title, "play it at your own risk." The British poster advertises the cinematic heritage of Jordan, while highlighting the masculine and political violence associated with Fergus's large image. The American poster conversely creates the dark atmosphere of sexual intrigue, notably offering audiences a participatory game rather than a serious political reality.

In the wake of the film's promotion and box-office success in the United States, the Internet continued to promote the film's initial participatory lure. Typically, dozens of Web sites about *The Crying Game* appeared in numerous languages. Some sites, such as *The Crying Game* Fan Page, feature photos, Boy George's rendition of the title song, and links to movie reviews. Others are devoted to a single star, such as Forest Whitaker or Jaye Davidson.

Ratings and, especially, word of mouth created specific expectations and interests in *The Crying Game*. It received an R rating in the United States (no doubt for its frontal male nudity), where such a rating would more likely suggest sexual content than violence. But, especially in the United States, word of mouth functioned as the most powerful strategy in the promotion of *The Crying Game*. Viewers, including movie reviewers, were urged to keep the secret of Dil's sexuality as a way of baiting new audiences to see the film. A widely announced word-of-mouth promotion—"Don't tell the secret!"—drew a continuous stream of audiences wanting to participate in this game of secrets. Word of mouth became part of a strategy to entice American audiences who, anticipating a sexual drama of surprises and reversals, would in most instances overlook the political tensions that complicated the film for British audiences.

Figure 1.38 *The Crying Game* (1992). British poster promoting political violence.

Figure 1.39 *The Crying Game* (1992). American poster promoting sexual games.

of mouth about a film by offering potential audiences the possibility of some participation in the making of the film, an approach that is more and more common today.

As they proliferate, promotional avenues like these deserve attention and analysis in terms of deciding how they add to or confuse our understanding of a film. Here, too, our different experiences of the movies take place within a complex cultural terrain where our personal interest in certain films intersects with specific historical and social forces to shape the meaning and value of those experiences. Here, too, the film experience extends well beyond the screen.

Movie Exhibition: The Where, When, and How of Movie Experiences

Distribution and promotion are called "extra-filmic dimensions" of the movie experience because they describe events that precede, surround, or follow the actual images we watch on a screen or television monitor. The final extra-filmic dimension of the movie experience is **exhibition,** the places where and the times when we can see films. Like distribution and promotion, we tend to take exhibition for granted as describing the normal cultural range of places and times for seeing movies: sometimes we watch films in theaters, sometimes on video monitors, or sometimes even on computer screens. However, the many ways that movies are exhibited mean much more than we realize to our feelings about a film and our interpretation of it.

The Changing Contexts of Film Exhibition

Film distribution, promotion, and exhibition are, not surprisingly, closely related in how they anticipate and condition our responses to movies. If distribution and promotion already work to anticipate, shape, and direct our tastes, exhibition practices can support or alter the intended aims and meanings of a movie. These exhibition practices include:

- the physical environment in which we view a movie
- the temporal frameworks describing when and the length of time we watch a movie
- the technological format through which we see the movie

Seeing the same movie at a cineplex or in a college classroom, watching it uninterrupted for two hours on a big screen or in thirty-minute segments over four days on a VCR can elicit very different kinds of experiences of that movie. A viewer may be completely bored by a film shown on an airplane, but, seen later in a theater, that film may appear full of visual surprises and interesting plot twists.

Movies have been distributed, exhibited, and seen in many different historical exhibition contexts. At the beginning of the twentieth century, movies rarely lasted more than twenty minutes and were often viewed in small, noisy **nickelodeon theaters,** storefront spaces where short films were shown continuously to audiences passing in and out, or in carnival settings that assumed movies were a passing amusement comparable to other carnival attractions **[Figure 1.40]**. By the 1920s, as movies grew

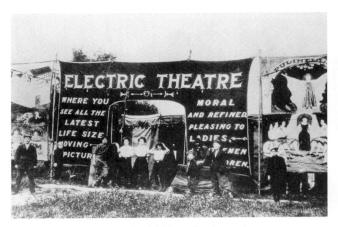

Figure 1.40 The carnival exhibition of early movies.

Figure 1.41 The lavish environment of movie palaces.

artistically, financially, and culturally, the exhibition of films moved to lavish **movie palaces,** like Radio City Music Hall, with sumptuous seating and ornate architecture **[Figure 1.41]**. By the 1950s, city centers gave way to suburban sprawl; as the theaters lost their crowds of patrons, widescreen and 3-D processes were introduced to distinguish the possibilities of film exhibition from its new rival, television at home. Today we commonly see movies at home, on a VCR or DVD player, where we can watch a movie in the normal 90- to120-minute period or extend our viewing over many nights in a series of episodes. In recent years, as movies continue to compete with home video, film exhibitors have countered with so-called megaplexes, theaters with twenty or more screens, more than six thousand seats, and over a hundred show times per day. These new entertainment complexes sometimes feature not just movies but also miniature golf courses, roller rinks, restaurants, and coffee bars.

These changing exhibition formats parallel many other changes in the ways in which we watch and respond to movies. Informing all of them is a **"sociology of exhibition space"**; how and where we watch a movie reflects or becomes part of specific social activities that surround and define moviegoing:

- Exhibition highlights a social dimension of watching movies because it gathers and organizes individuals as a specific social group.
- Our shared participation in that social environment directs our attention and shapes our responses in ways that influence how we enjoy and understand a film.

A movie such as *My Dog Skip* (2000) **[Figure 1.42]** will be shown and often be seen as a Saturday matinee in suburban theaters to attract families with children to its nostalgic story, set in the 1940s, of a southern boy and his dog. The time and place of the showing obviously coordinate with a period when middle-class families can usually share experiences together as recreation and amusement, making them more inclined perhaps to appreciate this lighthearted tale of family love and affection. Conversely, Peter

Figure 1.42 *My Dog Skip* (2000). A boy and his dog for Saturday matinees in the suburbs.

Watching Film and Television

When most of us see movies today, we watch them on television, which is not the way most films are first exhibited and seen. Although this way of viewing films is, for most of us, more common and natural than going out to a theater, it significantly alters the movie we see. With VCRs plugged into larger television monitors or home projection systems, the differences between television and film technology may seem less and less visible. However, important technological distinctions must be considered when comparing and contrasting the exhibition of films in a theater and the watching of movies on a television monitor.

The quality of the sound and image has always indicated a technological gap that impacts movies exhibited on television. Most accounts emphasize the loss of image and sound quality when moving from film projection to a television or videotape presentation [**Figure 1.43**]. Whether using 16mm film or the larger 35mm or 70mm film, movies offer between 3,500 and 4,000 lines of resolution. As an electronic transmission of pixels (dots containing information about color and brightness), television can offer a maximum of only 525 lines of resolution (although most home televisions can display between 300 and 400 lines). Both HDTV (high-definition television) and DVD (digital video disc) promise to improve the quality of the video image appreciably by creating higher resolutions of digital reproduction: HDTV offers 1,080 lines of resolution and DVD offers 480 lines. The popularity of elaborate stereo sound systems for the home may also offer high-quality sound to match the Dolby systems found in theaters, but in most cases film sound suffers significant deterioration when projects are transferred to television.

The size and format of the image has also distinguished film from television. Over the last four decades, movie theaters and television have developed changing aspect ratios (the ratio of the width of the frame to the height). Television monitors normally follow the "academy" ratio of 1.33:1, used traditionally in film projection. Modern movies commonly use widescreen ratios of 1.85:1 or 2.35:1. As a consequence, movies converted for television viewing are frequently subjected to a **pan-and-scan process** to allow the film image to fit the television format: with this process, a computer-controlled scanner determines the most important action in the image and then crops peripheral action and space so that the central action is reproduced as one image or perhaps re-edited to two images. Imitating the widescreen formats found in theaters, letterbox formats for video monitors are now regular options for videotapes and DVDs, and so the problems and solutions associated with the differences between film and television technology have become more complex and variable. Still, the questions remain: Because of these transformations and changes in the technology of exhibition, can we determine what an authentic or authorized experience of a film should be? Do contemporary exhibition and viewing practices suggest that most movies must be "amphibious"—that is, able to function and communicate through both theatrical and video exhibitions?

Figure 1.43 *Rear Window* (1954). The video image (left) is darker and has less contrast than the brighter, higher-contrast film image (right).

Greenaway's *The Pillow Book* (1996) **[Figure 1.44]**, a complex film about a woman's passion for calligraphy, human flesh, poetry, and sexuality, would likely appear in a small downtown theater frequented by single individuals and young couples who also spend time in the theater's coffee bar. This movie would probably appeal to an urban crowd with more experimental tastes in movies and time to gather over coffee to talk before or after films. Reversing the exhibition contexts of these two films should indicate how those contexts could generate wildly different reactions.

Our movie watching also includes the **technological conditions of exhibition,** the industrial and mechanical vehicles showing a movie. In a large theater, a movie can be shown with a 35mm or even 70mm movie projector that shows large and vibrantly detailed images. We might see another movie in a cineplex theater at a mall with a relatively small screen and a smorgasbord of other movies in the screening rooms surrounding it. We may watch a third movie on a VCR that uses tape rather than film and that we can stop, reverse, or fast forward. In the past, popular exhibition practices included inserting a short movie within a vaudeville performance or offering double features in drive-in theaters full of teenagers in cars. Today's movies are already beginning to be exhibited on a computer screen, where they share the monitor with other kinds of activities.

Different technological features of exhibition are sometimes carefully calculated to add to both our enjoyment and understanding of a movie. Cecil B. DeMille's epic film *The Ten Commandments* (1923) premiered in a movie palace, where the plush and grandiose surroundings, the biblical magnitude of the images, and the orchestral accompaniment supported the grand spiritual themes of the film. In most cases, the idea is to match, as here, the exhibition with the themes of the film so that the conditions for watching it parallel the ideas or formal practices in the movie. With a movie that uses special projection techniques for exhibition, such as 3-D glasses **[Figure 1.45]** for *Creature from the Black Lagoon* (1954), the form and technology of exhibition in which we are meant to watch the film can often relate to its subject matter. Here, the shocking appearance of the creature becomes even more shocking with more visual dimensions. Though a mostly nostalgic form of exhibition today, 3-D glasses and images create a perceptual illusion of three-dimensional space that places the audience more dramatically into the visual dynamics of *Creature from the Black Lagoon*'s suspense, involving those viewers more fully in the illusory danger of certain scenes (and so distinguishing this movie experience from that available on small-screen televisions, a major competitor at the time of its release).

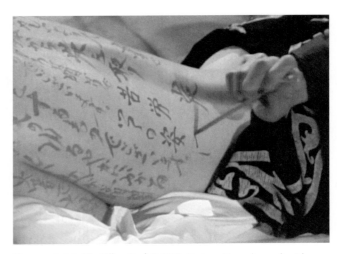

Figure 1.44 *The Pillow Book* (1996). Body calligraphy and art-house exhibition.

Figure 1.45 3-D exhibition.

IN FOCUS

Exhibiting *Citizen Kane* (1941)

The tale of a man obsessed with power and possessions, *Citizen Kane* is often considered one of the greatest films ever made. It is usually hailed for Orson Welles's portrayal of Charles Foster Kane and his direction of the puzzle-like story, and for the film's complex visual compositions. It is also a movie that ran into trouble even before its release because of its thinly disguised and critical portrayal of U.S. media mogul William Randolph Hearst. Less often is the film seen and understood according to its dramatic exhibition history, one that has colored or even decided the changing meanings of the film.

As the first film of a director already hailed as a "boy genius" for his work as a theater actor and director, *Citizen Kane* was scheduled to open with appropriate fanfare at the spectacular Radio City Music Hall in New York City. Besides the glamorous and palatial architecture of this building, exhibiting the film in New York first would take advantage of the fact that Welles's career and reputation had been made there. The physical and social context for this opening exhibition would combine the epic grandeur of the Radio City building and a New York cultural space attuned to Welles's artistic experimentation. Already offended by rumors about the film, however, Hearst secretly moved to block the opening at Radio City Music Hall. After many difficulties and delays, the film's producer and distributor, RKO, eventually premiered the film simultaneously at an independent theater in Los Angeles and at a refurbished vaudeville house in New York City **[Figure 1.46]**. As a final twist, when major theaters such as the Fox and Paramount chains were legally forced to exhibit the film, they sometimes booked *Citizen Kane* but did not screen it for fear of vindictive repercussions from Hearst. Where it was shown in Warner Bros. theaters, its short and tortured exhibition history overshadowed the film itself, making it appear for many audiences strange and unnecessarily confrontational. Clearly the intended opening exhibition would have generated a response quite different from the one that occurred. Would its association with a movie palace like Radio City Music Hall have highlighted the more traditional features of the film, like its comedy and star performances, and made its complex story less of an obstruction? Or might the scandal of the movie's exhibition problems have added to its notoriety and celebrity?

Changing sociological and geographical contexts for exhibition have continued to follow *Citizen Kane* as its reputation has grown through the years. After its tumultuous first exhibition in the United States, the film was rediscovered in the 1950s by the art-house cinemas of France. There, it became less a provocative commentary on an American mogul and his power politics than a brilliantly creative expression of film language. Today, most individuals who see *Citizen Kane* watch it in a classroom—say, in a college course on American cinema. In the classroom, we look at movies as students or scholars, and we are prepared to study

Figure 1.46 *Citizen Kane* (1941). A delayed premiere.

them. In this context, viewers may feel urged to think more about the film as an art object than as entertainment or thinly disguised biography. In the classroom, we may focus more on the importance of the serious tragedies in the film (such as Kane's real and visual alienation from his best friends) and less on the comic interludes (such as the vaudevillian dance number). This is not to say that someone watching *Citizen Kane* in an academic situation cannot see and think about it in other ways. It's clear, however, that exhibition context can, very importantly, suggest certain social attitudes through which we watch a movie.

Figure 1.47 *Citizen Kane* (1941). The supplementary material of DVD distribution and exhibition: Orson Welles and the script.

The exhibition history of *Citizen Kane* likewise describes significant differences in how the film is experienced through different technologies. Its original exhibition used a 35mm projection providing the rich textures and sharp images needed to bring out the imagistic details and stunning deep focus that made the film famous. The visual magnitude of scenes such as Susan Alexander's operatic premiere and Kane's safari picnic at Xanadu or the spatial vibrancy and richness of Kane, and Susan's conversation in one of Xanadu's vast halls arguably require the size and texture of a large theatrical image. Since its first theatrical exhibition, the film has been seen on 16mm film and later on videotape, and recently has been remastered as a DVD. The content of the film remains the same, but the different technologies often mute the visual power of such images and scenes because the lower quality or smaller size of the images redirect our understanding from the visual dramatics of single images to the events of the story.

The shift in the exhibition context from the theater to the television obviously affects other subtle and not-so-subtle changes in how we see and understand the movie. On television, the image becomes a different size and quality and our level of concentration changes, perhaps from intense concentration to distracted attention. A viewing experience on television or video, moreover, may be broken up because of commercials or because we can start and stop the movie. In the case of *Citizen Kane,* as with many other films that move between theaters and television, the basic action of the movie may appear the same, but how we engage that material can change in ways that determine the meaning of the film experience. Whereas the large images in the theater may direct the viewer more easily to the play of light and dark as commentaries on the different characters, a video player might not allow those observations but might instead allow the viewer to replay dialogue in order to note levels of intonation or wordplay. The DVD of *Citizen Kane* gives viewers the added opportunity to supplement the film with rare photos, documents on the advertising campaign, commentaries by filmmaker Peter Bogdanovich and critic Roger Ebert, and a documentary, *The Battle over Citizen Kane* (1996), that describes the history of its script and its exhibition difficulties **[Figure 1.47]**. To whatever degree these supplemental materials come into play, it is clear that a DVD exhibition of *Citizen Kane* offers possibilities for significantly enriching an audience's experience of the film. Viewers taking advantage of these materials would conceivably watch *Citizen Kane* prepared and equipped with certain points of view: more attuned perhaps to Welles's creative innovation and influence on later filmmakers like Bogdanovich or more interested in how the film re-creates the connections between Hearst and Kane detailed in the documentary supplement. That the DVD provides material on "alternative ad campaigns" for the original release of the film even allows viewers to investigate the way different promotional strategies can direct their attention to certain themes and scenes.

The Timing of Exhibition

Overlapping with distribution timing, the **timing of exhibition** is a more flexible but equally influential part of our movie experience. That is, when and for how long we see a film can shape our experience as much as where we see that film. Although most people see movies in the early evening, before or after dinner, audiences watch movies according to numerous rituals and in various time slots. Afternoon matinees, midnight movies, or the inflight movie on a long plane ride give some indication of how the timing of a movie experience can vary and how that can influence other considerations about the movie. In each of these situations, our experience of the movies includes a commitment to spend time in a certain way. Instead of time spent reading, in conversation, sleeping, or working on a business project, we watch a movie. That time spent with a movie accordingly becomes an activity associated with relaxing, socializing, or even working in a different way. On any particular occasion, reflect on the period of time you choose to watch a film. How else might that time be spent, and what is your rationale for using this time to watch a film? Does the choice of that specific day and time to see a film have any bearing on the film you choose to see? More importantly, how accurate are the conventional assumptions about the time spent watching films as a time to escape the so-called real world?

Traditionally, movie culture has emphasized **film exhibition as leisure time,** a time that is assumed to be less productive (at least compared to the time spent working a job) and that enforces assumptions about movies as the kind of enjoyment associated with play and pleasure. To some extent, leisure time is a relatively recent historical development. Since the nineteenth century, when motion pictures first appeared, modern society has aimed to organize experience so that work and leisure could be separated and defined in relation to each other. We generally identify leisure time as "an escape," "the relaxation of our mind and body," or "the acting out of a different self." Since the early twentieth century, movie exhibition has been associated with leisure time in these ways. Seeing a comedy on a Friday night promises relaxation at the end of a busy week. Playing a concert film on a VCR while eating dinner may relieve mental fatigue. Watching a romantic film on television late at night may offer the passion missing from one's real life.

Besides leisure time, however, we can and should consider **film exhibition as productive time,** meaning time used to gain information, material advantage, or knowledge. From the early years of the cinema, movies have been used to illustrate lectures or introduce audiences to Shakespearean performances. More strictly educational films, such as those shown in health classes or driver education programs, are less glamorous versions of this use of film. Although less widely acknowledged as part of film exhibition, productive time continues to shape certain kinds of film exhibition. For a movie reviewer or film producer, an early morning screening may be about "financial value" because this use of time to evaluate a movie will presumably result in certain economic rewards. For another person, a week of films at an art museum represents "intellectual value," as it helps explain ideas about a different society or historical period. For a young American, an evening watching *Schindler's List* can be about "human value" because that film aims to make viewers more knowledgeable about the Holocaust and more sensitive about the suffering of other human beings.

Film exhibitions usually try to provide a variety of time periods to accommodate many different temporal values, and different viewers can certainly find different values in the same exhibition. Still, the timings of exhibitions do tend to frame and emphasize the film experience according

Figure 1.48 *Moulin Rouge!* (2001). Premiering glamour in the glamour of Cannes.

to certain values. The Cannes International Film Festival introduces a wide range of films and functions both as a business venue for buying and selling film and as a glamorous showcase for stars and parties. The May timing of this festival and its Riviera location assure that the movie experience will be about pleasure and the business of leisure time. In contrast, the New York International Film Festival, featuring some of the same films, has a more intellectual or academic aura. That it occurs in New York City during September and October, at the beginning of the academic year, associates this experience of the movies more with artistic value and productive time. The premiere of *Moulin Rouge!* (2001) at Cannes exploited both the high-profile glamour of that festival's party atmosphere and a French context that would certainly draw the kind of attention it would not receive at the New York event **[Figure 1.48]**.

 VIEWING CUES: Exhibition

- Whether the next film you see in class is an older movie or a more recent one, consider—or better yet research—how the film was first exhibited. Would it have been shown in a nickelodeon? A movie palace? A cineplex? How would that exhibition context have been appropriate for the movie?

- How could the "sociology of exhibition" be more or less suited to this film? What would be the ideal audience for the film? Why? What kind of exhibition would most likely draw that audience?

- Imagine seeing this film at different times of the year or in the week. How would the timing of the exhibition affect your expectations about the movie? What would be the best time to exhibit the film? Why?

- Imagine watching this movie as two different uses of time, as a "leisure time activity" and as a "productive time activity." How would exhibiting the movie in those different kinds of time slots draw a viewer to different ways of looking at it? How might you view this film differently, for instance, if you saw it in a classroom versus if you saw it during a long airplane flight? What, if any, specific actions or themes would you recognize in one and not the other?

- Consider how different kinds of exhibition technologies might affect your response to this movie. How would a large-screen format versus a videotape change your experience of the film? If there is a DVD of this film, does it enhance or shape your understanding of the film in specific ways? If so, how?

Classroom, library, and museum exhibitions tend to emphasize understanding and learning as much as enjoyment. When students watch films in these kinds of situations, they are asked to attend to them somewhat differently from the way they may view films on a Friday night at the movies. They watch more carefully, perhaps; they may consider the films as part of historical or artistic traditions; they may even take notes as a logical part of this kind of exhibition. These conditions of film exhibition do not necessarily change the essential meaning of a movie, but in directing how we look at a film, they can certainly shade and even alter how we understand that film. Like other changes in viewing conditions, exhibition asks us to engage and think about the film not as an isolated object but as part of the expectations established by the conditions in which we watch it.

CRITICAL VOICES: DOUGLAS GOMERY ON EXHIBITION

Especially popular from 1905 to 1910, nickelodeons were the first viable form of commercial exhibition of the movies, showing a program of films lasting from a few minutes to perhaps twenty minutes each. In this excerpt, Douglas Gomery, a historian of film culture, examines the economic and social roots of movie culture and explains how promotion and exhibition almost inevitably intertwine. In this selection from *Shared Pleasures: A History of Movie Presentation in the United States* (1992), he demonstrates that critics can often learn as much about a movie by looking offscreen as by focusing on the images on the screen.

The nickelodeon functioned as a small and uncomfortable makeshift theatre, usually a converted cigar store, pawnshop, restaurant, or skating rink made over to look like a vaudeville theatre. In front, large, hand-painted posters announced the movies for the day. Inside, the screening of news, documentary, comedy, fantasy and shorts lasted about an hour. The show usually began with a song, a hit from the day illustrated with hand-painted, color magic lantern slides displaying the images and words of the song. Most entertainment, though, came from motion pictures. The front of the typical nickelodeon represented its most important and costly feature. Nickel theatres sold their wares to a public walking by, and so soon they developed a myriad of lights with a prominent ticket booth, usually accompanied by a barker, to hawk their latest entertainment. Theatre owners attempted, for as little cost as possible, to emulate legitimate theatre but in the end had to settle for a simple selling window in the manner of an arcade or dime museum. Huge paintings might cost the operator hundreds of dollars. Wood gave way to pressed metal as the nickelodeon owners prospered. . . . 1

With nickelodeon prices so much lower than a big-time vaudeville show, it is not surprising to learn that early devotees came from the poorer sections of the cities. This gave rise to the expression "democracy's theatre." But . . . a policy of catering to the poorer and lower-middle-class (. . .) patrons was not embraced by the theatre owners themselves. They could look down the street and see the monies being made by vaudeville entrepreneurs who sought out middle-class audiences. Movie entrepreneurs, once they felt safe with the nickelodeon formula, abandoned their original poorer patrons for a more selective audience, catering to a middle-class with more discretionary income and more time to spend in a movie house. . . . 2

By the mid-1910s the matrix of nearly twenty thousand theatres was in place, supplemented by traveling rural operations. Yet the evidence from the day indicates that as early as 1907 there were just "too many" theatres chasing too many nickels. *Moving Picture World* penned an editorial arguing that "the craze is on the wane" and ran it in June 1907: "Today there is 3 a cutthroat competition between the little nickelodeon owners, and they are beginning to compete each other out of existence." Although it would be two years before everyone agreed that the nickelodeon era was to be short-lived, the signs by 1907 were remarkably accurate.

The original ticket price soon gave way to admissions prices of ten cents and then more. Entrepreneurs seized the opportunity to increase their original prices. And with this new ten-cent price, still much less than the big-time vaudeville show, it is not surprising to learn that early devotees of the nickelodeon were keen to escape from average working days of ten hours or more, six days a week.

To lure the ideal family trade, the nickelodeon owner looked to the "New American woman" and her children. On a shopping break or after school, the theater owner set up special "tea hour" screenings; if women and children came, the owner had a stamp of respectability that could (and did) lead to more money and a more favorable image of the community. Thus women and children saw half-price afternoon specials. Stories in the movies catered to them. Filmmakers began to draw on respected authors such as Emile Zola, Edgar Allan Poe, Victor Hugo, Mark Twain, and even William Shakespeare for copyright-free inspiration for ten-minute capsulated versions of the classics. Owners of nickel shows saw [that] the popularity of such stories signaled the respectability that aspiring social climbers in the community sought.

By 1911 the nickelodeon was often misnamed. Moreover, newer theatres, designed as theatres and not made-over clothing stores, were rising. In the years preceding the second decade of the twentieth century, the trend was toward the movie show as a middle-class entertainment, held in a spacious theatre and costing as much as twenty-five cents.

THE NEXT LEVEL: ADDITIONAL SOURCES

Benjamin, Walter. "The Work of Art in the Age of Mechanical Reproduction." In *Illuminations*, edited by Hannah Arendt. New York: Schocken, 1969. This is an early and seminal essay on how the activity of viewing movies differs from the way we engage the traditional arts. Written originally in 1935, it remains a source of debates about how spectators perceive and think about movies.

Gomery, Douglas. *Shared Pleasures: A History of Movie Presentation in the United States.* Madison: University of Wisconsin Press, 1992. A history of the many changes in film exhibition from 1895 to 1990. Well researched and discriminating, this study provides a wealth of detail about the evolution of distribution in U.S. movies.

Lukk, Tiiu. *Movie Marketing: Opening the Picture and Giving It Legs.* Los Angeles: Silman-St. James, 1997. Less a scholarly work than a series of case studies, this book concentrates on a variety of contemporary movies—from *Four Weddings and a Funeral* (examined in this chapter) to *Mrs. Doubtfire*—and describes the different marketing and promotion strategies used today.

Mayne, Judith. *Cinema and Spectatorship.* New York: Routledge, 1993. This excellent book rethinks models of identification at the movies to develop more varied and dynamic descriptions that account for racial and sexual differences in viewers.

Williams, Linda, ed. *Viewing Positions: Ways of Seeing Film.* New Brunswick: Rutgers University Press, 1995. A varied collection of essays on spectatorship at the movies, with critical discussions ranging from the accounts of viewers of early cinema to the theoretical dynamics of postmodern spectators.

Compositions: Film Scenes, Shots, Cuts, and Sounds

I

A movie creates a world through its formal and technical powers, to some extent mimicking how we commonly use our senses to experience our real world. Most often, films activate our senses of sight and sound; to a lesser extent, films can also aim to stimulate our sense of touch. D. W. Griffith's *Broken Blossoms* (1919) re-creates the claustrophobic sensations of being trapped in a small room; in the Taviani brothers' Italian film *Padre Padrone* (1977), we hear the breezes whisper through tree limbs as if we were alone in a strange, almost mystical, landscape; in Rob Marshall's *Chicago* (2002), we again and again visually experience the robust energies and physical power of dance [Figure I.1]. A rare gimmicky movie, *Scent of Mystery* (1960), even engages an audience's sense of smell by releasing rose and tobacco odors from pipes under viewers' seats! Manipulating the senses, film images and sounds create experiences we recognize and respond to—physically, emotionally, and intellectually.

In the next four chapters, we will identify the formal and technical powers associated with the different elements of film form. In each chapter, we will provide a short historical, industrial, and cultural background for that formal element. We will then detail the specific elements and strategies of each particular aspect of film form. Finally, we will suggest some of the cultural values and traditions that have evolved around these formal mechanisms and that help determine our points of view on and interpretations of scenes, shots, cuts, and sounds at the movies.

◀ Figure I.1 *Chicago* (2002). The physical power of dance.

Exploring a Material World: Mise-en-Scène

If the average film-goer saw his favorite star on the screen last night, it is safe to wager that today he does not remember much about the settings in the picture. The story and the stars, he will tell you, were so interesting, he did not really notice anything else. Exactly. It was so interesting that he was not conscious of the background. Most people have the same experience, no matter how observant they may ordinarily be.

—Cedric Gibbons, art director for 1,500 films, including *Grand Hotel* (1932), *Gaslight* (1944), and *An American in Paris* (1951)

KEY OBJECTIVES

A film's sets and settings, costumes and make-up, and other elements depicted by its images are its mise-en-scène. This chapter describes how the mise-en-scène organizes and directs much of our film experience by putting us in certain places and by arranging the people and objects of those places in specific ways. Most mise-en-scènes orchestrate a rich and complex variety of formal and material elements inherited from theater. In this chapter, we consider

- how settings create meaningful environments for a film
- how the cultural and historical backgrounds of the mise-en-scène remain alive today
- how sets and props relate to the film's story
- how actors and performance styles function in a mise-en-scène
- how lighting is used to evoke certain meanings
- how costumes contribute to our understanding of a character
- how mise-en-scène puts in play values associated with specific film traditions

From the French term meaning "placed in a scene" or "onstage," **mise-en-scène** refers to those elements of a movie scene that are put in position before the filming actually begins and are employed in certain ways once the filming does begin. The mise-en-scène contains the scenic elements of a movie, including actors, lighting, sets and settings, costumes, make-up, and other features of the image that exist independent of the camera and the processes of filming and editing.

Outside the movies, mise-en-scène surrounds us every day. The architecture of a town might be described as a public mise-en-scène. How a person arranges and decorates a room could be called a private mise-en-scène.

Figure 2.1 *The Elephant Man* (1980). Recognizing the human beneath the power of make-up.

Courtrooms construct a mise-en-scène that expresses institutional authority. The placements of the judge above the court, of the attorneys at the bar, and of the witnesses in a partially sequestered area express the distribution of power in this mise-en-scène. The flood of light through the vast and darkened spaces of a cathedral creates an atmospheric mise-en-scène aimed to inspire contemplation and humility. The clothes, jewelry, and make-up a person chooses to wear are, in one sense, the functional costuming all individuals don as part of inhabiting a particular mise-en-scène: businessmen wear suits, clergy dress in black, and service people in fast-food restaurants wear uniforms with company logos.

In many ways, we live through our responses to these physical and material surfaces and objects and the sensations associated with them. Bright morning light might intensify the objects around us. A certain arrangement of furniture in a room might offer real comfort or discomfort. Whether these responses involve actually touching the materials or simply imagining their texture and volume, this tactile experience of the world is a continual part of how we engage and understand the people and places around us.

In the movies, too, we respond to the spaces and textures of mise-en-scène. Characters attract or repulse us through the clothing and make-up they wear: in *Some Like It Hot* (1959), Marilyn Monroe's eroticism is inseparable from her slinky dresses; *The Elephant Man* (1980) hinges on the deforming make-up of Joseph Carey Merrick and the drama of recognizing a sensitive human being inside a hideous shape **[Figure 2.1]**. Actions set in open or closed spaces can generate feelings of portent or hopelessness: in *Lawrence of Arabia* (1962), the open desert shimmers with possibility and danger; in the Japanese film *Woman in the Dunes* (1964), a woman and a man are trapped in a sandpit, gasping with desperation **[Figure 2.2]**.

A movie mise-en-scène can often approximate a tactile or corporeal experience of the world, whereby we encounter places, objects, and people through actual or imagined sensual contact. In simplified terms, the human nervous system transmits signals from the surface of the body (for instance, from the skin of the fingertips) to the brain where they are processed as different sensations and reactions, from the pain of a burn to the pleasure of a caress. Usually

Figure 2.2 *Woman in the Dunes* (1964). The arid heat of a sandpit.

this process involves actual physical contact, but scientific research also recognizes that tactile experiences can be indirectly triggered as a kinetic memory, in which the physical experience is provoked as an imagined contact or response. For example, a person with a missing limb may reexperience sensations associated with that part of the body (such as an itch). Similarly, in *Vertigo* (1958), the protagonist relives again and again the dizzying fear of heights that he first discovered when he watched a partner fall from a roof. The physiology of these tactile experiences can be culturally modified, influenced, or emphasized in very different ways by specific films. A taste for the texture and smell of food (especially chocolate) has rarely been re-created so intensely as it is in *Like Water for Chocolate* (1992) **[Color Plate 1]**.

The artistic precedent for cinematic mise-en-scène is primarily the theatrical stage, where our sensual and tactile engagement is naturally more real: the audience actually participates in the movements of real actors in real time. Film engages us in a different way. A film's material world may be actual objects and people set in actual locations, like the stunning slopes of the Himalayas in *Seven Years in Tibet* (1997). Or it may include objects and settings constructed by art designers to appear fantastic or realistic, such as the cramped spaces within a submarine in *U-571* (2000) **[Color Plate 2]**. In any case, mise-en-scène—a film's places and spaces, people and objects, lights and shadows—is a dimension of our movie experience that we always value but usually take for granted.

The Foundations of Mise-en-Scène

The first movies were literally "scenes." Sometimes they were quaint public or domestic scenes (a baby being fed or a couple kissing); often they were dramatic scenes re-created on a stage for a movie camera. The ancient sites and holy objects seen in *The Passion Play of Oberammergau* (1898) fascinated audiences with their realistic appearance. A mixture of slides and short films, *Old Mexico and Her Pageants* used native scenes and costumes to enliven and illustrate an 1899 lecture. While the first films usually presented what could be accomplished in a one-room studio or a confined outdoor setting, by 1907 mise-en-scène had become more elaborate. Movies like *The Automobile Thieves* (1906) and *On the Stage; or, Melodrama from the Bowery* (1907) began to coordinate two or three interior and exterior settings, using make-up and costumes to create different kinds of characters and exploiting the stage for visual tricks and gags. In D. W. Griffith's monumental *Intolerance* (1916), the sets that reconstructed ancient Babylon and other places in history were, in many ways, the main attraction **[Color Plate 3]**. In this section, we will identify the foundations of mise-en-scène, introduce some of the central terms and concepts underpinning the notion of mise-en-scène, and sketch some of the historical paths associated with the first cinematic use of mise-en-scène, from which were developed cinematic mise-en-scènes throughout the twentieth century.

Settings and Sets

Settings and sets are the most fundamental features of mise-en-scène. The **setting** refers to a fictional or real place where the action and events of the film occur. The **set** is, strictly speaking, a constructed setting, often on a studio soundstage, but both the setting and the set can combine natural and constructed elements. For example, one setting in *Citizen Kane* (1941) is a fictional mansion located in Florida (based on an actual Hearst estate in California), which, in this case, is a set constructed on an RKO soundstage.

Historically and culturally, the kinds and significance of sets and settings have changed with regularity. The first films were made either on stage sets or in outdoor settings, using the natural light from the sun. Films gradually began to integrate both constructed and natural mise-en-scènes into a single movie, where many sets and settings function as important backgrounds for the story. Today's cinematic mise-en-scènes continue to use elaborate stages, such as the studio re-creation of Vietnam battlefields for *Full Metal Jacket* (1987), as well as actual locations, such as the Philadelphia streets and neighborhoods of *The Sixth Sense* (1999). Models and computer enhancements of these mise-en-scènes are increasingly popular for many movies, including the recent *A.I.* (2001), which digitally re-creates a futuristic New York City after it has been destroyed by rising ocean waters **[Color Plate 4]**.

In creating a mise-en-scène for a film, settings and sets can establish scenic realism and scenic atmosphere. One of the most common, complicated, and elusive yardsticks for the cinema, **realism** is the term most viewers use to describe the extent to which a movie creates a truthful picture of a society, person, or some other dimension of life. Realism can refer to psychological or emotional accuracy (in characters), recognizable or logical actions and developments (in a story), or convincing views and perspectives of those characters or events (in the composition of the image). The most prominent vehicle for cinematic realism, however, is the **scenic realism** of the mise-en-scène, which enables us to recognize sets and settings as accurate evocations of actual places. A combination of selection and artifice, scenic realism is most commonly associated with:

- the physical accuracy of the backgrounds, objects, and other figures
- the cultural accuracy of the backgrounds, objects, and other figures
- the historical accuracy of the backgrounds, objects, and other figures

Indeed, our measure of a film's realism is often more a product of the authenticity of this scenic realism than of the other features of the film, such as the psychology or actions of characters. Movies like the animated *Beauty and the Beast* (1991) and the science fiction film *Twelve Monkeys* (1995) dramatize authentic human emotions (the blossoming of an unexpected love in the first and the relentless anxiety of the hunted in the second), but these films would probably not be considered realistic films because of the fantastic nature of their settings in magical castles and futuristic laboratories. Other movies, such as *Michael Collins* (1996), which depicts the Irish revolution at the turn of the century, establish a convincing realism through the physical, historical, and cultural verisimilitude of the sets and settings (in *Michael Collins*, Dublin and the Irish countryside), regardless of how the characters or story may be exaggerated or romanticized **[Figure 2.3]**.

Figure 2.3 *Michael Collins* (1996). The Irish countryside at the turn of the century creates a quiet scenic realism torn apart by equally realistic violence.

Recognition of scenic realism frequently depends, of course, on the historical and cultural point of view of the audience. *Risky Business* (1983), for example, set in an affluent white American suburb of expensive cars and

Figure 2.4 *The Shawshank Redemption* (1994). The close confinement of a prison cell offset with props and pictures of an outside world.

designer homes, may seem realistic to many affluent Americans but would appear as a fantastic other world to farmers living in rural China.

In addition to scenic realism, the mise-en-scène of a film also creates **scenic atmosphere and connotations,** those feelings or meanings associated with particular sets or settings in a film. The setting of a ship on the open seas might suggest danger and adventure; a kitchen set may connote comfortable, domestic feelings. Invariably these connotations are developed through the actions of the character and developments of the larger story: the early kitchen set in *Mildred Pierce* (1945) creates an atmosphere of bright, slightly strained warmth; in *E.T.* (1982), a similar set describes the somewhat chaotic space of a modern, single-parent family; in *The Shawshank Redemption* (1994), Andy's prison cell suggests a stifling confinement but also the signs of hope that predict his eventual escape [Figure 2.4].

A Short History of Mise-en-Scène

Called by some the greatest movie ever made, the French masterpiece *Children of Paradise* (1945) is set in Paris during the 1830s. Opening and closing with the spectacular sets of the Boulevard of Crime (a street named for the violent melodramas staged in the many popular theaters there), the film focuses on a soon-to-be-famous mime, Baptiste, and his love for the vivacious Garance, a woman also loved by Federick, Baptiste's friend and an aspiring Shakespearean actor. Shot almost entirely in studios in Nice and Paris, the constructed sets move between street scenes of romance and crime and the theatrical stages on which many of the characters act out their other passions, with the famous nineteenth-century Theatre des Funambule acting as a centerpiece for much of the drama. A film about one of the grand eras of theater life, *Children of Paradise* is essentially about the complexities of love set within the dramatic changes of its historical mise-en-scène [Figure 2.5].

Figure 2.5 *Children of Paradise* (1945). A film about the theatrics of life.

Like other formal elements of the movies, all cinematic mise-en-scènes are inseparable from their larger history. Indeed, understanding the evolution of mise-en-scène may be especially complicated because it involves the separate histories of painting and costuming; of the construction of social space, from houses to urban planning; and, more recently, of various lighting techniques. Here, we will limit our discussion to the theatrical heritage of mise-en-scène, emphasizing three specific motifs within that history:

- how mise-en-scène maps relations between different parts of society within a larger world or universe
- how mise-en-scène reflects social institutions
- how mise-en-scène describes the possibilities and the limits of human expression, both physical and verbal

The clearest heritage of cinematic mise-en-scène is the theatrical tradition that began with early Greek theater around 500 B.C. and evolved through the nineteenth century. The first stages appeared in and served as places where a community's religious beliefs and truths could be acted out for that community. Centuries later, European medieval theater would celebrate Christian stories as medieval mystery plays in which a small cast of characters would act out, with props or scenery, tales of Adam and Eve or of the shepherds who witnessed the birth of Christ. Both theatrical traditions present the mise-en-scène as a unique place apart from daily existence but open to the world around it, where theatrical figures are larger than life and the objects on stage are both real and symbolic. During the Renaissance of the late sixteenth and early seventeenth centuries, the sets, costumes, and other elements of mise-en-scène (of William Shakespeare's plays, for instance) began to reflect a secular world of politics and personal relationships through which individuals and communities fashioned their values and beliefs [Figure 2.6].

By the beginning of the nineteenth century, lighting and other technological developments rapidly altered the nature of mise-en-scène in ways that began to anticipate the cinema. Spectacular mise-en-scène expanded the pictorial background of plays in ways that often drew attention away from the dramatic action. David Garrick and others began to separate the audience more definitively from the stage and introduced artificial lighting to enforce that separation and highlight scenic sets on stage. In marked contrast to the drawing-room interiors of eighteenth-century mise-en-scène, sets and stages grew much larger; they could now support the sometimes massive panoramic scenery and machinery developed by innovators such as P. J. de Loutherbourg, who created optical scenic illusions that overwhelmed audiences with breathtaking spectacles. At about the same time, groups of interacting actors gave way to single individuals, frequently isolated before a vast scenic world. With this structural change to the stage, there also developed the rising cult of the actor as star (such as British actors Fanny and John Kemble and Ellen Terry) as the necessary center of the mise-en-scène.

As movies developed out of the nineteenth century, the theater would continue to be a central measure of the historical development for cinematic mise-en-scène. Whereas the subjects of the first films were limited by their dependence on natural light, by 1900 indoor stage melodramas became a popular source for filmmakers: *The Downward Path* (1901) was one of the more elaborate sets, using five tableaux converted from the stage play to tell the plight of a country girl who succumbs to the wickedness of the city. A more classical piece of stage drama, the 1904 *Damnation of Faust* was one of many early films that turned to famous playwrights for movie material. In 1912, one of the most famous stage actors of all time, Sarah Bernhardt, appeared in the films *Queen Elizabeth* and *La Dame aux Camélias*. Encouraging this theatrical direction in mise-en-scène in these early years was the implementation around 1906 of **mercury-vapor lamps** and **indoor lighting systems,** innovations that quickly encouraged experiments with lighting to shade and highlight action in a film.

Figure 2.6 *Henry V* (1944). Recreating the Shakespearean stage of the Globe Theatre.

Sets and Settings in
Meet Me in St. Louis (1944)

Vincente Minnelli's *Meet Me in St. Louis* is a frolicking musical that, in one sense, is about settings and sets: it foregrounds many of the elements of mise-en-scène that may appear less visibly in other movies. The setting is St. Louis in 1903, as the city prepares to host a World's Fair. Within this setting, the film concentrates on a family's large Victorian house whose elaborate stairways, porches, and parlors are the sets that contain most of the film's action. The narrative describes the family harmony of four siblings, their parents, a jovial cook, and a grandfather, and then follows the various crises precipitated when romances disturb this tranquility and the father's career threatens to move them all to New York City. The setting and sets for these actions become the film's center and its stabilizing context: the palpable hominess of the kitchen stove and pots, the comfortable chair that anchors the father, and the spaciously elaborate entryway and oak staircase that signal Victorian solidity and financial comfort.

Figure 2.7 *Meet Me in St. Louis* (1944). Tootie knocks the head off one of her family of snow people.

More so than many films, *Meet Me in St. Louis* creates a special self-consciousness about the importance of sets. During a party, for example, the parlor becomes an impromptu set for staging musical performances. Here Esther (played by Judy Garland) and her sisters and brother perform for their guests, and the creation of this stage in the home represents a way of bonding people through the entertainment value of a set. Later, when the family seems about to leave for New York, Tootie, the youngest sister, visits the staged scene of snow people she has built on the lawn. It is a family—snowmen, -women, and -children set in the yard outside the house. For Tootie, this set probably represents the harmony of her own family, but in her anger at the impending departure from St. Louis, she smashes and destroys the figures [**Figure 2.7**]. In both scenes, *Meet Me in St. Louis* underlines how important sets and settings are to the meaning of the characters' lives and the themes of the film.

However accurate they are in fact, the sets of *Meet Me in St. Louis* aim at historical and scenic realism. Besides the architecture of the house and

Elaborately constructed sets, carefully designed costumes, and the centrality of actors would define filmic mise-en-scène from early films like *Cabiria* (1914) and *Intolerance* to elaborate musicals like *Chicago* (2002). By 1915, **art directors** or **set designers,** those individuals responsible for supervising the conception and construction of movie sets, became an integral and important part of filmmaking (although in those early years, they were "technical directors" doing "interior decoration"). With the develop-the costumes of the characters, one set stands out: the trolley car. It creates the illusion of a set in motion and, at the turn of the century, was one of the many remarkable new mechanical and technological progressions in the history of cities. As the site of budding love and adolescent excitement, the crowded, clanging trolley suggests that the place of American progress can also easily accommodate the energy of young love.

Through its historical setting in 1903, *Meet Me in St. Louis* calls attention to the inherited history of mise-en-scène as a way of mapping different community relationships, of reflecting social institutions, and of measuring the powers of individuals to interact with their world—of creating, in short, certain scenic atmospheres and connotations. As a geographical place, St. Louis suggests the center of the United States, and the affluence of the house sets are, with unmistakable nostalgia, meant to connote the middle-class midwestern-America at the turn of the century. The film's location in the middle of the country also comes to represent a global centrality: as one character remarks during the opening of the World's Fair there, St. Louis has now become the center of the world. This movie, made in 1944, when Americans were spread around the world fighting World War II, is about the United States and the enduring institutions of the American mise-en-scène.

Within this setting, the splendor of the house serves to represent the institutional magnificence of the family, a large and varied family that, in this case, corresponds to the many rooms that act as a fluid set through which the characters, mostly women, sing, dance, cry, and love each other. Indeed, *Meet Me in St. Louis* is most intriguing as it weaves a group of confined, melodramatic mise-en-scènes (the rooms within the house) until they eventually open out as a spectacular mise-en-scène (at the harmonious gathering at the World's Fair). Between these two kinds of scenes, the female characters of the film learn, above all else, how to take control of their situations, to overcome fear, to act on desires—to, in short, stage their world to serve their emotions and needs. Esther's initial flirtation with John, for example, begins with her conscious and careful orchestration of mise-en-scène. After a party, she asks him to help extinguish the gas lamps in the foyer of the home, and as she moves him around the set, from lamp to lamp, she brings a new romance to light **[Figure 2.8]**.

Figure 2.8 *Meet Me in St. Louis* (1944). Esther setting the scene for romance.

Accordingly, the concluding mise-en-scène at the World's Fair becomes a marvelous spectacle that, in terms of the narrative, rewards the family for staying put in St. Louis with a stupendous light show and theatrical display of buildings, restaurants, and monuments. As all the characters rejoice, the setting of St. Louis now becomes, through the global connotations of this glowing World's Fair set, the figurative center of the world **[Color Plate 5]**.

ment and growth of various studio systems through the 1920s (both in Hollywood and Europe), **soundstages**—large soundproofed buildings designed to construct and move sets and props with a new efficiency—added to the rapid expansion of the movie industry. Evident in movies as diverse and historically distant as the futuristic film *Metropolis* (1926), constructed on the soundstage of the German Ufa studios, and *The Gangs of New York* (2002), which utilized the Italian Cinecittà studios, soundstages offer filmmakers the power to shape and control the mise-en-scène more precisely in supporting and expanding the themes of the film. As the movie business expanded through the 1930s, **costume designers,** who plan and prepare how actors will be dressed for parts, also played an increasingly larger role in films, assuring sometimes splendor and sometimes historical accuracy in the appearances of characters. Indeed, for those films in which costumes become central to the story—films about disguises or historical eras, for instance—one could argue that the achievement of the film becomes inseparable from the decisions about costuming.

In the 1930s and 1940s, when cinematic realism became a higher priority for many films, exterior spaces and actual places—identifiable neighborhoods and recognizable cultural sites—appeared more often as the primary mise-en-scène of many films. From Italian neorealist films (see p. 371) through the rise of contemporary documentary filmmaking, **location scouting** then determined places that would work as the most suitable mise-en-scène for different movie scenes. At this historical juncture the confines of a theatrical mise-en-scène opened more and more onto realistic sets and settings. Indeed, few films more explicitly demonstrate this transformation within the history of mise-en-scène than Laurence Olivier's 1944 *Henry V,* where the drama shifts from the stage of Shakespeare's Globe Theatre to the comparatively realistic sets of ships leaving for war in France **[Color Plate 6]**. In recent decades, the cinematic task of re-creating those realistic environments and mise-en-scène locations has shifted to computerized models, which become the location builders for many modern mise-en-scènes, and **computer-graphics technicians,** who design the models to be digitally transferred onto film.

If we recognize actors as one of the central features of mise-en-scène, the selection and identification of the most suitable actors for a film has been one of the most overlooked but important historical features of mise-en-scène since 1915. **Casting directors,** those who identify which actors would work best in particular roles, followed the advent of the star system around 1910—when the exceedingly popular "Biograph Girl," Florence Lawrence, first demanded to be named and given a screen credit—and be-

VIEWING CUES: Sets/Settings

- Describe, with as much detail as possible, one of the sets or settings in the next movie you watch for class. Other than the actors, which features of the film seem most important? Explain why.

- Examine the interaction of two important sets or settings in the film. What is their relationship? Does that interaction suggest important themes in the film?

- Consider the scenic connotations created by one of the most important sets or settings. Are there atmospheric or other suggestions attached to these sets that help you understand the scene in important ways?

- How do the sets or settings add to or detract from the realism of the film? What are the most conspicuous signs of that realism? Or, if the sets and settings seem fake, what most signals that artificiality? How does the realism of the mise-en-scène play a part in your understanding of the film?

- Can you identify any historical precedents for the primary mise-en-scène of this film? A specific kind of theater? A cityscape? An architectural style?

came bigger and bigger players in the determination of this dimension of mise-en-scène. **Agents** (and, today, so-called "super agents"), who negotiate roles for actors with a casting director or filmmaker, have often taken over this function, as they negotiate parts for stars and other actors. Since the 1970s, these super agents, such as Michael Ovitz during his time at Creative Artist Association in the mid-1970s, sometimes predetermine a package of stars and other personnel from which the film and its mise-en-scène must be constructed.

Throughout the twentieth century, the history of filmic mise-en-scène has included real and constructed locations around the world, movies mainly about costumes, and sets and scenes fabricated through computer technologies. Like the spectacular sets of crowded boulevards and the closeted balconies where lovers are reunited in *Children of Paradise*, movies build scenes of all shapes and sizes, mapping the places we live and our physical powers in those places.

The Elements of Mise-en-Scène: Props, Actors, Costumes, and Lights

Unlike other dimensions of film form such as editing and sound, mise-en-scène was in place with the first films. The early decades of film history were explorations in how to best use the materials of mise-en-scène. By 1906, mercury-vapor lamps for indoor lighting added new possibilities to the mise-en-scène, in that lighting could now be manipulated with the same flexibility as furniture and sets. Eventually, as in *Titanic* (1997), movies would travel the globe and search the seas for settings; set builders turned into computer model makers; and costuming became not only more elaborate but also obsessed with the historical accuracy of dresses, shoes, and even buttons. Here we will examine the multiple physical objects and figures that speak through cinematic mise-en-scène.

Props

Props (short for *property*) are objects that function as parts of the sets or as tools used by the actors. Props acquire special significance when they are used to express characters' thoughts and feelings, their powers and abilities in the world, or even the primary themes of the film. In *Singin' in the Rain* (1952), when Gene Kelly transforms an ordinary umbrella into a gleeful expression of his new love, an object whose normal function is to protect a person from rain becomes better used as an extension of a dance: the pouring rain makes little difference to a man in love [Color Plate 7]. In Alfred Hitchcock's *Suspicion* (1941), an ordinary glass of milk, brought to a woman who suspects her husband of murder, suddenly crystallizes the film's unsettling theme of malice hiding in the shape of innocence; in his *Spellbound* (1940), parallel lines in the pattern of a bathrobe trigger a psychotic reaction in the protagonist John Ballantine, and in this film too a glass of milk suddenly appears ominous and threatening [Figure 2.9]. Even natural objects or creatures can become props that concentrate the meanings of a

Figure 2.9 *Spellbound* (1940). An ordinary but ominous glass of milk.

movie: in the 1997 Japanese film *The Eel*, the main character's bond with the eel becomes the vehicle for his poignant redemption from despair about human society.

Props appear in movies in two principal forms. **Instrumental props** are those objects displayed and used according to their common function. **Metaphorical props** are those same objects reinvented or employed for an unexpected, even magical, purpose, like Gene Kelly's umbrella, or invested with metaphorical meaning. The distinction is important because the type of prop can characterize the kind of world surrounding the characters and the ability of those characters to interact with that world. In *Babette's Feast* (1987), a movie about the joys of cooking in a small Danish village, a knife functions as an instrumental prop for preparing foods; in *Psycho* (1960) that same prop is transformed into a hideous murder weapon. *The Red Shoes* (1948) might be considered a film about the shifting status of a prop, red dancing slippers: at first these shoes appear as an instrumental prop serving Victoria's rise as a great ballerina, but by the conclusion of the film they have been transformed into a darkly magical prop that dances the heroine to her death **[Color Plate 8]**.

In addition to their function within a film, props may acquire significance in two prominent ways. **Cultural props,** such as a type of car or a piece of furniture, carry meanings associated with their place in a particular society. The hero of *The Love Bug* (1969) drives a tiny Volkswagen Bug and the comedy revolves around the commonplace associations with this inexpensive and youthful car model and its remarkable magical powers; in *Easy Rider* (1969), the two protagonists ride low-slung motorcycles that clearly suggest a countercultural rebellion **[Color Plate 9]**. **Contextualized props** acquire a meaning through their changing place in a narrative. *The Yellow Rolls-Royce* (1964) and *The Red Violin* (1998) focus fully on the changing meaning of the central prop: in the first film, three different romances are linked through their connection to a beautiful Rolls-Royce; the second film follows the path of a Nicolo Bussotti violin from seventeenth-century Italy, to an eighteenth-century Austrian monastery, to nineteenth-century Oxford, to the Chinese cultural revolution in the twentieth century, and finally to a contemporary

Figure 2.10 *The Red Violin* (1998). The changing significance of a contextualized prop.

Montreal shop **[Figure 2.10]**. Some films play specifically with the meaning a contextual prop comes to acquire. In *Ronin* (1998), a mysterious briefcase unites a group of mercenaries in a plot about trust and betrayal, but its secret significance becomes ultimately insignificant; Alfred Hitchcock's famous "McGuffins"—props that only appear to be important, like the stolen money in *Psycho* and the uranium in *Notorious* (1946)—are props meant to move a plot forward but are of little importance to the real drama of love, fear, and desire.

Staging: Performance and Blocking

At the center of most mise-en-scènes is a flesh-and-blood **actor** who embodies and performs a film character through gestures and movements. Occupying a borderline region of the mise-en-scène, **performance** describes the actor's use of language, physical expression, and gesture to bring a character to life and to communicate important dimensions of that character to the audience. Because characters help us see and understand the actions and world of film and because performance is an interpretation of that character by an actor, many films are made or broken by an actor's performance. In a film like *Kind Hearts and Coronets* (1949), in which Alec Guinness plays eight different roles, the shifting performances of the actor may be its greatest achievement.

In a performance, we can distinguish two primary elements: **voice,** which includes the natural sound of an actor's voice along with the various intonations or accents he or she may create for a particular role, and **bodily movement,** which includes physical gestures and, especially important to the movies, eye movements and eye contact. (As in many elements of mise-en-scène, these two features of performance also rely on other dimensions of film form such as sound and camera positions.) Woody Allen has made a career of developing characters through the performance of a strident, panicky voice and bodily and eye movements that dart in uncoordinated directions. At the heart of such movies as *The Blue Angel* (1930) and *Shanghai Express* (1932) is Marlene Dietrich's sultry voice, drooping eyes, and languid body poses and gestures **[Figure 2.11]**.

Figure 2.11 *The Blue Angel* (1930). The body and eyes of Marlene Dietrich.

Additionally, different acting styles define performances. With **stylized acting,** an actor employs emphatic and highly stylized gestures or speaks in pronounced tones with elevated diction; the actor seems fully aware that he or she is acting and addressing an audience. Much less evident today, these stylized performances can be seen in the work of Lillian Gish in *Broken Blossoms* (1919), in Joel Grey's role as the master of ceremonies in *Cabaret* (1972) **[Figure 2.12]**, and in virtually any Monty Python movie. More influential since the 1940s, **naturalistic acting** asks an actor to fully and naturally embody the role that he or she is playing in order to communicate that character's essential self. Sometimes associated with a practice called "Method acting," it is famously demonstrated by Marlon Brando as Stanley in *A Streetcar Named Desire* (1951), a role in which the actor and character seem almost indistinguishable **[Figure 2.13]**.

Figure 2.12 *Cabaret* (1972). Joel Grey's stylized performance.

As part of the usual distribution of actors through mise-en-scène, **leading actors**—the two or three actors who appear most often in a film—play the central characters. Recognizable actors associated with particular character types or minor parts are sometimes referred to as **character actors.** They usually appear as secondary characters playing sinister or humorous roles, such as the bumbling cook in a western. **Supporting actors** play secondary characters in a film, serving as foils or companions to the central characters. Supporting actors and character actors add to the complexity of how we become involved in the action or pinpoint a movie's themes. In the hands of a strong actor, such as James Earl Jones in a supporting role in *Field of Dreams* (1989) or Robin Williams as the encouraging professor in *Good Will Hunting* (1997), these supporting

Figure 2.13 *A Streetcar Named Desire* (1951). Marlon Brando becomes Stanley.

Figure 2.14 *Field of Dreams* (1989). James Earl Jones as Terence Mann, the supporting character with opportunities unavailable to the protagonist.

roles frequently balance our perspective on the main characters, perhaps requiring us to rethink what the main character means and what distinguishes him or her. In *Field of Dreams*, the writer that Jones plays, Terence Mann, fulfills his fantasy of joining the baseball game that the lead actor Kevin Costner's character does not choose to enter because of a more important commitment to his family **[Figure 2.14]**.

The leading actors in many mise-en-scènes are, of course, **stars**—those individuals who, because of their cultural celebrity, bring a powerful aura to their performance, making them the focal points in the mise-en-scène. Unlike less famous actors, star performers

- center and often dominate the action and space of a mise-en-scène
- bring the accumulated history and significance of their past performances to each new film appearance
- acquire a status that transforms their individual physical reality into more abstract or mythical qualities, combining the ordinary and extraordinary

The star's performance focuses the action of the mise-en-scène and draws attention to important events and themes in the film. In *Casablanca* (1942), there are a multitude of individual dramas about different characters trying to escape Casablanca, but Humphrey Bogart's (as the character Rick Blaine) is, in an important sense, the only story: the many other stories become more or less important only as they become part of his life. In *The Bridges of Madison County* (1995), the story of a male photographer and a female immigrant who meet and fall in love in the isolated farmlands of Iowa, there are no characters other than the stars Clint Eastwood and Meryl Streep for most of the film, which tends to intensify the story by further emphasizing the focus on them. In a way, this film becomes the story of two stars creating an exclusive world of two people bracketed off from other lives and characters **[Figure 2.15]**.

Figure 2.15 *The Bridges of Madison County* (1995). A film about two star performances.

Moreover, in both those films, much of the power of the characters is a consequence of the star status of the actors, recognized and comprehended in relation to their other roles in other films—and in some cases, in relation to a life off the screen. Recognizing and identifying with Rick in *Casablanca* implies, especially for viewers in the 1940s, a recognition on some level that Rick is more than Rick, that this star-character in *Casablanca* is an extension of characters Bogart has portrayed in such films as *High Sierra* (1941) and *The Maltese Falcon* (1941). A similar measuring takes place as we watch Eastwood and Streep. With Streep especially, her performance in *The Bridges of Madison County* is remarkable because it is so unlike the characters she plays in *Sophie's Choice* (1982) and *Out of Africa* (1985); part of our appreciation and understanding of her role is the performative skill and range she embodies as a star. We understand these characters as an extension of and departure from other characters associated with the star.

As a result of this extended presence, stars acquire a mythical power whereby we understand and expect from their characters larger-than-life accomplishments and abilities. Star-performers are capable of astonishing acts of intelligence and physical or emotional strength; they can commit acts of kindness and acts of evil that typical individuals would be incapable of. Rick is nobler than the usual individual, more compassionate, braver, and ultimately able to sacrifice his merely human tendencies to the grander, mythical self that closes the film. Because he is a star, we accept Robin Williams in *Dead Poets Society* (1989) as both wittier and probably more passionate than the average high-school English teacher; in *It Happened One Night* (1934), we expect Clark Gable to be far more charming and self-confident than a regular reporter would be. Certainly this mythic stature is part of what drives us to identify desires and dreams with stars; it also allows movies to engage in particular confrontations with a viewer's expectations, such as when a film turns on stars' mythical immortality: in *Psycho*, star Janet Leigh is unexpectedly killed halfway through the movie; in *Arlington Road* (1999), the protagonist Jeff Bridges does not, as we expect, survive.

The meaning and importance of stars is only part of the process through which we come to comprehend films. Sometimes we come to films without knowledge of a featured star. Or a film may depart from this way of watching a movie by not featuring any stars or by featuring stars from another film culture, such as the French actor Juliette Binoche in the film *Chocolat* (2000). Some movies, such as Robert Altman's *Nashville* (1975), may populate the story with an ensemble of supporting actors rather than one or two stars. The result is a movie that is not so much a story as it is a collage of different episodes that parodies our desire for stars in the movies. In François Truffaut's *The 400 Blows* (1959), a then-unknown actor, Jean-Pierre Léaud, plays the main character, Antoine Doinel, and the innocence of the young actor matches perfectly with the story of a growing boy who must struggle to find an identity on the streets of Paris [**Figure 2.16**]. (Truffaut would continue the relationship between Léaud and Doinel through a series of films that matches the growth of the character with the growth of the actor.)

Whatever the status of the actor, mise-en-scène usually highlights **performative development:** changes in a character described through an

Figure 2.16 *The 400 Blows* (1959). An unknown Jean-Pierre Léaud (*right*) grows into his role.

actor's performance. An actor's performative development may take place from one movie to another or it may occur within the same movie. We may remark on how an actor changes or develops his or her performative style over the course of several movies as a way of understanding each different character. Alternatively, we may note how one performance allows us to comprehend the development of a character through one movie. Katharine Hepburn's many performances had developed a spectrum of characters, from *Stage Door* (1937) through *Long Day's Journey into Night* (1962); this stylistic flexibility in her acting allowed her to depict a host of personalities, from the saucy rebel to the weary, drug-addicted mother, a performative range that potentially comes into play in our expectations when we watch any of her roles. In a single film, *On Golden Pond* (1981), a sharp viewer may map Hepburn's development of several of these performative skills: her role as the aging wife of a lonely, confused man communicates, through the changing carriage of her body and facial expressions, a struggle to maintain the strength of a once-youthful rebel despite her own weariness **[Color Plate 10]**.

Actors are frequently cast for parts precisely because of their association with certain **character types** (see p. 227) that they seem especially suited to portray because of their physical features, acting style, or previous roles. Bogart often plays hard-boiled detectives, while Marilyn Monroe reappears in films as the sexy and seductive single woman. To appreciate and understand a character can consequently mean recognizing this intersection of a type and an actor's interpretation or transformation of it. Arnold Schwarzenegger's large and muscular physical stature and clipped, stiff acting style suit well the characters he plays in *The Terminator* (1984) and *Total Recall* (1990), but in *Kindergarten Cop* (1990) his performance and character become more interesting precisely because he must develop that performance type in the role of a kindergarten teacher.

Figure 2.17 *Little Women* (1994). Blocking the family tightly around the father.

Blocking refers to the arrangement and movement of actors in relation to each other within the single physical space of a mise-en-scène. **Social blocking** describes the arrangement of characters to accentuate relations between them. In *Little Women* (1994), family and friends gather around the wounded father who has just returned from the Civil War, suggesting the importance of the familial bonds at the center of this society **[Figure 2.17]**. **Graphic blocking** arranges characters or groups according to visual patterns to portray spatial harmony, tension, or some other visual atmosphere. Fritz Lang, for instance, is renowned for his blocking of crowd scenes: in *Metropolis* (1926), the oppression of individuality appears instantly in the mechanical movements of rectangles of marching workers **[Figure 2.18]**; in *Fury* (1936), a mob lynching in a small town creates graphic-blocked patterns whose directional arrow suggests a kind of dark fate moving against the lone individual.

Figure 2.18 *Metropolis* (1926). Rectangular masses of futuristic workers.

Costumes and Make-Up

Costumes are the clothing and related accessories that a character wears or that define that character. These can range from common fashions, like a dark suit or dress, to more fantastic costumes. Cosmetics, or **make-up** applied to the actor's face or body, highlight or even disguise or distort certain aspects of the face or body.

How actors are costumed and made up can play a central part in a film as well, describing tensions and changes in the character and the story. Sometimes a character becomes fully identified with one basic look or costume: through his many movie incarnations, James Bond has always appeared in a tuxedo; in *Crocodile Dundee* (1986), the singularity of Paul Hogan in New York City is underlined by his Australian bush hat, rugged clothing, and suntanned skin. Moreover, the dynamic of costuming can be highlighted in a way that makes costuming the center of the movie. *Pygmalion* (1938) and its musical adaptation as *My Fair Lady* (1964) are essentially about a transformation of a girl from the street into an elegant socialite [Color Plate 11]; along with language and diction, that transformation is indexed by the changes of costume and make-up from dirt and rags to diamonds and gowns.

Costumes and make-up function in films in three different ways. First, when costumes and make-up support scenic realism they reproduce, as accurately as possible, the clothing and facial features of people living in a specific time and place. Thus, Napoleon's famous hat and jacket, pallid skin, and lock of hair across his brow are a standard costume and the basic make-up for the many films featuring this character from Abel Gance's 1927 *Napoléon* to Sacha Guitry's 1955 *Napoleon*. Second, when make-up and costumes function as **character highlights,** they draw out or point to important parts of a character's personality. Often these highlights are subtle, such as the ascot a pretentious visitor wears; sometimes they are pronounced, as when villains in silent films wear black hats and twirl their moustaches. In Fellini's *Casanova* (1976), the title character wears thick white make-up and dresses in ornate, theatrical outfits to suggest the decadent and excessive nature of his character. In Fellini's *Roma* (1972), an autobiograhical panorama of the title city becomes a bombastic fashion show peopled by the fantasy characters and memories of childhood [Color Plate 12]. Finally, when costumes and make-up act as **narrative markers,** their change or lack of change becomes a crucial way to understand and follow a character and the development of the story. Often a film, such as *Citizen Kane* or *The Age of Innocence* (1993), develops through the aging face of the protagonist, gradually whitened and lined, and changing styles of clothing, appearing more modern, as the story advances. In Alan Rudolph's offbeat *Trouble in Mind* (1985), Coop's hairstyles grow increasingly outlandish as he becomes more and more absorbed in the surreal plot. In the adaptation *The Picture of Dorian Gray* (1945), the entire story concentrates on the lack of change in the facial appearance of the protagonist, who has sold his soul for eternal youth.

Costumes and make-up that appear as natural or realistic in films carry important cultural connotations as well. In *Rocky* (1976), the title character dresses to reflect his working-class background in South Philadelphia, and his somewhat clownish hat particularly accentuates his bumbling but likeable personality [Figure 2.19]. When Rocky boxes in the championship fight, however, he becomes

Figure 2.19 *Rocky* (1976). The hats and jackets of South Philadelphia.

a bare and powerful form whose simple trunks and cape contrast with the glitzy costumes of his opponent. As the bout progresses, facial make-up exaggerates the gruesome violence of the fight, yet he continues to deliver his lines with an almost humble dignity and determination. After he has fought for the championship, his plain girlfriend in nerdy eyeglasses becomes more attractive through the power of make-up and costuming.

Lighting

One of the most subtle and important dimensions of mise-en-scène is **lighting.** Our daily experiences outside the movies demonstrate how lighting can affect our perspective on a person or thing, as when a room hidden in dark shadows evokes feelings of fear, while the same room brightly lit suggests warmth and comfort. *Mise-en-scène lighting* refers specifically to light sources—both natural light and electrical lamps—located within the scene itself. It is used to shade and accentuate the figures, objects, and spaces of the mise-en-scène, but the primary sources of film lighting are usually not visible onscreen.

The interaction of lighting, sets, and actors can create its own drama within a specific mise-en-scène. How a character moves through light or how the lighting on the character changes within a single mise-en-scène can signal important information about the character and story. In *Back to the Future* (1985), the suddenly illuminated face of Marty McFly, from an unseen source, signals a moment of revelation about the mysteries of time travel. More complexly in *Citizen Kane,* the regular movement of characters, particularly of Kane, from shadow to light and then back to shadow might suggest Kane's moral instability.

A mise-en-scène can use both natural and directional lighting. **Natural lighting** usually assumes an incidental role in a scene; it derives from a natural source in a scene or setting, such as the illumination of the daylight sun or the lamps of a room. Spread across a set before more specific lighting emphases are added, **set lighting** distributes an evenly diffused illumination through a scene as a kind of lighting base. **Directional lighting** is more dramatically apparent; it may create the impression of a natural light source but actually directs light in ways that define and shape the object or person being illuminated. As illustrated in the accompanying scenes from *Sweet Smell of Success* (1957) **[Figures 2.20–2.26]**, the lighting used in mise-en-scène has developed an even more specific technical grammar to designate its variety of strategies:

Figure 2.20A *Sweet Smell of Success* (1957). High-key lighting in the glare of a city coffee shop.

Figure 2.20B Low-key lighting creates the shadowy atmosphere of a sexual encounter.

Figure 2.21A *Sweet Smell of Success* (1957). Fill lighting works to emphasize, naturally, Sidney Falco in a moment of crisis.

Figure 2.21B A dramatic use of fill lighting isolates the face of J. J. Hunsecker and, to a slightly lesser extent, Sidney Falco.

Figure 2.22 *Sweet Smell of Success* (1957). Subtle highlighting (along with the low angle of the camera) dramatizes the powerful figure of J. J. Hunsecker.

Figure 2.23 *Sweet Smell of Success* (1957). The backlighting of Frank and Sidney as they enter Rita's apartment.

- **Key lighting** is the main source of lighting from a lamp; it may be bright with few contrasts (or "high") or shadowy with sharp contrasts between light and dark (or "low"), depending on the ratio of key to fill lighting and the effect desired **[Figures 2.20A and B]**.
- **Fill lighting** can be used to balance the key lighting or to emphasize other spaces and objects in the scene **[Figures 2.21A and B]**.
- **Highlighting** describes the use of the different lighting sources to emphasize certain characters or objects or to charge them with special significance **[Figure 2.22]**.
- **Backlighting** (sometimes called **edgelighting**) is a highlighting technique that illuminates the person or object from behind; it tends to silhouette the subject **[Figure 2.23]**.
- **Three-point lighting** combines key lighting, fill lighting, and backlighting to blend naturally the distribution of light in a scene **[Figure 2.24]**.
- **Frontal lighting, sidelighting, underlighting,** and **top lighting** are used to illuminate the subject from different directions in order to draw out features or create specific atmospheres around the subject **[Figure 2.25 and 2.26]**.

Figure 2.24 *Sweet Smell of Success* (1957). Three-point lighting blends naturally various parts of the scene.

Figure 2.25 *Sweet Smell of Success* (1957). Sidelighting highlights Frank D'Angelo during his seduction of Rita, the cigarette girl.

Figure 2.26 *Sweet Smell of Success* (1957). Underlighting transforms a policeman into a threatening image.

The effects of lighting in the mise-en-scène range from a **hard** to a **soft** lighting surface that, in conjunction with the narrative and other features of the mise-en-scène, elicit certain responses. **Shading,** the use of shadows to shape or draw attention to certain features, can explain or comment on an object or person in a way the narrative does not. Hard and soft lighting and shading can create a variety of complex effects through highlighting and the play of light and shadow that enlighten viewers in more than one sense. The Italian romance *Enchanted April* (1991) depends on its soft natural lighting, and the shaded eyes of Jake in *Chinatown* (1974) indicate problems with his perspective well before the plot describes them. In a movie like *Barry Lyndon* (1975), the story is conspicuously inseparable from

 VIEWING CUES: Elements of Mise-en-Scène

- For your next assigned film, turn off the sound and analyze a single scene in the movie. What is communicated just through the elements of the mise-en-scène?

- Identify the single most important prop in this film. Why is it significant?

- Distinguish two props: one instrumental and the other metaphorical. Describe how the props reflect certain themes in the film.

- Focus on a central character/actor. How would you describe his or her acting style in the film? Does that style seem compatible with the story?

- If there are stars in this film, describe what you know about each star and the expectations associated with him or her. How does the presence of stars control the mise-en-scène and your understanding of the film? How do they contribute to the meaning of the movie?

- Are there specific scenes in which the blocking is especially important? How?

- How do costuming and make-up play a role in this film? Do they tend to add scenic realism, highlight character, or mark the narrative development? How so? Select a specific example, and make a short argument for why the costuming or make-up is important to understanding the movie.

- Where in the film does lighting dramatically add to a scene? Where does it work less obtrusively but in an equally important way?

From Props to Lighting in *Do the Right Thing* (1989)

In Spike Lee's *Do the Right Thing*, characters wander through the theatrical space of Bedford-Stuyvesant, a multicultural neighborhood in Brooklyn. Here, life becomes a complicated negotiation between private mise-en-scènes (apartments, bedrooms, and businesses) and public mise-en-scènes (city streets and sidewalks crowded with people). With Lee in the role of Mookie, who acts as a thread connecting the different characters, stores, and street corners, the film explores the different needs that clash within a single urban place by featuring a variety of stages—rooms, stores, and restaurants with personal and racial associations. On the hot summer day of this setting, lighting creates an intense and tactile heat, and this sensation of heat makes the mise-en-scène vibrate with energy and frustration.

However much it appears to use a real location, *Do the Right Thing* carefully constructs a setting of interlocking sets. Mother Sister, in her window frame, "sees all" of this highly public place, where interior lives are constantly on display and frequently in conflict when they meet on the street. Walls and windows become especially significant for the sets of this film: DJ Mister Señor Love Daddy's window is a window to the entire neighborhood; a bright-red wall acts as a backdrop for the lounging, fast-talking Sweet Dick Willie and his two pals, who rhetorically perform as if on stage; and other building walls are painted with political slogans ("Dump Koch," "Tawana Told the Truth," and "*Our* Vote Counts"). Most importantly to the plot, the movie's mise-en-scène contains the pizzeria's "wall of fame" where Sal hangs his photos of celebrated Italian Americans.

The central crisis of *Do the Right Thing* turns on the drama of instrumental props that become loaded with cultural meanings and metaphorical powers. Early in the film, Smiley holds up a photograph of Martin Luther King Jr. and Malcolm X as a call to fight against racism with both non-violence and violence. Shortly after, Da Mayor nearly instigates a fight because the Korean grocer has not stocked a can of his favorite beer, Miller High Life. It is the photographs of famous Italians in Sal's pizzeria—photos of Frank Sinatra, Joe DiMaggio, Liza Minnelli, Al Pacino, and others—however, that ignite the film. When Buggin' Out complains that there should be photos of African Americans on that wall because Sal's clientele is all black, Sal angrily responds that he can decorate the walls of his pizzeria however he wishes. Later, when Radio Raheem refuses to turn down his boom box (an object that has become synonymous with who he is), he and Buggin' Out confront Sal with the cultural significance of the photo-props and their social rights within this mise-en-scène: why, they demand, are there no photographs of African Americans on the wall **[Color Plate 13]**? Finally, at the climactic moment in the film, Mookie tosses a garbage can through the window of the pizzeria, sparking the store's destruction but saving the lives of Sal and his son.

The film's performances mobilize faces and bodies as active forces in the mise-en-scène. Rather than two or three star performers, *Do the Right*

Thing features numerous supporting roles: Ossie Davis as Da Mayor, John Turturro as Pino, Rosie Perez as Tina, Danny Aiello as Sal, Richard Edson as Vito, and Giancarlo Esposito as Buggin' Out, to name a few. Although they appear to work in a naturalistic style that accurately re-creates realistic figures from the streets of Brooklyn, the people in this neighborhood must constantly and consciously perform for each other in order to communicate and establish their identities. This leads to the often exaggerated stylized acting found in the gestures and grimaces of Turturro's portrayal of an angry Italian son and in Esposito's theatrical movements, declamatory speeches, and wild eyes as his character tries to provoke actions.

Lee's performance as Mookie is certainly the central role, one that draws on his then-emerging status as a star actor and a star filmmaker (a combination found in the work of such other director-actors as Clint Eastwood, Woody Allen, and Vincent Gallo). In fact, this double status as star and director indicates clearly that what happens in this mise-en-scène is about him. Physically unimposing, restrained, and cautious throughout the film, Lee's performance seems to shift and adjust depending on the character he is responding to: he is confrontational with Pino, defensive with Tina, and generous with the stuttering Smiley, for example. As the central performer in a neighborhood of performers, Lee's Mookie is a chameleon, surviving by continually changing his persona to fit the social scene he is in. By the end of the film, however, Mookie must decide which performance will be the real self he brings to the mise-en-scène—how, that is, he will "act" in a time of crisis by taking responsibility for the role he is acting.

Do the Right Thing features costumes that reflect the styles of dress in U.S. cities in the 1980s, and make-up that intends to suggest natural faces, thus adding to the scenic realism of the film. Yet their significance exceeds scenic realism because the costumes both highlight characters and mark the movie's narrative development. Da Mayor's dirty, rumpled suit contrasts sharply with the costumes that define the personalities of younger characters, such as Mookie's Brooklyn Dodgers shirt with the name and number of the legendary African American baseball player Jackie Robinson on the back [Figure 2.27], and Pino's white, sleeveless tee-shirt with its white working-class connotations. Jade, Mookie's sister, stands out in her dramatic hats, skirts, earrings, and noticeably more elegant make-up and hairstyles, calling attention perhaps to the individuality and creativity that allow her, uniquely here, to casually cross racial lines.

Two other examples in *Do the Right Thing* underline the cultural and political force of costuming. When a white man on a bicycle accidentally runs over Buggin' Out's Air Jordan sneakers, his apology doesn't sufficiently counter the effect of his Boston Celtics tee-shirt featuring the name of its white star-player, Larry Byrd, and the incident nearly results in a violent conflict. Besides the cultural play of clothing in instances like this one, among the more complicated pieces of costuming is Radio Raheem's hand jewelry, huge "love" and "hate" rings that recall *The Night of the Hunter* (1955), in which the central antagonist has those words tattooed on his knuckles. Among other resonances, Radio Raheem's rings transform the mysterious and psychotic connotations of the earlier movie into an explicit political message, akin to the opposing ideologies personified by Martin Luther King Jr. and Malcolm X.

Figure 2.27 *Do the Right Thing* (1989). Mookie in the heritage of Jackie Robinson.

Both social and geometrical blockings become dramatic calculators in a film explicitly about the "block" and the arrangement of people in this neighborhood. Mother Sister sits in her window looking down at Da Mayor on the sidewalk, suggesting her dominance over and distance from the confusion in the street. In one scene, Pino, Vito, and Mookie stand tensely apart in a corner of the pizzeria as Mookie calls on Vito to denounce his brother's behavior and Pino counters with a call for family ties; their bodies are quietly hostile and territorial simply in their arrangement and their movements around the counter that separates them. This orchestration of bodies climaxes in the final showdown at Sal's pizzeria. When Buggin' Out and Radio Raheem enter the pizzeria, the screaming begins with Sal behind the counter, while Mookie, Pino, Vito, and the group of kids shout from different places in the room. When the fight begins, the bodies collapse on each other and spill onto the street as a mass of undistinguishable faces. After the arrival of the police and the killing of Radio Raheem, the placement of his body creates a sharp line between Mookie and Sal and his sons on one side and the growing crowd of furious blacks and Latinos on the other. Within this blocking Mookie suddenly moves from his side of the line to the other and then calmly retrieves the garbage can to throw through the window. The riot that follows is a direct consequence of Mookie's decisions about where to position himself and how to shatter the blocked mise-en-scène that divides Sal's space from the mob.

Do the Right Thing employs an array of lighting techniques that at first may seem naturalistic but through the course of the film are directional in particularly dramatic ways. Especially through the lighting, heat becomes a palpable feature of this mise-en-scène. From the beginning, the film juxtaposes the harsh, full glare of the streets with the soft morning light that highlights the interior spaces of DJ Mister Señor Love Daddy's radio station, where he announces a heat wave for the coming day, and the bedroom where Da Mayor awakens with Mother Sister. Here, the lighting of the interior mise-en-scène emphasizes the rich and blending shades of the dark skin of the African American characters, while the bright, hard lighting of the exterior spaces draws out the sharp distinctions in the skin colors of blacks, whites, and Asians. This high-key lighting of exteriors, in turn, accentuates the color of the objects and props in the mise-en-scène as a way of sharply isolating them in the scene: for example, the blues of the police uniforms and cars, the yellows of the fruits in the Korean market, and the reds of the steps and walls of the neighborhood [Color Plate 14].

Other uses of lighting in the film are more specifically dramatic and complex. For example, the dramatic backlighting of Mookie, as he climbs the stairs to deliver the pizza, adds an almost religious and certainly heroic/romantic effect to the pizza delivery. When Pino confronts Vito in the storage room, the scene is highlighted by an overhead light that swings back and forth, creating a rocking and turbulent visual effect. In the final scene, Mookie walks home to his son on a street sharply divided between the bright, glaring light on one side and the dark shadows on the other.

More charged with the politics of mise-en-scène than many films, *Do the Right Thing* turns a relatively small city space into an electrified set where props, actors, costumes, and lighting create a remarkably dense, jagged, and mobile environment. Here, the elements of mise-en-scène are always theatrically and politically in play, always about the spatial construction of culture in a specific time and place. To live here, people need to assume, as Mookie eventually does, the powers and responsibilities of knowing how and when to act.

the lighting techniques that illuminate it: extraordinarily low and soft lighting, with sharp frontal light and little fill light on the faces, creates an artificial intensity in the expressions of the characters, whose social desperation hides their ethical emptiness [Color Plate 15]. One particular version of this play of light is referred to as **chiaroscuro lighting,** a pictorial arrangement of light and dark that can create the uneasy atmospheres found in German expressionist films such as Paul Wegener's 1920 tale of magic and supernatural creatures, *The Golem.*

None of the elements of mise-en-scène—from props to acting to lighting—can be assigned standard meanings because they are always subject to how individual films use them. They have also carried different historical and cultural connotations at different times. While the shadowy lighting of German expressionist cinema, as in the 1924 horror film *Waxworks,* may be formally similar to that found in 1950s film noir, such as in *Kiss Me Deadly* (1955), the lighting has a very different significance, reflecting the distinctive perspective of each film and the cultural context that produced it. The metaphoric darkness that surrounds characters like Dracula and Jack the Ripper in the first film suggests a monstrous evil that may also be psychological; in the second, that shadowy atmosphere describes a corruption that is entirely human, a function of brutal greed and sexuality.

Points of View: Values and Traditions of Mise-en-Scène

Whether it presents authentic places or ingeniously fabricates new worlds, mise-en-scène consistently engages audiences. From the miniaturized reenactment of Admiral Dewey's naval victory in *The Battle of Manila Bay* (1898) and Georges Méliès's fantastic stage for *The Man with the Rubber Head* (1901) to the futuristic ductwork of *Brazil* (1985) [Color Plate 16], located "somewhere on the Los Angeles–Belfast border," and the contemporary streets of Tehran in *The Circle* (2000), movie audiences have long prized both the views of real lands and landscapes as well as the sets, props, and costumes created with astonishing verve and style for fantasized worlds.

In this final section, we will describe two prominent sets of values that have been associated with cinematic mise-en-scène since the beginning of film history. We will then sketch two central traditions that have emerged from those values in different ways through different cultures. Whereas we earlier examined the historical foundations and formal strategies of mise-en-scène, in this third context we will argue how those formal elements impart emotional and intellectual values and meanings through a film. For most movie viewers, recognizing the places, objects, and arrangements of sets and settings has never been a formal exercise. The mise-en-scène has always been the site where viewers measure human, aesthetic, and social values, recognize cinematic traditions, and, in those interactions, identify and assign meaning to the changing places of films. In brief, values beget traditions, and traditions become the grounds for meanings.

To Condition and to Measure

The most fundamental value of mise-en-scène is that it defines our location in the material world: the physical settings and objects that surround us indicate our place in the world. Some people can live only in large cities with bright lights and active crowds; others find it important that their town

CULTURAL SPOTLIGHT

Movie Spectaculars

Throughout film history, audiences have often gone to the movies simply to see spectacular places and sights. IMAX theaters, where panoramas of nature and space appear through the extraordinary size and scope of the screen, are the most notable example of movies catering to this thirst for magnificent scenes. But the history of cinema and its use of mise-en-scène abounds with examples of movie spectaculars that aim, first and foremost perhaps, to thrill audiences with sights they have never before seen and can barely imagine.

Movie spectaculars are films in which the magnitude and intricacy of the mise-en-scène share equal emphasis with or even outshine the story, the actors, and other traditional focal points for a movie. Certainly, many kinds of films have employed spectacular sets and settings as part of their narrative, but what distinguishes a movie spectacular is an equal or additional emphasis on the powers of the mise-en-scène to create the meaning of the film or even overwhelm the story. If small art-house films usually concentrate on the complexity of character, imagistic style, and narrative, movie spectaculars attend to the stunning effects of sets, lighting, props, costumes, and casts of thousands.

The history of movie spectaculars extends back to the 1914 Italian film *Cabiria,* an epic about the Second Punic War [**Figure 2.28**], which became a clear inspiration for the making of Griffith's *Intolerance,* with its four historical tales and sensational sets of ancient worlds. Since then, there have been many successful movie spectaculars and many colossal failures. Some of the most notable successes include *Napoléon* (1927), *The Ten Commandments* (1923, 1956), *Metropolis* (1926), *Alexander Nevsky* (1938), *Gone with the Wind* (1939), *The Adventures of Baron Munchausen* (1943, 1989), *Lawrence of Arabia* (1962), *2001: A Space Odyssey* (1968), *Apocalypse Now* (1979), *Gandhi* (1982), *The Last Emperor* (1987), and *Gladiator* (2000).

Movie spectaculars fit squarely into two cultural traditions: that of the sublime and that of the epic. The aesthetic tradition of the sublime has a long history, beginning with the writings of Roman philosopher Longinus and continuing with late eighteenth-

century and nineteenth-century thinkers, poets, and painters—from Immanuel Kant and Edmund Burke to Samuel Taylor Coleridge and J. M. Turner. The sublime usually suggests the power of scenes and places to dizzy (or simply humble) the human mind before their breathtaking size, beauty, or magnificence. Epics, from poetry like John Milton's *Paradise Lost* to novels like Herman Melville's *Moby Dick,* tell heroic tales of nations or spiritual communities and the moments and events that defined them. More often than not, epics are about the importance of cultural place as a large national or spiritual mise-en-scène.

Movie spectaculars often set epic stories about the birth or salvation of communities in a sublime mise-en-scène whose magnitude of place overwhelms and supersedes individual desires and differences. Through the last century, these sublime epics have tended to expand from spectacles of cities (*Metropolis*) to visions of nationhood (*Gone with the Wind*) to the stellar landscapes that surround our globe (*2001: A Space Odyssey*). In all their differences, however, movie spectaculars exploit one of the central traditions of film viewing: the desire to be awed by sublime worlds beyond our normal views.

Figure 2.28 *Cabiria* (1914). In perhaps the first movie spectacular, the eruption of Mount Etna begins the cinematic tradition of mise-en-scènes of disaster.

have a church as the visible center of the community. Much the same holds true for cinematic mise-en-scène in which the place created by the elements of the mise-en-scène becomes the essential condition for the meaning of the characters' lives. As part of this larger cultural context, there are two primary values associated with cinematic mise-en-scène:

1. The mise-en-scène describes the physical conditions and limits of our natural, social, or imaginary worlds.
2. The mise-en-scène measures the ability of individuals and social groups to control and arrange their world in a meaningful way.

On the one hand, mise-en-scène describes the limits of human experience by indicating the external boundaries and contexts in which people live. On the other, it reflects the powers of the characters and groups that inhabit it by showing how people can impact the space in which they live. While the first set of values can be established without characters, the second requires the interaction of characters and mise-en-scène.

Mise-en-scène as an external condition indicates surfaces, objects, and exteriors that define the material possibilities in a place or space. Some mise-en-scènes are magical spaces full of active objects; others are barren landscapes with no borders. In *King Solomon's Mines* (1937) and *The African Queen* (1951), deserts and jungles create a threatening landscape of arid plains and dense foliage, whereas in films like *The Lady Vanishes* (1938) and *The American Friend* (1977), the interior of a train and subways offer long, thin passageways, multiple windows, and strange, anonymous faces where an individual's movements are restricted as the world flies by outside **[Color Plate 17]**. In each case, the mise-en-scène describes the material terms of a film's physical world; from those terms the rest of the scene or even the entire film must develop.

With the second value, **mise-en-scène as a measure of character,** the mise-en-scène dramatizes how an individual or group establishes an identity through interaction with (or control of) the surrounding setting and sets. For Robin Hood, the mise-en-scène of a forest becomes a sympathetic and intimate place where he can achieve justice and find camaraderie; for Little Red Riding Hood, a similar mise-en-scène becomes an environment fraught with unknowable dangers that test her resolve and courage. In *Young Guns* (1988), boyish cowboys find themselves in the freedom and violence of the frontier around them **[Figure 2.29]**. In *Donovan's Brain* (1953), the vision and the personality of a mad scientist is projected and reflected in a laboratory with twisted, mechanized gadgets and wires; essentially, his ability to create new life forms from that environment reflects both his genius and his insane ambitions. In both these interactions, the character and the elements of the mise-en-scène may sometimes determine more about each other's meaning than even the interactions between the characters do.

Keep in mind that our own expectations about the material world inevitably determine how we understand the values of different mise-en-scènes. To modern viewers, the mise-en-scène of *The Gold Rush* (1925) might appear crude and stagy; certainly the make-up and costumes might seem more like circus outfits than realistic clothing. For viewers in the 1920s, however, it is precisely the fantastical and theatrical quality of this

Figure 2.29 *Young Guns* (1988). Where western plains offer the freedom of violent expression.

mise-en-scène that makes it so entertaining: for them, watching the Little Tramp perform his balletic magic in a strange location is more important than the realism of the mise-en-scène.

Two Traditions: Naturalistic and Theatrical Mise-en-Scènes

Cinematic traditions represent historical variations on the implicit values. For cinematic mise-en-scènes, we can identify two prominent traditions, a naturalistic mise-en-scène and a theatrical mise-en-scène. A **naturalistic mise-en-scène** appears natural and recognizable to viewers. A **theatrical mise-en-scène** denaturalizes the locations and other elements of the mise-en-scène so that its features appear unfamiliar, exaggerated, or artificial. Throughout their history, movies have tended to emphasize one or the other of these traditions, although many films have moved smoothly between the two. From *The Birth of a Nation* (1915) to *Amadeus* (1984), settings, costumes, and props have been selected or constructed to appear as authentic as possible in an effort to convince viewers that the filmmakers had a clear window on a true historical place: the first movie re-creates the historical sites and elements of the Civil War, whereas the second reconstructs the physical details of Wolfgang Amadeus Mozart's life in eighteenth-century Europe. In other films, from *The Cabinet of Dr. Caligari* (1919) to *Edward Scissorhands* (1990), those same elements of mise-en-scène have exaggerated or transformed reality as most people know it: *Caligari* uses sets painted with twisted buildings and nightmarish backgrounds, while *Edward Scissorhands's* colorful suburban landscape erupts with the strange sculptures carved by a boy with scissors for hands.

Naturalism is one of the most effective and most misleading ways to approach mise-en-scène. If a mise-en-scène is about the arrangement of space and the objects in it, as we have suggested, then naturalism in the mise-en-scène means that how a place looks is the way it is supposed to look. We can, in fact, pinpoint several more precise characteristics of a naturalistic mise-en-scène:

- The world and its objects follow assumed laws of nature and society.
- The elements of the mise-en-scène have a consistently logical or homogeneous relation to each other.
- The mise-en-scène and the characters mutually define each other, although the mise-en-scène may be unresponsive to the needs and desires of the characters.

Naturalistic mise-en-scènes are consistent with accepted scientific laws and cultural customs. Thus, in a naturalistic setting, a person would be unable to hear whispers from far across a field, and a restaurant might have thirty tables and several waiters or waitresses. This kind of realistic mise-en-scène also creates logical or homogeneous connections among different sets, props, and characters. Costumes, props, and lighting are appropriate and logical extensions of the naturalistic setting, and sets relate to each other as part of a consistent geography. A movie set in Florence, Italy, such as *Hannibal* (2001), uses sets and locations that are more or less faithful to the layout of that city, and in the submarine film *Das Boot* (1981), the individual sets are necessarily small, cramped rooms and the characters wear the uniforms of World War II German sailors. Naturalism in the movies also means that the mise-en-scène and the characters mutually define or reflect each other. The gritty streets and dark rooms of a city reflect the bleak attitudes of thieves

Figure 2.30 *The Perfect Storm* (2000). The natural ferocity of the ocean as test and measure of the characters.

and femmes fatales in *The Killers* (1946); in *The Perfect Storm* (2000) **[Figure 2.30]**, the ferocious battle with the sea reflects the personal turmoil and struggles of the characters and allows them to reach their full physical and psychological potential as human beings.

Two more specific traditions have emerged from the naturalistic mise-en-scène. A **historical mise-en-scène** re-creates a recognizable historical scene, highlighting those elements that call attention to a specific location and time in history: *All Quiet on the Western Front* (1930) can still stun audiences with its brutally accurate representation of trench warfare in World War I; *A Man for All Seasons* (1966) re-creates the sumptuous robes and august chambers of Parliament in the sixteenth-century England of martyr Thomas More. Calling attention to the ordinary rather than the historical, on the other hand, an **everyday mise-en-scène** constructs commonplace backdrops for the characters and the action. In *Louisiana Story* (1948), a swamp and its rich natural life are the always-visible arena for the daily routines of a young boy in the Louisiana bayous. In the Brazilian film *Central Station* (1998), a railroad station in Rio de Janeiro and a poor rural area in the Brazilian countryside are the understated stages in a touching tale of a woman's friendship with a boy in search of his father.

In contrast, theatrical mise-en-scènes create fantastical environments that display and even exult in their artificial and constructed nature. Films in this tradition define themselves in one or more of these terms:

■ Elements of the mise-en-scène tend to violate or bend the laws of nature or society.
■ Dramatic inconsistencies appear within one or between two or more mise-en-scènes.
■ The mise-en-scène takes on an independent life that requires confrontations or creative negotiations between the props and sets and the characters.

Often violating the accepted laws of how the world functions, theatrical mise-en-scènes call attention to the arbitrary or constructed nature of that world. Horses change colors and witches melt in *The Wizard of Oz* (1939), and in movies from *Top Hat* (1935) to *Silk Stockings* (1957), Fred Astaire somehow finds a way to dance on walls and ceilings and transform spoons and brooms into magical partners. Dramatic inconsistencies within or between different mise-en-scènes in a film indicate the instability of those scenes, costumes, and props—and the world they define. The films of Monty Python offer innumerable examples. In *Monty Python's The Meaning of Life* (1983), a pirate ship sails through the streets of Manhattan and a darkly costumed grim reaper interrupts a classy dinner party to announce that all of the chatting friends have died of food poisoning. In a theatrical mise-en-scène, props, sets, and even bodies assume an independent (and sometimes contradictory) life that provokes regular confrontations or negotiations between the mise-en-scène and the characters [**Figure 2.31**]. Martin Scorsese's *After Hours* (1985) describes the plight of Paul when he finds himself lost at night in the SoHo neighborhood of New York City. Characters suddenly die, a woman surrounds herself with the objects and clothing of a 1960s lifestyle, and

Figure 2.31 *Monty Python's The Meaning of Life* (1983). A dinner party suddenly disturbed by the theatrical entry of Death.

a vigilante group mistakes Paul for a robber; in this film, each apartment or street corner seems to be another individual's personal stage and Paul becomes an unwilling participant in the play.

Two historical trends—expressive and constructive mise-en-scènes—are associated with the tradition of a theatrical mise-en-scène. In an **expressive mise-en-scène,** the settings, sets, props, and other dimensions of the mise-en-scène assert themselves independently of the characters and describe an emotional or spiritual life permeating the material world. Associated most commonly with the German expressionistic films of the 1920s, this tradition is also seen in surrealism, horror films, and in the magic realism of Latin American cinema. Since Émile Cohl's 1908 *Fantasmagorie* depicted an artist surrounded by sketches and drawings and whose life and activity are independent of him, expressive mise-en-scènes have enlivened the terrifying, comical, and romantic mise-en-scènes of *The Birds* (1963), in which birds become demonic; *Barton Fink* (1991), in which wallpaper sweats; and *The Secret of Roan Inish* (1994), in which the natural world of Ireland becomes a magical kingdom. In a **constructive mise-en-scène,** the world can be shaped and even altered through the work or desire of the characters. Films about putting together a play or even a movie are examples of this tradition as characters fabricate a new or alternative world through their power as actors or directors. In François Truffaut's *Day for Night* (1973), for example, multiple romances and crises become entwined with the project of making a movie about romance and crises, and the movie set becomes a parallel universe in which day can be changed to night and sad stories can be made happy. Other films, however, have employed constructive mise-en-scènes to dramatize the wishes and dreams of their characters. In *Batman* (1989), spectacular costumes and electronic gadgets create a comic-book mise-en-scène in which good and bad characters battle each other for control, whereas the mise-en-scène of *Being John Malkovich* (1999) constantly defies the laws of spatial logic, as Craig the puppeteer and his co-worker Maxine struggle for the right to inhabit the body of the actor Malkovich.

We rarely experience the traditions of naturalistic and theatrical mise-en-scènes in entirely isolated states. Naturalism and theatrics sometimes alternate within the same film, and like our experience of mise-en-scène in general, following the play and exchange between the two can be one of the more exciting and productive ways to watch movies and to understand the complexities of mise-en-scène in a film—of how place and its physical

Values and Traditions in
The Bicycle Thief (1948)

The setting of Vittorio de Sica's *The Bicycle Thief* is post–World War II Rome, a mise-en-scène whose stark and impoverished conditions are the most formidable barrier against the central character's longing for a normal life. Antonio Ricci finds a job putting up movie posters, a humble but adequate way to support his wife and his son Bruno in an economically depressed city. When the bicycle he needs for work is stolen, he desperately searches the massive city on foot, hoping to discover the bike before Monday morning when he must continue his work. The winding streets and cramped apartments of Rome appear as bare, crumbling, and scarred surfaces, describing a frustrating and impersonal urban maze through which Ricci walks asking questions without answers, examining bikes that are not his, and following leads into strange neighborhoods where he is observed with hostile suspicion. In what was once the center of the Roman Empire, masses of people wait for jobs, crowd onto buses, or sell their wares. The most basic materials of life take on disproportionate significance as props: the sheets on a bed, a plate of food, and an old bike are the center of existence. In this mise-en-scène, the mostly bright lighting reveals mostly blank faces and walls of poverty.

Individuals have little power to change or even fully understand this mise-en-scène. When Ricci reaches a point of extreme desperation, he visits a woman—"The Santona" or "the one who sees"—who is supposed to have visionary powers and who he hopes will tell him where to find his bike. Of course, in a room filled with more impressive furniture and props than anywhere else in the film, she can only offer bromidic and useless advice: "Find it now or not at all" **[Figure 2.32]**. Neither visionary nor even human powers can affect the material reality and force of this mise-en-scène. Characters must mostly watch without affecting the world around them.

The Bicycle Thief is among the most important films within the naturalistic tradition of mise-en-scène, associated specifically with the Italian neo-realist movement of the late 1940s. The laws of society and nature follow an almost mechanical logic that cares not at all for human hopes and dreams. Here, according to a truck driver, "Every Sunday, it rains." In a large city of empty piazzas and anonymous crowds, physical necessities reign: food is a constant concern; most people are strangers; a person needs a bicycle to get around town; and rivers are more threatening than bucolic. Ricci and other characters become engulfed in the hostility and coldness of the pervasive mise-en-scène, and their encounters with Roman street life follow a path from hope to despair to resignation. In the beginning, objects and materials, such as Ricci's uniform and his bed linens, offer promise for his family's happiness in a barren and anonymous cityscape. However, the promise of these and

Figure 2.32 *The Bicycle Thief* (1948). The Santona: distinguished more by her furnishings than her vision.

other material objects turns quickly to ironic emptiness: the bicycle is stolen; the marketplace overwhelms him with separate bicycle parts that could never be identified; and settings (such as the church into which he pursues one of the thieves) offer no consolation or comfort. Finally, Ricci himself gets caught in this seemingly inescapable logic of survival when, unable to find his bike, he tries to steal another one **[Figure 2.33]**. Only at the end of the day, when he discovers his son is not the drowned body pulled from the river, does he give up his search for the bicycle. Realizing that this setting and the objects in it will never provide him with meaning and value, he returns sadly home with the son he loves.

The Bicycle Thief is a superb accentuation of the common and everyday within a naturalistic tradition. Ricci and his neighbors dress like the struggling working-class population, and the natural lighting progresses from dawn to dusk across the various sets that mark Ricci's progression through the day. This film's everyday mise-en-scène is especially powerful because without any dramatic signals, it remains permeated by World War II. Even within the barest of everyday settings, objects, and clothing, *The Bicycle Thief* suggests the traces of history—such as Mussolini's sports stadium—that have created these impoverished conditions.

Along with these traces of history within its everyday mise-en-scène, we are reminded of a theatrical tradition that ironically counterpoints the film's realism. While performing his new duties in the first part of the film, Ricci puts up a glamorous poster of the movie star Rita Hayworth **[Figure 2.34]**. Later, the sets and props change when Ricci wanders from a workers' political meeting to an adjacent theater where a play is being rehearsed. In these instances, a poster prop and a stage setting become reminders of a world that has little place in the daily hardships of this mise-en-scène—a world where, as one character puts it, "Movies bore me." For many modern tourists, Rome might be represented by that other tradition—as a city of magnificent fountains, glamorous people, and romantic restaurants. For Ricci and his son, however, that tradition is only a strange place and a fake set like the restaurant filled with rich patrons eating ravenously before returning to face the reality of the streets. For Europeans who lived through World War II (in Rome or other cities), the glaring honesty of this mise-en-scène in 1948 was, understandably, a powerful alternative to the glossy theatrical tradition of Hollywood sets and settings.

Figure 2.33 *The Bicycle Thief* (1948). Bare streets and a bicycle to steal.

Figure 2.34 *The Bicycle Thief* (1948). Reminders of different values and traditions: the Rita Hayworth poster.

Figure 2.35 *Sullivan's Travels* (1941). Leaving Hollywood to explore the "real" world.

contours condition and shape most experiences. In this context, Preston Sturges's *Sullivan's Travels* (1941) is a remarkable example of how the alternation between these two traditions can be the very heart of the movie. In this film, Hollywood director John L. Sullivan, after a successful career of making films with titles like *So Long, Sarong,* decides to explore the realistic world of suffering and deprivation (as material for a serious realistic movie he intends to title *O Brother, Where Art Thou?*). He subsequently finds himself catapulted into a grimy world of railroad boxcars and prison chain gangs, where he discovers, ironically, the power of those fantastic places and people he once filmed to delight and entertain others **[Figure 2.35]**. The theatrical mise-en-scènes of Hollywood, he learns, are as important to human life as the ordinary ones people must inhabit.

VIEWING CUES: Mise-en-Scène Traditions and Values

- Examine the mise-en-scène of the film you are studying in class. Consider how it suggests fundamental values. Does it emphasize the force of the physical conditions of society or how those conditions can be transformed?

- Identify a tradition in which this mise-en-scène best fits: naturalistic or theatrical. How does thinking about the movie in terms of this tradition help you better understand it?

- In your own words, describe why this mise-en-scène fits best with a naturalistic or a theatrical tradition. If naturalistic, does it emphasize historical elements or everyday elements? Explain how this perspective helps you describe your experience of the film. Illustrate your position using two or three scenes as examples.

- Can you profitably compare the mise-en-scène of this film with that of other films in the same tradition? Select one other film that seems to use its mise-en-scène like this one does, and argue how these mise-en-scènes share certain traits. Do they end in similar visions of the world?

CRITICAL VOICES: BÉLA BALÁZS ON THE FACE OF GRETA GARBO

A scriptwriter, filmmaker, and professor, Hungarian Béla Balázs was an early film critic and theoretician. His *Theory of the Film,* first published in 1945, ranges over numerous topics, including the artistic complexity of the human face and body, reminding us of how important and complex these elements in the cinematic mise-en-scène can be. For him, an actor's face can carry much of the meaning of a film. Although his language is sometimes outdated and extravagant, he captures the almost mystical feeling we sometimes have gazing at film stars.

The hero, the paragon, the model . . . is an indispensable element in the poetry of all races and peoples, from the ancient epics to the modern film. This is a manifestation of the natural selection of the best, of the instinctive urge towards improvement, a postulate of biology, not of aesthetics. . . . In this age of film culture, when man has again become visible, he has again

1

become awakened to a consciousness of beauty, and the visual propaganda of beauty is again an expression of deep-seated biological and social urges.

The physical incarnation of the hero or heroine is beauty of a kind which 2 exactly expresses the ideologies and aspirations of those who admire it. We must learn to read beauty, as we have learned to read the face. A scientific analysis of what we call sex appeal, for instance, would greatly enrich our knowledge of social psychology. . . .

Art snobs often affect to despise the beauty of film stars and tend to re- 3 gard beauty as a disturbing secondary effect which rouses base instincts and has nothing to do with "real art." But such a universal cultural phenomenon as the film must not be measured solely by the standards of a purely artistic production. For beyond this the vital instincts and social tendencies of mankind manifest themselves in so significant a form in the film that they cannot be disregarded.

The film stars who have been most successful did not owe their popu- 4 larity to their histrionic gifts, even if they happened to be excellent actors. The most popular of them did not act at all, or rather acted only themselves. Not only Charlie Chaplin remained always the same Charlie in every film, without changing mask, costume or manner. Douglas Fairbanks, Asta Nielsen, Lillian Gish, Rudolph Valentino and others of the greatest also remained the same. They were no creators of characters. Their names, costumes, social positions could be changed in their various parts, but they always showed the same personality and this personality was their own. For the dominant element in the impression they made was their personal appearance. They turned up as old acquaintances in each new film and it was not they who assumed the mask of the character they played—on the contrary, the parts were written for them in advance, were made to measure for them so to speak. For what the public loved was not their acting ability, but they themselves, their personal charm and attraction. Of course to possess such charm is also a great thing. But as an art it most resembles lyrical poetry, which also expresses the poet's heart and not things external. These great film stars were great lyrical poets whose medium was not the word, but the body, the facial expression and gesture; the parts they played merely change opportunities of exercising this their art. . . .

Up to now Greta Garbo was the most popular star in the world. This is 5 said not on the basis of aesthetic considerations. There is a better, more exact, indeed absolutely accurate standard. This standard is the amount in dollars which was the reward of her popularity.

It was not the actress Garbo who conquered the hearts of the world. 6 Garbo is not a bad actress, but her popularity is due to her beauty. Though even this is not so simple. Mere beauty is a matter of taste, of sex appeal, and for this one reason alone cannot have the same effect on many millions of people in the whole world to the same degree. And then there are so many perfectly beautiful women that the harmony of Garbo's lines could not in itself have ensured such a unique privileged position for her.

Garbo's beauty is not just a harmony of lines, it is not merely ornamental. 7 Her beauty contains a physiognomy expressing a very definite state of mind.

Like the face of all other actors, Greta Garbo's face changes during a 8 scene. She, too, laughs and is sad, is surprised or angry, as prescribed by her part. Her face, too, may be once that of a queen and once that of a bedraggled drab, according to what character she has to play. But behind this variety of facial expression we can always see that unchanged Garbo face, the fixed unchanged expression of which has conquered the world. It is not mere beauty, but a beauty of peculiar significance, a beauty expressing one particular thing, that has captured the heart of half mankind. And what is this thing?

Greta Garbo is sad. Not only in certain situations, for certain reasons. 9
Greta Garbo's beauty is a beauty of suffering; she suffers life and all the surrounding world. And this sadness, this sorrow is a very definite one: the sadness of loneliness, of an estrangement which feels no common tie with other human beings. The sadness of reticent purity, of the shrinking of a sensitive plant from a rude touch is in this beauty, even when she plays a down-and-out tart. Her brooding glance comes from afar even then and looks into the endless distance. Even then she is an exile in a distant land and does not know how she ever came to be where she is.

But why should this strange sort of beauty affect millions more deeply 10 than some bright and sparkling pin-up girl? What is the meaning of the Garbo expression?

We feel and see Greta Garbo's beauty as finer and nobler, precisely be- 11 cause it bears the stamp of sorrow and loneliness. For however harmonious may be the lines of a face, if it is contentedly smiling, if it is bright and happy, if it can be bright and happy in this world of ours, then it must of necessity belong to an inferior human being. Even the usually insensitive person can understand that a sad and suffering beauty, gestures expressing horror at the touch of an unclean world, indicates a higher order of human being, a purer and nobler soul than smiles and mirth. Greta Garbo's beauty is a beauty which is in opposition to the world of today.

THE NEXT LEVEL: ADDITIONAL SOURCES

Affron, Charles and Mirella. *Sets in Motion: Art Direction and Film Narrative*. New Brunswick: Rutgers University Press, 1995. Concentrating on the work of set designers, this study examines a number of films to demonstrate how sets do far more than embellish a film, often becoming the center of its meaning.

Brewster, Ben, and Lea Jacobs. *Theatre to Cinema: Stage Pictorialism and the Early Feature Film*. Oxford: Oxford University Press, 1997. A careful scholarly investigation of the transition from stage to screen in early film history.

Dyer, Richard. *Stars*. Rev. ed. London: BFI, 1998. A landmark study of the many ways that stars organize and focus a reading of film, through both their onscreen presence and their offscreen activities.

Gibbs, John. *Mise-en-Scène: Film Style and Interpretation*. New York: Columbia University Press, 2002. A book devoted exclusively to the importance of mise-en-scène, it is a historical survey of this critical dimension of film and a detailed examination of its aesthetic powers.

Williams, Christopher. *Realism and the Cinema*. London: Routledge, 1980. A wide-ranging examination of the arguments about film realism, this book also looks at different filmic practices of realism and the ideological stakes implicit in those movies.

Seeing through the Image: Cinematography

As a generation of cinematographers, we represent all the cinematographers that have gone before us. . . . But even before that, there is a whole history of painting. Since the first graffiti was scratched on the walls of caves, since the first Egyptian drawings, since Piero della Francesca, we have had ways to express emotional stories and emotional figures in a particular style. There is no question that when you make a design, shoot a picture or photograph a movie, it is the representation of all two thousand years of history, whether you are conscious of it or not.

—Vittorio Storaro, cinematographer for
The Conformist (1970) and *Apocalypse Now* (1979)

KEY OBJECTIVES

What does a film look like—its images, its frames, its colors? This chapter describes that feature of movies at the center of most individuals' experiences of them: film images. Although film images sometimes seem like transparencies or open windows on the world, here we will detail the subtle and complex ways individual movie images compose perspectives in order to communicate feelings, ideas, and other meanings. We will examine

- how the film image draws on a long historical heritage
- how the frame of an image positions our point of view according to different distances and angles
- how film shots use the depth of the image in various ways
- how the film image moves according to certain patterns in order to achieve certain effects
- how color and other compositional features of the image can be employed in a movie
- how the movie image assumes different values and participates in different cinematic traditions

Most people today primarily experience the physical world visually: we look left and right for cars before we cross a busy street, we watch sunsets in the distance, we focus in on a face across the room. The visual dynamics by which we encounter that world vary. Sometimes we are caught up in the close-ups of a crowded sidewalk; sometimes we watch from a window high above the street. Vision allows us to distinguish colors and light, to evaluate the sizes of things near and far, to track moving objects, or even to invent shapes out of formless clouds. Vision allows us to project ourselves into the world, to explore objects and places, and to transform them in our minds. We make images of the mise-en-scènes that surround us and, in the cinema, we know the material world only as it is relayed to us through the images (and sounds) that we process in our minds.

We go to the movies, then, to enjoy sights, share other people's perspectives on the world, and explore that world through the activity contained in a film image. In Ingmar Bergman's *Persona* (1966), the details of a woman's tense and mysterious face suggest the complex depths of the person behind it. At the beginning of *Saving Private Ryan* (1998), we witness

Figure 3.1 *Saving Private Ryan* (1998). Extreme images: the dying on D-Day.

the eerie perspective of dead and dying soldiers as bullets zip across the ocean surface during a D-Day invasion **[Figure 3.1]**. In *Walkabout* (1971), an empty horizon in an Australian wilderness vibrates with heat and light, becoming a vision of a new and unknown world **[Color Plate 18]**.

Vision is a complex physiological process that begins when light rays reflected from an object in the outside world strike the retina of the eye and create an image of that object in the eye. Photography, which means "light writing," mimics vision in the way it registers light patterns onto celluloid film. Whereas vision is continuous, photography freezes a single moment in an image. Movies connect a series of photographic moments to create a moving image. Although in actuality a series of still images, film produces this illusion of movement because of a delay in human perception called **persistence of vision:** the human brain retains a visual imprint for approximately one-twentieth to one-fifth of a second. As a result, the continuous projection of a series of still images, overlapping when processed by the brain, appears as if it is the image of a single movement. This perception of motion is known as the **phi phenomenon** (discovered by psychologist Max Wertheimer in 1912).

Through these technological and physiological mechanisms, the magic of the film image becomes, in part, its power to re-create how we see the world. That magic also becomes, however, its power to change how we see the world through imagistic compositions that direct, expand, and even transform our natural vision. Today, new visual technologies offer perspectives that surpass the powers of human vision, such as in *Blade Runner* (1982), where Rick Deckard uses a computer to explore unseen spaces in a photograph **[Color Plate 19]**. Through that image, he sees a room in a way that traditional human perspective never could. Even the traditional film image, however, manifests similar power and art. Whether in the slow-moving precision and clarity of the one image of Michael Snow's *Wavelength* (1967) or in the glowing and nostalgic textures of Frederico Fellini's *Amarcord* (1974), the film image can bring us to see and understand the world with fresh eyes.

The Foundations of Cinematography

With the very first movies, there was simply a single moving image. The Lumieres' early film *Niagra Falls* (1897) is little more than a moving photograph of the famous falls and a group of bystanders, but its compositional balance of a powerful natural world and the people on its edge draws on a

Figure 3.2 *Niagra Falls* (1897). The wonder and balance of a single moving image.

Figure 3.3 *The Kiss* (1896). Regarding intimate moments.

long history of painting that infuses the film with remarkable energy and beauty **[Figure 3.2]**. Referred to in one newspaper as "The Anatomy of a Kiss," *The Kiss* (1896) titillated viewers by giving them a playfully analytical snapshot of an intimate moment **[Figure 3.3]**. With these early film images, the foundations of cinematography were laid.

The Shot: Frame, Depth, and Movement

Cinematography means motion-picture photography, literally "writing in movement." The basic unit of cinematography is the shot. The **shot** is the visual heart of the cinema: it is a continuous point of view (or continuously exposed piece of film); it may move forward or backward, up or down, but it does not change, break, or cut to another point of view or image. A film depicting a hotel room, the morning after a wild party, may "shoot" or employ cinematographic shots in many different ways. One version might show the entire room with its broken window, a fallen chair, and a man crouched in the corner as a single shot that depicts the scene from a calm distance. Another version might show the same scene in a rapid succession of images made by multiple shots—the window, the chair, and the man—creating a visual disturbance missing in the first version.

In cinematographic terms, **point of view** refers to the position from which a person, an event, or an object is seen (or filmed). All shots have a point of view: a **subjective point of view** re-creates the perspective of a character; an **objective point of view** represents the more impersonal perspective of the camera. To see a baseball game from directly behind home plate offers a different point of view on the game than to watch it from center field **[Figure 3.4]**. A point of view may be discontinuous when, for instance, in *The Natural* (1984) the perspective changes dramatically from the position behind home plate to a point of view positioned on the field, or it may change as part of a continuous point of view when, in that same film, the perspective from behind home plate shifts gradually to follow the ball into the stands. While the first is an edited cut, the second is a single shot whose point of view is

Figure 3.4 *The Natural* (1984). A point of view on the game.

Figure 3.5 *A League of Their Own* (1992). A mobile frame following the racing character.

continuous. The specific object highlighted within a point of view is the shot's **focus,** the point in the image that is most clearly and precisely outlined and defined by the lens of the camera. In our example, while the point of view may move continuously, the focus may remain constantly on a single player or even on the small baseball that appears in the image.

Every shot must orchestrate three important attributes of that image: framing, depth of field, and movement. The **framing** of a film shot contains, limits, and directs the point of view within the borders of the rectangular frame. Usually that framing is balanced, but sometimes it can appear unbalanced or askew, which is called a **canted frame.** Framing correlates with the camera's distance from its subject. In *A League of Their Own* (1992), the framing at one point contains only the face of the batter and, shortly after, the entire ballpark. Film images also create a **depth of field,** the range or distance before and behind the main focus and within which objects remain relatively sharp and clear: sometimes an image may create a short or shallow range and sometimes a long or deep focus. From a viewing position in the center-field bleachers, consequently, a film image may focus primarily on a play at second base but create a depth of field that keeps the players before and behind that action—the pitcher and an outfielder—in focus. Finally, a film image or shot may have **movement,** according to which the **mobile frame** of the image follows an action, object, or individual, or continuously moves to show a different action, object, or individual. (The movement of the image we watch obviously requires the camera or lens to move during filming.) During the championship game in *A League of Their Own,* the mobile frame of the shot moves with the younger sister as she races around the field on her way to scoring the winning run, the movement of the shot capturing the strength and dexterity of her strides in a single motion **[Figure 3.5]**.

A Short History of the Cinematic Image

Andrei Tarkovsky's *Andrei Rublev* (1966) is about a fifteenth-century religious icon painter who is devoted to his art but entangled in the political turmoil of his times. Devotion to images is the center of the world for this monk, but the barbarous society around him continually forces him to question that life and the value of those images he creates **[Color Plate 20]**. Set centuries before the cinema appeared, *Andrei Rublev* describes the crisis of a man straddling religious ideals and secular reality, a crisis of social, psychological, and historical pressures that surrounds and permeates every image he makes. As Tarkovsky knew well, cinematic images invariably bear and reflect their own historical pressures.

A history of the film image ought properly to begin when people first began to draw and to make images. Since ancient times, philosophers have remarked on the human need to represent and reproduce the world in images. From primitive cave drawings and early religious icons to modern film and computer images, the image has represented human vision engaging the world. Across this history, we can identify three cultural roles for the image:

- as a manifestation of power and control
- as a tool explaining the world
- as a form of amusement

Early images were often associated with magical or spiritual powers. Primitive societies painted scenes of a hunt to elicit good fortune or to placate a natural world that they did not understand. Religions created icons of gods and the spiritual world to honor those forces and to bring them into the community. By the sixteenth century, the power of images of Christ or the saints became a subject of dispute that led to the Reformation. Protestants accused the Roman Catholic Church of placing too much faith and power in images. In 1671, Athanasius Kircher's treatise *Ars magna lucis et umbrae* [The great art of light and shadow] described early experiments with projected images, including the magic lantern, whose "magical power" to re-create images is identified by many as a precursor of the film projector **[Figure 3.6]**.

By the nineteenth century, the discovery of photography introduced what the German essayist Walter Benjamin has called "the age of mechanical reproduction." In 1839, Louis Jacques Mandé Daguerre produced the first still photograph (although Joseph Niépce had created the prototype in 1826 through a "camera obscura" device that creates images by drawing light through an aperture with a lens). The photograph offered a new ability to mechanically produce images of reality and to make these images readily available to the growing masses who wished to have themselves and their world photographed.

During the nineteenth century, scientists photographed a range of different sociological or physical phenomena that this technological image could uniquely pinpoint and capture for investigation. Anticipating motion pictures, in 1872, Eadweard Muybridge began to make a series of photos of animals and humans in motion **[Figure 3.7]**, one of the great examples of how photography permeated the culture of the second half of the nineteenth century—from family photograph albums to private pornography collections. Combining amusement and science, a variety of contraptions explored the rudiments of the moving image. The Phenakistiscope (1832) and

Figure 3.6 A magic lantern. Historical precursor of the cinema.

Figure 3.7 Eadweard Muybridge's motion studies. Experimenting with photographs of motion. *Courtesy, the George Eastman House.*

the Zoetrope (1834), examples of such scientific toys presaging the cinema, allow a person to view a series of images through slits in a circular wheel, a view that creates the illusion of a moving image.

From these beginnings, the technology that drives cinematography accelerated during the twentieth century in ways that increased the power and artistry of the film image to control, explain, and entertain. Here we will sketch some of the principal features in the production of the cinematic image and its projection, as they historically developed.

Since the advent of the movies in 1895, advances in **film stock**—consisting of a flexible backing or base and a light-sensitive emulsion—gave film images improved texture and clarity by controlling the "grain" of the image (from grainy to clear and detailed). The **gauge** of films describes the width of the film stock. While most commercial movies are produced on gauges of 35mm film stock, since around 1950, gauges of 8mm, 16mm, and 65–70mm have been commonly used, respectively, for home movies, art films, and grand movie epics (although all these gauges had been introduced earlier in film history). Most early black-and-white films used an **orthochromatic** stock that was especially sensitive to greens and blues; the far superior **panchromatic** stock responded to a full spectrum of colors and became the standard for black-and-white movies after 1926. By the 1920s, **film speed**—the rate at which moving images are recorded (and later projected)—increased from sixteen frames to twenty-four frames per second, offering more clarity and definition to moving images. By the 1930s, color processes, by which a few or a wide range of colors become part of the film image, evolved from individually hand-painted frames or tinted sequences of silent films to the more modern and complex **Technicolor process.** First developed between 1926 and 1932 and effectively adjusted over the last seventy years, Technicolor uses three strips of film to transfer colors directly onto a single image. If hand-colored images added artistic atmosphere to silent films, then Technicolor offered both more realism and more artifice to films of the 1930s and has since been used for a spectrum of creative purposes.

From the 1930s through the 1960s, the **camera lens,** that piece of curved glass that redirects light rays in order to focus and shape images, changed significantly—in terms of both the speed at which an aperture allows light to be gathered (that is, the "f-stop") and the introduction of wide-angle, telephoto, and zoom lenses. Each lens produces a different **focal length**—the distance from the center of the lens to the point where light rays meet in sharp focus—that alters the perspective relations of an image. The range of perspectives offered by these advancements allowed for better resolution, more depth of field, wider angles, and more frame movement. During the 1920s, filmmakers used gauzy fabrics and, later, special lenses to develop a so-called **soft style,** through which the image could highlight the main action or character. From the mid-1930s through the 1940s, the development of the **wide-angle lens** (commonly considered a lens of less than 35mm in focal length) allowed cinematographers to explore a depth of field that could show different visual planes simultaneously. The early 1950s witnessed the arrival of several **widescreen processes,** which changed the size of the image—its aspect ratio (see p. 85)—by dramatically widening it (in part, to distinguish the cinema from the new competition of television). One of the most popular of these processes in the fifties, CinemaScope used an **anamorphic lens,** which squeezed a wide-angle view onto a strip of 35mm film and then "unsqueezed" it during projection. In the 1960s, cinematographers began to experiment more aggressively with ways to distort or call attention to the image through the use of **filters** (transparent sheets of glass or gels placed in front of the lens), **flares** (created by directing strong light at the lens),

telephoto lenses (a lens with a focal length of at least 75mm and capable of magnifying and flattening distant objects), and other special effects. Since 1980, the most dramatic change in the history of the film image has been the growing use and importance of **digital cinematography,** a computerized system of recording and storing information that is physically more flexible and economically more practical than film and offers much higher quality than previous formats (see pp. 102–3).

The history of film images is the history of film, cameras, and other recording and projection equipment. Because the movement of the film frame has always been one of the great powers of the film image, recording equipment quickly incorporated tripods and vehicles on which to swing or move the camera. Since the 1930s, more and better mobility has driven the technological development of the film image: from the camera's release from the bulky soundproofing equipment of the late 1920s to the appearance of **lightweight handheld cameras** (such as the Arriflex camera) in the 1950s, and, in the 1970s, the **Steadicam,** a camera stabilization device that allows the operator to make smooth, rapid movements. Since the early projectors that employed high-intensity lamps and carbon arcs, movie projection has advanced to modern **IMAX** and **Showscan** projection systems developed in the 1970s. Projected horizontally rather than vertically, IMAX stores approximately three times as much information as a 70mm film image. Developed by Douglas Trumball and marketed in 1983, Showscan projects at sixty frames per second (rather than twenty-four frames) and creates remarkably dense and detailed images.

Although the film image always develops in new directions, these traces of its past constantly resurface. Russian iconography permeates the images of Tarkovsky's *Andrei Rublev.* The Japanese tradition of *ukiyo-e* wood-block prints appears in the films of Kenji Mizoguchi, including *Utamaro and His Five Women* (1946). And in Raoul Ruiz's *Time Regained* (2000), rich color tones re-create the vibrancy of magic lanterns. In virtually every movie we see, in short, our experience of the film image is permeated by its history.

VIEWING CUES: Frame, Depth, and Movement

- While watching the next film shown in your class, choose what you consider the two or three most important shots. Describe them as precisely as possible. Why do you consider them so important?

- Examine a shot you consider especially rich in detail. What objects or individuals does the composition isolate in a significant way? How exactly does the composition of the image draw attention to those objects or individuals?

- Consider the framing and depth of field in one or two shots. How is framing used to comment on characters or objects in the shots? How does the depth of field become particularly important?

- Are there shots in which the movement of the frame stands out? For what purpose? Describe carefully the movement of the shot, and then explain how the movement adds to our understanding of what happens.

- Think about the cinematography of the film in relation to the larger history of the image. Are there shots that seem like paintings or other kinds of images from history? To what effect?

In Focus: Frames and Movements in *The Grand Illusion* (1937)

Jean Renoir's *The Grand Illusion*, set during World War I, focuses on a group of French aviators who are moved from one German prison camp to another. Certainly the horror, devastation, and loss of war impact the lives of these soldiers, but the achievement of the film is to reveal how a common humanity can transcend this war setting. *The Grand Illusion* demonstrates that its brutal and repressive mise-en-scène is only part of the drama and that the point of view from which events are revealed often tells the richer tale. Here, especially, it is possible to imagine the influence of Renoir's father, the French impressionist painter Pierre-Auguste Renoir, for whom the frame of a painting (such as *The Boating Party*) harmonized the points of view of so many kinds of people, watching each other's humanity unfold. In the catastrophes of war since the *belle époque* of his father's France, Renoir the son still finds the power of framing to portray human compassion.

Appropriate to this attention to the image, a smudge in a reconnaissance photograph opens the film and the two French officers who fly off to investigate that blur are soon captured. Brought to a German barracks after their plane is shot down, the captured officers are treated with the special deference due aristocrats: the German Captain von Rauffenstein meets them with the greeting, "I'm honored to have French guests."

Two main themes are apparent in *The Grand Illusion*. The first concerns the passing of one historical age, preoccupied with breeding and good manners, into another, characterized by less regard for family background. The first relationship between the French Captain de Boeldieu and his German captor, Rauffenstein, personifies the last flickerings of the old aristocratic order. The two captains agree about their predicament at Boeldieu's deathbed: whatever the outcome of the war, says Rauffenstein, "it will mean the end of the Rauffensteins and the Boeldieus." "We are no longer needed," replies the French officer. The new age, personified by the French soldiers Maréchal and Rosenthal, promises more than just a loss of social manners. As the vehicle for the second theme of the film, this group suggests that camaraderie, compassion, and love can transcend the differences of class, race, and nationality. Signaled throughout the film by the bonding of French, Russian, and English prisoners under duress, the theme crystallizes at the conclusion when working-class Maréchal returns to save the wealthy Jewish Rosenthal. As they cross through the snowy mountains into Switzerland, Rosenthal summarizes a key motif in the film: "You can't see borders; they're man-made."

Figure 3.8 *The Grand Illusion* (1937). Seeing beyond the frame.

These themes of a lost age and a new humanity shape the visual compositions of *The Grand Illusion*, where subjective point-of-view shots and framings designate the confrontations between personal perspectives and the world. Immediately after his capture, the wounded Maréchal dines with a German officer who tries to uphold the illusions of social etiquette, politely offering to cut his food while they chat about their pasts as auto mechanics. Suddenly, they both become silent and look beyond the film frame [**Figure 3.8**]. The next shot shows the object of the somber point of view—a funeral wreath for a French flier recently gunned down by the Germans.

Similarly, frame compositions describe subtle relations and tensions in the interaction of the characters. Late in the film, for instance, Boeldieu and Maréchal plan the latter's escape: Boeldieu stands on the right side of the frame, elevated to the top corner; Maréchal squats in the lower left-hand corner; and occupying the majority of the frame's center is a pet squirrel in a birdcage [**Figure 3.9**]. Here the composition suggests the breach between the two comrades ("we've got nothing in common," Maréchal claims), but it also connects them through the squirrel in the middle of the image, whose caged predicament, like theirs, supersedes social distinctions.

In *The Grand Illusion*, the flux of reality is best seen in the movement of the frame. Of course, depth of field creates powerful compositions as well. When Rauffenstein realizes, during the escape episode, that Boeldieu will not surrender and will have to be hunted down by his soldiers, one shot shows Rauffenstein climbing wearily and sadly up the castle steps in the background while lines of German troops race through the foreground in pursuit of Boeldieu [**Figure 3.10**]. More often, though, the movement of the frame, from side to side or front to back, makes the crucial points and renders the major themes. One powerful sequence begins with three village women at the gate of the prison, with men working in an open field in the deepest plane of the image. As the women stare past a wagon entering the gate, the camera follows their gaze to a group of young German soldiers marching in formation. One woman remarks, "Poor boys." In the next image, Boeldieu, Maréchal, and other French prisoners watch through a window frame as the same German soldiers march rapidly across the background of the image. With his men making costumes for a prison play, Boeldieu sighs, "Out there, children play soldier. In here, soldiers play children." In the foreground, inside the window frame now, the camera frame momentarily isolates several prisoners and each comments on what the war means to him. In the background, the Germans continue to exercise, suddenly drawing the French

Figure 3.9 *The Grand Illusion* (1937). Frame composition: commenting on the characters.

Figure 3.10 *The Grand Illusion* (1937). Rauffenstein fading into the depth of field.

Figure 3.11 *The Grand Illusion* (1937). Lovers moving beyond borders and frames.

prisoners to the window as they begin to march. As the frame moves, right to left, across the prisoners' faces, we watch as they recognize a dark and violent reality much greater than their private lives.

The Grand Illusion presents an intricate story rooted in the traditional human values of compassion and respect. The power of the film is its ability to dramatize those values in the context of modern war, where they are tested in ways that threaten their survival. At the heart of this drama, the film analyzes the many ways individuals and groups interact across different and often combative points of view. At the conclusion, Maréchal's chance meeting with a German countrywoman leads to a moment of unexpected love. Able to see outside the frames that have divided nations and individuals, this French man and German woman fall in love and, with her help, the two men escape to Switzerland, beyond the boundaries that confined them [**Figure 3.11**].

Framed and Focused: Elements of Cinematography

Although we rarely attend to single images in a movie, the cinematography in most movies involves careful construction by filmmakers and attentive observation by perceptive viewers. Abel Gance's *Napoléon* (1927) [**Figure 3.12**] orchestrates simultaneous and multiple images timed precisely to appear intermittently throughout the film; to shoot single scenes in *Dancer in the Dark* (2000), Lars van Trier uses numerous cameras placed at different angles and distances in order to capture the exact images he needs. In more conventional and common ways, films have experimented with and refined ways to manipulate and use the film image and its properties for over one hundred years. Here, we will examine and detail the numerous formal possibilities inherent in our experience of the cinematic image, possibilities that, when recognized, enrich all we see at the movies.

Figure 3.12 *Napoléon* (1927). Revolutionary image surrounding a new French leader.

The Spaces, Angles, and Distances of the Film Image

The three dimensions of the film image—the height and width of the frame and the apparent depth of the image—offer endless opportunities for representing the world and how we see it. One film image may frame a world from afar; another may place the action in the foreground and minimize the depth of field. These differences in the film image invariably affect our experience of a movie. A story seen as a large widescreen projection surely affects us differently than one seen on a television monitor. Indeed, even the proximity of the frame to a character in a movie will probably influence how we feel about that character. Here, we will examine the textures, angles, and shapes through which we enter that imagistic world of film.

Like the frame of a painting, the basic shape of the film image on the screen is central to the film composition. Called the **aspect ratio,** it describes the width and height of the film frame as it appears on a movie screen or television monitor. *The Grand Illusion, Citizen Kane* (1941), and other classic films employ the **academy ratio** of 1.33:1, standardized in 1932 by the American Academy of Motion Picture Arts and Sciences and used by most films until the 1950s. The standard U.S. **widescreen ratio** is 1.85:1, but Nicholas Ray's 1955 drama of teenage frustration and fear, *Rebel Without a Cause,* uses a widescreen ratio of 2.35:1 to create an even longer, more horizontal image. The standard European widescreen ratio is 1.66:1. Because these ratios describe the dimensions of the frame of the image we see, they often shape our experience to align with the themes and actions of the film. Thus, in *Rebel without a Cause,* the CinemaScope frame becomes a useful format for depicting the loneliness and isolation of Jim Stark (played by James Dean) and his friends, Judy and Plato. In a scene in the planetarium, Ray uses cinematography to express the vastness of an existential space for these small-town youths, one that is dark, wide, and unknowable **[Color Plate 21]**. While the more confined frame of *Citizen Kane* fits a film about a man driven to control the world, the widescreen space in *Rebel Without a Cause* suits the fitful search of restless teens. Although an aspect ratio may not be a crucial determinant in every movie, it never escapes the consideration of the filmmaker. For instance, Stanley Kubrick wanted his war film *Full Metal Jacket* (1987) to appear in academy ratio rather than widescreen, as one might expect. With this choice, Kubrick emphasizes a central theme: that the Vietnam war entered world consciousness through television, whose square aspect ratio approximates academy ratio.

Film ratios have gone through many changes over the years. One such change occurs when videotaped movies appear on television. Most television broadcasts of movies, as well as many videotape versions, now announce that they have been "formatted to fit your screen." A videotape or DVD version of a film is sometimes **letterboxed** by blocking off the top and bottom strips of the television frame to accommodate a smaller version of the widescreen image. But often widescreen movies converted to a television frame will have been altered through a **pan-and-scan process,** which either chops off outer portions of the image that are not central to the action or reconstitutes a single widescreen image into two consecutive television images. Reframing the image can certainly alter our perception of the film and its story. In movies like *Rebel Without a Cause* and *The Lord of the Rings: The Fellowship of the Ring* (2001), to name just a few, the surrounding space of the frame is an important part of the drama that helps us understand the characters and their actions. Even when these changes seem minor or barely noticeable, they can subtly influence our perceptions and responses to a film **[Color Plate 22]**. In *Badlands* (1973), a letterboxed image (rather than one formatted to fit the television frame) more appropriately displays the horizontal space so important to this road movie and the isolated wanderings of its criminal protagonist.

Whatever the proportions of the aspect ratio, a film frame can also be reshaped by various **masks,** attachments to the camera that cut off portions of the frame so that part of the image is black. Mostly associated with silent films—like D. W. Griffith's *Intolerance* (1916) **[Figure 3.13]**—or modern movies recalling that earlier period, a masked frame may open only a corner of the frame, create a circular effect, or leave

Figure 3.13 *Intolerance* (1916). A triangular mask isolating the triangular harp.

Figure 3.14 *The Night of the Hunter* (1955). Irising-out on a figure of evil.

Figure 3.15 *The Devil Probably* (1977). A frame surrounded by a spiritual life?

Figure 3.16 *The Passion of Joan of Arc* (1928). The intensity of religious faith in a close-up.

just a strip in the center of the frame visible. An **iris shot** masks the frame so that only a small circular piece of the image is seen: in Harold Lloyd's *The Freshman* (1925), a shot of a timid collegian **irises-in** (opening the circle to reveal more of the image) to show his seemingly safe location surrounded by a crowd of hostile football players. Conversely, a full image may be reduced, as an **iris-out** (closing the circle), to isolate and emphasize a specific object or action in that image: a shot of a courtroom, for example, might iris-out to reveal the nervous hands of the defendant's mother. In *The Night of the Hunter* (1955), an iris-out follows the demonic preacher as he walks toward the house of the children he threatens [**Figure 3.14**].

Onscreen space refers to the space visible within the frame of the image, whereas **offscreen space** is the implied space or world that exists outside the film frame. Usually the action in offscreen space is less important than the action in the frame (as when a close-up focuses on an intimate conversation and excludes other people in the room). Offscreen space does, however, sometimes contain important information that will be revealed in a subsequent image (as when one of the individuals engaged in conversation looks beyond the edge of the frame—toward a glaring rival shown in the next shot). Offscreen spaces in horror films like *Alien* (1979) seethe with a menace that is all the more terrifying because it is not visible [**Color Plate 23**]. In Robert Bresson's *The Devil Probably* (1977), that world outside the frame often suggests a spiritual one that pressures but eludes the fragmented and limited perspectives of the characters within the frame [**Figure 3.15**].

The proximity of the film frame to its subject determines much about the point of view of a shot and contributes a great deal to how we understand or feel about what is being shown. **Close-ups** show details of a person or object, such as the face or hands or a flower on a windowsill, indicating perhaps nuances about the character's feelings or thoughts or suggesting the special significance of the object. An **extreme close-up** moves in even closer, singling out, for instance, the person's eyes or the petal of the flower. Carl Dreyer's *The Passion of Joan of Arc* (1928) and Ingmar Bergman's *Persona* (1966) are well-known examples of films that use close-ups and extreme close-ups to depict religious fervor and existential agony, respectively, through the heroine's facial expressions [**Figure 3.16**].

At the other end of the compositional spectrum, a **long shot** places considerable distance between the camera and the scene, object, or person, allowing the latter to remain recognizable but to now be defined by the large space and background it is a part of. An **extreme long shot** creates an even greater distance

Figure 3.17A *Shane* (1953). Barely seen (through an attentive deer's antlers), Shane approaches through an extreme long shot.

Figure 3.17B The mysterious figure becomes more recognizable in a long shot.

between the camera and the person or object, so that the larger space of the image dwarfs small objects or human figures, such as with distant vistas of cities or landscapes. Most films feature a combination of these long shots, sometimes to show distant action or objects, sometimes to establish a context for action, and sometimes, as with the introduction and conclusion of *Shane* (1953), to emphasize the isolation and mystery of a character as he arrives in the distance **[Figure 3.17]**. Between close-ups and long shots, a **medium shot** describes a middle ground in which we see the body of the person from the waist up, as in *The Maltese Falcon* (1941) **[Figure 3.18]**, while a **medium long shot** increases distance between the camera and the subject somewhat farther, perhaps showing the character's entire body. A **medium close-up** shows a character's head and shoulders and is frequently used in conversation scenes. Melodramatic or romantic films about personal relationships often feature a predominance of medium close-ups and medium shots to capture the emotional expressions of the characters, such as the story of a new bride's haunting by the memory of a former wife in *Rebecca* (1940) **[Figure 3.19]**. Open-air adventures, such as *The Seven Samurai* (1954),

Figure 3.18 *The Maltese Falcon* (1941). A medium shot of Sam Spade (played by Humphrey Bogart).

Figure 3.19 *Rebecca* (1940). The melodramatic tension of a medium shot.

Figure 3.20 *The Seven Samurai* (1954). A long shot in an open-air adventure.

Figure 3.21 *The Piano* (1993). A high-angle long shot of the arrival on the beach.

Figure 3.22 *The Piano* (1993). An extreme low-angle shot, slightly canted, describes the farmer/husband as he furiously descends toward his unfaithful wife.

Figure 3.23 *The Piano* (1993). With this overhead shot, the film depicts a rare moment of contentment and harmony at the piano.

the tale of a sixteenth-century Japanese village that hires warriors for protection, tend to use more long shots and extreme long shots in order to depict the battle scenes **[Figure 3.20]**. Framing is defined relatively; there is no absolute cut-off point between a medium and a medium long shot, for example. As we have seen, the most common reference point for the scale of the image is the size of the human figure within the frame, a measure that is not a universal element of the cinematic image.

Film shots are positioned according to a multitude of angles, as demonstrated by the accompanying series of shots from Jane Campion's *The Piano* (1993), a powerful film about a mute Scottish woman who travels with her daughter to New Zealand to complete an arranged marriage. **High angles** present a point of view directed at a downward angle on individuals or a scene **[Figure 3.21]**, while **low angles** view the world from a position lower than its subject **[Figure 3.22]**. In either case, the exact angle of the shot can vary from very steep to very flat angles. An **overhead shot** (sometimes called a **crane shot** because of the machinery on which the camera is mounted) depicts the action or subject from high above, sometimes looking directly down on it **[Figure 3.23]**. In the Czech film *The Shop on Main Street* (1965) **[Figure 3.24]** a clever opening crane shot looking down on the town reflects the point of view of a stork nesting on a chimney.

Shots change their angle depending on the physical or geographical position or point of view, so that a shot from a tall adult's perspective may be a high-angle shot, whereas a child's view may be seen through low angles. Such shots are often **point-of-view shots,** which are defined as shots that re-create the perspective of a character and may incorporate camera movement or optical effects as well as camera angle in order to do so. The angles employed for these shots can sometimes indicate psychological, moral, or political meanings in a film, as when victims are seen from above and oppressors from below, but such interpretations must be made carefully because formal features like these do not automatically assume a symbolic or other meaning.

Not to be confused with depth of field (see p. 78), which is a measure that can be applied to any photographic image, **deep focus** means that multiple planes in the image are all in focus. A film about three physically and psychologically brutalized veterans returning home from World War II, William Wyler's *The Best Years of Our Lives* (1946) is a superior example of how deep focus can create relationships within a single image: the two grown children in the foreground frame the happy reunion of their parents in the background, all in harmonious balance and focus **[Figure 3.25]**. In

Figure 3.24 *The Shop on Main Street* (1965). A crane shot settles in a bird's nest.

shallow focus, only a narrow range of the field is focused, but here too the choice of a depth of field indicates what is significant in an image. A shot can direct its focus at a specific plane within the image, such as in this medium shot from *The Best Years of Our Lives*, in which the focused foreground of embracing lovers leaves the blurred background of the veteran's artificial arms barely visible and insignificant **[Figure 3.26]**. With a **rack focus** (or **pulled focus**), the focus shifts rapidly from one object to another, such as refocusing from the face of a woman to the figure of a man approaching from behind her. During a dramatic scene in *L.A. Confidential* (1997), a young self-righteous police officer, Ed Exley, assures his captain he can force the criminal suspect to confess, and the shot rack focuses from the captain to Exley to catch the latter's determined expression as he turns toward the interrogation room **[Color Plate 24]**.

Color profoundly affects our experience and understanding of a film shot. Most early movies (from 1895 to 1935) were black-and-white films,

Figure 3.25 *The Best Years of Our Lives* (1946). The deep focus and balance of the restored family harmony.

Figure 3.26 *The Best Years of Our Lives* (1946). Through this shallow focus, the lovers are absorbed in their private space.

Figure 3.27 *Nosferatu* (1922). A troubling atmosphere of black-and-white shadows and shades.

Figure 3.28 *The Third Man* (1949). Sharply contrasting blacks and whites, with scintillating greys, intensify the drama of good and evil in Vienna.

Figure 3.29 *Raging Bull* (1980). Black and white as bare violence.

but contrast and gradations of black and white, like color, can work carefully to create atmosphere or emphasize certain motifs. In F. W. Murnau's *Nosferatu* (1922), shades and tones of black and white create an ominous world where evil lives, not in darkness but in shadings **[Figure 3.27]**. In *The Third Man* (1949), black-and-white contrasts glisten on the damp surfaces of a morally slippery world **[Figure 3.28]**. No longer a necessity, the black-and-white format in modern films like *Raging Bull* (1980) and *Pleasantville* (1998) is used self-consciously. In the first film, it suggests the violent extremities in the life of prize fighter Jake LaMotta as well as the style of films of the period and milieu in which it is set **[Figure 3.29]**; in the second film, it parodies the superficial and simplistic lives of 1950s television, a world suddenly confused when emotional colors enter the characters' lives **[Color Plate 25]**.

Beginning with the colors of the mise-en-scène (natural colors, painted sets, locations, or actors' costumes), **color** describes the spectrum of color grades and hues used by a film, while **tone** refers to the shading, intensification, or saturation of those colors (such as metallic blues, soft greens, or deep reds) in order to sharpen, mute, or balance them for certain effects. Color film stocks—the kinds of emulsion affixed to a celluloid backing—allow a full range of colors to be recorded to film. Once colors are recorded on film stocks, that film can be manipulated to create **color and tone balances** that range from realistic to more extreme or unrealistic palettes of color: these may appear as either **noncontrasting balances** (sometimes called a **monochromatic color scheme**), which can create a more realistic or flat background against which a single color becomes more meaningful, or **contrasting balances,** which can create dramatic oppositions and tensions through color.

In the first decades after the 1895 arrival of the cinema, before color film stock was available, some movies, like the 1910 version of Shakespeare's *King Lear,* used laboriously hand-tinted colored frames that appeared like moving paintings **[Color Plate 26]**. In the 1930s, most notably with *Becky Sharp* (1935), the Technicolor revolution began as a way of creating not only more realistic worlds but also more fantastic worlds of people and places more colorful than normal life **[Color Plate 27]**. The 1950s introduced the successful but inferior Eastmancolor. Since then, color has become a key element in the composition of the image: *American Graffiti* (1973) uses bright and varied colors to intensify the memory of summer 1962 in California, bright with cars, romance, and teenage energy **[Color Plate 28]**. In his adaptation of the last volume of Marcel Proust's *Remembrance of Things Past, Time Regained* (1999), Raoul Ruiz uses rich and sumptuous pastels to represent the protagonist's sensual memory and vibrant imagination **[Color Plate 29]**.

The Moving Frame

When the film frame begins to move, a film shot re-creates a quality of vision that has always been a part of the human experience but that could be adequately represented only with the advent of film technology. In our daily lives, we anticipate these movements of a shot: when, for instance, we focus on a friend at a table and then refocus beyond that friend and toward another at the door; when we stand still and turn our head from our left shoulder to our right; or when we watch from a moving car as buildings pass. Like these adjustments within our field of vision, the film image can move its frame and focus through changes in the position of the camera frame (such as pans or tracking shots) or through changes in the focus of the camera lens (such as zooms).

Reframing refers to the movement of the frame from one position to another within a single continuous shot. One extreme and memorable example of reframing is an early shot in *Citizen Kane*. Here, the camera pulls back from the boy in the yard to reframe the shot to include the mother and the men observing him from inside the window; it then continues backward to reframe the mother as she walks toward a table **[Figure 3.30]**. Often such reframings are much more subtle, such as when the camera moves slightly upward to keep centered in the frame a character who is rising from a chair.

Two common types of mobile frames are pans and tracking shots. A **pan** moves the frame from side to side without changing the position or axis of the camera. In other words, the camera rotates, as if a character were turning his or her head. The fairly standard long shot that moves from left to right as the frame scans the skyline of San Francisco, for example, is a pan shot. Or a pan may re-create a character's point of view, beginning with a medium shot of a young woman in the doorway and then panning across to her companion sitting at a table. During the last scene of *Death in Venice* (1970), a slow pan leaves the main character, Gustav von Aschenbach, as he walks onto the beach and then swings past a jetty to settle the shot on the turbulent ocean and the glowing horizon. The movement of this pan suggests perhaps the romantic yearning and searching that characterize the entire film and that now culminate in von Aschenbach's death **[Color Plate 30]**. A **tracking shot** changes the position of the point of view by moving forward or backward or around the subject, usually on tracks that have been constructed in advance. In a similar **dolly shot,** the camera is moved on a wheeled dolly that follows a determined course. The term **traveling shot** is sometimes used interchangeably with both tracking and dolly shots. In the remarkable first shot of Jean-Luc Godard's *Contempt* (1963), a camera on tracks moves forward into the foreground of the image, following a woman reading. When the track reaches that foreground, the camera turns and aims its lens directly at us, the audience.

Figure 3.30 *Citizen Kane* (1941). Reframing to enlarge and complicate the drama.

Figure 3.31 *Goodfellas* (1990). The long and winding track of power behind the scenes.

When these two kinds of mobile frames follow an individual, they are sometimes called **following shots.** In *The 400 Blows* (1959), a single following shot tracks the boy, Antoine Doinel (for eighty seconds), as he runs from the reformatory school toward the edge of the sea. In *Goodfellas* (1990), a film about mobster Henry Hill, a famous tracking shot, lasting nearly three minutes, twists and turns with Hill and his entourage through a back door, a kitchen, and into the main room of a nightclub, suggesting the bravura and power of a man who can go anywhere, who is both onstage and backstage **[Figure 3.31]**. Less common, **tilts** move the frame up or down on a horizontal axis, as when the frame swings upward to re-create the point of view of a man following a skyscraper from the street into the clouds. In Wim Wenders's *Paris, Texas* (1984), a story about a father and son searching for the boy's mother, repeated tilt shots become a rhetorical action, moving the frame up a flagpole with an American flag, along the sides of Houston skyscrapers, and into the sky to view a passing plane. In this case, vertical tilts seem to suggest an ambiguous hope to escape or find comfort from the long quest across Texas.

Zoom lenses, which employ a variable focal length of 75mm or higher, accomplish a different kind of compositional reframing and movement.

Figure 3.32 *The Blair Witch Project* (1999). Handheld shots bring the viewer into the horror.

During **a zoom-in,** the camera remains stationary as the zoom lens changes focal length to narrow the field of view on a distant object, bringing it into clear view and reframing it in a medium shot or close-up. Less noticeable in films, a **zoom-out** reverses this action, so that objects that appear close initially are then distanced from the camera and reframed as small figures. One of the significant side effects of a zoom-in is that the image tends to flatten and lose its depth of field, whereas a track can call attention to the spatial depth that it moves through. Although camera movements (tracking shots) and changes in the lens's focal length (zooms) may look similar to contemporary viewers, zoom lenses were not widely available to filmmakers before the 1950s and were thus not employed in many classic films. In two very different films, *An Occurrence at Owl Creek Bridge* (1962) and Ján Kádar's *Adrift* (1969), zoom-outs are combined with forward tracking shots, so that the respective protagonists appear to be running forward but never making any progress.

Encouraged first by the introduction of lightweight 16mm cameras and later by the use of video formats, **handheld shots,** produced by an individual carrying the camera, create an unsteady frame that suggests the movements of an individual point of view. *The Blair Witch Project* (1999) uses handheld shots so that the audience participates in the characters' frightened flight through the haunted forest **[Figure 3.32]**. Thomas Vinterberg's *The Celebration* (1998) also employs handheld digital video techniques to express the tension, anger, and confusion at a family gathering. In both of these cases, the handheld point of view aims to involve the audience more immediately and concretely in the action.

Animation and Special Effects

Our visual experience is not just realistic and natural; it also contains fantastic images found in our dreams or imaginations. These kinds of images can be re-created in film through two important manipulations of the image, animation and special effects, which can be used to make film seem even more realistic or completely surrealistic.

Animation traditionally refers to moving images drawn or painted on individual animation **cels,** which are then photographed onto single frames of film. In fact, animation includes several variations on that formula, as witnessed in films like *Chicken Run* (2000), the comic story of a chicken rebellion, and Czech filmmaker Jan Svankmajer's *Alice* (1988), which combines live action, puppets, and stop-motion animation to re-create the dizzying events of Lewis Carroll's story. With both these films, **stop-motion photography** records, as separate frames in stop action, inanimate objects or actual human figures that are then synthesized on film to create the illusion of motion and action: **claymation** accomplishes this effect with clay figures, while **pixilation** employs this technique (or instead simply cuts out images from a continuous piece of filmed action) to transform the movement of real human figures into rapid jerky gestures. If films from *Snow White and the Seven Dwarfs* (1937) to *Shrek* (2001) create graphic cartoon narratives through traditional frame-by-frame drawings and colorizing, today's animation is accomplished more and more through **computer graphics.** Films such as *Toy Story* (1995) **[Color Plate 31]** and *Finding Nemo* (2003) are composed entirely of **computer-generated imagery (CGI).** The striking advances in animation represented by such sophisticated techniques have contributed to the wide popularity of such films. The renewed appreciation for the medium was reflected in the introduction in 2002 of a new Academy Award category: feature-length animated films. Recently Richard Linklater's *Waking Life* (2001) recorded real figures and action on video as a basis for painting individual animation frames digitally **[Color Plate 32].**

A term encompassing many practices, **special effects** includes such basic manipulations as **slow motion** or **fast motion** to make the action move at unrealistic speeds (achieved by filming the action faster or slower than normal and then projecting it at normal speeds); **color filters** that change the tones of the recorded image with different tinted lenses; and **miniature** or **gigantic models** used to stage disasters or fantastic landscapes of the kind seen in the monstrous seas of *The Perfect Storm* (2000), which combined the use of models with CGI. Another common special effect that remakes more than one shot into a single image is a **process shot,** a term that describes many different ways that the image can be set up and manipulated during filming. A process shot might project a background for the action on a screen in order to add another layer to the reality of the image (such as a large dinosaur bearing down on a screen behind an unaware scientist who appears to be only inches away) or to intentionally undermine the realism of the image by suggesting two or more competing realities. Hans-Jürgen Syberberg's film *Our Hitler* (1977), for example, shows Hitler quietly eating dinner while, in the background, Jews arrive at concentration camps **[Figure 3.33]**; at other

Figure 3.33 *Our Hitler* (1977). Puppets and process shots unravel the illusion of a fascist dictator.

From Angles to Animation in *Vertigo* (1958)

Alfred Hitchcock's suspense film *Vertigo* is a useful guide into the world of film images because the plot hinges so dramatically on "seeing" and on the attempt to "possess" the world through images. In this complex tale, a wealthy husband (Gavin) hires a retired police detective (Scottie), who suffers from acrophobia (or fear of heights), to watch his wife (Madeleine), whom he claims is troubled by her obsession with a woman from the past (Carlotta). After Scottie rescues Madeleine during an apparent suicide attempt, he falls in love with her, and, when his acrophobia later prevents him from stopping her as she races to leap from a mission tower, her death sends Scottie into a spiral of guilt. Later, he believes he sees his lost love on the streets of San Francisco, and his pursuit of a lookalike woman (Judy) entangles him in another twist to this psychological murder mystery in which the central crisis is distinguishing reality from fictive images of it.

In this story about Scottie being "framed" for failing to save a life, *Vertigo* brilliantly takes advantage of almost every possibility in the film frame. Employing a particular brand of widescreen projection called VistaVision, the aspect ratio of Hitchcock's film is one of its immediately recognizable and significant formal features: the especially open space that the widescreen frame creates becomes a fitting environment for Scottie and his anxious searches through the wide vistas of San Francisco. Although *Vertigo* does not employ masks in the artificially obvious way of older films, at times Hitchcock cleverly creates masking effects by using natural objects within the frame: at several points, for instance, the frame of the car windshield masks and so intensifies Scottie's perspective as he follows Madeleine; at other times the film uses doors or other parts of the mise-en-scène to create masking effects that isolate and dramatize Scottie's intense gazing at Madeleine **[Color Plate 33]**.

Like many other Hitchcock films, *Vertigo* continually exploits the edges of the frame to tease and mislead us with what we (and Scottie) cannot see. In Scottie's pursuit of Madeleine, she frequently evades his point of view, disappearing like a ghost beyond the frame's borders (as when Madeleine suddenly vanishes from the frame while she and Scottie visit the Sequoia forest). The mystery of Madeleine's fall to her death is especially shocking because it occurs offscreen, revealed only as the blurred body flashes by the tower window, which acts as a second frame limiting Scottie's perception of what has happened **[Figure 3.34]**.

Figure 3.34 *Vertigo* (1958). From offscreen: the flash of a falling body.

Scottie's fascination with the image of Madeleine also draws attention to the importance of the distance between the subject and the viewer. Specifically, the different distances between the frame and the object of Scottie's sight reflect his longing for Madeleine and his desire to know the mysteries she conceals, and his obsession with Madeleine's face creates a continual drama of close-ups and, often, extreme close-ups. Like many films, these close-ups concentrate on faces and significant objects, such as Madeleine's full face, her bouquet of flowers, or the twisted swirl in her hair [Color Plate 34].

The angles of shots are crucial in *Vertigo*. The hilly San Francisco setting naturally accentuates high and low angles as Scottie follows Madeleine through the streets, and the film's recurring motif about the terror of heights informs even the most commonplace scenes, as high angles and overhead shots ignite Scottie's panicked paranoia: whether attempting the steep steps of the church tower, looking down from the stepladder in Midge's apartment, or driving on a steep street, the angles trigger Scottie's anguish and suggest danger. Especially when these sharp angles reflect Scottie's point of view, they suggest complex psychological and moral concerns about power and control as well as about desire and guilt, perhaps dramatizing those moments when Scottie's desires leave him in positions where he is most out of control and threatened.

Deep focus and color are less flamboyant than other elements but equally important to the film. When Scottie discovers Madeleine on the shoreline, for instance, she appears as a small figure in the middle ground. The massive Golden Gate Bridge recedes into the background and the depth adds to her fragile appearance. *Vertigo* also uses shallow focus as a key feature. Whereas the deep-focus images may suggest mysterious relations and personal conflicts, *Vertigo* frequently uses images whose surfaces seem almost two-dimensional. When Madeleine leaves Ernie's restaurant, there is virtually no depth in the close-up as she turns her profile, so that her image becomes a kind of flat, moving portrait—certainly an appropriate way to introduce a character who is associated with a painted portrait and who will haunt Scottie's mind as a drifting image. Finally, while there is a realistic balance of rich colors in the skin tones of the characters and the hues of the buildings, reds, blues, and greens stand out sharply in exaggerated or unnatural ways, as when curtains seem to emanate a green glow that suffuses Judy's room. Like the repetition of red, this eerie green echoes throughout the film, as in Madeleine's metallic-green car and Scottie's green sweater. Indeed, one might go so far as to claim a symbolic or metaphoric meaning for this green in the film: one renowned admirer of Hitchcock, director François Truffaut, associates that color with death in his film *The Green Room* (1978).

Certainly among the more elaborate dimensions of *Vertigo* is its moving frame. One casual scene demonstrates how common shot movements not only describe events in a complex way but also subtly invest those events with nuance and meaning. The scene takes place early in the film in the business office of Scottie's former schoolmate Gavin. With the activity of the shipyard continuing outside the picture window, Gavin works to enlist Scottie's help to follow his wife. The scene begins with Gavin sitting in his chair, but Scottie soon sits and Gavin stands and moves around the room: a pan of Gavin walking to a higher position in the room is followed by a low-angle shot of Gavin and a complementing high-angle shot of Scottie; a backward track then depicts the more aggressive Gavin as he moves to the front of the image toward the stationary Scottie [Figure 3.35]. As the moving frame continues to focus on Gavin trying to convince Scottie to help him

Figure 3.35 *Vertigo* (1958). A backward track on the aggressive Gavin.

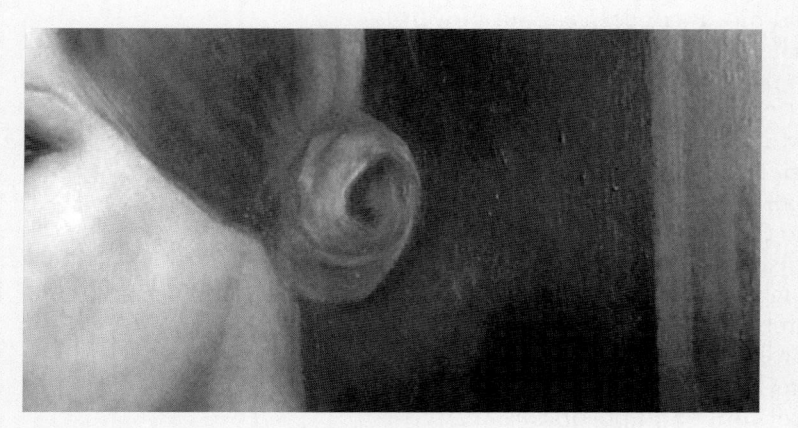

Figure 3.36 *Vertigo* (1958). Zooming-out and tracking to reframe the details of an obsession.

track his wife, the framing and its movement indicate that this is not quite a conversation between equals: the moving frame makes clear that Gavin directs the image and controls the perspective.

A more clearly central series of camera movements takes place when Scottie finds Madeleine standing before a portrait of Carlotta in an art museum. Here, the camera executes several complex moves that simulate Scottie's perspective: it simultaneously zooms-in and tracks first on the swirl in Madeleine's hair and then reframes by tracking and zooming-out on the same hair design in the painting of Carlotta **[Figure 3.36]**. Indeed, these reframings in the museum resemble the opening sequence in which Scottie hangs from the gutter and his frightened glances at the street below are depicted through a quick, distorting combination of zooming-in and tracking-out that describes his intense panic and spatial disorientation. Entirely through these camera movements, the film connects Scottie's original trauma and guilt with his mysterious attachment to Madeleine.

Although *Vertigo* seems to be a realistic thriller, it employs—dramatically and disconcertingly—both animation and special effects as a part of its story and description of Scottie's state of mind. An eerie matte shot re-creates a tower that is missing from the actual church at San Juan Bautista; its goal is perhaps largely to add a crucial element to the setting where Scottie's fear of heights will be exploited. Yet, along with the nightmarish significance of that tower, in the final scene the matted image appears as an eerily glowing surface and color as the surreal tower looms over yet another dead body. More obvious examples of special effects include the rear projections and animation when Scottie begins to lose his grip on one reality and become engulfed in another: in one scene, Scottie and Judy's kiss spins free of the background of the room and, earlier, during a nightmare triggered by his psychotic depression, an eruption of animation depicts the scattering of the mythical Carlotta's bouquet of flowers and a black abstract form of Scottie's body falling onto the roof of the church **[Color Plate 35]**.

Rather than mimicking or supplementing reality, these instances of animation and special effects in *Vertigo* point out how fragile the photographic realism of the cinematographic shot can be. *Vertigo* describes the obsessions of a man in love with the image of a woman (echoed from Carlotta to Madeleine to Judy). The film contains inordinately long periods without any dialogue, almost as a way to insist that Scottie's (and the film's) interest is primarily in images—in all their forms (from paintings to memories) and from many angles (high, low, moving, stationary, onscreen and offscreen).

VIEWING CUES: Elements of Cinematography

- Identify the original aspect ratio of the film you are studying in class. How is the aspect ratio appropriate or inappropriate to this film's themes and aims? If the film has been "panned and scanned" in order to be shown on a television screen, explain how that process might distort certain scenes.

- Are there any unusual masks employed in this film? What purpose do they serve?

- Consider the relation of onscreen and offscreen space in two or three shots from the film, and argue the importance of offscreen space in one of those shots. How does it add to your understanding of that shot?

- Look for a pattern of compositional distances in this film. Do there seem to be a large number of long shots? Close-ups? Some other pattern? Describe one such pattern, and explain how it reinforces one or more themes of the film.

- Select one or two shots in which depth of field seems especially important. Describe each shot as precisely as you can. How does depth of field distribute the objects or characters in a way that helps you better understand the shot?

- How is color or black and white used in the film? For more realism? For more specific purposes? Try to identify one color that strikes you as dominant. How would you explain the importance of that color?

- Examine one or two shots in which camera movements—tracks, pans, zooms, or others—are important. Why is a moving frame of a single shot used here instead of a series of shots? How does that movement comment on what is happening in the shot?

- Describe and analyze one important instance of special effects or animation in this film. Why is it used?

times the film reduces Hitler to a puppet onstage. Finally, a **matte shot,** such as the ominous church tower in *Vertigo* **[Color Plate 36]**, joins two pieces of film, one with the central action or object and the other with the additional background, figures, or action (sometimes painted or digitally produced) that would be difficult to create physically for the shot.

Points of View: Values and Traditions of the Film Image

From the chariot races in Enrico Guazzoni's 1913 *Quo Vadis?* to the spectacular descent of an alien spaceship in the 1977 *Close Encounters of the Third Kind,* movie images have been valued for their beauty and realism (often referred to as **production values** because of the skill and money invested). But film images carry other values in what they preserve and say about the world. French filmmaker Jean-Luc Godard's remark that film is truth at twenty-four frames a second suggests one way to describe the power and importance of the film image. Yet, as Godard's many films themselves demonstrate— from his iconoclastic depiction of a small-time hood in *Breathless* (1959)

Figure 3.37 *My Life to Live* (1962). Creating ideas about the image of a prostitute.

and his powerful portrayal of a meditative prostitute in *My Life to Live* (1962) **[Figure 3.37]** to his controversial search for spiritual meaning and truth in *Hail Mary* (1985)—this "truth" is not just the truth of presentation but also the truth of representation. Film images are prized and honored, in short, for their accuracy and artistry in showing or presenting us with facts as well as for how well they interpret or represent those facts.

Here, we will present two sets of primary values that inform how we see, understand, and judge film images. We will then explore two traditions that shape many of our expectations and responses to cinematography. In earlier sections of this chapter, we have investigated the cultural and formal structures of the film image. In this section, we will examine how we intellectually and emotionally interact with film images—even if we are not always aware of it. Having earlier addressed the historical background of the image and the compositional details we see, we turn to how we respond to film images according to the cultural and historical values and traditions that make images meaningful.

To Present or to Represent

Most of us value images as visual records of events that carry different personal and social meanings. We scrutinize television images for their truthfulness or absurdity. We honor old paintings in museums and churches. We carry pictures in our wallets that remind us of past feelings and relationships. Photographic and film images especially impress us as presences with enormous power to affect and provoke us. These images can replicate, extend, and distort how we usually perceive our lives and the world around us, and in them we have learned to look for and appreciate two primary values:

1. to present the world as a true record of events, people, and places
2. to represent that world for us in a way that suggests specific meanings or interpretations of those events, people, and places

Either by itself or in conjunction with other dimensions of the movie, such as the editing or the story, the film image thus assumes two different powers: one is the mimetic aim to straightforwardly present or document what is

Figure 3.38 *The Last Emperor* (1987). The value of an "authentic" image.

seen or how it is seen, and the other is the instrumental aim to control the meaning of what is seen as a "*re*-presentation."

The **image as presentation** reflects our belief that film communicates the details of the world realistically. The film image creates a true "second world," such as an image of past events and people or of an unknown reality. We prize the stunning images of the ancient Forbidden City in *The Last Emperor* (1987) **[Figure 3.38]** and the point-of-view shots of an insect in *Honey, I Shrunk the Kids* (1989) for their veracity and authenticity in depicting realities or perspectives. In pursuing this goal, cinematography may document either subjective images, which reflect the points of view of a person experiencing the events, or objective images, which assume a more general accuracy or truth in film images. In *Little Big Man* (1970), images from the perspective of a 101-year-old pioneer raised by Native Americans succeed, for many, in both ways: they become remarkably convincing displays of known historical events and characters—from the Battle of the Little Bighorn to General George Custer and Wild Bill Hickok—and they poignantly re-create the perspective of the pioneer as he lived through and now remembers those events.

Figure 3.39 *Blonde Venus* (1932). Calling attention to the power of representation with extreme images of race and gender.

Another value of the film image is an instrumental power, according to which the image influences or even determines the meaning of the events or people it portrays by "*re*-presenting" a reality through the mediating or interpretive power of cinematography. The **image as representation** recalls both the magical/religious impulse of the cave painter and the scientific power of the visual anthropologist; that is, how we depict individuals or actions implies a kind of control over them, knowledge of them, or power to determine what they mean. Accordingly, to frame (through a photograph or on film) means to capture and contain a person or object according to a point of view that, more or less, defines it. This imagistic value to represent permeates the drama of *Vertigo*, in which Scottie tries so desperately to define Madeleine as an image. It can also be found at the heart of films as diverse as *Blonde Venus* (1932) and *Fight Club* (2000), both about the ability of the film image to capture and manipulate a person or reality in the service of a point of view **[Figure 3.39]**. Depending on how an image uses its compositional power, from framing and distance to colors and special effects, a film image might represent an object or a character as, for instance, humorous, innocent, horrifying, or with significantly more complex meanings. In *Blonde Venus*, the film image makes Marlene Dietrich into a self-consciously erotic figure; in *Fight Club*, the main character projects and represents himself, undetectedly for much of the film, as a violently sado-masochistic alter-ego image.

Part of the art of film is that these two primary imagistic values are sometimes ambiguous and can be mobilized in intricate ways in a movie (as indeed they are in both *Blonde Venus* and *Fight Club*). An image that shows a child as witty or even beatific can be compositionally constructed as an objective presentation of the perspective of the mother or as an interpretive representation of the child by the film. Placed within the play of these values, a perceptive viewer must consider the most appropriate values and meanings for the shot—that, in short, it reflects the mother's position or the film's position. Watching closely how images carry and mobilize values, we thus encounter the complexity of making meaning in a film and the importance of our own activity as viewers.

Presence and Text: Two Traditions of the Film Image

Specific cinematographic traditions have emerged from the history of these values. Film traditions reflect expectations about the imagistic values encountered in different movies, and these expectations, in turn, influence how we respond to certain kinds of shots and framings in other movies. For some kinds of movies, like documentaries and historical fiction films, we have learned to see the film frame as a window on the world. For others, such as avant-garde or art films, we learn to approach the images as puzzles, perhaps revealing secrets of life and society. Here, we will designate two prominent traditions in the history of the film image: the tradition of image as presence and the tradition of image as text. In the first case, we identify with the image; in the second, we read it.

In discussing the compositional practices of the film image, what we call the **tradition of presence** implies the following:

- a close identification with the point of view of the image
- a response to the image that is primarily emotional
- an experience of the image as if it were a lived reality

Part of a varied history, images in this tradition fascinate us with a visual activity we participate in, overwhelm us with their beauty or horror, or comfort us with their familiarity. Although not entirely separable from the story and other elements of the film form, imagistic presence is what principally entertains us at the movies, what elicits our tears and shrieks. A shot of horses and riders dashing toward a finish line or of a woman embracing a dear friend communicates an immediacy or truth that engages us and leads us through subsequent images.

Figure 3.40 *9½ Weeks* (1986). A viscerally sensual image.

Two variations within this tradition are the traditions of the phenomenological image and the psychological image. The tradition of the **phenomenological image** refers to filmmaking styles that approximate, through images, the physical activity according to which we normally see the world and visually participate in it—such as a shot that re-creates the dizzy perspectives from a mountaintop. As old as film history itself, this tradition appears in vastly different movies: from the remarkably visceral and physically chaotic battle scenes in Orson Welles's *Chimes at Midnight* (1966) to the erotic film *9½ Weeks* (1986) **[Figure 3.40]**, phenomenological shots convey a sensual vitality in the image itself. The tradition of the **psychological image,** in contrast, creates images that reflect the state of mind of the viewer or a more general emotional atmosphere in a scene: in *10* (1979), a middle-aged man fantasizes the image of his dreams coming true as a beautiful woman running toward him in slow motion; in *Midnight Cowboy* (1969), disorienting, blurry images at a party re-create Joe's mental and perceptual experience after taking drugs **[Color Plate 37]**. Both traditions appear regularly in film history and in many different cultures, but certain film movements emphasize one over the other. Westerns—such as *High Noon* (1952)—tend to rely on phenomenological images to imbue movement and conflict with energy **[Figure 3.41]**, whereas movies that concentrate on personal crises—such as the melodramatic *Written on the Wind* (1956), a tale of wealth and happiness in which high-strung emotions and mental stress are everywhere—often employ psychological images to reflect the states of mind of the characters **[Color Plate 38]**.

Tradition of textuality refers to a different kind of film image, one that demands

- an emotional distancing of the viewer from the image
- a reaction to the image that is primarily analytic
- an experience of the image as artifice or as constructed like a written statement or an aesthetic object to be interpreted

We stand back to look at film images in this tradition from an intellectual distance. They seem loaded with signs and symbols for us to decipher. They impress us more for how they show the world than for what they show. So-called difficult, abstract, or experimental films—from *The Seashell and the Clergyman* (1928) to *Pi* (1998)—enlist viewers most

Figure 3.41 *High Noon* (1952). A shot that concentrates on bodies in motion and pain.

obviously within this tradition, but many films integrate images that test our abilities to read and decipher **[Figure 3.42]**. A tilted framing of an isolated house or a family reunion shot through a yellow filter may stand out in an otherwise realistic movie as a puzzling image that asks for more reflection: How do we read this image? Why is this unusual composition included? In *The Seashell and the Clergyman*, apparently about a priest in love with a beautiful woman, images resemble the cryptic language of a strange dream, requiring viewers to struggle to decipher them, perhaps as a way of understanding the film's complex drama of repression and desire **[Figure 3.43]**.

Two specific versions of the tradition of textuality are the traditions of the aesthetic image and the semiotic image. The **aesthetic image** asks to be contemplated and to be appreciated for its artistic re-creation of a world or a perspective as texture, color, and composition. A second offshoot of the tradition of imagistic textuality, the **semiotic image** presents images as signs to be interpreted presumably like language or to be read like a poem. While aesthetic images are usually found in art films like *The Seashell and the Clergyman*, they also surface in many other kinds of films: in the luxurious close-ups of Greta Garbo in *Queen Christina* (1933), in the elaborate imagistic composition of Busby Berkeley's musical *Dames* (1934), and in such recent films as *Run, Lola, Run* (1998) and *Requiem for a Dream* (2000).

Figure 3.42 *Pi* (1998). An ordinary image of cream in coffee becomes a visual and mathematical puzzle through the eyes of a fragile math genius.

Figure 3.43 *The Seashell and the Clergyman* (1928). Extreme angles, shadows, and highlighted patterns in the pavement suggest a complex dream image.

Digital Cinema

Watching movies during the last ten years has meant seeing a new type of image: the digital image. Historically, the film image was a celluloid image whose widths have ranged from 35mm to 70mm (in the first part of the twentieth century) to 16mm and 8mm (in the latter half of the twentieth century). During the 1970s, videotape, a flexible magnetic strip that registers sound and images, influenced not so much film production but the way films would be distributed (for home viewing). Today, however, video images created by digital technologies are having a powerful impact on both the production and distribution of movies. Digital image processing allows for faster and less expensive filmmaking, and digital signal processing will soon revolutionize the way films are distributed. It also promises to challenge viewers' assumptions about the inherent realism of film and photographic images because digital images are capable of creating remarkably realistic duplications of people and events.

Forrest Gump (1994) is a celebrated example of the integration of digital image processing with conventional filmmaking. Throughout this tale of a slow-witted character, digitized samples of historical footage of well-known figures (such as President Lyndon B. Johnson and Alabama Governor George Wallace) are blended with images of the fictional Forrest Gump (played by Tom Hanks) **[Figure 3.44]**. In one sense an extension of the tricks of traditional special-effects cinematography, the digital craft has expanded to generate convincing virtual realities. Future computer-generated manipulations of figures and space will continue to test what realism in cinema means to viewers.

Figure 3.44 *Forrest Gump* (1994). Gump with George Wallace: digitally blending fiction and history.

In *Run, Lola, Run,* for instance, a realistic shot of the mother watching a television tracks into the television itself, at which point it becomes an imaginatively animated tracking shot that follows the cartoon image of Lola as she dashes down the stairs. The transformation signifies the malleable world of this movie **[Color Plate 39]**.

Although the tradition of the semiotic image is predominantly associated with new-wave movies, such as Glauber Rocha's *Antonio das Mortes* (1969) and Jean-Luc Godard's *Numéro deux* (1975), it is also found in older films like Sergei Eisenstein's *The Battleship Potemkin* (1925) and Dziga Vertov's *The Man with the Movie Camera* (1929) in which realistic and unrealistic images form strange compositions that demand a reflective reading. In R. W. Fassbinder's *In a Year of Thirteen Moons* (1978), a medium close-up shows the transsexual Elvira being violently forced to look at herself in a mirror. This emotionally painful image—through its slightly askew angle, tilted planes, and doubling of the face—becomes inscribed with emotional and social divisions, hostilities, and imbalances **[Figure 3.45]**. Like Elvira herself, her reflection becomes a shredded text.

Certainly there are other traditions and other versions of these traditions in film images, but recognizing the dominance of either the tradition

Color Plate 1 *Like Water for Chocolate* (1992). Dark, luxuriant colors draw attention to the moist and thick texture of the food.

Color Plate 2 *U-571* (2000). Balancing dark and muted colors in an image where the faces are what stand out only adds to the realism of the claustrophobic mise-en-scène of a submarine.

◄ Color Plate 3 *Intolerance* (1916). Coloring specific film frames underlines the exotic in the lavish sets of Babylon.

Color Plate 4 *A.I.* (2001). A futuristic, submerged New York City where the color scheme is all the more disturbing because of its simplicity, moving from bright-blue skies to darker blue seas to a black-blue skyline.

Color Plate 5 *Meet Me in St. Louis* (1944). The World's Fair as the climactic stage and set, the vivid Technicolors now helping to create the fantasy.

Color Plate 6 *Henry V* (1944). Transforming the history of mise-en-scène from a Renaissance stage to Technicolor realism.

Color Plate 7 *Singin' in the Rain* (1952). An umbrella transformed as dancing prop; the dark, monochromatic tone works to draw attention to the gleeful activity of the character and his prop.

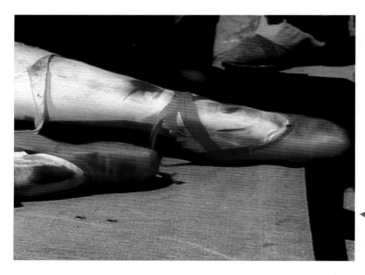

◀ Color Plate 8 *The Red Shoes* (1948). Brilliantly red shoes: a color and prop that dominate a tragic story of passion and obsession.

Color Plate 9 *Easy Rider* (1969). Against the naturalistic earthy tones of the setting (browns, oranges, yellows), the metallically gleaming motor-cycles stand out as countercultural icons.

Color Plate 10 *On Golden Pond* (1981). A career of different roles em-bodied in Katharine Hepburn's complex performance. Here, with co-star Henry Fonda, the low-contrasting browns and tans suggest both aging and enrichment.

Color Plate 11 *My Fair Lady* (1964). A flower girl transformed through costume and shimmering color. Most remarkable here is how the predominantly black-and-white costume colors actually draw more attention to the subtle brilliance of the colors in the image.

Color Plate 12 *Fellini's Roma* (1972). Brilliant colors and costumes define life as a memory and dream.

Color Plate 13 *Do the Right Thing* (1989). The political flashpoint of props: nostalgic black-and-white photos stand out from the colored wall.

Color Plate 14 *Do the Right Thing* (1989). The high-key lighting against a glaringly red wall adds to the intensity and theatricality of these otherwise casual commentators on the street.

Color Plate 15 *Barry Lyndon* (1975). Low candle lighting and a murky color scheme add an eerie atmosphere to the ghostlike appearance of the characters.

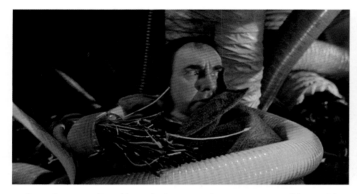

Color Plate 16 *Brazil* (1985). The twisted mise-en-scène of future life where the glowing oranges and blues of metals and plastics engulf a human face.

Color Plate 17 *The American Friend* (1977). The crowded anonymity of a subway: although the balance of colors results in a naturalistic image, the sheen and gloss of those colors (throughout this film) seem to denaturalize the world of the main character.

◄**Color Plate 18** *Walkabout* (1971). Somber blue-grays and dark browns almost erase the contrast between an open sky and an unknown world, barely highlighting the pale skin of a lost boy.

Color Plate 19 *Blade Runner* (1982). The original monochromatic colors of this photograph become, through the aid of a computer, electronically reframed and redrawn with glittering highlights and glowing blue neon lines.

Color Plate 20 *Andrei Rublev* (1966). Glorious gold, blue, and red transcend the wear of history in this Rublev icon.

Color Plate 21 *Rebel without a Cause* (1955). Angry teens lost in space: the blue haze of the cityscape in the background seems to surround and engulf the contrast between the white shirt and the black jacket.

◄Color Plate 22 *The Lord of the Rings: The Fellowship of the Ring* (2001). ▲ (left) An image formatted to fit a televised screen. (right) A widescreen image restored through letterboxing.

Color Plate 23 *Alien* (1979). Stalked by an alien creature, even close-ups—whose soft natural hues contrast sharply with the surrounding black—call attention to the menace offscreen.

Color Plate 24 *L.A. Confidential* (1997). A rack focus isolates a moment of determination, creating a blurred grey background and highlighting the facial skin tones.

Color Plate 25 *Pleasantville* (1998). Peering at life in black and white from a colored world.

Color Plate 26 *King Lear* (1910). Tinted frames embellish early cinematic Shakespeare.

Color Plate 27 *Becky Sharp* (1935). One of the first full Technicolor features whose bright primary colors embellish and bring to vivid life literary adaptation (of *Vanity Fair*).

Color Plate 28 *Time Regained* (1999). As with old and treasured photographs, soft and sumptuous sepia tones of yellow and tan suffuse this image of remembrance.

Color Plate 29 *American Graffiti* (1973). The gleam of starry blues and playful yellows as the markers of teenage memories.

Color Plate 30 *Death in Venice* (1970). Following a slow pan from shore to sea, the natural light of a sunset creates the airy and sparkling surface of browns, blues, and greys, a fittingly intense but ephemeral beauty.

Color Plate 31 *Toy Story* (1995). The exaggerated crayon colors of toys leap from the more balanced, natural tones of a background world.

Color Plate 32 *Waking Life* (2001). Stylized strokes of a digital ▶ palette: the complimentary gradations of greens and blues and distinct areas of color bring to life a series of reflections on where reality and the cinema intersect.

Color Plate 33 *Vertigo* (1958). In this stunning composition, Scottie's previously masked point of view becomes graphically juxtaposed with the mirror-image of the woman he pursues. The color scheme draws out three distinct planes in the image: the luxuriant colors of the flowers in the background, the pale hair and blue suit of Madeleine, and the copper shadow of Scottie's peeking face.

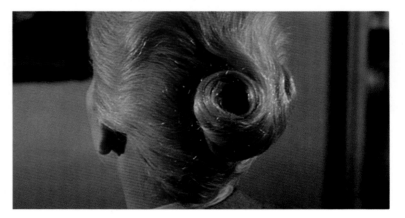

Color Plate 34 *Vertigo* (1958). A close-up of the vertiginous swirl, intensified by the bright hues that virtually whiten the blonde hair.

Color Plate 35 *Vertigo* (1958). The special effects of a nightmare: an abstracted black figure against equally abstracted brick and earth tones.

Color Plate 36 *Vertigo* (1958). The matte shot of the church tower, with pale whites against an artificially blue sky and unmoving clouds, is almost real but strangely unreal.

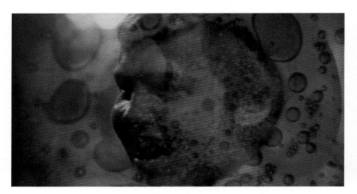

Color Plate 37 *Midnight Cowboy* (1969). Special effects and blurred, colored contrasts create the murky hallucination of cowboy Joe Buck.

Color Plate 38 *Written on the Wind* (1956). Suffused with wild emotions, the image displays the character's almost hysterical state of mind through the fiery-orange gown set against stunning blues.

Color Plate 39 *Run, Lola, Run* (1998). An aesthetic game where life is transformed into a colorful cartoon.

Color Plate 40 *Timecode* (2000). Fracturing real time with the digital image: a grid of edgy and metallic hues where even whites and flesh tones become digitally intensified colors.

Technically, the digital image offers advantages and disadvantages. Besides the economic advantage of lightweight and mobile cameras, the sharpness of the digital image suggests a kind of immediacy that distinguishes it from traditional celluloid images. The tale of a family gathering that is shattered through the horrifying revelation of a grown son, Vinterberg's *The Celebration* is an example of how the digital image dramatizes a stark reality with edgy directness. In addition, the digital image allows for nonlinear editing (even for movies that eventually appear as conventional film images), whereby connections, insertions, and changes can be made anywhere in the film through computer access to the master disc. Thus a filmmaker may readily experiment with multiple sequences. An ambitious use of digital technology is Mike Figgis's *Timecode* (2000). A director of Hollywood films, including *Leaving Las Vegas* (1995), Figgis made *Timecode* entirely with digital recording equipment. In a frame that contains four different quadrants, four stories are presented simultaneously in real time [Color Plate 40]. A dark comedy about murder and sex set in Hollywood, *Timecode* is a ninety-three-minute film that presents four continuous shots without any edits, sharing a single frame. Well outside mainstream film culture, "machinima" has become one of the more interesting offshoots of digital cinema. With this practice, filmmakers (such as Hugh Hancock, the creator of *Ozymandias* [2000]) manipulate the digital graphics of popular computer video games in order to create original images and stories (*Ozymandias* being a free interpretation of the Percy Bysshe Shelley sonnet).

Digital image processing also has several disadvantages. Digital images are recorded with pixels (densely packed dots), rather than the crystal array or grain produced by the celluloid emulsion used for film. When converted to a digital file, a 35mm film frame contains about ten million pixels. A sophisticated digital camera, such as the Sony Panavision HD 24 videocamera, records about two million pixels for each of the primary colors. This difference may not make one kind of image better than the other, but the digital image has less range to explore the grains and tones found in the film emulsion, which are further enhanced by light in film production. In addition, traditional film equipment outperforms digital equipment in difficult outdoor conditions.

Strictly speaking, digital cinema is actually digital video produced with increasingly sophisticated equipment. Yet as cinema and video overlap and interact more and more, the digital image—while unlikely to replace the celluloid image—will certainly redefine and expand the film experience. Already digital cinema has asked us to rethink our measure of reality on the screen, to re-conceive how stories can be told, and, in some cases, to recast how audiences can interact with films.

of presence or the tradition of textuality within a single film or part of a film is an important way to begin to appreciate and understand that movie. A romance like *Enchanted April* (1992), suffused with Italian sunshine, exudes exotic presence and wonder, and recognizing how it engages a larger tradition of presence allows us to see its distinctions and differences. A visually dense and complex film about an underground gang of Nazi "werewolves," Lars von Trier's *Zentropa* (1991) asks us to decipher images constructed with special effects and mixed media, but part of its success as a movie is attributed to how it innovates the complexities of a tradition of textuality. Film compositions communicate information and tell tales, yet we best experience and process—and enjoy—film images by recognizing the values and traditions that underpin them and our expectations of them. The initial hostile reception of *Bonnie and Clyde* in 1967, for instance, turned to admiration

Figure 3.45 *In a Year of Thirteen Moons* (1978). The problem of reading a sexual identity in crisis through its image.

In Focus: Values and Traditions in *M* (1931)

S et in Germany around 1930, Fritz Lang's *M* constantly calls attention to its powers to present both objective and subjective experiences. *M* tells the gruesome tale of a child murderer, Franz Becker, whom both police and criminals pursue in an attempt to regain each group's stable, if corrupt, social situation. Throughout the film, objective images alternate with subjective ones: images seem at some points to describe the facts of a dark and anxious German society in 1930; at other points they reproduce that world through the perspective of individual characters. Even in a fiction film such as this one, the images document a history of facial expressions, cultural products, and social activities, such as the uniforms of the German police and the raucous criminal dens. At still other points in this film, the images convincingly present personal perspectives, such as the anxiety of a mother as she waits for her daughter, glances at the clock several times, and stares at an empty seat before a table setting **[Figure 3.46]**.

In *M* the boundaries between these objective and subjective images regularly blur, and the film occasionally leaves unclear whether the images are a factual record of German street life or descriptions of anxious or even deranged minds. Early in the film, an extreme high-angle shot presents an apparently objective view of children playing in a courtyard, but the angle of the shot also suggests the uneasy and oppressive feeling that suffuses the atmosphere. Soon afterward a medium shot tracks laterally left to right as it follows the young girl, Elsie Beckmann, as she walks home bouncing a ball, straightforwardly depicting her carefree journey but also suggesting that someone might be following and watching her. Later, a descriptive tracking shot of a man walking with a young girl is transformed into a scene of chaos, fear, and anger because the shot suddenly becomes identified with the subjective perspective of a crowd that sees the man as the murderer.

There are numerous examples in *M* of the power of the image to represent individuals by assigning them meanings and values, often in a self-conscious fashion that dramatically calls attention to this power. These representations are sometimes the common kind one finds in many films: a dark low-angle shot defines a criminal as dangerous, whereas a close-up of a mother emphasizes her internalized sorrow and pain. At other times, the structure of an image suggests more elaborate commentary: the detective Karl Lohmann is shot from an extreme low angle that not only describes him sitting in a chair but also depicts him as a grotesque, slovenly, and comical

Figure 3.46 *M* (1931). Conveying personal anxiety through an image.

caricature. Sometimes, other, darker judgments and meanings appear through the image. As part of a complex maneuver in that early tracking shot of Elsie, the image shifts subtly from being a description of her perspective to an ominously threatening point of view. When Elsie stops and bounces her ball off a poster warning of the murderer, the low camera angle assumes her point of view, but when, suddenly, the dark shadow of a man drifts across the poster and her perspective, the image acquires a darker and more threatening point of view that literally takes over Elsie's perspective with its own [Figure 3.47]. In a more diabolical way than in most films, to see someone or something here means to control and designate them through the seer's image of them—and here the power of that perspective over Elsie anticipates her murder. When, at the conclusion of the film, Becker stumbles into a vacant warehouse,

Figure 3.47 *M* (1931). The imagistic shift from description to threat.

he ironically finds himself the object of the same representational power in the image, the source of the perspective now being a large crowd rather than a troubled individual. He suddenly finds himself literally captured by the gaze of a mob of street thieves and criminals prepared to judge him as the target of their eyes, just as he had done to Elsie.

M appears at the end of what is commonly called the "golden age" of German cinema, generally identified with two specific movie traditions: German expressionist films and German "street films." In street films, the movie image documents the tough and unglamorous social realities of criminals, prostitutes, or other desperate individuals. In German expressionism, film images often investigate emotional, psychological, and subconscious realities. What makes *M* so complex is that it engages both these German film movements: while its documentary-like shots of criminals, tools and weapons suggest the realism of street films, the expressionistic tradition allows Lang to explore a different kind of presence through the textuality of the image, one associated with desires and fears.

One set of images is especially indicative of expressionism: the images of spirals that appear throughout *M* suggest the power of an image to mesmerize and absorb the viewer. Early in *M*, a high-angle shot of a staircase from above (reflecting the point of view of the anxious mother) creates a dizzy perspective that draws the eye into the receding spiral composition; later, this same imagistic figure of absorption recurs in a shop window as a mechanical circle spins hypnotically [Figure 3.48]. These visual metaphors suggest a loss of consciousness that seems to describe Becker's madness, but other, less dramatic, images draw viewers into compositions that are similarly gripping and absorbing. Midway through the escalating drama, after the criminals pursue Becker into a factory, a medium close-up focusing on his face as he picks at the lock of a storeroom intensifies Becker's emotional desperation through the very proximity and size of the image, making it difficult for us not to empathize with the pain of this villainous character. Indeed, sometimes an image may point toward offscreen realities that are not fully shown but still fire the viewer's imagination with a powerful consciousness of that reality. When the criminals interrogate the factory guard, the camera pulls back from the room and stops outside, where we hear but cannot see the torture. The horrible presence of that torture

Figure 3.48A *M* (1931). German expressionism: dizzying overhead shot of a staircase.

Figure 3.48B *M* (1931). German expressionism: a spiral figure and the mesmerizing loss of consciousness.

becomes more immediate and disturbing through the suggestive force of the composition.

In addition, the characters and the film viewers of *M* encounter a tradition of textual images (also associated with German expressionism) that asks them to interpret the secrets and mysteries within the image. At one point, Becker examines his close-up reflection in a mirror, pulling his mouth down in a distorted frown, perhaps as a bizarre attempt to see and comprehend the madman inside himself. At another, a close-up of a note from Becker is examined closely in order to analyze "the very particular shape of the letters"; and several times, the police assemble images of fingerprints and maps to try to identify and locate the killer. In both cases, images become explicit instruments for investigating the crime and thus, the police hope, instruments with which to capture Becker. The plot turns dramatically when the criminals trailing Becker surreptitiously mark the back of his jacket with the letter *M*, thereby identifying this anonymous figure of a man on the street as the killer by making his image a legible text. Less directly, the film creates complex visual metaphors that ask viewers to decipher their significance: a balloon purchased by Becker for Elsie later appears in a medium shot tangled in telephone wires to suggest her death and perhaps the twisted person of Becker (whose body resembles the balloon figure) **[Figure 3.49]**.

Figure 3.49 *M* (1931). Reading a visual metaphor.

As with all films, the cinematic images in *M* bear different values and participate in different imagistic traditions, in this case creatively overlapping and intersecting. Like many excellent films, the cinematography in *M* cannot be reduced to a single value or pigeonholed in a single tradition. Carefully exploring the powers and limitations of the image as it puts in play different values and traditions, *M* makes clear that looking and seeing deeply matter in our lives and that the creation of meaningful images of self and others always has serious social implications.

VIEWING CUES: Values and Traditions of the Film Image

- In the film you will watch next in class, find two or three shots that aim "to present" certain experiences and two or three shots that aim "to represent" different realities. Analyze one shot of each type carefully, explaining how certain presentational and representational values appear in the image.

- Explain the relation of these imagistic powers to the film's themes. How do the images reflect some of the values at stake in the film?

- Identify the tradition that best aligns with this film: a tradition of presence or a tradition of text. Research the historical context for the film. Is there a more specific cinematic tradition informing the movie? How does locating the film in these traditions explain what is most important and distinctive about it?

several months later. One way of understanding the dynamics of this change is to note that viewers ultimately realized that the film's images belong not to a tradition of presence but to a tradition of textuality. At first, many may have seen the film as glamorizing 1930s violence; only later did they recognize the distance of those images as an ironic commentary on 1960s violence. Film, like chance, favors the prepared mind.

CRITICAL VOICES: JOHN BELTON ON THE WIDESCREEN IMAGE

As John Belton makes clear in his sketch of the history of Cinerama (in this excerpt from his 1992 book *Widescreen Cinema*), the connection between multiscreen or widescreen formats and the cultural and historical contexts in which this formal feature developed is central to how images are understood. Although many movies use the widescreen format, this particular aspect ratio may still bear traces of its epic and nationalistic origins.

Cinerama, like the cinema itself, traces its origins back to its dubious   1
antecedents in the fairground, where con men, pickpockets, sword-swallowers, Barnumesque showmen, Rube Goldberg–like inventors, and genuine scientists pitched their wares. The fanciest of fairgrounds is the "Exposition" or world's fair, and it is here, in the meeting ground for scientists and showmen, that the cinema was truly born, not in the privacy of some inventor's laboratory, toolshed, carriage house, or barn. . . .

The history of multiscreen or large-screen motion picture formats could   2
be written on the backs of a succession of world's fair ticket stubs, from the Chicago Exhibition of 1893 and Paris Exposition of 1900 to the Brussels World's Fair of 1958, where Disney's Circarama was introduced, and the Seattle World's Fair of 1962, which featured "Spacearium," a 70mm Cinerama-like process in which images shot with a fisheye lens were projected onto a huge curved dome, filling an angle of view 360 x 160 degrees. This history would extend from Expo '67 in Montreal, which boasted a 360-degree projection system, a 70mm multiple-image device, and a 35mm mosaic of vertical and horizontal images, to Expo '90 in Osaka, which featured the IMAX process; and from the recent world's fairs in Vancouver and Tokyo, where

Showscan was premiered, to Expo '85 in Tsukuba, Japan, where a black-and-white Omnimax 3-D system premiered, Expo '86 in Vancouver, Canada, where IMAX 3-D was demonstrated, and Expo '90 in Osaka again, where both IMAX Solido (a full-color, wraparound, 70 mm 3-D system) and IMAX Magic Carpet (a two-projector, two-screen, 70mm process) were unveiled. The last system consists of two IMAX projectors and two IMAX screens— "one in front of the audience and the other, visible through a transparent floor, underneath," which gives audiences the illusion that they are floating in space, "like the magic flying carpet of Arabian Nights." [Belton is quoting here from David Katz's "A Widescreen Chronology."]

World's fair exhibits typically present displays of a country's latest tech- 3
nological developments in science and industry through the use of entertainment programs designed to showcase its artistic achievements as well. These fairs serve as both trade shows and forums for individual nations to use in propagandizing their overall cultural progress. Motion pictures in general have long been regarded as a means of either direct or indirect propaganda, ranging from Sergei Eisenstein's didactic lessons in Russian history and Leni Riefenstahl's epic paeans to Nazi power to the (supposedly) more subtle American agitprop of Frank Capra and others. But large-screen motion pictures in particular have become associated over the years with the promotion of national identity either through their origins as exhibits in national pavilions at world's fairs or through their inherent ability to convey certain kinds of subject matter.

Though not developed for a world's fair, Abel Gance's multiscreen 4
process suggests one way in which widescreen has lent itself to ideological purposes. In 1926–27 Gance developed the three-screen system known as Polyvision in an attempt to create a canvas large enough to convey the epic nature of his subject matter—Napoleon. His hero, in turn, is integrally linked to the identity of the nation as a whole. Gance's tryptic screen not only draws upon (Catholic) religious numerology to deify his hero but recalls the French flag—the tricolor—as well. This allusion is driven home by the use of red, blue, and "white" tinting in adjacent panels of the triptych at certain moments in the film. The shape of the film echoes its content, and the dramatic changes in shape from one to three screens, which Gance orchestrates at crucial moments in his narrative, mirror the explosive energies of both Napoleon and France. Unfortunately, the video version of the film [*Napoléon*], though retaining the triptych, reduces it in size, optically zooming out to the letterbox format to accommodate the three panels within the same space initially occupied by one. This reduction in the image size reverses the impact of the sudden shift to three screens in the original version.

THE NEXT LEVEL: ADDITIONAL SOURCES

Belton, John. *Widescreen Cinema*. Cambridge: Harvard University Press, 1992. This book examines the technical, economic, social, and aesthetic forces that have been a part of widescreen cinema since 1896, shaping and reshaping the film image to respond to different cultures and audiences.

Berger, John. *Ways of Seeing*. Harmondsworth: Penguin, 1972. Small and well illustrated, Berger's book offers a remarkably broad perspective on how images of all kinds—from paintings to television advertisements—are informed by powerful historical and cultural values.

Schaefer, Dennis, and Larry Salvato. *Masters of Light: Conversations with Contemporary Cinematographers*. Berkeley: University of California Press, 1984. Fascinating discussions with acclaimed directors of photography give insight into their art and craft.

Smoodin, Eric. *Animation Culture: Hollywood Cartoons from the Sound Era*. New Brunswick: Rutgers University Press, 1993. An examination of not only the technical strategies in film animation (from 1930 to 1960) but also the complex political and ideological agendas that often drove those strategies.

Winston, Brian. *Technologies of Seeing*. London: BFI, 1997. A critical review of the development of the technological image—from 16mm film to HDTV to holography—this study emphasizes the logic behind these changes and how they engage other historical and social shifts.

Relating Images: Editing

The cutting of a scene into shots is a necessarily artificial operation, the same aesthetic calculation which made [William Wyler] choose to reduce the number of shots to the minimum necessary for the clarity of the narrative. In fact The Best Years of Our Lives *has no more than 190 shots an hour—approximately 500 shots in a film of 2 hours 40 minutes. Let's recall, for reference, that modern films comprise on average some 300–400 an hour, approximately double that number. . . . Shots of longer than 2 minutes are not rare in* The Best Years of Our Lives, *without even a slight re-framing to reduce their static nature. In reality, there is no longer any trace of the resources of montage in such mise-en-scène. Even the decoupage, considered as an aesthetic of the relation between shots, is singularly reduced: the shot and the sequence tend to become one and the same. Many of the scenes of* The Best Years of Our Lives *merge together with Shakespearean dramatic unity and are treated in a single fixed shot.*

—André Bazin, film critic and co-founder of the journal *Cahiers du Cinéma*

KEY OBJECTIVES

How does a film connect separate images to create or reflect certain patterns through which we see the world and think about it? This chapter describes what many consider the most unique dimension of the film experience: the editing or linking of different images to imitate how we see the world as a series of images or to create patterns that depart from our customary visual experiences. We will examine how edited images:

- are based on a material cut or break in the film
- construct spatial relationships between images
- construct temporal relationships between images
- establish continuity
- emphasize graphic or rhythmic patterns
- are organized into meaningful scenes and sequences
- encourage particular ways of thinking about images
- are used in filmic traditions of continuity or disjuncture

Whether a film bombards the viewer with images, as does *JFK* (1991), or uses relatively few shots, as does *The Best Years of Our Lives* (1946), editing allows film to bring us myriad views of its subject. Alexander Sokorov's *Russian Ark* (2002) made history by avoiding cutting altogether, making use of the latest digital recording technology. This film, structured as a tour of the Russian Hermitage Museum, uses mise-en-scène and movement to tell a story traversing several epochs of history. However, the capacity of film to transcend space, time, and perspective is more easily conveyed by editing.

All around us we witness images that are juxtaposed and overlapped: in a series of store windows in a shopping center, on the billboards of a highway, as we change television channels, even in the unpredictable logic of dreams. As we process these different sights as a series of related images, we experience something like the logic of film editing, the process through which different images or shots are linked together. In fact, the editing of film images departs from the way we normally see the world, for in everyday perception, even a series of discrete images remains unified by our singular position and consciousness. There are no such limits in editing. In the movie's finished version, a **shot** can be defined simply as a continuous length of film, regardless of the camera movement or changes in focus it may record. One shot is selected and joined to other shots by the editor to guide viewers' perception. The shot is the basic unit of film and of electronic media, such as television and video. Editing can produce meaning by combining shots in an infinite number of ways.

The first shot in Spike Lee's *Crooklyn* (1994) starts from a fire escape and begins moving down the Brooklyn block where the film is set. This single crane shot gives us an overview of the neighborhood and its inhabitants. Next, we see a collage of different images: men playing dominos, a child's hair being combed out, boys spinning tops [**Figures 4.1–4.3**]. When edited together, these multiple images, taken from different heights, angles, and distances, give us a much more detailed impression of the variety and vitality of the setting. If the film shot presents the film's mise-en-scène from a single perspective, film editing extends and redefines images by linking them together in various relationships. Some of these relationships mimic the way an individual looks at the world (for example, a shot of someone looking off in the distance linked to another shot of an airplane in the sky), but often these relationships exceed everyday perception. Edited images may leap from one location to another or one time to another and may show different perspectives on the same event.

One of the most fundamental processes in filmmaking, editing is not based in physiology. Human perception is continuous. Unless we consciously or externally interrupt our vision (as when we blink our eyes), we do not see the world as the construction of separate images linked together in selected patterns. However, we find it perfectly natural that a film consists of eight hundred or more discrete images, often not noticing the cuts. In terms of human experience, the activity of editing—moving sometimes randomly and rapidly between different images—may best approximate the visual activity

Figure 4.1 *Crooklyn* (1994). The overview provided by a moving crane shot contrasts with a variety of edited images of neighborhood activities in the opening scene.

Figure 4.2 *Crooklyn* (1994).

Figure 4.3 *Crooklyn* (1994).

Figure 4.4 *Living Playing Cards* (1903). Pioneer Georges Méliès anticipated later editing techniques with magical transformations like this one.

Figure 4.5 *Living Playing Cards* (1903).

of a dream, in which images and patterns in our unconscious are triggered in sleep and assert themselves in an unpredictable or illogical order. This similarity suggests that editing is fundamentally an intellectual or conceptual arrangement that constructs image patterns to access particular emotions or ideas.

Our responses build, of course, on the intricate and multiple dimensions of the film image itself, whose qualities are often highlighted by juxtapositions with other images. In this chapter, we will examine the different formal strategies through which we experience editing when we watch a film. Editing techniques often work in the service of narrative explication or realism but non-narrative and abstract films also use editing to create their systems. As with the other formal features that shape the film experience, we will place editing in its historical context and later examine how its various strategies reflect social and cultural aims and assumptions.

The Foundations of Editing

Editing is one of the most significant developments in the syntax of cinema because it allows for a departure from the fixed perspective on the scene and for the continuous duration characteristic of theater. The earliest films consisted of a single shot, which could run only as long as the reel of film in the camera. In the early trick films of pioneer Georges Méliès, this limitation was manipulated. Objects and people disappeared or transformed when he stopped the film in the camera and resumed after rearranging the mise-en-scène. Similar **in-camera editing** is often used by home video camera operators today. In his 1903 film *Living Playing Cards*, a magician, played by Méliès himself, seems to make his props come alive **[Figures 4.4 and 4.5]**. Méliès sometimes adjusted such transitions by actually cutting the film, thus employing editing in the very early history of film. The basic properties of editing quickly developed and were absorbed into the technical process of filmmaking.

Editing is integral to filmmaking from the planning stages. When a film is shot, the cameraperson provides many takes of the same action; only a fraction of the film that is shot and developed makes it into the finished product. The relationship between the length of film shot and that which is used in the finished project is referred to as the **shooting ratio,** which will vary considerably according to the nature of the film and its budget. The editor will choose among different takes of the same shot—in order to prevent continuity errors, such as changes in the position of figures or objects from shot to shot, or to highlight an actor's best performance or a preferred lighting effect. **Coverage** means ensuring that a number of shots of a particular scene are taken from different angles and distances, in order to show two different characters in a conversation through close-ups and over-the-shoulder shots, for example. These takes will be intercut with a continuous

master shot of the scene's entire action. Having adequate coverage ensures smooth editing of the finished scene.

All filmmakers shoot a film with some notion of its edited version in mind, breaking down a script in order to figure out the camera setups that will yield desired shots. Some filmmakers are very meticulous about planning for editing as they shoot. Alfred Hitchcock said he considered the actual process of shooting the film uninteresting; his **storyboards** already laid out each scene shot-by-shot [**Figure 4.6**]. Other filmmakers will shoot many more hours of footage than they could possibly use and create the finished film in the editing room. This is often true of documentarians, who cannot plan the action they film.

For fiction films, each day's shooting is printed and the filmmaker screens **dailies** in order to evaluate the available footage. Usually the editor is supplied with a number of filmed versions, or **takes,** of each shot that is to be incorporated in a scene. A camera take is a continuously exposed piece of film. During the period of a film's **post-production,** the editor begins to assemble the selected takes of a shot into a **rough cut,** juxtaposing one shot with the next and shaping these linkages into larger units that may correspond to narrative sections, rhythmic intervals, or descriptive sequences. The physical join in the film is called a **splice,** and the material that the editor works with is called **work print.** When all editing decisions have been made in consultation with the filmmaker, the film is said to have **locked picture.** The camera negative is edited according to the editor's **final cut** by a **negative cutter** and prints are made for distribution.

Most of this technical labor is obscured when we watch an ordinary film. Rarely can we describe or enumerate the edits. Learning to watch for this basic element of film language is a rewarding way to experience the specificity of film as a medium.

The Cut

The material foundation for film editing is a **cut,** which describes the break and common border that separate two shots from two different pieces of film. A single shot can depict a woman looking at a ship at sea by showing a close-up of her face and then panning to the right, following her glance to reveal the distant ship she is watching. A cut renders this action in two shots, the first showing the woman's face and the second showing the ship. While the facts of the situation remain the same, the single-shot pan and the cut joining two shots create different experiences of the scenario. The first might emphasize the distance that separates the woman from the object of her vision. The second might create a sense of immediacy and intimacy that transcends that distance. In a key scene from *The Best Years of Our Lives*, we first see several characters occupying different spaces of the same shot [**Figure 4.7**]. After the character on the right shifts

Figure 4.6 *The Birds* (1963). Alfred Hitchcock sketched out in advance what his edited films would look like in storyboards like this one. The details differ from the finished scene (see **Figures 4.51–4.54**).

Figure 4.7 *The Best Years of Our Lives* (1946). Using deep-focus cinematography, this scene presents foreground and background actions in the same shot.

Figure 4.8 *The Best Years of Our Lives* (1946). The man standing at the piano (played by Fredric March) turns his attention to the background character on the phone (played by Dana Andrews).

Figure 4.9 *The Best Years of Our Lives* (1946). A cut to a closer shot emphasizes his perspective without assuming his point of view.

his attention to the character behind him, we are presented with a cut isolating them **[Figures 4.8 and 4.9]**. As these examples illustrate, the use of a cut usually follows a particular logic, in this case emphasizing the significance of an action. The infrequently used **shock cut** juxtaposes two images whose dramatic difference aims to create a jarring visual effect. Samuel Fuller's *Shock Corridor* (1963) surprises viewers with color footage sequences in a black-and-white film. Later in the chapter we will investigate additional ways that editing may create logical or shocking links to different images.

Other Shot Transitions

Edits can be embellished in ways that attempt to guide our experience and understanding of the transition. For example, **fade-outs** gradually darken and make one image disappear, while **fade-ins** do the opposite. Hitchcock fades to black to mark the passing of time throughout *Rear Window* (1954). A **dissolve** (sometimes called a **lap dissolve** because two images overlap in the printing process) **[Figure 4.10]** briefly superimposes one shot over the next, which takes its place: one image fades out as another image fades in. Usually these devices indicate a more definite spatial or temporal break than do straight cuts and often mark breaks between sequences or larger segments of a film. A dissolve can take us from one part of town to another, while a fade-out, a more visible break, can indicate that the action is resuming the next day. A number of other transitions between shots or scenes are most often found in older films, especially silent films. The **iris-out** begins by masking the corners of the frame in black and gradually obscuring the image as if a camera shutter were closing; an **iris-in** opens on a small, usually circular, portion of the frame and gradually expands to reveal the entire image. The iris was often used in films by D. W. Griffith to highlight objects or faces **[Figure 4.11]**.

Figure 4.10 *The Scarlet Empress* (1934). Extended dissolves were a favorite device of director Josef von Sternberg. The layering of a conversation and the approach of a carriage appear almost as an abstract pattern.

Wipes join two images together by moving a vertical, horizontal, or sometimes diagonal line across one image to replace it with a second image that follows that line across the frame. Modern films from *Star Wars* (1977) to the independent feature *Desert Hearts* (1985) have used wipes to reference an obsolete film style **[Figure 4.12]**. These transitional devices are traditionally known as **optical effects** because before digital editing, they were created in the printing process with an **optical printer.**

Although editing can generate an infinite number of combinations of images, as we will see, rules have developed within the Hollywood storytelling tradition to limit the number of probable combinations. Other film traditions can be characterized by their interest in exploiting the range of possibilities of editing as a primary formal property of film.

Figure 4.11 *Broken Blossoms* (1919). The iris focuses our attention and emphasizes the vulnerability of Lillian Gish's character.

A Short History of Editing

Long before the development of film technology, different images were linked together to convey perceptions of the world. Soviet filmmaker Sergei Eisenstein claimed that much of the art of film editing was anticipated by nineteenth-century British writer Charles Dickens, whose novels shift back and forth among characters, scenes, and actions. Indeed, a long history of cultural practices anticipates the structures of editing, participating in a cultural impulse to see beyond the limitations of the human body. This brief history of juxtaposed images suggests several social functions that have left their traces on editing as it evolved into its modern film forms. We shall explore

- how these practices work to tell stories
- how they break down an experience into component parts in order to produce an attitude toward it
- how they aim to create intellectual or social comparisons
- how they create certain graphic and aesthetic effects

Images have been linked to storytelling since people began creating them. Ancient Assyrian reliefs show the different phases of a lion hunt, while the Bayeux tapestry, a 230-foot-long embroidery, chronicles the Norman Conquest of England in 1066 in invaluable visual and historical detail. Twentieth-century comic strips continue this tradition: each panel of a comic strip presents a moment of action—much like a storyboard used in creating a film sequence. As we read the strip in a particular order, the story unfolds. Many of these practices also break down the depicted subject matter into images representing its component parts. Our attention is focused on figures and objects that help us decipher the images and influence our response.

Very early in human history, religious icons juxtaposed or contrasted different images to create symbolic meanings through their interaction. Religious

Figure 4.12 *Desert Hearts* (1985). The 1950s setting of Donna Deitch's film is evoked by using old-fashioned wipes between scenes.

▲ **Figure 4.13** Ads are modern icons in Godard's films.

Figure 4.14 Photomontage ▶ by Hannah Höch. *Astronomy and Movement Dada* (1992).

triptychs, connecting three panels with different pictures, conveyed complex spiritual ideas. Such an allegorical use of juxtaposed images might still be encountered in an art or experimental film. In several of his films, Jean-Luc Godard comments on (and reproduces) the commodification of the female form by the iconic use of advertising images **[Figure 4.13]**. In each of these cases, the contrasts and similarities in the individual images direct and complicate the narrative or symbolic interactions between them.

In some practices, graphic interaction becomes the central quality of the connected images, as in the folk art of quilting, where separate units are matched and ordered to create graphic patterns. The abstract film *Ballet Mécanique* (Dudley Murphy and Fernand Léger, 1924) uses cutting to create graphic and rhythmic patterns by juxtaposing objects in motion. In one segment of this film, shots of detached female mannequin legs form a complex "dance."

In photography, many of the traditions anticipating film editing were expanded and exploited in new ways. One of the early mechanical and perceptual breakthroughs in the development of the cinema was Eadweard Muybridge's successful 1877 experiment to break down the movement of a galloping horse by taking a series of photographic images. Presented together, these images resemble an edited sequence of shots of a horse in motion. Such **chronophotography** was produced by Muybridge and by the French scientist Étienne-Jules Marey to study human and animal motion **[see Figure 3.7 on p. 79]**. Incrementally altered images comprise the individual frames of a projected film. The individual cells of animation are patterned after photographic records of movement. Recording such analytical images on a flexible, continuous filmstrip was one of the necessary conditions for the emergence of cinema.

By the first part of the twentieth century, photographs were often arranged to highlight the relation between the different images. Eugène Atget, for example, photographed specific views of Paris buildings and streets at different times or in different phases of construction in order to convey the lapse of time. As photography continued to evolve as an art medium, artists would often connect separate photographs by particular motifs or visual patterns. In the 1920s photomontages of German artist Hannah Höch, different images were combined into a new composition to suggest conceptual connections and establish novel visual effects [Figure 4.14]. More recently, artist David Hockney combined separate Polaroid photographs to create one overall image.

Cinema took its cue from the dynamics of linking separate photographic images and began to order them according to a specific temporal design. Early programs of one-shot films created an effect of juxtaposition by their sequence. Films quickly evolved from showing characters or objects moving within a single image to connecting different images. One of the most important and popular films in the historical development of cinema, Edwin S. Porter's *The Great Train Robbery* (1903) tells its story in fourteen separate shots, including a famous final shot of a bandit shooting his gun directly into the camera [Figure 4.15]. The film's last cut is used to enhance the shock effect of the image rather than to complete the narrative. However, Porter, a prolific filmmaker who worked for Thomas Edison, is often credited with introducing the editing techniques that would become the basis of standard filmmaking style. While some of these techniques were used earlier by other filmmakers, Porter synthesized and popularized these techniques and developed their artistic use.

The development of film editing practices and codes accompanied the development of the storytelling capacity of cinema. In Porter's *Life of an American Fireman* (1903), we see the same action—the firefighter's rescue of a mother and baby from a burning building—in its entirety from two different viewpoints, from inside and outside the house. Soon such repetitions would become less common as audiences learned to follow the action through the use of such editing patterns as **crosscutting,** which cuts back and forth between actions in separate spaces.

D. W. Griffith, who began making films in 1908, is a towering figure in the development of film editing style. Griffith is closely associated with the use of crosscutting or **parallel editing,** alternating between two or more strands of simultaneous action, which he used in the rescue sequences that conclude dozens of his films. In *The Lonely Villa* (1909), shots of female family members isolated in a house alternate with shots of villains trying to break in and with shots of the father rushing to rescue his family. The infamous climax of Griffith's *The Birth of a Nation* (1915) uses crosscutting to promote identification with the white "victims" of Reconstruction. Griffith cuts among a white family trapped in an isolated cottage and black soldiers trying to break in, a white woman threatened with rape by a mulatto politician, and the Ku Klux Klan riding to the rescue of both [Figures 4.16–4.18]. Here we can see the ideological

Figure 4.15 *The Great Train Robbery* (1903). The shocking final image *after* the bad guys are caught.

Figure 4.16 *The Birth of a Nation* (1915). Parallel editing between two different attacks and last-minute rescues at the end of the film adds to viewers' feelings of suspense and manipulation.

Figure 4.17 *The Birth of a Nation* (1915). Parallel editing.

Figure 4.18 *The Birth of a Nation* (1915).

implications of cutting, for the dramatic editing urges the viewer to root for the Ku Klux Klan to arrive in time, regardless of his or her actual antipathy for the group. The merging of technique and ideas exemplified in Griffith's craft is a strong (though controversial) demonstration of the power of editing.

Less than a decade later, Sergei Eisenstein's first film, *The Strike* (1924), developed the craft of editing in a different though equally dramatic fashion. Eisenstein's films and writings center on the concept of **montage,** the French word for editing that has come to signify a style emphasizing the breaks and contrasts between images joined by a cut. To depict the mass shooting of workers in *The Strike*, Eisenstein interspersed, or **intercut,** long shots of gunfire and of the fleeing and falling crowd with gruesome close-ups of a bull being butchered in a slaughterhouse [**Figures 4.19 and 4.20**]. The effect of his montage is visceral and provocative. Eisenstein and such other filmmakers as Lev Kuleshov, Vsevolod Pudovkin, and Dziga Vertov advanced montage as the key component of modernist, politically engaged filmmaking in the Soviet Union of the 1920s.

One of the most fascinating self-reflexive sequences in film history is the editing sequence in *The Man with the Movie Camera* (1929) [**see Figures**

Figure 4.19 *The Strike* (1924). The workers' massacre compared to the slaughter of a bull.

Figure 4.20 *The Strike* (1924).

Changing Pace, Changing Technology

Watching Vincente Minnelli's *An American in Paris* (1951) and Baz Luhrmann's *Moulin Rouge!* (2001), you would appreciate them as two spectacular musical romances based in two fantasy versions of Paris. You would also notice the differences between these two films made fifty years apart—differences in sensibility, use of genre conventions, decor, and musical choice, among other elements. But the most striking difference is pace, achieved primarily through different approaches to and techniques of editing. *An American in Paris* was edited by Adrienne Fazan on 35mm film and, like most Hollywood movies of the classical era, its cutting allows the film's action to unfold with clarity. Consistent with other aspects of the film, Jill Bilcock's editing of *Moulin Rouge!* can best be described as frenetic, encouraging visceral engagement rather than narrative clarity.

Overall, the pace we are accustomed to in contemporary films is considerably faster than that of Hollywood films in the classical period. What is behind this increase in speed? One factor is the use of new technology supporting nonlinear digital editing, which makes cutting less labor intensive and thereby encourages experimentation with rapid cutting of the kind we see in *Moulin Rouge!* and other recent films. Such experimentation also draws on multiple cinematic traditions and aesthetic influences, including Soviet montage and other avant-garde precedents. Broad cultural shifts such as the faster pace of communication and computing have also affected the movies. It might even be argued that the overall acceleration of contemporary life has spurred the development of new editing technologies and protocols. A comparison of these two films' editing strategies will help introduce the basics of nonlinear digital editing that shape our experiences as twenty-first-century film viewers.

An American in Paris is about the struggling painter of the film's title, played by Gene Kelly, who falls in love with a Frenchwoman played by Leslie Caron. The lengthy "American in Paris" ballet that ends the film moves from elaborately staged street scenes to a segment set in a Montmartre nightclub whose decor is based on the iconic Parisian café artwork of Henri de Toulouse-Lautrec. Kelly enters the club and begins to dance with one of the can-can dancers (played by Caron) and is incorporated into their routine. Lasting approximately two minutes, the segment contains six shots, none of them close-ups. The dance number is sparingly cut, preserving the integrity of the dancers' bodies and performances and displaying the sets, costumes, and choreography in full.

Near the beginning of *Moulin Rouge!*, the struggling writer, played by Ewan MacGregor, describes his introduction to the scandalous world of the Montmartre club Moulin Rouge, where he will meet his true love, the courtesan Satine, played by Nicole Kidman. The club's showman host, its bawdy dancers, and its lustful patrons are introduced in a rapidly edited, extended musical sequence. Accompanying a shift between songs, a montage series juxtaposes the faces and kicking legs of individual can-can dancers, wider shots of the dance, and the naive hero looking on [Figures 4.21 and 4.22]. Seventeen shots are presented in approximately thirteen seconds of screen time. From an average shot of twenty seconds in a scene from *An American in Paris*, we move to an average of less than one second in a comparable scene from *Moulin Rouge!*. The striking contrast in the editing is apparent in the very different handling of the can-can dancers' movements. In the climax of the

Figure 4.21 *Moulin Rouge!* (2001). The frenzy of the nightclub performers and patrons is conveyed by rapid cutting.

Figure 4.22 *Moulin Rouge!* (2001).

number in *An American in Paris*, the dancers circle around Gene Kelly [**Figure 4.23**], their figures forming a pattern within the high-angle shot. In the musical number from *Moulin Rouge!*, the bodies are fragmented and the graphic patterns and rhythms are established through editing. The cutting style is confrontational; we are disoriented spatially from shot to shot. The pace of the editing matches the frenzy of the club. Rather than clarifying the story, the cutting draws our attention to itself, making us participate viscerally in climactic action that comes within the first ten minutes of the film. Both sequences are part of elaborate numbers designed to impress the viewer with the resources of cinema and the energy of entertainment, but only *Moulin Rouge!* makes editing a primary vehicle of this engagement.

In general, the Hollywood musical is not a genre associated with fast cutting. Its vitality comes from song and dance and, consequently, the performers are given the space and time to dazzle the spectator. In part a homage to the classic Hollywood musical, Luhrmann's film also borrows some of its improbable excess from the astonishing musical numbers of the Bombay-based Hindi film industry. Yet the pace of *Moulin Rouge!* is fast even for a "Bollywood" musical. It is the influence of another recent genre—the contemporary music video—that is most palpable in the pace of the film's cutting. Music videos use the continuity of a popular song to give the visuals coherence as they defy spatial and temporal logic. This particular musical even incorporates an eclectic mix of popular songs, as if its score were culled from a program of music videos. It is difficult to imagine how Luhrmann's film could have been made earlier in film history, drawing as it does not only on historical avant-garde and popular global practices of montage but also on the increasingly rapid rhythms of commercial television and other forms of visual communication. Indeed, *Moulin Rouge!* represents a new kind of editing, not only in style but in practice as well.

The changing technology of film editing has had a direct effect on the speed of contemporary films. Recent years have seen a shift in the technological basis of the film editor's craft, which had remained quite stable over the course of film history.

4.95 and 4.96 on p. 155]. The film's editor, Yelizaveta Svilova, who appears in the sequence, was married to director Dziga Vertov and was one of the radical "kinoki" (Kino-Eye) documentary filmmaking group. In fact, an often-overlooked aspect of the social history of editing is its relative openness to the participation of women. As soon as fiction films began to be shot out of sequence, someone on set had to be responsible for maintaining continuity, and the overwhelmingly gendered perception of this role is clear in its now-obsolete job title **script girl.** Some script supervisors, as the position became known, went on to become editors themselves. It has been argued that the very invisibility that editing strives for in the narrative tradition makes it compatible with forms of labor traditionally performed by women that are so often effaced and unrecognized, and even that editing was allocated to women because it resembled sewing and other kinds of detail-oriented "women's work." Regardless of why they were admitted as editors to an otherwise male-dominated profession, women made significant contributions. Dorothy Arzner, the only woman director working in

Figure 4.23 *An American in Paris* (1951). The vitality of the dance is captured by a single shot.

Formerly, editors cut actual film footage by hand on a Moviola or flatbed editing table. Now, most editors use computer-based nonlinear digital editing systems.

In the past, highly skilled film editors and their teams would build up a cut from all of the available footage, selecting the best performances and technical values from all of the takes shot during production. Any change demanded physically recutting the footage. In nonlinear editing, film footage is stored as digital information on high-capacity computer hard drives. In contrast to the time-consuming process of looking for a particular scene by shuttling through a roll of film on the editing table, digitized shots and soundtracks can be easily organized and any part of them accessed instantaneously. Additionally, sound-editing options can be simultaneously combined with picture editing. Finally, optical effects such as dissolves and fades can be immediately visualized on the computer, whereas formerly they could not be tested until they were added much later at the laboratory. Because of the flexibility and efficiency of the new technology, the majority of feature films are now edited with nonlinear computer-based systems. *Moulin Rouge!* exploits digital editing as well as other digital technologies to their fullest capacity, even including montage within shots.

As our comparison of two films made a half-century apart suggests, the differences between traditional and nonlinear digital editing are not just technical matters to be debated by those responsible for the craft. A study comparing feature films edited on film and on computer systems noted a tendency for more rapid cutting in a nonlinear format. Our everyday interactions with images, sounds, and information via the Internet are nonlinear experiences. To some extent the new technologies that have developed and become incorporated into our culture correspond to our changing cognitive and sensory experience of the contemporary world. The more rapid pace of contemporary films, even if it cannot always be directly attributed to the capabilities of nonlinear editing technology, is a notable part of this sensory shift.

Hollywood in the 1930s, first impressed studio executives with her work as an editor on silent films, and she later employed women editors for many of the films she directed. Decades later, women such as Dede Allen, who cut *Bonnie and Clyde,* and Martin Scorsese's collaborator Thelma Schoonmaker finally received widespread recognition for editing.

The largely unobtrusive conventions we are familiar with in film and on television today were in large measure established and institutionalized by the peak of D. W. Griffith's career at the end of the 1910s. (With the addition of recorded sound a decade later, **sound editing,** which will be discussed in Chapter 5, became incorporated in this style.) Avant-garde movements continued to explore the more abstract and dynamic properties of editing employed by the Soviets, and eventually such montage techniques were incorporated into the mainstream via the quick cutting of music videos and commercials. Rather than always smoothing over cuts, editing techniques today often flaunt the novel effects of juxtaposing images of disparate content, duration, and scale, and they draw on new technology to do so.

Cutting to the Chase in *The General* (1927)

Buster Keaton's classic comedy *The General* is a tour-de-force demonstration of cinema as a medium of movement, and it is the film's editing, along with Keaton's own astonishing agility, that keep it going. Set during the Civil War, *The General* features Keaton as Johnnie Gray, a Confederate train engineer in pursuit of the Union raiders who have stolen his locomotive, named "the General," and unwittingly kidnapped the heroine Annabelle Lee, who is trapped inside. *The General* was produced at the end of the silent era when editing had already been developed in sophisticated ways. In the absence of dialogue, editing is even more heavily relied on as a narrative and visual language. The editing is not as fast-paced as that of a contemporary action film, but current films with chases at their core, like *Speed* (1994), are a tribute to Keaton's ingenuity. Johnnie's train moves inexorably on its tracks, pursuing another moving train. The camera, too, is constantly moving—on tracks or in vehicles like those it films. And it is the film's editing that dynamically juxtaposes these shots, keeping the film itself in motion.

This comical pursuit takes place primarily on Johnnie's locomotive. But as with any chase film, crosscutting shapes the central action of *The General*, pacing the audience's response to Johnnie's misadventures by returning constantly to the object he pursues. Johnnie chases the locomotive first in a handcart and next on an old-fashioned tricycle (which he jumps on just as its owner parks it). The humor comes from the parallel editing between the powerful engine and these lowly human-powered conveyances.

Figure 4.24 *The General* (1927). An impending mishap with the cannon.

Figure 4.25 *The General* (1927).

In the first chase sequence, a long shot from the side shows a cannon, which Johnnie had commandeered and loaded, separating from his engine [Figure 4.24]. When it stalls on the tracks, the increasing distance makes it seem inevitable that the cannonball will hit Johnnie instead of the enemy. The film makes this point by cutting to a threatening straight-on angle of Johnnie from the cannon [Figure 4.25]. During this part of the chase, Johnnie gives the thieves the impression that they are outnumbered. A fortuitous bend in the road diverts the cannon blast and the Union soldiers believe they are under attack. However, the film's cutting gives us a picture of the actual situation [Figure 4.26]. It is again through editing that we learn when the Union soldiers realize their mistake; a cut to an extreme long shot shows their train passing over a trestle bridge, while Johnnie, alone with his diminutive locomotive, is visible on a track far beneath.

Figure 4.26 *The General* (1927). A miraculous turn of events as the engine rounds a bend in the track.

In *The General*, many sequences are hilarious precisely because the subtlety of their editing complements Keaton's performance, as when Johnnie continues to chop wood atop his train as the Confederate army marches behind him. When the Union army appears on the other side of the tracks, Johnnie finally turns and notices what he has gotten himself into [Figures 4.27 and 4.28]. Much later, Johnnie pretends he is a Union soldier and hides Annabelle in a gunnysack [Figure 4.29]. A long shot shows him being ordered to load the sack slung over his shoulder on the train [Figure 4.30]. In a view of the same action from the rear, we see that Annabelle has been busy behind Johnnie's back uncoupling the train car so that they can both escape with the General [Figure 4.31]. Again, the editing delivers the punchline. Often a seemingly inevitable situation is miraculously averted, such as when a cannon Johnnie fumblingly shoots straight into the air destroys a dam and thwarts the enemy, rather than falling directly down on Johnnie's head as he anticipates. The execution of each of these gags depends on a very clear

Figure 4.27 *The General* (1927). Oblivious to everything but the chase, Johnnie (played by Buster Keaton) finally notices the tide of history.

Figure 4.28 *The General* (1927).

Figure 4.29 *The General* (1927). Hiding Annabelle in a gunnysack.

Figure 4.30 *The General* (1927). Pretending to assist the Union soldiers in loading the train.

Figure 4.31 *The General* (1927). The editing shows us Annabelle uncoupling the train cars.

setup defined by editing between the various elements: the upright cannon, Johnnie's quizzical gaze up waiting for the cannonball, a cut to the dam.

Most of the film follows editing conventions and relies on straight cuts between shots and on fades between segments. For example, the first fade is motivated by the train entering a dark tunnel. A later transition humorously illustrates the temporal ellipsis implied by a fade. A tableau of Johnnie with his arms around Annabelle in the rain fades out for the night, only to fade in on the two figures in the exact same posture the next morning. The conventional use of the fade-out to indicate the passage of time is upheld, while the narrative conventions to which it corresponds, the discreet handling of a love scene, are disappointed.

The General celebrates the kinetic nature embodied in the words *motion picture* and *cinema* (from the Greek "I move"), proceeding as an almost nonstop action sequence. It sums up the fluidity of silent-era filmmaking and, in the continuous space and time demanded by the chase framework, illustrates the principles that would continue to govern studio filmmaking. The entire film is organized around trains moving relentlessly forward on a mechanical path—like film itself, in which one edited shot follows another past the projector's beam.

VIEWING CUES: Cuts and Other Edits

- Train yourself to be attuned to editing. During a scene from the film you will watch next in class, clap or count each time there is a cut. Look at the scene again. What difference would it make if any one of the cuts were missing or replaced by camera movement?

- Make a list of other transitional devices used in the film. Could a cut be substituted? If so, what effect(s) would it have? What spatial, temporal, or conceptual relationship is being set up between scenes joined by a fade, dissolve, iris, or wipe?

- Construct a set of storyboards for a specific sequence. How do editing choices break a situation down into its component parts?

- What symbolic relationships among images are set up by the film's editing patterns? How do these relationships influence the possible interpretations of certain scenes or the films as a whole?

The Patterns and Logic of Editing

Our eyes are trained to make sense of a series of discontinuous, linked images by conventional ways of handling space, time, story, and image patterns in the movies. We understand the action sequences in *Mission: Impossible II* (2000) despite the improbable feats performed by the hero. Likewise, we make connections among the three separate narratives from three separate time periods in *The Hours* (2002). As noted earlier, most of these patterns were established early in the course of film history. In this section, we will explore the spatial and temporal relationships set up by editing and introduce the rules of the Hollywood continuity editing system, a dominant method of editing narrative films. Patterns of editing images based on graphics, movement, and rhythm will then be examined in order to show how different techniques provide very different experiences.

Editing Narrative Space and Time

In both narrative and non-narrative films, editing is a crucial strategy for ordering space and time. Two or more images can be linked together to imply spatial and temporal relations to the viewer. **Verisimilitude,** literally "having the appearance of truth," is that quality of fictional representations that allows readers or viewers to accept a constructed world, its events, its characters, and the actions of those characters as plausible. In cinematic storytelling, clear, consistent spatial and temporal patterns greatly enhance verisimilitude (although dialogue, acting, sets, and costumes, and other elements are also important). In the commercial U.S. film industry, these patterns are constructed through conventions of editing that form part of **Hollywood continuity style.** Because its constructions of space and time are so codified and widely used, we will devote special consideration to this style.

Continuity editing is a system that uses cuts and other transitions to establish verisimilitude and to tell stories efficiently, requiring minimum mental effort on the part of viewers. The basic principle of continuity editing is that each shot has a continuous relationship to the next shot. Two particular strategies are at the heart of this style:

- using an establishing shot to construct an imaginary 180-degree space in which the action will develop
- approximating the experience of real time by following human actions

Continuity editing has developed and deployed these patterns so consistently that it has become the dominant method of treating dramatic material, with its own set of rules that narrative filmmakers are taught. Minimizing the perception of breaks between shots, and so familiar in itself, it is often called **invisible editing.** The "rules" of continuity can be broken, however. Such variations may appear less "realistic" simply because they allow us to notice the editing that is normally hidden.

Spatial Continuity

Spatial patterns are frequently constructed by the use of an **establishing shot,** generally an initial long shot that establishes the setting and orients the viewer in space to a clear view of the action. Establishing shots quickly became a standard way of introducing scenes in a wide variety of films. A scene in a western, for example, might begin with an extreme long shot of wide-open space and then cut in to a shot that shows a stagecoach or saloon, followed by other, tighter shots introducing the characters and action.

The standard practice for filming a conversation presents a relatively close shot of both characters (also known as a **two-shot**) in a recognizable spatial orientation and context, and then displays the character who is speaking in the next shot before cutting again to show the other character. The editing may proceed back and forth, with periodic returns to the initial view. Such **reestablishing shots** restore a seemingly "objective" view, making the action perfectly clear to the spectator. Early in Howard Hawks's *The Big Sleep* (1946), when detective Philip Marlowe (played by Humphrey Bogart) is hired by General Sternwood, the scene opens with an establishing shot and their conversation follows this pattern. The simple interview, which provides a great deal of plot information, is broken down by many imperceptible cuts that eventually focus our attention on the protagonist's face before reestablishing the space [**Figures 4.32–4.39**]. Many conversations from contemporary

Figure 4.32 *The Big Sleep* (1946). Conversation in continuity style: the establishing shot.

Figure 4.33 *The Big Sleep* (1946). The two-shot.

Figure 4.34 *The Big Sleep* (1946). Alternating shots of the two characters cut in closer and closer.

Figure 4.35 *The Big Sleep* (1946).

Figure 4.36 *The Big Sleep* (1946).

Figure 4.37 *The Big Sleep* (1946).

Figure 4.38 *The Big Sleep* (1946).

Figure 4.39 *The Big Sleep* (1946). The reestablishing shot.

daytime soap operas are handled in much the same way. We have learned to expect the coordination of conversations with medium close-ups of characters speaking and listening, just as we expect that these figures will be situated in a realistic space.

Another device that is used in continuity editing is the **insert,** a brief shot, often a close-up, such as a shot of a hand slipping something into a pocket or a smile another character does not see. The use of inserts helps transcend viewers' spatial separation from the action, pointing out details significant to the plot or underscoring verisimilitude—for example, showing us a ringing telephone. An insert that breaks continuity is referred to as a **nondiegetic insert** (such as the display of printed text in a Jean-Luc Godard film). More specifically, a nondiegetic insert introduces an object or view from outside the film's world or makes a comparison that transcends the characters' perspectives. A famous nondiegetic insert in which a shot of housewives chatting cuts to another of chickens clucking is used by Fritz Lang to illustrate the concept of gossip in *Fury* (1936).

Exceptions tend to prove the rules of continuity editing. In *Natural Born Killers* (1994), extraneous and disorienting cuts interrupt character interactions. The film's opening sequence dispenses with an establishing shot: a shot of a pot of coffee introduces the location and is followed by some exterior shots of the diner. The waitress's response to Mickey's order is repeated and the second shot is in black and white. In this example of **overlapping** editing, we are shown two shots of the same action, a technique that violates continuity [**Figures 4.40 and 4.41**]. This disorienting introduction conveys a skewed perception of the diner's space, foreshadowing the eruption of violence later in the scene.

In continuity editing, after the establishing shot provides the initial view of a scene, subsequent shots follow the logic of spatial continuity in scale or size of the image and figure orientation. It is unlikely that an extreme close-up of a character's face will appear without having been set up by a shot showing that character in a particular setting. If a character appears at the left of the screen looking toward the right in the establishing shot, it is likely that he or she will be shown looking in the same direction in the medium shot that ensues. Movements that carry across cuts will also adhere to a consistent screen direction. A character exiting the right of a frame will probably enter a new space from the left. Similarly, a chase sequence covering great distances is likely to provide spatial cues. The breakdown of a scene will proceed as if the action were traversed by an imaginary line that the camera will not cross.

This practice of editing follows what is known as the **180-degree rule,** the primary rule of continuity editing and one that many films and tele-

Figure 4.40 *Natural Born Killers* (1994). Overlapping editing is a violation of continuity. A medium close-up in color as the waitress speaks.

Figure 4.41 *Natural Born Killers* (1994). A close-up in black and white immediately follows a the line is repeated.

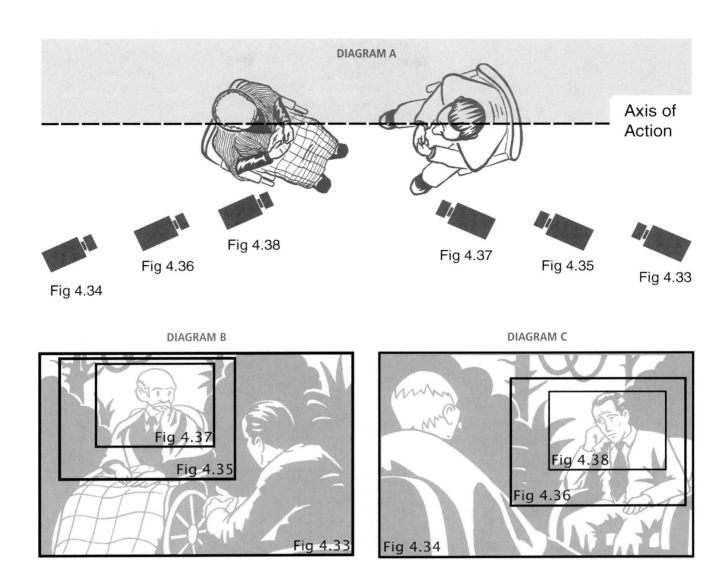

Figure 4.42 Diagrams illustrating the 180-degree rule in the conversation from *The Big Sleep*. **Diagram A** shows how the space of the scene is set up as if it were bisected by an imaginary line called the axis of action that the camera cannot cross. The camera positions of the two-shot and subsequent shots alternating between the two characters are labeled to correspond with still images 4.33–4.38. **Diagrams B and C** show how each character is framed in progressively closer shots.

vision shows consider sacrosanct. The three diagrams in **Figure 4.42** illustrate the 180-degree rule with reference to the scene from *The Big Sleep* discussed earlier in this chapter. Marlowe and the general are consistently filmed as if bisected by an imaginary line known as the **axis of action,** visible in **Figure 4.42A.** All of the shots illustrated by the still images in **Figures 4.32–4.39** were taken from one side of this axis, and the camera positions from which the shots were filmed are depicted in the figure and labeled accordingly. In general, any shot taken from the same side of the axis of action will ensure that the relative positions of human figures and other elements of mise-en-scène and the directions of gazes and movements will remain consistent. If the camera were to cross into the 180-degree field on the other side of the line (represented in **Figure 4.42A** by the shaded area), the characters' onscreen positions would be reversed. Although many shots are edited together in the conversation scene from *The Big Sleep,* the transitions remain largely invisible because the angle from which each character is filmed remains consistent.

Diagrams B and C of **Figure 4.42** illustrate the relationship among progressively closer shots of each character from the same angle. The frames are labeled to correspond with the still images in **[Figures 4.33–4.38]**.

During the unfolding of a scene, however, a new axis of action may be established by figure or camera movement. In the opening scene of *Johnny Guitar* (1945), spatial consistency is maintained by following the 180-degree rule as the title character arrives at the empty saloon owned by the film's heroine, Vienna, and exchanges glances with the silent bartender and casino dealers. But when Vienna steps onto the balcony overlooking the saloon, the axis of action shifts dramatically to highlight her exchange with Johnny. Some directors break the 180-degree rule and cross the line, either to signify chaotic action or because conventional spatial continuity is not their primary aim.

Although less frequently reiterated, the **30-degree rule** illustrates the extent to which continuity editing attempts to preserve spatial unity. This rule specifies that one shot must be followed by another shot taken from a position greater than 30 degrees from that of the first. The rule aims to emphasize the motivation for the cut by giving a substantially different view of the action. The transition between two shots less than 30 degrees apart might be perceived as unnecessary or discontinuous—in short, visible. Joseph Cornell's experimental film *Rose Hobart* (1936) is a re-editing of the Hollywood film *East of Borneo* (1931); the original film's continuity editing principles are broken in Cornell's reassemblage, defying spatial and temporal logic **[Figures 4.43 and 4.44]**.

One of the most common spatial practices within continuity editing, and a regular application of the 180-degree rule, is the **shot/reverse-shot** (sometimes called shot/counter-shot) pattern. Often used during conversations, such as in the example from *The Big Sleep*, this pattern begins with a shot of one character taken from an angle at one end of the axis of action, continues with a shot of the second character from the "reverse" angle at the other end of the line, and proceeds back and forth.

Figures 4.33–4.38 and **diagrams B and C** of **Figure 4.42** illustrate this pattern of alternating shots in the conversation scene from *The Big Sleep*. A

Figure 4.43 *Rose Hobart* (1936). Joseph Cornell re-edited and re-scored the 1931 Hollywood adventure film *East of Borneo,* naming his film after its star.

Figure 4.44 *Rose Hobart* (1936). Mismatched eyelines, abrupt changes in mise-en-scène, and violations of the 30-degree rule wreak havoc with continuity.

Figure 4.45 *Clueless* (1995). This scene follows the 180-degree rule and favors the film's heroine, Cher (played by Alicia Silverstone), as it alternates among characters.

Figure 4.46 *Clueless* (1995).

Figure 4.47 *Clueless* (1995).

Figure 4.48 *Clueless* (1995).

scene from *Clueless* (1995), in which the protagonist, Cher, and her friends, Dionne and Tai, converse in a coffee-shop booth provides another example of a shot/reverse-shot sequence. The scene begins with a tracking establishing shot that depicts the overall environment and shows who is sitting where **[Figure 4.45]**. Then the scene cuts back and forth across the booth, usually to depict the character who is speaking **[Figure 4.46]**. Cher has the majority of the scene's shots, indicating that she is the focal point of our identification **[Figure 4.47]**. Sometimes Dionne and Tai, sitting opposite, are depicted in a two-shot; occasionally these secondary characters receive individual shots **[Figure 4.48]**.

Frequently the shots and reverse shots used in conversation scenes are taken over the shoulder of the character who is looking, which helps to remind us of their shared physical space. In general, continuity editing often implies spatial contiguity; in other words, it gives the impression that consecutively depicted spaces are adjacent ones. If a character looks offscreen toward the left, the next shot will likely show the character or object that the character is looking at in a screen position that matches the gaze. This is referred to as an **eyeline match [Figures 4.49 and 4.50]**. Shot/reverse-shot sequences of characters in conversation often use eyeline matches. Eyelines give the illusion of continuous offscreen space into which characters could move beyond the left and right edges of the frame.

Many of Alfred Hitchcock's most suspenseful scenes are edited to highlight the drama of looking. Often a character is shown looking, and the next shot shows the character's optical point of view, as if the camera (and hence the viewer) were seeing with the eyes of the character. Such point-of-view

Figure 4.49 *The Silence of the Lambs* (1991). An eyeline match establishes the position of Clarice (played by Jodie Foster) in relation to Hannibal Lecter (Anthony Hopkins) in his cell.

Figure 4.50 *The Silence of the Lambs* (1991). The reverse shot.

shots are often followed by a third shot in which the character is again shown looking, which reclaims the previous shot as his or her literal perspective. In a tense scene from *The Birds* (1963) in which the heroine, Melanie, sits on a bench outside a school as threatening crows gather on the playground equipment behind her, Hitchcock uses both eyeline matches and point-of-view sequences. Eventually a bird flying high overhead catches her attention **[Figure 4.51]**. When she turns her head to follow its flight, the shots are matched by her eyeline **[Figure 4.52]**. Next comes a point-of-view sequence in which Melanie—and the viewer who shares her perspective—is horrified by the sinister sight of congregating birds **[Figures 4.53 and 4.54]**. The ed-

Figure 4.51 *The Birds* (1963). A low-angle shot of a flying bird is matched to Melanie's eyeline.

Figure 4.52 *The Birds* (1963).

Figure 4.53 *The Birds* (1963). Following its flight, she registers shock at what she sees.

Figure 4.54 *The Birds* (1963). A point-of-view shot of the gathered birds.

Figure 4.55 *The Way We Were* (1973). Barbra Streisand's face registers her character's emotion in this reaction spot.

iting of this scene serves both to construct a realistic space and to increase our identification with Melanie by focusing solely on the act of looking.

Elsewhere in the film, Mitch's point of view is conveyed by partially masking the frame as if we were looking along with him through his binoculars. Similarly, when we share the point of view of a character waking from a knock on the head, we may see a blurry image. In contrast, over-the-shoulder shots used in a shot/reverse shot sequence are not point-of-view shots because they do not show exactly what the characters see. However, if, as the conversation intensifies, the scene proceeds in tighter framings of characters' faces as if from the direct perspectives of the participants, the film has introduced point-of-view shots.

These components of the continuity system—shot/reverse-shot-patterns, eyeline matches, and point-of-view shots—construct space in order to highlight human subjectivity. An emphasis on human perspective is also visible in the **reaction shot,** which depicts a character's response to something that viewers also see [Figure 4.55]. The cut back to the character "claims" the view of the previous shot as subjective. Continuity editing constructs spatial relationships to create a plausible and human-centered world on-screen.

Although continuity editing strives for an overall effect of coherent space, films can reject continuity and use editing to construct less predictable spatial relations. For example, in Michelangelo Antonioni's film *L'Avventura* (1960), cuts join spaces that are not necessarily contiguous. The landscapes the characters move through express their psychological state of alienation; a realistic use of space is rejected.

Temporal Relations

Editing is one of the chief ways that temporality is manipulated in the time-based medium of cinema. A two-hour film may condense centuries in a story. By **chronology** we mean the order according to which shots or scenes convey the temporal sequence of the story's events. Sequences of shots or scenes may describe the linear movement of time forward as one event follows another in temporal order. Often human activity directs the selection and ordering of events in this way. Editing may also create nonlinear patterns in which events are juxtaposed out of their temporal order. Within the continuity system, such nonlinear constructions are introduced with strict cues about narrative motivation. A **flashback** follows one or more images of the present with one or more of the past; it may be introduced with a dissolve conveying the character's memory or with a voiceover in which the character narrates the past. In one sense, *Citizen Kane* (1941) uses a linear structure, organizing itself around a series of interviews and investigations conducted by a reporter looking for an angle on a great man's death. However, the story of Kane's life is provided in a series of lengthy flashbacks that make the film's chronology complex. Like the typical film noir that relies on the instability of appearances, *Sunset Boulevard* (1950) uses flashbacks motivated by voiceover narration. The film presents a particularly interesting case: continuity is maintained even though the protagonist-narrator is shown to be dead in the first sequence.

The less common **flashforward** connects an image of the present with one or more future images. Flashforwards present a serious challenge to realistic motivation: how can the characters we are asked to identify with "see" the future? The technique is thus usually reserved for works that intentionally challenge our perceptions. In the countercultural film *Easy Rider* (1969), for instance, the protagonist has a brief flashforward vision of an aerial image of the accident that will be his demise at the end of the film. In Nicolas Roeg's *Don't Look Now* (1973), a couple is tormented by the recent death of their daughter and haunting images of a small figure in a red rain slicker prove to be flashforwards to a revelatory encounter. In *Memento* (2000), the chronology of scenes is completely reversed, but the maintenance of continuity within each scene allows us to follow the film.

An **achronological** sequence is one that cannot be identified temporally. The purpose of such a sequence is often descriptive, such as a series of shots identifying the setting of a film. In *An American in Paris,* as one character describes the heroine to another, we see a series of shots depicting her different qualities (with different outfits to match). These little vignettes are achronological.

Art films often manipulate temporality through editing, defying realism in favor of psychological constructions of time. French novelist and director Alain Resnais makes time the subject of his film *Hiroshima Mon Amour* (1959), which constantly relates the present-day story set in Japan to a character's past. An image of her lover's hand sparks the female protagonist's memory of being a teenager in France during the war, and the flashback begins with a matching image of another hand. But temporality is such an important dimension of film narration that even more traditional narratives explore the relationship between the order of events onscreen and those of the story. Steven Soderbergh's *The Limey* (1999) ingeniously inserts shots **[Figures 4.56 and 4.57]** of the activities of the protagonist, played by Terence Stamp—including images from *Poor Cow* (1967), a film in which Stamp

Figure 4.56 *The Limey* (1999). Shots of indeterminate chronology punctuate a conversation scene.

Figure 4.57 *The Limey* (1999).

appeared many years before—into the narrative but out of sequence, keeping us guessing about temporal relations.

Mike Figgis's *Timecode* (2000) unfolds in real time with continuously running cameras and thus would not seem to provide a good example of editing time. However, the division of the frame into four smaller frames creates an effect of juxtaposition not unlike that set up by sequential cuts; within a temporal relation of simultaneity, the spectator's attention makes linear choices [Figure 4.58].

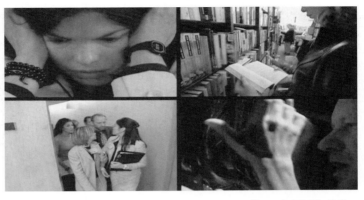

Figure 4.58 *Timecode* (2000). Shifting attention among the frame's four quadrants tells a linear story without editing.

Timecode is an experiment in filmic **duration,** a term that denotes the temporal relation of shots and scenes to the amount of time that passes in the story. In *Timecode* the story time is identical to the screen time, whereas in most narrative films the story time is radically condensed and temporal relations constructed through editing are complexly related to the temporality of the film's story. Temporal continuity is maintained by cutting that constructs a sequence of cause-and-effect events. Editing is one of the most useful techniques for manipulating narrative time. Although actions may seem to flow in a continuous fashion, editing allows for significant temporal abridgement or **ellipsis.** Cutting strategies both within scenes and from scene to scene attempt to cover such ellipses. Grabbing a coat, exiting the front door, and turning the key in the ignition might serve to indicate a journey from one locale to the next. As we have seen, transitional devices such as dissolves and fades also manipulate the duration of narration. Without the acceptance of such conventions, time would be experienced in a disorienting fashion. A specific continuity editing device used to condense time is the **cutaway:** the film interrupts an action to "cut away" to another image or action—for example, a man trapped inside a burning building—before returning to the first shot or scene at a point further along in time. We are so accustomed to such handling of the duration of depicted events that a scene in real time, such as the central character's taking a bath in *Jeanne Dielman, 83 quai du Commerce, 1080 Bruxelles* (1975) seems unnaturally long. Less frequent than the condensation of time, the extension of time through overlapping editing occurs with the repetition of an action in several cuts [see Figures 4.40 and 4.41]. In *The Battleship Potemkin,* a sailor, frustrated with the conditions aboard ship, is shown repeatedly smashing a plate he is washing. The onscreen passage of time in this scene is longer than that of the action. Overlapping editing is a violation in a continuity system and while it can be used for emphasis or for foreshadowing, it often appears strange or "gimmicky."

The duration of individual shots helps determine the **pace** of a film's editing. What defines relative shot length and hence the experience of pacing can be personally subjective and culturally relative. The quick pacing characteristic of action sequences has become more prevalent in contemporary cinema. One obvious example of controlling pace is the use of **long takes,** or shots of relatively long duration; the image is sustained for what can seem an inordinate amount of time. In Claude Lanzmann's nearly ten-hour-long documentary about the Holocaust, *Shoah* (1985), the camera films an interview subject speaking and then holds on the subject while an onscreen translator conveys his or her words to Lanzmann, who is also present. The long take, often filmed in deep focus with a wide-angle lens, became a significant aesthetic tool in William Wyler's *The Best Years of Our Lives* and

Figure 4.59 *Dog Star Man* (1964). Graphic patterns are enhanced through editing.

other films striving for a particular kind of realism. In the opening quote to this chapter, film theorist André Bazin claims "there is no longer any trace of the resources of montage" in this film's long takes. For Bazin, an advocate of the **sequence shot,** in which an entire scene plays out in one take, this type of filmmaking more closely approximates human perception and is thus more realistic than montage. Because of the preponderance of long takes, such films rely more heavily on mise-en-scène, including acting, and camera movement than editing to focus viewers' attention. Yet the extended duration of shots fundamentally affects the film's rhythm and pace, which is a key "resource of montage." Most films use shot duration to follow a rhythm that relates to the particular aims of the film. In *Flowers of Shanghai* (1998) by contemporary Taiwanese filmmaker Hou Hsaio-hsien, long takes evoke the city's past and vanished way of life. In contrast, the notorious shower murder sequence from *Psycho* (1960) uses seventy camera setups for forty-five seconds of footage, the many cuts launching a parallel attack on viewers' senses.

As we have seen, continuity editing strives for a realistic space and time that approximates recognized perspectives, such as the crowded movement of a city street. Some narrative films aim to construct psychological space and time, creating such emotional and imaginative perspectives as the anxiety and suspense associated with horror films. In some films, the two may overlap: in *The Crowd* (1928), for example, images of New York City convey a specific setting as well as the hero's psychological impression of an overwhelming, disorienting sensory experience.

Earlier in this chapter, we introduced the term *montage* in relation to Soviet filmmaking of the 1920s. In the Hollywood tradition, montage is usually reserved to denote thematically linked sequences and sequences that show the passage of time by using quick sets of cuts or other devices, such as dissolves, wipes, and superimpositions, to bridge spatial or temporal discontinuities. In studio-era Hollywood, Slavko Vorkapich specialized in such sequences and lent them his name. For example, a Vorkapich sequence might show a series of opening-night triumphs of an actress in a "success montage"; a "roaring twenties montage" might show flappers, beaver coats, and model Ts; or a "dairy industry montage" might depict cows being milked, conveyor belts transporting milk cartons, and schoolchildren drinking milk in quick succession. In this specialized sense and in its use simply as a synonym for editing (Alfred Hitchcock, for example, often discussed it in this way), montage emphasizes the creative power of editing—especially its potential to build up a sequence and augment meaning, rather than to remove the extraneous as the term *cutting* implies.

Abstract Editing: Shapes and Surfaces, Movements and Rhythms

In addition to temporal and spatial narrative patterns, editing may link images according to more abstract similarities and differences that make creative use of space and time. Here, we distinguish among three abstract patterns in editing: graphic editing, movement editing, and rhythmic editing. Often these patterns will work together to support or complicate the action being shown.

Linking or defining a series of shots in **graphic editing** are such formal patterns as shapes, masses, colors, lines, and lighting patterns within images. Graphic editing may be best envisioned in abstract forms: one pattern of images may develop according to diminishing sizes, beginning with large shapes and proceeding through increasingly smaller shapes; another pattern may alternate the graphics of lighting, switching between brightly lit shots and dark, shadowy shots; yet another pattern might make use of lines within the frame by assembling different shots whose horizontal and vertical lines create specific visual effects. Many experimental films highlight just this level of abstraction in the editing. Among Stan Brakhage's hundreds of experimental films, *Dog Star Man* (1964) **[Figure 4.59]** uses graphic matches and superimposition extensively. Frequently, narrative films employ graphic editing as well. Graphic elements of the mise-en-scène such as arches are incorporated in Eisenstein's editing design for *Ivan the Terrible, Part One* (1945) and *Part Two* (1946) **[Figure 4.60]**. Coherence in shape and scale often serves a specific narrative purpose, as in the continuity editing device called a **graphic match,** in which a dominant shape or line in one shot provides a visual transition to a similar shape or line in the next shot. One of the most famous examples of a graphic match is Stanley Kubrick's shock cut from a prehistoric bone tossed in the air toward a spaceship in *2001: A Space Odyssey* (1968) **[Figures 4.61 and 4.62]**.

To connect images through *movement* means that the direction and pace of actions, gestures, and other movements are linked with corresponding or contrasting movements in one or more other shots. Cutting on action, or editing during an onscreen movement, quickens a scene or film's pace. A common version of this pattern is the continuity editing device called a **match on action,** whereby the direction of an action (such as the tossing of a stone in the air) is edited to a shot depicting the continuation of that action (such as the flight of that stone as it hits a window). Often a match on action obscures the cut itself, such as when the cut occurs just as a character opens a door; in the next shot, we see the next room as the character shuts the door from the other side. In *Meshes of the Afternoon* (1943), Maya Deren depicts a continuous movement across diverse backgrounds by strictly matching the action of her character walking forward. The character's first stride is on the beach; her next strides are on dirt, among tall grasses, on concrete, and finally on carpet **[Figures 4.63 and 4.64]**. As an example of graphic matching as well, because the scale and distance are precisely matched in each shot, this series of cuts demonstrates film editing as a unique way of seeing.

Figure 4.60 *Ivan the Terrible, Part Two* (1946). Strong graphic components of Sergei Eisenstein's image create forceful impressions in juxtaposition.

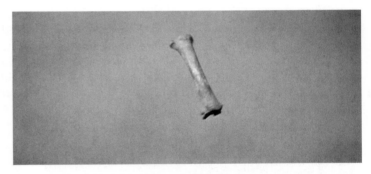

Figure 4.61 *2001: A Space Odyssey* (1968). A famous match cut transcends millennia of history.

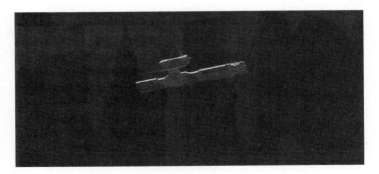

Figure 4.62 *2001: A Space Odyssey* (1968).

Figure 4.63 *Meshes of the Afternoon* (1943). The power of cinema illustrated by matching the protagonist's steps across changing backgrounds.

Figure 4.64 *Meshes of the Afternoon* (1943).

(Similarly, the example from *2001: A Space Odyssey,* cited in the preceding paragraph, is also a match on action following the movement of the bone through the air.) Leni Riefenstahl's extraordinary editing of the swimming sequence in her documentary *Olympia* (1938) has become a model for editing athletic performances, associating the superhuman mobility of athletes with that of the cinema. Movement editing can, however, resist matching and instead create other patterns of movement in a series of images: rapid and slow movements, movements into various spaces of a shot, or different styles of movement can be edited together for visual effects. This is often the case in music videos. In pioneering experimental filmmaker Shirley Clarke's *Bridges-Go-Round* (1958), bridges—stationary structures—come alive and achieve a balletic movement *through* the editing. In the climactic sequence of *Strangers on a Train* (1951), the movements of a carousel around, up and down, and finally out of control are intercut chaotically with the two characters' physical struggle **[Figures 4.65 and 4.66]**. Action sequences such as fights and chases also exploit the possibilities of movement editing.

Figure 4.65 *Strangers on a Train* (1951). Chaotic movement editing in the film's climax.

Figure 4.66 *Strangers on a Train* (1951).

When a film following continuity editing breaks spatial consistency by varying the direction of movements in such sequences, viewers are temporarily disoriented.

Finally, **rhythmic editing** describes the organization of the editing according to different paces or tempos determined by how quickly cuts are made. Like the tempos that describe the rhythmic organization of music, editing in this fashion may link a rapid succession of quick shots, a series of slowly paced long takes, or shots of varying length to modulate the time between cuts. Since rhythm is a fundamental property of editing, it is often combined with graphic or movement or continuity aims. The early French avant-garde filmmaker Germaine Dulac defined film as "a visual symphony made of rhythmic images." *Fantasia* (1940) makes obvious how editing follows the rhythms of the music that is its subject. Frequently, experimental films find their formal coherence in a rhythmic editing pattern, as in Hollis Frampton's *Zorn's Lemma* (1970), which is structured around repeating and varying cycles of twenty-four 1-second shots. However, narrative films also depend on editing rhythms to underpin the emotion and action of a scene. The harrowing opening sequence of *Vertigo* (1958), for example, uses almost no dialogue, relying on the rhythmic alternation of shots of Scottie looking down from the rooftop, where he hangs from his hands, and shots of the view below **[Figures 4.67 and 4.68]**. Directors in different genres and traditions work with their editors to achieve distinctive editing rhythms in their films.

Figure 4.67 *Vertigo* (1958). Shots of Scottie (played by Jimmy Stewart) hanging from a rooftop alternate rhythmically with shots of the ground below, enhancing (and literalizing) suspense.

Figure 4.68 *Vertigo* (1958).

As we have stressed, these different editing patterns are not easily separated: continuity principles are found in many traditions; realistic and psychological editing perspectives commonly overlap; and spatial, temporal, and abstract patterns are often successfully combined.

Editing from Scene to Scene

The coordination of temporal and spatial editing patterns beyond the relationship between two images results in a larger level of cinematic organization found in both narrative and non-narrative films. The shot is the single length of film, and combining it with another shot leads to an edited unit. The conjunction of these units in a narrative may constitute either a scene or a sequence. While these two terms are not always strictly distinguished, one can think of a **scene** as one or more shots that can be described in terms of a continuous space, time, and action, such as the return of Ethan Edwards at the beginning of *The Searchers* (1956). Edwards's brother's family spies his arrival on the horizon and gathers on the porch to await his approach. He arrives, dismounts, and enters the homestead with them, at which point the scene ends. In contrast, a **sequence** is any number of shots that are unified as a coherent action (such as a walk to school), or as an identifiable motif (such as the expression of anger), regardless of changes in space and time. Later in *The Searchers*, one sequence covers several years' time as Ethan and Martin Pawley search for their abducted relative Debbie in a series of shots of them traversing different landscapes at different seasons.

IN FOCUS

Patterns of Editing in *Bonnie and Clyde* (1967)

Arthur Penn's *Bonnie and Clyde* represented a new kind of filmmaking in the late 1960s, in part because of its complex spatial and temporal patterns of editing. Based on the famous outlaws from the 1930s, the film describes the meeting of the title characters and their violent but clownish crime wave through the South. Clyde enlists Bonnie in her first robbery because she is bored with her small-town life. As their escapades continue, they are naively surprised by their notoriety. Soon the gaiety of their adventures gives way to bloodier and darker encounters: Clyde's accomplice-brother is killed, and, eventually, the couple is betrayed and slaughtered.

Dede Allen's editing of this tragicomedy creates both realistic and psychological patterns of time and space. The film's opening shots are presented as snapshots edited together as a documentary photomontage, freezing time rather than making images move [**Figure 4.69**], almost as if to suggest that only by animating these images can the history come alive.

Indeed, temporal and spatial realism are constructed by the links between moving images. The scene depicting the outlaw couple's first small-town bank robbery begins with a long shot of a car outside the bank [**Figure 4.70**]. The next shot, from inside the bank, shows the car parked outside the window [**Figure 4.71**]. Spatially, this constructs the geography of the scene; temporally, it conveys the action that takes place within these linked shots. This scene creates verisimilitude.

At other points in *Bonnie and Clyde*, the logic of the editing describes psychological or emotional patterns. When Bonnie is introduced, for example, the first image we see of her is an extreme close-up of her lips; the camera pulls back as she turns right to look in a mirror. This is followed by a cut on action as she stands and looks back over her shoulder to the left in a medium shot and then by another cut on action as she drops to her bed,

Figure 4.69 *Bonnie and Clyde* (1967). Still photographs will come alive in the course of the film.

Figure 4.70 *Bonnie and Clyde* (1967). Spatial and temporal continuity during the first robbery.

her face visible in a close-up through the bedframe, which she petulantly punches. With another cut, she rises from the bed with her back turned toward us and reaches to the right for her dress. Not only is this central character described by a series of jerky shots, but her boredom and frustration are also built into the editing. Bonnie's restless movements back and forth while dressing are mimed by a moving camera and by cutting on action. The lack of an establishing shot combines with the multiple framings to emphasize the claustrophobic mise-en-scène, taking us right into the character's psychologically rendered space [**Figures 4.72 and 4.73**]. Although standard continuity editing devices are used throughout the film, its pace, style, and decor allow for shortcuts like this one. Next Bonnie goes to her window and, in a point-of-view construction, spots a strange man near her mother's car. She comes downstairs to find out what he is doing and

Figure 4.71 *Bonnie and Clyde* (1967).

her conversation with Clyde is handled in a series of shot/reverse shots, starting with long shots as she comes outside and proceeding to closer pairs of shots. The two-shot of the characters together is delayed. The way this introduction is handled emphasizes the inevitability of their pairing.

Because *Bonnie and Clyde* is a gangster film in which cars and guns figure prominently, complex spatial connections are repeatedly set up between the pursuers and the pursued. Editing on movement pervades the film; its stop-and-go rhythm is probably one of its most striking features. As the Barrow gang flees from the police in one car chase, shots alternate between the police and the gang. Intercut, as a parallel action, are interviews with witnesses to the robbery (who brag about having been part of a Bonnie and Clyde caper). The temporal and spatial organization of the chase is interrupted by the interviews, whose setting is ambiguous [**Figures 4.74 and 4.75**].

As a summary of the patterns and logic of editing, the strategies used in the climactic sequence of *Bonnie and Clyde* are instructive. At the film's conclusion, Bonnie and Clyde are in hiding at the home of the father of their accomplice, C. W. Moss. In the scene immediately preceding the ambush, the couple waits in their car for C. W. to finish up some errands in town. A complex series of cuts, several bridged by graphic matches on the actions

Figure 4.72 *Bonnie and Clyde* (1967). Restless editing conveys character psychology.

Figure 4.73 *Bonnie and Clyde* (1967).

Figure 4.74 *Bonnie and Clyde* (1967). Linear action is crosscut with achronological images as the outlaws' reputation spreads.

Figure 4.75 *Bonnie and Clyde* (1967).

of opening and shutting of car doors, depicts Bonnie and Clyde spotting a police car and pulling out, while C. W. hides behind a shop door, watching them go; their departure is intercut with C. W.'s point-of-view shots as we realize he is up to something. Two discrete scenes, distinguished by changes in action and characters, are edited together to form the concluding sequence of the film. Bonnie and Clyde see C. W.'s father beside his broken-down truck and pull up next to him. His anxiety about being a part of the frame-up is signaled by his quick glance at the bushes, followed by a point-of-view shot in which a flock of birds suddenly rises. Bonnie and Clyde are each shown following his gaze in eyeline matches. As he takes cover, a remarkable series of rapid-fire shots ensues, alternating rhythmically between close-ups of the lovers' faces as they look at each other in alarm, realizing they are surrounded **[Figures 4.76 and 4.77]**. Then the shooting begins.

The final scene of the sequence is the film's most famous and influential. Accompanied by the staccato of machine-gun bullets, Bonnie's and Clyde's deaths are filmed in slow motion, their bodies reacting with almost balletic grace to the impact of the gunshots and to the rhythm of the film's shots, which are almost as numerous. In nearly thirty cuts in approximately forty seconds, the film alternates between the two victims' spasms and re-

Figure 4.76 *Bonnie and Clyde* (1967). Quick, rhythmic close-ups convey the characters' realization that they have been caught.

Figure 4.77 *Bonnie and Clyde* (1967).

Figure 4.78 *Bonnie and Clyde* (1967). The famous death sequence uses slow-motion cinematography with movement and overlapping editing.

Figure 4.79 *Bonnie and Clyde* (1967).

establishing shots of the death scene. Clyde's fall to the ground is split into three shots, overlapping the action **[Figures 4.78–4.81]**. The hail of bullets finally stops, and the film's final minute is comprised of a series of seven shots of the police and other onlookers gathering around, without a single reverse shot of what they are seeing. Like most films, *Bonnie and Clyde* matches the duration of scenes and editing rhythms to the actions and themes of the story, yet one of the more creative and troubling dimensions of the film is the striking combination of slow, romantic scenes and fast-paced action sequences, which culminate in this memorable finale.

For linking sex with violence, glamorizing its protagonists through beauty and fashion, and addressing itself to the anti-authoritarian feelings of young audiences, *Bonnie and Clyde* is among the most important U.S. films of the 1960s. Together with other countercultural milestones, such as *The Graduate* (1967) and *Easy Rider*, it heralded the end of studio-style production and the beginning of a new youth-oriented film market, one that revisited film genres of the past with a modern sensibility. However, as we have seen, it was not only the film's content that was innovative; *Bonnie and Clyde*'s editing and the climactic linkage of gunshots with camera shots also influenced viewers—ranging from French new-wave filmmakers to the American public.

Figure 4.80 *Bonnie and Clyde* (1967).

Figure 4.81 *Bonnie and Clyde* (1967).

Sequences can be constructed of one or more scenes, such as parallel actions during a chase or characters conversing in a restaurant, hailing a cab, and continuing their conversation, with continuity editing condensing the time of the actions. Editing using cuts or other transitions governs the immediate juxtaposition of shots as well the relationship between such larger units as scenes and sequences.

One way to relate editing on a micro level to editing on a macro level is to attempt to divide a film into large narrative units, a process referred to as narrative **segmentation.** A film may have forty scenes and sequences but only ten large segments. Often locating editing transitions such as fades and dissolves will point to these divisions, which occur at significant changes in narrative space, time, characters, or action. Tracing the logic of a particular film's editing on this level also gives insight into how film narratives are organized. For example, the setting of a film's first scene may be identical to that of the last scene, or two segments showing the same characters may represent a significant change in their relationship. Sometimes the "seam" between segments will itself reveal something significant to viewers about the larger organization of the film. In *Imitation of Life* (1959), director Douglas Sirk starkly contrasts a very upsetting scene in which Sarah Jane is beaten by her boyfriend after he discovers her mother is black with another scene in which her mother massages the feet of her white employer, Lora. Lora's exclamation—"That feels so good!"—acquires sickening irony in the juxtaposition. Here, two scenes of black and white intimate relationships, one violent, one apparently benevolent, are deliberately contrasted. Once again, the connections among narrative units demonstrate how editing extends from the juxtaposition of shots to structure the film as a whole.

VIEWING CUES: The Patterns and Logic of Editing

- Do a shot-by-shot breakdown of one scene from a film screened in class. What is the motivation behind each cut? What overall effect do these cuts have on the scene and the film?

- How is space constructed in this scene? Does the film follow continuity patterns, such as the 180-degree rule? Can you identify other ways that spatial continuity is maintained?

- How is the film's temporal organization structured by its editing? Does the film follow a strict chronology? How does the editing abridge or expand time?

- What graphic patterns are constructed through the editing of this film? What effects do these patterns have on your viewing of the film?

- What is the relationship between figure and camera movement within specific shots and the film's cutting?

- Time the shots of a specific sequence. How does the rhythm of the editing in the sequence contribute to the film's mood or meaning?

- Focus on the editing between scenes and sequences by segmenting the entire film into large narrative units. Often fades and dissolves can help you locate these breaks.

Points of View:
Values and Traditions of Film Editing

As we have seen, editing conventions developed early in the history of cinema. Cutting to a close-up in a silent film such as *The Cheat* (1912) was an innovative way of smoothly taking the viewer inside the world of the film's story without resorting to an intertitle (in which descriptive words or dialogue are inserted into the body of a film **[Figure 4.82]**. Early documentary films—*Song of Ceylon* (1934), for example—developed conventional editing patterns based on associations between images linked through the voiceover narration and, later, the illustration of interviews with archival footage. Experimental films like *The Flicker* (1965) employed various patterns of alternation or progression for aesthetic and structural purposes. The continuity editing that evolved in Hollywood during the 1910s remains the dominant "language" of narrative cinema (including animation) and television today. Far from a logical and inevitable progression, the development of editing conventions in Hollywood films serves specific purposes: they provide a sense of spatial and temporal coherence and they help tell a story with clarity. The very word *continuity* represents a value served by this system.

Figure 4.82 *The Cheat* (1912). An early use of the close-up to increase audience involvement.

Nevertheless, over time, there have been striking modifications to these dominant editing principles. In the 1960s, a "jumpy" kind of editing was introduced, one that simulated the freewheeling style of pop icons like The Beatles in Richard Lester's *A Hard Day's Night* (1964). Commercials are edited to enhance the associations generated by the product being marketed, which is often decontextualized in flattering close-ups that are juxtaposed with metaphorically related imagery. By the 1980s, the influence of advertising made its mark on the music videos shown on MTV, and these, in turn, influenced feature films from *Flashdance* (1983) to *Do the Right Thing* (1989). Even more recently, such films as Quentin Tarantino's *Pulp Fiction* (1994), which presents its narratiave out of chronological sequence, systematically depart from the spatial and temporal predictability of the narrative films of the past. Nevertheless, such films still rely on audiences' knowledge of these conventions; their innovations are then felt precisely as the breaking of those expectations.

Although we may not "naturally" perceive the world in a succession of images, our experience of audiovisual media would be profoundly different were it not organized in this way. Hence, it is useful to reflect further on the values served by particular film editing practices.

To Generate Emotions and Ideas,
To Move Beyond Individual Perception

In contemporary culture, images provide a collage of different perspectives, figures, and objects. Disparate billboards create a montage of images on highways to attract us to products and places, while television generates a rhythmic collage of violence and comedy as we surf through different channels. As a concentrated and careful version of these different experiences of

Figure 4.83 *Stagecoach* (1939). Editing encourages identification with the film's white characters.

Figure 4.84 *Stagecoach* (1939).

the dynamics of images in our lives, film editing can assume one or both of the following general aims:

- ■ to generate emotions and ideas through the construction of patterns of seeing
- ■ to move beyond the confines of individual perception and its temporal and spatial limitations

In John Ford's *Stagecoach* (1939), for instance, we experience the approach of pursuing Indians and the subsequent battle and escape from the perspective of the stagecoach's white passengers [**Figures 4.83 and 4.84**]. Audience members almost involuntarily hope for the vanquishing of the pursuers, who are shown in long shots. We feel palpable relief, along with the surviving passengers, when their pursuers give up the chase. The editing also constructs feelings of tension. Since we are not confined to the interior of the stagecoach, we see the initial threat and the close calls that the characters cannot see. Through logic and pacing, the editing does more than just link images in space and time; it also generates emotions and thoughts.

This potential of editing is well illustrated in the legendary editing experiments led by Soviet filmmaker Lev Kuleshov in the 1920s. A shot of an actor's face followed by a bowl of soup signified "hunger" to viewers, while the link between the same face and an image of a baby created feelings of delight. In the absence of an establishing shot, viewers took these pairs of images as linked in space and time. Editing a shot of a powerful leader with a shot of a peacock encouraged the audience to identify the leader with the concept of vanity, a more specifically conceptual association. Eisenstein referred to this intentional juxtaposition of two images in order to generate ideas as **intellectual montage.** In an example from his *October* (1927), the slogan "In the Name of God" is followed by a series of images from different religious traditions to show the relativity of the concept of the divine and the hypocrisy of the depicted action.

In addition, editing has the power to move beyond the temporal and spatial confines of the individual's perception. With a full array of editing techniques and strategies, film may allow a viewer to see the world, not just from other angles but also more quickly and with greater complexity than normal human vision allows. Vision overcomes the physical limitations of human perception, such as great separations in time and space, so that viewers might be treated to a series of shots showing observers all over the world awaiting a visitation from outer space. In *2001: A Space Odyssey*, no individual character's consciousness anchors the film's journey through space and time. Instead, our experience of the film is largely governed by the film's editing—including its long-shot images that show crew members floating outside the spaceship accompanied by Johann Strauss's *The Blue Danube* waltz and its montage of psychedelic patterns that erases all temporal borders. Our almost visceral response to action sequences is a result of the cinema's ability to defy our perceptual limits.

Of course, the two central aims of film editing often overlap. The abstract images in *2001: A Space Odyssey* make us think about the boundaries of humanity and the vastness of the universe—and, perhaps, about cinema as a manipulation of images in space and time. Many of Alfred Hitchcock's climactic sequences generate emotions of suspense—achieved in *Saboteur* (1942) by literally suspending his character from the Statue of Liberty's torch, hanging on for dear life **[Figure 4.85]**—and transcend the confines of perception—in the same sequence by showing us close-ups of his face and of the threads of his jacket sleeve coming undone **[Figure 4.86]**.

Our responses to these editing patterns are, of course, never guaranteed. We may feel emotionally manipulated by a cut to a close-up or cheated by a cutaway. Additionally, across historical periods and in different cultures, editing styles can seem vastly different and audience expectations vary accordingly. Older transitional devices such as irises and wipes might generate laughter from audiences today. The slow, meditative editing of Iranian director Abbas Kiarostami's *A Taste of Cherry* (1997) may appear boring to a viewer who has been raised on Hollywood action film sequences. However we respond, editing generates an experience unique to film and television.

Figure 4.85 *Saboteur* (1942). Emotional tension is created while transcending human perspective.

Figure 4.86 *Saboteur* (1942).

Two Traditions: Continuity and Disjunctive Editing Styles

Since the beginning of the twentieth century, continuity editing has been paralleled and sometimes directly challenged by various alternative practices that we refer to collectively as disjunctive editing. It is useful to distinguish these two traditions to give us more precise ways of discussing film form and to remark on philosophical differences in editing styles. However, in modern filmmaking, it is quite possible to find these two traditions converging in the editing style of a single film.

As noted earlier, continuity editing is not an inevitable or a "correct" style of cutting films. Rather, it creates shot patterns that

■ shape space and time to approximate a closed fictional world
■ construct a logic and rhythm that mime human perception

In *Vertigo,* a close-up of Scottie staring off to the right of the frame, followed by a medium long shot of Madeleine, constructs the illusion of continuous space despite the cut and derives its logic from the human look. It is something of an irony that emulating human perspective entails departing from it—most notably to show the person who is looking. Continuity editing seems to proceed as a continuous action organized around human perception—even if there is no clearly identified person driving that perception, as in a series of establishing shots of decreasing distance. In the opening shots of *Rear Window,* Hitchcock makes a kind of joke about how cinematic vision mimes human vision. An elaborate camera movement shows us the courtyard view from L. B. Jefferies's room while his protagonist sleeps. When Jefferies later wakes up and looks out the window, Hitchcock cuts from images of him to isolated views of the windows opposite, using editing to re-map the space with which we have already been made familiar in accordance with Jefferies's now alert gaze.

Here, we will focus on the dominant Hollywood tradition and a specific practice of continuity called analytical editing, and we will also show how art cinema creates a different variant of continuity through editing. Hollywood film editing is part of a systematic approach to filmmaking. **Continuity style** refers to an even broader array of technical choices that support this principle of effacing technique to clarify the narrative and its human motivation. Lighting highlights the face. Mise-en-scène is scaled to the human figure and generally does not distract from the action. Plot is oriented to the perceptions and goals of a clearly drawn protagonist. The soundtrack also plays a major role, as we will see in Chapter 5. But it is editing that best exemplifies the principle of seamlessness in continuity style by incorporating many other aspects. Lighting must be consistent from shot to shot, and other aspects of mise-en-scène—such as costumes and make-up, props, and figure behavior—must be meticulously monitored from setup to setup by following the **continuity script.** (For example, the person in charge of continuity would ensure that a cigarette almost burned down in one shot is not freshly lit in a later shot.)

In a Hollywood film, editing a scene in the service of narrative continuity and clarity is called **analytical editing.** In other words, the scene is analyzed or broken down by the camera to direct spectators' attention from the general perspective of an establishing shot to increasingly more specific views. Closer shots show character speech (shot/reverse-shot sequences) or denote the position of significant props or gestures (inserts, cutaways, reaction shots). Again, it is paradoxical that "continuity" traditionally depends on a large number of cuts. Indeed, this paradox prompted André Bazin's praise for William Wyler's use of long, continuous takes. Despite Bazin's claim that such choices heighten realism, cuts in films using long takes are often especially noticeable. Hitchcock reflects on these questions in *Rope* (1948), in which he allows the camera to run out of film before cutting, resulting in a feature film with only ten shots, in many ways an "unnatural" viewing experience.

Spatially, the relationships set up in the Hollywood continuity tradition follow the logic of human interaction. Analytical editing cuts the world to the measure of the body and camera distance is measured in anthropomorphic scale (a close-up is a shot in which the human face would be seen in its entirety). Point-of-view editing registers the impact of the world on humans, literally sandwiching a view between two shots of a person looking. The 180-degree rule outlines a field of interaction well illustrated by the shot/reverse-shot sequence, in which the camera takes turns "seeing" from different characters' perspectives.

becomes a reflection on the process of viewing a film. How can we assume that the action we are viewing is happening now, when recording, editing, and projection/viewing are all distinct temporal operations? In one shot [Figure 4.91], we see the female protagonist played by Delphine Seyrig on a staircase; in the very next shot, she appears outside, along the balustrade of a garden. Her body remains in an identical position while the background changes; however, the temporal relationship between the shots is unexplained.

The jump cut can also be used to explore the magical properties of the medium, an aim that goes back to the trick films of Georges Méliès at the beginning of the twentieth century. Maya Deren's *Meshes of the Afternoon*, for example, begins with a hand lowering a flower into the frame. In the film's second shot, the hand abruptly disappears. Later, a hand reaches forward to remove a key from the table; then the key suddenly reappears in its original position. This action is repeated; we are invited to engage in existential reflection, enhanced by the fact that the disjunctive nature of these cuts is underscored in the film by a distinctive, synchronized note on the soundtrack.

Figure 4.91 *Last Year at Marienbad* (1961). Delphine Seyrig strikes poses against various backgrounds, challenging our perception of time and place. This same technique was later used in music videos.

In addition to jump cuts, other distantiation devices are highlighted throughout the films of Jean-Luc Godard. By foregrounding the ideological effects of continuity breaks, Godard assaults viewers' complacency and asks them to understand disruption as an opportunity for critical thinking. Godard's work emphasizes fragmentation and distance on many levels, from shot and sound/image juxtaposition to the organization of the narrative into "chapters." (The device of introducing chapters with text or numbers is borrowed directly from Brecht's plays.) For example, Godard's *Two or Three Things I Know about Her* (1966) disrupts continuity by cutting between images and printed texts, by having characters and bystanders address the camera directly in the middle of sequences, and by cutting to ever-closer views of a cup of coffee during a meditative voiceover, until finally the entire widescreen image is engulfed by espresso. Calling attention to the editing in film through distantiation foregrounds both the actual labor that goes into constructing the piece and the conventions and assumptions being challenged in the work.

The aim of grabbing viewers' attention through collision is at the center of Sergei Eisenstein's work on montage, which is the heart of the second subtradition. Eisenstein's writings, undertaken until his death in 1945, have secured him a place as one of the foremost theorists of cinema. He first developed his concept of montage in conjunction with his work in theater before beginning his film experiments with *The Strike* in 1924. For Eisenstein, montage is a dialectical process. Two shots linked dialectically (that is, contrasted or opposed to one another) become synthesized into something greater, a visual concept. In *The Battleship Potemkin*, the shots of stone lions juxtaposed in sequence suggest that one stone lion is leaping to life [Figures 4.92–4.94]. According to Eisenstein, the concept of awakening, connected to revolutionary consciousness, is thus formed in spectators' minds even as they react viscerally to the lion's leap. The association of aesthetic fragmentation with a political program of analysis and action has persisted in many uses of disjunctive editing.

Figure 4.92 *The Battleship Potemkin* (1925). Sergei Eisenstein rouses stone lions through montage.

Figure 4.93 *The Battleship Potemkin* (1925).

Figure 4.94 *The Battleship Potemkin* (1925).

Whereas Hollywood films traditionally avoid a disjunctive style, alternative and experimental films often employ it as the foundation of the film. The fragmentation of time and space (which is germane to editing) is an important aesthetic aim of artistic **modernism.** (Think, for instance, of cubism in painting, which aims to show different facets of an object through a distorted depiction of its shape, color, and composition, a very cinematic concept.) Experiments in film using distantiation, montage, and other alternative practices characterize modernist filmmaking; in contrast, Hollywood **classicism** strives for balance and wholeness. Modernist filmmaking—like that of Godard and Eisenstein—may have a political agenda, seeking to use art to promote a critical consciousness and to break with the status quo. But editing that goes against the grain of continuity values is central to avant-garde film movements that have primarily aesthetic aims. In the 1920s, for example, experimental filmmakers in France organized their films' montage around the rhythms of poetry and music. In Germaine Dulac's surrealist film *The Seashell and the Clergyman* (1928), the central figure is as surprised as we are when his head suddenly appears on the seashell. During the same period, an international genre of "city symphony" films emerged. Walter Ruttmann's *Berlin: Symphony of a City* (1927) and Dziga Vertov's *The Man with the Movie Camera* (1929) each creates a conceptual whole through montage. In both films, the life of the metropolis is depicted through rhythmic patterns of images that emulate the condensed time and space of modernity. Vertov's film even combines footage from different cities. A central sequence shows the film-within-the-film being constructed on the editing table **[Figures 4.95 and 4.96]**. Similarly, in the documentary film style developed by British producer John Grierson in such films as *Drifters* (1929), images were cut together in a poetic montage.

Later modernist filmmakers also used montage. American filmmaker Kenneth Anger explores the ritual aspects of film in *Scorpio Rising* (1964), which edits the cult behavior of bikers to a rock-and-roll soundtrack. (In contrast, Andy Warhol's films are distinct for their lack of editing. *Empire* [1964], an eight-hour shot of the Empire State Building using a stationary camera, might be seen as a very prolonged homage to the first films of the Lumière brothers.) The structural film movement eschewed narrative and mise-en-scène and explored properties specific to film, including the potential of editing. Ernie Gehr's *Serene Velocity* (1970) renders a surprisingly visceral viewing experience by cutting together shots of the same hallway taken with different focal lengths **[Figure 4.97]**. Part of the experience of watching such films is reflecting on their

Figure 4.95 *The Man with the Movie Camera* (1929). Montage under construction, from still frame to moving image.

Figure 4.96 *The Man with the Movie Camera* (1929).

principles of construction. The very title of Trinh T. Minh-ha's *Reassemblage* (1982) references the process of editing. In this short experimental documentary shot in Senegal, Trinh critiques ethnographic film-making's presumption that an image can tell the truth of another culture to an outsider. Her film makes use of disjunctive editing by repeating shots, using jump cuts, and refusing to synchronize the picture to a complex soundtrack. Films made from found footage, such as Bruce Conner's *A Movie* (1958), rely on montage to create humorous, sinister, or thought-provoking relationships among seemingly random images.

Video art has also made significant use of disjunctive editing through montage. With the use of effects, video editing can be layered as well as sequential, developing one of Eisenstein's principles: "each shot is a montage cell." In other words, relationships of contrast and opposition exist not only between shots, but within shots as well. Cecelia Barríga's low-budget video art piece *Meeting of Two Queens* (1991) is ingeniously constructed by recutting brief clips from the films of Greta Garbo and Marlene Dietrich. The montage creates comparisons between the glamorous movie star rivals, engineers a meeting, and suggests a romance between the two by making use of our expectations of continuity editing and altering mise-en-scène through superimposition **[Figure 4.98]**. Barríga thereby introduces disjunction to classical films originally edited for continuity.

Converging Traditions

It is important to stress that many films and videos employing disjunctive editing are obliged to employ continuity editing techniques as well. More and more frequently, commercial film and television incorpo-

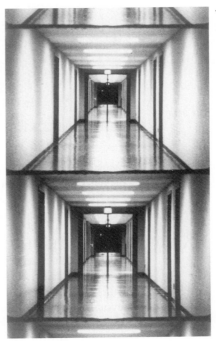

◀**Figure 4.97** *Serene Velocity* (1970). Variations in focal length with a single setup are experienced viscerally through editing.

Figure 4.98 *Meeting of Two Queens* (1991). Re-editing on video puts Greta Garbo and Marlene Dietrich, stars from rival studios, in the same film.▼

Figure 4.99 *Dancer in the Dark* (2000). The use of many digital cameras permits the intercutting of close shots from multiple perspectives.

Figure 4.100 *Dancer in the Dark* (2000).

rate disjunctive editing techniques, including those formerly restricted to the avant-garde. It is no longer possible—if indeed it ever was—to assign specific responses, such as passive acceptance or political awareness, to specific editing techniques.

As digital video cameras and editing equipment become more commonly used for theatrical features, different kinds of juxtapositions will also become more common. Lars von Trier's use of one hundred small digital video cameras to film *Dancer in the Dark* (2000) presented an editing challenge that an editor working with footage from one film camera would never face. Fortunately, nonlinear digital editing on a computer system allows for many possibilities to be sampled by the editor and director without affecting the original materials. Von Trier's film breaks down actions much more minutely than standard analytical editing, so that the arbitrariness of the cutting becomes apparent rather than hidden [**Figures 4.99 and 4.100**]. However, there is no clear indication that the audience's distantiation is intended.

It is evident from all of the examples just cited that a great deal of the formal expressive potential of moving-image media such as film and video lies in the exploitation of the disjunctive powers of editing. While this capacity has been emphasized in non-narrative traditions, it is also key to mainstream forms such as the television commercial. Disjunctive editing is an extremely useful tool in the condensed timeframe and gut-level appeal of advertising, helping viewers make associative connections between the products and values. In music videos, such as David Fincher's video for Madonna's 1990 hit song "Vogue," space and time are defied for a more immediate effect, as the cutting interacts with the music and the rhythms of the dancers. We remain unable to orient ourselves in space. Music video's contribution to contemporary editing conventions in feature films and television is profound, and directors such as Fincher (who went on to make *Fight Club* and *SeFen* among other films) have used their experience creating music videos to make some of the most aesthetically innovative contributions to recent commercial cinema, routinely dispensing with establishing shots, breaking the 180-degree rule, and otherwise bending the rules of continuity editing. As the two formal traditions of continuity and disjunctive editing converge, the values associated with each tradition become less distinct. For Eisenstein, calling attention to the editing was important because it could change the viewer's consciousness. For contemporary filmmakers, disjunctive editing may serve more as an innovative "look."

One filmmaker, Oliver Stone, is closely associated with both Hollywood filmmaking and disjunctive editing. A major source of controversy over his *JFK* (1991) is the way the film cuts back and forth among diverse "sources"—historical footage, re-created black-and-white scenes, and the investigation, which was filmed in color—to support his fictionalized vision of a conspiracy behind the presidential assassination—a real event that was experienced to an unprecedented degree through the media. An 8mm home movie was the most reliable witness, and the footage, recorded by bystander Abraham Zapruder, has received more frame-by-frame analysis than film scholars have given *The Battleship Potemkin*. Stone's film draws on the "authenticity" lent by newsreel-like footage. Still, if one attends to the disjunctive editing of *JFK*—its seemingly random range of film stocks and bafflingly high number of cuts—it is evident that far from presenting a seamless conspiracy theory or evidence that the image does not lie, the form of Stone's film testifies to the mediated nature of all recent historical events.

To summarize, editing is perhaps the most distinctive feature of film form. Editing leads an audience to experience images through particular emotions and ideas, and it remains one of the most effective ways to create meanings from shots. These interpretations can vary from the almost automatic inferences about space, time, and narrative that we draw from the more familiar continuity editing patterns to the intellectual puzzles posed by the unfamiliar spatial and temporal juxtapositions of disjunctive editing practices.

 VIEWING CUES: Editing Traditions and Values

- Note the main editing techniques used in the film. What different emotional and intellectual responses are evoked by these choices? Be sure to jot down specific examples from the film to support your response.

- How is the film's cutting used to extend your perspective?

- When does the film use continuity editing? Are human agency and temporal and spatial coherence reinforced by this practice?

- Does the film's editing call attention to itself in a disjunctive fashion, setting up conflicts or posing oppositional values? If so, how and to what end?

- If both continuity and disjunctive editing are present, how do they interact?

Montage from *The Battleship Potemkin* (1925) to *The Untouchables* (1987)

Soviet filmmaker Sergei Eisenstein's *The Battleship Potemkin* is one of the most renowned examples of daring and innovative editing in film history. A 1925 silent classic based on an actual historical event, *The Battleship Potemkin* describes the revolt of maltreated sailors aboard their ship, the sympathetic response of townspeople on shore, and the violent repression of those people by czarist soldiers. Although the story itself is quite direct and relatively brief, Eisenstein employs a variety of disjunctive cutting techniques to charge specific incidents with powerful energy and meanings, emphasizing the breaks and contrasts between images joined by a cut.

In a film with no single protagonist, numerous cuts join small groups to show the participation of the masses in anti-czarist sentiment, moving our perspective beyond the confines of individual perception and its temporal and spatial limitations. To give heightened drama or dynamic tension to an action, Eisenstein uses more shots than a Hollywood film would find necessary, sometimes overlapping the same action from one shot to the next in several points of view. When the ship's doctor is thrown overboard by sailors, the gesture is repeated from overhead and side angles, expanding the screen time of the action and "showing the seams" of the editing through distantiation in order to engage viewers' emotions and to lead them to a particular idea: the desperation of the sailors resulting in a mutinous act **[Figures 4.101 and 4.102]**. After the doctor hits the water, Eisenstein employs an insert of the maggot-infested meat that the doctor had approved for the sailors' consumption. Appearing out of temporal sequence, this shot reminds us of the narrative justification of the doctor's treatment and underscores the intertitle: "now he'll feed the fishes."

Figure 4.101 *The Battleship Potemkin* (1925). Overlapping cuts of the same action.

Figure 4.102 *The Battleship Potemkin* (1925).

The centerpiece of *The Battleship Potemkin* is the famous Odessa steps sequence in which innocent citizens are shot and trampled by the czar's soldiers. The sequence is justly celebrated for its dynamic cutting, which makes dramatic use of movement and graphic patterns within shots to bring about Eisenstein's favored interaction between shots: collision. The sequence begins with the intertitle "Suddenly"; townspeople then begin to run from the imperial soldiers down the vast steps toward the camera. This action moves generally from left to right. Several different figures are isolated and intercut throughout the sequence: a boy without legs propelling himself forward with his arms, a group of women, a mother running with her child. When the orderly rows of troops are shown entering from top left, the shot provides a dramatic graphic contrast to the chaos of the mass of people. In the first major crosscutting episode within the sequence, the mother becomes separated from her son in the crowd and shots of her turning back for him are intercut with shots of him falling and being trampled by the crowd. Her movement against the crowd to retrieve his body in her arms, from right to left across the screen, is vigorously contrasted with shots of the oncoming crowds and with shots of the soldiers' inexorable progression behind them. Finally, she climbs high enough and enters a shot from the bottom left, which positions the soldiers across the top. The film cuts to peasants looking on, and in the next shot, she is fired on and falls as the troops continue marching down. The use of movement in opposing directions is one of the key elements that organizes this complicated editing sequence [Figures 4.103–4.106].

As if this dramatic episode has not raised enough tension and pathos, after an intertitle announces the arrival of the Cossacks, Eisenstein embarks on one of

Figure 4.103 *The Battleship Potemkin* (1925). The conflict between the organized troops and the frightened masses is heightened by graphic collisions among shots showing different screen directions, patterns of light and shadow, and figure movement in the first part of the Odessa steps sequence.

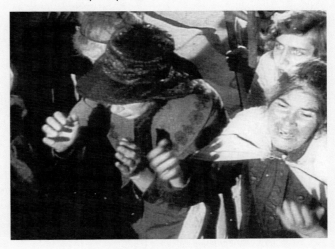

Figure 4.104 *The Battleship Potemkin* (1925).

Figure 4.105 *The Battleship Potemkin* (1925). The Odessa steps sequence.

Figure 4.106 *The Battleship Potemkin* (1925).

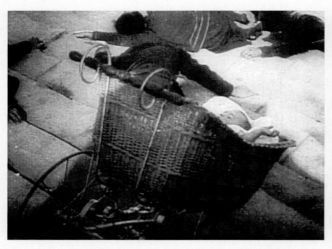

Figure 4.107 *The Battleship Potemkin* (1925). Horrified onlookers and repeated details of the baby carriage's descent convey our help-lessness in one of the most famous editing sequences in film history.

Figure 4.108 *The Battleship Potemkin* (1925).

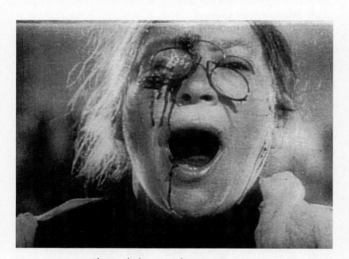

Figure 4.109 *The Battleship Potemkin* (1925).

the most famous editing sequences in film history. A young mother is shot and falls in several overlapping cuts. The baby carriage she had been clutching begins to roll down the stairs. Intercut with its descent (in changing screen directions) are repeated shots of onlookers who seem to be miming our own powerless, horrified gaze. No establishing shot puts these figures in spatial context. Just as the carriage reaches the bottom and begins to overturn, Eisenstein cuts to quick shots of a Cossack striking directly at us and then to the briefest of shots of the face of a woman wearing pince-nez. In a famous shock cut, her glasses are instantly shattered and bloodied. The sequence fades out [Figures 4.107–4.109]. As our vision is assaulted by the shock cut, the image of shattered glasses mirrors our "injury," even as it stands in for an even more horrific, absent image of the baby's fate.

The Battleship Potemkin, Eisenstein's second film, made a similarly strong impact when it was released in the West in 1926. Threatened with political censorship, it was hailed by artists, activists, and intellectuals as a significant advance in film art. It brought international acclaim to Eisenstein and to the extraordinary Soviet cinema of the 1920s. In the long term, Eisenstein's stylistic legacy has survived even as the revolutionary purpose he associated with his aesthetic innovations has become questioned or abandoned. His work has provided the occasion for more than one homage.

Director Brian De Palma emerged among a generation of U.S. filmmakers who were trained in film schools and familiar with film history. He is particularly well known for paying tribute to—or stealing from, depending on your perspective—other great directors in his films. His *Obsession* (1976) borrows motifs from Alfred Hitchcock's classic *Vertigo,* for example. In his tale of Chicago's crime world in the 1930s, *The Untouchables,* De Palma fashions a tense showdown in a train station that "quotes" the Odessa steps sequence from *The Battleship Potemkin,* sometimes shot for shot. Audiences familiar with the original sequence recognize the endangered baby carriage at the top of the steps [Figure 4.110]. Some see a tour de force of suspenseful editing; others think the sequence a distracting self-indulgence.

Figure 4.110 *The Untouchables* (1987). Despite exact quotations of Eisenstein's shots, the last-minute rescue of the baby is more consistent with Hollywood traditions and values than with Soviet montage.

In De Palma's "version" of the sequence, federal agent Eliot Ness (Kevin Costner) and his sharpshooter sidekick George Stone (Andy Garcia) are collecting evidence of Al Capone's financial mismanagement by intercepting his bookkeeper as he attempts to catch the 12:05 train. Cutting from the station's giant clock, to Ness scoping out the staircase, to a mother struggling to climb the stairs with her luggage and her child in a carriage, De Palma and his editor, Jerry Greenberg, set up what will be a most effective action sequence in continuity style. They carefully establish a believable space and a linear, "deadline"-oriented time frame.

Tension mounts as the clock nears noon. The mother makes her way laboriously up the vast staircase. At one point a trainload of passengers sweeps down, stepping over her. A few sailors cross her path, De Palma's nod to the subject matter of Eisenstein's film. After an extreme close-up of the clock at noon, Ness finally goes to help the mother, but as he pulls the carriage up the stairs (a sequence punctuated by several shots of the boy smiling up at him), Capone's men begin to descend. Ness, almost at the top and sensing himself surrounded, turns to shoot at one of the goons. A detail shows Ness as he lets go of the carriage; then, amidst the chaotic gunfire that ensues, De Palma exploits the carriage's slow descent, intercutting shots of the mother failing to catch the handle and of her view of the carriage from the top of the stairs, an overhead shot of the boy, a shot of the wheels hitting the stairs, and a shot of one of the bad guys shooting at Ness right over the top of the carriage. Finally, Ness runs down, still shooting, to try to catch the carriage, but Stone arrives in the nick of time, diving to stop it with his body at the last step [Figures 4.111–4.113]. The boy smiles calmly up at Ness. In the final phase of the action, Stone aims his gun at the final gang member even as he is bracing the carriage from beneath. "You got him?" Ness asks, his question referring both to the boy and to the villain, summing up the way the scene's

Figure 4.111 *The Untouchables* (1987).

Figure 4.112 *The Untouchables* (1987).

visual elements play off each other as well as the individual heroism that contrasts so markedly with the ethos of Eisenstein's film. Stone makes the shot. We never see the boy returned to his mother.

Like the sequence from *The Battleship Potemkin,* the protracted climax of *The Untouchables* proceeds nearly without language through several peaks of action by way of its complex editing. The dynamism of contrasting upward and downward movement is also retained, as is the pathos of the mother confronted by gunfire at the top of the stairs (elements of both movements of the *Potemkin* scene are incorporated into this one). But De Palma's set piece differs from Eisenstein's in that it serves the film's narrative goals through spatial and temporal coherence and, in particular, emphasizes its focus on the perceptions and motivations of individuals.

In Eisenstein's film, the conflict was between state power/the righteousness of the people and the cutting reinforces this objectively rendered polarity. In *The Untouchables,* tension is raised by Ness's struggle with the choice between helping the mother (and later attempting to save the child) and completing his single-minded quest to bring down Capone by apprehending the only man who can give evidence to convict the mob boss. This centrality of character psychology is conveyed by relying on subjective points of view that "suture" our perspective to that of the protagonist. Ness's face is seen before the first shot of the mother and carriage: his gaze conveys the danger of her being on the stairs at the wrong time. Again, it is Ness who looks into the carriage after its fall has been broken to see a smiling child. The individuals whom Eisenstein singles out are types; their faces

CRITICAL VOICES: VSEVOLOD PUDOVKIN ON EDITING

Soviet filmmaker Vsevolod Pudovkin is known for his films *Mother* (1926), *The End of St. Petersburg* (1927), and *Storm over Asia* (1928). Written in 1926, the following remarks on "editing of the scene" were published in his collection *Film Technique.* Although Pudovkin was, like Eisenstein, a student of Kuleshov and a champion of montage, he saw editing as more constructive than contrastive; this passage describes a system similar to the one used in Hollywood films of the period.

In order to make clear to oneself the nature of the process of editing a scene, one may draw the following analogy. Imagine yourself observing a scene unfolded in front of you, thus: a man stands near the wall of a house and turns his head to the left; there appears another man slinking cautiously through the gate. The two are fairly widely distant from one another—they

Figure 4.113 *The Untouchables* (1987).

are not rendered in close-ups marking a subjective point of view. Eisenstein's film makes us helpless witnesses like the massacred people, whereas De Palma's version gives us the illusion of agency. Through its spatial construction, the Odessa steps sequence makes the slaughter of innocents a public spectacle. In the train station shootout, strict spatial continuity is preserved in rendering the virtuosic performance of the heroes. Temporality is also oriented to human goals as we watch the clock and study Ness's expression. Eisenstein's temporal scheme emphasizes disruption: the abstract but urgent caption "suddenly" introduces the extraordinary event and the disjunctive editing sequence that renders it. Repetition in *The Battleship Potemkin* seems to have a didactic function, underscoring the unjust suffering of the people. In *The Untouchables*, multiple shots of the boy's face as his carriage bumps down the steps through the crossfire blatantly, and almost humorously, manipulate our emotions.

More than sixty years after Eisenstein used montage in a modernist film to shock and prod his viewers to action, De Palma incorporated the central image of threatened innocence provided by a baby carriage tumbling down stairs into a genre film, showing off all of the resources of continuity editing. Eisenstein's political objective lay as much in his subject matter as in the editing techniques he innovated to convey them. De Palma's style has been called postmodernist because it emphasizes surface effects over subject matter and borrows from other styles. Editing in the disjunctive tradition is about opening up multiple meanings, whereas the continuity tradition favors closure. In *The Untouchables*, the baby survives the precipitous plunge.

stop. The first takes some object and shows it to the other, mocking him. The latter clenches his fists in a rage and throws himself at the former. At this moment a woman looks out of a window on the third floor and calls, "Police!" The antagonists run off in opposite directions. Now, how would this have been observed?

1. The observer looks at the first man. He turns his head. 2
2. What is he looking at? The observer turns his glance in the same direction 3
   and sees the man entering the gate. The latter stops.
3. How does the first react to the appearance on the scene of the second? A 4
   new turn by the observer; the first takes out an object and mocks the second.
4. How does the second react? Another turn; he clenches his fists and throws 5
   himself on his opponent.

5. The observer draws aside to watch how both opponents roll about fighting.   6

6. A shout from above. The observer raises his head and sees the woman   7 shouting at the window.

7. The observer lowers his head and sees the result of her warning—the   8 antagonists running off in opposite directions.

The observer happened to be standing near and saw every detail, saw it   9 clearly, but to do so he had to turn his head, first left, then right, then upwards, whithersoever his attention was attracted by the interest of observation and the sequence of the developing scene. Suppose he had been standing farther away from the action, taking in the two persons and the window on the third floor simultaneously, he would have received only a general impression without being able to look separately at the first, the second, or the woman. Here we have approached closely the basic significance of editing. Its object is the showing of the development of the scene in relief, as it were, by guiding the attention of the spectator now to one, now to the other separate element. The lens of the camera replaces the eye of the observer, and the changes of angle of the camera—directed now on one person, now on one detail, now on another—must be subject to the same conditions as those of the eyes of the observer. The film technician, in order to secure the greatest clarity, emphasis, and vividness, shoots the scene in separate pieces and, joining them and showing them, directs the attention of the spectator to the separate elements, compelling him to see as the attentive observer saw. From the above is clear the manner in which editing can even work upon the emotions. Imagine to yourself the excited observer of some rapidly developing scene. His agitated glance is thrown rapidly from one spot to another. If we imitate this glance with the camera we get a series of pictures, rapidly alternating pieces, creating a *stirring scenario editing-construction*. The reverse would be long pieces changing by mixes, conditioning a calm and slow editing-construction (as one may shoot, for example, a herd of cattle wandering along a road, taken from the viewpoint of a pedestrian on the same road).

We have established, by these instances, the basic significance of the   10 constructive editing of scenes. It builds the scenes from separate pieces, of which each concentrates the attention of the spectator only on that element important to the action. The sequence of these pieces must not be uncontrolled, but must correspond to the natural transference of attention of an imaginary observer (who, in the end, is represented by the spectator). In this sequence must be expressed a special logic that will be apparent only if each shot contains an impulse toward transference of the attention to the next. For example: (1) A man turns his head and looks; (2) what he looks at is shown.

THE NEXT LEVEL: ADDITIONAL SOURCES

Burch, Noel. *Theory of Film Practice.* Translated by Helen Lane. Princeton: Princeton University Press, 1981 (1973). In this influential study, a contemporary French theorist and filmmaker considers the construction of space and time in Hollywood and avant-garde films.

Dancyger, Ken. *The Technique of Film and Video Editing: Theory and Practice.* 2d ed. Boston and London: Focal Press, 1997. Aimed at directors and focusing on the history, theory, and practice of film editing, this clear and readable book is designed as an update to Karel Reisz's 1953 classic, *The Technique of Film Editing*, and to its 1968 revision by Gavin Miller.

Eisenstein, Sergei. *The Eisenstein Reader*. Edited by Richard Taylor. London: British Film Institute Publishing, 1998. A collection of shorter writings by the Soviet filmmaker that illuminate his film practice and his theories of montage, covering his entire career from 1923 to 1947.

Metz, Christian. *Language and Cinema*. The Hague: Mouton de Gruyter, 1974. Outlining the field of film semiotics in this dense but influential work, Metz presents his framework for analyzing the syntagmatic components of the narrative film (the *grand syntagmatique*). Editing is crucial to supporting the comparison of film with language via the definition of a grammar of film.

Oldham, Gabriella. *First Cut: Conversations with Film Editors*. Berkeley: University of California Press, 1992. Editors share secrets of their craft.

Listening to the Cinema: Film Sound

When a sound can replace an image, cut the image or neutralize it.
The ear goes more toward the within, the eye toward the outer.

—Robert Bresson, director of *Diary of a Country Priest* (1950), "Notes on Sound"

KEY OBJECTIVES

Does sound add its own meaning to a film or is it there to supplement the images? Listening to movies defines the filmgoing experience just as watching them does. Too often given secondary status, sound engages spectators perceptually, gives key spatial and story information, and affords an aesthetic experience of its own. This chapter explores how speech, music, and sound effects are constructed and how they are perceived by the film's "auditor." We will examine

■ how sounds convey meaning in relationship to images

■ how sounds are recorded, combined, and reproduced

■ the functions of the voice

■ the principles and practices that govern the use of music

■ the principles and practices that govern the use of sound effects

■ the values determining the traditional relationships between images and sounds

The cinema is an audiovisual medium, one among many that saturate our contemporary experience. Many of the visual technologies we encounter in daily life are also sound technologies: your computer informs you that "you've got mail," the beeps from your little sister's Game Boy drive you from the room, or you notice that your television's volume soars when a program is interrupted by a commercial. These devices all use sound to encourage and guide interaction, to complement the visuals, and to give rhythm and dimension to the experience. The cinema works similarly, using complex combinations of voice, music, and sound effects.

Seeing and hearing, though often experienced together, are distinct dimensions of sensual experience. These differences affect our perceptions of these dimensions of cinema. We can take in an image all at once but must wait for sound to unfold over time. This durational property of sound is palpable as Public Enemy's "Fight the Power" plays in the opening credits sequence of *Do the Right Thing* (1989) over Rosie Perez's dance, bridging frequent and abrupt changes in costume, sets, and lighting. The first shot of the film's story shows a ringing alarm clock held in front of a microphone, as the DJ, Mister Señor Love Daddy, begins his rap. His voice and the music he's playing are heard as the camera takes us into the street and finally emerge from a character's bedside radio, another use of the duration of sound. Seeing is more directional than hearing. We must all face forward and open our eyes in order to watch a movie, but even if we cover our eyes during the shower sequence in *Psycho* (1960), we will still be assaulted by the high-pitched string theme that Bernard Herrmann composed for the scene, which seems to come from behind and around us. Our binaural hearing can give us important clues about the distance and position of a sound source, however, and this capacity is active in cinema audition as we interpret the images we see. Sound adds to our sense of place in the series of vignettes that opens *Barry Lyndon* (1975), all introduced by the narrator's rich tones that seem to be reading to us: a duel is seen in a long shot and heard at a distance; a courting scene is accompanied by birdsong; Lyndon's thwarted romance is set to a haunting Irish song; British troops parade to martial music; characters dance a country jig.

Sounds are identified by their frequency or pitch, their amplitude or volume, and their harmonics—the subtones that give a sound its particular quality—though rarely do we pause consciously to notice these qualities. Similarly, the soundtrack is rarely the first aspect that we reflect on after "seeing" a film. Yet we may be impressed enough by the score to find ourselves humming it or even purchasing the soundtrack CD. Sound factors into our expectations of films as well. We anticipate how a summer blockbuster or a heartwarming Christmas movie will sound, and we would be disoriented if the film departed from these expectations. The aural dimension of the film experience can be all the more rewarding to explore through film analysis because it can be so naturalized and hard to grasp in our ordinary experience.

The Foundations of Film Sound

Despite our habitual references to motion *pictures* and to film *viewers*, sound is fully integrated into the film experience. In fact, one aspect of sound, human speech, is so central to narrative comprehension and viewer identification that we can often follow what happens even when the picture is out of sight. (Television aesthetics rely heavily on sound to make contact with "viewers" who may be outside the visual range of the TV set.) Sounds can interact with images in infinite ways, and strategies used to combine the two fundamentally affect our understanding of film. The song "We'll Meet Again"—a nostalgic 1940s song used to boost troop morale during World War II—that accompanies footage of H-bombs dropping in *Dr. Strangelove, or: How I Learned to Stop Worrying and Love the Bomb* (1964) makes it impossible to read these images as noble or tragic; instead, a frame of black satire determines our view of war **[Figure 5.1]**. Sound is also important in the moviegoer's perception because of the fascinating relationship between the original sound and its reproduction. Although a sound is altered when it is recorded, engineered, and reproduced, we feel that we are hearing a real sound in

Figure 5.1 *Dr Strangelove, or: How I Learned to Stop Worrying and Love the Bomb* (1964). An image of aggression set to nostalgic 1940s music sets the film's dark satiric tone.

real time. With images, we readily recognize that we see only a two-dimensional copy of the original. Sound effects accompanying footsteps are not really necessary to convey that a character is walking; such an image is easily interpreted. However, the sound of footsteps increases the sense of immediacy and presence. In recent years, improvements in sound technology and developments in sound recording practices have pursued goals of ever-greater "realism" and intensity, making contemporary films sound much richer than those of the past. Sound has also led the way toward digitization, with digital image manipulation and picture editing following in turn. In this chapter, we will consider more fully the technology and aesthetics of film sound while exploring the relationship of sound and image and the often unperceived meanings of sound.

The three major elements used to build a soundtrack—the human voice, music, and noise or sound effects—will be discussed in our analysis. A single image is often combined with a variety of soundtrack elements. Sound can make the illusions of film viewing even more perfect or introduce unexpected perceptions. In the following sections, we will first consider the ways that sound and image may interact onscreen and then turn to the practical consideration of how sounds are gathered, combined, and reproduced.

Sound and Image

Any consideration of sound in film entails discussion of the relationship between sounds and images. Some filmmakers, such as the comic actor and writer-director Jacques Tati, have consistently given equal weight to the treatment and meaning of sound in their films. In *Playtime* (1967), as in Tati's other films, comic gags take place in long shots, and sounds cue us about where to look [**Figure 5.2**]. Derek Jarman's *Blue* (1993), made after the filmmaker had lost his vision through an AIDS-related illness, combines an image track consisting solely of a rich shade of blue with a soundtrack featuring a complex mix of music, effects, and voices reading diaries and dramatic passages. Gazing into a vast blue screen allows viewers to focus more carefully on a soundtrack that conveys particular emotions and ideas.

For many filmmakers, however, as for viewers, sound functions more as an afterthought, there to enhance the impact of the image. Many possible reasons exist for this disparity. Film is generally considered to be a predominantly visual medium rather than an aural one, following a more pervasive hierarchy of vision over sound. The artistry of the image track is perceived to be greater, as the image is more clearly a conscious rendering of the object being photographed than the recording is of the original sound. The fact that sound came later in the historical development of cinema has also been offered as an explanation of its secondary status. Yet the importance and variety of aural experiences at the movies were great even before the introduction of synchronized soundtracks. Since the early years of sound cinema, certain directors and composers have struggled against a too literal, and too limited, use of sound in film, arguing that the infinite possibilities in image and sound combinations are germane to the medium and its historical development. French filmmaker René Clair feared that the introduction of sound would kill the visual possi-

Figure 5.2 *Playtime* (1967). Sound directs viewers' attention to an unusual degree in the films of Jacques Tati.

bilities of the medium and reduce it to "canned theater." In his musical film *Le Million* (1931), for example, in which crowds pick up and sing songs integral to the plot, Clair demonstrates that sound's potential is more than additive; it transforms the film experience viscerally, aesthetically, and conceptually **[Figure 5.3]**.

Because sound and image always create meaning in conjunction, film theorists attentive to sound have looked for ways to talk about the possibilities of their combination. In his 1960 *Theory of Film*, Siegfried Kracauer emphasizes a distinction between **synchronous** and **asynchronous sound.** The former has a visible onscreen source, such as when dialogue appears to come directly from the speaker's moving lips, while the latter does not. (Some analysts prefer to call this distinction **onscreen** versus **offscreen sound.**) Kracauer goes on to differentiate between **parallelism** in the use of sound, which occurs when the soundtrack and image "say the same thing," and **counterpoint** (or contrapuntal sound), when two different meanings are implied by these elements. The two pairs of terms are distinct from each other. A shot of a teakettle accompanied by a high-pitched whistle is both synchronous and parallel. The teakettle accompanied by an alarm bell would be a synchronous yet contrapuntal use of sound. A voiceover of a nature documentary may explain the behavior of the animals in an asynchronous use of parallel sound. Idyllic images accompanied by a narration stressing the presence of toxins in the environment and an ominous electronic hum would be a contrapuntal use of asynchronous sound. A familiar example of the multiple meanings that film sound–image relationships can achieve comes at the end of *The Wizard of Oz.* The booming voice and sound effects synchronized with the terrifying image of the wizard are suddenly revealed as asynchronous sounds produced by the ordinary man behind the curtain. When we see him speaking into a microphone, the sound is in fact synchronous, and what was intended as a parallel has now become a contrapuntal use of sound.

Figure 5.3 *Le Million* (1931). Songs convey the plot in René Clair's early sound film.

In 1928, the dawn of the motion-picture sound era, radical Soviet directors embraced the creative possibilities of sound. Sergei Eisenstein, Vsevolod Pudovkin, and Grigori Alexandrov wrote in their "Statement on Sound" that "only a contrapuntal use of sound in relation to the visual montage piece will afford a new potentiality of montage development and perfection." This endorsement of counterpoint, invoking principles of musical composition, can be opposed to filmmaking practices that emphasize parallelism—the mutual reinforcing or even the redundancy of sound and image. In Hollywood films, for example, it seems remiss not to accompany a shot of a busy street with traffic noises, although viewers immediately understand the locale through the visuals. This parallelism is also an aesthetic choice, one striving for clarity and harmony.

Sound and image always generate meaning in relation to each other, often increasing the effect of verisimilitude. Even when there is no logical connection between what we see and what we hear, the simultaneity of the experience creates a connection. The acceptance of stock sound effects, such as the use of the thud of a watermelon to convey bodily impact during a fight sequence, emphasizes how readily we match or, in the language of sound technicians, "marry" sounds to imagined sources. Regardless of the terms theorists use to characterize sound–image relationships, we can see a concern with naming both the spatial and temporal relationships of images and sounds and their aesthetic purpose.

One of the most frequently cited and instructive distinctions is between **diegetic sound,** which has its source in the narrative world of film, and **nondiegetic sound,** which does not belong to the characters' world. Materially, the source of film sound is the actual soundtrack that accompanies the image, but diegetic sound refers to a visible onscreen source. **Diegesis** (a term derived from literary analysis but now more commonly used in film studies) refers to the world of the film's story, including not only what is shown but also what is implied to have taken place. (*Diegesis* comes from the Greek work meaning "telling" and is distinguished from *mimesis* meaning "showing." The implication is that while mimetic representations imitate or mimic, diegetic ones use particular devices to tell about or imply events and settings.) One question offers a simple way to distinguish between diegetic and nondiegetic sound: can the characters in the film hear the sound? If not, the sound is likely to be nondiegetic. This distinction can apply to voices, music, and even sound effects. Conversations among on-screen characters, the voice of God in *The Ten Commandments* (1956), a voiceover that corresponds to a confession a character is making to the police, and the radio music that accompanies the morning routines of Jeffries's neighbors in *Rear Window* (1954) are all diegetic. Nondiegetic sounds do not follow rules of verisimilitude. For example, the voiceover narration that tells us about the characters in *The Magnificent Ambersons* (1942), background music that accompanies a love scene or journey, or sound effects such as a crash of cymbals when someone takes a comic fall are all nondiegetic. Audio prac-

Figure 5.4 *Written on the Wind* (1956). Source music indicated here by the record player becomes a dramatic soundtrack when Marylee's dance is intercut with her father's heart attack.

titioners refer to diegetic music, such as a shot of a band performing at a party or characters listening to music, as **source music [Figure 5.4]**.

However useful, this distinction can sometimes be murky. Certain voiceovers, though not spoken aloud to other characters, can be construed as the thoughts of a character and thus as arising from the narrative world of the film. Film theorist Christian Metz has classified these as **semi-diegetic sound;** they can also be referred to as **internal diegetic sound.** The uncertain status of the dead character's voiceover in *Sunset Boulevard* (1950) is an example. Diegetic music—such as characters' singing "Happy Birthday"—is often picked up as a nondiegetic theme in the film's score. Such borderline and mixed cases, rather than frustrating our attempts to categorize, are illustrative of the fluidity and creative possibilities of the soundtrack as well as of the complex devices that shape our experience of a film's spatial and temporal continuity.

A Short History of Film Sound

Topsy-Turvy (1999) tells the story of the collaboration between Gilbert and Sullivan, the late-nineteenth-century British lyricist-composer duo, as they brainstorm, quarrel, and finally witness the first production of their operetta *The Mikado*. The behind-the-scenes story culminates in a performance of the operetta that brings together sound and image for the theater audience within the film and extends this experience to the film's viewers. That our visual experience of the movies is enhanced and complemented by acoustic experiences is not surprising; many of the traditions and technologies that became synthesized in the institution of the cinema involved sound. The nineteenth-century symphonic repertoire was drawn upon heavily in compiling scores to accompany so-called silent films; these same works greatly influenced the conventional practices of scoring narrative films made in Hollywood and elsewhere. One finds precursors of the experience of sound cinema in phenomena that join sound, especially music, to a public visual spectacle as well as in inventions such as the phonograph that made synchronized sound possible.

Figure 5.5 *The Umbrellas of Cherbourg* (1964). The mise-en-scène of the film matches the intensity of experience in a world in which all dialogue is in song.

Our automatic acceptance of the music that accompanies motion pictures is rooted in the ancient tradition of combining music with forms of visual spectacle, which goes back at least as far as the use of choral odes in classical Greek theater. It is difficult to think of a theatrical tradition that does not have its own distinctive musical conventions. Opera, which integrates story and song, appears directly in film—from the memorable integration of recognizable nineteenth-century classics into the scores of such films as *Diva* (1982) and *The Godfather* (1972) to the operatic films of Luchino Visconti and Werner Schroeter. As in opera, every aspect of a film production—sets, costumes, lighting, and sound—is integrated in the service of a narrative. In his unique films *The Umbrellas of Cherbourg* (1964) and *The Young Girls of Rochefort* (1967), filmmaker Jacques Demy pursues a vision of film's musicality **[Figure 5.5]**. All of the dialogue is sung to Michel Legrand's music, while the sets and costumes are designed to harmonize with this heightening of experience.

Melodrama is arguably as important a resource for filmic storytelling as is realism. Literally meaning "music plus drama," melodrama originally designated a theatrical genre popularized in eighteenth-century France that combined spoken text with music. In England, the category of melodrama permitted the mounting of popular theatrical spectacles when laws restricted "legitimate" theater to particular venues. Stage melodrama became increasingly more spectacular throughout the nineteenth century; dominating the American stage, melodrama had an incalculable influence on cinematic conventions. Not only was the aural component of the form very important, but the up-and-down rhythms of melodrama's sensational plots also drew on the strongly felt but inexpressible emotions that music so powerfully conveys. All of these qualities are present in film melodramas, from D. W. Griffith's *Way Down East* (1920) to James Cameron's *Titanic* (1997). In the latter film, the melodrama is enhanced by diegetic musical accompaniment that the orchestra famously plays even as the ship goes down **[Figure 5.6]**.

Figure 5.6 *Titanic* (1997). Diegetic music for the melodrama.

Figure 5.7 Early nickelodeon programs interspersed films with sing-alongs. Slides like this one from *Ramona* (1928) provided the lyrics.

Other nineteenth-century theatrical traditions influenced not only cinema storytelling but also the social role it would eventually play. These traditions drew on sound as well as on image. Contemporary distaste for the minstrel tradition often makes us overlook its importance as the most popular entertainment in the nineteenth-century United States. But this highly codified musical form left an indelible mark on the cinema. Al Jolson performed songs in blackface in the film that popularized synchronized sound, *The Jazz Singer* (1927). Music halls in Great Britain and vaudeville theaters in the United States lent cinema popular talents, proven material, and formats such as the review, delivering audiences with specific expectations of sound and spectacle to the new medium. Because of the preexisting popularity of specific performers and styles, many ethnic voices were heard in cinema that might otherwise have been excluded from entertainment directed at mass audiences.

It was only after recorded synchronized sound had thoroughly saturated the film industry that the movies of the preceding years began to be seen as lacking something in comparison with sound films. The term *silent drama* was sometimes used during the period to distinguish the movies from stage dramas that used spoken language. But in fact, so-called silent cinema was not only a distinct art form; it was often loud and noisy as well. Loudspeakers lured customers into film exhibitions accompanied by lecturers, pianos, organs, small ensembles, or, later, full orchestras. In nickelodeons and other movie venues, audiences themselves customarily made noise, joining in sing-alongs between films [Figure 5.7] and talking back to the screen. Often sound effects were supplied by someone standing behind the screen or by specially designed machines. Occasionally, actors even provided dialogue to go along with the picture. Though each of these sound performances was unique, a standardized form of soundtrack to go with films in mass distribution was already in the works.

As far back as the end of the eighteenth century, inventors were engaged in the problems of sound reproduction. Edison's phonograph, introduced in 1877, had an irreversible impact on the public and on late-nineteenth-century science. As film theorist James Lastra notes in *Sound Technology and the American Cinema*, such inventions were often spoken about in terms of writing. *Phonography* means "sound writing" and Edison first thought of recorded sound as a way to record business letters. Such analogies helped the public incorporate unfamiliar technologies into their experience. The fact that Edison was also one of the primary figures in the invention of the motion-picture apparatus shows that the eventual coming together of film and sound haunted the medium from its inception. One of the films made by Edison Studios in 1895 is a sound experiment in which Edison's chief inventor, W. L. K. Dickson, plays a violin into a megaphone as two other employees dance. In 2000, after the original sound cylinder that accompanied this seventeen-second fragment of film was discovered and repaired, prominent Hollywood editor Walter Murch put its image and sound back together for the Library of Congress [Figure 5.8]. Sound cylinders provided a way

Figure 5.8 Edison Studios' Sound Experiment (1895). A rare film fragment with synchronized sound from the dawn of cinema.

of synchronizing image and sound very early in film history, and inventors continued to experiment with means of providing simultaneous picture and sound throughout the silent-film era. The early technique of recording sound on a separate disk remained linked to the film apparatus in the late 1920s, when Warner Bros.' Vitaphone process became the first widely adopted technology to link sound to a projected image.

No event in the history of Hollywood film was as cataclysmic as the rapid incorporation of synchronized sound in the period 1927–1930. Many dynamics were at work in the introduction of sound, from the relationship of cinema to radio, theater, and vaudeville to the economic position of the industry as the United States headed into the Great Depression to the popularity of certain film genres and stars. Yet exhibitors needed to be convinced to adopt the relatively untested new technology. The expense of converting a sufficient number of theaters to make the production of sound films feasible was considerable, and the studios had to be willing to make the investment. One impetus was the prospect of gaining a competitive edge in uncertain economic times. Inevitably, competition arose over solutions to technical problems, with significant financial gain in store for the company whose system was adopted.

In the 1926–1927 period, two studios actively pursued competing sound technologies. Warner Bros. aggressively invested in sound and, in 1926, premiered its Vitaphone sound-on-disk system with a program of shorts, a recorded speech by Hollywood censor William Hays, and the first feature film with a recorded score, *Don Juan.* Fox developed its Movietone sound system, which recorded sound optically on film and, in 1927, introduced its popular Movietone newsreels, which depicted everything from ordinary street scenes to exciting news (such as aviator Charles Lindbergh's take-off for Paris) and were soon playing in Fox's many theaters nationwide [Figure 5.9]. The new technology became impossible to ignore when it branched out from musical accompaniment and sound effects to include synchronous dialogue. Public response was enthusiastic.

Warner Bros. second feature film with recorded sound, *The Jazz Singer,* released in October 1927, is credited with convincing exhibitors, critics, studios, and the public that there was no turning back. Starring vaudevillian Al Jolson, the country's most popular entertainer of the time, the film tells a story, similar to Jolson's own, of a singer who must turn his back on his Jewish roots and the legacy of his father, a cantor in a synagogue, in order to fulfill his show-business dreams. The film proceeds much like a silent film, using conventional intertitles and a continuous score, until Jolson's musical numbers are accompanied by synchronous diegetic music and singing. Here, the film makes its greatest impact; when Jolson ad-libs during his performance, he introduces dialogue to the movies with a famous promise that soon after came true: "You ain't heard nothing yet!" [Figure 5.10].

The Jazz Singer thus inaugurated a brand-new genre, the musical, one that would capitalize on the convention already in place of presenting movies and music together. Performers of all ethnic groups, including African American singers and dancers, were soon featured in shorts that carried over the

Figure 5.9 Program for Fox Movietone News. Fox Studios developed a system to record sound optically on the film itself and then produced newsreels to show it off in its vast theater holdings.

Figure 5.10 *The Jazz Singer* (1927). Warner Bros.' Vitaphone sound-on-disk system achieved success because of Al Jolson's singing and spontaneous dialogue.

variety of the vaudeville stage. For his sound film debut at MGM, director King Vidor chose to make *Hallelujah!* (1929), a musical with an all-black cast, capitalizing on the cultural association of African Americans with the expressive use of song. Not only musical talent but also stage performers with training and experience were now in demand in Hollywood and they would displace many of the silent screen's most beloved stars. Writers who could provide dialogue were also desperately needed, and Broadway playwrights, respected novelists, and celebrated wits such as Dorothy Parker and Anita Loos moved to California to try their hand at the new medium. In the wake of *The Jazz Singer*'s phenomenal success, the studios came together and signed with Western Electric (a subsidiary of AT&T) to adopt a sound-on-film system in place of the less flexible Vitaphone sound-on-disk process. The studios also invested in the conversion of their major theaters and in the acquisition of new chains to show sound films.

The transition to sound was not entirely smooth, of course. The troubles with exhibition technology were more than matched by the difficulties posed by cumbersome sound recording technology. In the very early years of sound recording, great precautions were needed to prevent noise in the studio from being picked up in the recording process. Recorders worked in specially constructed sound booths. Performers and cameras were rooted to their positions, and critics and filmmakers bemoaned that the cinema had lost much of its kinetic quality. Some filmmakers overcame the stasis when moveable sound blimps were developed. Despite such problems, the transition was extremely rapid: by 1930, silent films were no longer being produced by the major studios; only a few independent filmmakers, such as Charlie Chaplin, whose art grew from the silent medium, held out.

The ability of films to cross national borders in many directions, a much-celebrated property of the early medium, was also changed irrevocably by the addition of monolingual spoken dialogue. Film industries outside the United States acquired national specificity, and Hollywood set up European production facilities. Exports were affected by conversion-standard problems and patents disputes. For a time, films were made simultaneously in different languages. Marlene Dietrich became an international star in *The Blue Angel* (1930), produced in Germany in French, English, and German versions. Comparing variations in these films is fascinating, for they demonstrate material dimensions not only of language but also of music and other sounds on the different soundtracks. The Spanish-language *Dracula* (1931), directed by George Melford, used the same sets and the translated script of Tod Browning's Hollywood classic but with a Spanish-speaking cast and more provocative female costumes [**Figures 5.11 and 5.12**]. With adequate dubbing technology and other strategies, Hollywood's dominance of foreign markets was eventually reestablished and foreign films, already dwindling on U.S. screens, became increasingly rare.

By this period, radio had thoroughly transformed the public into a mass audience linked by standardized products and technology and had intro-

Figure 5.11 *Dracula* (1931). Tod Browning's classic is one of a cycle of early sound-era horror films made by Universal.

duced engineering models that would influence sound cinema. In part to utilize its sound technology, the Radio Corporation of America entered the motion-picture production business in 1928, joining with the Keith-Orpheum chain of vaudeville theaters. The new studio, RKO, quickly became one of five studios known as the "majors" that would dominate sound-era cinema, and its releases provide us with several key examples of sound films. For example, Fay Wray's screams cannot be forgotten by anyone who has seen RKO's *King Kong* (1933). This effect was created by **looping**—recording on a loop of film that is replayed and layered, filling in the sound and exceeding realistic reproduction [**Figure 5.13**]. This relatively early sound film also includes a creative blending of effects and music to give presence to Kong—who is merely a mechanical model. Max Steiner's score does not commence until the characters arrive at Skull Island, home of Kong. The music helps us enter a fantasy world as a music cue on the radio might do. Long sequences on the island remain without dialogue, as nearly constant musical accompaniment and effects convey the drama.

Figure 5.12 *Dracula* (1931). The Spanish-language version was shot on the same sets, with cast and costumes for the export market. This version was directed by George Melford.

One of the most innovative directors in the history of sound cinema, Orson Welles, was invited to make his first film, *Citizen Kane* (1941), at RKO. Welles's reputation in theater and radio was achieved most notoriously with the 1938 *The War of the Worlds* broadcast that many listeners mistook for a report on an actual Martian invasion. In *Citizen Kane*, Welles draws on his background and makes innovative use of sound, working with composer Bernard Herrmann throughout the production phase of the film and bringing the distinctive quality of his own voice to his performance in the title role. Welles experiments with sound mixing techniques and uses abrupt adjustments in volume and quality of sound at scene changes. For example, as we begin to hear the butler's version of Kane's dying days, the cut to the flashback is accompanied by the shriek of a cockatoo [**Figure 5.14**], calling attention to a shift that other films would hide. *Citizen Kane* also exploits the spatial properties of its sound to work against the two-dimensional quality of the screen. For example, the bustle of the newspaper offices is conveyed

Figure 5.13 *King Kong* (1933). Fay Wray's screams were looped to increase their effect in this RKO classic film.

Figure 5.14 *Citizen Kane* (1941). Sounds, such as this cockatoo's screech, punctuate rather than smooth over scene transitions in Orson Welles's stylistically innovative film for RKO.

in layers of sounds; likewise, conversations in cavernous Xanadu echo ominously. Both those techniques complement the film's use of deep-focus cinematography.

As we have seen, the traditions of spectacle enhanced by music and the human dream to "store" sounds converged in the sound practices that the cinema adopted. The establishment of representational norms in sound recording and mixing practices proceeded rapidly after the introduction of sound. How movies sound—the crispness of voices, the lush quality of orchestral background music, the use of sound effects in conjunction with what is onscreen—supports ideas about the complementary relationship of sound and image, listening and viewing, and about the value of verisimilitude. Further technological innovations in the 1950s (stereophonic sound), the 1970s (Dolby and surround sound), and the 1990s (digital sound) brought the aural experience of Hollywood cinema to the fore but did little to challenge these ideas. More than simple technological "improvements," these changes corresponded with historical shifts in film's social role as television, home video, and computer games became competitive entertainments. In place of a detailed historical account of how the use of sound has strived to preserve the uniqueness of cinema, a brief overview of sound recording, mixing or re-recording, and reproduction will help us understand the technical processes while we keep in mind the experiential and critical implications of their evolution in film.

The Techniques of Film Sound

As early as the preproduction phase of a contemporary film, a **sound designer** may be involved to plan and direct the overall sound through to the final mix. One of the most prominent sound designers, Walter Murch, worked with Francis Ford Coppola to create a soundscape for *Apocalypse Now* (1979) that is as responsible for the film's surreal horror as the film's visuals **[Figure 5.15]**. During production, **sound recording** takes place simultaneously with the filming of a scene. When the slate is filmed at the beginning of each take, the **clapboard** is snapped; this recorded sound is used to synchronize sound recordings and camera images **[Figure 5.16]**. Microphones for recording synchronous sound may be placed on the actors (radio microphones), suspended over the action outside of camera range on a device resembling a fishing pole called a **boom,** or in other locations on set. The placement of microphones is often dictated by the desire to emphasize clarity and intelligibility of dialogue, especially the speech of the stars, in

Figure 5.15 *Apocalypse Now* (1979). The sound of the ceiling fan evokes the memory of helicopters on this film's influential soundtrack.

the final version of a film. **Direct sound** is sound captured directly from its source, but some degree of **reflected sound,** captured as sounds bounce from the walls and sets, may be desired to give a sense of space. The **sound recordist** or **production mixer** combines these different sources during filming, adjusting their relative volume or balance. In the **multitrack sound recording process,** introduced in Robert Altman's *Nashville* (1975), as many as twenty-four separate tracks of sound can be recorded on twelve tracks.

When a cut of the film is prepared, the crucial and increasingly complex phase of **postproduction sound** work begins. **Sound editing** interacts with the image track to create rhythmic relationships, establish connections between sound and onscreen sources, and smooth or mark transitions. When a sound carries over a visual transition in a film, it is termed a **sound bridge.** For example, music might continue over a scene change or montage sequence, or dialogue may begin before the speaking characters are seen by the audience. The director consults with the composer and the picture and sound editors to determine where music and effects will be added, a process called **spotting.** Sound effects may be gathered, produced by sound-effects editors on computers, retrieved from a sound library, or generated by **foley artists.** Named for the legendary sound man Jack Foley, these members of the sound crew watch the projected film and simultaneously generate live sound effects—footsteps, the rustle of clothing, a key turning in a lock—on what is called a foley stage. These effects are eventually mixed with the other tracks. The film's composer begins composing the score, which is recorded to synchronize with the film's final cut **[Figure 5.17]**. The composer may actually conduct the musicians in time with the film. **Postsynchronous sound,** recorded after the fact and then synchronized with onscreen sources, is often preferred for the dialogue used in the final mix—**natural sound** recorded during production may be indistinct due to noise, perspective, or other problems, and much of the actor's performance will depend on intelligibility of dialogue. During **automated dialogue replacement (ADR),** actors watch the film footage and re-record their lines to be dubbed into the soundtrack (a process also known as looping because actors watch a continuous loop of their scenes). Although dubbing can violate verisimilitude, in Italy and other countries it is used for all of a film's dialogue. Dubbing often replaces the original language of a film for exhibition in another country. Other common practices, such as assembling extras to approximate the sound of a crowd (known as **walla,** the word they were instructed to murmur) or recording **room tone** (the aural properties of a location when nothing is happening), may be used to cover any patch of pure silence in the finished film. Such practices show the extent to which the sound unit goes to reproduce "real-seeming" sound.

Sound mixing or **re-recording,** an important stage in the postproduction of a film, can occur only after the image track, including the credits, is complete (this is referred to as **locking picture**). All three elements of the

Figure 5.16 Clapboards are used to synchronize sound and image takes.

Figure 5.17 *Far from Heaven* (2002). Director Todd Haynes and composer Elmer Bernstein recording the film's score, which re-creates the sound of 1950s Hollywood movies.

Cinematic Sensations

The success of synchronized sound in the late 1920s provided evidence of the public's desire for a multifaceted sensory experience at the cinema. Nevertheless, the incorporation of sound was denounced by many respected film artists and theorists, who saw it as a betrayal of the potential of film as a specifically *visual* art form. Rudolf Arnheim regarded sound as a first step toward the "complete film," an attempt to reproduce reality of which he was critical. He feared that the successive addition of properties such as color, sound, and widescreen technology would carry the imitation of nature to such a degree that film as an art form would be ignored. "Film is on its way to the victory of wax museum ideals over creative art," Arnheim lamented. But is it reproduction or sensation that such inventions serve? While the metaphor of the wax museum recalls cinema's affinity with earlier popular spectacles, it does not suggest the dynamism of our urge to experience a range of sensory stimuli at the cinema. In *Brave New World* (1932), Aldous Huxley imagines "feelies" that would totally immerse viewers in the spectacle. In fact, a number of actual inventions in the history of film go beyond sound and vision to stimulate the other senses. Usually part of the exhibition phase, they transform our theater experience.

In 1905, very early in film history, Hale's Tours and Scenes of the World exhibited travel films in theaters that looked like railway cars. In some venues the cars would rock to simulate movement and the films would be accompanied by train noises. This tradition of linking films to amusement park rides continues in present-day attractions such as Disney World's Star Tours, and in films based on rides, such as *Pirates of the Caribbean* (2003). In the 1950s, film impresario William Castle appealed directly to viewers' sense of touch with his film *The Tingler* (1959) **[Figure 5.18]**. Castle wired selected seats in the movie theater to a motor that vibrated when the film's creepy creature escaped, ostensibly to stalk the aisles. Many film theorists argue that even without such gimmicks, the cinema makes a palpable appeal to our sense of touch. The vastness of the image, the sensual surface of the screen, the rhythms of editing, and the vibrations of sound all have visceral effects, which the IMAX and 3-D formats enhance.

What of the other senses? In 1960, Smell-O-Vision premiered with the film *Scent of Mystery*. Plastic tubes hidden under the seats emitted smells such as garlic and pipe smoke. Much later, filmmaker John Waters introduced Odorama in an

soundtrack—music, sound effects, and dialogue—that have been recorded on separate tracks will now be combined. As the tracks are mixed, they are cut and extended, adjusted and "sweetened" by the sound editor with the input of the director and perhaps the sound designer and picture editor. There are no objective standards for a sound mix. Besides making sure it is complete and clear, the director and technicians will have specific ideas for the film's sound in mind. The final mix might place extra emphasis on dialogue, modulate a mood through the volume of the music, or punch up sound effects during an action sequence. In a film like *Barton Fink* (1991), much of the sense of inhabiting a slightly unreal world is generated by a sound mix that incorporates sounds such as animal noises into the effects accompanying creaking doors **[Figure 5.19]**. At a film's final **mix,** a sound mixer produces a master track to match the final cut of the film. Optical tracks are "married" to the image track on the film print, whereas digital tracks may be printed on the film or recorded on separate disks.

Sound reproduction is the stage in the process when the film's audience (literally, those who listen) experiences the film's sound. During pro-

WHEN THE SCREEN SCREAMS YOU'LL SCREAM TOO... IF YOU VALUE YOUR LIFE!

PERCEPTO! newest and most startling gimmick on the screen!...

COLUMBIA PICTURES presents

The Tingler

GUARANTEED

starring VINCENT PRICE
with JUDITH EVELYN
DARRYL HICKMAN · PATRICIA CUTTS
Written by ROBB WHITE · Produced and Directed by WILLIAM CASTLE
A WILLIAM CASTLE PRODUCTION

Figure 5.18 *The Tingler* (1959). The advertisement recognizes that the theater experience is as important as the film.

homage to such gimmicks and to showmen like Castle. Synchronized to his film *Polyester* (1981), scratch-and-sniff cards featured an array of smells including those of a rose, pizza, and an old tennis shoe. The sense of taste is stimulated in movies about food, such as *Like Water for Chocolate* (1992) and *Eat Drink Man Woman* (1994).

Smell and taste are generally satisfied more directly at the snack bar, but the fact that exhibitors make most of their revenue from the sale of popcorn and other concessions attests to how integral sensory gratification is to moviegoing. Because theaters need to be wired for the Tingler or Smell-O-Vision or specially built for Cinerama or IMAX, technologies that enhance sensory experience remain novelties. Such provisions are costly investments and the existence of few outlets make films in these formats less profitable to produce. Yet the drive for the "complete film" seems to have persisted throughout the history of the medium. In Plato's parable of the cave, the prisoners did not realize that everything they saw was an illusion. With technologies that perfect sound reproduction, build characters from computer code, diffuse smells throughout the cinema, and literally give us "movies" in theme park rides, have we reached "the fulfillment of the age-old striving for the complete illusion," as Arnheim put it? Or do we enjoy these simulations precisely because we remain so very keenly aware of their artifice?

jection, optical soundtracks are illuminated and read by a solar cell that transfers the light to electrical energy, which is then amplified and transferred to the speaker system. Magnetic and digital soundtracks are also converted back to sound waves by the sound system during projection.

The reproduction of sound gives a strong impression of the presence of the sound source. However altered they might be, photographic images refer to their originals in the world. Although we might not think about it when we are watching a movie, the presence of the image always implies the absence of the object. Listening to cinema sound affords a somewhat different experience. The reproduction of a sound is undoubtedly a copy. But it seems to have the same presence or effect on the ear as the original sound, even if its source, directionality, tonality, or depth has changed. We believe we are hearing the

Figure 5.19 *Barton Fink* (1991). Unusual sounds in the mix add to the film's odd atmosphere.

sound right here, right now, and indeed we are, but we are hearing a recording of an actual airplane engine, not an actual airplane engine. Sound perspective enhances this impression of presence and can be manipulated with great nuance in digital sound mixing.

The placement of speakers in the actual three-dimensional space of the theater may be used to suggest sounds emanating from the left or right of the depicted scene or from behind or in front of the audience. In 1979, the exhibition of *Apocalypse Now* introduced what became a standard configuration of three channels of sound behind the screen, and sound to the left and right behind and surrounding the audience. The technology utilizes sound's capability of reaching the viewer/auditor in a more immediate way than the visual. Also in the 1970s, Dolby sound, an improved stereo recording system that reduced noise and allowed the reproduction of high frequency sound, was introduced. The release of *Star Wars* (1977) ushered in an explosion of films with stereo soundtracks using Dolby technology.

The most recent and radical change in playback, **digital sound,** has yet to be standardized into one system, and the competitive formats recall the period of sound's introduction in the late 1920s. In 1993, Steven Spielberg's *Jurassic Park* pioneered digital theater sound (DTS) with sound recorded on a separate disk. Basically, digital sound reproduces a sound wave through sampling the source and converting the data digitally. It allows for extremely high-resolution recording and playback and complex mixing. Genres such as science fiction and action blockbusters that rely heavily on the excitement generated by a dynamic and high-volume sound mix take full advantage of digital sound capabilities. With the marked improvement of sound technology in film recording, mixing, and exhibition introduced by digital sound, filmgoers have become much more aware of and interested in film sound. Just as in the 1950s, when new film technologies such as CinemaScope and stereophonic sound were used to lure customers back to the theaters, today's digital sound systems attract audiences to theatrical exhibition. Audiophiles lead the companion trend toward **home theaters** with digital sound systems and speakers configured like those of movie theaters to emulate surround sound. Although cinema's mimetic capacity to reproduce images and sounds from the natural world is one of its strongest appeals, the perpetual quest for images and sounds that are bigger, louder, better indicates that part of cinema's appeal is its ability to provide a heightened sensory experience that intensifies the ordinary.

VIEWING CUES: Elements of Film Sound

- Isolate a single scene in the movie you will screen next in class. Make note of as many aspects of its sound as you can.

- Are you aware of the direction of particular sounds that you hear in the film? Are the words of major actors the most audible elements of the film's sound mix? Is the mix full or are there relatively few sounds?

- Turn off the sound and see if you can follow the action as readily. Is your emotional response altered? How?

- Try substituting a scene's score with one or two different pieces of music. Does your experience of the scene change substantially?

- How did the format and venue in which you watched the film affect your experience of its sound?

 **IN FOCUS**

Sound and Image in *Singin' in the Rain* (1952)

As noted earlier, no event in the history of Hollywood film was as revolutionary as the synchronized sound introduction in the 1920s. Hollywood has even furnished its own myth about this fascinating chapter in the cultural history of film in the great musical *Singin' in the Rain*.

Directed by Stanley Donen and Gene Kelly, *Singin' in the Rain* demonstrates a delightfully escapist use of sound in film while also being *about* how sound in film achieves such effects. A beloved movie myth, it addresses the relationship of sound to image, the history of film sound technologies, and the process of recording and reproducing sound. In the 1940s and 1950s, MGM's "Freed Unit," working under the supervision of producer Arthur Freed (a former songwriter whose songs are used in *Singin' in the Rain*), produced a series of lavish and inventive musicals. Set in Hollywood at the end of the 1920s, *Singin' in the Rain* follows efforts at the fictional Monumental Pictures to make the studio's first successful sound film. Although the film's self-consciousness about the filmmaking process invites the audience into a behind-the-scenes perspective, the film itself continues to employ every available technique to achieve the illusionism of the Hollywood musical. One of the lessons of the film is that a "talking picture" isn't just "a silent picture with some talking added" as the studio producer assumes it to be. The film shows that adding sound to images enhances them with all the exuberance of song and dance, comedy, and romance.

From the very beginning of *Singin' in the Rain*, the technology responsible for sound reproduction—technology that is usually hidden—is displayed. The film opens outside a Hollywood movie palace where crowds have gathered for the premiere of the new Lockwood and Lamont picture. Our first orientation is aural: "Ladies and gentleman, I am speaking to you from. . . ." The asynchronous announcer's voice carries across the crowds and seems to address us directly. The second shot opens directly on a loudspeaker, underscoring the parallelism of image and soundtrack, and then begins to explore the crowd of listeners. When we first see the radio announcer, the source of the synchronous voice, the microphone is very prominent in the mise-en-scène **[Figure 5.20]**. Referring to the bygone days of radio and silent movies, the film celebrates its modern audience's opportunity to watch sound and image combined in a sophisticated MGM musical.

Singin' in the Rain immediately begins to exploit the resources and conventions of studio-era sound cinema. When star Don Lockwood (Gene Kelly) begins to tell the story of his past in a diegetic voiceover to

Figure 5.20 *Singin' in the Rain* (1952). A concern with sound recording technology is evident in the microphone's prominence in the first scene.

Figure 5.21 *Singin' in the Rain* (1952). The illusion of romance is visibly created on the soundstage, but the music the characters dance to has no apparent source.

the assembled crowds and the radio listeners at home, this is a contrapuntal use of sound because the series of flashback images belie his words. When his onscreen image gives way to his offscreen voice speaking of studying at a conservatory, we see him and his buddy, Cosmo Brown (Donald O'Connor), performing a vaudeville routine instead. The scene shows that images and voices can be out of sync, a theme that will become prominent in the film as a whole. It also shows the multiple ways the sound-track can interact with the images. The virtuosic and comic vaudeville routine is, in turn, accompanied by lively music and humorous sound effects—the diegetic sound of the flashback world—encouraging our direct appreciation of the number. Next we hear the crowd's appreciative reactions to Lockwood's narra-tion, a narration that we know to be phony. However, we do not experience these two different levels of sound—Don's self-serving narration and the debunk-ing synchronized sound of the flashbacks—as confusing. It is clear that the film's unveiling of the mechanisms of sound technology will not limit its own reliance on the multiple illusions of sound and image relationships.

Later, when Don wants to express the depth of his feelings to Kathy Selden (Debbie Reynolds), he takes her to an empty soundstage. Ironically, his sincerity depends on the artifice of a sunset background, a wind ma-chine, and a battery of mood lights, which together render the very picture of romance [**Figure 5.21**]. Yet the corresponding sound illusion is conjured without any visible sound recording or effects equipment. Instead, each of Don's touches, such as switching on the wind machine, is synchronized with an "invisible," nondiegetic musical flourish. The richly orchestrated musical accompaniment to the ensuing dance number does not originate from an onscreen source. It is possible to ask us to suspend our disbelief in this way because, in the film's world, music is everywhere.

The film pits the stilted, overblown style of silent costume drama against the rhythms of a vital, contemporary musical—a form so spontaneous that song even erupts backstage. In the "Make Them Laugh" sequence, Cosmo extemporizes a dance with props available on the set. When he begins to sing, an unseen orchestra starts up; when he takes a pratfall, cymbals crash in a parallel but asynchronous use of sound. The world in which illusions are made is itself illusory. In the course of the film, Don Lockwood will learn to incorporate his true self—the one who enjoys "singin' and dancin' in the rain"—into his onscreen persona. Lina Lamont (Jean Hagen), who repre-sents image without the animating authenticity of sound (she's a beautiful woman with a comical accent and, ironically, her hilarious performance is one of the greatest aural pleasures of the film), will be replaced by Kathy who dubs Lina's voice. Kathy is depicted as genuine *because* she can sing. Image and sound go together.

Nothing illustrates the film's paradoxical acknowledgment of the sound–image illusions constructed by Hollywood and its indulgence in them better than the contrast between the disastrous premiere of the nonsinging *The Dueling Cavalier*, and the film's final scene at the opening night of the mu-sical *The Dancing Cavalier*, in which the truth of Lina's imposture comes out. In the former, a noisy audience laughs at and heckles the errors of poor synchronous sound recording: the actors' heartbeats and rustling costumes

Figure 5.22 *Singin' in the Rain* (1952). The dubbing deception is revealed.

Figure 5.23 *Singin' in the Rain* (1952). The film's final reflexive moment is accompanied by an invisible chorus on the soundtrack.

drown out their dialogue (of course for us, the laughter and the heartbeats are both sound effects, the latter mixed at comically high levels). The film they have created fundamentally misunderstands the promise of "talking pictures." Don's lines "I love you, I love you, I love you" are vapid and roundly mocked. The falseness is fully on display when the film goes out of sync: the villain nods his head as Lina's high-pitched "No, no, no" comes out, suggesting that men and women are as different as *yes* and *no*. The potential deceptiveness of technology is mocked. At the premiere of *The Dancing Cavalier*, in contrast, the film finally makes the proper match, not only between sound and image (thus correcting the humorous synchronization problems of the first version) but also between Don and Kathy. After she's forced to dub Lina "live" at the premiere, and the hoax is exposed when the curtains are drawn for all the audience to see **[Figure 5.22]**, the humiliated Kathy runs from the stage. Don gets her back by singing "You Are My Lucky Star" to her from the stage (thus demonstrating before the audience in the film that, unlike Lina, he used his own singing voice during the film within a film). Cosmo conducts the conveniently present orchestra (the premiere is of a sound film that should not require accompaniment), and Kathy joins Don in a duet. The core characters finally have both a public stage for a "live" performance of their formerly behind-the-scenes musical and emotional sincerity. Lest we read the film as suggesting that the onscreen orchestra is more genuine than the romantic background music of the earlier scenes because it is synchronous, we must note that the film ends triumphantly with asynchronous music. A full, invisible chorus picks up "You Are My Lucky Star" as the camera takes us out into the open air, to pause on the billboard announcing the premiere of *Singin' in the Rain*, starring Lockwood and Selden (who, of course, are represented by images of the stars of the movie by the same name that we are watching, Gene Kelly and Debbie Reynolds) **[Figure 5.23]**. This chorus, which cries out "movie convention," and the billboard advertising the title of the film we are watching, are the culmination of the film's effort to render Hollywood illusionism—so aptly represented by extravagant musicals such as *Singin' in the Rain*—natural. *Singin' in the Rain* dramatizes the arrival of sound in Hollywood as the inevitable and enjoyable combination of sound and image.

Elements of the Film Soundtrack:
Voice, Music, Sound Effects

Glengarry Glen Ross (1992), adapted by David Mamet from his own play, is dominated by the sound of actors' voices. *The Terminator* (1984) keys us to events in its futuristic world by the sound of noise, while the title of *The Sound of Music* (1965) announces what one can expect to hear on its sound-track. Voice, music, and sound effects are the three elements of the film soundtrack, and they are often present simultaneously. In some sense a film's image track, composed of relatively discrete photographic images and text, is simpler and more unified. Nevertheless, although the three sound elements can all be present and combined in relation to any given image, conventions have evolved governing these relationships. Usually dialogue is audible over music, for example, and only in special cases does a piece of music dictate the images that accompany it. (Disney's *Fantasia* [1940] was an experiment in allowing the music to "go first.") Here we shall examine each of the basic elements and its potential to make meaning in combination with images and other sounds. We will uncover conventional usages and how they have shaped the film experience and given direction to theorists' inquiries into the properties and potential of film sound.

Voice in Film

Human speech is often central to narrative film's intelligibility, primarily in the form of dialogue (film scenarios became known as scripts when there were words for the actors to say). Acoustic qualities of the voices of actors make a distinct contribution to a film: Jimmy Stewart's drawl is relaxed and reassuring; Robin Williams's cadences let us know we are watching something more antic and comic. But of course *what* actors say is crucial: speech establishes character motivation and goals and conveys plot information.

Making an intelligible record of an actor's speech quickly became the primary goal in early film sound recording processes, although this goal required some important concessions in the otherwise primary quest for realism. For example, think about how we hear film characters' speech. While the image track may cut from a long shot of a conversation to a medium shot of two characters to a series of close-up, shot/reverse-shot pairings, the sound-track does not reproduce these distances accurately through changes in volume or the relationship between direct and reflected sound. Rather, actors are miked so that what they say is recorded directly and is clear and intelligible and uniform in volume throughout the dialogue scene. **Sound perspective,** which refers to the apparent distance of a sound source, remains close. A great deal of humor is derived from the depiction of early solutions to the miking of actors in *Singin' in the Rain*. First only every other word is caught as the actress Lina Lamont moves her head while speaking; then hiding the microphone in her bodice amplifies the sound of her heart, drowning out the words she speaks. Director Robert Altman's innovations in multitrack film sound recording in *Nashville*, mentioned earlier in this chapter, allowed each character to be miked and separately recorded. One stylistic feature of this technique is Altman's extensive use of **overlapping dialogue,** mixing characters' speech simultaneously, a technique Orson Welles had attempted with less sophisticated recording technology. In *Nashville*, characters constantly talk over each other [**Figure 5.24**]. This technique, which may make individual lines less distinct, is often used to approximate the everyday experience of hearing multiple, competing speakers and sounds at the same time.

Figure 5.24 *Nashville* (1975). Robert Altman's twelve-track recording process captures each character individually, and overlapping dialogue is used in the final mix.

Dialogue is also given priority when it carries over visual shifts, such as shot/reverse-shot patterns of editing conversations. We watch one actor begin a line and then watch the listener as he or she continues. Sound preserves temporal continuity as the scene is broken down into individual shots. As commentators on film sound have noted, in the Western philosophical tradition, speech is endowed with the capacity to signify presence, and films defer to this capacity. Speech occurs here and now, and thus it is a key support of verisimilitude. Sometimes the most outlandish plot premises and settings can be anchored by dialogue. Given the importance and authority we accord the spoken word, it is interesting that film sound often has second-class status in relation to the image.

The voice can be seen to originate from an onscreen speaker, or it may originate from a speaker who can be inferred to be present in the scene but who is not currently visible. This technique is referred to as **voice-off,** and it is a good example of the greater spatial flexibility of sound over image. The opening shot of *Laura* (1944) follows a detective looking around a fancy apartment as a narrator introduces the film's events. Abruptly, the same voice addresses the detective from an adjacent room, telling him to be careful what he touches, a striking use of voice-off. It may also be used in a genre such as the horror film to generate suspense. Early in the film *M* (1931), the murderer's offscreen whistle is heard, followed by an onscreen shadow of a man, combining the expressive possibility of sound (just recently introduced when the film was made) with that of lighting and mise-en-scène (which had already been available to silent cinema) **[Figure 5.25]**.

In an experimental film, voice-off may also serve to make the viewer/listener think about different levels of the film's fiction. How do we know that an offscreen voice shares the same space and time as the onscreen figures? Yvonne Rainer's *The Man Who Envied Women* (1985) uses an array of voice/image juxtapositions **[Figure 5.26]**. In one scene, we see a hand arranging and rearranging pictures pinned on a wall and hear a voice interpreting the juxtapositions. We cannot determine to whom the voice belongs, to whom it is addressed, or even what its spatial or temporal relationship to the image might be, although all of these questions are raised by the juxtaposition. In Jean-Luc Godard's *Two or Three Things I Know about Her* (1966), characters frequently address the camera

Figure 5.25 *M* (1931). Use of off-screen sound and space imply the murderer's presence.

Figure 5.26 *The Man Who Envied Women* (1985). The voices we hear may or may not belong to the story world in this film, which experiments with the relationship between sound and image.

directly as if they are being interviewed. In fact, they are responding to questions from Godard that are inaudible to us, but the lack of a voice-off makes the sequences function on a different level than the film's more obviously fictional (although equally verbose) episodes.

While use of the voice-off in a classical film is a strong tool in the service of film realism, implying that the mise-en-scène extends beyond the borders of the frame, the illusion of realism can be challenged if the origins of the voice-off are not clear. The voice-off of HAL 9000, the computer in *2001: A Space Odyssey* (1968), is consistent with realism because the voice has a known source. However, the regularity of its volume makes it seem to pervade the spaceship even as it retains its intimate quality. In its uncanny combination of humanity and technology, it suggests how the voice-off can introduce distance into the customary match of sound and image.

Although both are uses of the human voice whose source is not visible in the frame, a voice-off is distinguished from the familiar technique of **voiceover** by the simple fact that characters within the diegesis cannot hear the latter. The voiceover is an important structuring device in film: a text spoken by an offscreen narrator can act as the organizing principle behind virtually all of the film's images, such as in a documentary film, a commercial, or an experimental video or essay film. The unseen narrators of the classic documentaries *Night Mail* (1936) and *The Plow That Broke the Plains* (1936) offer a poem about the British postal service and an account of the U.S. government's agricultural programs, respectively **[Figure 5.27]**. The voiceover device soon became the cornerstone of the documentary tradition, in which the voiceover "anchors" the potential ambiguity of the film's images. The sonic qualities of such voiceovers—usually male, resonant, and "unmarked" by class, regional, or foreign accent or other distinguishing features—are meant

Figure 5.27 *Night Mail* (1936). Classic documentary accompanied by verse read in voiceover.

to connote trustworthiness (although today they can sound propagandistic). The traditional technique of directing our interpretation of images through a transcendent voiceover is sometimes referred to as "the Voice of God." A similar confident male voice can still be heard in nature shows, commercials, and trailers seen in movie theaters.

The "March of Time" series, combining documentary and newsreel styles, screened in cinemas in the 1940s. In the newsreel segment early in *Citizen Kane*, Orson Welles emulates, and gently mocks, this genre's characteristic sound. The volume even increases notably at the start of the segment to emphasize the voiceover's booming authority. This sanctioned story of Kane's life remains impersonal, in contrast to the multiple on-camera narrators whose recollections organize the film's other segments. In the introduction to *History of the World: Part I* (1981), Mel Brooks casts Orson Welles himself as God the narrator, parodying precisely the theological transcendence with which voiceovers have been associated.

In the 1960s, documentary filmmakers began to reject voiceovers that allowed for little or no questioning of the interpretation of events or of the sound–image correlation. In effect, the multiple meanings of the image had been reduced to a singular meaning conferred by the voiceover. Hence, asynchronous voices were eschewed altogether in documentary styles such as **cinéma vérité,** which instead used onscreen voices to advance the action. Attributed to filmmakers or subjects participating in events, these voices left the interpretation of images up to the viewer. This documentary movement started in France, using unobtrusive lightweight cameras and sound equipment to capture a real-life situation as well as whatever change or conflict might be provoked by the filming. The closely related U.S. movement, **direct cinema,** in the hands of filmmaker Frederick Wiseman in *High School* (1969) and *Domestic Violence* (2001), aims to observe an unfolding situation as unobtrusively as possible.

For some filmmakers, even a voice-off interview of onscreen subjects is considered intrusive because it calls attention to the presence and intention of the filmmaker and draws it away from the documentary's subject matter. Other documentarians consider the on-camera or voice-off interview to be an important marker of the limitations of any film's perspective; for example, filmmaker Michael Moore has made his on-camera filmmaking persona an important part of his films. The connotations of the voiceover tradition have been modified by identifying the filmmaker's voice or introducing a voice with distinct, embodied qualities, what some theorists call "grain." Because female or youthful or regionally or nationally distinct voices are not culturally granted the same authoritative status as the white, male, educated voice, such voiceovers can remind viewers of the subjective qualities of the documentary. Any voiceover text is only a partial take on truth, an aspect that is hidden in the abstract qualities of the traditional voiceover. When a filmmaker's own voiceover narration is used in a work that is autobiographical, or in one that reflects on the filmmaking process, it may increase documentary "truth" even as it eschews objectivity. Lourdes Portillo structures her documentary about her family members in Mexico and California, *The Devil Never Sleeps* (1994), as an investigation, using her own unfolding perspective to guide its structure. Trinh T. Minh-ha's strategy in *Reassemblage* (1982) is to use her own voice, whose softness and accent require the

viewer's close attention, to record questions about the film's subject and process. She scripts the voiceover in fragments that refuse to explain or "cover" the images. Such experiments have begun to blur the boundaries between documentary and other film genres. They encourage a focus on the way the soundtrack participates in the overall structure of a film. Isaac Julien's *Looking for Langston* (1988) is about poet Langston Hughes but is by no means a conventional documentary **[Figure 5.28]**. Its soundtrack is crowded with voices reciting poetry by a number of contemporary black gay male authors, and it does not claim to provide definitive information about Hughes.

Theorist Bill Nichols looks at the different ways the voices of filmmakers and subjects can be used in documentaries to discuss what he terms the "voice" of the film itself. At one end of the spectrum is the authoritative, anonymous voiceover that sets up and interprets the film's images. At the other, **talking heads**—on-camera interviews—usually shot in medium close-up—tell the documentary's story, such as in Lynne Fernie and Aerlyn Weissman's documentary about lesbian

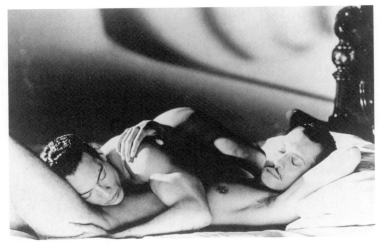

Figure 5.28 *Looking for Langston* (1988). Poets' voices are heard on the soundtrack of Isaac Julien's meditation on black gay male culture.

life in the 1940s to 1960s, *Forbidden Love* (1992), and there is no voiceover, printed text, or on-camera presence to lead the viewer through the material. The interviewed subjects are the authorities. In between lie a spectrum of possibilities. In *Roger and Me* (1989), director Michael Moore's own voiceover is heard, and he interacts on camera with his subjects, while in other documentaries filmmakers may interview subjects on camera but not attempt to draw attention to themselves. In his documentary *Lumumba: Death of a Prophet* (1992), Raoul Peck speaks about the process of making his film, showing black leader (the strip attached to the beginning of a reel of film sometimes used to project a black image onscreen) as he speaks about how the images that he needs to tell his story about the controversial death of the African leader are missing. Given this broad spectrum, "voice," in Nichols's sense of the work, then refers to how the film's overall perspective correlates with the status of specific speakers in the film.

In their book *Unthinking Eurocentrism*, Robert Stam and Ella Shohat introduce "voice" as an analytic category in order to challenge both the primacy of the visual in film theory and the Eurocentric perspective of film history. They argue that traces of non-European voices and cultures persist in documentaries and fiction films in such elements as music or performance styles. This **dialogic** or double-voiced quality means that films convey multiple messages. For example, a film like Spike Lee's *Do the Right Thing* relies as much on the verbal styles of its characters and the emotions and meanings of its music as on its visual elements, and neither of these levels is definitive.

Voiceover narration is also used in fiction films, often as a way to introduce us to the story world. *The Royal Tenenbaums* (2001) begins with a "once upon a time" voiceover. Voiceovers can also render characters' subjective states. Much of the humor of *Bridget Jones's Diary* (2001), for instance, comes from our access to the heroine's internal (semi-diegetic) comments on the situations she encounters [Figure 5.29]. But voiceover can also be an important structural device in narration, orienting viewers to the temporal organization of a story by setting up a flashback or providing a transition back to the film's present. The sound and image tracks can relate to each other with considerable temporal complexity. For example, a voiceover narration in the present can accompany a scene from the past that uses both images and sounds from within the depicted world. Use of voiceovers to organize a film's temporality is prevalent in certain genres such as film noir, in which the voiceover imitates the hard-boiled, first-person investigative style of the literary works from which many of these stories are adapted. Sometimes, in keeping with the murky world of film noir or the limited perspective of the investigator, such voiceovers prove unreliable. For example,

Figure 5.29 *Bridget Jones's Diary* (2001). Bridget's wicked comments about her co-workers are audible only to us.

Figure 5.30 *Laura* (1944). Waldo Lydecker (played by Clifton Webb) opens the film with a voiceover narration and then calls to the detective in a voice-off. The next shot shows him writing in the tub.

Figure 5.31 *Mildred Pierce* (1945). The voiceover of Mildred (played by Joan Crawford) increases our sympathy for her situation as a wife and mother in the flashback.

the account of the heroine's death given by the narrator in voiceover in the opening scene of *Laura*, which is interrupted by the striking voice-off described on page 185, is contradicted later in the film when she proves to be alive **[Figure 5.30]**. At the end of *Laura*, the villain's offscreen voice is heard on a radio broadcast, tricking the characters about his whereabouts, a plot twist that seems to refer to this unreliability of the voice.

Michael Curtiz's *Mildred Pierce* (1945) is a "woman's film"—featuring a female star whose character faces exaggerated versions of the problems many women encounter—but it is given a film noir framework, and the voiceover is an important element in this clash of styles. In the beginning, Mildred (played by Joan Crawford) confesses to a crime we eventually learn she did not commit. However, her voiceover's credibility is compromised by her gender as well as by genre conventions. Several flashbacks are introduced by scenes in which Mildred is interrogated by the police. "It seems as if I was born in a kitchen," she narrates, and the film depicts her life as a wife and mother **[Figure 5.31]**. These voiceovers are quickly abandoned as the flashback segments revert to and play out in synchronized sound. Eventually, Mildred's version of events is discredited by the police, who use her words to convict her daughter; her voiceover ultimately confirms their point of view. In fact, critics note that in women's pictures such as *Mildred Pierce* and Hitchcock's *Rebecca* (1940), female voiceovers rarely carry films through to closure, violating the symmetry we have come to expect from a classical Hollywood film.

Synchronization, the visible coordination of the voice with the body from which it is emanating, tends to be a valued practice in Hollywood films. It anchors sound that might otherwise seem to be autonomous or even call into question the seamless illusion of reality that Hollywood films strive for. Film theorist Kaja Silverman argues that synchronization is especially enforced for characters who are culturally more closely identified with the body, such as women and African Americans; these characters have not been allowed to achieve authoritative presence through speech alone. Thus Morgan Freeman's voiceover narration of *The Shawshank Redemption* (1994) is unusual precisely because it validates the experience of an African American character. *Eve's Bayou* (1997) is narrated by a child, a device that infuses the film with wonder and a sense of having to decipher the narrative; the fact that Eve is female and African American makes the film's emphasis on untold stories even more urgent [Figure 5.32].

Ever since "the talkies" were introduced, the human voice has organized systems of meaning in various types of film: narrative films are frequently driven by dialogue, documentaries by voiceover, and experimental films often turn voice into an aesthetic element. As noted earlier in this chapter, some writers suggest that a theory of "voice" can open up cinema analysis to more meanings than a model devoted to the image alone. Although we have stressed how frequently film sound is subordinated to the image, certainly the realm of the voice shows us how central sound is to cinema's intelligibility. In fact, the prevalence of the human voice is a measure of just how focused the universe of classical cinema is on depicting human experience. From recording to mixing to reproduction, sound practices privilege the human subject. Contrasting a Hollywood drama with a film whose dialogue is dubbed demonstrates how sound mixing favors the human voice. The flatness of the postsynchronized sound used in dubbed films confirms our belief in a more "natural" way of synching up voices and bodies. Ironically, the Hollywood soundtrack is likely to have used postsynchronized dialogue in the form of ADR, a technology that strives for an illusion more perfect than the original sound it replaces.

Figure 5.32 *Eve's Bayou* (1997). A little girl's version of events is given credence by the voiceover device.

Music in Film

Music is a crucial element in the film experience; among a range of other effects, it provides rhythm and deepens emotional response. Music has rarely been absent from film programs and many of the venues for early film had been musical ones first. The piano, an important element of public and private amusements at the turn of the twentieth century, quickly became a cornerstone of film exhibition [Figure 5.33]. Throughout the silent-film period, scoring for films steadily developed from the distribution of collections of music cues that accompanists and ensembles could play to correspond with appropriate moments in films to full-length compositions for specific films. When D. W. Griffith's *The Birth of a Nation* premiered in 1915, a full orchestra, playing Joseph Carl Breil's score in which the Ku Klux Klan rallied to Wagner's "Ride of the Valkyries," was a major audience attraction. The architecture of the large movie palaces constructed during this period was acoustically geared to audiences familiar with listening to orchestral music in a concert setting. *The Jazz Singer* and other early sound films were conceived to show off the musical performances of their stars. As we mentioned previously, speech made it to the screen as an afterthought—and thus the introduction of dialogue presented problems of scale and volume in the movie palaces.

Figure 5.33 So-called silent films were almost always accompanied by musicians.

Although the term *talkies* for the new sound films soon took over, movies of every genre—westerns, disaster films, science fiction films—relied on music from the beginning. Often this music contributes to categorizing

Figure 5.34 *Blazing Saddles* (1974). Soundtrack music finds its onscreen source in Count Basie's orchestra playing in a desert in Mel Brooks's spoof.

such films *as* genre films. Vangelis's music for *Blade Runner* (1982), for example, distinctly marks it as a science fiction film. In contrast, Max Steiner's score for *Gone with the Wind* (1939) sets its nostalgic, romantic tone.

Narrative Music When we think about the conventions of film sound, background music comes most immediately to mind. Music is the only element of cinematic discourse besides credits that is primarily nondiegetic. It can also move easily back and forth from the level of the story world to the nondiegetic level on which that world can be commented upon. In the back of our minds, we are aware that the practice of scoring films with music that has no source in the story violates verisimilitude, and yet we readily accept this convention. The gag in Mel Brooks's *Blazing Saddles* (1974), in which the musical soundtrack turns out to be coming from Count Basie's jazz orchestra playing in the middle of the desert, is entertaining because it shows the absurdity of the convention **[Figure 5.34]**. Occasionally we are jolted out of absorption in a film because the music is simply too overblown, its commentary on the action too obvious. Nevertheless, normally we value the musical score as a crucial element of our affective, or emotional, response to a film. The scoring for narrative films thus presents a notable paradox: much of what is valued in classical cinema—verisimilitude, cause-and-effect relationships—is completely ignored in even the most admired examples of film music.

The conventions of musical scoring, composition, orchestration, and mixing contribute to a particular kind of experience at the movies. Film music encourages us to be receptive to the information being conveyed by the visual as well as by the other acoustic dimensions of the film. It opens us to experience the movie as immediate and enveloping. It encourages us to let our barriers down. Many commentators speculate that these effects are psychologically related to the fact that the earliest human sensory experience is auditory. Because music is nonrepresentational—it is not a copy of something specific in the world the way an image is—it can be more suggestive. Set apart from the diegesis and taking place right there in the theater, music eases our transition into the fictional world.

Because many of the practices of musical scoring were developed in tandem with the dominant form of narrative film, we shall focus this discussion on narrative film music. In Hollywood and related mainstream film practices, the musical score has a direct connection to the story. However complex or lush it may be, it serves a dramatic purpose. The term **background music,** also referred to as **underscoring** (in contrast to source music, which is diegetic), already emphasizes this status. Music quite literally underscores what is happening dramatically. A piece of music composed for a particular place in a film is referred to as a **cue.** When recording the score, the conductor watches the film for the "cue" to begin playing that particular piece of music. Often music reinforces story information though recognizable conventions. Action sequences in the *Indiana Jones* series are introduced by the inescapable "dum da-dum dum" as a parody of and a tribute to these recognizable themes. Through the use of **motives,** themes assigned to particular figures, music also participates in characterization. We know when the main character has entered the scene not only visually but also aurally, because principal characters usually have a musical motif. The presence of "bad girl" Marylee Hadley in *Written on the Wind* (1956) is signaled by a distinctive sultry theme. Most notably, music is subordinate to that part of the narrative which competes in the realm of sound, the dialogue. A music cue will usually be audible during sequences in which there is no dialogue, often helping to smooth a spatial or temporal transition. When dialogue predominates, however, it will fade, its volume will drop, or it will change to be less "competitive."

Composers for classical cinema, such as Erich Korngold, Dimitri Tiomkin, and Max Steiner, generated their own set of musical styles to suit the accepted function of film music, and many of these principles are still dominant in contemporary practice. In Steiner's more than three hundred scores, including those for *King Kong, Gone with the Wind, Now, Voyager* (1942), and *Mildred Pierce,* musical accompaniment was notable for being almost continuous. He composed using a **click track**—holes punched in the film to keep the beat of the action—and his style was highly illustrative, emphasizing what happens on the screen through music.

Much of Hollywood film music composition is derived from nineteenth-century, late romantic orchestral music. Here the term *classical* is undoubtedly appropriate for studio-era Hollywood style, for popular music was rejected in favor of classical music. The work of such composers as Wagner and Strauss was rich in its ability to convey narrative information; reliant on compositional principles such as motives assigned to different characters, settings, or actions; and lushly emotive, tonal, and euphonic. As such, it was perfectly suited to the musical experience that Hollywood was striving for with the integration of sound. This type of music was compatible with Hollywood storytelling not only because of its purely musical qualities, but also because of the associations and values this music carried for audiences. These associations ranged from the high cultural status conferred on symphonic music of European origin (as opposed to the status of American jazz or pop) to the recognizable connotations of a particular instrumentation, such as somber horns for a funereal mood, violins for romance, and a harp for an ethereal or heavenly mood.

In her book *Unheard Melodies: Narrative Film Music,* Claudia Gorbman lists the "principles of composition, mixing, and editing" that classical film music follows. The first is **invisibility,** which refers to the predominance of nondiegetic music (over the actual depiction of musicians) and to the fact that the technical apparatus that produces film music, like the camera and the projector responsible for the image we see, is never seen. The boom mikes visible in a film like *Red Rock West* (1992) violate this principle and are clearly accidental. The principle of **inaudibility** is analogous to the "invisible" editing style of the continuity system. This principle dictates that conscious attention should not be paid to the score. Volume does not interfere with dialogue, the mood and rhythm of the music do not contradict that of the action, and compositions are matched to narrative flow rather than allowed to follow their own progression. Ironically, screen music is at its best if we do not "hear" it.

Gorbman next stresses film music's function as a **signifier of emotion.** Dialogue and action fall short in their capacity to convey not only particular feelings but also the experience of feeling itself. Music is subjective, whereas the image is perceived as objective. A close-up of the heroine's face matched with a great swell of music in *Now, Voyager*, a convention readily seen today in the soap opera, provides a good example of how music supplements visuals when emotions are at stake. Gorbman isolates three common ways music's connotation of emotion are used. First, music conveys the irrational. In Hitchcock's *Spellbound* (1945), for example, the mental state of the hero is conveyed by the sound of the theremin, an unusual electronic instrument whose spooky sound is also used in science fiction films **[Figure 5.35].** Second, music is associated with women, who are already culturally associated with emotion. Our pejorative idea of sappy music is derived from the sound of women's genres, where tears and musical notes fall with the same abundance. The music accompanying a brief scene in an empty bedroom in Gillian Armstrong's *Little Women* (1994) gives the viewer time to cry after Beth's death. Third, lush orchestration ennobles the ordinary and makes the specific timeless. In *The Cider House Rules* (1999), the milestones of one young man's coming of age are made grand by Rachel Portman's score.

Figure 5.35 *Spellbound* (1945). The use of the theremin in Miklós Rózsa's score connotes psychological distortion in Alfred Hitchcock's film about psychoanalysis.

The next principle Gorbman discusses, **narrative cueing,** refers to how music tells us what is happening in the plot. It is heavily relied on in classical scores. Cues may be denotative: a return of the main theme signifies that *Gone with the Wind* is about to conclude; a western song over the credits of *Rancho Notorious* (1952) signifies the setting of a film of that genre. Narrative cueing is also connotative: violins on the soundtrack may indicate that the characters are falling in love; a few notes of "Deutschland über alles" in the score of *Casablanca* (1942) signifies the looming Nazi threat. Music's role in relation to narrative may be to point something out or emphasize its significance; the most noticeable examples are called **stingers,** sounds that force us to notice the significance of something onscreen, such as the ominous chord struck when the villain's presence is made known. The highly effective soundtrack of *The Shining* (1980) includes a stinger when a mirror held up to letters written backwards on the wall reveals the word *murder*. Scores can also musically imitate what happens on the screen—a soufflé falls, a doorbell rings. Over-illustrating the action through the score, such as accompanying a character walking on tip-toe with plucked strings, is referred to as **mickey-mousing.** (This term is a reference to the way cartoons often use the musical score to follow or mimic every action in synchronization, narrating through music rather than language.) Max Steiner is particularly noted for his habit of pointing out everything in his soundtracks in this manner.

We have already indicated how important the soundtrack as a whole is to a film's **continuity,** another principle of film music. Continuity is also valued in the music itself. Discontinuities in visual information represented by cuts and scene changes are frequently bridged by the durational aspect of sound, and this function is most easily served by music. Various arrangements of the theme song of *High Noon* (1952) carry characters across space and help bridge transitions between scene changes. Critics of studio-style film music complain that the composer's job is nothing more than filling up any gaps in the film with the soundtrack.

Gorbman notes that musical scores follow the principle of **unity,** which is also a basic tenet of classical film style. Composing a score around themes provides built-in unity through its structure of repetition and variation. Often critics attribute the classical film score's stress on unity to the influence of composer Richard Wagner's notion of the *Gesamtkunstwerk* or "total work of art." Finally, Gorbman concludes her list of principles for narrative film scores with the acknowledgment that any one of these rules may be violated, but only, she emphasizes, in the service of another rule. Her list of points is extremely helpful in identifying what makes narrative film scores, despite considerable range, so consistent and recognizable.

Although musical scoring conventions have evolved and changed since the classical era of studio filmmaking, we can hear in the orchestral scores of John Williams, the most well-known composer of films of the 1980s and 1990s, an homage to the romantic styles of the studio composers of earlier decades. Williams composes heroic, nostalgic scores that support and sometimes inflate the narrative's significance in films from *Star Wars* to *Home Alone* (1990). His five Academy Awards and more than forty nominations suggest that the film industry recognizes his style's consistency with Hollywood studio practice.

In Hollywood cinema of the studio era, nonclassical musical styles, such as jazz, popular, and dance music, might be used as source music and featured in musicals, but their incorporation into background music was gradual. One of the effects of the neglect of American musical idioms in favor of European influences was that African American artists and performers were rendered almost as inaudible as they were invisible in mainstream movies. African American performers were frequently featured in musicals, but they were there to provide entertainment and were rarely integrated into the narrative. Lena Horne's talent, for example, was shamefully underutilized because there were almost no leading roles for African American women at the time **[Figure 5.36]**.

Figure 5.36 Most of Lena Horne's appearances in mainstream films were restricted to cameo numbers.

As jazz music became more popular, jazz themes began to appear in urban-based film noirs of the 1940s. Henry Mancini's music for Orson Welles's *Touch of Evil* (1958) effectively connotes themes of crime, violence, and sexuality in the exaggerated border-town setting. Occasionally, dissonance appeared in studio scores, but usually only when diegetically motivated—for example, to signify a psychological disturbance. In keeping with this connotation, the first atonal score was composed by Leonard Rosenman for *The Cobweb* (1955), a movie set in a home for the mentally ill. With other changes in the U.S. film industry in the postwar period, musical conventions shifted as well. Modernist and jazz-influenced scores, such as Leonard Bernstein's score for *On the Waterfront* (1954), became more common as different audiences were targeted through more individualized filmmaking practices. At the end of the studio era, the great tradition of the Hollywood musical also began to wane, but a closer look at the genre will underscore how central music is to the narrative film experience, even at the cost of verisimilitude.

The Hollywood Musical   It was fitting that the last effort of the studios to dominate movie screens was the big-budget, spectacular musical, because in many ways the musical epitomizes Hollywood entertainment. Despite the phenomenal success of *The Sound of Music* in 1965, however, further attempts at studio-produced blockbuster musicals, such as *Doctor Dolittle* (1967) and Francis Ford Coppola's *Finian's Rainbow* (1968), were box-office disappointments, their failures indicative of a change in movie culture.

The musical had been a perennial favorite, from the early sound era's backstage musicals featuring elaborate Busby Berkeley numbers [**Figure 5.37**] to later musicals that integrated songs and narrative, such as *An American in Paris* (1951) and Rogers and Hammerstein's *Oklahoma!* (1955), forming abiding myths of the U.S. character. The musical genre often followed the principles of classical narrative film scoring with the addition of production numbers that positively reveled in film music's audibility. The opening tune of Rouben Mamoulian's early sound film *Love Me Tonight* (1932) is picked up by character after character, as if they can all actually hear the background music. The manner in which music connotes emotion or "spirit" in Hollywood films is perhaps best illustrated by the musical genre, in which this feeling erupts in a story world where song and dance are expected.

Even as the studios tried to prolong their dominance with spectacular musicals, Richard Lester's films with the Beatles, *A Hard Day's Night* (1964) and *Help!* (1965), successfully revised the genre for an era geared toward youth and dominated by popular music. At the end of the twentieth century, films from directors notable for their stylization, such as Todd Haynes's *Velvet Goldmine* (1998), the Coen brothers' *O Brother, Where Art Thou?* (2000), Lars von Trier's *Dancer in the Dark* (2000), and Baz Luhrmann's *Moulin*

Figure 5.37 *42nd Street* (1933). Busby Berkeley choreographed outrageous musical numbers designed for the unique perspective afforded by the movie camera.

Rouge! (2001), updated the genre. But by this time, songs had found their way onto soundtracks through means that often did not require the suspension of disbelief demanded by the often utopian world of the musical.

Prerecorded Music   Popular songs have long had a place in the movies, promoting audience participation and identification by appealing to tastes shared by age or ethnic groups. Sheet music and recordings sales were profitable tie-ins even before sound cinema. In the 1980s, however, the practice of tying the affective (and commercial) response of the audience to popular music on a film's soundtrack was so well established that the pop score began to rival originally composed music. *American Graffiti* (1973) helped inaugurate this trend with its soundtrack of nostalgic 1960s tunes, and *The Big Chill* (1983) captures the zeitgeist of its characters' and viewers' generation through popular music. The centrality of prerecorded music is reflected in the increasing importance of the **music supervisor,** who selects and secures the rights for songs to be used in films. In these youth-oriented, MTV-influenced films with pop music scores, such as *Flashdance* (1983), the promotion of the soundtrack is as important as that of the film. In the 1990s, the proliferation of the pop soundtrack drew the film experience outside the theater to the record store, and music videos began to include scenes from upcoming films. Although theme songs have been composed for and promoted with films for decades, as in *Love Is a Many-Splendored Thing* (1955) to name one hit, the contemporary movie and recording industries have such close business relationships that even films without pop soundtracks often feature a tie-in song in their end-credits sequences. The extremely successful film careers of musicians like rapper-actor Will Smith demonstrate the increasing symbiosis of these entertainment media.

Sound Effects in Film

Although the movies can represent the world in many ways, their capacity for successful mimesis, or imitation, has always fascinated audiences. Much of the mimetic impression in cinema comes from the use of sound effects, although like other aspects of the soundtrack they may not be consciously noticed by viewers. Dialogue in film is deliberate; it tells a story and gives information. Background music is a clear enhancement, "unrealistic" if we pay attention to it. But sound effects appear unmanufactured, even accidental. This sense of the naturalness of effects is ironic because the sound texture of a film is so deliberately crafted and because in daily life we hardly notice such ubiquitous sounds as fluorescent lights humming, crickets chirping, and traffic going by, sounds that might appear to be added to achieve a "realistic" sound mix.

In most films, every noise that we hear is selected and these effects generally conform to our expectations of movie sounds. Virtually nothing appears onscreen that does not make its corresponding noise: dogs bark, babies cry. A spaceship that blows up in outer space will usually produce a colossal bang even though there is no sound in space. If a recording of a .38 revolver sounds like a cap gun on film, it will be dubbed with a louder bang. These expectations vary according to film genre. Traffic noise will be loud in an action film, in which we remain alive to the possibilities of the environment. In a romance, the sound of cars will likely fade away unless traffic is keeping the lovers apart. Furthermore, our sense of the role of sound effects in films has changed over time. In an interview with film scholar Elisabeth Weis, soundman Michael Kirchberger comments that an "older film like *Casablanca* has an empty soundtrack compared with what we do today. Tracks are fuller and more of a selling point." The extraordinary density of contemporary soundtracks does not necessarily mean that they are more "realistic"; they simply make more extensive use of the particular properties of sound to convey a visceral experience of the cinema. The change in the texture of contemporary soundtracks is based in new technological capabilities, but, as in other instances of "improved" technologies, this progress is not inevitable but rather a development that follows particular ideas and goals, although these are likely to remain unstated.

Sound effects are one of the most useful ways of giving an impression of depth to the two-dimensional image when they are reproduced in the three-dimensional space of the theater. Although the screen is itself only an illusory space of action, film presentation makes use of the directional properties of sound—a gunshot may come from the lefthand side of the screen, for example. In the mix, additional diegetic sounds such as thunderclaps can be added that were not present on set at all, adding significantly to a film's illusionism. Asynchronous sound effects, such as the hoot of an owl in a dark-woods setting, both expand the sense of space and contribute to mood, often in very codified, even clichéd ways. Adding the clank of utensils and snatches of offscreen conversation to the soundtrack when two characters are shown at a table conjures a restaurant setting without having to shoot the scene in one.

The very manner in which noises are produced for a soundtrack illustrates their function in constructing, rather than reproducing, a particular experience. As we detailed earlier, incidental sounds—footsteps, the rustle of clothing, a punch in the stomach—are not even recorded at the same time as the film's dialogue. Rather, they are added later by the foley artist by walking on gravel, rubbing different pieces of fabric, hitting a rolled-up telephone book, and so on. Our acceptance of these simulated synchronous sounds testifies to the strength of our impulse to perceive effects realistically.

Subjectivity through Sound in *The Piano* (1993)

The fact that Jane Campion's film about a nineteenth-century woman who travels from Scotland to New Zealand with her young daughter to marry a man she's never met takes its title not from the central character but from an object, a musical instrument, cues us into the importance of sound in this film. The heroine Ada McGrath's grand piano, which she transports on her long journey, is a central element in the film's plot and mise-en-scène. Not surprisingly, piano music on the soundtrack echoes this importance, carrying a great deal of the film's emotion, sensuality, and drama. Because Ada is mute, our understanding of voice as a medium of subjectivity extends to the metaphor of music as voice, powerfully conveying the story of a headstrong woman shaping her own experience. In addition, sound effects are used expressively to make Ada's psychological experience accessible to us.

Although Ada cannot speak, the film paradoxically begins with her voiceover: "the voice you hear is not my speaking voice; it is my mind's voice." This innovative use of the voiceover device allows us access to Ada's inner world even before we have seen her, powerfully connecting us to her subjectivity. The voiceover will not return until the very end of the film, when she speaks of the silence of her piano, lying at the bottom of the sea, as a "weird lullaby" [Figure 5.38]. In the interim, Ada's "voice" makes itself heard through written notes and sign language, which her daughter, Flora, translates so that others

can understand. Flora also uses her own voice to express a will as strong as her mother's. She makes up stories to shock the women in their new town and she eventually reveals to her stepfather, Stewart, that her mother is having an illicit affair. Ada's lover, George Baines, the overseer on her husband's plantation, indicates another level of the film's use of voice by speaking with the Maori in their own language.

Ada's voiceover declares, "I don't think of myself as silent because of my piano." She speaks most directly and expressively through her music. When Ada and Flora first arrive in New Zealand, they are stranded on the beach overnight. Ada breaks open the piano's wooden

Figure 5.38 *The Piano* (1993). The mute heroine's voiceover describes the piano's underwater grave.

crate just enough to reach in to play with one hand. The music fills the soundtrack, although we hear the sound effects of a key plunking and of waves lapping at the shore in the mix. The piano is associated with Ada's desire and individuality and with the freedom of the seascape. As she is led away by her husband the next day, the piano is temporarily abandoned on the beach. Ada looks back at the instrument, and her visual point of view is accompanied by nondiegetic music, which then provides continuity during the shots of

Figure 5.39 *The Piano* (1993). Nondiegetic music accompanies the heroine's thoughts of her piano.

their progress across the lush but difficult terrain, always connecting her back to the piano on the beach even when she can no longer see it. Later, during a rainstorm when she goes to the window of her new home, we see a shot of the piano on the beach **[Figures 5.39 and 5.40]**. Obviously, this is not a literal point-of-view shot but a subjective insert. The nondiegetic piano music that accompanies the shot reprises the piece Ada had begun on the beach, following the principle of unity. As space seems to be transcended by the soundtrack, the close interplay between nondiegetic and diegetic music helps to make Ada the subjective center of the film.

The Piano's nineteenth-century setting motivates the use of a romantic musical idiom that functions, as it would in the score of a classical Hollywood film, to signify emotion. For example, in the dramatic scene in which her husband brutally punishes Ada for her affair with Baines, music swells (the theme from her journey away from the beach), only to terminate abruptly when Flora screams out, "Mother!" Interestingly, however, Ada plays music not by well-known nineteenth-century composers but her own original compositions. This strengthens both the metaphor of music as voice and its association with female transgression in the film. As a town busybody comments, "She does not play music as we play it. . . . To have a sound creep inside you is not at all pleasant." Early in the film, Baines takes Ada back to the beach and to her piano. Music comes in as a sound bridge before the scene transition. We then see Ada playing on the beach, as the sounds of waves, birds, and Flora's voice reinforce the fact that the music is now diegetic. Although these sound effects add realism, they also have psychological dimensions, conveying Ada's passion as well as her connections with her daughter and with the wildness of the waves and the freedom of birds in flight. It gets dark; Flora joins Ada at the keyboard, but the music remains continuous over the ellipsis.

The process is a meticulous reconstruction of some but not all of the sounds that would have been present on set. The sounds selected are those that are deemed significant, if only because they establish a particular mood. Dramatic effects such as explosions are quite deliberately placed, and often enhanced, because of their narrative significance.

At the same time that they serve a mimetic function, sound effects have become part of how the cinema experience is distinguished from the ordinary. THX is a standards system, devised by director George Lucas and named after his first feature film, *THX 1138* (1971), for evaluating and ensuring the quality of sound presentation. THX theaters promise to deliver an intense aural experience that is identical in each certified venue. Sound effects, like visual effects, draw in viewers. How crucial a film's sound is to the Hollywood illusion is marked in the relatively recent Academy Award category for sound effects editing. Audiences are increasingly trusted to discern things aurally. In the films of master action film director John Woo, for example, each character may have a particular gunshot noise assigned to him or her so that the action can be followed throughout a protracted sequence without dialogue.

After witnessing this scene, Baines purchases the piano from Stewart and makes a proposition to Ada. In exchange for erotic favors, he will give the piano back to her, key by key. Music remains associated with eroticism when their attraction becomes mutual. Ada's husband eventually catches her with Baines (he overhears and then spies on them). But what the film shows us at this point is a scene in which reciprocal passion, removed from Baines's initial objectification and Stewart's voyeurism, is indicated by the beautiful nondiegetic piano accompaniment.

Figure 5.40 *The Piano* (1993). The music seems to conjure this insert of the piano, abandoned on the beach.

Throughout *The Piano* the heroine's point of view and audio perspective are central. This is powerfully conveyed by the soundtrack even though Ada never uses the synchronized speech that is usually associated with characters' desires and intentions. The film's soundscape is filled with the rich noises of the New Zealand landscape. The suck of mud on the characters' shoes combines with the rustle of petticoats. Birds sing and screech, rain and wind clamor for attention. These wild elements are associated with Ada's wildness and the sharpness of her hearing. When she leaves Stewart and orders her piano thrown overboard, these sounds culminate with quiet, mysterious underwater noises as she is pulled into the sea. She breaks free and surfaces as her voiceover returns to narrate the film's ending. She has followed her desires; she and Flora go to live with Baines, and she teaches piano and begins learning to speak. But most important, the music Ada feels compelled to play—when she hears Baines is leaving, when she walks in her sleep—and the music that accompanies significant moments in the film, assisting transitions and narration, are associated with her own will and sensuality. In a medium that often visually objectifies women, Campion uses soundtrack elements to endow her heroine with subjectivity.

The distinctive soundtrack of *Jaws* (1975) lent us not only what has now become the cliché of the shark's musical motif, but also a rich new standard of sound-effects use. The film acknowledges a predecessor in the genre—and in the ingenious use of sound—when the death of the shark is accompanied by a sound effect of a prehistoric beast's death from *King Kong*. In these monster movies, sound effects take us beyond everyday events while also relying on their capacity to refer to familiar experience.

As with music, the animated film illustrates the deliberately designed nature of film sound effects particularly well. In fact, most cartoon soundtracks are prepared in advance of the images, the reverse of live-action filmmaking. Cartoons thus demonstrate especially well the synchronization of sound effects to onscreen actions. Drawings do not "naturally" make sounds of their own; every sound in an animated film is conventionalized. In *Duck Amuck* (1953), for example, Daffy Duck is baffled by the cartoon he finds himself in and cannot follow the logic of his mischievous animator. All sorts of mishaps befall him, and the abrupt termination of the soundtrack is one of the most disturbing of these mishaps. So unused are we to complete silence, that we

VIEWING CUES: Voice, Music, and Sound Effects

- Identify specific uses of voice in the film you will screen next in class. Is dialogue abundant? Genre-specific? If voiceovers are used, what is their function and diegetic status?

- Try to recall as much as you can of the film's score after a single viewing. Then, watch the film again and pay particular attention to its music. Is the film's score drawn from the classical tradition? Is popular music used? How do scoring choices contribute to the film's meaning?

- To what extent do sound effects add to the film's sense of realism? Can you locate an example in which sound effects are primarily responsible for creating a particular impression of location, action, or mood?

- Isolate a particular scene in which sound seems especially responsible for conveying information to the spectator. How do voice, music and sound effects work together?

are likely to look around us to see whether the theater's sound system really has gone out. Daffy holds up a sign demanding "Sound please!" and begins to play the guitar with which his animator has provided him. But the sound it "emits" is that of a machine gun, demonstrating with this synchronization error the arbitrary nature of the standard of matching image and sound. As Daffy's misadventures suggest, sound effects appeal to the audience subtly and viscerally.

Points of View:
Values and Traditions of Film Sound

The sounds of the film experience build on audiences' everyday social and leisure activities to contribute to the movies' immediacy and sensory richness. Whether it is the pathos lent by Louis Gottschalk's score for D. W. Griffith's *Broken Blossoms* (1919), the stimulating interactions between the musical quotations of *2001: A Space Odyssey* and Alex North's original music for the film, the indelible aural record of Laurence Olivier's performance of *Hamlet* (1948), or the comical sounds of Jacques Tati's *Playtime*, movie soundscapes intensify our experience of what the world sounds like while attesting to sound's power to convey what seem like essential truths.

To Authenticate and to Feel

Sound is all around us. While vision depends on an objective distance between the viewer and the viewed, sound comes to meet us. Although our philosophical tradition puts a premium on seeing over the other senses, as in "seeing is believing," within this tradition there is also a strong current of mistrust: "the eyes deceive." Hearing can then seem more reliable, especially when it is associated with the voice. The voice comes from within, and this interiority gives it depth and authenticity. We tend to trust what we hear, to enter into the perceptual experience fully. In this framework, we can recognize two primary values associated with the use of sound in film:

- As a set of indicators of a real, multidimensional world, film sounds give the viewer/auditor the impression of being authentically present in space.
- As a less "literal" sign than the image and a more immediately perceived experience than the visual, sound encourages the viewer to experience emotion.

Each of these values exploits specific aspects of film sound. The sense of authenticity depends in part on the technique of sound reproduction. The emotive capacity depends on the kind of sound that we experience, such as a particular piece of music. Film sound seems to permeate the body of the viewer in a way that images alone cannot, a quality that contributes to its authenticity and emotion.

The assumption that sound gives the viewer/auditor the impression of being authentically present in space is supported by the preferences established in the standard techniques of sound recording, mixing, and reproduction. As we have mentioned, though the cinematic images and sounds that we see and hear were both captured at some other moment and are being reproduced for us, sounds feel immediate. Hearing the taps on Eleanor Powell's shoes in *Born to Dance* (1936) makes us witnesses to her virtuosity [**Figure 5.41**]. This perceptual immediacy anchors us in space and makes the human subject seem central to the film experience. Foregrounding actors' voices through close miking and sound perspective and mixing that emphasizes dialogue also authenticates our perception. We are "in on" the characters' most intimate conversations. Sounds that are synchronized with the action by the depiction of their sources in the image, or even sounds that support the action while not being themselves "authentic"—for example, background music—all give us a central place in the fictional world that begins to seem present and real. The zither theme of *The Third Man* (1949) makes us feel disoriented in the streets of postwar Vienna, just as the film's characters are.

Through the very properties that make it hard even to notice or to describe concretely, sound encourages the viewer to experience emotion. Sound tends to connote interiority and the ineffable. When the lovers in *Now, Voyager* cannot really say what they mean to each other, the string section, performing Max Steiner's score, eloquently takes over. Sound reaches the viewer viscerally, seeming to involve the body directly. Excruciating suspense is generated in *Jurassic Park* when, on the digital soundtrack, the T-Rex's footsteps can be heard approaching the truck where the children are hiding [**Figure 5.42**]. Simply watching the dinosaur progress would be a less emotional experience.

The film environment attempts to duplicate our acoustic experience of the world, to orient us in this new space in a way that feels genuine and genuinely gets us to *feel*. This is not necessarily measured by strict realism. The sense of presence at the dance contest in *Saturday Night Fever* (1977) is better achieved through a sound mix that sacrifices background noise to focus on the Bee Gees' music.

Figure 5.41 *Born to Dance* (1936). Eleanor Powell's tap dancing is a perfect display of synchronized sound.

Figure 5.42 *Jurassic Park* (1993). The film's digital soundtrack generates keen suspense.

Although film sound can have a great deal of complexity, and realism is thrown out the window every time background music appears, authenticity and emotion are often served by a subordination of the autonomy of sound to the cues given by the image. In contrast to this practice of sound–image continuity, however, a competing approach explores the concrete nature of sounds and their potential independence of the images and of each other. This practice of sound montage, which characterizes the films of Jean-Luc Godard and others, does not *serve* the values of authenticity and emotion; rather, it makes us conscious of their violation by calling attention to the actual sound recording process or asking us to be aware of and reflect on emotional cues.

Two Traditions: Sound Continuity and Sound Montage

Sound continuity describes the range of scoring, sound recording, mixing, and playback processes that strive for the unification of meaning and experience by subordinating sound to the aims of the narrative. **Sound montage** reminds us that just as a film is built up of bits and pieces of celluloid, a soundtrack is not a continuous gush of sound from the real world, but is composed of separate elements whose relationship to each other can be creatively manipulated and reflected upon. The theme song from *Doctor Zhivago* (1965) is extremely lush and romantic, but it reinforces the big emotions of the film's characters at appropriate points in the plot and thus achieves continuity. In Andrei Tarkovsky's *Nostalgia* (1983), though the sound of an electric saw can be heard at different times and in different settings, the source is never revealed. This ambiguous sound functions as an element of montage. Most assumptions, shared by technicians and viewers, about what constitutes a "good" soundtrack emphasize a continuity approach. However, since the introduction of sound, many filmmakers have used it as a separate element for a montage effect. With the increasing sophistication of audio technology, it is possible that sound montage will find more practitioners.

Analyzing a film that adheres to sound continuity can be rewarding precisely because really hearing the soundtrack demands such attentiveness. As we have seen, matching up actors' voices with their moving lips and ensuring the words are intelligible were among the early goals of sound technology. Audiences were thrilled just to *see* the match. Despite our familiarity with film sound, the degree of redundancy between image and sound in the continuity tradition still makes it difficult to analyze the soundtrack autonomously. From the priority granted to synchronization, we can define several compatible continuity practices.

- The relationship between image and sound and among separate sounds is motivated by dramatic action or information.
- With the exception of background music, the sources of sounds will be identifiable.
- The connotations of musical accompaniment will be consistent with the images (for example, a funeral march is unlikely to accompany a high-speed chase).
- The sound mix will emphasize what we should pay attention to.
- The sound mix will be smooth and will emphasize clarity.

Films that adhere to the principles of verisimilitude will use sound to amplify, as it were, what is taking place on the screen. Attention will be directed back to the characters, actions, and mise-en-scène by sound that supports it. In *The Big Sleep* (1946), a conversation in a car between the two protagonists, Marlowe and Vivian, begins with engine noise in the background. We see that there is a dog on the porch in the opening scene of *The Searchers* (1956), but when we hear it bark, the image comes alive. The relationship between image and sound and among separate sounds will also be motivated by dramatic action or information. In *The Big Sleep*, the engine noise will soon disappear so we can focus on the characters' avowal of love. The continuous use of music to cover a sequence of character activity draws our attention away from discontinuity in the image track. For example, continuous orchestral music links the "research montage" in *Se7en* (1995).

It may be easier to think of what sound continuity seeks to avoid than what it positively pursues. Sound should not intrude on the narrative. Unmotivated or unidentified sounds will not have a prominent place on the soundtrack. Nor will unidentified speakers be heard, unless in a conventional context such as a documentary, in which the voiceover explanation will demonstrate its own continuity with the content of the image. Characters' speech will not break with the diegesis to offer commentary or *non sequiturs*. Technology and techniques have developed in consort with these aims. Dolby noise-reduction technology improves frequency response and gives an almost unnatural clarity. Noise interferes with the sound signal and can call attention to the fact that the sound was recorded and thus, to how the film was made. These are goals of continuity rather than of strict realism. As film scholar John Belton has observed, film conventions have developed in accordance with what the *image*, not the world, sounds like. Both documentary and narrative traditions tend to rely on sound continuity.

Exploring the infinity of sound and image interactions, and interactions among sounds and images, is the province of montage. Often deriving its practices in direct opposition to the principles of sound continuity, sound montage calls attention to the distinct, autonomous elements that make up a film. Because sound continuity is so pervasive, many of the examples of its violation are from less familiar art and experimental films and from very recent cinema. Bertolt Brecht, whose writings about theater are discussed in Chapter 4, called for "the separation of elements" that would make audiences aware of each element of a theatrical production and thus of the work that went into creating it. Separating sound from image in film is one of the most concrete illustrations of Brecht's principle. Like disjunctive image-editing practices, sound montage does not smooth over juxtapositions. In sound montage,

- sound may "come first"
- the borders between the nondiegetic and the diegetic may be difficult to establish
- the expectation that every element of the mise-en-scène will make a naturalistic noise is frustrated
- voices, whether diegetic or nondiegetic, do not always preserve the illusion of a closed world
- music might appear and disappear, giving it a more material presence
- effects can be "synchronized" to arbitrary sources

When motivated relationships—for example, the image of a dog motivates the sound effect of barking—are given up, we see and hear something different onscreen than an attempt at an extension of our natural world. This can be directly critical, as in a disturbing sequence in *Natural Born Killers* (1994), when Mallory's life at home with her abusive father is presented as if it were a situation comedy, complete with laugh track, applause, and perky theme music, directly commenting on how the media uses sound

Figure 5.43 *La Jetée* (1962). Voice-over narration and music render the film's succession of still images moving.

to manipulate emotion. In a very different use of sound montage, the succession of still images that comprises Chris Marker's *La Jetée* (1962) is anchored by a voiceover that tells of the time experiments in which the protagonist is participating, identifying the film as science fiction **[Figure 5.43]**. Prioritizing sound makes us listen to the film's structure; the image track accompanies or provides counterpoint to what we hear.

The use of the voice can be opened up to include direct address to the spectator or the use of recitation or reading instead of naturalistic dialogue, as in Godard's *Weekend* (1967) or Julien's *Looking for Langston*. The sensual quality of sounds can be explored as it might be in a musical composition, or poetic effects can be achieved by combining different sound "images." Voices are layered in Marguerite Duras's *India Song* (1975). A film can deliver ideas through multiple channels; the sound can contradict the image. Interview texts printed on the screen are read aloud with slight alterations by the voiceovers in Trinh T. Minh-ha's *Surname Viet Given Name Nam* (1989). The qualities of these voices—they are of heavily accented nonactors clearly reading aloud—convey information that could not be gathered from images **[Figure 5.44]**.

Overall, sound montage stresses the fact that images and sounds communicate on two different levels; rather than trying to make them equivalents, montage calls attention to what each contributes differently. Sergei Eisenstein, the primary theorist of montage, extended his ideas to sound even before the technology was perfected. In his first sound film, *Alexander Nevsky* (1938) **[Figure 5.45]**, he experimented with what he called "vertical montage," which emphasized both the simultaneity of and the difference between image

Figure 5.44 *Surname Viet Given Name Nam* (1989). The stories of Vietnamese women's lives are told through printed text and voice-overs, both of which compete with additional sound and visual elements in filmmaker Trinh T. Minh-ha's experimental documentary.

Figure 5.45 *Alexander Nevsky* (1938). The editing of Sergei Eisenstein's first sound film was planned with the score in mind.

and sound. He also collaborated closely with composer Sergey Prokofiev to make a film in which every picture edit was influenced by the accompanying soundtrack. German filmmaker Ulrike Ottinger's *Madame X: An Absolute Ruler* (1977) makes ingenious use of postsynchronous sound. Her film's motley crew of female pirates do not speak; instead, their movements are "synchronized" with noises like animal growls or metallic clanking **[Figure 5.46]**.

Experimentation with sound montage began with the introduction of sound and has followed different subtraditions, two of which we will consider here. Filmmakers such as Jean Vigo and René Clair in France and Rouben Mamoulian and King Vidor in the United States are identified with the **poetic use of sound montage** in the early sound era. In films such as Mamoulian's *Applause* (1929), music and effects do not duplicate the image but create a more subjective setting. French director Robert Bresson takes apart the usual fit between sound and image by a minimalist use of sound. In spare films such as *Pickpocket* (1959) and *L'Argent* (1983), which explore themes of predestination and isolation through scrutiny of details, Bresson achieves an uncanny presence of select sounds while refusing realistic indicators of space **[Figure 5.47]**. In his writings on sound, Bresson sums up his ideas: "what is for the eye must not duplicate what is for the ear." Belgian filmmaker Chantal Akerman also achieves a hyperrealist use of sound in films such as *Jeanne Dielman, 23 Quai du Commerce, 1080 Bruxelles* (1975), where the echo of the protagonist's high heels resonates long after the film's images fade. Without the use of room tone or other techniques to give spatial cues or to make sounds warmer, the minimalist sounds in the films of Bresson and Akerman become very concrete.

Dziga Vertov's early sound film *Enthusiasm* (1931) innovates the collection of documentary sounds and exemplifies a **collage approach.** A clock ticks over the image of a tolling bell, for example. The Soviet filmmaker was keenly interested in sound, and his work in radio and even his poetry showed a fascination with industrial noise. Jean-Luc Godard's many experiments with sound collage, which began early in his career, are indebted to Vertov's (for a time, Godard worked in a collective called the Dziga Vertov group). Godard emphasizes music in the organization of many of his films; a favorite technique is to interrupt a music cue so that it literally cannot fade into the background. In *First Name: Carmen* (1983), we actually see a string quartet playing without knowing what its relationship to the story space might be. The abrupt cessation of a soundtrack element may be extended to voices and effects as well. In the café scene in *Band of Outsiders* (1964), one of the characters suggests that if the friends in the group have nothing to say to each other, they should remain silent. This diegetic silence is conveyed by the complete cessation of sound on the soundtrack, something that is rare indeed. By using nonauthoritative or noncontinuous voiceovers as well as frequent voice-offs, and

Figure 5.46 *Madame X: An Absolute Ruler* (1977). This feminist pirate film parody uses postsynchronous sound inventively to make the ship's figurehead "speak" in sound effects coordinated with her gestures.

Figure 5.47 *L'Argent* (1983). Robert Bresson's films rely on a minimal yet heightened sound design.

Figure 5.48 *Tout va bien* (1972). Jean-Luc Godard's interest in sound is underscored by sound equipment in the diegesis.

by having on-camera characters address the camera, read, or make cryptic announcements, Godard challenges the natural role of the human voice in giving character and narrative information. Instead, language becomes malleable, an element in a collage of meaning.

Several examples from *Tout va bien* (*All's well*) (1972), made by Godard and Jean-Pierre Gorin, illustrate these strategies. The film opens with an unidentified male voice-off declaring his intention of making a film. A female voice responds that that will require money. The image shows a hand writing checks for the production of the film *Tout va bien*. In another sequence, one of the film's protagonists speaks directly to the camera about his career as a political filmmaker turned director of commercials, and he is seated next to a camera as he does so. The speech makes us think about Godard's own position. Another memorable scene is set in a supermarket as it is taken over by anarchists. The cacophony of this setting is interrupted by the internal diegetic monologue of the other main character, a journalist played by Jane Fonda **[Figure 5.48]**. To add another element, her words are introduced by loudspeaker tones, such as those that would normally direct shoppers to a special bargain. This sound element confuses internal and external sound, layering sound in a collage effect. A measure of Godard's emphasis on sound can be detected in the name of his production company, Sonimage (which means either his image or sound/image), and in the release of an audio version of his television series *Historie(s) du cinéma* (1988–1998). Over a more than forty-year career, Godard has earned a reputation as probably the most exemplary practitioner of sound montage.

Other experimental filmmakers such as Yvonne Rainer have developed very interesting collage styles in their work with sound. In Rainer's *Journeys from Berlin/1971* (1980), we are engaged by a voiceover narration that does not correspond to the images we see and by the words on the soundtrack that often sound like unattributed quotations. In German filmmaker Alexander Kluge's *The Patriot* (1979), the narrating voiceover is attributed to a knee.

 VIEWING CUES: Film Sound Traditions and Values

- As you view and listen to the film you will screen next in class, observe whether and how the soundtrack "authenticates" the image by reinforcing the reference to the real world. If there were no sound in the film, how would it feel less "real"?

- How is emotion introduced to the viewing experience through auditory qualities?

- Sound continuity can be achieved using many different elements of sound and image. How do background sound, voices, and music work to achieve continuity? How might this effect be disrupted by changing the relationship among elements?

- Is sound used to create meaning through sound montage? If so, how and to what effect?

Values and Traditions in *The Conversation* (1974)

In the 1970s, some of the most innovative U.S. films were produced by Francis Ford Coppola's Zoetrope Studios—from George Lucas's *American Graffiti* to Coppola's own *Apocalypse Now*. Among the director's most inspired collaborations with sound designer and editor Walter Murch, *The Conversation* is also notable because its very topic is the exploitation of sound technology. While the film's own sound conforms to the principles identified with the continuity tradition, by virtue of its foregrounding of how sound is created and transmitted, it can also illustrate the aims of sound montage practice.

The film, set in San Francisco, follows the activities of a surveillance expert, Harry Caul (played by Gene Hackman), as he goes about what seems to be a routine job: eavesdropping on a pair of lovers in the park. Harry's expertise and interest in technology leave little space for human contact and complement his rather paranoid character. In an early scene, he rebuffs his landlady's request for keys to his apartment in case of fire. There would be nothing personal to rescue; as he says, "I have nothing personal *except* my keys." Interestingly, Harry's hobby is playing the saxophone. The warm sound of this instrument foreshadows his eventual awakening to the more human dimensions of the sounds he records for a living.

The first sequence of the film is a tour de force of sound and image counterpoint, which makes us partake in the activity of surveillance as we actively attempt to decode what is happening on the screen. Eavesdropping enhances the sound's quality of presence; we feel we are *right there* in the scene. Yet the activities of the on-camera sound recordists make us aware of those of the recordist, mixer, and director behind the scenes, just as a sound montage would do.

The film opens with a slow crane shot over San Francisco's Union Square, which is accompanied by jazz music whose sound perspective remains constant. As the music shifts from an instrumental theme to the banter of two singers, and as the hubbub of the busy square and then the applause become audible, we recognize that the music is diegetic, coming from the scene even though we cannot at first see the source. The music's festive and emotional connotations are immediately recognizable. Yet electronic interference comes in very early on; we begin to suspect that we are hearing the music through a device "within" the film as well as through the loudspeaker in the theater, and the emotional register turns slightly sinister.

In the next few shots it remains difficult to tell who the object of the surveillance is and who the object of our attention should be, in part because the sound is not mixed to emphasize the action. Indeed, it is the gestures of a mime, taunting through his mimicry a figure whose crumpled raincoat suggests a desire for anonymity, that we must "listen" to in the first aerial shot if we want to pick out Harry in the crowd. The silent stalker is stalked. Finally, when Harry enters a van where his assistant is stationed, we learn that the target is a young couple, Ann and Mark, played by Cindy Williams and Frederic Forrest [**Figure 5.49**].

Figure 5.49 *The Conversation* (1974). We eavesdrop on characters that the plot never brings us to know better.

Figure 5.50 *The Conversation* (1974). Audio technology becomes a pervasive presence in the film.

The sound mix in the scene is quite complicated. The cut to the first shot taken at ground level corresponds to a notable shift in sound perspective with an increase in the diegetic music volume. Quickly a snatch of random conversation is heard, followed by a snippet of another—this time, the targeted couple—but the succession has already identified for us the arbitrariness of continuity sound mixing practices that isolate immediately what we should pay attention to. The closeness of our sound perspective is then given technical justification when we see both Harry and a man with a hearing aid in close proximity to the couple. We stay with Ann and Mark as they continue a conversation about a drunk passed out on the park bench; the volume of the conversation does not change as Harry climbs into the van. Here, the continuity in sound perspective signals the importance of this apparently trivial conversation. And once again, what seemed like the film's sound—we hear the conversation—is revealed as sound produced within the story—what we hear is the recording of the conversation as we see the reel-to-reel tape recorder spinning **[Figure 5.50]**. At other moments, electronic interference comes in, constantly reminding us that what we are hearing is filtered through several sets of equipment and through the aural perspective of other listeners.

In the next scene, as Harry begins to listen to his recording for more than just the quality of the reproduction, he will play these few lines of recorded conversation over and over again, discovering in the captured sounds clues to a suspicious event. Is the "guilty" party the couple, presumably engaged in an affair, or those who pay to have them watched? And what is the ethical role of the "invisible" bystander, the hired sound recordist, and by extension the film viewer? The opening scene of *The Conversation* functions like a puzzle. Harry and the viewer will strive to find the truth behind the sounds

Because of the possibilities of mixing sound electronically, and because of the music and performance traditions on which it draws, video art has also explored sound montage to a great extent. But even in Hollywood films, sound montage can dominate. Although it is narratively motivated by the futuristic setting, the soundscape of Ridley Scott's *Blade Runner* resembles that of an experimental film. Sound is at least as responsible as the mise-en-scène and the storyline for the theme of anxiety in a synthetic, syncretic world. Director David Lynch's sound designs are similarly integral to his disorienting onscreen worlds.

captured in the square. We powerfully feel sound's ability to testify to presence in a particular space and time by the emphasis on the value of Harry's recording.

Toward the end of the scene a new sound element is introduced. A nondiegetic moody piano theme begins as the couple parts; the music continues, with some street noise in the mix, as Harry starts home. The piano carries over the dissolve to the next scene and ends just as Harry turns the key in his door, when it is abruptly replaced by a shrill sound effect, his alarm being set off. Our newly honed attention to the concrete nature of each sound element encourages us to evaluate this nondiegetic musical theme. Associated almost exclusively with long shots of Harry making his way around town, the wandering theme played on a single instrument underscores his alienation, inviting us as viewers to feel the emotion Harry attempts to keep at bay. After Harry arrives home we see him playing the sax. The sound of the saxophone is very solitary; it connects Harry to the piano theme we've just heard as well as to the musicians in the park. All three of these musical elements, though distinct, are jazz. Jazz's connotations of the urban night world establish the film in the genre of film noir, although it begins in broad daylight. Interestingly, however, Harry plays his sax along with a record player, synching up his own performance of the expressive qualities of music with prerecorded sound. This is emphasized by a shot of the record spinning. Such close-ups of sound technology are frequent in the film and remind us of the source of film voices, music, and effects. Often these cutaways are unmotivated by any character's specific attention to the sounds being emitted at that moment.

As the film progresses, Harry becomes increasingly suspicious of his employer's intentions, and it is to the evidence gathered in the first scene, in the form of the tape, that he returns again and again. The film's theme of paranoia finds a perfect echo in its setting in the world of sound technology, eavesdropping, and surveillance. Because of the claims to presence of sound, the incriminating audiotape, with the accidental music and noises it captures, appears "real" and convincing even in a film that is constantly showing off the paraphernalia of sound recording, mixing, and playback. By emphasizing that truth lies in the words spoken in that first conversation, the film upholds the privileged relationship between the voice and inner nature, while also facilitating Harry's (and the audience's) identification with other humans *through* technological mediation. Sound is used in service of narrative, but the narrative is about the uses of sound. Despite the period quaintness of the now-obsolete machines the film lingers on—reel-to-reel tape recorders and oversized headphones, the squeaky sound of rewinding, and the mechanical click of old-fashioned buttons—*The Conversation* remains an apt commentary on the values and practices of sound technology.

In their richness, contemporary soundtracks draw more and more on montage traditions of layering sounds without necessarily encouraging reflection on the discrete functions of sound and image. The continuity tradition that subordinates sound to image and accords with screen realism is still dominant. One of the most interesting films to confront questions of sound practice in Hollywood film is *The Conversation* (1974). Although it does not depart from sound continuity in ways that an experimental film might do, the film asks viewers to consider the meanings and effects of sound as an autonomous element.

The relationship of sound to image is a constructed one. In this excerpt from "Ideology and the Practice of Sound Editing and Mixing" (1985), Mary Ann Doane argues that there is an ideological dimension to this relationship. She pinpoints the values that are upheld in the actual practices of sound technicians working the classical Hollywood system. Her vocabulary draws on linquistics; "syntagmatic" means the sequential ordering of elements.

My assumption is that not only techniques of sound-track construction but the language of technicians and discourses on technique are symptomatic of particular ideological aims. . . . The disregard of the sound track on the level of theory . . . does not have its counterpart on the level of practice. Hollywood has recognized the extent to which the "supplement," that is to say, sound, can infiltrate and transform that which is supplemented. In an industry whose major standard, in terms of production values, might be summarized as "the less perceivable a technique, the more successful it is," the invisibility of the work on sound is a measure of the strength of the sound track. . . . 1

Symptomatic of th[e] repression of the material heterogeneity of the sound film are the practices which ensure effacement of the work involved in the construction of the sound track. Cuts in the track are potential indicators of that work. In the editing of optical tracks, it was discovered that the overlapped lines of a splice caused a sharp noise in playback. The technique of "blooping" was developed to conceal what could only act as an irritating reminder that syntagmatic relationships are not "found" or "natural" but manufactured. Blooping is the process of painting or punching an opaque triangle or diamond-shaped area over a splice and results in a fast fade-in, fade-out effect. The ideological objective of these techniques doubles that of continuity editing—the effect desired is that of smoothing over a potential break, of guaranteeing flow. Abrupt cuts on music or sound effects are avoided in favor of the homogenizing effects of the fade or dissolve. Obviously. . . . since the absence of sound would signal a break in an otherwise continuous flow, it has become a major taboo of sound-track construction. . . . 2

Ernest Walter's prescriptions for sound in the screening of rough cuts indicate the extent to which the values of continuity and fullness govern techniques: 3

> It can be very disturbing to all concerned [in the screening of rough cuts] when the sound track of sequences incorporating mute shots suddenly goes dead on the cut. It is better to incorporate even a temporary sound effect to cover these shots so that the normal flow of sound is uninterrupted. 4

"Normality" is established as a continuous flow, and the absence of sound, in the language of the sound technicians, is its "death." When a sound track goes "dead on the cut," the transgression is one of theological nature. "Death" and "life" are consistently metaphors associated with sound. A room or stage with low reverberation potential is "dead" and in postsynchronization, reverberation must be added to give "life" to the recording. Sound itself is often described as adding life to the picture. And the life which sound gives is presented as one of natural and uncodified flow. 5

Altman, Richard, ed. *Sound Theory, Sound Practice*. New York: Routledge, 1992. An anthology that addresses the undertheorizing of film sound introduced by the editor and including perspectives on the history of film sound and on practices other than narrative film.

Chion, Michel. *Audio-Vision: Sound on Screen*. Edited and translated by Claudia Gorbman. Foreword by Walter Murch. New York: Columbia University Press, 1990. In this translated work by a leading theorist of film sound, Chion stresses the inseparability of sound and image and introduces original terminology to interrogate the experience more precisely.

Gorbman, Claudia. *Unheard Melodies: Narrative Film Music*. Bloomington: Indiana University Press, 1987. A thorough examination of how music works in narrative cinema, drawing on narratology and semiology. Introduces important theories of film music with extensive examples.

Lastra, James. *Sound Technology and the American Cinema*. New York: Columbia University Press, 2000. Linking practices and rhetoric of film sound in the 1920s and 1930s with nineteenth-century technologies, Lastra demonstrates persistent ways of speaking about the aural dimension and tracks social and sensorial changes wrought by modernity.

Weis, Elisabeth, and John Belton, eds. *Film Sound: Theory and Practice*. New York: Columbia University Press, 1985. A comprehensive anthology covering history, technology, aesthetics, and classical and contemporary sound theory. A section on practice includes essays on the work of directors who have used sound innovatively, from the early sound period to New Hollywood.

Organizations: From Stories to Genres

PART II

Our experience of films is not just as elaborate scenes, brilliant images, dramatic cuts, and rich sounds. We also go to the movies for the gripping suspense of a murder mystery, the fascinating revelations of a documentary, the poetic voyage of a musical score set to abstract images and sounds, and the delight of seeing life as if it were a 1930s musical. However our interest in a movie is piqued, we turn to films like *Se7en* (1995) for the gruesome twists and turns of its story, to *Hoop Dreams* (1994) for the disturbing facts behind sports recruiting, to *Fantasia* (1940) for rhythms and sounds made into creative animated images, and to *Dancer in the Dark* (2000) for a somber, contemporary reworking of an old genre, the musical [Figure II.1].

Besides the stylistic details found in the mise-en-scène, cinematography, editing, and the composition of sound, movie experiences are also encounters with larger organizational structures and attractions. Some of us may look first for a good story; others may prefer experimental or documentary films. Some days we may be in the mood for a melodrama; other days we may feel like watching a horror film. Part II explores the principal organizations of movies—narrative films, documentary and experimental films, and movie genres—each of which, as we will see, arouses certain expectations about the movie we are viewing. Each shapes and turns the world for us into a distinctive kind of experience, offering a particular way of seeing it, understanding it, and enjoying it.

◀ **Figure II.1** *Dancer in the Dark* (2000). The contemporary shape of the musical.

Telling Stories about Time: Narrative Films

Stories give people the feeling that there is meaning, that there is ultimately an order lurking behind the incredible confusion of appearances and phenomena that surrounds them. . . . [Yet] for me I totally reject stories, because for me they only bring out lies . . . and the biggest lie is that they show coherence where there is none. . . . Stories are impossible, but it's impossible to live without them.

—Wim Wenders, director of *Paris, Texas* (1984) and *Wings of Desire* (1988)

KEY OBJECTIVES

What makes for an interesting story on film? Narrative film developed out of a long artistic and literary tradition of characters pursuing goals and confronting obstacles to those goals. Traditionally, narrative follows a three-part structure—a beginning, a middle, and an ending. At its core, narrative maps the different ways we have learned to organize patterns of time and history in our lives. We will examine

- how different historical practices create the foundations for film narratives
- how film narratives construct a plot that is different from a story
- how film characters motivate actions in a story
- how plots create different temporal and spatial schemes
- how the power of narration and narrative point of view determine how we understand a story
- how film narratives can be differentiated as either classical or alternative, two narrative traditions with different assumptions and values

Virtually everyone loves stories, those descriptions of characters in action. Most people grow up listening to stories—about parents and grandparents, about the fantasy characters who inhabit our dreams, about events that have become part of our national history. We recount the highlights of a weekend with friends as a spontaneous anecdote, and we warn our siblings about future dangers with a cautionary tale of what could happen down the road. Descriptions of actions and events as they develop in time, stories permeate our lives and help us situate human experience within the changing movements of life. Indeed, from those first movie sketches about bandits and explorers in *The Great Train Robbery* (1903) and *A Trip to the Moon* (1902) to the elaborate tales of political history and personal crises in

Tomás Gutiérrez Alea's narrative of 1960s Cuba, *Memories of Underdevelopment* (1968), and John Sayles's story of a 1920 West Virginia labor union, *Matewan* (1987) **[Figure 6.1]**, movies have thrived on **narrative,** the art and craft of constructing a story with a particular plot and point of view.

Stories spring from both personal memories and communal memories, through which we reconstruct the events, actions, and emotions of the past through the eyes of the present. We all live our lives and experience our relationships with the help of stories that provide some level of coherence and logic to the flux of life. We often recall the events of the last year as a story that highlights or reconstructs different encounters according to a chronology in which we each play the main character. Sometimes, of course, those memories provide our "memories of the future," imagined narratives of our lives as they will exist in the years ahead. A clever version of this kind of narrative, *The Terminator* (1984) tells the story of a cyborg who returns to the present from the future in order to kill a woman who will, in later years, give birth to the leader of his adversaries.

Figure 6.1 *Matewan* (1987). Retelling the story of labor rebellion and violence.

The first bonds between movies and stories served what we will call an **economics of leisure time.** In the first decades of the twentieth century, the budding movie industry recognized that stories take time to tell and that an audience's spending time watching stories makes money for the industry. In 1900, most individuals went to the movies to spend an afternoon with friends or an hour away from work. If, at first, this way of spending time offered simple and short sights and shocks, by 1913 moviemakers recognized that by making simple images into more complex stories, they could attract larger audiences, keep them in their seats for longer periods, and charge more than a nickel for admission. Along with the growing cultural prestige of offering movies that told serious stories, movies could now sell more time for more money through the power of longer stories.

The Foundations of Narrative Film

While the first movies were usually content to show simple moving images (such as a train arriving at a station), often these images referred to a story behind them. As early as 1896, the actor Joseph Jefferson represented Rip van Winkle in a brief short. By 1903 there appeared a variety of similar film tableaux—Shakespeare's *King John* (1899), *Cinderella* (1900), *Robinson Crusoe* (1902), *Uncle Tom's Cabin* (1903), and *Ali Baba and the Forty Thieves* (1905)— that assumed audiences would know the larger story behind the few images shown on the screen **[Figure 6.2]**. As the artistic, economic, and technological potential for movies grew, filmmakers aimed to tell those stories, and, from then on, worked expeditiously to develop the cinematic structures and styles that could creatively accommodate original stories.

Figure 6.2 *Ali Baba and the Forty Thieves* (1905). An early tableaux narrative.

Stories and Plots

As a starting point, let us identify the main features of any kind of narrative: story, character, plot, and narration. (Later in this chapter, we will explore and develop each of these four features in more detail.) A **story** is the subject matter or raw material of a narrative, the actions and events, usually perceived in terms of a beginning, a middle, and an end and focused on one or two **characters,** those individuals who motivate the events of the story. Stories tend to be summarized easily, as in "the tale of a man's frontier life on the Nebraska prairie" and "the story of two women fighting for equal rights in Pakistan." The **plot** orders the events and actions of the story according to particular temporal and spatial patterns, selecting some actions, individuals, and events and omitting others. The plot of one story may include the smallest details in the life of a character; another may highlight only major, cataclysmic events. One plot may present a story as progressing forward step by step from the beginning to the end; another may present that same story by moving backward in time. One plot may describe a story as the product of the desires and drives of a character, whereas another might suggest that events take place outside the control of that character. Thus, one

Figure 6.3A *Life of an American Fireman* (1903). A simple story with a cinematic plot.

Figure 6.3B *Life of an American Fireman* (1903).

Figure 6.3C *Life of an American Fireman* (1903).

Figure 6.3D *Life of an American Fireman* (1903).

plot of President John F. Kennedy's life could describe all the specifics of his childhood through the details of his adulthood; another plot might focus only on his combat experience during World War II, the major events of his presidency, and his shocking assassination in 1963. The first might begin with his birth, and the second with his death. Finally, how the plot is formulated can also differ significantly: one version of this story might depict Kennedy's life as the product of his energetic vision and personal ideals, whereas another version presents his triumphs and tragedies as the consequence of historical circumstances.

From early films like Edwin S. Porter's *Life of an American Fireman* (1903) to recent movies like Christopher Nolan's *Memento* (2000), movies have relied on the narrative tension between story and plot to create suspense, mystery, and interest, indicating that the construction of the plot may be as important to the meaning of the film as the story itself. In the Porter film, the story proceeds from a fire alarm sounded [Figure 6.3A], to the racing of the fire fighters through the streets [Figure 6.3B], to the rescue [Figure 6.3C and 6.3D]. Yet even in this short and simple narrative, some incidental details are omitted, such as the actual raising of the ladders, to add to the urgency and energy of the narrative. In *Memento*, the tension between plot and story is more obvious and dramatic: this unusual plot, about a man without a short-term memory, begins with a murder and proceeds backward in time through a series of short episodes, as the film unveils fragments of information about who the man is and why he committed the murder [Figure 6.4]. In other films, we know the story (of President Kennedy's life, for instance) or the outcome of the story (that Kennedy was assassinated); in these cases, what interests us is discovering the story through the construction of the plot.

In addition to character, story, and plot, narration is essential to our understanding of film narrative. **Narration** refers to the emotional, physical, or intellectual perspective through which the characters, events, and action of the plot appear. Sometimes, narration is associated just with the action of the camera and occasionally reinforced by verbal commentary on that action. In other instances, as in *Memento*, the narration becomes identified with the voiceover commentary of a single individual, usually (but not always) someone who is a character in the story; this perspective is called **first-person narration,** often recognized as the reflection of one person's subjective point of view. In still other films, such as the epic *Gone with the Wind* (1939), the narration may assume a more objective and detached stance vis-à-vis the plot and characters, seeing events from outside the story; this is referred to as **third-person narration** (which we will later refine as "omniscient" or "restricted"). Even in cases of third-person narration, a presiding attitude or

Figure 6.4 *Memento* (2000). A crisis of memory becomes a crisis of plot.

Figure 6.5 *Gone with the Wind* (1939). The triumphant vision of a third-person narration.

perspective defines the narration as it controls the plot. With third-person narrations like *Gone with the Wind*, it still may be possible to describe a more specific kind of attitude or point of view. Rather than "detachment," this film's narration might be described as "triumphant," given that its intense focus on the personal dignity and determination of individuals like Scarlett O'Hara counterpoints and redeems the sweeping range of its historical perspective on the tragedy of the Civil War **[Figure 6.5]**.

None of these dimensions of film narrative—story, plot, and narration—functions independently of historical, cultural, and industrial issues. Many narratives in Western cultures, for instance, center on individuals, their fates, and their self-knowledge, and many Western narrative models—such as the Judeo-Christian one that assumes a progressive movement from a fall to a redemption—reflect our basic cultural belief in individual and social development. Of course, cultural alternatives to this popular logic of progression and forward movement do exist, and in some cultures individual characters may be less central to the story than the give-and-take movements of the community or the passing of the seasons. In the movies of African filmmaker Sembène Ousmane, such as *Xala* (1975), the influence of an oral tradition—associated with the "griot" storytellers who in some African cultures would, at public gatherings, recount the many tales that bound the community together—creates narrations that seem more like layers of music and song, moving around space rather than forward through history. When following a film narrative, it is crucial always to question not just the pattern according to which it organizes events, but also the cultural values implied or addressed by that pattern.

A Short History of Narrative Film

The movies did not invent narrative. All film narratives inherit a long cultural history, and some films, like *Little Big Man* (1970) and *Contempt* (1963), make explicit references to the narrative history that precedes them. *Little Big Man*, for instance, acts out the heritage of Native American storytellers gathered around the fire telling the history of their people; *Contempt*, on the other hand, struggles with the narrative differences found in Homer's *Odyssey* and those demanded by commercial filmmaking, between telling a tale as an epic poem and as a Hollywood blockbuster **[Figure 6.6]**.

Figure 6.6 *Contempt* (1963). A film about the struggle to narrate Homer's *Odyssey* with film.

Japanese Cinema and the *Benshi*

Whether or not we are aware of it, our viewing experiences at the movies are guided by the narration of the film (and sometimes by a clearly defined narrator). Movies may not always call attention to their narration and even less often to an individual narrator, but these narrative elements always direct our attention and attitude toward a story. Although viewers are not usually attentive to film narration and narrators, films regularly signal the presence of different kinds of narrators and narrations as they establish different relations with spectators. Early silent films and even recent sound films sometimes use intertitles or subtitles to comment on or add information about the action of the story, and modern movies like *Reservoir Dogs* (1992) and *The Piano* (1993) use voiceover narrations and screen titles to comment on or describe the action of their unfolding stories.

One of the most dramatic instances in which film narration is made visible is the Japanese tradition of the *benshi*. Originally associated with the Kabuki theater, which evolved from the feudal period to the beginning of the modern era in Japan, the *benshi* is an actor who stands to the side of the stage and narrates the action that occurs on the stage. Because of the importance and power of this theatrical tradition, the *benshi* became a major figure in Japanese cinema at the start of the twentieth century. In early silent films, the *benshi* provided different voices for the main characters, explained changes in location and time, and often commented on events and actions. After 1912, with the steady increase in the number of imported foreign films in Japan, the *benshi* primarily translated intertitles from Hollywood or other foreign films; by 1920, however, the *benshi* had resumed a more active connection to the film's story, both explaining the plot and commenting on the action and characters. According to some film scholars, the sound revolution of the late 1920s was slow to arrive in Japan principally because of the political and social importance of the *benshi*. Nevertheless, the *benshi*'s central role in film narration was eventually usurped by the new narrational range offered by sound cinema.

Throughout the twentieth century, the tradition of the *benshi* continued to affect film narrative in Japan, where such films as Kenji Mizoguchi's geisha tale *Sisters of Gion* (1936), Hiroshi Inagaki's samurai epic *Chushingura* (1962), and Masaki Kobayashi's loosely related group of four ghost tales in *Kwaidan* (1964) often imply or clearly present a meditative and mobile narration that bears traces of the *benshi* tradition **[Figure 6.7]**. According to celebrated Japanese director Akira Kurosawa, the freedom of modern Japanese films to shift locations dramatically, to make unpredictable jumps between times or places, and to move the plot through only vague or underdeveloped character motivations suggests the heritage of the *benshi* in presuming a more dynamic interaction between the film and its narrative voice.

Figure 6.7 *Kwaidan* (1964). The heritage of the *benshi* in contemporary Japanese narrative.

To appreciate the richness of film narrative, viewers must keep in mind the vast history of other kinds of cultural narratives that underpin the stories we see on the screen.

Storytelling has always been a central part of societies and cultures. For hundred of years, stories have aimed to

- entertain individuals and audiences
- teach or convey practical, spiritual, and other important information
- remember different facts and truths

The many stories of the Bible, the Greek epics, the oral tales of indigenous cultures around the world, and the well-known stories of historical events (such as the Civil War) and people (such as Abraham Lincoln) are all driven by these aims. Stories pass time, they entertain children before bed and sailors at sea, they communicate ideas about social behavior, and they strengthen both the memory and imagination of a society. In a sense, stories are the historical center of culture and the bonds of a community are often the stories that individuals share and discuss.

Throughout history, stories have appeared in a myriad of material forms and served innumerable purposes, many of which reappear in movie narratives. Spoken or recited aloud, oral narratives represent a tradition that extends from the Greeks to the performance artists on today's stages. Written narratives, such as Charles Dickens's *Bleak House* (1853), appear as printed languages in books or magazines, while visual narratives develop through a series of graphic images, such as the stories told through lithographs in the eighteenth century and in modern comic books like *Spider-Man*. Musical narratives communicate stories through arrangements that might identify characters by certain musical motifs, as in *Peter and the Wolf* (1934). In these and other examples, the form and material through which a story is told opens some possibilities and closes others, allowing certain unique expressions and prohibiting others. Just as an oral narrative might offer more direct and flexible contact with listeners, allowing a story to change from one

 VIEWING CUES: Story, Plot, and Narration

- For the film you will watch next in class, describe as much as you can about the story. What are the main events, the implied events, and the significant and insignificant details of that story?

- Next, attempt to distinguish the film's story and plot. How do they differ? What significant omissions distinguish the two? Does the plot present the events of the story chronologically, from beginning to end, or in some other way?

- How do the differences between the film's plot and story suggest certain themes? In what ways do they inform your understanding of the film?

- Reflect on the film's narration. Is it prominent or not? How would you describe the perspective of the narration? Objective? Satirical? Humorous? In some other terms? If not controlled by an individual, how might the narration reveal certain attitudes about the story's logic?

- What traces of older narrative traditions can be found in this film? Are these historical precedents from novels, plays, or oral storytelling? Does the film use or transform them in ways that are important to your understanding of the movie?

Plot and Narration in *Apocalypse Now* (1979)

Francis Ford Coppola directed *Apocalypse Now,* one of Hollywood's most ambitious film narratives, not long after his blockbuster successes *The Godfather* (1972) and *The Godfather: Part II* (1974) and his ingenious *The Conversation* (1974). Coppola and his first successful films were part of an American renaissance in moviemaking during the 1960s and 1970s, revealing the marked influence of the French new-wave filmmakers Jean-Luc Godard, François Truffaut, and others who brought decidedly experimental and ironic attitudes to film narrative. *Apocalypse Now* is also one of the first serious attempts by a U.S. director to confront the lingering anger and pain of the Vietnam War, a then-recent and traumatic memory that Americans struggled to make sense of.

The film's story is deceptively simple: during the Vietnam War, Captain Willard (played by Martin Sheen) and his crew journey into the jungle to find a maverick and rebellious U.S. army colonel named Kurtz (Marlon Brando). The story describes Willard's increasingly strange encounters in the war-torn jungles of Vietnam and Cambodia. Eventually, he finds and confronts the bizarre rebel Kurtz at his riverside encampment in Cambodia.

As in other film narratives, *Apocalypse Now* constructs its story through a particular plot with a particular narrative point of view. The story of Willard and Kurtz could be plotted in a variety of other ways—by offering more information about the crew that accompanies Willard, for instance, or by showing events from an objective point of view rather than from one man's perceptions and thoughts. However, the film's plot concentrates less on the war or Kurtz (who is the main topic of the characters' conversations) than on Willard and his quest to find Kurtz. The plot begins with the desperate and shell-shocked Willard being given the assignment to seek out and kill Kurtz, to "terminate with extreme prejudice," and then follows Willard on his journey as he encounters a variety of strange and surreal people, sights, and activities [Figure 6.8]. In one sense, the plot's logic is

Figure 6.8 *Apocalypse Now* (1979). Willard's narrative point of view.

linear and progressive: for Willard, each new encounter reveals more about the Vietnam War and about Kurtz. At the same time, the plot creates a regressive temporal pattern: Willard's journey up the river takes him farther and farther away from a civilized world and a rational truth, returning him to his most primitive instincts.

The mostly first-person narration of *Apocalypse Now* focuses primarily on what Willard sees around him and on his thoughts on those events. At times, the narration extends beyond Willard's perspective, showing actions from the perspective of other characters or from a more objective perspective, while still representing these other characters and events as part of Willard's confused impressions. Bound mostly to Willard's limited point of view, the narration colors events and other characters with a tone that appears alternately as perplexed, weary, and fascinated. As a function of the film's narration, Americans, Vietnamese, and Cambodians appear increasingly bizarre, unpredictable, and even inhuman: rock music merges with the sounds of helicopters; soldiers surf during a violent attack on a village; tigers explode from the jungle; U.S. soldiers riot during a Playboy Bunny extravaganza in the depths of Vietnam. In these and other ways, the narration, linked to Willard's control of the narrative point of view, communicates not just what happens but also the disturbing sense of a world gone awry. In *Apocalypse Now*, the traditional narrative pattern of personal progress and development is both acknowledged and severely challenged.

Indeed, as part of its exploration of the tragedies and horrors of the Vietnam War, *Apocalypse Now* continually raises questions about its own narrative debts and historical influences. Characters tell each other stories about their lives, use the musical narrative of a Wagnerian opera as background for a vicious attack on a village, and (toward the end of the film) even act out a mythic narrative of ritual sacrifice as a bull and Kurtz are simultaneously slaughtered. The film makes no secret of its loose adaptation of Joseph Conrad's novella *Heart of Darkness* (1902), a masterpiece of British literature set in the nineteenth-century African Congo. Throughout

telling to another, a visual narrative might be able to describe the appearance of characters more concretely without being able to represent their thoughts. In the context of these differences, we must attend to how a particular film narrative might employ an oral form or how a musical narrative (say, from an opera) may work alongside the visual narrative of a movie.

As narrative film developed into the twentieth century, two important industrial events stand out—the introduction of film scripts to prepare movie narratives and the advancement of narrative dialogue through sound. Whereas many early silent movies were produced with little advanced preparation, the growing number and increasing length of movies from 1907 onward required the use of **scriptwriters,** who create film scripts, either original stories or adaptations from short stories, novels, or other sources. (A 1907 copyright lawsuit regarding an early movie version of *Ben-Hur* underlined the importance of scriptwriters who could develop original narratives.) A crucial industrial piece within the development of narrative cinema, the **film script** is the written narrative from which a movie is made. It first appears as a **treatment,** which succinctly describes the story as a constructed plot, and then proceeds through numerous revisions of the **screenplay,** another name for the film script that includes dialogue and

Figure 6.9 *Apocalypse Now* (1979). The literary history of a cinematic narrative.

the movie, passing references are made to various literary practices that question whether a traditional narrative can make sense of the brutality and emptiness of modern life, such as Joseph Campbell's well-known studies of narrative myths and T. S. Eliot's dark meditation in "The Hollow Men" (his 1925 poem that begins with a quote from Conrad's *Heart of Darkness,* "Mistah Kurtz—he dead") **[Figure 6.9]**. Deep in Kurtz's dark jungle cavern we catch glimpses of Campbell's books and hear Kurtz reciting Eliot's poems, as if Coppola is acknowledging a narrative lineage that extends from Conrad's novella to *Apocalypse Now,* each mapping the difficult relationship of narrative, modern history, and the darkness of the human heart. Almost a compendium of these narrative materials and traditions, *Apocalypse Now* seems to suggest that the history of war and conquest may well be bound up by a long history of attempts to control life and other people through the power of narrative.

each chronologically ordered scene in the plot. Called a **shooting script,** the final version of the screenplay also contains camera positions for each scene of the narrative.

While dialogue had an obviously limited function in silent movies (appearing only as **intertitles,** printed words inserted between the images), the marriage of **sound technology** and **dialogue** in the late 1920s proved to be one of the most significant advancements in the history of film narrative. While sound impacted the cinema in numerous ways, it allowed, most importantly perhaps, for film narratives to create and develop more intricate characters, whose often rich dialogue and vocal intonations signaled new psychological and social dimensions. More intricate characters could, in turn, propel more complex movie plots through the 1930s and thereafter.

Although movies expanded their narrative powers throughout the twentieth century, the older narrative heritages and events continue to permeate modern movies, as in the explicit use of the oral narrative in *Little Big Man,* in the tension among entertainment, instruction, and memory found in *Contempt,* and in the many creative ways that sound and dialogue are now used to create modern movie characters.

Narrative Characters

The first characters portrayed in films were principally bodies on display or in motion: a famous actor posing, a person running, a figure performing a menial task. When movies began to tell stories, however, characters naturally became the central vehicle for the actions, and with the advent of the Hollywood star system around 1910, distinctions in characters developed rapidly. From the 1896 *Lone Fisherman* to the 1920 *Pollyanna* (featuring Mary Pickford), film characters evolved from amusing moving bodies to adored mythic figures. With the introduction of sound films in 1927, complex psychologies and social categories began to identify characters and their relations. Today the evolution of characters continues with digitalized figures threatening to replace real-life actors. Through all these historical incarnations, narrative characters have remained one of the most intricate yet underestimated dimensions of the movies.

Character Motivation

As indicated earlier, characters are either central or minor figures (usually, but not always, human beings) who anchor the events in a film. They are commonly identified and understood as a product of their appearance, gestures and actions, dialogue, the comments of other characters, as well as such incidental but important features as their names or clothes. Characters' thoughts, personalities, expressions, and interactions focus the action of most films and propel their narratives. In this sense characters "motivate" the actions of a film's story. Their wishes and fears produce events that cause certain effects or other events to take place; thus, the actions, behaviors, and desires of characters create the **causal logic** of a film narrative, whereby one action or event leads to or "causes" another action or event to follow. In the 1939 classic film *The Wizard of Oz,* Dorothy's unrelenting desire to "go home"—to find her way back to Kansas—leads her through various encounters and dangers that create friendships and fears; these events, in turn, lead to others, such as Dorothy's fight to retrieve the witch's broom. In the end, she returns home joyfully. The character of Dorothy is thus defined first by her emotional desire and will to go home and then by her persistence and resourcefulness that eventually allow her to achieve that goal [**Figure 6.10**]. A character's emotional and intellectual make-up motivates specific actions that subsequently define that character.

Figure 6.10 *The Wizard of Oz* (1939). Narrative cause-and-effect logic on the Yellow Brick Road.

Even though movies commonly aim to create largely realistic characters, most film characters are a combination of both ordinary and extraordinary features. This blend of fantasy and realism has always been an important movie formula: it creates characters that are recognizable in terms of our experiences and exceptional in ways that make us interested in them. Often the differences and complexities of certain film characters can be attributed to this blending and balancing. For example, the title characters of *Julia* (1977), *Gandhi* (1982), and *Malcolm X* (1992)—the spy and friend of Lillian Hellman, the humble lawyer who became the leader of India [**Figure 6.11**], and the street hustler who spearheaded a movement

Figure 6.11 *Gandhi* (1982). Characters: balance of the ordinary and extraordinary.

for social justice, respectively—all combine extraordinary and ordinary characteristics. Even when film characters are entirely fictional, as with the tough but vulnerable heroine of *Alien* (1979), understanding them means appreciating how that balance between the ordinary and the extraordinary is achieved.

Character Coherence

No matter how realistic characters may appear and no matter how well the ordinary and extraordinary are blended in characters, their behavior, emotions, and thoughts are usually consistent and coherent. **Character coherence** is the product of different psychological, historical, or other expectations that see people as fundamentally consistent and unique. We usually evaluate a character's coherence according to one or more of the following three assumptions or models.

1. The character coheres in terms of one or more abstract values, such as when a character becomes defined through his or her overwhelming determination or treachery.
2. The character acts out a logical relation between his or her inner or mental life and visible actions, as when a sensitive character suddenly acts in a remarkably generous way.
3. The character reflects social and historical assumptions about normal or abnormal behavior, as when a fifteenth-century Chinese peasant woman acts submissively before men with power.

Thus, the character Charles Foster Kane in *Citizen Kane* (1941) appears inexplicable in many ways: he madly seeks more and more art objects, rejects his friends, and changes from an idealistic and energetic young man into a bitter and reclusive old man [**Figure 6.12**]. A closer examination of his character, however, might suggest that he is unusually complicated but still coherent by virtue of his obsessive determination to control his world, his need for unconditional love, or the historical image of masculine wealth and power in U.S. society in the 1940s.

Inconsistent, contradictory, or **divided characters** subvert one or more patterns of coherence. While

Figure 6.12 *Citizen Kane* (1941). A complex but coherent character.

Figure 6.13 *All About Eve* (1950). Character doubling.

inconsistent characters may sometimes be the result of poor characterization, a film may intentionally create an inconsistent or contradictory character as a way of challenging our sympathies and understanding. In films like *Desperately Seeking Susan* (1985)—about a bored suburban housewife, Roberta, switching identities with an offbeat and mysterious New Yorker—characters tend to complicate or subvert the traditional images of coherence by displaying personalities that are excessively unstable. *All About Eve* (1950) dramatizes a version of this instability through **character doubling**—whereby two characters become mirror images of each other—in its tale of an aging theater star whose life and personality become absorbed by an adoring younger actress. In the ensuing drama, the line between the real self and the mask of self becomes turned and twisted in a way that undermines fundamental notions about character coherence and stability **[Figure 6.13]**.

Film characters inevitably reflect certain historical and cultural values. In Western cultures, the most common movie character is "the singular character," distinguished by one or more features that isolate the character as a unique personality. Like John Wayne as Ethan in *The Searchers* (1956), the unique character is a product of a complex mixture of traits. The broad scope of these traits reflects a modern notion of the advanced individual as one who is emotionally and intellectually complex and one-of-a-kind. The consequent **character depth** associated with the unique character becomes a way of referring to personal mysteries and intricacies that deepen and layer the dimensions of a complicated personality, such as Louise in *Thelma and Louise* (1991), whose surface actions clearly hide a deep trauma (a sexual assault) that she tries unsuccessfully to repress. At other times, the unique character may be a product of one or two attributes, such as exceptional bravery or massive wealth, that separate him or her from all the other characters in the film. We should acknowledge that, at least in part, singularity represents a social system that prizes individuality and psychological depth in ways that are open to question. After all, Hannibal Lecter, in *The Silence of the Lambs*

Figure 6.14 *The Silence of the Lambs* (1991). The dark depth of character.

(1991) and its prequel and sequel is one of the most singular and exceptional characters in film history **[Figure 6.14]**; our troubling identification with him (at least in part) goes right to the social heart of our admiration for such uniqueness.

Character grouping refers to the social arrangements of characters in relation to each other. Traditional narratives usually feature one or two **protagonists,** characters we identify as the positive forces in a film, and one or two prominent **antagonists,** characters who oppose the protagonists as negative forces. As with the sympathetic relationship between a German officer and a French prisoner in *The Grand Illusion* (1937), this oppositional grouping of characters can sometimes be complicated or blurred. Surrounding, contrasting, and supporting the protagonists and antagonists, **minor** or **secondary characters** are usually associated with specific character groups. In *Do the Right Thing* (1989), Da Mayor wanders around the edges of the central action throughout most of the film. Although he barely impacts the events of the story, he becomes importantly associated with an older generation whose idealistic hopes have been dashed but whose fundamental compassion and wisdom stand out amidst racial anger and strife.

Social hierarchies of class, gender, race, age, and geography, among other determinants, also come into play in the arrangements of film characters. Traditionally, movie narratives have focused on heterosexual pairings in which males have claimed more power and activity than their female partners. Another traditional character hierarchy places children and elderly individuals in subordinate positions. Especially with older or mainstream films, characters from racial minorities have existed on the fringes of the action and of social ranks markedly below the protagonists: in *Gone with the Wind,* character hierarchy describes a structure that moves downward from white adult men and women to African Americans. When social groupings are more important than individual characters, the **collective character** of the individuals in the group is primarily defined in terms of the

Figure 6.15 *Erin Brockovich* (2000). Character as class representative.

group's action and personality. Sergei Eisenstein's *The Battleship Potemkin* (1925) explicitly fashions a drama of collective characters, crafting a political showdown among the czarist oppressors, the rebellious sailors, and the sympathetic populace in Odessa. Modern films, such as *Erin Brockovich* (2000) **[Figure 6.15]**, may shuffle those hierarchies noticeably so that classes like blue-collar workers or groups like women and children assume more new power and position, as in this story about a woman's fight against a corporate polluter.

Character Types

Character types share distinguishing features with other, similar characters. A single trait or multiple traits may define character types. These may be physical, psychological, or social traits; tattoos and a shaved head identify a character as one type (a "skinhead" or punk, perhaps), while another character's use of big words and a nasal accent may represent another type (a New England socialite, perhaps).

We might recognize the singularity of Warren Beatty's performance as Clyde in *Bonnie and Clyde* (1967), yet as we watch more movies and compare different protagonists, we might come to recognize him also as a character type who—like James Cagney as gangster Tom Powers in *The Public Enemy* (1931) and Bruce Willis as John McClane in *Die Hard* (1988)—can be described as a "tough yet sensitive outsider." Offering various emotional, intellectual, social, and psychological entrances into a movie, character types include such figures as "the innocent," such as Velvet Brown in *National Velvet* (1944); "the villainous," such as the title character in Fritz Lang's *Dr. Mabuse* (1922); and "the comic," such as Jerry/Daphne (played by Jack Lemmon) in *Some Like It Hot* (1959) **[Figure 6.16]**. These and other character types can often be subclassified in even more specific terms—such

Figure 6.16 *Some Like It Hot* (1959). A traditional comic character type.

as "the damsel in distress," "the psychotic killer," or the "class clown," for example. Usually, character types bring clear psychological or social connotations and imply cultural values about gender, race, social class, or age that a film engages and manipulates. In *Life Is Beautiful* (1997), the father (played

Figure 6.17 *Life Is Beautiful* (1997). The comic character type transformed into a hero.

by director Roberto Benigni) jokes and pirouettes in the tradition of comic clowns from Chaplin and Buster Keaton to Jacque Tati and Bill Murray, outsiders whose love of the physical undermines the social and intellectual pretensions around them. In *Life Is Beautiful*, however, this comic type must live through the horrors of a Nazi concentration camp with his son, and in this context that type becomes transformed into a different figure, a heroic type who physically and spiritually saves his son [**Figure 6.17**].

Film characters are also presented as **figurative types,** characters so exaggerated or reduced that they no longer seem at all realistic and instead seem more like abstractions or emblems. In some movies the figurative character appears as an **archetype,** a reflection of a spiritual or abstract state or process, such as when a character represents evil or oppression. In *The Battleship Potemkin,* a military commander unmistakably represents social oppression, while a baby in a carriage becomes the emblem of innocence oppressed. In different ways, figurative types present characters as intentionally flat, without the traditional depth and complexity of realistically drawn characters, and often for a specific purpose:

- for comic effect, as with the absentminded professor in *Back to the Future* (1985)
- for intellectual argument, as in *The Battleship Potemkin*
- for the creation of an imaginative landscape, as in *The Wizard of Oz* and *The Princess Bride* (1987)

Figure 6.18 *Imitation of Life* (1934). The distortions of stereotypes.

When a film reduces an otherwise realistic character to a set of static traits that identify him or her in terms of a social, physical, or cultural category—such as the "black mammy" character in *Imitation of Life* (1934) [**Figure 6.18**] or the vicious and inhuman Vietnamese in *The Deer Hunter* (1978)—this figurative type becomes a character **stereotype.** Stereotypes are usually offensive even when not overtly negative, because they tend to be applied to marginalized social groups who are not represented by a range of character types.

Character Development

As we have seen, characters are a product of certain physical, psychological, or cultural elements that describe them as individuals and that audiences must attend to and recognize. In addition, certain character types reflect recognizable traits and actions that have evolved through cultural and film history. Finally, film characters change over the course of a film and thus require us to evaluate and revise our understanding of them as they develop. We are charmed by Jimmy Stewart's character George Bailey in *It's a Wonderful Life* (1946) not simply because of his boyish and awkward good looks or because he represents a type of clownish and compassionate everyman. We also learn to admire and understand Bailey through the traumatic crisis he experiences and overcomes. Here, our interest in the character may be related to notions of growth, stability, patience, and remorse—human qualities that we see tested and developed throughout the course of the film.

Characters are often understood or measured by the degree to which they change and learn from their experiences in a story. Both the changes and the character's reaction to them determine much about the character and the narrative as a whole. We follow characters through this process of **character development,** the patterns through which characters move from one mental, physical, or social state to another in a particular film. In Hitchcock's *Rear Window* (1954), under the stress of a murder mystery, the beautiful Lisa changes from a seemingly passive socialite to an active detective. In *Clueless* (1995), the spoiled Cher's change is really a self-discovery: that she has all along loved the man she thought she despised [**Figure 6.19**].

Figure 6.19 *Clueless* (1995). Changing into a new self with new knowledge.

Character development follows four general schemes: external and internal changes and progressive and regressive developments. **External change** is typically a physical alteration, as when we watch a character grow taller or gray with age. Commonly overlooked as merely a realistic description of a character's growth, exterior change can signal other key changes in the meaning of a character. As in *Pygmalion* (1938) and *My Fair Lady* (1964), the main character in *Pretty Woman* (1990) is an uneducated and rather crass girl who changes into a sophisticated woman with fashionable clothing, better speech, and a stylish coiffure; these external changes become markers of other changes in the character's social and personal sense of self and ability to evaluate others. **Internal change** measures character changes from within, such as when a character slowly becomes bitter through the experience of numerous hardships or becomes less materially ambitious as he or she gains more of a spiritual sense of the world. In *Mildred Pierce* (1945), though there is minimal external change in the appearance of the main character besides her costumes, her consciousness about her identity dramatically changes—from a submissive housewife, to a bold businesswoman, and finally to a confused, if not contrite, socialite. Furthermore, as part of these external and internal developments, **progressive character development** occurs with an improvement or advancement in some quality of the character, whereas **regressive character development** indicates a loss of or return to some previous state or a deterioration from the present state. For most viewers of *Pretty Woman*, Vivian grows into a more complex and perhaps more powerful woman; for others, Mildred Pierce's path resembles a return to her originally submissive role.

Using these schemes to understand character development can be a complex and sometimes even contradictory process. Some characters may seem to progress materially, but regress spiritually, for instance. Other characters may not develop at all or may resist development throughout a film. Character development is frequently symptomatic of the larger society in which characters live. When the boy Oskar in Volker Schlöndorff's *The Tin Drum* (1979) suddenly refuses to grow at all, his distorted physical and mental development reflects the new Nazi society then being born in Germany [**Figure 6.20**].

Figure 6.20 *The Tin Drum* (1979). Arrested character development as a symptom of the new Nazi society.

Characters in *Casablanca* (1942)

The Academy Award-winning film *Casablanca* offers an unusually varied and accomplished group of actors and characters. Humphrey Bogart as Rick creates a realistic portrait of an American businessman whose nightclub in Casablanca, in the neutral French Morocco, is the meeting place for expatriates and the Nazi soldiers who quietly intimidate them. Weathered and tough looking, rather than glamorously handsome, Rick acts and dresses like a successful nightclub owner: appropriately calm and careful and seemingly in control of all situations. This realistic physical demeanor is both complemented and complicated by Rick's psychological character, which convincingly alternates between his cool cynicism (about life and people in general) and his understated but passionate idealism (about his deep love for Ilsa, the former lover who arrives in town with her freedom-fighter husband) **[Figure 6.21]**. In fact, Rick develops a complex relationship between his physical character and our glimpses of his psychological make-up that adds considerable depth to his overall character.

Character realism in *Casablanca* is clearly both historical and cultural. Not only might Rick's physical features, such as his hairstyle and gestures, seem outdated today, but his psychological and emotional behavior, like his rugged and restrained masculinity, might also seem like an archaic description of a male character to contemporary viewers. These historical and cultural differences can complicate or trouble our identification with and understanding of a movie.

Rick and other characters in *Casablanca* effectively and skillfully dramatize the balancing of the two dimensions of the ordinary and the extraordinary. Although Rick presents himself as part of the heterogeneous crowd he oversees, it is clear to us that he is distinguished from them by his superior intelligence and his exceptional physical and mental strength. Ingrid Bergman as Ilsa is both more beautiful and more sophisticated than the other women in the film (including the attractive but timid Bulgarian Annina whom Rick saves from the clutches of Captain Renault). Ilsa stands out because of her stunning beauty and her extraordinary devotion to the noble cause of her resistance-fighter husband, Victor Laszlo, an aristocratic European **[Figure 6.22]**. Yet a central crisis of the movie reveals Ilsa's deep love for the tough and unsophisticated Rick, so that a part of her character also includes the basic and enduring passion of all lovers. With minor characters less central to the story—such as Sascha the bartender and Major Strasser the Nazi commander—the balance between the ordinary and the extraordinary tends to swing one way or the other, making these minor characters appear more simplistic and less interesting.

Figure 6.21 *Casablanca* (1942). Rick's psychological character alternates between the cynical and the passionate.

Particularly rich characters like Rick and Ilsa can be evaluated according to any one of the three models of character coherence listed earlier in this chapter. Both characters exhibit many different character traits, some of which may seem contradictory: they are at once aloof and caring, loyal and suspicious, quick to anger and to reconcile. For some viewers, Rick may represent the eternal values of quiet nobility and heroism, while Ilsa may stand for endurance and self-sacrifice. For still other viewers, these characters make sense only according to 1940s mores and social codes, when to protect their emotions, men acted tough and bitter and women acted haughty and defensive. Rick and Ilsa might also be explained by the elaborate relationship of their internal and external lives: they have had to develop two sides to their characters, one as public survivors and the other as private lovers. Although those two sides are never really brought together, they remain humanly coherent as two, albeit painfully coexisting, sides of the human character.

It is difficult to find an incoherent or divided character in *Casablanca* (although the changing allegiances of Captain Renault shade him in that way). But, character groupings and hierarchies do play central roles in this film. For instance, the positive values in Rick's singularity come into view, through his hostile relationship with his main antagonist, Major Strasser, and even more so through his barely visible competition with Victor. Moreover, the many secondary characters create a particularly dynamic field of groupings, including the local north Africans, the American and European refugees and expatriates, and the French colonialists. Signor Ferrari, Ugarte, Sam, and Mr. and Mrs. Leuchtag are among a panorama of minor characters who act as background and give depth to the social fabric of the film.

Much of the patriotic force of *Casablanca* lies in how these minor groupings give way to the larger distinction of Nazis versus resisters. Occasionally, our engagement with the private drama of Rick and Ilsa shifts to the community of Rick's nightclub—such as when the resisters dramatically confront the Nazis by rising to sing the French national anthem, "La Marseillaise" **[Figure 6.23]**. Indeed, we can understand *Casablanca* as a drama of character by following Rick's transformation from a singular to a collective character ready to sacrifice his individuality for a larger political cause.

Figure 6.22 *Casablanca* (1942). The extraordinary and the real in Ilsa.

Figure 6.23 *Casablanca* (1942). Characters as collective resistance.

VIEWING CUES: Narrative Characters

- Examine carefully one or two characters in the film you will watch next for class. How is each character constructed and identified? By a name? By his or her clothing? By other important traits?

- Does the character appear realistic? Why or why not? For what reasons—physical, psychological, or historical? In what ways does the character's historical or cultural realism seem at odds with your own cultural or historical situation?

- Focusing on a single character in the film, test the assumption that all central film characters are a mix of the ordinary and the extraordinary. What seems ordinary about the character? What is extraordinary? Are these traits balanced or do they fall more in one direction than the other?

- Choose a character in the film to analyze in terms of singularity and coherence. Can the protagonist be defined as singular? In what way? Does that singularity indicate something about the human values in the film? Does the character seem coherent? In what ways?

- Do any characters seem divided or contradictory? How can you explain the contradictions in these characters? Do they reflect a theme of the movie?

- Turn your attention to the film's minor characters. What do the most important minor characters represent?

- What kinds of social hierarchies are suggested by the collective characters or character groupings in this film?

Narrative Times and Places: Shapes and Strategies in Film Narrative

Since the beginning of movie history around 1900, narrative films have experimented with new ways to tell stories. One of the first such films, Edwin S. Porter's *The Great Train Robbery* (1903), though primitive by today's standards, manipulated time and place by shifting from one action to another and coordinated different spaces by jumping between exterior and interior scenes. Since then, movie narratives have contracted and expanded times and places according to ever-varying patterns and well-established formulas, spanning centuries and traveling the world in Sally Potter's *Orlando* (1992) or confining the tale to two hours in one town in Agnès Varda's *Cleo from 5 to 7* (1962). Intricate temporal organizations and spatial shapes have thus become the art of storytelling on film.

Diegetic and Nondiegetic

Most narratives involve two kinds of materials, those related to the story and those not related to the story. The entire world that a story describes or infers is called its **diegesis,** a Greek word that refers to the characters, places, and events shown in the story or implied by it. The diegesis of Steven Spielberg's *Amistad* (1997) includes characters and events explicitly revealed in the narrative, such as a rebellion on a slave ship in the first part of the nineteenth century and the subsequent defense trial featuring John Quincy Adams. However, the film's diegesis also includes our knowledge of other unseen figures and events from American history, including a victorious war for independence and a near future that would erupt in the Civil War. The extent to which we find the film realistic or convincing, creative or manipulative, depends on our recognition of the richness and coherence of the diegetic world surrounding the story. Some films intentionally leave the diegesis unclear or misleading as a way of complicating our understanding of the story. *In the Realm of the Senses* (1976) is a story of passionate and all-consuming sexuality that takes place in 1930s Japan **[Figure 6.24]**; that the diegetic context of a society preparing for war is only glimpsed once or twice in this film adds to the isolated intensity and surreal quality of its story.

Figure 6.24 *In the Realm of the Senses* (1976). The barely visible diegetic context of Japan at war.

The notion of diegesis is critical to our understanding of film narrative because it forces us to consider those elements of the story that the narration chooses to include or not include in the plot—and to consider *why* these elements are included or excluded. Despite the similarity of information in a plot and a story, **plot selection and omission** describes the exchange by which plot constructs and shapes a story from its diegesis. Take, for instance, a film about the social unrest and revolution in Russia at the beginning of the twentieth century: since the diegesis of that event includes a number of events and many characters, what should be selected and what should be omitted? Faced with this question for his film on the 1905 revolution, Sergei Eisenstein reduced the diegesis to a single uprising on a battleship near the Odessa steps and called the film *The Battleship Potemkin*.

Nondiegetic information in the narrative includes material used to tell the story that does not relate to the diegesis and its world, such as background music and credits. These dimensions of a narrative indirectly add to a story and affect how we participate in or understand it. With silent films, nondiegetic information is sometimes part of the intertitles—those frames that usually print the dialogue of the characters but can occasionally comment on the action—as when D. W. Griffith inserts a line appropriated from Walt Whitman, "Out of the cradle endlessly rocking," into his complex narrative *Intolerance* (1916). As we discussed in Chapter 5, **nondiegetic soundtracks** are commonly musical scores or other arrangements of noise and sound whose source is not found in the story, as opposed to **diegetic soundtracks** whose source can be located in the story. Most moviegoers are familiar with the ominously thumping soundtrack of *Jaws* (1975) that announces the unseen presence of the great white shark: in this way the story punctuates its development to quicken our attention and create suspenseful anticipation of the next event.

Credits are another nondiegetic element of the narrative. Sometimes seen at the beginning and sometimes at the end of the movie, credits introduce the actors, producers, technicians, and other individuals who have worked on the film (with Hollywood movies today, famous stars, the director, and the producers usually appear at the beginning, while the closing credits name the secondary players and technicians). How this information is presented can often suggest ways of looking at the story and its themes as the story unfolds or as we look back at it after it has ended. In *Psycho* (1960), for instance, the opening credits graphically anticipate a story about fragile identities torn apart by psychic and actual violence. To the sound of the intense musical theme that accompanies much of the anxiety and violence in the film, the credits present names that are formed by lines running

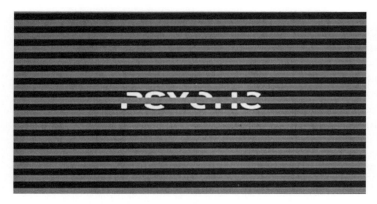

Figure 6.25 *Psycho* (1960). Signaling motifs in the opening credits.

together from opposite sides of the screen; the names are then torn apart to make way for the next credit. Although we tend not to consider this dimension of the narrative, motifs signaled in the credits can resonate through the entire film **[Figure 6.25]**.

Temporal Schemes

A narrative can be organized according to a variety of **temporal schemes.** Individuals and societies create patterns of time as ways of measuring and valuing experience. Repeating holidays once a year, marking births and deaths with symbolic rituals, and rewarding work for time invested are some of the ways we organize and value time. Similarly, narrative films develop a variety of temporal patterns as a way of creating meaning and value in the stories and experiences they recount.

Most commonly, plots follow a **linear chronology** in which the selected events and actions proceed one after another through a forward movement in time. The logic and direction of a linear plot commonly follows a central character's motivation—that is, the ideas or emotions that make a character choose a course of action. In these cases, a character pursues an object, belief, or goal of some sort, and the events in the plot are constructed according to some causal logic that follows a cause-and-effect pattern centered on that character's motivation. The linear chronology of the plot will thus show how that character's motivating desire affects or creates new situations or actions: put simply, past actions generate present situations and decisions made in the present will create future events. The narrative of *The African Queen* (1951) structures the linear action precisely in this way: as the two main characters try to escape hostile Germans and the dangers of the African jungle, their cunning and growing affection for each other push them to pass each new obstacle **[Figure 6.26]**.

Linear narratives most commonly structure their stories in terms of beginnings, middles, and ends. As a product of this structure, the relationship of the **narrative opening** and **closing** is normally central to the temporal logic of a plot. How a movie begins and ends and the relationship between those two poles explain much about a film. Sometimes this relation can create a sense of closure or completion, as happens when a romance ends with a couple united or with a journey finally concluded. Other plots provide less certain relations between openings and closings. Michelangelo Antonioni's *Blowup* (1966) begins with a photographer at work developing pictures and concludes with his retrieving an imaginary tennis ball for an imaginary tennis match played by mimes **[Figure 6.27]**. From the opening, the film's narrative follows the photographer's search for reality (in photos that suggest a possible murder); the conclusion therefore offers only ambiguity, suggesting perhaps the impossibility of that search.

One of the most common temporal schemes in narrative films, the **deadline structure** adds to the tension and ex-

Figure 6.26 *The African Queen* (1951). Moving a narrative down the river.

citement of these plots, accelerating the action and plot toward a central event or action that must be accomplished by a certain moment, hour, day, or year. These narrative rhythms can create suspense and anticipation that summarize the entire narrative and the characters who motivate them. In *The Graduate* (1967), Benjamin must race to the church in time to declare his love for Elaine and stop her from marrying his rival. In the German film *Run, Lola, Run* (1998), Lola has twenty minutes to find 100,000 Deutschmarks to save her boyfriend; and this tight deadline results in three different versions of the same race across town in which, like a game, Lola's rapid-fire choices result in three different conclusions **[Figure 6.28]**.

The deadline structure points to another common temporal pattern in film narrative: the doubled or parallel plot line. **Parallel plots** refer to the implied simultaneity of or connection between two different plot lines, usually with their intersection at one or more points. Quite frequently with film narratives, a movie will alternate between actions or subplots that take place at roughly the same time and that may be bound together in some way, such as by the relationship of two or more characters. One standard formula in a parallel plot is to intertwine a private story with a public story. *The Graduate* develops the story of Benjamin's entry into the adult world of careers, social rituals, and sexual power; concurrently it follows his developing romance with Elaine, the daughter of a woman with whom he is having an affair. In some crime films, such as *Double Indemnity* (1944), a murder mystery (in this case, involving insurance money) frequently parallels and entwines with a torrid love story (here, about seduction and manipulation) **[Figure 6.29]**. In addition to recognizing parallel plots, we need to consider the relationship between them. In any particular movie, does one part of this doubled plot have more force and meaning than the other?

Despite the dominance of various versions of linear chronologies in movie narratives, most films deviate, to some extent, from straight linear chronologies to create different perspectives on events in order to lead viewers toward an understanding of what is or is not important in a story or to disrupt or challenge viewers' notions of the film as a realistic re-creation of events. **Plot order** describes how events and actions are arranged in relation to each other to create a chronology of one sort or another. A linear chronology is the most dominant temporal order that movies can adapt. Either within a linear chronology or as a variation of it, actions may appear out of chronological order, as when a later event precedes

Figure 6.27 *Blowup* (1966). Anticipating an ambiguous closure.

Figure 6.28 *Run, Lola, Run* (1998). Different choices and different deadlines.

Figure 6.29 *Double Indemnity* (1944). Parallel plots of love and crime.

Figure 6.30 *The Godfather: Part II* (1974). A retrospective plot woven into a contemporary tale.

an earlier one in the plot. One of the most common nonlinear plot devices is the narrative **flashback,** whereby a story shifts dramatically to an earlier time in the story. When a flashback describes the perspective on the whole story, it creates a **retrospective plot,** which tells of past events from the perspective of the present or future. In *The Godfather: Part II* (1974), the modern story of mobster Michael Corleone periodically alternates with the flashback story of his father, Vito, many decades earlier; this counterpointing of two different histories draws parallels and suggests differences between the father's formation of his mafia family and the son's later destruction of that family in the name of the mafia business **[Figure 6.30]**. Conversely and less frequently, a narrative chronology may **flashforward,** leaping ahead of the normal cause-and-effect order to a future incident. Thus, a film narrative may show a man in an office and then flashforward to his plane leaving an airport before returning to the moment in the plot when he sits at his desk. In *They Shoot Horses, Don't They?* (1969), the plot flashes forward to a time when Robert is on trial; the unexplained scene creates a mysterious suspense that is not resolved until we later discover that he shoots Gloria at her request.

Other nonlinear chronological orders might interweave past, present, and future events in less predictable or logical patterns. *Hiroshima Mon Amour* (1959) mixes documentary photos of the nuclear destruction of Hiroshima at the end of World War II, a modern story of a love affair between a French actress and a Japanese architect, and flashback images of the woman growing up in France during the previous war, when she had her first relationship with a German soldier **[Figure 6.31]**. Only gradually, and certainly not in chronological order, is the story of her past revealed. Conversations with her lover and images of Japan during World War II seem to provoke leaps in her memory, and as the film narrative follows these flashbacks, we become involved in the difficulty of memory as it attempts to reconstruct an identity across a historical trauma. When a narrative violates linear chronology in these ways, the film may be demonstrating how subjective memories interact with the real world; at other times, as with *Hiroshima Mon Amour,* these violations may be ways of questioning the very notion of linear progress in life and civilization.

Movie narratives also rely on various other temporal patterns, through which events in a story are constructed according to different time schemes. **Narrative duration** refers to the length of time an event or action is presented in a plot, whereas **narrative frequency** describes how often those plot elements are repeatedly shown. *Die Hard: With a Vengeance* (1995) features a now standard digital countdown for a bomb that threatens to blow up New York City; the narrative suspense is, in large part, the amount of time the plot spends on this scene, dwelling on the bomb mechanism. Thus, the thirty plot seconds for this event in the film narrative take much longer than thirty real seconds, the temporal duration being not simply a real but also

Figure 6.31 *Hiroshima Mon Amour* (1959). A nonlinear mix of past and present.

an extended time. At the other end of the spectrum, a plot may include only a temporal flash of an action that really endures for a much a longer period

Figure 6.32 *Claire's Knee* (1970). Knee fetishes and narrative repetitions.

Figure 6.33 *My Dinner with Andre* (1981). Multiple narratives spread across a single space.

of time: in *Citizen Kane*, a series of short scenes lasting only moments describes the dissolution of Kane's first marriage over several years. Instead of representing the many complications that extend an actual duration of an event, the plot condenses these actions into a much shorter episode. How often an event, person, or action is depicted by a plot—its narrative frequency—also determines the meaning or value of those events within a narrative. That is, when something is shown more than once, its value and meaning to the story increase. A movie may, for instance, return again and again to an exchange of glances between two specific characters, leaving no doubt that this relationship is central to the plot. In Eric Rohmer's *Claire's Knee* (1970), the witty plot returns again and again to the knee of the title and the frequency of this return suggests both the main character's obsession with this part of the young woman's body and, at the same time, how potentially comic that obsession can become through time [**Figure 6.32**]. In repetitions like this, it is important to recognize narrative frequency as a way of drawing our attention to significant events, gestures, phrases, places, or actions.

Placing Stories

Along with the temporal patterns of narrative, plot constructions also involve a variety of spatial schemes, spaces constructed through the course of the narrative as different mise-en-scènes (see pp. 44–51). These **narrative locations**—indoors, outdoors, natural spaces, artificial spaces, outer space— define more than just the background for stories. Stories and their characters explore these spaces, contrast them, conquer them, inhabit them, leave them, build on them, and transform them. As a consequence, both the characters and the stories usually change and develop.

Narrative space thus functions as a second prominent formal feature of plot. Louis Malle's *My Dinner with Andre* (1981) is, for many, a strange and unusual film because it tells story after story but takes place in a single visible space. The film occurs at a dinner table, where Andre Gregory and Wallace Shawn exchange anecdotes and memories, dreams, and second-hand stories [**Figure 6.33**]. That this film infuses a single mise-en-scène with such energy testifies to the imaginative power of stories to use and transform space. Although movies generally take advantage of their visual powers to present plots and narratives as simply "taking place" in different locations, a narrative develops those spaces through various meanings and connotations.

As a product of narrative action and characters, space may be developed in four different ways. Whether actual places or constructed settings, the **historical location** abounds in film narratives as the recognized marker of a historical setting that can carry meanings and connotations important to the narrative. A character in *Roman Holiday* (1953) visits the monuments

Figure 6.34 *Roman Holiday* (1953). Exploring historical locations.

of Rome, where she discovers a sense of human history and a romantic glory missing from her own life **[Figure 6.34]**. Films from the 1925 *Ben-Hur* to the 2000 *Gladiator* use the historical connotations of Rome to infuse the narrative with grandeur and wonder. An **ideological location** in a narrative describes spaces and places inscribed with distinctive social values or ideologies. Sometimes these narrative spaces have unmistakable political or ideological significance, such as the slave galleys of *Amistad* or the oppressive grandeur of the czar's palace in Eisenstein's *October* (1927). Less obviously, the politics of gender can underpin the locations of a film narrative in crucial ideological ways: in *9 to 5* (1980), the plot focuses on how three working women successfully transform the patriarchal office space of their jobs into a place where the needs of women are met **[Figure 6.35]**. **Psychological location** in a film narrative suggests an important correlation between a character's state of mind and the place he or she inhabits at that moment in the story. In Antonioni's *The Eclipse* (1962), empty modern streets become the eerie and disturbing correlatives to the mind and feelings of the alienated protagonist, Vittoria. Less common, **symbolic space** is a space transformed through spiritual or other abstract meanings related to the narrative. In different versions of the Robinson Crusoe story—from Luis Buñuel's *The Adventures of Robinson Crusoe* (1954) to *Robinson Crusoe on Mars* (1964) and the recent *Castaway* (2000) **[Figure 6.36]**—the space of an island might become symbolic of the providential ways of life or of the absurdity of the human condition.

Complex narratives often develop and transform the significance of one or more locations, making this transformation of specific places central to the meaning of the movie. In *The Battleship Potemkin*, for example, narrative infuses the Odessa steps with historical, psychological, ideological, and symbolic significance. In this case, the realistic mise-en-scène represents a famous location in the 1905 Russian Revolution, a psychological place of

Figure 6.35 *9 to 5* (1980). Gendered locations.

Figure 6.36 *Castaway* (2000). The island as symbolic location.

terror, an ideological location of oppression, and a symbol of the revolutionary uprising. In Jim Jarmusch's *Mystery Train* (1989), the narrative interweaves the stories of two Japanese tourists, an Italian woman on her way home to bury her husband, and three drifters who hold up a liquor store **[Figure 6.37]**. All happen to seek refuge in a sleazy Memphis hotel. Although they never meet, the narrative location of the hotel becomes gradually infused with the meanings of their individual dramas: the hotel becomes simultaneously a place of historical nostalgia for 1950s America and of blues music

Figure 6.37 *Mystery Train* (1989). A hotel transformed through multiple lives and meanings.

for the Japanese couple, a comically ritualistic and spiritual location for the Italian woman who takes leave of her husband's ashes after meeting Elvis Presley's ghost, and a weird debating hall where the drifters discuss contemporary social violence.

Narration and Narrators

Plots are organized according to the perspective that informs them. Whether this perspective is explicit or implicit, we refer to this dimension of a narrative as its **narration**—the point of view that emotionally and intellectually shapes how plot materials appear and what is or is not revealed about them. Narration carries and creates attitudes, values, and aims that are central to understanding any movie. Sometimes narrations might reflect the attitudes clearly identified with a filmmaker. In movies like John Sayles's *Lianna* (1983), *The Brother from Another Planet* (1984), and *Lone Star* (1996), the narration moves around the fringes of society, quietly meditating on the loneliness and compassion that make individuals human **[Figure 6.38]**. Tim Burton's *Beetlejuice* (1988) and *Sleepy Hollow* (1999) also tell stories of isolation and longing, but his narrations assume a more exaggerated and often comic point of view, finding the human spirit in the most distorted actions and figures. Sometimes these narrative perspectives suggest the historical period when they were made; the narrations of 1930s Hollywood films re-create a theatrical point of view inherited from the New York stage. Other times these narrational positions are cultural, as in the films of Yasujiro Ozu, whose slow explorations of family life show the traces of traditional Japanese conceptions of space and time.

Interestingly, film narration may be more transparent when we watch silent films, in which the narration must often speak through intertitles that

Figure 6.38 *Lone Star* (1996). Narration across different cultures and dramas.

provide both dialogue and commentary. When a narrative intertitle in *Foolish Wives* (1922) introduces a scene with the text "Woman's Vanity . . . Idle—Foolish—Wives," the narration speaks clearly the somewhat bitter and patriarchal prejudices that inform the perspective of the story. In *2001: A Space Odyssey* (1968), the narration covers thousands of years of human evolution, from apes to computer intelligence in outer space. It selects, as part of its narrative perspective, incidents that mark transitions in human knowledge, power, and perhaps violence: apes learning to kill to conquer land, and computers learning to kill to survive. Does this narration assume a position of divine wonder at the span of human development? Or could that narrative stance be better described as a satirical vision, quietly mocking that history of human desire? Deciding which position controls that narrative will determine how we understand the movie.

Narrators and narrative frames are frequently used to signal the specific perspective of the narration. Both of these describe formal tactics for drawing us into a story and both direct and create the arrangement of the plot as a specific position implying attitudes, standards, or powers. The most common narrative perspectives are first-person narration, omniscient narration, and restricted narration.

Some films, as noted earlier, use a **narrator,** a character or other person whose voice and perspective describe the action of a film from a point of view outside the story. A **first-person narrator** has some relation to the story he or she is telling, signaled by the pronoun "I" in written or spoken texts. Especially with first-person narrators, a standard device to mark the presence and perspective of that narrator is the **voiceover** commentary, a soundtrack commentary in which the narrator introduces the story and may occasionally make observations about it. First-person narration is an especially tricky notion for film narratives because this use of the voiceover to guide movie images can usually only approximate the full subjectivity of a first-person point of view. To attempt a literal first-person narration with film would require the film frame to become the narrator's eyes, re-creating only what the narrator sees. Narrated entirely through the first-person

point of view of the detective Philip Marlowe, *Lady in the Lake* (1947) demonstrates how tiresome such a narration can become. The more common strategy is, accordingly, to signal a first-person narration through a voiceover narrator.

Appearing at the beginning and end of a narrative, a narrative frame is often a vehicle for introducing a first-person narration but serves many other narrative functions as well. A **narrative frame** describes a context or person positioned outside the story to bracket the film's narrative in a way that helps define its terms and meaning. Sometimes signaled by a voiceover, this frame may indicate the story's audience, the social context, or the time period from which the story is understood. The frame may, for instance, indicate that the story is a tale told to children, that it is being told to a detective in a police station, that it is the memory of a dying woman. In each case, the narrative frame indicates the crucial perspective and logic that define the narration.

In *Sunset Boulevard* (1950), the presence of the narrator is announced through the voiceover narration of the screenwriter-protagonist who introduces the setting and circumstances of the story [**Figure 6.39**]. His voice and death become the narrative frame for the story. Through the course of the film, his voiceover disappears and reappears, but we are aware from the start that the story is a product of his perspective; how we understand the story is at least as dependent on this narrator and his attitudes as it is on the story's events. For this reason, viewers realize that, though the story and plot seem focused on a delusory movie star whose glory has long past, the narrative (as opposed to the story) is perhaps even more about this writer's experience of her. That we learn from the start that this first-person narrator is dead becomes an unsettling irony. What does this suggest about why the narrator is telling this story? As a memorial? To justify his actions in the story? How do the narrator's attitudes—cynical and fatigued—color the narration and hence inform the story? Does his death before the narration begins undermine the whole story, suggesting how in Hollywood even writer-narrators are not dependable authorities?

Figure 6.40 *The Ice Storm* (1997). Frozen and framed: the memory of childhood.

The Ice Storm (1997) also uses a narrative frame. The narrator in this case is a young man whose commuter train has stopped en route to his home because of a heavy ice storm. The narrative begins as he waits in the night for the tracks to be cleared of ice and debris, while he reflects on his family; this isolated moment and compartment frame the flashback narration that follows. Although he too disappears as a narrator until we return to the train and his voice at the end of the movie, his salient position as a narrator makes clear that this tale of a pathetically dysfunctional family in the 1970s is, most importantly, about this young man at a turning point in his life **[Figure 6.40]**. Indeed, both these examples suggest a question to ask about narrators: does it make a difference if the narrator is seen as part of the story?

Most film narrators are not so visible and the majority of film narratives employ some version of a third-person narration. The standard form of classical movie narration is **omniscient narration,** a version of third-person narration in which all elements of the plot are presented from many or all potential angles. An omniscient narrative perspective not only knows all; it also knows what's important and how to arrange it to reveal the truth about a life or a history. **Restricted narration** organizes stories by focusing on one or two characters. Even though this narration also assumes objectivity and is able to present events and characters outside the range of those primary characters, it largely confines itself to the experiences and thoughts of the major characters. The historical source of restricted narration is the novel and short story; as such, its emphasis on one or two individuals reflects a relatively modern view of the world (since the eighteenth century) that is mostly concerned with the progress of individuals. Buster Keaton's *The General* (1927), for example, limits what is shown or included in the plot to the experiences of the main character, Johnny Gray, as he rescues his locomotive and his girlfriend from the Northern army during the Civil War **[Figure 6.41]**. Limiting the narration in this way allows the movie to attend to large historical events and actions (battles or family meetings, for instance) while also prioritizing the problems and desires of Johnny.

Figure 6.41 *The General* (1927). Restricted narration: Johnny in the Civil War.

Narrative Space and Time in *The Searchers* (1956)

John Ford's *The Searchers* is a remarkable film narrative whose construction is as dramatic as it is unobtrusive. Its diegesis is quickly but clearly indicated: its world is the small settlements in a mostly open-range Texas not long after the Civil War, including the U.S. frontier where Ethan Edwards and Martin Pawley search for Edwards's nieces, Debbie and Lucy, who were captured by a renegade band of Comanche. There are a variety of minor characters within the story, such as Ethan's brother, Aaron, and sister-in-law, Martha, the feeble-minded Mose Harper, Reverend Samuel Clayton, and Ethan's Native American nemesis, Chief Scar. Additionally, some diegetic information is not shown yet as part of the narrative: the facts behind Ethan's cloudy and perhaps criminal past and his affectionately tense relationship with his brother's wife. Perhaps the most important part of the diegesis, which the story refuses to show explicitly, is the relationship between Debbie and Scar. Although this relationship drives the narrative and Ethan's vengeance, we know very little about it, including whether it is consensual or not. More importantly, why is it not more directly addressed by the diegesis? Implied by the invisibility of this relationship is a historical fear of, and fascination with, miscegenation or interracial relationships.

The narrative of *The Searchers* features crucial nondiegetic material. The credits appear in a fairly standard manner: most prominently, the title and the names, in large letters, of the producer C. V. Whitney, the star John Wayne, and the director John Ford. Yet three other features of these credits stand out: the titles are set against a drawing of a flat brick (probably adobe) wall, the final title pinpoints the time and place as "Texas 1868," and the overture song "The Searchers" is introduced ("What makes a man to wander? . . ."). Minor though these details may seem, they announce *The Searchers* as being about the walls of home, with the weight of a precisely dated post–Civil War historical epic permeated by the existential questions of the cowboy ballad. The use of nondiegetic sound also supports our understanding of the narrative at other points. When serious encounters or revelations occur, such as Ethan's announcement that he will not return to the canyon where he discovered something unspeakable, sharp and ominous chords on the symphonic soundtrack punctuate his exclamation [**Figure 6.42**].

The plot is clearly linear. The quest to find two young girls, Debbie and Lucy, kidnapped by Scar and his tribe, leads Ethan and Martin across the

Figure 6.42 *The Searchers* (1956). Nondiegetic sound announces the unspeakable event.

plains, where they must encounter and overcome various obstacles (hostile Comanche, the heat of the desert, winter hardships, and even Ethan's own tortured mind). After Lucy is found dead, Debbie becomes the sole object of their successful search, and, through the condensation of several years, this linear chronology returns the two men to the home from which they began their quest. Note that the resulting circularity of the linear plot suggests that even though the central character has moved forward through his quest, he has simultaneously circled backward.

Along the way, the plot introduces the precarious plight of the homesteaders, as well as extends the crisis of the kidnappings and Ethan's interior and exterior struggles through the majority of the film, and finally resolves that crisis with Debbie's rescue, her homecoming to her new family, the Jorgensens, and the successful reunion of Martin and the girl he left behind, Laurie. Framing this plot, the home lost at the beginning is figuratively restored at the end, although both these homes/houses are, somewhat disturbingly, associated with a darkened doorway. In *The Searchers*, some elements of the plot are necessarily shown: the attack on the homestead, various encounters along the trail as the men seek information about Scar's whereabouts, and the climactic battle with Scar and his men. Other elements omitted from or selected by the plot might seem more arbitrary and less obvious choices, yet it is often these choices that suggest most about the perspective and meaning of the narration. The omission of information about Ethan's past and his relationship with Martha, for instance, obliquely creates a "hero" with scars on his own moral character, thus complicating significantly his moral righteousness in pursuit of Debbie and Scar. Conversely, the inclusion of a sequence in which Ethan and Martin comically barter trinkets, mistakenly resulting in a Native American wife for Ethan, seems, at least at first glance, a strange addition to the plot.

Although *The Searchers* may not seem determined by a deadline structure, such a temporal logic underlies it in two ways: (1) Martin must rescue Debbie before Ethan finds her if he is to save her from Ethan's plans to murder her, and (2) he must return home in time to marry Laurie and save her (and him) from the wrong marriage.

This deadline temporality of *The Searchers* points to another common temporal structure in film narrative: the parallel plot. The central plot of Ethan and Martin's relentless pursuit of Debbie and Scar is counterpointed by the romantic plot of the budding love between Martin and Laurie. Clearly, the two are related both thematically and temporally: the two plots cross paths as the search commences and continues, and in this film the search and restitution of social order must be completed before the personal romance can be resolved. The relationship of these two plot lines seems to suggest that Ethan's bitter need for vengeance must be stopped or redeemed if more compassionate and loving relations are to be allowed to develop.

Although *The Searchers* has a fundamentally linear plot, it does introduce an extended flashback within the linear chronology. As Martin's anxious girlfriend back home reads a letter from him in the present tense in the narrative chronology, the film narrative flashes back to earlier events retold in Martin's letter: his accidental acquisition of Look as a wife, a buffalo hunt in the deep of winter, the massacre of an Indian village by U.S. soldiers. Why this shift in the linear chronology of the plot? Perhaps it is a critical reminder of the domestic sanctuary of home and marriage that Martin has forsaken through his desperate drive toward a future goal. Though Martin's letter lasts only minutes, it is meant to describe many months of the story. Through this temporal condensation, Laurie's few minutes with the letter appear, on one level, to be more emotionally significant than Martin's many

Figure 6.43 *The Searchers* (1956). The dark threshold of the cave.

months of physical endurance on the plains.

Narrative frequency also becomes key to our understanding of *The Searchers*. Ethan's regular retort "That'll be the day!" may make that repeated comment more important than it seems, especially when he counters all its cynical expectations with the generosity of his final actions. More clearly central to the film's plot is the frequent return to the darkened threshold that opens the film, concludes the film, and is re-created twice in the dark threshold of the cave into which Ethan, Martin, and, later, Debbie flee **[Figure 6.43]**. One interpretation of the repetition of this place or its image might begin by noting that the doorway and cave entrance describe the divide between interior safety and exterior danger, a key theme in the film.

The narrative of *The Searchers* presents, develops, and coordinates a variety of central spaces. Most noticeably, the home of Aaron and Martha Edwards, with its domestic interiors, contrasts with the open expanses of the western frontier, with its stunning vistas and dramatic plateaus. Through the course of the narrative, moreover, the open spaces reveal a variety of different spatial connotations: the rugged terrain of deserts and valleys, river crossings, and snowy winter mountains. These open spaces then feature a number of more specific locations with more definite narrative significance: the cabin of the sinister traders, two different Native American encampments, the Mexican hacienda, and, most importantly, the cave in which Ethan and Martin hide and into which Debbie later flees. Thinking about the relation of these different geographies to the narrative, one might argue the following: the narrative of *The Searchers* explores these different places for the signs of a common humanity; the darkened cave, like the darkened doorway of the lost home, becomes that place where humanity is most threatened—possibly from within as well as from without—and where the troubled humanity of Ethan finally redeems itself in an act of forgiveness.

As a result, Johnny's ingenuity becomes apparent and seems much more honorable—and funny—than the grand epic of war that stays in the background of the narrative. With these and other restricted narrations, the logic and attitude of the narration determine why some characters receive more or less attention from the limited narrative point of view.

While omniscient narration and restricted narration are the most common kinds of classical narration, some films use variations on these models. **Reflexive narration** describes movies that call attention to the narrative point of view of the story in order to complicate or subvert their own narrative authority as a consistent perspective on the world. Robert Wiene's *The Cabinet of Dr. Caligari* (1919) is a well-known early example of reflexive narration that fractures the veracity and reliability of its narrative point of view when, at its conclusion, we discover that the narrator is a madman.

In *The Searchers,* Texas just after the Civil War—indeed, the entire U.S. frontier—works as a historical space central to the film's narrative. The many explicit narrative references to the history of this place make it the recognized site of a crossroads between European whites, Mexicans, and Native Americans, precisely at that time when U.S. identity attempted to recover from the national violence of the Civil War, fought in part over the racial divide between whites and blacks. Other places bear the marks of racial politics, such as the room where Ethan sees the white girls raised by Native Americans and notes that "they're not white anymore." Less intentionally, gender politics imbues various locations of this film (the washrooms of cabins, the teepees of Native Americans) that define women as subservient to men. Finally, the darkened cave and darkened doorway to the home both bear enormous psychological connotations in regard to Ethan and his darkened, alienated psyche.

Figure 6.44 *The Searchers* (1956). The first-person narration of Martin's letter and voiceover.

The narration in *The Searchers* is far more complicated than it may first seem. Because the narrative point of view includes events both connected to Ethan's search and outside of it, the narration is technically third-person omniscient, capable of embracing all characters and actions within its purview. For most of the film, however, it develops a limited third-person focus on Ethan's and Martin's efforts to find Debbie. Even this dominant dimension of the narration becomes complicated because its limited concentration is implicitly divided between Ethan and Martin, characters with significantly different attitudes and goals. Within the main narrative, as we have seen, the film also interjects Martin's first-person narration as a letter to Laurie [Figure 6.44]. One way to think about this narrational mobility is to argue that the western epic here is told not as one person's story, but as a story stretched and experienced from competing perspectives. This would explain how the tone and logic of the film's narration skillfully alter its perspective from that of a determined quest to a more meditative inquiry.

Contemporary and experimental films commonly question the very process of narration at the same time that they construct the narrative. **Unreliable narration** raises, at some point in the narrative, crucial questions about the very truth of the story being told: in *Fight Club* (1999), the bottom falls out of the narration when, toward the conclusion of the film, it becomes clear the first-person narrator has been hallucinating the entire existence of a central character, around whom the plot develops.

Multiple narrations are found in films that use several different narrative perspectives for a single story or for different stories in a movie that loosely fits these perspectives together. The 1916 *Intolerance* weaves four stories about prejudice and hate from different historical periods ("the modern story," "the Judean story," "the French story," and "the Babylonian story") and could be considered a precursor to the tradition of multiple narration.

Figure 6.45 *Germany in Autumn* (1978). A compilation of narratives: Germany and terrorism.

A more recent comic version, Woody Allen's *Zelig* (1983), parodies the objectivity proposed by many narratives by presenting the life of Leonard Zelig in the 1920s through the onscreen narrations of numerous fictional and real persons (such as Saul Bellow and Susan Sontag). **Compilation films** or **anthology films,** movies that feature the work of different filmmakers, such as *Germany in Autumn* (1978) **[Figure 6.45]**, *Aria* (1987), and *New York Stories* (1989), are more extreme versions of multiple narratives. This type of movie features a number of stories, each made by a different filmmaker. Although the stories may share a common theme or issue—a political crisis in Germany, operatic arias, or living in New York City—they intentionally replace a singular narrative perspective with smaller narratives that establish their own distinctive perspectives.

VIEWING CUES: Narrative Times and Places

■ For the film you will watch next in class, present a descriptive sketch of its diegesis. Which events are then excluded or merely implied when that diegesis becomes presented as a narrative? How can you explain the selection and omission of material from the film's diegesis?

■ What are the most important nondiegetic materials in the movie? Try to analyze how some of those materials (such as the credits and soundtrack) emphasize certain themes or ideas that are important to the film.

■ How is time shaped in this film narrative? What especially important instances of frequency or duration can you point to in the time scheme of this narrative?

■ Identify the three most significant narrative locations in the movie. How does the narrative construct different meanings for different locations? Distinguish the historical, ideological, psychological, and symbolic places in the narrative. How do they add to your understanding of the story?

■ Is the film's narration primarily an omniscient, a restricted, or a first-person narration? If there is a first-person narrator, does the narrative become more about the narrator than the story itself? How so? If the narration is omniscient or restricted, how does it determine the meaning of the story?

Points of View:
Values and Traditions of Film Narrative

Early narrative films moved quickly to establish values and traditions. Building on their relation with nineteenth-century novels, early films gravitated to historical events and characters for their subjects. Showing images of famous events and people soon led to more extended narratives about historical figures and actions, and even when fictional stories were the topic, film narratives grew increasingly fascinated with the many ways time and temporality could be organized to communicate certain meanings and values. From historical epics *The Birth of a Nation* (1915) and *The Charge of the Light Brigade* (1936) to a film about crises in the daily lives of three women, *The Hours* (2002), narrative movies have been prized as both public and private histories, as records of celebrated events, personal memories, and daily routines. In their reflections of time, change, and loss, film narratives show viewers how to make time meaningful.

To Shape Memory and to Make History

Film narratives organize human experience, through moving images and sounds, in order to describe how individuals or communities change with time. Film, video, and computer narratives today saturate our lives with flashes of insight or events repeated again and again from different angles and at different speeds. As such, film narratives create two prominent values that suggest why they are so important to us:

1. Narratives describe the different temporal experiences of individuals.
2. Narratives reflect and reveal the shapes and patterns of larger social histories (of nations, communities, and cultures).

The first value, that *film narratives describe individual temporal experiences,* suggests how stories aim to re-create recognizable patterns of personal experience that convincingly describe our lives or the real lives of other individuals. Film narratives thus commonly portray the changes in a day, a year, or the life of a character or community. Such narratives are not necessarily actual real-time experiences (although such is the case in the two hours of *Cleo from 5 to 7*). However, they do aim to approximate the patterns through which different individuals experience and shape time: time as endurance, time as growth, time as loss, and so on. In *Hoosiers* (1986), which concentrates on the rise of a basketball coach, narrative time becomes about anticipation and action, the tense excitement summarized by a championship basketball game. In the Dutch film *Antonia's Line* (1995), time becomes about

Figure 6.46 *Antonia's Line* (1995). Time becomes the generational bond between mothers and daughters.

women remembering and sharing experiences as their family expands in the years after World War II, about the generational bonds of the love between mothers and daughters **[Figure 6.46]**.

The second value, that *film narratives reflect and reveal social history,* suggests that narratives order the various dimensions of time—past, present, and future events—in ways that are similar to models of history used by nations or other communities. Consequently, narratives create public perceptions of those histories and ways of understanding them. The extent to which narratives and public histories are bound together can be seen by noting how many historical events—such as the Civil War and World War II—become the subject for narrative films. But narrative films also can reveal public history in smaller events, where personal crisis or success becomes representative of a larger national or world history. A movie about J. Robert Oppenheimer and the Los Alamos detonation of July 16, 1945, Roland Joffé's *Fat Man and Little Boy* (1989) is a grippingly constructed account of the start of the U.S. atomic age. The tale of a heroic African American regiment, *Glory* (1989) **[Figure 6.47]** tells a history of the Civil War left out of

Figure 6.47 *Glory* (1989). A different narrative and different history.

such other narratives as *The Birth of a Nation* and *Gone with the Wind*. In these cases, film narratives are about cultural origins, historical losses, and national myths.

Two Traditions: Classical and Alternative Narratives

Based on how movies engage or re-create narrative values, two prominent traditions of narrative movies have emerged: classical film narrative and alternative film narrative. Usually presenting a close relationship between individual lives and social history, **classical film narratives**

■ are centered on one or more central characters who propel the plot with a cause-and-effect logic (whereby an action generates a reaction)
■ develop plots with linear chronologies directed at certain goals (even when flashbacks are integrated into that linearity)
■ employ an omniscient or a restricted narration that suggests some degree of realism

Classical narrative often appears as a three-part structure: (1) the presentation of a situation or a circumstance; (2) the disruption of that situation, often as a crisis or confrontation; and (3) the resolution of that disruption. Its narrative point of view is usually objective and realistic, including most information necessary to understand the characters and their world.

Since the 1910s, the U.S. **classical Hollywood narrative** has been the most visible and dominant form of classical narrative, but there have been many historical and cultural variations on this narrative model. Both the 1925 and 1959 *Ben-Hur* films develop their plots around the heroic motivations of the title character and follow his struggles and triumphs as a former citizen who becomes a slave, rebel, and gladiator, fighting against the cruelties of the Roman Empire. Both movies spent inordinate amounts of money on large casts of characters and on details and locations that attempt to seem as realistic as possible. Yet even if both these Hollywood films can be classified as classical narratives, they can also be distinguished by their variations on this narrative formulas. Besides some differences in the details of the story, the first version attends more to grand spectacles (such as the sea battles) and places greater emphasis on the plight of the Jews as a social group; the second version concentrates significantly more on the individual drama of Charlton Heston as Ben-Hur, on his search to find his lost family, and on Christian salvation through personal faith [**Figure 6.48**].

Figure 6.48 *Ben-Hur* (1959). A classical vision of history.

Two important variations on the classical Hollywood narrative tradition are the **classical European narrative,** films made in Europe since 1910 and flourishing in the 1930s and 1940s (see pp. 367–71), and the **postclassical narrative,** a global body of films that began to appear after World War II and that strained but maintained the classical formula for coherent characters and plots. This latter tradition remains visible to the present day (see pp. 357–64). Although it is difficult to offer broad or definitive models for these two classical narratives, the European model tends to situate the story in large and varied social contexts that dilute the singularity of a central protagonist and is usually less action-oriented than its U.S. counterpart. Conversely, the postclassical model frequently undermines the power of a protagonist to control and drive the narrative forward in a clear direction. Thus, in Jean Renoir's *Rules of the Game* (1939), a diverse milieu of many classes and social types (from servants to aristocrats) interact on a large estate to create a narrative that seems less like a single plot than a collage of many stories about sexual escapades and bankrupt social mores. An exchange between two characters summarizes the range of this satiric narrative: one character exclaims "Stop this farce!" and the other replies, "Which one?" [Figure 6.49]. As a postclassical narrative, Martin Scorsese's *Taxi Driver* (1976) works with a plot much like that of *The Searchers*, but in Travis Bickle's strange quest to rescue a New York City prostitute from her pimp, he wanders with even less direction, identity, and control than his predecessor, Ethan; Bickle, a dark hero, becomes lost in his own fantasies, erupting into senseless violence and seemingly bent on his own destruction [Figure 6.50].

Figure 6.49 *Rules of the Game* (1939). The European tradition of classical narrative.

Figure 6.50 *Taxi Driver* (1976). The postclassical narrative.

Although **alternative film narratives** also tell stories, their narrative constructions often dramatize the disjunction between how individuals live their lives according to personal temporal patterns and how those patterns conflict with those of the social history that intersects with their lives. More radical departures from both classical and postclassical models, these narratives

- deviate from or challenge the linearity of the narrative
- undermine the centrality of a main character
- question the objective realism of classical narration

Most visible in foreign and independent film cultures, these movies tell stories while also revealing information or perspectives traditionally excluded from classical narratives in order to unsettle audience expectations, provoke new thinking, or differentiate themselves from more common narrative structures (see pp. 372–04 and 403–08).

Both the predominance and motivational control of characters in moving a plot come into question with alternative films. Instead of the one or two central characters we see in classical narratives, alternative films may

Figure 6.51 *A Taste of Cherry* (1997). Vague motivations and random encounters.

Figure 6.52 *Rashomon* (1950). Four narratives within one film.

Figure 6.53 *Pather Panchali* (1955). The shape of an Indian narrative.

put a multitude of characters into play, their stories perhaps not even connected. In Jean-Luc Godard's *La Chinoise* (1967), the narrative shifts among three young people—a student, an economist, a philosopher—whose tales appear like a series of debates about politics and revolution in the streets of Paris. A visually stunning film, Abbas Kiarostami's *A Taste of Cherry* (1997) contains only the shadow of a story and plot: a middle-aged Mr. Badii wishes to commit suicide for no clear reason; after a series of random encounters and requests, his fate remains uncertain at the conclusion **[Figure 6.51]**. Freed of the determining motivations of classical characters, the plots of alternative film narratives tend to break apart, omit links in a cause-and-effect logic, or proliferate plot lines well beyond the classical parallel plot. As an extreme example, Antonioni's *Red Desert* (1964) seems to completely abandon its original story midway through the film when it becomes clear that its protagonist, Giuliana, is too alienated and unmotivated to live her life with a beginning, middle, and end.

Many kinds of alternative film narratives question, in various ways, the classical narrative assumptions about an objective narrational point of view and about the power of a narrative to reflect universally true experiences. In *Rashomon* (1950), four people, including the ghost of a dead man, recount a tale of robbery, murder, and rape four different ways, as four different narratives **[Figure 6.52]**. Ultimately, the group that hears these tales (as the frame of the narrative) realizes that it is impossible to know the true story.

By employing one or more of their defining characteristics, alternative film narratives have also fostered more specific cultural variations and traditions, including non-Western narratives and new-wave narratives. (With both these traditions, it should be noted, more state support and less commercial pressure have often abetted the experimentation with alternative narrative forms.) Alternative **non-Western narratives,** such as those found in the cinema of Japan, Iran, and China, swerve from classical narrative by drawing on indigenous forms of storytelling with culturally distinctive themes, characters, plots, and narrative points of view. Indian filmmaker Satyajit Ray, for example, adapts a famous work of Bengali fiction for his 1955 *Pather Panchali*, the story of a boy named Apu and his impoverished family; although heavily influenced by European narrative films, such as Renoir's *The River* (1951), Ray's film is suffused with the native tones, symbols, and slow-paced plot of the original novel, as it rediscovers Indian history from inside India [**Figure 6.53**]. The tradition of **new-wave narratives** describes the proliferation of narrative forms that have appeared around the world since the 1950s; often experimental and disorienting, these narratives interrogate the political assumptions of classical narratives by overturning their formal assumptions. Italian new-wave director Bernardo Bertolucci's *The Conformist* (1970) is indicative: it creates a sensually vague and dreamy landscape where reality and nightmares overlap; through the mixed-up motivations of its central character, Marcelo Clerici, the film explores the historical roots of Italian fascism, a viciously decadent world of sex and politics rarely depicted in the histories of classical narrative [**Figure 6.54**].

Both these broad categories contain many narrative cultures that differ sharply from each other and both suggest not so much a complete opposition to classical narrative as much as a dialogue with that tradition. In this context, Indian film narratives are very different from African film narratives and the new waves of Greece and Spain represent divergent issues and narrative strategies. All, however, might be said to confront, in one way or another, the classical narrative paradigm.

Figure 6.54 *The Conformist* (1970). Narrative disorientation of a fascist's history.

VIEWING CUES: Film Narrative Tradition and Values

- For the film you will watch next in class, examine the values that are implicitly or explicitly presented in the narrative. Is this film primarily about an individual's history or a public history? If it depicts an individual's history, what does the narrative say about the meaning of time and change in the lives of the characters? If it is a public history, what events are presented as most important? How are different events linked to suggest a meaningful pattern for that community? Is the film about the origin of the community or about an overlooked piece of its history?

- Consider the traditions that this film's narrative seems closest to. Would you describe this film as a classical Hollywood narrative, a classical European narrative, or a postclassical narrative? What defines it as such? Argue why it fits the model you choose.

- If you believe this film is an example of an alternative narrative, explain why. Does it work within a non-Western or new-wave tradition? What specific features of this film define it as part of one tradition or another?

Narrative Value in *Mildred Pierce* (1945) and *Daughters of the Dust* (1991)

Certainly there are many movies that operate between the classical and alternative narrative traditions, and many other movies that draw on parts of each tradition. Although pure examples may not exist, here we will examine *Mildred Pierce* and *Daughters of the Dust* as representative of the main features of these two traditions. They offer decidedly different ways to remember experiences and conceive of history.

Figure 6.55 *Mildred Pierce* (1945). A classical heroine with fatal ambitions.

Figure 6.56 *Mildred Pierce* (1945). A private life recovered as public.

Very much a part of the classical movie tradition, the narrative of Michael Curtiz's *Mildred Pierce* is an extended flashback covering many years—from Mildred's troubled marriage and divorce, her rise as a self-sufficient and enterprising businesswoman, and her disastrous affair with the playboy Monty. After the opening murder and the accusation of Mildred (its narrative frame), the narrative returns to her humble beginnings with two daughters and an irritating husband who soon divorces her. Left on her own, Mildred works determinedly to become a financial success and support her daughters [Figure 6.55]. Despite her material triumphs, her youngest daughter, Kay, dies tragically and her other daughter, Veda, rejects her when that daughter falls in love with Mildred's lover, Monty. The temporal and linear progressions in Mildred's material life are thus ironically offset in the narrative by her loss along the way of her emotional and spiritual life.

In *Mildred Pierce* we find all three cornerstones of classical film form. The title character, through her need and determination to survive and succeed, drives the main story. The narrative uses a flashback frame that, after the opening murder, proceeds linearly, from Mildred's life as an obsequious housewife to a wealthy and vivacious socialite to her final sad awareness of the catastrophe of life. Finally, the restricted narration follows her development as an objective record of those past events.

Set in the 1940s with little mention of World War II, *Mildred Pierce* is not a narrative located explicitly in public history, yet it is a historical tale that visibly embraces a crisis in the public narrative of America. While focused on Mildred's personal confusion, the film delineates a critical period in U.S. history. In the years after World War II, the U.S. nuclear family would come under intense pressure as independent women with more freedom and power required changing social structures. *Mildred Pierce* describes this public history in terms of personal experience, but like other classical narratives, the events, persons, and logic of Mildred's story reflect a national story in which a new politics of gender must be admitted and then recuperated into a tradition centered on the patriarchal family. *Mildred Pierce* aims directly at the recuperation of the private life (of Mildred) into a patriarchal public history (of the law, the community, and the nation): Mildred presumably recognizes the error of her independence and ambition and, through the guidance of the police, is restored to her ex-husband [Figure 6.56].

A very different kind of narrative, Julie Dash's *Daughters of the Dust* recounts a period of a few days in 1902, when an African American community prepares to move from Ibo Landing, an island off the coast of South Carolina, to settle in the North. The members of the Peazant family meld into a community whose place in time oscillates between their memories of their African heritage (as a kind of cyclical history) and their anticipation of a future on the U.S. mainland (where time progresses in a linear fashion) [Figure 6.57]. *Daughters of the Dust* avoids concentrating on the motivations of a single character. Instead it drifts among the perspectives of many members of the Peazant family—Nana the grandmother, Haagar, Viola, Yellow Mary, the troubled married couple Eula and Eli, and even their unborn child.

Figure 6.57 *Daughters of the Dust* (1991). Narrative time as cyclical.

For many viewers, the difficulty of following this film is related to its nontraditional narrative, which does not move its characters forward in the usual sense but instead creates individuals who live in a time that seems more about communal rhythms than personal progress, where the distinction between private and public life makes little sense [Figure 6.58]. The plot of *Daughters of the Dust* is structured as a denial of the dramatic turn of events that organizes the three-part movement of a classical plot. A fundamental question or problem appears quietly at the beginning of the film: will the Peazant family's move to the U.S. mainland remove them from their roots and African heritage? Yet the film is more about presentation and reflection than about any drama or crisis emerging from that question. Eventually, that question may be answered when the characters move to the mainland where they, presumably, will be recast in a narrative more like that of *Mildred Pierce*. But for now, in this narrative, they and the film embrace different temporal values.

In *Daughters of the Dust*, the shifting voices and perspectives of the narration have little interest in a unified or objective

Figure 6.58 *Daughters of the Dust* (1991). Rhythmically moving communities where past and present intersect.

Figure 6.59 *Daughters of the Dust* (1991). A story narrated through many voices.

perspective on events **[Figure 6.59]**. Besides voiceovers by Nana and Eula, the narrational point of view appears through Unborn Child, a mysterious figure who is usually invisible to the other characters and who narrates as the voice of the future. Interweaving different subjective voices and experiences, the film's narration disperses time into the communal space of its island world, an orchestration of nonlinear rhythms. Certainly, a public history is being mapped in this alternative film, but it is one commonly ignored by most other American narratives and classical films. Especially with its explicit reflections on the slave trade that once passed through Ibo Island, *Daughters of the Dust* maps part of African American history, perhaps best told through the wandering narrative patterns inherited from the traditions and styles of African storytellers.

CRITICAL VOICES: MANTHIA DIAWARA ON RACE IN NARRATIVE FILM

Manthia Diawara is among a growing number of film scholars concerned with how ethnic and racial differences shape films and our responses to them. In the following passage from *Black American Cinema* (1993), he argues that the presence of characters of different races does not necessarily guarantee or adequately reflect the significance of those characters; rather, the narrative construction of time and space distinguishes recent African American films from the classical Hollywood narrative. For Diawara, these narrative organizations are the most important determinants of the social and ideological world in which characters live.

The way in which a filmmaker selects a location and organizes that location in front of the camera is generally referred to in film studies as mise-en-scène. Spatial narration in classical cinema makes sense through a hierarchical disposition of objects on the screen. Thus space is related to power and powerlessness, in so far as those who occupy the center of the screen are usually more powerful than those situated in the background or completely absent from the screen. . . . When Black people are absent from the screen they read it as a symbol of their absence from the America constructed by Hollywood. When they are present on the screen, they are less powerful and less virtuous than the White man who usually occupies the center. Hollywood films have regularly tried to resolve this dilemma, either through token or symbolic representations of Blacks where they are absent— for instance, the mad Black scientist in *Terminator 2;* or through a substitution of less virtuous Blacks by positive images of Blacks—for instance, *Grand Canyon* or *The Cosby Show*. But it seems to me that neither symbolic representations nor positive images sufficiently address the specificity of Black

1

ways of life, and how they might enter in relation to other Americans on the Hollywood screen. Symbolic representation and positive images serve the function of plotting Black people in White space and White power, keeping the real contours of the Black community outside Hollywood.

The construction of time is similarly problematic in the classical narra-   2
tive. White men drive time from the East to the West, conquering wilderness and removing obstacles out of time's way. Thus the "once upon a time" which begins every story in Hollywood also posits an initial obstacle in front of a White person who has to remove it in order for the story to continue, and for the conquest ideology of Whiteness to prevail. The concept of beginning, middle, and end, in itself, is universal to storytelling. The difference here is that Hollywood is only interested in White people's stories (White times), and Black people enter these times mostly as obstacles to their progress, or as supporting casts for the main White characters. "Once upon a time" is a traditional storytelling device which the storyteller uses to evoke the origin of a people, their ways of life, and the role of the individual in a society. The notion of *rite de passage* is a useful concept for describing the individual's separation from or incorporation into a social time. The classical narrative in cinema adheres to this basic ideological formula in order to tell White people's stories in Hollywood. It seems that White times in Hollywood have no effect on Black people and their communities: whether they play the role of a negative or a positive stereotype, Black people neither grow nor change in the Hollywood stories. Because there is a dearth of Black people's stories in Hollywood that do not revolve around White times, television series such as *Roots*, and films such as *Do the Right Thing*, which situate spectators from the perspective of a Black "once upon a time," are taken out of proportion, celebrated by Blacks as authentic histories, and debunked by Whites as controversial. . . .

[With films such as Bill Gunn's 1972] *Ganja and Hess*, it is easy to see   3
how important time and space are to defining the cinematic style they each extol. The preponderance of space in films such as *Ganja and Hess* reveals the hierarchies of power among the characters, but it also reveals the preoccupation of this style of Black cinema with the creation of space on the screen for Black voices, Black history, and Black culture. . . . Black films use spatial narration as a way of revealing and linking Black spaces that have been separated and suppressed by White times, and as a means of validating Black culture. In other words, spatial narration is a filmmaking of cultural restoration, a way for Black filmmakers to reconstruct history, and to posit specific ways to being Black Americans in the United States.

The emphasis on time, on the other hand, reveals the Black American as he/she engenders himself/herself amid the material conditions of every-   4
day life in American society. In films like *Sweet Sweetback* and *Boyz N the Hood*, where a linear narrative dominates, the characters are depicted in continuous activities, unlike the space-based narratives, where the past constantly interrupts the present, and repetitions and cyclicality define narration. Crucially, whereas the space-oriented narratives can be said to center Black characters on the screen, and therefore empower them, the Black-times narratives link the progress of time to Black characters and make time exist for the purpose of defining their needs and their desires. Whereas the space-based narratives are expressive and celebratory of Black culture, the time-based narratives are existentialist performances of Black people against policing, racism, and genocide.

Branigan, Edward. *Narrative Comprehension and Film*. New York: Routledge, 1992. An analytical account of the structures of narrative cinema and of how audiences learn to identify and process them.

Elsaesser, Thomas, and Adam Barker, eds. *Early Cinema: Space/Frame/Narrative*. London: British Film Institute, 1990. Representing leading British, American, and European scholars, this collection of essays explores the first twenty years of the cinema, including the exciting multitude of filmic practices and experiments that fashioned early narrative cinema.

Fell, John L. *Film and the Narrative Tradition*. Norman: University of Oklahoma Press, 1974. A collection of essays tracing the many different historical and cultural backgrounds of narrative cinema.

Kawin, Bruce F. *Mindscreen: Bergman, Godard, and First-Person Film*. Princeton: Princeton University Press, 1978. A deft and insightful study of self-conscious or reflexive narrative films, taking into account their literary heritage and philosophical/psychological underpinnings.

Turim, Maureen. *Flashbacks in Film: Memory and History*. New York: Routledge, 1989. A complex and theoretical investigation of how flashbacks have structured narratives from silent films to the present.

Other Cinematic Shapes: Documentary and Experimental Films

All current cinema is romantic. . . . Let us forget all this, and consider, if you please: a pipe—a chair—a hand—an eye—a typewriter—a hat—a foot. . . . Let us consider these things for what they can contribute to the screen for what they are—in isolation—their value enhanced by every known means.

—Fernand Léger, painter and director of *Ballet Mécanique* (1924)

KEY OBJECTIVES

Although most people know narrative films best, there are numerous other kinds of films and moving images in our culture. How are these other films different from narrative movies? What attracts us to them? How do they organize their material? What makes them popular, useful, and uniquely illuminating? Here we will describe documentary and experimental films and introduce both the features and strategies that they share and those that make them distinctive. We will examine

- how documentary and experimental films are best distinguished

- how these films employ nonfictional and non-narrative images and forms

- how documentary and experimental movies draw on historical heritages

- how and where the strategies and aims of these different kinds of films overlap

- how documentary and experimental films have become associated with cultural values and traditions

Our life experiences are, of course, not simply narrative experiences. For instance, the center of our days can be a series of unrelated impressions or snatches of conversations, while our memory of a city that we once visited may be largely a matter of the colors of buildings and the movements of crowds. However central narratives are to our lives, we also encounter the world in many other ways. We read a factual report about a political protest in the morning newspaper; we check a textbook for assistance in writing an essay for class; we admire the graphic designs of a magazine advertisement; and we watch a series of interviews about jazz trumpeter Miles Davis on television.

Although most people associate movies with stories, a large body of the films we encounter and enjoy do not tell stories or organize themselves primarily as stories. Narrative patterns can play a part in these other movies, yet these films usually minimize, disguise, or even avoid entirely such narrative features as plot and character. *The Children of Chabannes* (1999), for example, describes the gripping plight of four hundred Jewish refugee children, aged two to seventeen, protected by a small French village in the summer of 1942. Most fascinating and moving about this film, however, is not a well-crafted or intricate plot but its immediacy and realism, presented through a collage of archival footage, talking head interviews, and journal entries recited over old photographs. We witness events we have never seen before, perhaps perceiving them as unarguable facts that distinguish them from the fictional events of narrative films.

Two kinds of films whose organizations often differ significantly from narrative cinema are documentary films and experimental films. **Documentary films** present (presumably) real objects, persons, and events—from sensational news to everyday routines. **Experimental films** concentrate on or "experiment with" unconventional forms and actions—from abstract image and sound patterns to strange visionary worlds found in dreams or hallucinations. Both categories suggest important ways to think about and distinguish movies whose principal shape is not a narrative organization. Although each, strictly speaking, identifies very different kinds of film practice, we will discuss them together here because these they share many common formal strategies and, especially in recent years, have often blurred the lines that traditionally divided them.

If narrative films are about memory and the shaping of time, the experiential core of both documentary and experimental movies is **intellectual and imaginative insight,** an enlarging of what we can know, feel, and see. Certainly narratives can enlarge and intensify the world for us in these ways as well, but without the primary task of telling a story documentary and experimental movies—whether they are newsreels or abstract explorations of light and shadow—can concentrate on leading our intellectual and imaginative activities down new paths. For our purposes, intellectual insight describes how these films offer new facts and information, while imaginative insight suggests how these films urge new ways of experiencing the world through the mind and senses. Indeed, these two kinds of knowledge can often intersect in a single documentary or experimental film, offering information, ideas, and a new appreciation of the world to an audience. A movie about the rise of skateboarding in southern California, *Dogtown and Z-Boys* (2001) communicates, on the one hand, ideas and facts about the birth of a sport and the individuals who help develop it; on the other hand, it creates a poetic collage of still photos, music, and talking heads, capturing the emotional energy and visual ballet in skateboarding that many of us may not have previously appreciated **[Figure 7.1]**.

If narrative films are at the heart of commercial entertainment, documentary and experimental movies operate according to what we will call an **economics of information.** Many of the first films made in the 1890s and early 1900s, such as the traveling exhibitions and shows of Lyman H. Howe in America and Walter Haggar in England, were part of lectures, scientific presentations, or visual illustrations of the art of motion. Churches, schools, and cultural institutions supported and financially subsidized these presentations, usually in the name of intellectual, spiritual, or cultural development. In a less obvious way, many early experimental films, such as Hans Richter's abstract *Rhythmus* series (1921–1924)

Figure 7.1 *Dogtown and Z-Boys* (2001). The facts and poetry of skateboarding.

or Jean Cocteau's surreal *The Blood of a Poet* (1932), appeared as part of an art exhibition or cine-club where they developed their art in the service of "information" about motion and perspective, the activity of the unconscious, the creative process, or even spiritual awakening. Since then, documentaries and experimental films have remained, to some extent, tied to and often financially dependent on museums, government agencies, local social activists, and cultural foundations—from the Works Progress Administration (WPA) projects that funded U.S. documentaries in the 1930s to the National Endowment for the Arts (NEA) grants that support some artistic and experimental films today. Although these films often claim and sometimes deserve the title "independent films," their survival has depended on a public culture that promotes learning as a crucial part of the film experience. Outside of or on the fringes of the commercial cinema, this "other" culture of films has endured and often triumphed through every period of film history and in virtually every world culture. Here, we will explore the many ways these films have expanded how we see, listen, and think.

The Foundations of Documentary and Experimental Films

At the end of the nineteenth century, the search for empirical and spiritual truths produced new educational practices, technological tools, colonial expeditions, and secret societies as the vehicles to new experiences, pragmatic thought, and better worlds. When films first appeared in the midst of these trends around 1895, they illustrated lectures, offered cinematic portraits of famous people, and guided audiences through short movie travelogues. For many, film was not an art but a tool for exploring and explaining the physical and social world. British filmmaker Cecil Hepworth's *Explosion of a Motor Car* (1901) experiments with stop-action filming to create a humorous and gruesome explosion of a car whose passengers then fall in pieces from the sky **[Figure 7.2]**. In 1897, factual and fabricated images of the Spanish-American War attracted large audiences everywhere; in 1901, the Edison Company stunned viewers with a series of short films documenting the assassination of President William McKinley and the transition of power to President Theodore Roosevelt. Just as narrative films spring from cultural foundations and histories that preceded the cinema by centuries, so too are documentary and experimental films rooted in a long history.

Nonfiction and Non-Narrative

The cornerstones for documentary and experimental films are two key and often debated concepts: nonfiction and non-narrative. Although non-narrative has commonly been applied to both documentary and experimental films, nonfiction has been primarily associated with documentary films. As we shall see, however, some experimental films also employ nonfictional strategies and the creative relationship between non-narrative and nonfictional practices is part of what has made many films so dynamic and exciting.

Nonfiction in films refers to the (presumed) factual descriptions of actual events, persons, or places,

Figure 7.2 *Explosion of a Motor Car* (1901). Comic experiments with early cinema.

Figure 7.3 *Elizabeth* (1998). Mixing nonfiction and narrative.

rather than their fictional or invented re-creation. In most cases, facts are malleable and debatable, just as every person's image of an attractive person differs slightly. Yet a basic distinction throughout human history (and much of film history) has been the difference between the truth of facts and the questionable truth of fiction. The precariousness of this distinction has provoked heated debates throughout film history, but movie culture has nonetheless often assumed a fundamental distinction between, say, a PBS documentary about the life of Queen Elizabeth I of England and the 1998 feature film *Elizabeth*. The first film uses the accounts of scholars and historians, old paintings and artifacts, and the written accounts of her contemporaries to show the complex facts and issues in the life of one of the great women of history. The second film uses some of that same information, but constructs it as an entertaining and easily comprehensible story [Figure 7.3]. If the notion of nonfiction usually defines documentary films, it is important to recognize that it can also illuminate certain experimental films. For example, *The Man with the Movie Camera* (1929) creates a dazzling array of cinematic experiments in order to present a seemingly factual record of a Russian city. Similarly, Raoul Ruiz's *Of Great Events and Ordinary People* (1979) turns an assignment to conduct nonfictional interviews in a Paris neighborhood into a complex and humorous reflection on the impossibility of the interview process's revealing any truth or honesty.

For both documentary and experimental films, **non-narrative** indicates the organization of films in a variety of ways that eschews or de-emphasizes stories and narratives, while employing such other organizational forms as lists, repetitions, or contrasts as the organizational structure. Whether these films concentrate on abstract forms, events, objects, or individuals, they may choose—rather than to develop a story—to create a visual list (of objects found in a old house, for instance), to repeat a single image as an organizing

Figure 7.4 *Koyaanisqatsi* (1983). Non-narrative images.

pattern (returning to an ancient carving on the front door of that house), or to alternate between objects in a way that suggests different fundamental contrasts (contrasting the rooms, clothing, and tools used by the men and the women in that house). A non-narrative movie may certainly embed stories within its presiding organization, but those stories usually become secondary to the non-narrative pattern. In *Koyaanisqatsi* (1983), slow-motion and time-lapse photography capture the open vistas of an American landscape and their destruction against the drifting tones of Philip Glass's music: pristine fields and mountains, rusty towns, and garbage-strewn highways [Figure 7.4]. Through these images one may detect traces of a story about the collapse of America in what the Hopi Indian title declares is "a life out of balance," but that simple and vague narrative is not nearly as powerful as the emotional force of the film's accumulating repetitions and contrasts. Diane Keaton's *Heaven* (1987) intersperses clips from old movies with angels and other images of heaven and presents a litany of faces and voices to answer such questions as "Does heaven exist?" and "Is there sex in heaven?" Although we may sense a religious mystery tale behind these questions and answers, this movie is better understood as a playful list of unpredictable reactions to the possibility of a life hereafter.

Nonfiction and non-narrative clearly suggest distinctive ways of seeing the world. Although they often overlap in both documentary and experimental films, one form of presentation does not necessarily imply the other. A non-narrative film may be entirely or partly fictional, as when a pseudo-documentary movie pretends to be a scientific report about an undiscovered people. Conversely, a nonfiction film can be constructed as a narrative, as in a film about Eleanor Roosevelt that tells the story of her life from old photos, home movies, and newsreel film footage. Complicating these distinctions, is the fact that both kinds of practices can become less a function of the intentions of the film than of our perception of them; what may seem nonfictional or non-narrative in one context may not seem so in another. For many Germans in 1934, Leni Riefenstahl's *Triumph of the Will* was a nonfictional account of Adolf Hitler's public popularity and power, filmed at a Nazi Party congress [Figure 7.5]. For most contemporary viewers, however, it looks like a highly manipulative work of fictional propaganda. Likewise, for some viewers, Alain Resnais's *Last Year at Marienbad* (1961) seems primarily a non-narrative study in the structural repetition and geometry of the rooms, hallways, and gardens of a baroque estate; for others, the film contains an elusive plot about a woman and a man's efforts to seduce her. Keeping in mind the different meanings of nonfiction and non-narrative and how they can historically shift should, however, only make them more useful in judging the strategies of a particular documentary or experimental movie as part of changing cultural contexts.

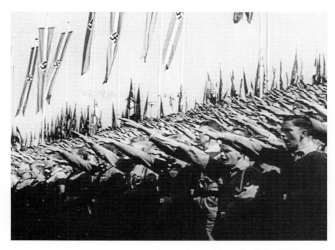

Figure 7.5 *Triumph of the Will* (1934). Fictional propaganda in nonfictional form.

A Short History of Documentary and Experimental Film Practices

Errol Morris's film portrait *Mr. Death: The Rise and Fall of Fred A. Leuchter, Jr.* (1999) is an extraordinary gathering of the insights and energies that have propelled documentary and experimental film practices. Its nominal subject is Fred Leuchter, an inventor/engineer/investigator who establishes his dubious reputation by refurbishing and modernizing electric-chair equipment for the Massachusetts penal system [Figure 7.6]. Against this background, most of the film describes Leuchter's enlistment by neo-Nazis who draw Leuchter and his pseudo-scientific expertise into a plan to prove that the Holocaust did not take place, specifically at the concentration camp in Auschwitz. With techniques that seem to alternate between news reportage and dreamscape, this film creates a portrait of an individual absurdly disengaged from history and social space; in doing so, it draws on a long history of scientific writings, literary essays, photographic portraits, and surrealistic paintings.

Figure 7.6 *Mr. Death: The Rise and Fall of Fred A. Leuchter, Jr.* (1999). Alternating between news reports and dreamscapes.

Just as narrative films have a complex history of different cultural activities and strategies, so do documentary and experimental films. As with narrative, these practices and their purposes have varied in different cultures and at different points in history. Since human beings began to think about and organize the world, documentary and experimental practices have aimed to

- accurately portray facts and realities
- communicate new knowledge and information
- alter ways of seeing and thinking

From ancient government records to family videotapes, from charts of new territories to school textbooks, from religious tracts to abstract paintings, we have described and learned about the world in ways that stories cannot fully explore. The journals describing Marco Polo's travels through China, the early nineteenth-century treatise by Sir Humphry Davy on the discovery of electricity, and the Cubist painting *Guernica* by Pablo Picasso on war in Spain have all, in their own ways, recorded a lost world, offered new ideas, or changed how we see society.

Indeed, documentary and experimental practices may offer more possibilities and variations than narrative practices do: oral practices such as sermons, political speeches, and academic lectures; visual practices such as maps, photographs, and paintings; musical practices such as folk songs and symphonies; and written practices such as letters, diaries, poems, scientific treatises, and newspaper reports. Sermons, guides to social behavior, and instruction manuals range from oral addresses to visual descriptions. With the late-sixteenth-century writings of Michel de Montaigne, the essay form appeared as a new kind of writing, addressing personal and everyday subjects as a fragmented commentary on life and ideas. Throughout the eighteenth and nineteenth centuries, journalism developed as a public forum for expressing ideas, announcing events, and recording daily happenings around town.

By the end of the eighteenth century, the rationality of science and technology was poised to offer unlimited powers for people to improve what they knew and how they used that knowledge to change society. The industrial revolution was underway, offering economic and material growth; railroads made the world smaller; and more efficient printing presses made much of that world more literate. Mary Wollstonecraft and Thomas Malthus wrote books, pamphlets, and lengthy essays describing the current state of society and insisting on practical ways that social science could improve the lives of colonized people, especially women and the poor. In 1851, in one of the most famous gatherings of scientific truths and social entertainments, the Crystal Palace in London demonstrated much of the century's scientific developments in an entertaining exhibition of lectures, inventions, and visual demonstrations.

As the middle class moved to the center of Western societies, people demanded more information about the world. Photography and photojournalism, evolving from new printing and lithographic technologies, became widespread and popular ways to record and comment on events. Unlike narrative practices, such as realistic novels or short stories, photojournalism presented virtually instantaneous and seemingly uncontestable records, factual representations of people and events frozen in time. One of the most dramatic combinations of social science and photography, Jacob Riis's *How the Other Half Lives* (1890) is part lecture, part photoessay; its pseudo-scientific sermon exposes and condemns living conditions in New York City's tenement housing.

Some resisted the scientific and utilitarian bias of these documentary trends. In the first half of the nineteenth century, Percy Bysshe Shelley proclaimed that poets were the unacknowledged legislators of the world. In the second half, Walter Pater argued for the power of art, in and of itself, to reveal the importance of the human imagination and create experiences unavailable in the practical world of commerce and science: "To burn always with this hard, gemlike flame, to maintain this ecstasy," he claimed of art and poetry, "is success in life." For those committed to these aesthetic positions, new kinds of paintings—from the other-worldly visions of Pre-Raphaelites like Dante Gabriel Rossetti to the glimmering impressionist paintings of Claude Monet—turned their attention away from the facts of the world to the states of mind and visual feelings that could be captured in poems and on canvas. At stake here was clearly not practical knowledge but sensibility and creativity.

Through the course of the twentieth century, these precursors of documentary and experimental practices developed according to both separate and overlapping film histories and traditions. In their preoccupation with film as a unique art form and as a powerful tool for revealing the world, respectively, the avant-garde film movements in France in the 1920s (see pp. 369–70) and the British social documentaries of the 1930s both grew out of these earlier histories. Even more so than other film practices, the introduction of **optical sound recording** in 1927 catapulted documentary films forward, as it provided that crucial dimension whereby newsreels, documentaries, and propaganda films could add educative or social commentary to accompany their images. In the 1950s, minor revolutions in both practices followed the technological development of lightweight, **handheld cameras** (such as the Arriflex models) allowing filmmakers a new kind of spontaneity and personal inventiveness. The rise of television in the 1950s brought an important expansion of documentaries through that medium (most famously identified with the work of television journalist Edward R. Murrow), just as video and digital video production continue to promise that kind of creative control for both documentary and experimental practices at the beginning of the twenty-first century.

Finally, **public and private institutional support** has played a central role in documentary and experimental practices. Examples include the various cine-clubs in the United States and Europe, New York City's Film and Photo League and President Roosevelt's Resettlement Administration in the 1930s, the National Film Board of Canada since the 1940s, and numerous public, or state-run, television networks in more recent decades (such as the American PBS, the British Broadcasting Corporation, and the German ZDF). Indeed, the histories of documentary and experimental film can never really be divorced from these critical sources of funding and distribution.

Although *Mr. Death* and other contemporary documentary or experimental films might seem far from these earlier historical traditions, in fact they are not. *Mr. Death* is a moving portrait, part of the heritage of portraits handed down from painting and photography. It analyzes and, in an oblique manner, argues the facts of a historical truth—just as an essay on social science does. With its strange, surreal images, the film even reminds us that the darkest and most disturbing of historical realities can sometimes appear most honestly as the imaginary projection of a fragile mind. Funded in part by television backers at England's Channel Four Films and the U.S. Independent Film Channel, *Mr. Death* demonstrates, in short, that even the most daring and original non-narrative and nonfiction films are part of a long history of complex strategies.

Nonfiction and Non-Narrative in *Man of Aran* (1934) and *Meshes of the Afternoon* (1943)

Robert Flaherty's documentary film *Man of Aran* and Maya Deren's experimental film *Meshes of the Afternoon* are early, incisive examples of how such films employ, albeit in different ways, both nonfictional and non-narrative practices. *Man of Aran,* a documentary about a small community living on islands off western Ireland, does not identify the characters or explain their motivations; instead, it lists and describes the activities that make up their daily lives and records the hardships of living on a barren, isolated island. The members of this seemingly primitive community cart soil to grow potatoes on their rocky plots and struggle against the ferocious sea to fish and survive [Figure 7.7]. In an important sense, the film is a historical and cultural record: it documents the routines of their existence without the drama of a narrative beginning, climax, or conclusion. Adding to the distant atmosphere of a place that seems newly discovered by this film, the characters are not named and the force of the sea constantly overwhelms their meager attempts to create order and meaning in their lives. Well beyond learning about the customs of a distant way of life, audiences find in *Man of Aran* a dignity of living far removed from common experience and knowledge.

Meshes of the Afternoon is not about distantly real places and cultures; it is about the near but mysterious reality of our dream worlds and unarticulated feelings. A woman in black enters a house and falls asleep in a chair. After images of her sleeping eyes alternate with a window to the outside world, we see keys, knives, and mirrors begin to take on a life of their own [Figure 7.8]; objects suddenly disappear and scenes are repeated without explanation. Following the laws not of reality but of the imagination, the film transforms the outside world into a visionary exploration of an internal world, becoming

Figure 7.7 *Man of Aran* (1934). The hard realities of life on an isolated island.

a puzzle of shapes and lines that never come completely together as a clear picture. From the perspective of the film, this internal world of the unconscious mind may be less recognizable than fishermen and boats, but no less factual than those wild islands off the coast of Ireland. Though not practical information, we learn something about the less predictable laws of the unconscious.

Both these films are challenging because stories and narratives are not their primary organizational feature. Instead, they mostly accumulate, repeat, and contrast images as their main form of organization. In *Man of Aran,* the facts of the brutal lifestyle on the island are ordered as a list of tasks that

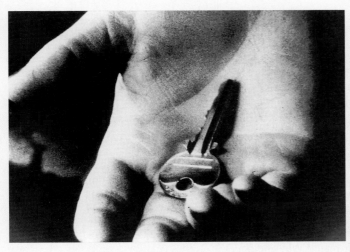

Figure 7.8 *Meshes of the Afternoon* (1943). The mysterious realities of a dream world.

Figure 7.9 *Meshes of the Afternoon* (1943). The surfacing face of repressed desire?

contrast human activities with natural forces: preparing meals, planting a garden, and repairing fishing nets alternate with images of crashing waves, barren rock coasts, and empty horizons. Although in *Meshes of the Afternoon* the organization is less clear, the images and objects can be grouped according to patterns that contrast interiors and exteriors, punctuated by the repetition of certain images, such as windows, beds, mirrors, keys, and the knife.

Although they are subsumed under these alternative organizational patterns, traces of fiction and narrative are still visible in both films. In *Man of Aran,* some situations are fabricated, such as the episode in which the men are nearly lost at sea in the hunt for a basking shark (an activity that was part of life two generations earlier but that, in 1934, no longer took place on the Aran Islands); the episode thus relies on the dramatic suspense that drives any good adventure story. *Meshes of the Afternoon* likewise suggests a story; one about a woman's repressed desires, fears, and struggle to escape through the work of this dream film **[Figure 7.9]**. When one of the figures of the woman approaches her sleeping double with a dagger in her hand, each of the five different steps she takes is placed in a space that moves from outside to inside: a step by the ocean, another on the earth, the next on grass, the fourth on the pavement outside the house, and the last on the rug inside the room. As we discussed in Chapter 4, this editing transforms space and time. Later events reveal the threat of violence to be connected to the appearance of a mysterious man.

However innovative and distinctive these two films are, they also remind us of their cultural heritage. *Man of Aran* adapts the tradition of the travel essay or travelogue, found in the works of writers from Henry James to Bruce Chatwin. While James describes the sights and sounds of his visits to Venice and Chatwin his encounters in Patagonia, Flaherty's film shows us a culture on the far reaches of modern civilization. Similarly, in *Meshes of the Afternoon,* we see a history of poetry and visionary painting that aims to transform reality through the interior power of the imagination and thereby reveal the facts of that interior world. Like William Blake's illustrated poems about the dark side of the imagination or Odilon Redon's pictorial voyages into the subconscious, Deren's film explores the complex spaces of desire and fantasy.

VIEWING CUES: Nonfiction and Non-narrative

- Is the film you have just seen in class best described as nonfiction or non-narrative? Does one of these categories seem more appropriate to the film than the other? Why or why not, and for what purpose?

- If it is primarily a nonfiction film, describe three facts or realities that are among its primary focus. Does the film aim to make you see these realities in new ways? What specific information or knowledge is the film trying to communicate?

- If it is primarily a non-narrative film, describe one or two of its non-narrative forms and patterns. What is the film trying to communicate through the presentation of those patterns?

- Look into the film's historical background: Would it have been viewed differently at the time it was made? Why and how?

- What historical precedents might explain the strategies used in this film? Scientific treatises? Essays? News reports? Abstract art? Does aligning the film with one or more historical precedents shed light on its aims? Explain.

Expositions, Imaginings, and Rhetorics: Formal Strategies in Documentary and Experimental Films

In the first quarter of the twentieth century, documentary and experimental films were overshadowed by narrative cinema. During this period, short cinematic portraits of famous people, such as *Joan of Arc* (1895), began to turn into longer narratives, from Alice Guy Blaché's *The Life of Christ* (1906) to Louis Mercanton's *Queen Elizabeth* (1912). Since that time, the fringe status of documentary and experimental cinema has been both a cultural disadvantage and an advantage, limiting the commercial possibilities and audiences for these kinds of film but also allowing a great deal of freedom and creativity. Whereas narrative films explored different techniques for telling stories, documentary and experimental movies developed just as vigorously in other directions: from Émile Cohl's 1910 *Automatic Moving Company*, in which household items like spoons magically pack themselves away, to Frederick Wiseman's 1969 exposé of U.S. education in *High School*, these films have developed an array of complex strategies of their own to portray the secret fantasies of individuals or reveal realities hidden in the corners of history.

Elements of Science and Art

Narrative films might be said to merge science and art, as they shape the material realities of life into imaginative histories. Traditionally, however, documentary and experimental films have emphasized one or the other, with documentaries concentrating on and developing a scientific and materialist approach to life and experimental films focusing on an artistic and imaginative approach. A narrative film might tell the story of a young girl in Thailand longing to leave an isolated island and describe her adventurous escape to Bangkok. A documentary film, in contrast, might examine the details of her daily chores, interspersed with interviews in which she explains her frustrations and tells of her hopes and wishes for another life. Finally, a daring experimental film might transform the island into a fantasy landscape in which, as the girl walks along the shore, she unexpectedly takes flight in the form of a seagull whose acrobatic movements turn the gray rocks into brilliant colors. While the narrative film relies on specific patterns that organize a plot around the actions and motivations of the girl, the documentary and experimental versions represent her through strategies and forms that resemble scientific and artistic methods. One deciphers her according to a number of characteristics and behaviors; the other re-creates her emotions as metaphors and symbols. Portrayed through these various strategies, the girl may be the same girl, but our experience of the character is that of three very different people.

Documentaries are not always scientific investigations; nor are experimental films always artistic expressions. Yet, however their borders may shift, we can identify two formal strategies available to both documentary and experimental movies: **expositional practices,** which show or describe experiences according to a certain arrangement, logic, or order, and **imaginative practices,** which present experiences according to inventive and creative organizations that commonly defy realistic or rational logic. These strategies also appear in narrative films, but in documentary and experimental films they become the central, rather than a subsidiary, organizational form. In fact, some documentary and experimental movies use both practices in different proportions; here we will isolate their distinctive characteristics as they might appear in different kinds of films or as they might be orchestrated through a single film. We will then describe how these formal practices, operating alone or together, are often presented through a presiding point of view or rhetorical position.

Expositional Practices

Both documentary and experimental films use expositional strategies to present information or perspectives without the temporal logic of narrative and with little explicit explanation or commentary. These are movies that observe the facts of life from a distance and organize their observations as objectively as possible or to suggest some definition of the subject through the exposition itself. Three common forms of exposition are cumulative, contrastive, and developmental exposition.

Cumulative exposition accumulates a catalog of images or sounds throughout the course of the film. It may be a simple series with no recognizable logic connecting the images. Joris Iven's *Rain* (1929) thus presents images from a single rainstorm, showing the rain falling in a multitude of different ways and from many different angles. We do not sense that we are watching this downpour from beginning to end; rather, we see this rain as the accumulation of its seemingly infinite variety of shapes, movements, and textures. Although for most of us rain is a general, commonplace phenomenon, this film dissects and collects it as a collage of textures. Part documentary and part experimental film, *Thirty-Two Short Films about Glenn Gould* (1993) describes, as the title suggests, a series of performances and moving snapshots of the renowned pianist Glenn Gould. Although some viewers may expect a kind of biography of Gould, the film intentionally fragments his life into numerical episodes focused on his playing, on his acquaintances

Figure 7.10 *Thirty-Two Short Films about Glenn Gould* (1993). A portrait as a series of performances.

discussing him, and on reenactments of moments in his life [**Figure 7.10**]. There is finally little story here, only a series of intense glimpses of a man whose genius has made him notoriously evasive.

A variation on cumulative exposition, **contrastive exposition** organizes its presentation as a series of contrasts or oppositions meant to indicate the different points of view on its subject. Thus, a film may alternate between images of war and peace or between contrasting skylines of different cities. Sometimes, these contrasts may be evaluative, distinguishing positive and negative events. At other times, contrastive exposition may suggest a more complicated relationship between objects or individuals. Among the most ambitious versions of this technique is a group of films by Michael Apted, beginning with his documentary *7 Up* (1963) and followed by successive films made every seven years; the films track the changing attitudes and social situations of a group of children as they grow into the adults of *42 Up* (1998) [**Figure 7.11**]. With a new film appearing every seven years, these films contrast not only the differences between developing individuals in terms of class, gender, and family life but also the differences in their changing outlooks as they grow older.

Developmental exposition presents places, objects, individuals, or experiences through a pattern or development with a specific non-narrative logic or structure. For example, an individual or object may be presented according to a pattern that proceeds from small to large, as part of a developmental pattern from passive to active events, or as developing from the physical to the spiritual. Kenneth Anger's experimental *Scorpio Rising* (1964) can be considered an expositional film that presents a series of stylized images of motorcycle culture. With only pop songs as background (such as the opening "Fools Rush In"), we see a series of motorcycles being assembled, young men dressing in leather and chains, and groups of bikers gathering to race or party [**Figure 7.12**]. More than a catalog, however, the logic of these images may be partly described according to the "rising" action of the movie's title as the bikes are prepared and the narcissistic young men get ready for the evening. Complicating this de-

Figure 7.11 *42 Up* (1998). Contrasting different faces through different generations.

scription are references to Nazi Germany, Marlon Brando in *The Wild One*, and comic books; fulfilling the demonic reference of the title, the film ends with flashes of racing bikes, sirens, and police lights. The exposition itself thus becomes more than a description of the surfaces of biker life, because it also describes some of the forces and directions driving the fascination with motorcycles—including homoeroticism and the dark shadows of a generation of young men embracing their own doom.

Imaginative Practices

Numerous artistic practices have influenced and shaped documentary and, especially, experimental cinema, from the linguistic forms of poetry to the graphics of abstract painting. Even films that choose a seemingly typical documentary topic can employ imaginative strategies to capture the essence of that experience: John Grierson's *Night Mail* (1936) describes the delivery

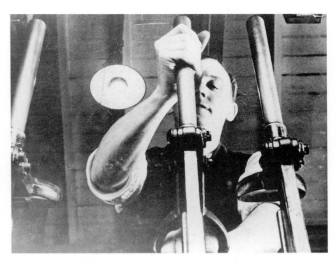

Figure 7.12 *Scorpio Rising* (1964). The development of a "rising."   **Figure 7.13** *Night Mail* (1936). A poetic re-creation of social life.

of mail across England, but through a rich style, visual and aural, the film becomes a magnificent paean to the precision and teamwork involved in what many would consider an unremarkable effort **[Figure 7.13]**. Imaginative strategies are organized creatively through metaphoric forms, symbolic forms, and structural or abstract forms.

Metaphoric forms link or associate different objects, images, events, or individuals in order to generate a new perception, emotion, or idea. In a film, this might be done by linking two different images, by indicating a connection between two objects or figures within a single frame, or by creating metaphors in the voiceover commentary as it responds to and anticipates images in the film. Juxtaposing images of workers being shot and a slaughtered bull, as Sergei Eisenstein does in his 1924 *Strike*, metaphorically describes the brutal dehumanization of those workers. Likewise, an entire film might be primarily a series of linked associations or metaphors presenting, for instance, numerous images of urban decay, Wall Street brokers, and gluttonous diners as metaphors for the dangers of a capitalist economy. Although some metaphoric practices typically appear in all movies, Derek Jarman's *Blue* (1993)—perhaps best described as an experimental autobiography—is a full metaphoric meditation on the color of the title and its chain of associations in the life of a man (the filmmaker) dying of AIDS. With only a single blue image shown, a voice drifts among the blue flashes on a retina, the blue skies from youth, the blue moods of depression, and so on. Across this meditation, blue becomes associated with the "blue funk" created by a doctor's news, the "slow blue love on a delphinium day," and "the universal love in which all men bathe."

Unlike the concrete associations that bind metaphoric images, **symbolic forms** isolate discrete objects or singular images that can generate or be assigned abstract meanings, either meanings already given those objects or images by a culture or ones created by the film itself. The symbolic significance may be spiritual (as with the Christian cross), or political (such as the flag of a particular country), or it may be tied to some other concept that has been culturally and historically grafted onto the meaning of a person, event, or thing. In consciously poetic films, such as *Meshes of the Afternoon* or *The Blood of a Poet*, mirrors become symbolic of self-knowledge or self-confrontation. Building on his earlier work with puppet films, Czech filmmaker Jirí Trnka created a remarkable modern experimental film, *The Hand*

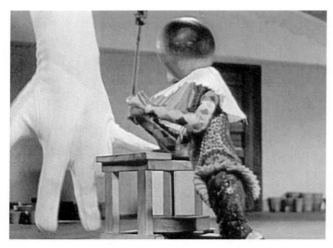

Figure 7.14 *The Hand* (1965). A symbolic figure of power and authority.

Figure 7.15 *Wavelength* (1967). The movement of a frame crossing space.

Figure 7.16 *Berlin: Symphony of a City* (1927). The structural ballet of a city.

(1965), around the symbolic weight it associates with a hand: under the domination of the single, live-action hand, a puppet struggles against the hand's demand that he make only other hands and not flowerpots **[Figure 7.14]**. In this case, the symbol suggests tyrannical power in general as well as specific totalitarian regimes in Eastern Europe.

Finally, **structural forms** and **abstract forms** foreground patterns, rhythms, movements, shapes, or colors that are abstracted from real actions and objects or created independently from recognizable figures to depict a more purely formal art. Michael Snow's *Wavelength* (1967) is a forty-five-minute image that slowly moves across a room in an extended zoom-in and ends with a close-up of a picture of ocean waves **[Figure 7.15]**. Punctuated with vague references to a murder mystery, this movie is almost a pure investigation of the vibrant textures of space: as flat, as colored, as empty, and, most of all, as geometrically tense. Another blurring of documentary and experimental categories, *Berlin: Symphony of a City* (1927) is an early example of how an organization that emphasizes abstract patterns can transform even everyday activity: here, the daily comings and goings, the traffic, and the people of Berlin are arranged according to various movements, lines, and rhythms that remake the city as a musical structure **[Figure 7.16]**.

Rhetorical Positions: Cinematic Investigators and Poets

Expositional and imaginative practices, whether they appear alone or together in a film, are often subject to the organizational point of view or rhetorical position that uses them. Just as narrative cinema uses narrators and narration, documentary and experimental films employ their own **rhetorical positions,** which shape those formal practices of the films according to certain perspectives and attitudes. Sometimes, these films avoid allowing a speaker to articulate the positions and attitudes of the film and assume instead the neutral stance of the uninvolved observer. At other times, the neutral observer takes a more investigatory and analytical stance. At still other times, a singular or collective voice is used to define the rhetorical perspective of a film, one that may be both emotional and expressive. Whether clearly visible and heard or merely implied by the film's organization, the rhetorical positions of documentary and experimental films generally articulate their attitudes and positions according to two principal frameworks, which often mix in a single film: the first is associated with a scientific perspective to interrogate and analyze, the second with artistic efforts to express or persuade. For example, the voice of Peter Davis's 1974 *Hearts and Minds* is both biased and analytical as it tears apart, with strategically placed interviews and news-

Figure 7.17 *Bowling for Columbine* (2002). Taking a stance on gun violence in the United States.

reel footage, the myths supporting the Vietnam War. In *Bowling for Columbine* (2002), a film about director Michael Moore's perspective on the media's obsession with violence, the tragic killings at Columbine High School, and Charlton Heston's promotion of the National Rifle Association, Moore assumes the stance of partly humorous satirist with a serious message about U.S. gun culture **[Figure 7.17]**.

Interrogative or **analytical positions** rhetorically structure a movie either in terms of an implicit or explicit question-and-answer format or by other techniques that identify a subject as under investigation. One of the most common interrogative techniques is the use of a voiceover or an on-camera voice that asks questions of individuals or objects that do or do not respond to the questioning, much like television news. With Trinh T. Minh-ha's *Surname Viet Given Name Nam* (1989), a question or problem may only be implied, and succeeding images may either resolve the problem or not. In this film, Vietnamese women living in the United States act the roles of interviewees living in Vietnam, responding to questions about gender and cultural differences in time of war. The film complicates both the identities of these women and any effort to portray accurately or authentically their experiences. As a result, it raises more questions than it answers. A film may also make the implied question even more complicated by comparing and contrasting different images so layered and complex that they are difficult to explain or respond to. Bruce Conner's experimental film *A Movie* (1958) contrasts wild races and chase scenes with images of refugees, an execution, and air crashes as an elusive questioning of what it means to watch a movie. Interrogative and analytic forms may, in short, lead to more knowledge about an experience or may make the question of how we know the different cultures of the world the essential question of the film. One of the simplest and subtlest examples of the interrogative or analytical form is Alain Resnais's *Night and Fog* (1955): as images of the Nazi concentration camps when the survivors were liberated are alternated with contemporary images of the same empty camps, the complex organizational refrain of the film becomes "Who is responsible?" **[Figure 7.18]**.

Expressive or **persuasive positions** articulate a perspective either as the expression of emotions, beliefs, or some other personal or social position or as an attempt to persuade an audience to feel a certain way.

Figure 7.18 *Night and Fog* (1955). Images without answers.

Expositional, Imaginative, and Rhetorical Strategies in *Sunless* (*Sans soleil*, 1982)

Chris Marker's *Sunless* is a global travelogue that moves through a dizzying catalog of different places and people, with commentary by a voice reading letters sent from the unnamed traveler to a friend in Europe. What makes this such a beautiful and difficult movie is the precision and care with which scientific and artistic strategies confront each other throughout the film, moving back and forth to parallel the correspondence between the traveler and his friend. On the one hand, the film explores, like social science or ethnography, the cultures of Japan and the African countries of Guinea-Bissau and the Cape Verde Islands. On the other, it enacts a poetic meditation on different conceptions of time and memory in the twentieth century.

The film is unusually rich in expositional and imaginative techniques. Indeed, the whole of *Sunless* can be considered a contrastive exposition given its display of different cultures and peoples from around the world. As a kind of travelogue, the film moves, often abruptly, among Japan, Iceland, Guinea-Bissau, the Cape Verde Islands, Isle-de-France, Okinawa, and the island of Sal. The contrasts that these places dramatize, however, are less about evaluations and surface differences than about contrasting senses of time and the commentator's efforts to comprehend them. As the commentator puts it, this is "not a search for contrasts but a journey to the two extreme poles of survival."

In *Sunless* even conventional accumulative expositions seem to have a twist or a sense of irony running through them. At one point, we see a series of more than twenty faces of African women. Each face has its own expression and shape and, as the series accumulates one face after another, each seems to shine forth with more individual personality and intensity: one stares, another turns away; one smiles, another glares hostilely. While the presentation appears to offer a collective representation of African women, almost a sampling of types of faces, the specific expressions undermine any generalities that might otherwise describe the exposition [Figure 7.19].

One of the central themes of *Sunless* is the power and isolated integrity of "things"—or in the voice-over's quotation of an eleventh-century Japanese woman writer, "things that quicken the heart." In one way, the film follows a cumulative organization by presenting different examples of these "things," from Japanese pachinko games to dogs on the beach. Yet in the film's meditation on this world of things, one possible and extremely subtle pattern that develops is the increasing intensity of objects and images as they grow more and more expressive of their own being and essence. Across its wide and varied exposition, *Sunless* moves from the many sleeping bodies on the ferry and the expressive

Figure 7.19 *Sunless* (1982). The accumulation of individual expressions.

faces of children to the abstract shapes of computer technology, where each thing becomes visual poetry in itself.

Just as it interrogates the scientific methods that have explored and colonized people of other cultures, *Sunless* also questions the artistic methods used to romanticize those cultures, presenting metaphors and simultaneously reflecting on them. Perhaps the most dramatic and important example occurs at the beginning and again toward the end of the film: at both points, the image of three children in Iceland appears, and the commentator, acting as the spokesperson for the unnamed letter writer, says about the effort to create a metaphor with this image, "He said that for him it was the image of happiness . . . and he has often tried to link it to other images but it had never worked." The image then becomes black and is replaced by three stationary U.S. fighter jets before the commentator continues, over another black image, with "One day I'll have to put it at the beginning of a film with a long piece of black leader. If they don't see happiness in the picture, at least they'll see the black." With this admittedly complex association, the film seems self-consciously to struggle to create a metaphor from one image of happiness and innocence that could attach itself to other experiences (in this case, perhaps the images of the entire film). But even in creating the metaphor, the commentator seems to recognize that all film metaphors disappear and fade to black as one image replaces the previous, sometimes fully alien, image.

There is similar attraction and doubt about the symbolic powers of this film. *Sunless* tends to avoid clear symbols, but they do crystallize in the more poetic moments of the film. At times the film seems to tease the viewer with symbolic significance that is just not there. Cats and owls permeate the film, sometimes appearing as symbols of patience and wisdom; at other times, they are simply described as the favorite animals of the traveler/commentator. Other cultural and cinematic symbols also beckon in this film: a statue of a faithful dog in Tokyo or the spiral image that recurs in many forms in Alfred Hitchcock's *Vertigo* (1958). Certainly these figures become part of a series of symbols about time and history: how people devote themselves to symbols of time or how time turns us constantly in its twists. Yet in this film, the regular presentation of symbols is always about why and how we make and need symbols—to help us anchor and explain living in a world so vexed by time and history [**Figure 7.20**].

Figure 7.20 *Sunless* (1982). Honoring fragile symbols.

Although not an abstract film, *Sunless* makes continual use of the texture and structures of representation—often in isolation. One section of the film shows a group of images filled with television sets whose multiple rectangular patterns fill the film frame. In its most abstract moments, Marker's film shifts to abstract computer designs, or what the voiceover refers to as images from "The Zone," where previously real images are now translated into quivering colors and lines. Here, the shift into abstract representation suggests an almost utopian purity or intensification that the real world will never have.

In *Sunless*, the voiceover is that of a commentator rather than a narrator. This is an intricate example of how powerful and complex a non-narrative voice can be—whether it is actually heard or is simply implied by the perspective of the film. The unidentified voice of a woman reads letters sent by another fictionalized person, Sandor Krasna (named only in the closing credits), who may be a cameraperson, the filmmaker, or simply a traveler. As these voices shift from one to another and merge one into another, they describe what they see, analyze its meaning, urge a certain understanding, or

Figure 7.21 *Sunless* (1982). A "poetry born of insecurity."

simply speak their amazement out loud. A scientifically inquiring voice moves through multiple questions and the unresolved analysis of these questions: What is the experience of happiness? What is memory? Is there a social politics to the experience of time? How can time be organized in life and on film? Meanwhile, the same voice grows poetically expressive, counterpointing its more analytic questions with expressions of delight, meditative reflections, and occasional efforts at gentle persuasion. Sometimes, the commentator verbally describes the emotionally drifting attitude of the film in its descriptions of its world: "poetry is born of insecurity . . . wandering Jews, quaking Japan . . . moving in a world of appearances, fragile, fleeting." At other times, the film silently describes that attitude: moving through still images of dead animals in the desert to frenetic and gay street festivals in Japan and Africa **[Figure 7.21]**.

Sometimes frustrating and sometimes sublime, *Sunless* stands out as a remarkable orchestration of the many strategies and formal tools available to documentary and experimental filmmakers. Just as these different films refuse the dominance of narrative organizations, Marker's movie refuses the distinctions that each of those two practices can claim in relation to the other. The result is a travelogue of a world that explodes into a poem of discrete particulars, which always fascinate us and always elude our attempts to contain them.

Expressive forms may emphasize a personal voice or vision as the main subject of the film dramatizes that personal presence through such techniques as voiceovers, handheld camera movements, or documents (old pictures or letters). In *Lost, Lost, Lost* (1976), Jonas Mekas portrays his fears and hopes in an autobiographical film about his growing up as an immigrant in New York. Counterpointing home movies, journal entries, and a fragmented style that resembles a diary, the rhythmic interjections of the commentator-poet express feelings ranging from angst to delight **[Figure 7.22]**. In Ross McElwee's *Sherman's March* (1986), the filmmaker sets out on a journey to document the conquest of the south by the famous Civil War general; along the way, how-

Figure 7.22 *Lost, Lost, Lost* (1976). The film as diary: expressive meditations.

Figure 7.23 *Titicut Follies* (1967). To expose and influence attitudes about the criminally insane.

ever, this witty film becomes more about the filmmaker's own failed attempts to start or maintain a romantic relationship with the many women he meets.

When a movie attempts to persuade or convince, it may downplay the presence of the personal perspective and instead use images and sounds to influence viewers through argument or emotional appeal, as in propagandistic movies that urge certain political or social views. Persuasive forms can use the power of documentary images themselves, set up revealing contrasts (say, between certain images or between what is said and what is seen), or use voices and interviews in an attempt to convince viewers of a particular truth or cause. Frederick Wiseman's *Titicut Follies* (1967), for example, works as an exposé of a Massachusetts prison for the criminally insane; much of the film's power resides solely in shocking images meant to provoke and outrage an audience about the institutional abuses of the prisoners **[Figure 7.23]**. With such movies, what we are being persuaded to do or think may not be immediately evident, yet it is usually obvious that we are engaged in a rhetorical argument that involves visual facts, intellectual statements, and sometimes emotional manipulation.

VIEWING CUES: Expositions, Imaginings, and Rhetorics

■ Examine carefully the formal organization of the film you will view next in class. Does the way this film is put together follow a clear formal strategy? Is its strategy expositional, imaginative, or a combination of both? Explain.

■ If the film's strategy is primarily expositional, does it use one or more of the associated techniques—cumulative, contrastive, or developmental exposition? Which one seems more important than the others? What experience or facts does the film present?

■ If the film's strategy is primarily imaginative, which of the associated techniques is most important to the film: metaphoric, symbolic, structural, or abstract forms? Identify the most representative shot or sequence and its meaning.

■ Compare the subject matter and formal strategies of the film. Do the dominant techniques seem appropriate to the presentation of the subject? Can you imagine another way of filming this subject? Explain.

■ Can the perspective or "attitude" of this film be described as a rhetorical position? Would you describe the presiding voice or attitude that shapes the perspective of the film as scientific or artistic? Why?

Points of View: Values and Traditions of Documentary and Experimental Films

More than with narrative cinema, the value of documentary and experimental movies to early audiences was unmistakable. Although amusement has always been a main attraction of the movies, as early as the 1890s, nonfiction movies called "actualities" presented sporting events, political speeches, and dramatic presentations of Shakespeare for their cultural and

Figure 7.24 *Leaving Jerusalem by Railway* (1896). Early cinema as education.

educational value. In 1896, the Lumière brothers took audiences on an educational railway trip with the "phantom ride" of *Leaving Jerusalem by Railway* [**Figure 7.24**]. In 1898, Thomas Edison presented an early ethnographic film about Native Americans called *Wand Dance, Pueblo Indians* (1898). *The Assassination of the Duke of Guise* (1908), an early product of the film d'art movement, proclaimed that the cinema could both bring respected dramas to the screen and offer the same larger cultural and aesthetic benefits of art and literature. According to these traditions, then, movies could presumably offer unmediated truths or artistic insights unavailable through other experiences. However much these values changed during the next century, they remained the foundations on which the different meanings for documentary and experimental films were built.

To Reveal and to Expand

Like narrative films, documentary and experimental movies suggest important relationships between themselves and society. First and foremost perhaps, these films suggest that the world is more varied and complex than a story often allows us to see. Because we see mostly narrative movies, these other films are probably always in this sense differential: successful documentary and experimental films offer different kinds of truth and creativity than narrative movies can communicate or provide. Sometimes this means assuming to offer *more* truth or *more* creativity or to offer those realities and experiences unavailable through narrative. Pursuing these aims, documentary and experimental films often question the basic terms of narratives, such as the centrality of characters, the importance of a coherent chronology, or the necessity of a narrative point of view. Documentary and experimental movies thus work according to two primary differential values:

1. They reveal new or ignored realities typically not seen in narrative films.
2. They expand ways of seeing and hearing beyond what narrative films can offer.

Assuming the *power to reveal new or ignored realities,* many documentary and experimental movies work to present realistic images through certain perspectives or techniques that might seem out of place in a narrative movie. Sometimes this means showing people, events, or levels of reality we have not seen before because they have been excluded from our social experience or from our movie experiences. Perhaps those images will place us closer to reality by showing us an object or a place from angles and points of views beyond the range of human vision: we see the bottom of a deep ocean through the power of an underwater camera or the war-torn plains of Serbia from the perspective of a child. Perhaps the object will be presented for an inordinately long amount of time, showing minute changes rarely seen in our usual experiences: one movie condenses the gestation of a child in the womb, while another shows the dread and boredom of a homeless person in Miami. David and Albert Maysles's *Grey Gardens* (1975) portrays the quirky extremes of two women, both relatives of Jacqueline Kennedy

Onassis, living in a dilapidated mansion in East Hampton, Long Island, working to slowly develop our capacity for understanding and feeling about individuals we rarely encounter [Figure 7.25]. For most viewers who have never witnessed these people and events, these sorts of films reveal realities that could never be accurately represented as a narrative drama.

Complementing their ability to reveal unknown realities, documentary and experimental films also assume the *power to challenge and expand how we see, feel, and hear*. Such movies press us to open our senses and our minds in unaccustomed ways: Hollis Frampton's *Lemon* (1969) presents only a lemon in changing light and Andy Warhol's *Empire* (1964) creates the illusion of a single shot of the Empire State Building that lasts eight hours. For those who have seen these films, a lemon and that New York building will never look the same.

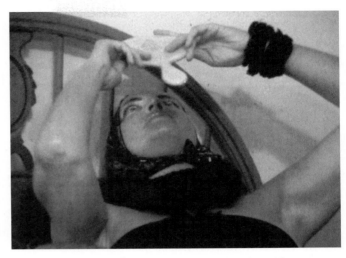

Figure 7.25 *Grey Gardens* (1975). Understanding the quirky.

An experimental movie might use unusual filmic techniques or materials, such as abstract graphic designs and animation, as vehicles for seeing and thinking in fresh ways. It might present a rapid series of images that seem to skip about randomly—much like the experience of a dream. Shirley Clarke's *Bridges-Go-Round* (1958) uses unexpected camera angles and zooms to turn the massive structures of various bridges into an ethereal dance.

As with narrative movies, the relationship between documentary and experimental films and the cultural and historical expectations of viewers plays a large part in how these movies are understood and what meanings are assigned to them. Some viewers might watch a film for scientific, social, or some other kind of conceptual information. Others might look at it as a formal or aesthetic experience, like a fine painting in a museum. Luis Buñuel's *Land without Bread* (1933) might seem to be a documentary about a poor region of Spain, and its bitingly ironic soundtrack commentary was an obvious social criticism at the time—so unmistakable, in fact, that the Spanish government banned the film. Without its cultural context, this film might be incomprehensible to some viewers today, reminding us of the importance of cultural context to the meaning and value of films.

Two Traditions: Social Documentaries and Avant-Garde Films

Two cinematic traditions are associated with documentary and experimental films: namely, the social documentary and avant-garde traditions. **Social documentaries** examine and present both familiar and unfamiliar peoples, cultures, and social activities from around the world. Using a variety of expositional practices, this tradition emphasizes one or both of the following goals:

■ authenticity, in representing how people live and interact
■ discovery, in representing unknown environments and cultures

The social documentary tradition is long and varied, stretching from Robert Flaherty's 1922 *Nanook of the North*, about the daily routines of an Inuit man and his people, and Pare Lorentz's 1937 *The River*, made for the U.S.

Cinéma Vérité

Although we most often go to movies for fun and entertainment, sometimes our main objective in watching a movie is to search for the truth about a person or event. This search for truth has been persistent in film history, though most viewers realize that discovering truth through the movies can be a complex process. Some films communicate truth and reality more convincingly than others because of the techniques they used. One of the most important and influential schools for investigating and presenting a true picture of the world is known as *cinéma vérité*, French for "cinema truth." This film movement arose in the late 1950s and 1960s in Canada and France before quickly spreading to film cultures in the United States and other parts of the world. Related to the Russian *Kino-Pravda* ("cinema truth") of the 1920s, cinéma vérité insists on filming real objects, people, and events in a confrontational way, in which the reality of the subject continually acknowledges the reality of the camera recording it.

Aided by the development of lightweight cameras, filmmakers like Jean Rouch created in their images a jerky immediacy to suggest their participation and absorption in the events they were recording. Rouch and Edgar Morin's *Chronicle of a Summer* (1961) is a series of interviews with individuals on the streets of Paris; Rouch's *Moi un noir* (1958), filmed in Treichville, Africa, stands back and simply lets the people of this town reveal themselves. In this version of cinéma vérité, rules of continuity and character development are willfully ignored. Here, reality is not just what objectively appears; it is also the fictions and fantasies that these individuals create for and about themselves and the acknowledged involvement of the filmmaker as interlocutor.

Figure 7.26 *Don't Look Back* (1967). The lucid reality of young Dylan.

Department of Agriculture about the Mississippi, through Indian filmmaker Nalin Pan's 2001 *Ayurveda: Art of Being,* about the Indian system of holistic medicine. Two important spin-offs from the social documentary tradition are the political documentary and the ethnographic film.

Partially as a result of the social crisis of the Depression in the United States and the more general economic crises that invaded most other countries after World War I, **political documentaries** aimed to explore human suffering and struggle or to celebrate the activities of common men and women. Contrasting themselves with the lavish Hollywood films of the times, these documentary films worked for a balance of aesthetic objectivity and political purpose. Their audiences sought a new honesty about human experience and often would leave these films with the will to reform social systems. Considered by some scholars and filmmakers the father of documentary, John Grierson made his first film, *Drifters* (1929), about

Moreover, unlike its American counterpart, French cinéma vérité draws particular attention to the subjective perspective of the camera's rhetorical position: in *Moi un noir,* a voiceover frequently makes ironic remarks about what is being shown; in *Chronicle,* the lingering camera seems consciously to provoke confessional admissions from its subjects.

The American version of cinéma vérité, referred to by its practitioners as **direct cinema,** is more observational and less confrontational than the French practice. Its landmark film, *Primary* (1960), follows Democratic candidates John F. Kennedy and Hubert H. Humphrey through the Wisconsin state presidential primary. D. A. Pennebaker and the Maysles brothers continued to work in this tradition, gravitating toward social topics in which the identity of the subjects is inseparable from their role as performers: Pennebaker made numerous cinéma vérité–like films such as *Don't Look Back* (1967), **[Figure 7.26]**, a portrait of the young Bob Dylan, and *The War Room* (1993), about the 1992 political campaign of Bill Clinton. In addition to *Grey Gardens,* Albert and David Maysles made numerous films in the direct cinema style, including *Salesman* (1969), about itinerant Bible salesmen, and *Gimme Shelter* (1970), a powerful and troubling record of the 1969 Rolling Stones tour across the United States.

Since then, a collective of Danish filmmakers known as Dogme 95 has appeared as the most notorious variation on the practice of cinéma vérité. Announcing themselves in the spring of 1995, they have translated the program into a radical call for new

Figure 7.27 *Italian for Beginners* (2000). From cinéma vérité to the immediacy of Dogme 95.

kinds of fiction films. Best known through such films as Lars von Trier's *The Idiots* (1998) and Thomas Vinterberg's *The Celebration* (1998), the Dogme 95 movement clearly echoes earlier attempts to bring more reality to filmmaking. The demands of the Dogme 95's "manifesto" include that films should always be made on location using handheld cameras and available light, that no special effects be added, that genre movies are unacceptable, and that directors must never be credited. Other films associated with this group are Danish Søren Kragh-Jacobsen's *Mifune* (1997) and Lone Scherfig's *Italian for Beginners* (2000) **[Figure 7.27]**, and films made outside Denmark, such as American director Harmony Korine's *Julien Donkey Boy* (1999). Cinéma vérité techniques continue to be used in documentary films such as *Hoop Dreams* (1994).

North Sea herring fisherman; another early British filmmaker, Humphrey Jennings, continued this tradition with *Listen to Britain* (1942), a twenty-minute panorama of British society—from soldiers in the fields to women in factories—at war. Since those first years, political documentaries have grown more varied and occasionally more militant. In 1968, Argentinian filmmakers Fernando Solanas and Octavio Getino produced *Hour of the Furnaces,* an examination of the colonial exploitation of Argentina's culture and resources. A contemporary version of this tradition, Robert Epstein and Richard Schmiechen's *The Times of Harvey Milk* (1984) describes the assassination of an activist who was the first gay supervisor elected in San Francisco **[Figure 7.28]**.

With roots in early cinema, **ethnographic documentaries** became a prominent part of the social documentary tradition after World War II in France. Closely related to the cinéma vérité movement, these documen-

Figure 7.28 *The Times of Harvey Milk* (1984). The tragic death of a gay politician.

taries aim to reveal cultures and peoples in the most authentic terms, without imposing the filmmaker's interpretations. Beginning with Jean Rouch's work in the 1940s and 1950s, such as *The Magicians of Wanzerbé* (1949), these documentaries transform film into an extension of anthropology, searching out the social rituals and cultural habits that distinguish the people of particular, often primitive, societies. Robert Gardner's *Dead Birds* (1965), for example, examines the war rituals of the Dani tribe in New Guinea, maintaining a scientific distance that draws out what is most unique and different about the people. The scope and subject matter of ethnographic documentaries have expanded considerably over the years, sometimes finding lost cultures in one's own backyard. Using found footage or archival prints of home movies made before 1950, Karen Shopsowitz's *My Father's Camera* (2001) argues that reality is sometimes best revealed by amateur filmmakers capturing everyday life though home movies and snapshots.

Associated especially with experimental cinema, **avant-garde films** also span film history with various aims, assumptions, and audiences. These films are primarily interested in:

- a self-conscious reflection on how human senses and consciousness work
- an exploration of and experimentation with film forms and techniques

Different avant-garde movements have evolved from the surrealist films of the 1920s through the postwar U.S. experimental cinema of the 1960s. Often these movies break with conventional or orthodox forms and subject matter; their audiences tend to be like the small and devoted groups who gathered at the cine-clubs in Paris or New York film societies like Cinema 16.

One of the most influential avant-gardes, **surrealist cinema** was a driving force in Europe of the 1920s, especially in France. Early works include René Clair's *Entr'acte* (1924) and Germaine Dulac's *The Seashell and the Clergyman* (1928), but certainly the most renowned surrealist film is Salvador Dali and Luis Buñuel's *Un chien andalou* (*An Andalusian Dog*, 1928). The latter begins with a close-up of an eye being slit by a razor; while teasing the viewer with the possibility of a story about a woman and her relationship with one or more men, the film drifts between unexplained objects (like a recurring striped box) and never emerges from its dream state. Through the powers of film to manipulate time, space, and material objects, surrealist filmmakers confronted middle-class assumptions about normalcy and, as in films like *Un chien andalou*, often reconstructed the world to resemble a dream driven by dark desires [Figure 7.29].

In the United States, **postwar experimental cinema** flourished in a climate of existential philosophy, new, lightweight 16mm cameras, and an in-

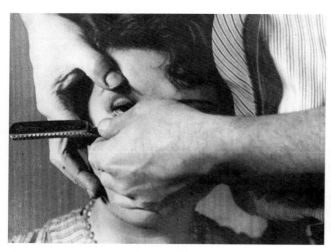

Figure 7.29 *Un chien andalou* (1928). The shocking visions of the surreal.

tensification of pop culture. These influences, together with an intimate community of viewers, helped create an unusually personal cinema about the intricacies of the human mind or the eccentricities of particular communities. Maya Deren, Stan Brakhage, Jonas Mekas, Kenneth Anger, Bruce Conner, Hollis Frampton, Michael Snow, and Yvonne Rainer stand out as major figures in the development of postwar experimental cinema. Perhaps the most poetic and most prolific, Brakhage's output stretches from the 1950s until his death in 2003. Across topics that include suicide (the 1958 *Anticipation of the Night*), the material used to make films (the 1963 *Mothlight*, which used actual moth wings), and a Pittsburgh morgue (the 1971 *The Act of Seeing with One's Own Eyes*), themes of insight and blindness run through many of his films, whose lengths range from the nine-second-long *Eye Myth* (1967) to the five-hour *The Art of Vision* (1965).

In recent years especially, the line between different documentary and experimental traditions has wavered and shifted, as the foundational structures of narrative, non-narrative, nonfiction, and fiction have increasingly exchanged tactics and topics, interrogating the values associated with their respective traditions. Increasingly visible and debated today, **documentary reenactments** use documentary techniques that present the reenactment of presumably true or real events. An early example of this blurring of boundaries, Sergei Eisenstein's fictional *Strike* (1924) uses documentary-style realism and avoids concentrating on individual characters in a narrative tale of a 1912 factory workers' strike in czarist Russia. *The Battle of Algiers* (1965) similarly constructs an account of the Algerian revolt against the French occupation (1954–1962) as a re-creation, a film about a real historical event that uses documentary techniques while developing the story with fictional events or characters [**Figure 7.30**]. *The Thin Blue Line* (1988) is, in part, a documentary about a man, Randall Adams, convicted of killing a Dallas police officer in 1976, but it also becomes a mystery drama about discovering the real murderer. While it uses the many expository techniques of documentary film (such as close-ups of evidence and interviews), *The Thin Blue Line* alternates these with staged reenactments of the murder evening, invented dialogue, an eerily musical soundtrack, courtroom drawings, and even clips from old movies. Popular movies like *This Is Spinal Tap* (1984) [**Figure 7.31**] and *Best in Show* (2000) create fictional documentaries as satirical comedies, the first a "rockumentary" about an invented heavy metal band and the second about the pretensions and absurdities of a famous dog competition in Philadelphia.

In **poetic narratives,** another hybrid movie tradition, a narrative organization exists but it is subjected to (and often disappears within) the more abstract or imaginative shapes and experiences associated with experimental and avant-garde films. As early as René Clair's *The Crazy Ray* (1925) and later with Jean Cocteau's *Orpheus* (1950), movies used stories as mere skeletons on which to elaborate and explore novel cinematic techniques and special effects.

Figure 7.30 *The Battle of Algiers* (1965). Reenacting historical realities.

Figure 7.31 *This Is Spinal Tap* (1984). The fine line of documentary reenactments.

Values and Traditions in *The Man with the Movie Camera* (1929)

Dziga Vertov's *The Man with the Movie Camera* appeared toward the end of the silent film era and amidst the most daring and powerful period in Russian cinema. At that time, Vertov's film theories and practices had moved in two directions, which, to a certain extent, culminated in this landmark movie. Vertov insisted on the use of actual people and events and the dynamics of daily living—what he called a function of the *Kino-Glaz* ("cinema eye")—and claimed that the cinema could extend the powers of the human eye to show the greater experiential and political truths of life—what he designated the power of *Kino-Pravda* ("cinema truth").

The Man with the Movie Camera is both a documentary exploration and an experimental montage celebration of a generic Russian city (a composite of Moscow, Kiev, Odessa, and a region in the Ukraine). The beginning of the film intertwines three sets of images. First, a theater opens for an audience: empty seats flip down to welcome the crowd that will soon arrive, an orchestra prepares its instruments, and a camera projector is being set up to show a film to the arriving audience. Second, the city awakens through a series of images: a woman stirs in bed; a sleeping man moves on a bench; and the immobile facades of buildings appear braced for activity. Finally, in the third part of this overture, a cameraman leaves a building, climbs in an open car, and begins his travels through the streets of the city, recording all the people and activities that describe the life of this city, from dawn until dusk **[Figure 7.32]**. This is not, in brief, a story; rather, it is a city coming to life, and bringing that city to life for the viewer is a cameraman and his film.

Figure 7.32 *The Man with the Movie Camera* (1929). Combining documentary and experimental values.

From one point of view, this film is a breathtaking revelation of the variety and energy of modern urban life. Movement is everywhere. As the day breaks, we witness empty streets coming alive with more and more people until crowds appear in many different shapes and sizes: workers burst through the gates of a factory, crowds jostle through intersections, and athletes gather to race and test their skills. Trolleys crisscross; flocks of pigeons burst in the air; and coal miners push large carts through industrial yards. Interspersed with these sights of continual public life are a multitude of more personal activities: a woman climbs out of bed and dresses, couples apply for marriage licenses, and groups gather at the end of the day for bubbling bottles of beer. A central theme of this Marxist film is "the people," rather than any one individual, and what *The Man with the Movie Camera* works most assiduously to reveal is that the people consists of individuals in all their many capacities to work and play together.

Alongside these revelations, the film challenges us to see this world with fresh eyes, to recognize the multiplicities and harmonies that escape perceptions dulled by daily routines. At several points, an image superimposes a human eye on a camera lens (in which we can see the reflection of a cameraman), suggesting how both forms of vision see and embrace the city before them. In the film, everyday life becomes a work of art seen through the movie camera, allowing us to see and perceive more than just images of an imaginary Russian city in 1929. The rapid pace and dynamic movements of the film demand that we engage the raw energy and excitement of city life as a utopian vision of modern life, as a political ideal that we are capable of creating with our own eyes. It aims to open our eyes to what we normally do not notice, to force us to look outside of ourselves at the world we participate in [Figure 7.33].

Figure 7.33 *The Man with the Movie Camera* (1929). To see an ordinary revolving door with newly opened eyes.

The Man with the Movie Camera remains important today because it is one of the earliest films to anticipate and combine the social documentary and avant-garde traditions, both of which would continue to appear, often on different tracks, throughout the rest of the twentieth century. An experimental documentary, this film attempts to show the essence of a society that, until the cinema, could never be fully represented. Its authenticity resides in the velocity of the life it represents and in the vast range of the everyday urban world it uncovers. After the awakening of this city, the speed of objects and people seems to accelerate according to the pace of modern life and the breadth of its new populace: a horse and buggy carrying refined women races the cameraman and his car, shoppers swing nonstop through a revolving door, factory machines and workers rapidly assemble cartons of cigarettes, and women run back and forth on a basketball court.

In addition to its place in the documentary tradition, *The Man with the Movie Camera* participates in the rise and centrality of avant-garde art in the 1920s, especially cubism and futurism, which aimed to represent the energy of visual action rather than the immobile depiction of objects. Like these avant-garde strategies, Vertov's film explores both how human vision moves and how the movies offer the unique means to capture the mechanics and imagination of human vision in motion. Throughout, *The Man with the Movie Camera* transforms inanimate objects and routine activities into abstract visual patterns full of life and harmony: images of traffic splitting into two parallel, contrapuntal spaces; images of telephone operators constructing webs of lines and angles at their switchboards; and a collage of images of a streetcar twirling around in a whirlwind of lines and movements. Indeed, this futuristic intensification and activation of human vision is, as the film suggests regularly, available especially through the modern mechanics of the movies. At one point in the film, alternating with shots of the work of a seamstress, a woman (the film's editor Elizaveta Svilova) works at her editing table; she examines several images of faces and selects certain ones to insert into a crowd sequence before the flow of film begins again [Figure 7.34]. Here, as in the cubist art of Georges Braque, Pablo Picasso, and others, vision is a dynamically "constructed" reality. Just as the film constantly calls attention to its making of images of the city with a film camera, it also implies that people working together can reconstruct their lives and

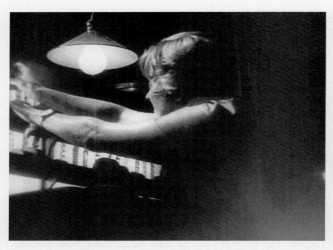

Figure 7.34 *The Man with the Movie Camera* (1929). The construction of vision.

Figure 7.35 *The Man with the Movie Camera* (1929). The city, the cinema, and modern life.

communities to be more efficient and humane visions of the social world. A tiny figure of the cameraman rises from a glass of beer; elsewhere his gigantic image looms over masses of people moving through the city [**Figure 7.35**]. The figure of the cameraman becomes the avant-garde guiding angel for remaking the modern world through new eyes.

The Man with the Movie Camera is an avant-garde documentary in which new visions remake the realities of everyday people and activities into a utopian city. Born in a 1920s Russian society in which art and politics necessarily coexisted, the film demands viewers' involvement in its realities and dynamic techniques: at its beginning and end, viewers are welcomed into the movie theater and encouraged to participate in and re-create the world along with their guide, the man with the movie camera. Though far removed from today's cinema, this film presents values that would shadow documentary and experimental films for the next seventy years.

Figure 7.36 *Street of Crocodiles* (1986). A poetic narrative about the life of porcelain and thread.

Werner Herzog's *Heart of Glass* (1976) is based on a Bavarian legend about the death of a glassblower and the subsequent loss of a secret formula that supported the village industry, but with its characters wandering directionless and speaking in poetic non sequiturs, the heart of the film explores the hypnotic images floating through a world that has lost its sense of time. Stephen and Timothy Quay's *Street of Crocodiles* (1986), constructed through stop-motion photography and based on the memoirs of Polish author Bruno Schulz, is a dark tale of a porcelain doll trapped in a sinister, nightmarish environment of animate screws and threads. Here, the remarkable life of thread and other objects—and not the thread of a story—shapes and organizes the film [**Figure 7.36**].

As we have seen, documentary and experimental films create movie experiences markedly different from

those of narrative cinema. While some of these experiences are non-narrative portraits that envision individuals in ways quite unlike the narrative histories of the same people, others are about the truth of events or about other imaginative spaces. Narrative movies encourage us to enjoy, imagine, and think about our temporal and historical relationships with the world and to consider when those plots and narratives seem adequate according to our experiences. Documentary and experimental movies remind us, however, that we have many other kinds of relationships with the world that involve us in many other insightful ways—through debate, through fantasy, and through analysis.

VIEWING CUES: Documentary and Experimental Film Traditions and Values

■ Examine the aims and values of an experimental or documentary film shown in class. Why is this film important? How is it meaningful? Does it present materials or actions that are not typically used in film to show us new facts or truths? Or does it aim to confront, perhaps even offend, our assumptions about the world in some way? How specifically does it achieve these aims and make its values apparent?

■ Investigate the historical background of this film. Argue why you think it best fits into the social documentary or avant-garde tradition. Can you locate it within a more specific category of that tradition, such as surrealist or postwar experimental? Or does it participate in another cinematic tradition? How is it similar to or different from other films that you may know from those traditions?

■ Consider how the film's historical context influences its values and meanings. Does seeing it in a different historical or cultural context distort or change the aims and assumptions of the film? Why or why not?

CRITICAL VOICES: MAYA DEREN ON "THE CREATIVE USE OF REALITY"

One of the most important contributors to avant-garde cinema, writer and filmmaker Maya Deren insists on the creative power of film to transform reality and move beyond what she considers the literary heritage of narrative films. Her films include *Meshes of the Afternoon* (1943), *A Study in Choreography for Camera* (1945), *Ritual in Transfigured Time* (1946), and *The Very Eye of Night* (1958). As she notes in this excerpt from "Cinematography: The Creative Use of Reality" (*Daedalus,* Winter 1960), her films pursue the creative manipulation of the image rather than its documentary powers.

Once we abandon the concept of the image as the end product and con- 1 summation of the creative practice (which it is in both the visual arts and the theater), we can take a larger view of the total medium and can see that the motion-picture instrument actually consist of two parts, which flank the artist on either side. The images with which the camera provides him are like fragments of a permanent, incorruptible memory; their individual reality is in no way dependent upon their sequence in actuality, and they can be assembled to compose any of several statements. In film, the image can and should be only the beginning, the basic material of the creative action. . . .

Whether the images are related in terms of common or contrasting 2 qualities, in the causal logic of events which is narrative, or in the logic of ideas and emotions which is the poetic mode, the structure of film is sequential. The creative action of film, then, takes place in its time dimension; and for this reason the motion picture, though composed of spatial images, is primarily a *time form*.

A major portion of the creative action consists of a manipulation of 3 time and space. By this I do not mean only such established filmic techniques as flashback, condensation of time, parallel action etc. These affect not the action itself but the method of revealing it. In a flashback there is no implication that the usual chronological integrity of the action, itself is in any way affected by the process, however disrupted, of memory. Parallel action, as when we see alternately the hero who rushes to the rescue and the heroine whose situation becomes increasingly critical, is an omnipresence on the part of the camera as a witness of action, not as a creator of it.

The kind of manipulation of time and space to which I refer becomes itself part of the organic structure of a film. There is, for example, the extension of space by time and of time by space. The length of a stairway can be enormously extended if three different shots of the person ascending it (filmed from different angles so that it is not apparent that the identical area is being covered each time) are so edited together that the action is continuous and results in an image of enduring labor toward some elevated goal. A leap in the air can be extended by the same technique, but in this case, since the film action is sustained far beyond the normal duration of the real action itself, the effect is one of tension as we wait for the figure to return, finally, to earth. . . .

Similarly, it is possible to confer the movement of the camera upon the 4 figures of the scene, for the large movement of a figure in a film is conveyed by the changing relationship between that figure and the frame of the screen. If, as I have done in my [1958] film *The Very Eye of Night*, one eliminates the horizon line and any background which would reveal the movement of the total field, then the eye accepts the frame as stable and ascribes all movement to the figure within it. The hand-held camera, moving and revolving over the white figures on a totally black background, produces images in which their movement is as gravity-free and as three-dimensional as that of birds in air or fish in water. In the absence of any absolute orientation, the push and pull of their interrelationships becomes the major dialogue. . . .

These are but several indications of the variety of creative time-space 5 relationships which can be accomplished by a meaningful manipulation of the sequence of film images. It is an order of creative action available only to the motion-picture medium because it is a photographic medium. The ideas of condensation and of extension, of separateness and continuity, in which it deals, exploit to the fullest degree the various attributes of the photographic image: its fidelity (which establishes the identity of the person who serves as a transcendent unifying force between all separate times and places), its reality (the basis of the recognition which activates our knowledges and values and without which the geography of location and dislocation could not exist), and its authority (which transcends the impersonality and intangibility of the image and endows it with independent and objective consequence). . . .

If cinema is to take its place beside the others as a full-fledged art form, 6 it must cease merely to record realities that owe nothing of their actual existence to the film instrument. Instead, it must create a total experience so much out of the very nature of the instrument as to be inseparable from its means. It must relinquish the narrative disciplines it has borrowed from literature and its timid imitation of the causal logic of narrative plots, a form

which flowered as a celebration of the earthbound, step-by-step concept of time, space and relationship which was part of the primitive materialism of the nineteenth century. Instead, it must develop the vocabulary of filmic images and evolve the syntax of filmic techniques which relate those. It must determine the disciplines inherent in the medium, discover its own structural modes, explore the new realms and dimensions accessible to it and so enrich our culture artistically as science has done in its own province.

THE NEXT LEVEL: ADDITIONAL SOURCES

Barnouw, Erik. *Documentary: A History of Non-Fiction Film.* 2d rev. ed. New York: Oxford University Press, 1993. This survey of major twentieth-century documentary films distinguishes kinds of nonfiction films by the rhetorical stances they initiate (such as those of the "explorer," the "prosecutor," and the "guerilla").

Barsam, Richard M., ed. *Nonfiction Film Theory and Criticism.* New York: Dutton, 1976. One of the first and still most important collections on the aims and distinctions of nonfiction filmmaking, this book features essays by John Grierson, Joris Ivens, and others.

Le Grice, Malcolm. *Abstract Film and Beyond.* Cambridge: MIT, 1977. An important experimental filmmaker himself, Le Grice begins by comparing these films to avant-garde paintings and then maps their development from the futurist movement through various post–World War II movements in the United States.

Nichols, Bill. *Blurred Boundaries: Questions of Meaning in Contemporary Culture.* Bloomington: Indiana University Press, 1994. An ambitious investigation that explores the "blurred" middle ground between fiction and nonfiction films; its historical scope moves from Sergei Eisenstein's *Strike* to the infamous Rodney King videotape to the work of a host of exceptional contemporary filmmakers.

Rees, A. L. *A History of Experimental Film and Video.* London: British Film Institute, 1999. Ranging from Jean Cocteau to Stan Brakhage and contemporary avant-garde video, this meticulous, smart, and readable account of twentieth-century experimental film and video brings the many diverse efforts up to date.

Rituals, Conventions, Archetypes, and Formulas: Movie Genres

I was always fascinated with the kind of picture which is called a melodrama. . . .
Melodrama in the American sense is rather the archetype of a kind of cinema. . . .

—Douglas Sirk, director of *All that Heaven Allows* (1956),
Written on the Wind (1956), and *Imitation of Life* (1959)

KEY OBJECTIVES

Why do so many movies repeat formulas and conventions? How do those repetitions affect our responses to films? This chapter argues that genres are not merely formulaic categories but practices connected to the human need for archetypes and rituals. The film industry has made this need part of an economic strategy in order to draw audiences back again and again to experience the genres they enjoy. Narrative, documentary, and experimental films have each created particular genres associated with their respective organization, but in this chapter we will focus specifically on six narrative film genres: comedy, western, melodrama, musical, horror, and crime films. For each genre we will identify its primary conventions and formulas and consider how it reflects and regulates its specific cultural and historical experiences. We will examine

- why film genres attract audiences
- how film genres spring from a long historical heritage
- which conventions and formulas identify a specific genre
- how genres change over time
- how values and traditions direct audiences to certain meanings in film genres

We all organize our days and years with routines: we read the newspaper in the morning or jog each evening; we gather with family every Thanksgiving or take a ski trip each February. We watch certain sports again and again. Tuning in regularly to specific television shows, such as *The Sopranos* and *Everybody Loves Raymond*, can shape our weeks and months. When these routines do offer a variation—say, when a sporting event features a new star player or a television show introduces a new character—the novelty of it is enjoyable partly because it remains circumscribed in the overall dependability of the ritual.

Movies also rely on repetitions and rituals that allow audiences to share expectations and routines. Besides the myriad characters and stories we

find at the movies, we frequently experience these movie repetitions in a film genre, an organization and categorization of film according to repeated subjects, icons, and styles. Grounded in audience expectations about characters, narrative, and visual style, a **film genre** is a set of conventions and formulas, repeated and developed through film history. We thus enjoy science fiction films—from the 1927 *Metropolis* to the 1958 and 1986 versions of *The Fly*—because we recognize and appreciate some version of a "mad scientist" who works in a mysterious laboratory setting in which new technology leads to strange and dangerous discoveries **[Figure 8.1]**. We

Figure 8.1 *The Fly* (1986). Revitalizing genre through film history.

return to genre films because we know and appreciate them. Indeed, we sometimes choose to see a movie because we identify it with a particular genre, and how we understand that movie is, to some degree, a function of the expectations it creates as part of that genre. One viewer may decide to rush out to see Wes Craven's *Scream* (1996) for the very same reason that another viewer may resolutely choose not to see it: because it is a horror film whose formulas and images—dark nights, large houses, and vulnerable young women—are part of a well-known genre. In an important sense, these different responses to particular genres define the film community to which we belong.

Like other social routines, genres describe **cultural rituals,** the repetition of formulas that help coordinate our needs and desires. For our purposes, rituals are both formal and ideological practices: they organize our lives according to certain repeatable patterns and thereby designate those patterns as enacting the values and beliefs we hold dear. Frequently, these rituals become a therapeutic means of responding to a crisis that is too traumatic, confusing, or irrational to resolve in a simple or pragmatic way. Many religions celebrate a child's coming-of-age (around the age of thirteen) through ritualized ceremonies involving family and friends. During autumn, many communities acknowledge the transition into winter by acting out serious and playful rituals—such as those associated with Halloween—that testify to the coming months of darkness and death. As we shall see, film genres carry their own specific cultural values.

Film genres follow an **economics of predictability**—that is, the production, regulation, and distribution of materials in ways that anticipate the desire for those materials and the efficient delivery of them. In this context, the movie industry's model for genre parallels the industrial model for the Ford Motor Company. Fordism, the economic model that defined U.S. industry through much of the twentieth century, worked to increase the amount and quality of production (of a kind of car) through the division of labor and the mass multiplication of parts. As a result of that increased production, cost would decrease and, ideally, consumption of the product would increase. Tied to a studio system that adapted this industrial system of mass production (see pp. 335–38), film genres enabled movie producers to reuse script formulas, actors, sets, and costumes to create, again and again, many different modified versions of a popular movie. In the same way that a consumer might buy a Ford automobile in a new color or different style every seven years, an audience might return every weekend to see the latest version of a swashbuckler adventure film like *Pirates of the Caribbean: The Curse of the Black Pearl* (2003). Returning to familiar film genres, audiences know what to expect and how to respond.

The Foundations of Film Genre

Early cinema knew immediately about genres from the lessons of its predecessors in photography, literature, art, and musical halls. Nineteenth-century portrait photography repeated standardized poses and backgrounds, and musical halls developed formulas that would, for instance, predictably alternate a musical number with a comic skit, both of which would often feature recognizable conventions and rhythms. Although the first films of the 1890s searched out new subject matter, objects, and events, rough generic patterns quickly developed. Common formulas for short films included panoramic views such as *Panoramic of Niagara Falls in Winter* (1899), historical events as in *Carrie Nation Smashing a Saloon* (1901), and, less often acknowledged, semi-pornographic scenes in "blue movies," such as *From Show Girl to Burlesque Queen* (1903) **[Figure 8.2]**. As the film industry and its audiences expanded through the 1900s, other types of films filled the catalog of early genres: scenes from the theater, sporting events, slapstick comedies, and, as outdoor filming increased, the first westerns became common subjects.

Figure 8.2 *From Show Girl to Burlesque Queen* (1903). Soft-core pornography: an early film genre.

Conventions, Formulas, and Expectations

Genres identify group, social, or community activity, and in this sense they seem opposed to the individual creativity we associate with many art forms, including the art film (see pp. 432–36). A film may work creatively and individually within its genre, but the work must begin within the framework of acknowledged conventions and formulas that audiences expect. Our recognition of these formulas represents a bond between filmmakers and audiences, determining a large part of how we see and understand a film. Film genres thus describe a kind of social contract, one that allows us to see a film as part of both a historical evolution and cultural community. We might recognize a western by the open plains and lone cowboys; certainly for much of the twentieth century, that genre engaged audiences' common knowledge about and interest in U.S. history and "how the West was won."

A definition of genre can be derived from its root, meaning "kind": it is a category or classification of a group of movies in which the individual films share similar subject matter and similar ways of organizing the subject through narrative and stylistic patterns. The most conspicuous dimensions of film genres are the conventions, formulas, and expectations through which we identify certain genres and distinguish them from others. **Generic conventions** are isolated properties or figures that identify a genre through such features as character types, settings, props, or events that are repeated from film to film. Cowboys often travel alone and crime films commonly have a seductive woman who is a foil to the hard-boiled detective. Generic conventions also include **iconography,** images or image patterns with specific connotations or meanings. Dark alleys and smoky bars are staple images in crime movies; musicals are frequently set in the world of the theater and entertainment industry. These conventions and iconographies can sometimes acquire larger meanings and connotations that

align them with other social and cultural **archetypes**—that is, spiritual, psychological, or cultural models expressing certain virtues, values, or timeless realities. Thus, a flood may represent the end of a corrupt life and the beginning of a new spiritual life, an archetypal meaning used in some disaster films but not in others. A meditative version of this kind of film, Peter Weir's *The Last Wave* (1977) describes ominous visions of a tidal wave that will destroy Australia, according to the Aborigines who predict it, as part of a spiritual process **[Figure 8.3]**.

Figure 8.3 *The Last Wave* (1977). Archetypal images underpinning generic conventions.

When generic conventions are put in motion as part of a plot, they become **generic formulas,** the patterns for developing stories in a particular genre. If generic conventions depend on a principle of selection, generic formulas describe a principle of arrangement for organizing those conventions through a plot: some conventions may appear in a particular film and others may not, while generic formulas suggest that those elements can be arranged in a standard way or in a variation on the standard. With horror films, such as *Jaws* (1975), we immediately recognize the beginning of one of these formulas: an attractive young woman or couple goes into the woods, an abandoned house, or in this case, the ocean, alone and is attacked there **[Figure 8.4]**. The rest of the formula proceeds as follows: an intrepid search for the cause of the horrific event (in *Jaws*, a great white shark) follows a wake of bodies; eventually, the protagonist confronts and usually conquers the evil, but there is often a suggestion that the evil will return.

In some cases, these generic formulas can also become associated with **myths**—spiritual and cultural stories that describe a defining action or event for a group of people or an entire community. All cultures have important myths that help secure a cultural identity. One may celebrate a national event associated with a particular holiday, such as the Fourth of July; another culture may see the birth and rise of a great hero from the past as the key to its cultural history. From *Young Mr. Lincoln* (1939) to *Patton* (1970), historical epics often re-create an actual historical figure as a cultural myth in which the character's actions determine a national identity—in these cases, a great nineteenth-century president who emancipated

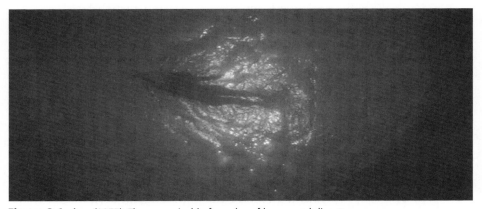

Figure 8.4 *Jaws* (1975). The recognizable formulas of horror and disaster.

Figure 8.5 *Patton* (1970). The mythic power of historical epics.

African Americans and a U.S. army commander who turned the tide of World War II [Figure 8.5]. The formulas of other genres also participate in this mythic function: science fiction films, such as Stanley Kubrick's *2001: A Space Odyssey* (1968), frequently recount explorations or inventions that violate the laws of nature or the spiritual world. The narrative formulas of these science fiction films can be related to broader myths, such as the Faustian myth of selling one's soul for knowledge and power or the story of Adam and Eve's eating from the tree of knowledge and their subsequent punishment.

Both conventions and narrative formulas depend on the activation of generic expectations for their success. Triggered by a film's promotion or by the film itself, **generic expectations** describe the experience and knowledge that a viewer activates while watching a film, so that he or she anticipates the meaning of particular conventions or the direction of certain narrative formulas. Thus, a narrative's beginning, characters, or setting can cue certain expectations about the genre that the film then satisfies or frustrates. The beginning of *Jaws* leads viewers to anticipate shock and danger, participate in the unfolding of the genre, and respond to any surprises this particular film may offer. In the case of *Jaws*, that much of the plot takes place on a sunny beach and open ocean, rather than in the darkened, confined houses of the usual horror film, becomes a clever variation that keeps the formula fresh and expectations attentive.

Indeed, generic expectations underscore the important role of viewers in determining a genre and how that role connects genres to a specific social, cultural, or national environment. Partly because of Hollywood's global reach and the extensive group of genre films it has produced, most audiences around the world will, for instance, quickly recognize the cues for a horror film or a western. Other non-Hollywood genres may not generate such clear expectations outside their native culture. Expectations about the formulas and conventions for a martial arts film are much more sophisticated in China than the United States. Likewise, the religious films, or *cine de sacerdotes*, of the 1940s and 1950s were well known in Spain but would hardly be recognized by viewers from other cultures (even those international viewers familiar with Luis Buñuel's 1961 attack on this national genre, *Viridiana*) [Figure 8.6]. Indeed, even within a culture the popularity of certain genres depends on the shifting tastes and expectations of an audience: musicals proliferated in the United States

Figure 8.6 *Viridiana* (1961). Genre and audience expectations.

in the 1930s; film noir crime films were especially visible in the 1940s and early 1950s; and the heyday of science fiction films occurred in the 1950s. If audience expectations signal the social vitality of a particular genre, that vitality changes as genres move from culture to culture or between historical periods within a single culture. In this sense, genres usually tell us something about community or national identity.

Figure 8.7 *Singin' in the Rain* (1952). Genre embedded in history.

A Short History of Film Genre

Among the most inventive musicals of all time, *Singin' in the Rain* (1952) is as much about history as it is about music. It begins in 1928, with two silent film stars concluding one generic film, a historical romance drawn from the pages of a literary work like *The Three Musketeers*, and follows them as they try, unsuccessfully, to adapt that genre to the new historical demands of "talking pictures" **[Figure 8.7]**. In the narrative confusion, failures, and frustrations that follow this clash of genre and history, they re-create their movie as a different film genre, the musical. Along the way a romantic melodrama involving the two protagonists, Kathy and Don, sneaks into the musical, while the wacky antics of Don's sidekick, Cosmo, recall the slapstick comedies of the Keystone Kops, Charlie Chaplin, and Harold Lloyd. In short, *Singin' in the Rain* reminds us more directly than most films that a film genre always carries the traces of an older and varied history.

Well before the advent of the movies, genres were used to classify works of literature, theater, music, painting, and other art forms. Literature offered large genres such as tragedy and comedy as well as more specific genres like poetic ballads, pastoral and epic poems, and dime novels. Musical genres included classical sonatas and symphonies as well as popular love songs or children's lullabies. The seventeenth-century Dutch painter Pieter de Hooch created genre paintings, which depicted scenes of domestic life and daily social encounters. In the eighteenth-century and early nineteenth-century paintings of David Wilkie, William Hogarth, and others, genre came to suggest an image of a "slice of life" or scenes aimed at familiarity, recognition, and shared (if heightened) human emotions. This combination of domestic realism and theatricality linked genres to the stage, particularly to the staging of melodramas, the most popular genre of the nineteenth century. In these different forms, three functions for genre began to take shape:

1. to provide models for producing other works
2. to direct audience expectations
3. to create categories for judging or evaluating a work

For painters in the eighteenth century, for example, historical paintings would need to follow certain generic rules about what objects to include in a painting about a naval victory; audiences would learn to expect all epic poems to begin with a generic invocation to the gods or a muse.

Since the beginning of film history, the importance of genre and the popularity of specific genres have waxed and waned depending on the historical period and culture. Although films have repeated subjects and formulas from their very beginnings, the rise of the studio system through the 1920s and 1930s provided extraordinarily fertile grounds for movie genres.

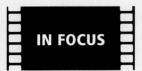
Conventions and Expectations in *The Gold Rush* (1925)

Made at the height of the silent film era, Charlie Chaplin's *The Gold Rush* signals, along with *The Kid* (1921), this important star-director's transition into longer narrative films and anticipates much of the future history of film comedy. The film takes place in the snowy and barren regions of the Yukon in the late nineteenth century. Structured as a series of vignettes or scenarios, the film begins with the arrival of Chaplin, the Lone Prospector, and proceeds through a series of misadventures as he seeks his fortune in gold, barely survives the dangers of the wilderness, and falls in love with a dance-hall girl, Georgia.

Conventions abound in *The Gold Rush*. Many of the characters are stereotypes: Georgia is the hardened bar girl with a heart of gold; Black Larsen is a "predatory scoundrel" whose massive and gruff appearance makes him the ideal counterpoint to the diminutive Chaplin; Chaplin's rival, Jack, is the handsome, suave bully whom he must battle for Georgia's heart. Here, as in many comic films, the comic conventions can often be described as "gags," visual jokes based on incongruity or the mismatching of things, people, and places. A dapper little aristocrat in the hostile north, Chaplin and his clothing always seem out of place: his baggy pants, bowler hat, and cane fit him oddly and fit oddly into this rough mining town in the Yukon [**Figure 8.8**]. From this start, gag after gag follows. A bear arrives in his cabin kitchen; Chaplin mistakenly uses a rope with a dog tied to it as a makeshift belt during a dance; and no matter how Chaplin jumps and moves around

Figure 8.8 *The Gold Rush* (1925). Reinventing conventional gags.

Figure 8.9 *The Gold Rush* (1925). Comedy as the triumph of life.

Big Jim and Black Larsen's fight for a gun, the barrel always seems directly pointed at him.

The narrative of *The Gold Rush* describes a fundamental formula for film comedy: the triumph of life. Regardless of how out of sync Chaplin seems with his world, he manages to overcome all these incongruities through his casual grace: an old shoe becomes a sophisticated dining experience to the starving man; a cabin teetering on the edge of a cliff becomes the set of a clownish skit of slipping and sliding that, after a balletic escape, lands Chaplin and Big Jim on their lost gold mine; stood up at his own New Year's party, Chaplin turns two forks with potatoes into a remarkable little dance number **[Figure 8.9]**; and, however physically mismatched, the couple, the "Lonely Prospector" finally wins the heart of the beautiful Georgia. In the end, this particular version of the comic formula—about an "undaunted Lone Prospector . . . somewhere in that nowhere"—resonates with other myths of human endurance, like the tales of Sisyphus and Job, where humility and patience triumph against a hostile world.

Although Chaplin himself now represents a comic icon and, for some, an archetype, his character was built from a history of generic emblems and signs. Carried over from earlier films, Chaplin's "Little Tramp" character bears traces of earlier archetypes such as the Pierrot figure of the *commedia dell'arte* theatrical tradition that flourished from the sixteenth to the eighteenth centuries **[Figure 8.10]**. Even Shakespeare's fools and Picasso's many painted clowns are echoed in the Little Tramp and Lonely Prospector: living on the edge of society, silly in most every way, Chaplin's clown, like those other theatrical, poetic, and painted clowns, represents a wisdom and creativity that more powerful and conventional members of society lack. Through this and other films, Chaplin adds to an enduring archetype for comic films, whose heritage would continue, for all their differences, with the comic characters found in the films of Jacques Tati, Woody Allen, and Roberto Benigni.

Generic expectations are, naturally, crucial to this comedy. They are the foundation of the gag itself: an audience must recognize that a joke is coming in order to appreciate it. With the first appearance of a shuffling little man in the snowy wilderness, audiences sense a comic situation that determines their reactions throughout the film. Despite the larger men and more attractive women, expectations suggest that Chaplin will not be defeated. As in all genres, however, audience expectations direct our attention to how conventions will be varied in this individual film. Of course Chaplin will triumph, but the means and degree of his triumph become the source of our fascination with this film. If the comic hero often wins the girl, the concluding surprise of *The Gold Rush* is that he wins not only his love but, unlike in his other comedies, his fortune in gold as well. Chaplin did not invent these comic conventions and formulas; rather, as in most successful genre films, *The Gold Rush* turns and twists those generic materials in ways that reinvigorate them with his personal touch.

Figure 8.10 Pierrot (1857) as early comic archetype.

The **studio system** describes the industrial practices of those large production (and, until 1948, distribution and exhibition) companies responsible for the kinds and quality of movies made in Hollywood (see pp. 335–38). The most famous studio system around the world, Hollywood studios differed in size, strategies, and styles—from the smaller United Artists to the massive MGM—but each used a production system based on the efficient recycling of formulas and conventions, stars, and sets. The system was headed by a mogul who assigned a producer, who in turn oversaw those many moveable parts that a studio had at its disposal. In this environment, individual studios refined their production line techniques, established their association with specific genres, and used and refined that expertise to develop those genres. Thus, by the 1930s, Warner Bros. was identified with gangster films, Paramount with sophisticated comedies, MGM with musicals and melodramas, RKO with literary adaptations, Columbia Pictures with westerns, and Universal with horror films.

However, the **Paramount decision of 1948,** in which the Supreme Court ruled that the major studios violated antitrust laws by monopolizing the film business, undid the studio system and thus a cornerstone of movie genres. Without control of a distribution network of theaters to ensure the profitability of its production decisions, the studio system gradually began its decline and, with it, the golden years of American film genres. Certainly, genre movies continued to be made and enjoyed (some, like film noir, appeared during this waning and others, like blaxploitation, came about in the ensuing fragmentation), but independent and less formulaic movies started to challenge the supremacy of genre films. To some extent, the popularity of genre films in the 1960s and 1970s was a **recycling of genres** through other cultures and within American culture. These recycled genre films, like Robert Altman's western *McCabe and Mrs. Miller* (1971) and Wim Wenders's German film noir *The American Friend* (1977), often returned to the earlier conventions and icons but with an ironic and self-conscious perspective on those formulas and their relation to a changing world.

In *Singin' in the Rain,* the characters recognize from the start that the success of a movie is inseparable from its historical predicament and place—and dependent on finding a film genre that will balance commercial prospects

VIEWING CUES: Film Genre Conventions

- Try to identify the genre of the film you will watch next in class. What specifically distinguishes this film as part of that genre? If the film resists being categorized this way, explain why.

- Reflect on the generic expectations that this film triggers. What exactly creates those expectations? The title? The opening scenes? An actor or character?

- Briefly explain those expectations. Then analyze how they are met or redirected.

- Describe three conventions typically associated with this genre.

- Does this genre rely on an identifiable iconography? Does it suggest certain archetypes or myths? Explain.

- Consider the historical precedents for this genre. Do they come from literary or theatrical history? From a cultural or religious ritual? Analyze how the genre's historical background sheds light on this film.

with the individual creativity of Don, Kathy, and Cosmo. As these characters discover, history renews some genres and demands the invention of new ones. Because genre is always a historical negotiation, an awareness of the vicissitudes of cultural history only makes movie genres more vital and meaningful.

Constellations of Movie Genres: Six Paradigms

From their first days, movies organized themselves as genres determined by subject matter: films about a famous person, films about panoramic views, and so on. As movies became more sophisticated, however, genres grew into more complex narrative organizations with recognizable formal conventions. By 1923, one poll of high school boys and girls identified their two favorite movies as Rex Ingram's epic war story *The Four Horsemen of the Apocalypse* (1921) and the exotic romance *The Sheik* (1921), featuring Rudolph Valentino. What attracted these young people, two or three times a week, to the movies were clearly identified generic preferences for westerns, comedies, detective stories, romances, and melodramatic tragedies. As films developed and differentiated stylistic and formal conventions, these generic preferences would change and grow.

Creating a list of movie genres can be more daunting and uncertain than it appears. Because genres are a product of a perspective that groups individual movies together, that perspective can construct genres in many different ways. To be extremely idiosyncratic and subjective, one could construct genres of "movies about Chicago" or "films with music tracks featuring David Bowie." As we will discuss in Chapter 11, for some scholars or viewers, film noir is an important movie genre that surfaced in the 1940s, whereas for others, film noir is less a film genre than a film style. A particular genre may, moreover, offer unusually wide boundaries or unusually narrow ones: comedies might appear too grand a category for some critics, and screwball comedies may seem too limited a group to be termed a genre. Here, we will focus on six important genres. Our aim is to define each genre as it has appeared in different cultures and at different points in history as part of its changing social contract with different audiences.

We will use the figure of a **generic constellation** to suggest how genres are best defined within a multidimensional field that, like the outlines that group different layers of stars in the sky, produces two major subsets for film genres. **Hybrid genres** are those film genres produced by the interaction of different genres to produce fusions, such as romantic comedies or musical horror films. **Subgenres** are those genres that define a specific version of the genre by refining it with an adjective, such as the spaghetti western or slapstick comedy. A generic constellation thus suggests how genres, as distinctive patterns, can overlap and shift their shape depending on their relation to other genres or as extensions of a primary field. From different perspectives, *Blazing Saddles* (1974) is a comedic western or a western comedy; seeing that film from one perspective or the other can make a difference in how we appreciate it [**Figure 8.11**]. For each central genre, we will highlight a selection of defining characteristics that have surfaced through film history, including

- the distinguishing features of the characters, narrative, and visual style
- the reflection of social rituals in the genre
- the production of certain historical hybrids or subgenres out of the generic paradigm

Figure 8.11 *Blazing Saddles* (1974). Comedic western or western comedy?

Although these generic blueprints will inevitably be reductive and the generic distinctions will overlap, they help isolate our responses to comedies, westerns, melodramas, musicals, horror films, and crime films. Maps of each of these generic constellations should guide our explorations of specific films and of how they engage particular social rituals.

Comedies

Film comedy has flourished since 1895, as comic actors of the vaudeville stage took their talents to the screen. Rooted in the *commedia dell'arte,* Punch and Judy, and the vaudeville stage acts that would later produce Buster Keaton and a host of other early comedians, film comedy is one of the first and most enduring of film genres. Its many variations can be condensed into these main traits:

- central characters who are often defined by distinctive physical features, such as the size of their bodies or their manner of speaking
- narratives that emphasize individual episodes more than plot continuity or progression and that usually conclude happily
- theatrical acting styles in which characters physically and playfully interact with the mise-en-scène that surrounds them

From the early silent comedies of producer Mack Sennett to the awkward and stumbling Woody Allen as Alvy Singer in *Annie Hall* (1977), comic characters stand out physically because of the shapes of their bodies, the expressions on their faces, or the gestures with which they move. Although comedies can develop intricate plots, their focus is usually on individual vignettes. In Sennett's *Saturday Afternoon* (1926), Harry Langdon balances between moving cars and hangs from telephone poles. In *Annie Hall,* Alvy jumps around a kitchen where he chases lobsters and later squirms at a family dinner table where he imagines himself as a Hassidic Jew **[Figure 8.12]**. In these episodic encounters, the comic world becomes a stage full of unpredictable gags and theatrical possibilities.

Comedies celebrate the harmony and resiliency of social life. Although many viewers associate comedies with laughs and humor, comedy is more fundamen-

Figure 8.12 *Annie Hall* (1977). The unpredictable comic stage.

tally about social reconciliation and the triumph of the physical over the intellectual. In comic narratives, obstacles or antagonists—in homes, marriages, communities, and nations—are overcome or dismissed by the physical dexterity or verbal wit of a character, or perhaps by luck, good timing, or magic. In *Bringing Up Baby* (1938), Katharine Hepburn is a flighty socialite who moves and talks so fast that she bewilders the verbally and physically bumbling Cary Grant, who will inevitably forsake his scientific priorities for the joys of this improbable romance. In *Groundhog Day* (1993), Bill Murray

Figure 8.13 *Home Alone* (1990). Comic resiliency.

plays a weatherman with many social and professional flaws, who falls into a magical world where he can relive each day with the ability to correct his previous errors and romantic blunders. Thus, perhaps the most obvious convention in comedies is the happy ending, in which couples or individuals are united in the form of a family unit or the promise of one to come. Very often, traditional comedies begin with some discord or disruption in social life or in the relationship between two people (lovers are separated, for instance); after various trials or misunderstandings, harmony is restored and individuals are reunited. In *Home Alone* (1990), for example, a family going on a trip to Paris mistakenly leaves the youngest and underappreciated boy behind. After the diminuitive but clever child trips up a pair of gruff but inept burglars again and again [Figure 8.13], the family happily returns home.

Historically, Hollywood film comedies experience numerous permutations and structural changes as they respond to audience expectations in changing contexts. The result is three salient subgenres: slapstick comedies, screwball comedies, and romantic comedies. Some of the first films were **slapstick comedies:** arriving in the first decade of the twentieth century, the first versions of this subgenre used printed intertitles rather than spoken dialogue and developed from a few minutes to about fifteen minutes long. Early films like those of Mack Sennett's Keystone Kops developed around physical moments and stunts set within fairly restricted social spaces. Later, feature-length slapstick—such as Sennett's *Tillie's Punctured Romance* (1914) [Figure 8.14], Harold Lloyd in *The Freshman* (1925), and Stan Laurel and Oliver Hardy in *The Music Box* (1932)—emphasized the humorous stunt and the dexterity of characters who maintain a balance despite the imbalance of their world. By the 1920s, comedy had integrated its gags and physical actions into a story that allowed physical games to develop new twists and turns over the course of narrative time within a social arena. Yet even within these longer versions of slap-

Figure 8.14 *Tillie's Punctured Romance* (1914). Slapstick stunts.

stick comedy, the singular slapstick moments stand out as most memorable: when Buster Keaton misfires the cannon vertically into the air in *The General* (1927), the cannonball fortuitously misses him and just happens to destroy an enemy bridge. Slapstick comedies remain popular today, although the

Figure 8.15 *Monty Python's The Meaning of Life* (1983). Metaphysical slapstick.

Figure 8.16 *The Shop around the Corner* (1940). The comedy of romance.

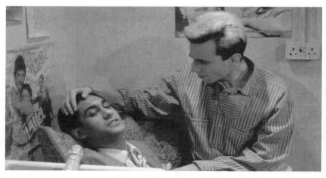

Figure 8.17 *My Beautiful Laundrette* (1985). Remaking romantic comedy in contemporary London.

ingenuity of the physical comedy has to a large extent given way to the most basic scatological or sexual jokes, as in *Porky's* (1981), *Police Academy* (1984), and *Austin Powers in Goldmember* (2002). In *Monty Python's The Meaning of Life* (1983) **[Figure 8.15]** and *Monty Python and the Holy Grail* (1975), slapstick becomes a much more complicated and intelligent ingredient of nonstop social satire.

In the 1930s and 1940s, **screwball comedies** transformed the humor of the physical into fast-talking verbal gymnastics that displaced the sexual energy of the drama with barbed verbal exchanges between men and women. In effect, these films usually redirected the comic focus from the individual clown to the confused heterosexual couple. *It Happened One Night* (1934), *Bringing Up Baby, His Girl Friday* (1940), and *The Philadelphia Story* (1940) are among the best-known examples of screwball comedies; each features independent women who resist, mock, and challenge the crusty rules of the world. When the right man arrives, one who can match these women in charm and physical and verbal skills, confrontation leads to love.

In **romantic comedies,** humor takes a second place to happiness. Popular since the 1930s and 1940s, romantic comedies like *Small Town Girl* (1936), *The Shop around the Corner* (1940) **[Figure 8.16]**, and *Adam's Rib* (1949) concentrate on the emotional attraction of a couple, but in a consistently light-hearted manner. This subgenre draws attention to a peculiar or awkward social predicament—in *Adam's Rib*, for example, the husband and wife lawyers oppose each other in the courtroom—that romance will eventually overcome on the way to a happy ending. More recent examples include *Sleepless in Seattle* (1993) and *You've Got Mail* (a 1998 remake of Ernst Lubitsch's *The Shop around the Corner*), where the comic predicaments have contemporary twists—in the first example, a woman falls in love with a man she hears on a radio talk show—but the formula and conventions remain fairly consistent. Stephen Frears's romantic comedy *My Beautiful Laundrette* (1985) suggests, however, the range of possibilities in the creative (and here political) reworking of any genre. In this case, the social complications include a wildly dysfunctional Pakistani family in London and the romance that blossoms between the entrepreneurial son and a white man, his childhood friend and a former right-wing punk **[Figure 8.17]**.

Westerns

Like film comedies, westerns have become a staple of Hollywood movies, although their popularity has waxed and waned in different historical eras. Growing out of nineteenth-century stories, dime novels, and journalistic accounts of the wild American West (more directly than out of famous novels of the frontier, such as James Fenimore Cooper's *Leatherstocking Tales*), this

Local Genres

Although most of us are familiar with the major Hollywood genres, we also see and recognize film genres connected to more specific times, places, events, and cultures. Modern American "teen films"—such as *The Breakfast Club* (1985), *Heathers* (1989), *Clueless* (1995), *She's All That* (1999), and *Bring It On* (2000)—can be considered part of a genre that relates in very particular ways to the characters, crises, and rituals of modern American youth. Local genres such as this one have appealed to specific movie audiences throughout film history. Although they are usually overlooked in discussions of movie genres, these rich and complicated genres illustrate the vital connection between a film genre and specific cultural values.

In a sense, all genres are local because they first take shape to reflect the interests and traditions of a particular community or nation. But history has tended to disregard national film borders, creating international or universal genres that are understood and enjoyed by many different kinds of people from many different places. Although westerns may be essentially an American genre, they have traveled successfully to Australia, Italy, Spain, and many other countries. While horror films may have their roots in the expressionistic cinema of Germany around 1920, horror is now a global genre.

Of the many local genres that have appeared around the world, two clearly stress the connection between genre and a particular culture: the Japanese *jidai-geki* films and the Austrian and German *heimat* films. Popular since the 1920s, the Japanese *jidai-geki* **films** are period films or costume dramas set before 1868, when feudal Japan entered the modern Meiji period. Movies such as *Revere the Emperor* (1927) and *A Diary of Chuji's Travels* (1927) work as historical travelogues to resurrect the customs and glory of times long past. Like most nations' relation to their preindustrial past, the Japanese view this period with curiosity, nostalgia, and pride, often seeing in these early films a kind of cultural purity that was lost in the twentieth century. Through the years, however, this genre, like all successful genres, has assimilated current affairs into its conventions and formulas: besides feudal courts and sword battles,

jidai-geki films develop plots about class unrest and social rebellion. Akira Kurosawa's *Ran* (1985) is an interesting engagement with this essentially Japanese genre: a feudal Japanese costume drama replete with many of the *jidai-geki* conventions, it is a film adapted from Shakespeare's *King Lear* that, ultimately, describes the end of an ancient world.

Set in idyllic countrysides, Austrian and German ***heimat* films** depict a world of traditional folk values in which love and family triumph over virtually any social evil and communities gather around maypoles and sing traditional German folk songs. Hailed by Austrian and German audiences throughout the first half of the twentieth century, this genre thrived in both countries with films from *The Priest from Kirchfeld* (1914) and *Heimat* (1938) to *The Trapp Family* (1956). As German filmmakers became more self-conscious about their historical background and the connection between this political history and the movies, modern films resurrected the *heimat* genre, now reinterpreted as complicitous in the social history of Germany. Peter Fleischmann's *Hunting Scenes from Bavaria* (1969), Volker Schlöndorff's *The Sudden Wealth of the Poor People of Kombach* (1971), Edgar Reitz's sixteen-hour *Heimat* (1984) **[Figure 8.18]**, and Stefan Ruzowitzky's *The Inheritors* (1998) are all explicit attacks on the mythology of this genre or reexaminations of its social meaning and power.

Figure 8.18 *Heimat* (1984). The traditional values of German home life subjected to postwar occupation.

Figure 8.19 *Butch Cassidy and the Sundance Kid* (1969). Tough and energetic western protagonists.

genre began to take shape in the first years of the movie industry, acting as a kind of travelogue of a lost historical period. From *The Great Train Robbery* (1903) to *American Outlaws* (2001), the western has grown into a surprisingly complex genre while also retaining its fundamental elements:

- characters whose physical and mental toughness separate them from the crowds of modern civilization
- narratives that follow some version of a quest into the natural world
- a stylistic emphasis on open, natural spaces and settings, such as the western frontier regions of the United States

According to this scheme, John Wayne as the Ringo Kid in *Stagecoach* (1939) has a physical energy and determination that would echo in Paul Newman and Robert Redford as *Butch Cassidy and the Sundance Kid* (1969) [**Figure 8.19**]. Never at ease with the law or the restrictions of civilization, these men find themselves on vague searches for justice, peace, adventure, freedom, and perhaps a treasure that offers all these rewards. Taking them through a western landscape filled with natural and man-made violence (like marauding Native Americans), quests through wide-open canyons and deserts seem at once to threaten, inspire, and humble these western heroes.

Through the trials of a lone protagonist, rugged individualism becomes the measure of any social relationship and of the values of most Western communities. Even when they are part of a gang, as in *The Magnificent Seven* (1960), these individuals are usually loners or mavericks rather than representative leaders. More so than in historical epics, violent confrontations are central to these narratives, and this violence is primarily measured by the ability and will of the individual rather than the mass, nation, or community, even when it is directed against Native Americans. In *High*

Figure 8.20 *High Plains Drifter* (1972). The social fabric of individual justice.

Plains Drifter (1972) **[Figure 8.20]**, the moody Clint Eastwood must protect a frightened town from the vengeance of outlaws. When a violent showdown concerns two groups—as in the gunfight at the OK Corral, between the Earps and the Clantons, in John Ford's 1946 *My Darling Clementine*— the battle is often about individual justice or revenge (of sons and brothers) or about who has the rightful claims to nature.

Like most film genres, westerns have responded to changing audiences. With several significant exceptions, including *The Covered Wagon* (1923), westerns were not a particularly respected genre in the 1920s and early 1930s, when they were still associated with their popularity with the mass audiences of early cinema and such popular forms as Wild West shows. Since then, however, three hybrids or subgenres have distinguished the western: the western epic, the existential western, and the political western. Within the constellation of westerns, the **western epic** concentrates on action and movement, developing a heroic character whose quests and battles serve to define the nation and its origins. With its roots in literature and epic paintings, this genre appears early and often in film history, foregrounding the spectacle of open land and beautiful scenery. An early instance of the western epic, *The Covered Wagon* follows a wagon train of settlers into the harsh but breathtaking frontier, where their fortitude and determination establish the expanding spirit of America. Years later, *Dances with Wolves* (1990) describes a more complex struggle for national identity: a traumatized Civil War veteran learns that being an American also means understanding and commiserating with Native Americans **[Figure 8.21]**.

In the 1950s, one of the most interesting decades for westerns, the **existential western** took shape. In this introspective version of the genre, the traditional western hero is troubled by his changing social status and his self-doubts. Here too, the frontier tends to grow more populated and civilized and the self-assurance and righteousness of the hero begins to suffer some doubts. *The Searchers* (1956), *The Furies* (1950), *Johnny Guitar* (1954), *Shane* (1953), and *The Left-Handed Gun* (1958) are existential westerns with protagonists who are troubled in their sense of purpose. The traditionally male domain of the West is now contested by women, evil is harder to locate and usually more insidious, and the encroachment of society complicates life and suggests the end of the cowboy lifestyle. Even into the 1990s, this subgenre has endured, most notably with *Unforgiven* (1992): here, the once unbendable Clint Eastwood is now financially strapped, somewhat hypocritical, and disturbingly aware that killing is an ugly business.

By the 1960s and 1970s, the **political western** had evolved out of the troubled territory of existential westerns: in this more contemporary and critical western, the ideology and politics that have always informed the

Figure 8.21 *Dances with Wolves* (1990). A modern western epic.

Figure 8.22 *The Wild Bunch* (1969). Westerns and the politics of aging cowboys.

genre are foregrounded; the heroism associated with individual independence and the use of violence naturalized in epic westerns become precisely what is questioned. In *The Man Who Shot Liberty Valance* (1962), the heroic myth of the American West is exposed as a lie. With only communities rather than frontiers to conquer in *The Wild Bunch* (1969), aging cowboys are less interested in justice and freedom than in indiscriminate and grotesque killing **[Figure 8.22]**.

Melodramas

Movie melodramas are one of the more difficult genres to define because melodramatic characters and actions can be part of many other kinds of movies. The word itself indicates a combination of the intensities of music (*melos*) and the interaction of human conflicts (*drama*). Indebted to a nineteenth-century theatrical heritage in which social and domestic oppression created heightened emotional dramas, film melodramas arrived virtually simultaneously with the first developments toward film narrative. Some fundamental formulas and conventions of this genre include

■ characters who struggle, often desperately, to express their feelings or emotions
■ narratives that build toward emotional or physical climaxes
■ a visual style drawn to interior scenes and close-ups

From D. W. Griffith's *Way Down East* (1920) to Kimberly Peirce's *Boys Don't Cry* (1999), the central character (often female) is restrained, repressed, or victimized by more powerful forces of society. These forces may pit a dominating masculinity against a weaker femininity. In Griffith's film, a city villain threatens an innocent virgin, and in *Boys Don't Cry* Nebraska country boys assault and murder Brandon Teena when they discover that he was born female (and named Teena Brandon) and has been living as a male. In the first film, the claustrophobic confines of rooms and buildings dramatize this victimization **[Figure 8.23]**. In the second, medium shots and close-ups of the protagonist emphasize the strains and contradictions of mistaken identity **[Figure 8.24]**. In each of these films, true to the conventions of melodrama, the story reaches a breaking point with the threat of death: one character almost drifts away on ice floes; the other is shot to death.

As social rituals, melodramas parallel and contrast westerns. Individualism and private life anchor this genre as well, but the drama of this life is not about conquering a frontier and finding a home, but rather about the strain on and often failure of the individual to act or speak out within that already established home and its family. Melodramas thus develop a conflict between interior emotions and exterior restrictions, between yearning or loss and satisfaction or renewal. One or more women are typically at the center of melodrama, illustrating how historically women have been excluded from or limited in their access to public powers of expression. Mise-en-scène and narrative space also play a major stylistic role in melodrama: individuals, traditionally female, retreat into smaller and smaller private spaces while some obvious or implied hostile force, often male, threatens and drives them further into a desperate internal sanctuary. These rituals are often graphically acted out. In Elia Kazan's film version of *A Streetcar Named Desire* (1951), confined in a run-down, claustrophobic home in New Orleans, Blanche and Stella also confine and repress their memories of a lost family history; their desires to escape are, for both, channeled through their sexuality. For Stella, that means accepting her husband Stanley's violent control of her; for Blanche, it means becoming a victim of Stanley's power and, after he rapes her, retreating into madness.

Figure 8.23 *Way Down East* (1920). The claustrophobic confines of melodrama.

Whereas early melodramas followed formulas around female distress and excessive emotions trapped by time and space, those formulas have grown subtler or at least more realistic over the years. Three subgenres of melodramas that usually overlap and rarely appear in complete isolation from one another can be distinguished: physical, family, and social melodramas. **Physical melodramas** focus on the physical plight and material conditions that repress or control the protagonist's desires and emotions; these physical restrictions may be related to the places and people that surround that person or may simply be a product of the person's physical size or color. One of the first great film melodramas, D. W. Griffith's *Broken Blossoms* (1919) is also one of the most grisly: in an atmosphere of drugs and violence, a brutal boxer, Battling Burrows, hounds and physically terrifies his illegitimate and frail daughter, Lucy. He eventually beats her to death (as she retreats into smaller and smaller rooms) and is himself killed by Lucy's one friend, a Chinese immigrant identified in the subtitles only as the Yellow Man (who then commits suicide). Although most melodramas do not so definitively emphasize the physical plight of the heroine, viewers can still recognize this generic focus on bodily or material strain in such melodramas as *Dark Victory* (1939), about a woman with a terminal brain illness; *Magnificent Obsession* (1954), about a blind woman whose vision is restored; and *Boys Don't Cry* and Rainer Werner Fassbinder's *In a Year of Thirteen Moons* (1978), more contemporary melodramas about sexual identity and physical violence.

Although physical arrangements play a part in them, **family melodramas** elaborate the confines and restrictions of the protagonist by investigating the psychological and gendered forces of the family. For many viewers, this is the quintessential form of melodrama, in which women and young people especially must struggle against patriarchal authority, economic dependency, and gender roles. In Douglas Sirk's *Written on the Wind* (1956), a Texas millionaire marries a beautiful but naive secretary and then

Figure 8.24 *Boys Don't Cry* (1999). The strain of gender, identity, and expression.

Figure 8.25 *Written on the Wind* (1956). The explosive tensions of the family melodrama.

Figure 8.26 *Mississippi Masala* (1991). Negotiating the multicultural family through melodrama.

tortures himself wondering whether the baby they are expecting is his or his best friend's (the man she should have married); the corruption and confusion of this household grows more intense and manic through the constant baiting and manipulations of a sister whose restlessness is expressed as sexual promiscuity **[Figure 8.25]**.

Social melodramas extend the melodramatic crisis of the family to include larger historical, community, and economic issues. In these films, the losses, sufferings, and frustrations of the protagonist are visibly part of social or national politics. Earlier melodramas fit this subgenre—for example, John Stahl's *Imitation of Life* (1934), remade by Douglas Sirk in 1959, makes the family melodrama inseparable from larger issues of racism as a black daughter passes for white. Yet modern melodramas commonly explore social and political dimensions of personal conflicts: in Mira Nair's *Mississippi Masala* (1991), the romance between an Indian woman born in Uganda and an African American man from Greenwood, Mississippi, must negotiate the family and cultural traditions of African Americans, South Asian immigrants, and local white Americans **[Figure 8.26]**.

Musicals

As we noted in Chapter 5, when synchronous sound came to the cinema in 1927, films quickly worked to design plots exclusively for music. Before then, music had always surrounded movies through piano or orchestral accompaniments of a film's projection. With the new sound technology, however, films began to focus exclusively on music or to integrate music and song into the stories. Precedents for film musicals range from traditional opera to vaudeville and musical theater, in which songs either supported or punctuated the story. Since the first musicals, the most common components of the musical have been

- characters who act out and express their emotions and thoughts through song and dance
- plots interrupted or moved forward by musical numbers
- spectacular sets and settings, such as Broadway theaters, fairs, and dramatic social or grand natural backgrounds, or animated environments

In *Gold Diggers of 1933* (1933) and *The Sound of Music* (1965), groups of characters escape the complexities of the situation (Depression-era society and Austria threatened by Nazis, respectively) by breaking into song **[Figure 8.27]**. Whether on a Broadway stage or against the beauty of an

Figure 8.27 *The Sound of Music* (1965). Salvation through song.

Alpine setting, characters in musicals speak their hearts and minds most articulately through music and dance.

As social markers, musicals are the flip side of melodramas, highlighting the joy of expression rather than the pain of repression. With musicals, the tearful cries of melodrama give way to the beautiful articulations of music. Both focus on personal emotions, but in musicals, song and dance become the longed-for vehicles for the repressed and inexpressible emotions of the melodrama. In musicals, the present easily usurps the past. There are certainly romantic crises, social problems, and physical dangers in the narrative, but in most cases, these obstacles are secondary and any difficulties can be remedied or at least put into perspective by the immediacy of song, music, and dance. With more plot than most musicals, *West Side Story* (1961) features all the tragedy and violence found in Shakespeare's *Romeo and Juliet* (on which it is based): gangs fight, lovers are separated, and horrible deaths happen. But even during the most troubling situations, a song and dance transform battle cries into gaiety ("Here Come the Jets") **[Figure 8.28]**, patriotic idealism into comic satire ("America"), and even a tragic death into a peaceful vision ("Somewhere").

After the first feature-length musical, *The Jazz Singer* (1927), musicals changed to reflect different cultural predicaments. Of the many types of musicals, we can identify three subgenres: theatrical, integrated, and animated musicals. No doubt the best known, **theatrical musicals** situate the musical convention onstage or "backstage"; here, it is unmistakable that the fantasy and art of the theater supercede the reality of the street. One of the finest early musicals, *42nd Street* (1933) is partly about the complicated love lives of its characters: a Broadway director who wants one last hit play, the starlet Dorothy Brock who juggles lovers offstage, and the chorus girl Peggy Sawyer who substitutes for the star and saves the show. What ultimately gathers all these hopes and conflicts is, of course, the musical show itself: through the remarkable choreography of Busby Berkeley and hit tunes like "Shuffle off to Buffalo," jealousies and doubts become a spectacular celebration of life on Broadway **[Figure 8.29]**. Although theatrical musicals later waned in popularity, *All That Jazz* (1979) resurrected this subgenre as an exaggerated and, frankly, self-indulgent staging of the autobiography of choreographer Bob Fosse. Most

Figure 8.28 *West Side Story* (1961). The joy of expression amidst social crisis.

Figure 8.29 *42nd Street* (1933). The musical as theater.

Figure 8.30 *Beauty and the Beast* (1991). Animation and the utopian possibilities of the musical.

recently, *Chicago* (2002) weaves the drama of abused and downtrodden women into an energetic musical in which the theatrics of song and dance burst open prison cells.

When musicals began to integrate musical numbers into more common situations and realistic actions, they became **integrated musicals.** Here, the idyllic and redemptive moments of song and dance are part of everyday lives. In *My Fair Lady* (1964), the grueling transformation of a street girl into a glamorous aristocrat is described by song; in the case of numbers like "The Rain in Spain," songs actually assist that transformation. *Dancer in the Dark* (2000) and *Pennies from Heaven* (1981) are more ironic versions of this subgenre. In both films, musical interludes allow the characters (a blind woman accused of murder and a sheet-music salesman during the Depression, respectively) to unexpectedly transcend the tragedies and traumas of life.

Beginning with *Snow White* (1956) and appearing more frequently within the last twenty years, **animated musicals** use cartoon figures and stories to present songs and music. Moving in the opposite direction of integrated musicals, these films—from *Fantasia* (1940), *Mary Poppins* (1964), and *The Yellow Submarine* (1968) to *The Little Mermaid* (1989), *Beauty and the Beast* (1991) **[Figure 8.30]**, and *Shrek* (2001)—fully embrace the fantastic and utopian possibilities of music to make animals human, nature magical, or human life "practically perfect in every way."

Horror Films

Horror has been a popular literary and artistic theme at least since Sophocles's account of Oedipus's terrifying realization of his fate, the horrifying suicide of his mother, and his ghastly self-blinding. The supernatural mysteries of Gothic novels, such as *The Monk* (1796), were followed in the nineteenth century by tales of monsters and murder, such as *Frankenstein* (1818). Occasionally overlapping with science fiction, horror films have crossed cultures and appeared in various forms throughout film history. The fundamental elements of horror films include:

■ characters with physical, psychological, or spiritual deformities, sometimes existing together in one character
■ narratives built on suspense, surprise, and shock
■ visual compositions that move between the dread of not seeing and the horror of seeing

In Carl Boese's *The Golem* (1920) **[Figure 8.31]** and Ridley Scott's *Alien* (1979) **[Figure 8.32]**, monstrous characters terrify the humans around them with their grotesque shapes and actions, lurking on the fringes of the visible world. Each film is infused with a nervous tension at the mere prospect of seeing a horror that exists just out of sight, a suspense that explodes when the creatures suddenly appear.

Horror films are about fear—physical fear, psychological fear, sexual fear, even social fear. The social repercussions of dramatizing what we fear are often debated, but regardless of whether showing horror on film has any effect on society, the genre's widespread popularity suggests that it is a central cultural ritual. Like scary stories around a campfire, horror films dramatize our personal and social terrors in their different forms, in effect allowing us to admit them and attempt to deal with them in an imaginary way and as part of a communal experience. Horror films make terror visible and, potentially, manageable. An eerie tale about alien invaders taking over bodies in an American town, *Invasion of the Body Snatchers* (1956) **[Figure 8.33]** acts out the prevalent fears in the 1950s about military and ideological invasion. The frightening story of a high school misfit with telekinetic powers, *Carrie* (1976) unveils all the anxiety and anger of female adolescence.

Figure 8.31 *The Golem* (1920). Physical terror.

Within this genre, horror and fear have taken many shapes in many different cultures, addressing audiences in specific historical terms throughout the twentieth century. Here, we call attention to three subgenres characterized by dominant elements: supernatural, psychological, and physical horror films.

Figure 8.32 *Alien* (1979). The suspense of not seeing.

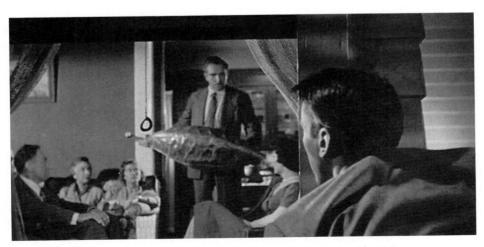

Figure 8.33 *Invasion of the Body Snatchers* (1956). Making visible the fear of invasion.

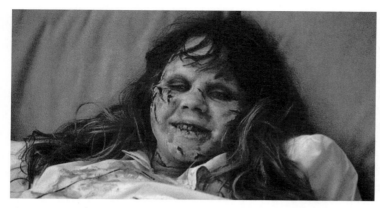

Figure 8.34 *The Exorcist* (1973). Supernatural horror.

Figure 8.35 *The Texas Chain Saw Massacre* (1974). The physical horror of the cannibalistic.

With **supernatural horror films,** a spiritual evil erupts in the human realm, sometimes to avenge a moral wrong and sometimes for no explainable reason. This subgenre includes such movies as Henrik Galeen's *The Golem* (1920), about a clay monster brought to life to save the persecuted Jews; the Japanese film *Kaidan* (1964), which features four tales based on the writings of Lafcadio Hearn about samurai, monks, and spirits; and *The Sixth Sense* (1999), about a boy able to see the dead. In *The Exorcist* (1973), Satan possesses a young girl's body, deforming it and speaking obscenities through it **[Figure 8.34]**. *The Exorcist* is typical of supernatural horror in that how and why this evil has invaded the life of this modern and affluent family is never made entirely clear, but the character of Father Damien Karras, the exorcist, may hold the answer: doubting the real horrific presence of evil in a modern age, he and that age suffer its vengeance.

Another variation on the threat to modern life, **psychological horror films** locate the dangers and distortions that threaten normal life in the minds of bizarre and deranged individuals. A variety of films—including *Psycho* (1960), *Whatever Happened to Baby Jane?* (1962), *Don't Look Now* (1973), *The Stepfather* (1987), and *The Hand That Rocks the Cradle* (1992)—participate in this subgenre. *The Silence of the Lambs* (1991) is characteristic: although it clearly features scenes of nauseating physical violence, it is Hannibal Lecter's diabolically brilliant mind and his empathetic bond with the protagonist, Clarice Starling, that make this film so mentally, rather than physically, horrifying.

Films in which the psychology of a character takes second place to the depiction of graphic violence are examples of **physical horror films,** a subgenre with a long pedigree and a consistent place in every cycle of horror film. Notable examples of contemporary physical horror films include *The Texas Chain Saw Massacre* (1974) **[Figure 8.35]**, the story of a cannibalistic Texas family who attacks lost travelers, and *Halloween* (1978), the first of a sequence of so-called slasher films about ghastly serial killings. Cut and banned in many countries, Tod Browning's 1932 *Freaks* testifies to both the longevity and the more intelligent potential of this subgenre. A morality tale of rejection and revenge, *Freaks* uses performers from actual carnival sideshows who, despite their shocking appearance and the repulsive revenge they perpetrate, ultimately act in more generous and humane ways than the physically "normal" villains.

Crime Films

Like other genres, crime films represent a large category that describes a wide variety of films. From the mysteries of Edgar Allen Poe and the tales of Sherlock Holmes to the pulp fiction of the 1920s, such as Dashiell Hammett's 1929 *Red Harvest*, crime stories have been a staple of modern culture. When early movies searched for good plots, criminal dramas that contained physical action and relied on keen observation were recognized as a genre made for the cinema, where movement and vision are central. A crime film's chief characteristics include

- characters who live on the edge of a mysterious or violent society, either criminals or individuals dedicated to crime detection
- plots of crime, increasing mystery, and often ambiguous resolution
- urban, often dark and shadowy, settings

From *Underworld* (1927) to *The French Connection* (1971), the principal characters of crime movies are usually either criminals or individuals looking for criminals. In *Underworld*, gangster Bull Weed flees and then faces his relentless police pursuers in the mean streets of Chicago. In *The French Connection*, detective Popeye Doyle becomes entangled in the narcotics underworld of New York. In the first film, the law triumphs but the tantalizing attraction of underworld life remains. In the second, legal victory is only partial and the glamour of the international drug market far outshines the tattered life of a New York cop **[Figure 8.36]**.

In crime films, deviance becomes a barometer of the state of society. If the outsiders in horror films represent what we most physically and psychologically fear and repress, crime films describe what we socially reject as outside the laws upholding the status quo. As with horror films, the illegitimate groups and illegal behaviors of crime movies fascinate us as much as the savvy and determination of the detectives and other guardians of the law who track them; perhaps the foundation for this fascination is that most people are capable of both social and antisocial inclinations at one time or another. Two of the most gripping and socially complex crime movies in film history, *The Godfather* (1972) and *The Godfather: Part II* (1974), offer a picture of twentieth-century America that culminates in the transformation of Michael Corleone from a respectable son and war hero into a ruthless mob boss willing and able to destroy any enemies or competitors **[Figure 8.37]**. The films reveal both sides of the mafia cult: its familial dedication and loyalty and its vicious thirst for power at any cost. Echoing this duality, these films suggest that U.S. society has grown from a struggling immigrant community into a rich and intimidating nation.

The different incarnations of crime films, from the 1920s to the present, include three prominent and popular subgenres: the gangster film, the hardboiled detective film, and film noir. **Gangster films** are typically (but not necessarily) set in the 1930s, when underworld criminal societies thrived; in these films, criminal activity characterizes a social world continually threatened by the most brutal instincts of its outcasts. *Scarface* (1932) **[Figure 8.38]** depicts a vicious mob war in which rivals coolly manipulate and shoot each other, while *The Public Enemy* (1931) follows Tom Powers's rise from a juvenile

Figure 8.36 *The French Connection* (1971). A tattered cop facing the glamour of crime.

Figure 8.37 *The Godfather: Part II* (1974). Organized crime, power, and family values.

Figure 8.38 *Scarface* (1932). Gangsters in the underbelly of society.

Figure 8.39 *Touch of Evil* (1958). The shady corruption of film noir.

delinquent to a bootlegging killer who terrorizes Chicago. More recent versions of gangster films—the 1983 *Scarface*, *Goodfellas* (1990), and *Reservoir Dogs* (1992), for example—tend to escalate the violence and explore the peculiar personalities of the criminals or the strained rituals that define them as a subculture.

Moving their narrative perspectives more toward the side of the law, **hard-boiled detective films** focus on a protagonist who represents the law or a more ambiguous version of it, such as a private investigator. Usually these individuals must battle a criminal element (and sometimes the police) to solve a mystery or resolve a crime. In one of the most renowned films of this type, *The Maltese Falcon* (1941), detective Sam Spade pursues both a mysterious treasure (the falcon statue) and the murderers of his partner (killed for the statue); suspected by the police, Spade embarks on a personal quest not so much for the treasure but, through his loyalty to his partner, for truth and integrity. Reinterpreted and reinvented in different cultures and with protagonists other than white males, this subgenre remains visible in such unusual movies as Jean-Luc Godard's meditation on crime detection, *Détective* (1985), and Lizzie Borden's feminist story of a sex crimes investigation in Georgia, *Love Crimes* (1992).

Although regularly discussed as a film style of shades and shadows, **film noir** can be considered a subgenre of crime films that emerged in the 1940s and distinctly elevates the legal, moral, and atmospheric ambiguity and confusion found in earlier examples of the genre. No longer simply about law versus crime or the ethical toughness of a detective, these films uncover darkness and corruption in virtually all people and places and never seem fully resolved. Orson Welles's *Touch of Evil* (1958) is one of the most powerful examples of film noir. Arriving in a Mexican town wild with drugs, prostitution, and murders, lawman Mike Vargas searches the dark alleys and filthy canals in pursuit of a murder mystery; he discovers that the heart of the corruption is Hank Quinlan, "a good detective but a lousy cop" **[Figure 8.39]**. In David Lynch's contemporary vision of a film noir world, *Blue Velvet* (1986), the naive Jeffrey Beaumont takes on the role of detective to solve the mystery of a decaying ear found in a field. Soon he finds himself a participant in the kinky sexual world of Dorothy Vallens **[Figure 8.40]**. His girlfriend, Sandy, wonders whether he is "a detective or a pervert," and after his nightmarish wanderings through an underworld that he keeps returning to, Jeffrey can do no better than repeat that "it's a strange world, isn't it?"

Figure 8.40 *Blue Velvet* (1986). Detective or pervert?

Generic *Chinatown* (1974)

Set in the 1930s Los Angeles of crime writers Dashiell Hammett and Raymond Chandler, Roman Polanski's *Chinatown* is a crime film that features elements of the gangster film, film noir, and especially the hard-boiled detective film. It opens in the offices of private investigator J. J. (Jake) Gittes, a location and a character that immediately recall such classics of the genre as *The Maltese Falcon* and *The Big Sleep* (1946). The room is scattered with light and shade from partially closed venetian blinds, and the tough but cool Gittes, wearing a white suit, controls the scene in every way, as he presents pictures of an unfaithful wife to the distraught husband who has hired him **[Figure 8.41]**. A former police officer who worked the Chinatown district of Los Angeles, Gittes now operates between the legitimate law and the underworld, seeking out the seedy, dark side of human nature and exposing "other people's dirty laundry."

Familiar conventions and formulas are everywhere in this modern version of the crime-film plot; some of these conventions, including the exotic and mysterious connotations of the title, are clearly clichés (this one bordering on racism). Bitter, smart, and attractive, Gittes, played by Jack Nicholson, takes what he believes is an everyday assignment to follow a husband, Los Angeles Water Commissioner Hollis Mulwray, who is suspected of having a sexual affair. Gittes becomes entangled, however, in events that are more complicated and devious than he can quite understand, events that "half the city is trying to cover up." The woman who hired him to spy on Mulwray turns out not to be his real wife, and the real Evelyn Mulwray becomes the foil that both attracts Gittes and makes it clear that, in this case, he is no longer in control. Like other crime-film detectives who survive with their independent moral vision, Gittes gradually and painfully uncovers the twisted

Figure 8.41 *Chinatown* (1974). Jake Gittes, the hard-boiled detective.

and complicated truth that underlies this plot: that Noah Cross, Mulwray's former partner and Evelyn's father, has killed Mulwray as part of a vast scheme to exploit the water shortage in Los Angeles. Indeed, it slowly becomes clear that the cryptic title of the movie refers to a section of urban life—and by extension, to all of life in this film—where conventional law and order have little meaning, where, in Gittes's words, "you can't always tell what's going on." As Cross tells him, "You may think you know what you're dealing with, but you don't." Shades and shadows, specialities of classic film noir, line the faces and spaces in this unclear world, and the addition of rich yellows, reds, and browns to the Los Angeles urbanscape creates a sickly, rather than sunny and natural, climate.

As in other crime films, the shadowy haze of corruption and violence appears also as a sexual darkness. Whereas in older crime films, sexuality regularly takes the form of a femme fatale whose aggressive sexuality threatens the men in the film, the sexual danger and disorder in *Chinatown* is far more horrifying. Here, the femme fatale is Evelyn, who seduces the hard-boiled detective Gittes, but the power of her sexuality poses little threat compared to the reality that he discovers behind it: that she has been raped by her own father, Cross, and that her daughter, the mysterious "other woman" involved with Hollis Mulwray, is also her sister. All these facts are climactically revealed in the dark streets of Chinatown when Evelyn is killed trying to flee with her daughter/sister **[Figure 8.42]**. True to the unsettling resolutions of this genre, the powerful and malevolent Cross walks away with his illegitimate daughter, the police stand idly by, and Gittes's only consolation is that "this is Chinatown." Although the resolutions of other crime films offer tentative and sometimes personal solutions to crime and corruption, here the ambiguity is considerably darker and seamier.

Like the ending to *Chinatown*, many of the variations in these crime-film formulas may be the product of changing times. Although this mysterious world of crime and corruption seemed an appropriate generic barometer for 1930s America, in the 1970s its connection to social and historical contexts was less apparent. With the Great Depression, Prohibition, and urban crowding and unrest, the crime film of the 1930s acted out its social instabilities through the marginal success of a marginal detective, like Sam Spade and others. In the 1970s, after the government corruption of Watergate, the moral ambiguities of the Vietnam War, and the confused sexual legacy of the 1960s, the genre returned with a new relevancy. In *Chinatown*, hard-boiled detectives are less confident than before, femme fatales are more neurotic, and corruption is more sickly and widespread.

Figure 8.42 *Chinatown* (1974). The unsettled and unsettling resolutions of a crime film.

VIEWING CUES: Categorizing Films by Genre

- Identify the generic paradigm of the film you will watch next in class. Which characteristics of this genre are most apparent in the film? Which are least apparent? If this film does not fit one of the paradigms discussed in this chapter, describe the genre in which it belongs.

- Can you identify this film as a particular hybrid or subgenre? Define the chief characteristics of the subgenre that are most clearly manifested in this movie.

- Differentiate the film from its genre: How does it engage or subvert the generic paradigm in which it operates? How do these variations on specific generic conventions or formulas help you understand the meaning of this film?

- Consider whether the cultural or historical context seems to shade and shape the generic formulas used in this film. How does the intersection of a specific culture and a film genre help illuminate the meaning of the movie?

Points of View: Values and Traditions of Film Genres

Since the beginning of the twentieth century when chase films were an international fashion, generic values at the movies were tied to the economics of the industry. Fashioned in accordance with the assembly line productions of other industrialized businesses, standardized formulas meant increased efficiency. Generic traditions thus became the foundation for movie studios as they emerged through the 1920s; predictable scripts, sets, and actors allowed the major studios to define themselves through one or more genres. Gradually, audiences learned what to expect from a film genre and the studio associated with it. Although film genres have changed and spread considerably since the 1930s, they remain a critical measure of audience expectations and of the ability of a film to satisfy or disappoint, surprise or bore, those movie viewers.

To Prescribe or to Describe

Broadly defined, genre represents a system of classification that can be used with many forms of human activity. In addition to literary and artistic classifications, science organizes plants and animals according to generic groupings; similarly, human society might be said to utilize generic categories when it characterizes individuals or activities as part of a class ("an upper-middle-class attitude"), gender ("a typically male response"), or region ("a Tuscan pasta specialty"), for example. This process of generic classification assumes that general or repeated patterns are the first measure of a phenomenon and that an object's (or person's or activity's) uniqueness or singularity is best understood as a variation on that determined pattern.

In this way, film genres imply values about how viewers experience and understand a movie (as well as how some directors approach making a genre film). Specifically, a generic perspective on the movies may derive from either prescriptive values or descriptive values. **Prescriptive values** assume that

- a model for a genre preexists any particular films in that genre
- a successful genre film deviates as little as possible from that model
- a viewer can and should be objective in determining a genre

Approaching a genre film prescriptively, a viewer might stand back from or outside of the many specific musicals that have been made and formulate, inductively and objectively, the main characteristics, rules, and conventions of that genre to determine "what this genre should be." With this model in mind, he or she can then evaluate any specific musical film in terms of whether it achieves or does not achieve that ideal. In this sense, Kenneth Branagh's *Love's Labour's Lost* (2000) may be seen as a terrific accomplishment, whereas *That's Entertainment* (1974) may seem to be a confused aberration of the prescribed terms of a musical.

With **descriptive values,** viewers prize genres for different reasons. From this perspective

- a genre develops and changes over time
- a successful genre film builds on older films and develops in new ways
- a viewer can and should acknowledge that his or her subjectivity helps determine a genre

A filmgoer, looking at film descriptively, surveys the history of a particular genre—say, melodrama—and deduces how its chief characteristics have altered through history. Admitting that such an exercise will necessarily depend on a person's particular perspective (such as which films he or she

Figure 8.43 *All That Heaven Allows* (1955). Descriptive generic values help link this film to its remakes.

has access to and the assumption that a particular genre exists), this viewer will value specific films for how they develop, change, and innovate within a generic pattern. From this perspective, a film like *Ali: Fear Eats the Soul* (1974), about the social prejudices that hound the relationship between a young Arab migrant worker and an older German woman, may be a remarkable variation on the melodramatic formula, which in the different cultural context of the 1950s produced *All That Heaven Allows* (1955), a version of the story in which a gardener and wealthy socialite fall in love [**Figure 8.43**]. With Fassbinder's "remake" in mind, Todd Haynes's *Far from Heaven* (2002) then reshapes and develops that same basic story and generic formula into a contemporary film in which the melodramatic crisis turns on a married man's discovery of his gay identity and his wife's threatened interracial affair with their gardener.

Both prescriptive and descriptive values can point viewers to particular readings of films. A studio, journalist, or filmmaker may, for instance, prescribe a particular genre as the framework for how a specific movie should be seen and evaluated. A studio may promote *In the Bedroom* (2001), a film about domestic violence and revenge, as a melodrama, whereas a journalist may urge audiences to see it as a murder mystery. Following one or the other of those prescribed genres will most likely result in different understandings of the film. Conversely, a movie historian may examine a number of similar films in order to describe the basic laws of a genre (say, science fiction), but if the body of films that generate his or her description is limited to Hollywood movies since 1950, that generic model will emphasize and overlook generic features that a wider survey (one including silent or Asian films, for example) might not. In both instances, the resulting model of a film genre reflects the perspective prescribing or describing the genre and generates meanings that limit or focus a viewer's understanding accordingly.

Two Traditions: Classical and Revisionist Genres

Two traditions have developed as ways of viewing and using genre to derive meanings from particular movies—one defines films within and against a classical tradition and the other according to a revisionist tradition. Related to prescriptive values, the **classical genre** tradition sees a film in relation to a structural paradigm that transcends historical variations, a paradigm that a genre film either successfully follows or not. Closer to descriptive values, the **revisionist genre** tradition sees a film as a function of changing historical and cultural contexts that modify the conventions and formulas of that genre. A particular western, for example, will be understood differently from a classical perspective than from a revisionist one. Together these two traditions identify one of the central paradoxes of any genre: genres can appear to be at once timeless and time bound, to create patterns that transcend history and to be extremely sensitive measures of history.

Classical generic traditions establish relatively fixed sets of formulas and conventions, associated with certain films or with a specific place in history. Classical genres can be viewed as both historical and structural paradigms. If **classical historical paradigm** presumes that a genre evolved to a point of perfection at some point in history and that one or more films at that point describe the generic ideal. For some viewers and critics, John Ford's *Stagecoach* is the historical paradigm for the western that reached its pinnacle in the United States in 1939; for others, F. W. Murnau's 1922 *Nosferatu the Vampire* is the historical paradigm for the horror film, achieving its essential qualities in the climate of 1920s Germany [**Figure 8.44**]. A **classical structural paradigm** relies less on historical precedent than on a formal or structural ideal that may or may not be actually seen, in a complete or pure form, in any specific film. For example, regardless of the many variations on science fiction films, a viewer familiar with the genre may develop a structural paradigm for the classic science fiction film. After viewing a wide spectrum of films—from *The Day the Earth Stood Still* (1951) to *The Man Who Fell to Earth* (1976)—a viewer may understand that the paradigm for the genre requires a visual and dramatic conflict between earth and outer space, the centrality of special effects, and a deadline plot structure. Some films will then fit this paradigm easily, whereas others, such as the frolicking *Repo Man* (1984) (about teenage angst, the repossessing of cars, and a mad scientist), may seem less convincing participants in the genre.

Figure 8.44 *Nosferatu the Vampire* (1922). A historical paradigm for horror films.

With an alternative perspective on the same films, the tradition of generic revisionism assumes that a genre is a product of historical and cultural flux, continually changing as part of a dialogue with films of the same genre. Within this tradition, two related perspectives have developed: generic displacement and generic reflexivity. Seen as part of a **generic displacement,** films within a genre change to reflect different cultural and historical communities. From this perspective, Fred Schepisi's 1982 *Barbarosa* is as much a western as *Stagecoach*, but it is adapted to a contemporary climate that sees outlaws and their myths in a more fantastic light. Films within the more modern tradition of **generic reflexivity** are unusually self-conscious about their generic identity and clearly and visibly comment on the generic paradigms. *Young Frankenstein* (1974) and *L.A.*

Values and Traditions in *Vagabond* (1985)

A fairly recent and less critically evaluated film genre, the road movie demonstrates many of the challenges and benefits of the concept of genre to shape and direct our responses to a movie. A prescriptive definition of the **road movie** would doubtless focus on automobiles or motorcycles as the center of narratives about wandering or driven men who are or eventually become buddies. Structurally, the narrative develops forward, usually along a linear path, as an aimless odyssey toward an undefined place or freedom. Encounters are episodic and disconnected and traveling shots of open roads and landscapes are the stylistic heart of the genre.

If this sketch succeeds as a structural prescription for the genre, locating a historical paradigm proves difficult because no single road movie has achieved the critical attention or achievement that could designate it as a paradigm. For some, *Easy Rider* (1969) represents the historical center of the genre, not only because of its celebrity but also because it introduced a long stretch of generic imitations. In *Easy Rider*, two disaffected bikers go searching for "the real America" and ride, directionless, into violence, drugs, rock and roll, and eventually death; the movie and its progeny crystallize the restless social mood of American youth in the sixties and seventies.

A descriptive definition of road movies would supplement this classical moment, showing how the road movie arrived at this point in 1969 and how it

Figure 8.45 *The Wages of Fear* (1953). The sullen and angry men of the road movie.

has evolved since then. From this perspective, the road movie genre has its origins in the 1930s, where the central motif of road travel occurs in such precursors as *Wild Boys of the Road* (1933), *You Only Live Once* (1937), and *The Grapes of Wrath* (1940), films that make traveling on the road the underpinning of the story. By the 1940s and 1950s, the more serious and existential dimensions of the road movie surface in *They Drive by Night* (1940), *Detour* (1945), and *The Wages of Fear* (1953), in which a lone male or male camaraderie (frequently inflected with anger and violence) moves to the center of the genre **[Figure 8.45]**. (This new dimension is summed up in the celebrated motorcycle movie, *The Wild One* [1953], in which, ironically, a road is rarely traveled.) During the 1950s in the United States, the social turbulence associated with the road movie began to spread (especially to adolescent angst directed at the family). That the automobile became the country's social and industrial backbone only added to the pertinence of the central convention of this genre.

The 1960s and 1970s featured both classical road movies like Monte Hellman's *Two-Lane Blacktop* (1971) and, more often, revisionist versions such as *Weekend* (1967), *Duel* (1972), *Paper Moon* (1973), *Badlands* (1973), *Road Movie* (1974), and *The Car* (1977). If *Two-Lane Blacktop* is a straightforward account of two young men racing across America to a romantically apocalyptic end, the latter movies revised those central themes and icons to reflect the changing times and styles: irony and pathos now permeate the adventure and junk and garbage strew the highways. In the 1980s and 1990s, both displaced and reflexive versions of road movies appeared: *Mad Max* (1979), *Mad Max 2: The Road Warrior* (1981), *Paris, Texas* (1984), and *Thelma & Louise* (1991). In *The Living End* (1992), which resurrects the genre with searing relevancy, the two HIV-positive road buddies have more on their minds than the direction of the road. More recently, the witty and self-conscious *O Brother, Where Art Thou?* (2000) returns the genre to its historical roots, reappropriating its title and certain scenes from the 1941 comic road movie *Sullivan's Travels* as it remakes Homer's *Odyssey* into the frolicking road adventure of three escaped convicts.

Figure 8.46 *Vagabond* (1985). Looking backward down the road.

As part of this historical development, French filmmaker Agnès Varda's 1985 *Vagabond* is one of the most radical contemporary revisions of the road movie. At first glance, this film about a hitchhiking vagrant only partly resembles a road movie, lacking that prominent icon of a car, motorcycle, or other motorized vehicle. Moreover, rather than moving forward down the road, this film moves backward, beginning with the corpse of the female protagonist, Mona, in a roadside ditch. In order to explain how her body ended up there, the narrative presents a series of flashbacks, tracing her wanderings as she hitchhikes through the French countryside **[Figure 8.46]**. It recounts forty-seven different episodes, eighteen of which describe individual meetings with Mona on the road. A migrant worker, a tree specialist named Landier and her assistant Jean-Pierre, a maidservant named Yolande, and her temporary boyfriend David are some of the different people who befriend Mona and try to stop her wanderings or just understand her. Throughout, Mona remains an enigma, often refusing help and companionship, explaining herself only with quips like "being alone is good" and "I move."

Figure 8.47 *Vagabond* (1985). An incomprehensible female road warrior.

An undefined search for identity propels the protagonists of most road movies and usually leads to some version of self-knowledge. *Vagabond*, however, changes the terms of that search. Instead of following the protagonist's point of view as she searches the horizon or the rear-view mirror for some insight into her present and past self, the film assumes the points of view of the eighteen people along the road, hoping their roadside perspectives will provide the key to this road warrior. Again and again, Mona's movement confuses and angers them: she is physically repulsive to some, verbally unresponsive to most, and consistently impenetrable to all **[Figure 8.47]**. Her movement becomes a refusal to have an identity or a claim to a self, knowable either to herself or others.

The key to the generic detours in this road movie is clearly that a woman has now taken the road traditionally claimed by men. If road movies commonly focus on male anxiety and desire, *Vagabond*, like the later *Thelma & Louise*, alters that central feature and with this change, maps a new road and explores different questions about identity. Men may attack Mona or be put off by her, but on this road they will not contain or control her. As in the classic road movie, the narrative and the film image continually move and progress in *Vagabond*. Here, however, progression and movement are the means of staying alive to the mobility of one's true self, rather than a way to search for some uncertain goal at the end of the road. Like many other road movies, the end of the road here is death, but for this woman that ending reveals nothing about the journey.

Figure 8.48 *Nosferatu the Vampyre* (1979). Generic reflexivity: re-creating and manipulating the paradigm.

Confidential (1997) surely fit this tradition, the first a goofy look at one of the most famous models for a horror film and the second a serious self-conscious reworking of the crime film. Less obviously perhaps, Werner Herzog's *Nosferatu the Vampyre* (1979) does not simply re-create the original *Nosferatu*, but also returns to many of its conventions and icons as a way of commenting on the continuing relevancy of the vampire myth and how it still reveals much about contemporary society [Figure 8.48].

VIEWING CUES: Film Genre Traditions and Values

- For the film you will watch next in class, consider how the genre allows you to perceive different values and meanings. If you understand film genres as having descriptive values, how would you evaluate this film according to those values? If you believe film genres have prescriptive values, what would be the particular generic strengths or weaknesses of the film?

- Place this film in a generic tradition. Would you characterize it as part of a classical or revisionist tradition? If it fits a classical tradition, is it within a historical or structural paradigm? If it fits a revisionist tradition, is it best described as displaced or reflexive?

- Write a two-paragraph description of how the meaning of this film depends on the values and traditions of its genre.

CRITICAL VOICES: CAROL J. CLOVER ON GENDER AND SLASHER FILMS

Carol J. Clover's *Men, Women, and Chain Saws* (1992) is a daring and demanding evaluation of one of the most popular genres in modern film culture, the slasher film. Concerned with both the conventions of this subgenre of the horror film and its target audience of young men, Clover investigates in this excerpt the rituals of identification put in play by slasher films and the implications for a feminist perspective on film.

At the bottom of the horror heap lies the slasher (or splatter or shocker or stalker) film: the immensely generative story of a psychokiller who slashes to death a string of mostly female victims, one by one, until he is subdued or killed, usually by the one girl who has survived. Drenched in taboo and encroaching vigorously on the pornographic, the slasher film lies by and large beyond the purview of the respectable (middle-aged, middle-class) audience. It has lain by and large beyond the purview of respectable criticism. Staples of drive-ins and exploitation houses, where they "rub shoulders with sex pictures and macho action flicks," these are films that are "never written up." . . .

On the face of it, the relation between the sexes in the slasher films could hardly be clearer. The killer is with few exceptions recognizably human and distinctly male; his fury is unmistakably sexual in both roots and

1

2

expression; his victims are mostly women, often sexually free and always young and beautiful. Just how essential this victim is to horror is suggested by her historical durability. If the killer has over time been variously figured as shark, fog, gorilla, birds, and slime, the victim is eternally and prototypically the damsel. . . . But what this line of reasoning does not take into account is the figure of the Final Girl. Because slashers lie for all practical purposes beyond the purview of legitimate criticism, and to the extent that they have been reviewed at all have been reviewed on an individual basis, the phenomenon of the female victim-hero has scarcely been acknowledged.

It is "on the face of it" that most of the public discussion of film takes place—from the [proposed] Dworkin-MacKinnon legislation [linking sexual violence to pornography] to Siskel and Ebert's reviews to our own talks with friends on leaving the movie house. Underlying that discussion is the assumption that the sexes are what they seem; that screen males represent the Male and screen females the Female; that this identification along gender lines authorizes impulses toward violence in males and encourages impulses toward victimization in females. In part because of the massive authority cinema by nature accords the image, even academic film criticism has been slow—slower than literary criticism—to get beyond appearances. Film may not appropriate the mind's eye, but it certainly encroaches on it; the gender characteristics of a screen figure are visible and audible given the duration of the film. To the extent that the possibility of cross-gender identification has been entertained, it has been that of the female with the male. . . . But if it is so that all of us, male and female alike, are by these processes "made to" identify with men and "against" women, how are we then to explain the appeal to a largely male audience of a film genre that features a female victim-hero? The slasher film brings us squarely up against fundamental questions of film analysis: where does the literal end and the figurative begin? how do the two levels interact and what is the significance of the interaction? and to which, in arriving at a political judgment (as we are inclined to do in the case of low horror and pornography in particular), do we assign priority? 3

A figurative or functional analysis of the slasher begins with the processes of point of view and identification. The male viewer seeking a male character, even a vicious one, with whom to identify in a sustained way has little to hang onto in the standard example. On the good side, the only viable examples are the boyfriends or schoolmates of the girls. They are for the most part marginal, undeveloped characters. More to the point, they tend to die early in the film. If the traditional horror plot gave the male spectator a last-minute hero with whom to identify, thereby "indulging his vanity as protector of the helpless female" [here Clover is quoting Morris Dickstein, a fellow theorist of horror films], the slasher eliminates or attenuates that role beyond any such function; indeed, would-be rescuers are not infrequently blown away for their trouble, leaving the girl to fight her own fight. . . . 4

The one character who does live to tell the tale is in fact the Final Girl. She is introduced at the beginning and is the only character to be developed in any psychological detail. We understand immediately from the attention paid it that hers is the main story line. She is intelligent, watchful, level-headed; the first character to sense something amiss and the only one to deduce from the accumulating evidence the pattern and extent of the threat; the only one, in other words, whose perspective approaches our own privileged understanding of the situation. We register her horror as she stumbles on the corpses of her friends. Her momentary paralysis in the face of death duplicates those moments of the universal nightmare experience—in which she is the undisputed "I"—on which horror frankly trades. When she downs 5 the killer, we are triumphant. She is by any measure the slasher film's hero. This is not to say that our attachment to her is exclusive and unremitting, only that it adds up, and that in the closing sequence (which can be quite prolonged) it is very close to absolute.

An analysis of the camerawork bears this out. Much is made of the use 6 of the I-camera to represent the killer's point of view. In these passages— they are usually few and brief, but striking—we see through his eyes and (on the soundtrack) hear his breathing and heartbeat. . . . We are linked, in this way, with the killer in the early part of the film, usually before we have seen him directly or before we have come to know the Final Girl in any detail. Our closeness to him wanes as our closeness to the Final Girl waxes— a shift underwritten by story line as well as camera position. By the end, point of view is hers; we are in the closet with her, watching with her eyes the knife blade pierce the door; in the room with her as the killer breaks through the window and grabs her. . . . And with her, we become if not the killer of the killer then the agent of his expulsion from the narrative vision. If, during the film's course, we shifted our sympathies back and forth and dealt them out to other characters along the way, we belong in the end to the Final Girl; there is no alternative. When Stretch eviscerates Chop Top at the end of *Texas Chain Saw II*, she is literally the only character alive, on either side. . . .

That the slasher film speaks deeply and obsessively to male anxieties 7 and desires seems clear—if nothing else from the maleness of the majority of the audience. And yet these are texts in which the categories masculine and feminine, traditionally embodied in male and female, are collapsed into one and the same character—a character who is anatomically female and one whose point of view the spectator is unambiguously invited . . . to share. The willingness and even eagerness (so we judge from these films' enormous popularity) of the male viewer to throw in his emotional lot, if only temporarily, with not only a woman but a woman in fear and pain, at least in the first instance, would seem to suggest that he has a vicarious stake in that fear and pain. If it is also the case that the act of horror spectatorship is itself registered as a "feminine" experience—that the shock effects induce in the viewer bodily sensations answering the fear and pain of the screen victim—the charge of masochism is underlined. This is not to say that the male viewer does not also have a stake in the sadistic side; narrative structure, cinematic procedures, and audience response all indicate that he shifts back and forth with ease. It is only to suggest that in the Final Girl sequence his empathy with what the film defines as the female posture is fully engaged, and further, because this sequence is inevitably the central one in any given film, that the viewing assumption hinges on the emotional assumption of the feminine posture.

THE NEXT LEVEL: ADDITIONAL SOURCES

Altman, Rick. *Film/Genre.* London: British Film Institute, 1999. A balanced survey of genre theories since Aristotle, this study addresses the importance of film genres for both the industry and for movie audiences, examining the historical variations of genres and their relationship to social life.

Browne, Nick, ed. *Refiguring American Film Genres.* Berkeley: University of California Press, 1998. This collection features articles by many top scholars on film genre today and gathers pieces on particular films and genres (including the war film and the jury film) that develop new theoretical stands on film genre.

Grant, Barry, ed. *Film Genre Reader II*. Austin: University of Texas Press, 1995. An indispensable anthology of essays on film genre, this volume covers a range of theoretical issues and analyzes numerous film genres. Contributors represent a range of traditional and contemporary critical methods.

Neale, Steve. *Genre*. London: British Film Institute, 1980. This brief but intellectually provocative account of film genres emphasizes the institutional and textual contract between the movie industry and the audiences that genre films crystallize and require in order to create systems of meaning.

Shatz, Thomas. *Hollywood Genres: Formulas, Filmmaking, and the Studio System*. New York: Random House, 1981. A lucid and carefully organized introduction to how film genre operates as an organizing principle for movies, with special attention given to westerns, gangster and hard-boiled detective films, screwball comedies, musicals, and family melodramas.

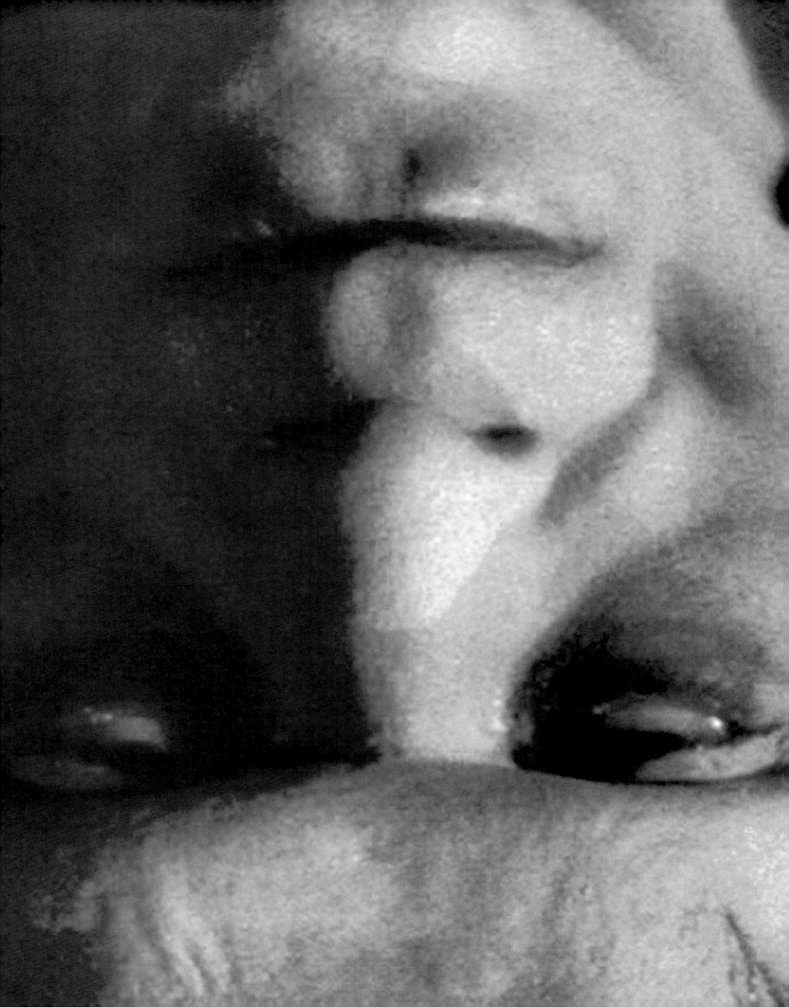

Histories: Hollywood and the World

Historical knowledge and information help our thinking about any subject—and movies are no exception. Watching films made in another era inevitably requires us to consider them, to some degree, as documents whose style and subject matter need a historical context in order to be appreciated. For example, without a sense of film history, many contemporary viewers of James Whale's *Franken-stein* (1931) might find its story simplistic, the acting clumsy, and its audiovisual style primitive. With a historical perspective on acting styles and techniques in the 1930s, however, a contemporary viewer could understand the film as a product of certain historical constraints and possibilities **[Figure III.1]**. The Great Depression, for ex-ample, inspired the dark views of reality and humanity that *Frankenstein* and other horror films seemed especially suited to address in an indirect way, while the advent of sound technology meant actors and film crews were still experimenting with ways to integrate and use this new dimension of cinematic storytelling.

There is no single way to view the history of cinema. Like other histories, movie history takes many shapes and can include many different kinds of materials and infor-mation. For some critics, this history appears evolutionary, with the course of movies developing forward and achieving increasingly advanced forms. Within this historical framework, Sam Peckinpah's *The Wild Bunch* (1969)—a story about outlaws terroriz-ing the border between the United States and Mexico—might make most sense as a stylistically advanced version of older westerns, such as *In Old Arizona* (1929) and

◀ Figure III.1 *Frankenstein* (1931). Within the historical context of fears and darkness.

Viva Zapata! (1952). Other notions about film history might shape our understanding and thinking about this movie in different ways. We could, for instance, view the film as a direct or indirect reflection of its larger historical context, revealing an intersection of social, technological, and cultural forces. Through this perspective, *The Wild Bunch* represents a cross-section of a historical moment: the violence brought home by the Vietnam War, the stylistic influence of European cinema in the 1960s, and the economic power of younger and more rebellious audiences all become important factors in understanding the film **[Figure III.2]**.

Whichever way we use history to help us think about movies, it is important to remember two points: (1) that our knowledge of film history invariably colors our perception of a particular movie and (2) that there is more than one way to envision film history. Introducing film history according to these guidelines, we aim not only to present key information about movie history (such as important dates, names, and events), but also to indicate how our sense of that history becomes richer and more insightful through an awareness of **film historiography,** the study of the methods and principles through which the past becomes organized according to certain perspectives and priorities.

In Chapters 9 and 10, we will look at a selection of historical models used to see and understand the movies: one group based in conventional models of history (and directed at Hollywood films) and the other in inclusive historical approaches (which extend the reach of history well beyond Hollywood and around the world). Each of these models offers certain advantages and disadvantages; a sophisticated movie history is likely to combine several models. In the context of these multiple perspectives on film history, determining a "correct" history of the cinema may be less important than recognizing the assumptions about film history that help shape our understanding and enjoyment of individual movies and film movements.

Figure III.2 *The Wild Bunch* (1969). At the crossroads represented by the 1960s.

Conventional Film History: Evolutions, Masterpieces, and Periodization

The year 1931 in the film industry, as was the case with the latter months of 1930, will continue to be a test of courage. . . . Artists who can only stand pleasant times and pleasant words are not of lasting value. This year will be a splendid year for the industry, for during it we see much of the purging effect of that greatest of all natural laws: the survival of the fittest.

—Cecil. B. DeMille, director of *The Ten Commandments* (1923 and 1956),
The Plainsman (1936), and *Reap the Wild Wind* (1942)

KEY OBJECTIVES

If our sense of film history inevitably shapes our experience of the movies, what are the best-known and most influential historical models for approaching and making sense of a film? With a focus on Hollywood film history, we will look at the most traditional and often dominant histories that have determined why we value certain movies. We will also suggest some of the cultural assumptions that have supported these histories and examine how these perspectives enrich our approach to film, while sometimes concealing certain complexities in specific films and in the film industry. Our emphasis will be on three kinds of traditional or conventional movie history:

■ history that describes the development of film as an evolutionary growth

■ history that focuses on the power of individuals and exceptional works

■ history that concentrates on and distinguishes different stylistic periods

Since the first days of moving pictures, movies have attempted to make history—that is, to establish a correct history of the past or at least to document a history that most of us can agree on. At one end of the twentieth century, *The Birth of a Nation* (1915) was reportedly hailed by President Woodrow Wilson as "writing history with lightning." At the other end, *JFK* (1991) would claim to correct the assumed facts of the Kennedy assassination by presenting the truth of that infamous event on film. The first movies, with their remarkable ability to present events and individuals as living images, began immediately to record actual historical happenings or to re-create fictionalized versions of historical moments. Seeing a celebrated boxing match in *The Corbett-Fitzsimmons Fight* (1897) or a scene from the Spanish-American War in *Wreck of the Battleship "Maine"* (1898) astonished audiences with the illusion of witnessing or participating in history itself. Film

Figure 9.1 *The Scarlet Empress* (1934). History in the movies: a very glamorous Catherine the Great.

history became, in one sense, the representation and actualization of true events. Since those early years, the history of the cinema has become one of the most common and pervasive ways people encounter the figures of the past. From the tale of the eighteenth-century Russian monarch Catherine the Great in *The Scarlet Empress* (1934) **[Figure 9.1]** to the story of John Reed and the Greenwich Village leftist movement in *Reds* (1981), the history of the movies has so powerfully and convincingly reconstructed the past that it has become the dominant framework through which many of us see and understand that past.

Just as the movies construct visions of history for us, how we look at film history is the product of certain formulas and models. Most commonly, film cultures from around the world have relied on what we will call conventional models of movie history. These **conventional histories** claim traditional and logical formulas for connecting events or persons in a single course through time. Historical changes might thus appear as a function of economic forces or be seen as following the will of powerful individuals who, by their acts, determine the direction of history. Based on judgments of aesthetic value or inherited opinions about who and what is most important, historical perspectives such as these necessarily prioritize and omit people, films, and issues in favor of traditional assumptions or evaluations. The 1941 *Citizen Kane* will appear in virtually every conventional history of the movies; the 1941 *The Face behind the Mask* will probably never be found there.

Of the conventional film histories from around the world, Hollywood history has been the most dominant. Our focus in this chapter on that Hollywood history should not be mistaken for a belief that "dominant" means most important. Rather, the Hollywood emphasis in this chapter is practical: because of its economic success, widely accepted artistic strategies, and global popularity, Hollywood cinema has provided the most universally recognized and influential framework for conventional histories of the movies. (Not surprisingly, these conventional histories of Hollywood invariably highlight those films that perpetuate and perfect the classical Hollywood narrative examined in Chapter 6.) Here, we will examine three of the most prominent ways that Hollywood history has been constructed: film history as evolution, film history as masters and masterpieces, and film history as periodization.

Film History as Evolution

The first movies to arrive, in 1895, were already part of a historical evolution that developed from science, the arts, and other cultural precedents. They appeared as a revolutionary moment in that history, astonishing the world with two-dimensional images that suddenly could move. Seeking the shock of the new, viewers flocked to see the race film *The Derby* **[Figure 9.2]** in 1896 and, later, the magic of Georges Méliès's 1902 *A Trip to the Moon*. Since then, each generation of films has identified its revolutionary and evolutionary moments. *The Jazz Singer* (1927) stunned audiences with talking images, *The Best Years of Our Lives* (1946) rocked viewers with its hard realism, and *The Godfather* (1972) announced the arrival of a Hollywood renaissance. This model of film history is one of gradual change, punctuated by dramatic and sweeping paradigm shifts.

Both scientific and human history have, at least for the last two centuries, been drawn toward evolutionary models of development. Evolution, made famous in the nineteenth century by Charles Darwin, theorizes that all biological species develop from earlier forms, following a logic of adaptation to their environment. In the popular understanding, evolution is seen as a progressive "survival of the fittest." In societies, we often equate it with better lifestyles, more material comforts, and more sophisticated attitudes.

Figure 9.2 *The Derby* (1896). The beginning of cinema's evolution.

Given the wide impact of evolutionary thought outside the realm of biological history, it is no surprise that one of the most common perspectives on movie history follows this formula. According to **evolutionary film history,** film culture develops through advancing forces that, over time, create more efficient, powerful, attractive, or sophisticated films. In this history, Hollywood films move through the twentieth century by financially and artistically conquering or dominating all other film cultures because the former are supposedly the most highly developed products and practices. This perspective on film history suggests that

- movies have grown out of the primitive practices of optical toys and jerky film images to mature into the lavish special effects of today
- movies attest to the survival and advancement of the best and most powerful film forms

We might admire early silent films like *A Trip to the Moon* **[Figure 9.3]** as defining the origins of movies, but we see them as crude and unsophisticated compared to the many artistic and technological advancements seen in *Star Wars* (1977) or more recent high-tech movies such as *The Matrix Revolutions* (2003).

Like scientific models of evolution, evolutionary film histories incorporate revolutionary events, punctuating slow progress with sudden disruptions and significant transformations. On the one hand, events or films proceed forward in a logical order that links one to the next, suggesting historical progression. On the other hand, that progress is often signaled by a disruptive or revolutionary change that directs movie advances in a particular way. The progress and disruptions of an evolutionary/revolutionary film history can involve any and all of the dimensions of movies: technological, economic, artistic, and so on. Using such a model, one can argue that movie history progresses through such revolutionary advances as the arrival of sound technology in 1927 and of new acting styles in the early 1950s.

In this section, we will follow some of the ways evolutionary models have been used to organize movie history by (1) identifying different cinematic

Figure 9.3 *A Trip to the Moon* (1902). Special effects in early cinema.

origins and (2) creating specified patterns of progression and conquest. Within these evolutionary origins and patterns, certain movies necessarily appear more valuable or important than others.

Points of Origin

Evolutionary movie histories establish points of origin—movies or events that mark the beginnings of cinema. For these histories, beginnings often determine the essential nature and terms of the milestones that follow. Here, we will highlight three kinds of historical origins commonly identified with early cinema:

1. scientific and technological origins
2. artistic origins
3. economic origins

One influential path for an evolutionary history of the cinema begins with scientific and technological origins. With this kind of emphasis, the evolution of the cinema begins as a search for scientific knowledge (particularly in the field of optics) and proceeds on a path of ever-increasing technological proficiency. As early as 1640, Athanasius Kircher's magic lantern—a mechanical device for directing light and shadows to reproduce images of the world—appears as a precursor of cinematic technology. Over the next two hundred years, a stream of technological toys and scientific instruments demonstrated new ways to generate images. As the industry, science, and technology of the image expanded into the nineteenth century, more central and recognizable technological sources for the cinema emerged from those devices and experiments. In 1839, Louis Jacques Mandé Daguerre developed early forms of photography (almost simultaneously with William Henry Fox Talbot's photographic discoveries in the 1840s). By 1877, Eadweard Muybridge had demonstrated how a series of photographic images could create the illusion of movement. Muybridge's work, most notably, exploited that physiological fact called the "persistence of vision," which Peter Mark Roget had scientifically verified in 1824 (see pp. 76–80). This phenomenon, involving the delayed processing of images between the retina and the brain, meant that images presented every one-twentieth to one-fifth of a second would overlap and so create the illusion of movement. By 1892, Thomas Edison and W. K. L. Dickson's work in the practical sciences took these experiments further to produce the Kinetoscope. Building on earlier experiments with a projection technology that ran a filmstrip with sprocket holes past the opening of a synchronized shutter, Edison's device allowed a single person to view continuously moving images through a peephole mechanism.

As the starting point for the movies we recognize today, the first films of the brothers Auguste and Louis Lumière represent another major moment in these scientific origins by rejecting the peephole technology of the Kinetoscope to project movies for public viewings. On March 22, 1895, the Lumière brothers showed *Workers Leaving the Lumière Factory* to a small group of acquaintances. On December 28 of the same year, they projected a number of other short films for the public, including *Arrival of a Train at a Station* [**Figure 9.4**]. For many historians, this is the beginning of cinema history as we know it (although some

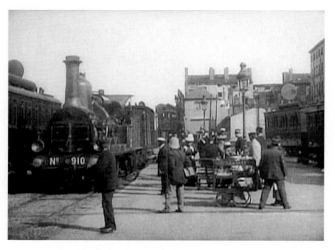

Figure 9.4 *Arrival of a Train at a Station* (1895). The beginnings of cinema history.

historians note that the German brothers Emil and Max Skladanowsky had also projected movies in Berlin two months earlier). These and other films by the Lumière brothers documented small, seemingly incidental social and historical realities, sometimes with wit and humor. Most of the movies that followed associated themselves more with the entertainment and artistic origins of cinema, but these earlier scientific and documentary impulses would remain an important lineage in film history throughout the evolution of classical film.

From a slightly different perspective, another common historical narrative traces cinema's **artistic origins.** According to this beginning, cinematic images are foreshadowed in cave drawings, Egyptian hieroglyphics, and stories found on tapestries. Depicted on the famous Bayeux tapestry, for example, is a series of images re-creating the 1604 battles between the Normans and King William of England. In these origins, one witnesses the ritualistic, artistic, and entertainment powers that the movies would develop in later years. Through these artistic traditions, human society represents itself and its world through beautiful images that honor that world, its myths, and its energy, reflecting the creativity of individuals and societies and providing the pleasure of seeing oneself re-created in pictures and words. Clearly, drama is part of this path, and it begins to draw closer to the cinema in the nineteenth century when the public begins to seek not only theatrical spectacles but also dioramas and panoramas **[Figure 9.5]**, the exhibition of large, sometimes circular paintings relying on special effects to re-create great events of history, such as the defeat of Napoleon at Waterloo.

1895 is the year most often designated as the beginning of the cinema, and original artistic and entertainment films followed fast on the heels of this technological start with short movies depicting theatrical scenes. By the beginning of the twentieth century, such movies as Méliès's *The Impossible Voyage* (1904), the Pathé brothers' production of *Alibaba and the Forty Thieves* (1907), and Edwin S. Porter's *The Dream of a Rarebit Fiend* (1906) used various special effects and imaginative stories to extend those first efforts to exploit the new artistic and entertainment possibilities of the cinema **[Figure 9.6]**. By the time of the 1908 film *The Assassination of the Duke de Guise,* the French *film d'art* movement forcefully announced the unique potentials of film as a creative art, absorbing painting, literature, and theater.

Related to both the scientific and artistic origins of the cinema are its **economic origins,** a third starting point in an evolutionary history of movies. Since the rise of a middle class in the eighteenth century, art, entertainment, and technology have had an important economic dimension. As popular entertainments expanded to address the rising middle class, cultural shows, books, and exhibitions generated more and more profits, which, in turn, attracted more and more economic investment. Throughout the nineteenth

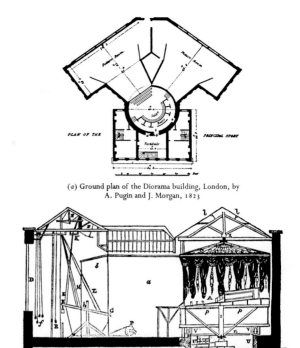

(*a*) Ground plan of the Diorama building, London, by A. Pugin and J. Morgan, 1823

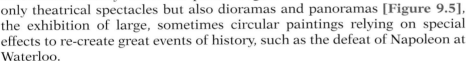

THE DIORAMA.

(*b*) Cross-section of the auditorium and picture emplacement of the Diorama, London

Figure 9.5 Nineteenth-century diorama: a point of origin.

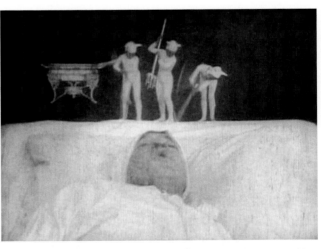

Figure 9.6 *The Dream of a Rarebit Fiend* (1906). The birth of art film.

century, numerous institutions, such as vaudeville halls and popular literature, identified a growing public appetite for amusements, encouraged by the increased leisure time and disposable incomes of the middle and lower classes. In 1893, in keeping with this trend, Edison started marketing his Kinetoscope, selling it for about $200. Entrepreneurs then charged individuals twenty-five cents for admission to Kinetoscope parlors where patrons could view short filmstrips of vaudevillian entertainment, historical tableaux, and re-created sporting events. In 1896, Edison began to employ Thomas Armat and Charles Francis Jenkins's Vitascope—a projection system that competed with the Lumière brothers' public projector, the Cinematographe. With largely commercial aims, the Vitascope showed short vaudevillian subjects—like *Butterfly Dance* (1896) and *Skirt Dance* (1898)—in amusement halls to a public whose enthusiasm for new entertainments and curiosities seemed economically boundless.

Progress and Conquest: More Reality, Money, and Sophistication

Along with points of origin, an evolutionary scheme requires progress through the conquest of old realities by new realities. According to this model of film history, movies get better with time because old problems are solved and former obstacles are overcome. Moving images become, it is assumed, more technologically proficient and entertaining, while the cultural force of movies becomes increasingly powerful. Let us look here at three ways that Hollywood history can be mapped as an evolutionary series of improvements or advances:

1. as an advancing realism
2. through its increasing economic importance as an entertainment industry
3. in terms of the growing sophistication of its audiences

One of the central notions about Hollywood history is that historical progress means an **advancing realism,** according to which the depiction of reality on film becomes more accurate as film technology becomes more advanced. This evolutionary prejudice is something we experience with older films whose stories or portrayals seem antiquated or unrealistic to our contemporary eyes. One way of differentiating war movies such as *From Here to Eternity* (1953) **[Figure 9.7]** and *Saving Private Ryan* (1998) has been to hail the powerful realism of the D-Day landing in the latter, while remarking, with hindsight, on some of the visual and narrative clichés of the former tale about army life on the eve of the Pearl Harbor attack.

We can distinguish several paths and stages through which films have claimed increasing amounts of realism. Once a movie mechanism had been developed to record real actions, one of the first major steps in the advancing realism of film was the development of more realistic characters and narrative actions to replace the stagy scenes presented on artificial sets. The early films *The Lonedale Operator* (1911) **[Figure 9.8]** and *The Battle at Elderbush Gulch*

Figure 9.7 *From Here to Eternity* (1953). The realism of war grown dated.

(1914) employed such editing techniques as cross-cutting and alternating close-ups and long shots to convincingly approximate how actions may occur simultaneously in two or more places or how two individuals may exchange a series of looks within a span of several minutes. From 1913 through the 1930s, Hollywood grew increasingly fluent with the language of narrative and the visual depiction of character psychology, no doubt, in part, because silent movies had to rely on images without dialogue. This path toward a greater realism has, moreover, continued to progress as movies explore a growing range of characters and stories. If the 1895 *Feeding the Baby* provided a familial glimpse of a father (film pioneer Auguste Lumière) feeding a baby daughter and the 1938 *You Can't Take It with You* follows the zany interaction of a single household, the 1996 *Lone Star* suggests a more elaborate family drama as it investigates the complex interracial bonds that twist and turn across two generations of Mexican American history **[Figure 9.9]**.

Figure 9.8 *The Lonedale Operator* (1911). Advancing film realism through editing.

In tandem with the evolution of realistic narratives and characters, a major technical advance in cinematic realism—the arrival of realistic sound—is related to the scientific and technological origins of the cinema. As we discuss in Chapter 5, early silent movies often were accompanied by sound effects or live music; there were also numerous early experiments with sound, such as Edison's Kinetophone system, a combination of the Kinetoscope and the phonograph developed in the early 1890s. In 1926, however, Warner Bros. introduced the Vitaphone system, which synchronized sound on discs with the moving images on film. It was a significant advancement in the integration of the moving image and sound, and, after a number of low-key releases, its triumph was announced with the premiere of *The Jazz Singer* on October 6, 1927. In the 1930s, the fascination with sound resulted in a cycle of musicals, from *The Broadway Melody* (1929) through *Gold Diggers of 1933* (1933) and *Top Hat* (1935), that overwhelmed the story with sound. Although another unintended consequence of this new sound technology was impeded camera movement, gradually both quality and mobility of sound recording equipment (from optical recording devices to magnetic to digital) improved steadily to advance the ways sound could promote realism in the movies. Now, synchronous sound could enhance visual realism (the sound of a screeching tire as we see a tire come to a sudden halt) and, as sound developed from the 1930s into the 1940s, asynchronous sound (the sound of screeching as two bitter enemies meet in a

Figure 9.9 *Lone Star* (1996). The new realities of cultural complexity.

Figure 9.10 *A Clockwork Orange* (1971). Dolby: enriching the reality of sound.

Figure 9.11 *Gone with the Wind* (1939). The new ranges and hues of Technicolor.

room) could create complex psychological realities. By the mid-1960s, Dolby digital sound systems were used in films, such as *A Clockwork Orange* (1971), to layer and enrich sound in more sophisticated ways **[Figure 9.10]**. Recently, in keeping with an evolutionary scheme that insists that more sound means more realism, films have been exhibited with increasingly loud sound systems. Movies like *Armageddon* (1998) and *The Avengers* (1998) commonly register sound at unusually high decibels in order to make loudness a measure of the realism of certain violent scenes.

Color processes, which began to appear in the 1920s, offered, if not more reality, at least a greater range of visual realities and particularly the realities of fantasy (see the color plates). Although hand-tinted color images had been used since early silent films and Technicolor had appeared in some movie sequences in the 1920s (such as DeMille's 1923 *The Ten Commandments*), the continual improvement of Technicolor processes in the 1930s set a new benchmark for cinematic realism. The 1935 *Becky Sharp* (adapted from William Makepeace Thackeray's novel *Vanity Fair*) became the first "three-color" Technicolor feature film. By the end of the decade, movies like *The Wizard of Oz* (1939) and *Gone with the Wind* (1939) **[Figure 9.11]** fully established color as a powerful part of creating fantastic and historical realism. Although World War II slowed the advancement of color, by 1954, over half of the movies made by Hollywood were in color (as opposed to only 12 percent of feature films in 1947). Today, color is, to some extent, so taken for granted that its reduction or elimination can be used, in an ironic historical turn, to suggest more realism. *The Man Who Wasn't There* (2001) is a recent example of an expensive Hollywood film challenging the progressive status of color by appearing (in the United States) as a black-and-white film.

Along with the evolution of realism, it is commonly supposed that Hollywood history has evolved as an **entertainment and economic venture.** If the movies originally appeared as a simple amusement or novelty, their entertainment and cultural value increased enormously as they began to assimilate narrative forms. Here again, Méliès is frequently credited with advancing this stage of movie history by developing film's ability to create illusions and present imaginative stories through such techniques as dissolves and stop-motion photography. His early films, like *Twenty Thousand Leagues under the Sea* (1907), construct fantastic or adventure tales taken from literature or current events. These were immensely popular around the world and stimulated the transition of film from a novel distraction to an entertainment based in narrative forms. After 1905, nickelodeons, the small storefront theaters showing programs of short movies (each about fifteen minutes long), would expand their immigrant and working-class clientele to include middle-class viewers (see pp. 30–31). By 1910, films were drawing a larger audience on the basis of their ability to tell stories that made movies appear a more respectable form of cultural entertainment. With new audiences and commercial possibilities before them, movies would develop their entertainment range by adapting great works of literature and, with movies

Figure 9.12 *The Robe* (1953). The wider worlds of CinemaScope.

like D. W. Griffith's *Intolerance* (1916), would gradually present themselves as a unique narrative form able to entertain and enlighten on a level equal with other artistic forms. Between 1914 and 1920, movie palaces supplanted nickelodeons and the movies evolved into an entertainment form at the center of American cultural life.

Special effects, those methods for manipulating or adding new dimensions to the film image, have always been a part of the evolution of movies as entertainment (see pp. 93–97). Since the first movies, tricks with sets, cameras, film, and even projection techniques were used to create effects to startle audiences or impress them with new realities. In the first decades of the cinema, disasters at sea could be created in miniature or with matte paintings in the background. In the 1950s, however, special effects—from widescreen formats like CinemaScope to 3-D images—became an increasingly important factor in distinguishing film from the newly arrived medium of television. CinemaScope, successfully pioneered in 1953 in both *The Robe* [Figure 9.12] and *How to Marry a Millionaire,* used technology to claim greater image size, especially width. The 3-D format, common between 1952 and 1954, was used in movies like *It Came from Outer Space* (1953) to claim more realistic depth. Since then, more and better special effects have served the historical advancement of films, each becoming the newest round in more astonishing entertainment.

Related to the evolution of film as entertainment, filmmaking grew into an increasingly large and complex economic force. The admission price of early movies was about a nickel, reflecting film's low production costs. As movie production began to emulate a factory system with stars, directors, camera operators, and other workers participating in the rapid assembly of short films, the cost of making movies rose and admission prices increased proportionately. Beginning around 1910, the star system (see pp. 54–55) marked a major shift in the history of cinema as it exploited the entertainment value of the movies to glamorize individual actors and later, to a lesser degree, directors. Since then the economics of this system have accounted for enormous increases in the cost of movies: put simply, while star actors and directors require unusually large salaries, they draw large box-office profits that far exceed those salaries. The movies thus took full advantage of rising costs throughout the twentieth century to inflate the attraction of films. *Ben-Hur,* the costliest film of 1959 and winner of numerous Oscars, is superceded by *Titanic* (1997), whose costs far surpass earlier films and whose Oscar-total equals that of *Ben-Hur.*

One crucial piece of the entertainment and economic history of Hollywood is its evolution into and out of the studio system. With the growth of film's power as commercial entertainment, financial competition intensified

Film Preservation and Archives

More frequently today than in the past, we see movies introduced as "recently restored" or "remastered from original print." Sometimes a film is re-released in theaters because some lost scenes have been put back in or because the sound quality has been corrected or adjusted. A DVD release of an older film can mean the resurrection of a movie that would have otherwise been unavailable for viewing. In cases like these, audiences experience an important and growing dimension of film culture, one that aims to preserve or resurrect pieces of film history that are in danger of being lost. Even when we are not fully aware of their activities, film archives and film preservationists can play a major role in a viewer's film experiences by determining the quality and range of what audiences see.

The history of silent films is an especially disturbing example of the importance of archives and preservation. Scholars estimate that more than 80 percent of the films made before 1930 have disappeared, being routinely destroyed (movies were considered as ephemeral as newspapers) or simply neglected (the chemical instability of film's cellulose-nitrate base means that they can self-combust or deteriorate quickly if not properly cared for).

Film preservation takes many forms. Videotape transference is the most common, but videotape deteriorates even more quickly than film and never adequately transfers the qualities of celluloid. Preserving the original film with a celluloid-acetate base is preferable, although the work is complicated and cannot fully halt eventual deterioration. In recent years, digital imaging has offered a new way to prevent works from deteriorating, but this process can alter the color tones of the original film and does not preserve the physical object.

Kevin Brownlow and David Gill's 1981 restoration of Abel Gance's *Napoléon* (1927) is a complex and particularly sensational example of restoration. Frustrated with the tattered versions of this silent French classic, Brownlow pursued the confused history of the film, searching out different versions from private and public archives and eventually patching together an accurate reproduction of the film. More recently, contemporary filmmakers, in recognition of the fragile history and heritage of film, have supported restoration efforts for American and foreign classics. In 2001, Martin Scorsese presented a restored version of *Night of the Hunter* (1955)—a dark, offbeat tale of a religious con man pursuing his two stepchildren and a hidden stash of

the stakes of evolutionary survival. In 1908, a monopoly of the industry leaders organized as the Motion Picture Patents Company (MPPC) to claim and protect their patents and copyrights on film equipment and technology and movie production, distribution, and exhibition. The MPPC also quickly established standard pricing for films and quite effectively reduced foreign competition (before the organization was declared illegal by the Supreme Court in 1915). From this early attempt to consolidate power, a variety of important studios emerged, many still prominent today. Following the movie industry's gradual move to Hollywood around 1910, Jesse L. Lasky and Adolph Zukor's Famous Players Film Company would unite to create the Lasky Corporation in 1916, eventually evolving into Paramount Pictures by 1935. In 1915, Louis B. Mayer began merging various production companies that became MGM (Metro-Goldwyn-Mayer) in 1924. William Fox's 1915 studio would become Twentieth Century Fox in 1935. Restructured from First National Pictures, Warner Bros. would come together in 1923. The smallest of the major studios, RKO (Radio-Keith-Orpheum) was formed in a 1929

Figure 9.13 *Night of the Hunter* (1955). This dark fable was restored with the support of Martin Scorsese.

Archives have also become among the most notable film archives in the world. These institutions not only preserve older films from decay but also offer film programs and research materials.

Many consequences have followed from these efforts to resurrect or preserve older films. Now widely ridiculed, the recent fad to colorize older black-and-white films, for instance, represents a misguided effort to secure a film's popularity with modern audiences while ignoring its historical authenticity. An exciting and far more respectable development in archival preservation is the DVD distribution of rare movies that viewers would previously never have been able to see: the five-disc collection *The Movies Begin—A Treasury of Early Cinema,* released in 2002, offers a variety of restored films from 1894 to 1913; and the four-disc *Treasures of American Film Archives,* released in 2000 by the National Film Preservation Foundation, taps U.S. archives and makes available such fascinating films as J. Stuart Blackton's *Princess Nicotine; or The Smoke Fairy* (1909) and James Sibley Watson's *The Fall of the House of Usher* (1928). More publicized, different versions of older films—such as Fritz Lang's *M* (1931) or Orson Welles's *Touch of Evil* (1958)—pieced together from materials found in archives and collections, are generating debates and investigations about which version appeared when and why. Indeed, one interesting question is whether some movies exist in a definitive version or whether the original experience of a particular film can ever be accurately re-created.

money—as part of a larger film-preservation effort he has helped to propel **[Figure 9.13]**.

Film archives, which are key to the efforts of film preservation, became central institutions beginning in the 1930s. Most notable has been the work at the Cinémathèque Française by Henri Langlois and at New York's Museum of Modern Art by Iris Barry. (As early as 1898, however, Polish scholar Boleslaw Matuszewski argued the need for film archives to preserve early imagistic records.) Since then, the British Film Institute, Pacific Film Archives, and Berlin Film

merger. Three so-called minor studios also figure largely in the evolution of Hollywood as an entertainment machine: Carl Laemmle formed Universal Studios in 1912; Columbia Pictures emerged in 1924; and competing with the studio goliaths was United Artists, formed by D. W. Griffith, Douglas Fairbanks, Mary Pickford, and Charlie Chaplin in 1919.

Identifying themselves with specific genres, stars, and styles that they could efficiently reproduce, these eight studios varied in size and strength, but they had enormous control over the kinds of movies made as well as how and where movies were seen. Thus, Warner Bros. developed a fast, modern style, claimed Bette Davis and Jimmy Cagney, and often produced films addressing social problems, whereas MGM created a rich, sumptuous style and was the home of Elizabeth Taylor, Clark Gable, and musicals. Especially for the majors, one crucial feature of their power was block booking: in a **system of vertical integration,** the major studios owned both the production companies and the theaters and could dictate that exhibitors book less desirable films to get the ones they wanted to show.

Figure 9.14 *Star Wars* (1977). The rise of the conglomerate block-buster.

The Paramount decision of 1948—in which the Supreme Court declared that studios formed a monopoly that had to be dismantled—began the decline of the studios as the primary entertainment engine for Hollywood movies. As a result, independent film production increased dramatically, accounting for disturbing and sometimes challenging films like *Kiss Me Deadly* (1955). In the 1960s, the most recent chapter in the evolutionary history of Hollywood begins with the conglomerate takeovers of the traditional studios: Universal Studios was bought by MCA (Music Corporation of America) in 1962, Paramount by Gulf & Western in 1966, United Artists by TransAmerica in 1967, Warner Bros. by Kinney National Services in 1969, and MGM by business mogul Kirk Kerkorian in 1970. The profits from blockbuster movies drew these companies to the movies, and today, the profits needed to maintain the interests of the media giants ensures blockbusters' survival. All these remade entertainment companies would, in restrospect, pursue the 1977 *Star Wars* investment multiples: $27 million invested to return well over $500 million by 1980, for a 1,855 percent profit within three years **[Figure 9.14]**.

Another, less common way, to trace the evolutions and revolutions in classical Hollywood history is through the **growing sophistication of audiences.** When the word *primitive* is applied to early films and their audiences, it is not meant to carry a pejorative meaning; but it does signal an evolutionary perspective, one that assumes movie viewers have advanced over the years as movies have grown more aesthetically and economically sophisticated. This developing sophistication presumably reflects an exchange whereby movies historically progress as their audiences' knowledge and film literacy grow, each promoting the other.

The first American audiences of the movies are characterized as predominantly working-class and immigrant viewers. While this is partly an overstatement that neglects viewers from other classes and backgrounds, it does identify early audiences that often sought out silent films for relief from tiresome jobs; since many of these immigrants did not know English, silent movies likewise provided an escape from the difficulties of a foreign language. In 1922, the studios hired Will Hays to head the newly formed Motion Pictures Producers and Distributors of America (MPPDA). Commonly known as the Hays Office, it was intended to monitor the effects of movies on their growing audiences. By the 1930s, the average family attended films three times a week, suggesting the continuing social evolution of movies and their audiences into mainstream culture. Consequently, these audiences were carefully monitored by institutions like the Payne Fund, which studied movies' supposed deleterious effects on children, minorities, and women. The attempt to promote films as wholesome entertainment continued under the Production Code, enforced from 1934 to 1968.

By the late 1950s and 1960s, younger audiences came to the forefront of movie culture: drive-ins and teenage audiences are one example; another is the college and urban audiences of art films and other alternative cinemas that proliferated after 1960. By this time, movies could be considered complex artistic objects. With films like Ingmar Bergman's *The Seventh Seal* (1957) and Federico Fellini's *8½* (1963) **[Figure 9.15]**—two very different

Figure 9.15 *8½* (1963). The second coming of the European art cinema.

meditations on death and existential meaning—movies seemed to justify aesthetic appreciation and academic study by college students. As the movie industry followed students out of the classroom in the late 1970s, the introduction of the VCR and other domestic viewing possibilities marked the beginning of another revolutionary phase of film literacy, intersecting with changes in the entertainment and technological histories of the movies. From that period to the most recent developments in new media and computer technologies, new viewing possibilities have allowed movie spectators more control over which movies they watch and how they watch them, thereby increasing the potential for viewer activity in unprecedented ways.

 VIEWING CUES: A Film's Place in Film History

- For the film you will watch next in class, try to place it within a chronology of film history. Does it seem connected to particular origins of the movies? What describes its primary justification for this association with those cinematic origins? Its technology? Its artistic achievement? Its contribution to the entertainment industry?

- If this film is not part of the origins of film history, how would you describe its place in film history? Is it an important part of a specific historical evolution in the cinema? A specific revolution of the cinema?

- Consider how best to view this film as part of an evolutionary history. Does it stand out historically as an advancement of realism, make a contribution to the entertainment and economic evolution of the movies, or address an audience in terms of some development in film language and literacy?

- How does placing this film in a historical context help you understand it better or differently? Does it appear more original and daring when seen historically? Or does its seem more commonplace?

Constructing Origins in
The Birth of a Nation (1915)

At the intersection of all three evolutionary paths stands D. W. Griffith's *The Birth of a Nation*, a famous example of the conjunction of these different evolutionary forces creating a long-celebrated historical origin. However repugnant the racism of this adaptation of *The Clansman* (which should raise questions about its progressive status), Griffith's film pushed the evolution of cinema to a level that still defines the characteristics of classical narrative. This story of two families divided by the Civil War and the postwar Reconstruction of the South has become the emblem for a major, revolutionary turn in film history.

From an evolutionary perspective, *The Birth of a Nation* can be considered part of the historical origin of mainstream cinema's technological, artistic, and economic sophistication. Technologically, it required an unprecedented number of sets and locations, with both natural and artificial lighting techniques and special effects [Figure 9.16]. It also employed more than 1,544 separate shots, when even the most advanced films during this era commonly needed less than one hundred shots. Moreover, these technological leaps extended into the realm of sound. Unlike the majority of silent films at the time, for *The Birth of a Nation* Griffith worked with composer Joseph Carl Breil to create an elaborate musical score that was performed with the film, including and orchestrating as needed work from Wagner, Beethoven, Verdi, and a variety of American folk tunes.

Figure 9.16 *The Birth of a Nation* (1915). A technological revolution, exemplified in this reenactment of Lincoln's assassination.

Building on this new technological sophistication, *The Birth of a Nation* also marks an artistic turning point in the evolution of cinema. Setting new standards for longer, more complex narrative films, it serves as the most famous example of a historical origin for the Hollywood feature film. At a time when most feature films were made within a month, this movie was rehearsed for six weeks and filmed over another nine weeks. The result is considered an artistic landmark in film history for two main reasons. First, the film extended the reach and prestige of American film to encompass an epic subject (nothing less than the purported birth of the modern United States, sprung from the violence and politics of the Civil War). Second, its narrative structure develops a complex parallel plot that intertwines U.S. history in the 1860s with the family dramas of the Camerons and the Stonemans, presenting a new spectrum of melodramatic emotions (ranging from intimate close-ups of women in distress to the tragic losses of lavish battle scenes) against a vast panorama of celebrated historical events. *The Birth of a Nation* also stands out as a major leap forward in the development of narrative structure and continuity editing because of its use of flashbacks to explain actions or a character's thoughts, framing devices such as irises to highlight information or perceptions, and alternating shot lengths, angles, and distances to create emotional effects (as in a typical chase sequence) **[Figure 9.17]**.

Economically, *The Birth of a Nation* signaled the start of movies as big business. Produced for the then-massive sum of $110,000, the film had an unprecedented run of forty-eight weeks, charged a two-dollar admission (for the first time in film history), and within five years of its opening, returned more than $15 million, making it one of the top-grossing films of all time.

Although it appeared early in film history, *The Birth of a Nation* already represents an evolutionary advance in realism, entertainment, and audience literacy. Despite its grossly distorted depiction of African Americans (most of whom were portrayed by white actors in blackface), the film overwhelmed many viewers with the accuracy of its battle scenes (with some shots based on the Civil War photography of Mathew Brady), its re-creations of famous historical events (such as the assassination of Lincoln and the surrender at Appomattox), and the realistic representation of subjective emotions **[Figure 9.18]** (including the insert during a marriage proposal of Margaret Cameron's dead brother as a description of her psychological state). Paralleling these advances in film realism, the status of movie entertainment also altered with *The Birth of a Nation*. After this film, the standard length of movies grew from about twenty minutes to over ninety minutes, while films continued to identify themselves with a literary and artistic heritage that situated them within mainstream culture. For its public premiere, Griffith appropriately rented a Broadway stage, the Liberty Theater, to reflect the newly elevated cultural status of the movies.

The original audiences for *The Birth of A Nation* were large and varied, most of them seeing for the first time a visual spectacle of this size and magnitude. Their reactions to this film, moreover, were vocal and contentious in discussions of the movie, suggesting an awareness of how a film of this kind impacts audiences and reverberates through society. Reportedly hailed by President Woodrow Wilson as "writing history with lightning" and condemned by the National Association for the Advancement of Colored People (NAACP) for its racist portrayal of African Americans, *The Birth of A Nation* announced not only new film forms but also new audiences, ones more responsive to and engaged with the movies than ever before.

Figure 9.17 *The Birth of a Nation* (1915). Advancing narrative structures through crosscutting and varying camera angles and distances.

Figure 9.18 *The Birth of a Nation* (1915). The psychological power of close shots.

Film History as Masters and Masterpieces

If film history seems to make sense according to an evolutionary scheme, it can also be seen as the result of the cumulative contributions of talented people and the great works they have produced. In this context, Thomas Edison, D. W. Griffith, and Charlie Chaplin become some of the most prominent movers and shakers of early cinema history; Orson Welles and David O. Selznick reshape film culture in the mid-twentieth century; and today, the future of the movies appears to be in the hands of such powerful and creative personalities as director Steven Spielberg and superagent/Disney president Michael Eisner. This perspective assumes that the direction and achievements of film history are the product of individual wills and ideas, from which is generated a history of singular achievements, cinematic masterpieces that stand out from the mass of other movies.

Other branches of human history have been similarly conceived of as the story of great men and women who have mastered particular problems or obstacles. This vision of the past becomes the historical record of the great actions and works of these individuals, who are like the rest of us but perhaps more daring, intelligent, or simply more fortunate. Queen Elizabeth I, George Washington, Napoleon Bonaparte, Winston Churchill, Susan B. Anthony, and Martin Luther King Jr. thus figure prominently in different world histories as individuals whose actions and accomplishments changed the world. From these individuals, events like the signing of the Magna Carta, the discovery of America by Columbus, the French Revolution, the movement for women's suffrage, and Civil Rights laws become monuments that measure how world history has progressed.

A cinematic history of great individuals and their works is a history driven by human desires and ideas. It can be defined as a history of singular expression and achievement. History becomes humanized and dramatic, and identified with specific people and the superlative artistic works they create. These acclaimed works then become recognized for their

- unique artistic value that transcends their historical context
- unique role as key moments in film history

To spotlight the filmmaker Orson Welles implies that his personal perspective altered the course of movie history. To designate *Citizen Kane* as a masterpiece is to claim that it stands above the many more common films made in 1941, or that it highlights the specific issues informing film culture at that time, such as leaps forward in camera technology or the shift to more complex narratives [Figure 9.19].

Despite the popularity and attractiveness of this way of seeing films (pp. 424–31), it does romanticize the historical meaning of movies. Movies are, in fact, the products of many individuals (from technicians and writers to stars and accountants) working together, and to designate one person as the primary source of a film is always a dubious proposition. Selecting a list of the best films is likewise a debatable and subjective task. The standards that produce those lists can vary considerably from list to list. For example, given Hollywood's mirroring of society as a whole and consequently its prejudices, for example, it should not be too surprising that histories such as this include few films by or about women or people of color.

Figure 9.19 *Citizen Kane* (1941). A distinguished masterpiece.

Conversely, there are advantages to this kind of history, especially in its willingness to differentiate and evaluate the achievements that have most impacted movie history. Here, we follow a traditional history of masters and masterpieces, pinpointing films and filmmakers often considered as particularly accomplished or as uniquely important reflections of particular historical issues. We will limit our survey to a selective number of commercial feature films that stand out in Hollywood history, recognizing that there are many great masterpieces and masters outside that tradition. Because such histories are always selective, it is important to consider why certain films and filmmakers are included, while others are excluded.

Pioneers, Silent Masters, and European Influences: 1900–1920s

At the origins of the cinema, pioneers such as Eadweard Muybridge, Thomas Edison, Auguste and Louis Lumière, and Georges Méliès were responsible for propelling the medium forward. These prominent individuals are credited, though their creativity and responsibility is sometimes overstated, with advancing the technology and art of the cinema to the next historical phase. Following them is Edwin S. Porter, noted for his achievements in *The Great Train Robbery* (1903) and many other films. Porter stands out as a transitional figure between the early experimenters with the film image and the makers of later narrative movies, and his *The Great Train Robbery* represents one of the earliest and most successful developments of narrative form and cinematic language [**Figure 9.20**]. In this film about a group of outlaws holding up a train, Porter cuts from one scene to another so that the movie both follows and creates the narrative action, rather than simply showing the entire action in one scene and then moving onto the action in another scene.

Figure 9.20 *The Great Train Robbery* (1903). A narrative leap forward.

The first masterpiece of American cinema is generally acknowledged to be *The Birth of a Nation*. Griffith, often called the father of narrative film, is the most celebrated of the silent masters of Hollywood cinema. Charlie Chaplin and Buster Keaton expand this group of prominent silent film directors, with their slapstick vignettes and early narratives extending Hollywood's power into the 1920s. Although Chaplin and Keaton each created distinct styles and stories, both replaced the clownish and chaotic gymnastics of early film comedies (such as Mack Sennett's Keystone comedies) with nuanced and acrobatic gestures that dramatized serious human and social themes. Chaplin's *The Kid* (1921), his first of many feature-length films, is a tale about his Little Tramp character befriending an impoverished orphan boy. It combines Chaplin's ingenious ability to make his seemingly awkward body a vehicle for poetic improvisation motivated by human need and companionship [**Figure 9.21**]. Keaton's works contrast Chaplin's theatrical style with a more carefully considered use of the film medium. As would *The General* (1927) a few years later, Keaton's *Sherlock, Jr.* (1924) forefronts his stoically subtle

Figure 9.21 *The Kid* (1921). From slapstick to comic narrative.

Figure 9.22 *Sherlock, Jr.* (1924). Buster Keaton's comic masterpiece.

Figure 9.23 *The Ten Commandments* (1923). The silent movie spectacular.

Figure 9.24 *Foolish Wives* (1922). European nuance in Hollywood.

face and acrobatic body movements in this intellectually intriguing story is about a film projectionist whose ghostly image leaves his sleeping body and enters the action of a movie he's showing in the theater **[Figure 9.22]**. While Keaton uses many traditional comic falls and chases here, he incorporates the film image itself into this play—creating an almost philosophical depth—as the character stumbles and wanders between the reality of film and the reality of life.

Providing a bombastic counterpoint to these silent comedies, DeMille's *The Ten Commandments* (1923) is a lavish spectacle that marks another direction in silent film history **[Figure 9.23]**. Extremely expensive to produce at that time (costing $1.5 million) and technically advanced (using an early Technicolor process), this film about Moses's biblical journey stands at the crossroads of 1920s film culture, when the excesses of movies began to provoke social concern about their ethics. Perhaps the most interesting balancing act in this film is in its portrayal of lurid sex and violence, scenes that are continually reframed by a clear and strong moral perspective.

From the 1920s onward, European influences began to appear in Hollywood. The aesthetic visions of an older culture produced two especially important filmmakers in Hollywood history: Ernst Lubitsch and Erich von Stroheim. Lubitsch's adaptation of Oscar Wilde's *Lady Windermere's Fan* (1925) is one of many films that became associated with "the Lubitsch touch," a phrase that indicates an urbane and world-weary visual and narrative style. In this film about upper-class social arrangements and manipulations, the sets and other elements of the mise-en-scène became elaborate, highly charged environments in which small details and gestures—a bedroom door closing or a furtive look—resonate with explicit meaning or symbolic overtones. In a similar vein, von Stroheim's *Foolish Wives* (1922) **[Figure 9.24]** presents a sordid vision of humanity in a drama about the seduction of wealthy Americans on the French Riviera, while his monumental adaptation of Frank Norris's naturalist novel *McTeague,* retitled *Greed* (1925), is one of the most stunningly ambitious and creative works of silent cinema. Although surviving versions are less than half of its original 315 minutes, *Greed* retains much of its power and brilliance. Set in San Francisco, this epic account of a dentist, McTeague, and his obsessive wife, Trina, painstakingly re-creates in naturalistic detail the social and psychological forces that lead to the characters' destruction. From the 1920s to today, directors from Europe, Asia, and other world cultures—Otto Preminger, Billy Wilder, Douglas Sirk, Louis Malle, Jane Campion, and Ang Lee, to name a few—have continued to distinguish themselves in Hollywood history.

Studio Classics and Classicists: 1930s

In the 1930s, an exceptional number and variety of studio classics and classicists emerged (consequently, any selective highlighting of major directors and movies will appear especially reductive). With this group of masterpieces, the term *classical* suggests movies that work efficiently within established formulas while also infusing those formulas with an unusual degree of creativity and artistry. Of the many accomplished directors and celebrated films, of this decade, three classicists and classics can be culled out as representative: Lewis Milestone with *All Quiet on the Western Front* (1930), Frank Capra with *It Happened One Night* (1934), and John Ford with *Stagecoach* (1939).

Never truly within the mainstream of Hollywood, Lewis Milestone in *All Quiet on the Western Front* **[Figure 9.25]** created the premier antiwar film of all time. Among the last of the great silent films, this story of the horrors of World War I describes brutal trench warfare through mobile cameras and graphic images, which make the drama seem like a documentary of human loss and political blindness in a wasteland of mud and darkness. Following the gaiety of the 1920s, this film is one of a multitude of movies that turned toward trenchant social issues with realism and honesty, relating it to such dissimilar classics as William Wellman's *The Public Enemy* (1931)—in which gangster violence and despair become a moral indictment of society as a whole—and German emigré director Fritz Lang's *Fury* (1936)—the dark tale of a lynch mob and a man wrongly accused of murder.

Of the many grand and popular movies made by Frank Capra—including *Mr. Deeds Goes to Town* (1936), *You Can't Take It with You, Mr. Smith Goes to Washington* (1939), and *Meet John Doe* (1941)—*It Happened One Night* is one of his first and best: a rollicking story of a rebellious socialite (Claudette Colbert) who flees her wealthy father and takes up, reluctantly, with a reporter (Clark Gable) who hopes to use her scandalous behavior as a news "scoop." Despite their antagonism as they travel the back roads to hide from detectives, they eventually fall in love **[Figure 9.26]**. Like George Cukor's later *The Philadelphia Story* (1940) in its verbal and physical wit, *It Happened One Night* gathers much of the energy in the 1930s that was making its way from the New York theatrical stages to the Hollywood screen. The film's social allegory about the common man correcting the greed and egotism of the rich would continue to define Capra's vision throughout this decade and into the 1940s.

Although John Ford worked successfully from the 1920s into the 1960s, *Stagecoach* is considered his watershed film. While his adaptation of *The Grapes of Wrath* (1940) is recognized as a brilliant example of the ethical consciousness-raising undertaken by films in the 1930s, *Stagecoach*, as we note in our discussion of the genre in Chapter 8, represents the structural perfection of the western **[Figure 9.27]**. The spare, tight narrative describes

Figure 9.25 *All Quiet on the Western Front* (1930). The first great antiwar film.

Figure 9.26 *It Happened One Night* (1934). One of Frank Capra's many extraordinary movies.

Figure 9.27 *Stagecoach* (1939). John Ford's perfect western?

the plight of a group of stagecoach passengers across a frontier plain threatened from without by Native Americans and from within by their social differences (the passengers include a corrupt banker, a prostitute with a heart of gold, and a remnant of the fragile gentry). With grand, sweeping vistas its background and the Ringo Kid (played by John Wayne) as its reluctant hero, *Stagecoach* documents the struggle for a national identity across a uniquely American terrain of violent frontiers and dramatic personal conflicts.

Many other movies stand out during these years. Although their artistic distinctions are debated, the 1939 triumvirate of *Gone with the Wind*, *The Wizard of Oz* and *Young Mr. Lincoln* would certainly be part of many surveys, representing the astonishing diversity achieved within the rigorous standards of classic Hollywood cinema.

Transitional and Turbulent Visions: 1940s–1950s

In a period of transitional and turbulent visions from 1940 through the 1950s, some of the most celebrated work in film was produced. John Ford's westerns—from *My Darling Clementine* (1946) to *The Searchers* (1956)—continue to be regarded as historical barometers: the first re-creates the prototypical western as a meditation on the power of nature and a communal individualism to overcome evil; the second is a morally ambivalent tale about where violence resides and how it troubles the motives of an older and darker John Wayne as Ethan Edwards (see pp. 242–45). Other important films of this dynamic Hollywood period include Preston Sturges's *Sullivan's Travels* (1941), William Wyler's *The Best Years of Our Lives* (1946), Elia Kazan's *A Streetcar Named Desire* (1951), and Billy Wilder's *Some Like It Hot* (1959). Spanning this variety, moreover, is the consistently brilliant work of Alfred Hitchcock, stretching from *Shadow of a Doubt* (1943) to the film some scholars and critics consider his greatest masterpiece, *Vertigo* (1958). Here, we highlight only a few of the most salient masterpieces of these years.

Regularly canonized in film history's hierarchies are Orson Welles and *Citizen Kane,* a film that is admired in part because it challenges the realism, continuity, and clarity of classical Hollywood cinema. The film offers a parable of the great American individual through the story of Charles Foster Kane, whose idealism turns into egotism and greed, blinding him to the importance of the people around him. The narrative structure and style reflect the fragmentations and divisions of this character through the use of multiple points of view and complex shots that create tensions and contradictions within single images (see pp. 34–35 and 481–83).

Although not as self-consciously coherent or formally complex, Michael Curtiz's *Mildred Pierce* (1945) and Howard Hawks's *The Big Sleep* (1946) both concentrate on this period's social and personal instability, most notably through questions surrounding female sexuality. As if reflecting their troubled characters and actions in their form, these films exhibit narratives that seem to lose their direction or visual styles overwhelmed with gloom. Along with its superb performances (notably that of Joan Crawford in the title role) and compelling narration, *Mildred Pierce* stands out in its trenchant depiction of a cultural crisis for 1940s women **[Figure 9.28]** (see pp. 252–54). Hawks made a number of renowned screwball comedies including *Bringing Up Baby* (1938), *His Girl Friday* (1940), and *Monkey Business* (1952), and one

Figure 9.28 *Mildred Pierce* (1945). A searing look at gender roles in the World War II period.

Figure 9.29 *The Big Sleep* (1946). The chemistry of Howard Hawks, Humphrey Bogart, and Lauren Bacall.

of the charms of *The Big Sleep* is Humphrey Bogart's and Lauren Bacall's banter, a characteristic derived from those films. But their electric characterizations of tough, independent individuals on the edges of right and wrong and a twisting story that's all the more powerful for its failure to remain focused make this detective film unforgettable **[Figure 9.29]**.

The World War II and postwar decade also features some of the greatest musicals in Hollywood history, Vincente Minnelli's *Meet Me in St. Louis* (1944) and Stanley Donen and Gene Kelly's *Singin' in the Rain* (1952) being the most notable. Set at the beginning of the twentieth century, Minnelli's film is a Technicolor musical tale of a happy family put in crisis by the possibility of having to leave their beloved St. Louis. Despite its lively and romantic tunes, the film also features darker elements that suggest it is more than a nostalgic story. Although Donen and Kelly are usually not described as among Hollywood's great directors, *Singin' in the Rain* figures on most lists of Hollywood masterpieces, both for its musical and choreographic ingenuity and the clever twists of a romantic plot set against the backdrop of 1927 and Hollywood's conversion to sound (see pp. 48–49 and 181–83).

Appearing in the mid-1950s, Nicholas Ray's *Rebel without a Cause* (1955) and Douglas Sirk's *Written on the Wind* (1956) document, in very different ways, a new tragedy at the heart of the American family. Perhaps Ray's most celebrated film, *Rebel without a Cause* gives a then-shocking depiction of a generational crisis in America in which teenagers drift aimlessly beyond parental guidance **[Figure 9.30]**. Directed by German emigrant Sirk, *Written*

Figure 9.30 *Rebel without a Cause* (1955). The cinematic triumph of teenage angst.

Figure 9.31 *Written on the Wind* (1956). A trenchant marriage of melodrama and politics.

on the Wind presents the epic collapse of a wealthy family torn apart by violence and sex. Its exaggerated emotions and visual style both elicit and undermine the intense pathos at the heart of a gigantic melodrama **[Figure 9.31]**.

Rebels and Visionaries, Dealers and Deals: 1960s–2000s

In the 1960s through the 1970s, rebels and visionaries move to the fore of our humanist history of powerful and influential filmmakers. Many of these young filmmakers learned their craft in film schools and went on to make movies steeped in the masterpieces and genres that preceded them. They include mostly men: Arthur Penn, Robert Altman, John Cassavetes, Stanley Kubrick, Francis Coppola, Steven Spielberg, and George Lucas. From these and other directorial superstars came *The Graduate* (1967), *The Godfather* and *The Godfather: Part II* (1972; 1974), *Jaws* (1975), and *Star Wars* (1977)—movies that redefined the masterpiece as an art film, a blockbuster, or both. Stylistically, these directors took chances with both content and form, exposing social hypocrisies and exploiting cultural fantasies and fears, while also experimenting with narrative structures, the reinterpretation of film genres, and new audiovisual technology.

Three 1960s films are regularly acknowledged as masterpieces among this decade's host of superior films: Arthur Penn's *Bonnie and Clyde* (1967), Stanley Kubrick's *2001: A Space Odyssey* (1968) **[Figure 9.32]**, and Sam Peckinpah's *The Wild Bunch* (1969). The first stands out for its timely exploration of naive gangsters as modern anti-heroes and its complex and jarring editing style, climaxing in the bloody ambush discussed in Chapter 4. *2001* startles its audiences with a tale of space exploration that soon becomes a searing investigation of the dark drive for power and the perils of technology in human history. Just as *2001* dismantles the popular genre of science fiction, *The Wild Bunch* uses the genre formula for westerns to bring out the disturbing political undertones of America's westward expansion. Besides their powerfully contemporary themes and issues, each of these films brilliantly challenged expectations about narrative form, film genre, and imagistic composition at the time.

Figure 9.32 *2001: A Space Odyssey* (1968). Combining art, intellect, and science fiction.

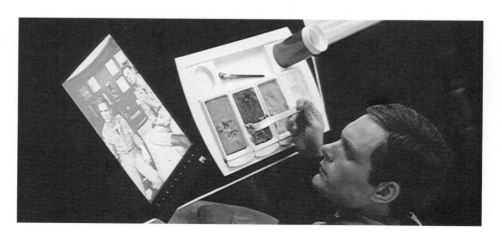

Figure 9.33 *Blue Velvet* (1986). A contemporary classic.

As with other periods in this abridged history, or short list of contemporary masterpieces could and should be expanded to include other remarkable films and filmmakers. For example, the work of Martin Scorsese, extending from this period through the present, includes several films that qualify as contemporary masterpieces: *Taxi Driver* (1976), *Raging Bull* (1980), and *Goodfellas* (1990), to name a few important examples.

Overlapping with the careers of these filmmakers, the most recent era of Hollywood moviemaking, from about 1980 to the present, has been driven by deals and deal makers, individuals whose commercial and entrepreneurial expertise, as much as or more than their artistic ability, accounts for the success of a movie. The central names and forces in this group are, curiously, a combination of high-profile industry leaders and individuals traditionally marginalized from the center of Hollywood power, such as African Americans and women. Along with the continued rise and expansion of power for movie directors like Spielberg and Lucas, producers, agents, and studio CEOs like Michael Ovitz and Michael Eisner assert themselves as key makers of movies, without actually directing films. In this context, Spike Lee deserves special attention not only for directing and starring in a modern masterpiece, *Do the Right Thing* (1989), but also for his savvy in using his reputation and business skills to create an important place for African American filmmakers in contemporary Hollywood.

Although recent history is always difficult to evaluate, we can propose three classics: Ridley Scott's *Blade Runner* (1982), David Lynch's *Blue Velvet* (1986) **[Figure 9.33]**, and Quentin Tarantino's *Pulp Fiction* (1994). Each of these films is a dramatic visual and narrative experiment that investigates the confusion of human identity, violence, and ethics at the end of the twentieth century. In *Blade Runner*, Dekker (played by Harrison Ford) hunts down human replicants in a fascinatingly dark and visually complex dystopia where technology creates figures "more human than human." With *Blue Velvet*, Lynch fashions a characteristically nightmarish version of small-town America in which Jeffrey, the protagonist, discovers violence seething through his everyday community and his own naive soul. In *Pulp Fiction*, where violence is also a measure of human communication, the narrative follows, unpredictably, the twisted actions and reflections of two hit men who philosophically meditate out loud about the Bible, loyalty, and McDonald's hamburgers. In all three of these exceptional films, we find not only the imaginative quality of the movies themselves, but also the professional skill and innovativeness of the filmmakers in both producing such daring and disturbing projects and successfully distributing them across mainstream film culture.

An important development in this recent Hollywood history of masters and masterpieces is the emergence of female and African American perspectives,

The Mastery of Alfred Hitchcock

The long career of Alfred Hitchcock parallels in many ways the history of Hollywood masters and masterpieces, emerging in the silent era of the 1920s and continuing into the rebellious innovations of the 1960s. Through this career, Hitchcock stands out as one of the most distinctive and flexible directors in cinema history. Just as he placed himself in his films (through short cameo appearances as different, briefly glimpsed characters), as a director, he reinvented his cinematic powers through a variety of different but equally accomplished films. Indeed, beyond the notable achievements of the films, Hitchcock shrewdly assisted the cultural construction of himself as a cinematic master. From his self-promotion through his own television series and film advertisements to his famous book-length interview with French director François Truffaut, Hitchcock worked to create a masterly image of himself to complement his filmic masterpieces. His artistic dexterity allowed him, perhaps more than any other filmmaker, to create a long line of cinematic achievements held together by his singular vision and personality. Of all the creative and prolific Hollywood filmmakers, Hitchcock claims the most films on lists of the greatest Hollywood films.

Even before he arrived in Hollywood, the British Hitchcock created one of the first sound masterpieces in the 1930s, *The 39 Steps* (1935). Immediately identifying Hitchcock as a master of suspense, this espionage drama made the new cinematic technology of sound a key element in the mystery of the plot: a music-hall tune, screams, train whistles, and cryptic dialogue create the dense fabric behind an assassination attempt. Even in this early phase of Hitchcock's career, his work demonstrates a remarkable ability to create carefully crafted stories that take unusual advantage of the formal and technological possibilities of film.

In the 1940s, Hitchcock made *Rebecca* (1940), *Suspicion* (1941), *Shadow of a Doubt* (1943), *Spellbound* (1945), *Notorious* (1946), and *Rope* (1948), films that combine artistic achievement and box-office success with a very personal sensitivity to topical social issues. A literary tendency, pronounced through the 1930s and early 1940s, appears in many of these films—most obviously in *Rebecca*, an adaptation of Daphne du Maurier's best-selling novel—as a subtle and poetic dialogue that often skims over the surface of a sinister reality. Brilliantly attuned to the social and global unrest of the 1940s, each film concentrates on melodramatic situations vaguely connected to a political or public threat that will potentially corrupt traditional romantic, family, and community structures. In *Shadow of a Doubt,* for instance, the picture of a cozy, happy family begins to crumble when the mysterious Uncle Charley visits. Shortly thereafter, his young niece, nicknamed Charley, begins to suspect that her favorite uncle (and linguistic double) is a serial killer **[Figure 9.34]**.

Figure 9.34 *Shadow of a Doubt* (1943). Hitchcock masters the family movie.

Many film historians argue that Hitchcock produced his greatest films in the 1950s and early 1960s: *Strangers on a Train* (1951), *Dial M for Murder* (1954), *Rear Window* (1954), *Vertigo* (1958), *North by Northwest* (1959), *Psycho* (1960) **[Figure 9.35]**, and *The Birds* (1963). Throughout this period, Hitchcock's work continues to explore the turbulent worlds and minds beneath the surface of normalcy, but gradually those explorations begin to shape his plots and characters into more radical and rebellious figures. Especially in the later films, Hitchcock begins to appear less like a brilliant Hollywood classicist and more like a confrontational rebel aiming to shock audiences and twist traditional film forms. As early as *Rear Window,* he experiments with unpleasant subject matter, making a movie almost exclusively about voyeurism. Immobilized by a broken leg, a photographer spies on his neighbors' escapades as if watching them on television sets; in the process, he discovers a murder—and the sordidness of his own imagination. By the time he made

Figure 9.35 *Psycho* (1960). Visual daring entwined in a masterpiece of horror.

Psycho, Hitchcock had grown even more confrontational and visually complex. Halfway through this film, the main character is murdered in a short edited sequence that is recognized as one of the most memorable in film history. It begins with a dramatic close-up of Norman Bates's eye spying on Marion Crane as she prepares to take a shower; it then explodes in a montage of rapid shots that, through the illusory power of editing, describe Marion's brutal murder. The sequence then concludes with a close-up of Marion's eye and the parallel image of water and blood washing down the hole of a drain. With stunning economy, the main character of the narrative is lost, and the audience's point of identification becomes strangely aligned with the murderous gaze of a psychotic killer.

upsetting the traditional hierarchy. Women directors have struggled to enter the traditionally male pantheon of mainstream film history, but the recent directorial work of women like Amy Heckerling, Barbara Kopple, Kathryn Bigelow, and Martha Coolidge (pp. 384–87) ensures that Hollywood history will continue to feature more than just white men. Similarly, the gradual appearance of African American directors—Spike Lee, John Singleton, the Hughes brothers, Carl Franklin, and others—as part of this history of masters and masterpieces highlights both the limitations and modern changes in this tradition.

Film History as Periodization

Another important and conventional way to organize film history is through historical **periodization.** With this method, we divide the timeline of Hollywood history into segments that describe groups of years during which movies share thematic and stylistic concerns. Cinemas other than Hollywood have often been described according to periods. For instance, the German expressionist period (roughly, 1919–1926) encompasses films that address psychic horror and social chaos through artificial and exaggerated sets and lighting. The period of Italian neorealism (1945–1952) produced movies that depict the dark and bare social realities of post–World War II Italy stripped of intricate plots and visual glamour. Both periods are discussed further in Chapter 10. Similarly, Hollywood history can be organized according to specific dates that define shared assumptions and perspectives. Unlike a history of unique masterpieces and masters, periodization is a history of stylistic and thematic similarities, a history of the typical.

Like our other two conventional models of film history, organizing movies by periods has many precedents outside the cinema. Historians of English history describe the Renaissance period, the Augustan era, the Victorian period, and other periods that share a common ground in artistic practices, political leadership, religious ideas, or other aspects. American history identifies such periods as the colonial age, the antebellum period before the Civil War, and the Depression era. In all these cases, there is an assumed or defined "spirit of the age" that either reflects a dominant event or institution (such as the reign of a specific queen or an economic crisis) or describes a cultural atmosphere made from the combination of various forces.

Two cornerstones of periodization are standardization and differentiation. With Hollywood films especially, this formula suggests the following:

■ Certain standard forms and styles become associated with a specific historical period or span of years.
■ Individual films then create variations on those standards as a way of differentiating themselves.

Most films use not only historically recognizable themes, plot devices, characterizations, genres, and visual styles but also the costuming, casting, editing, and sound practices of many kinds of movies made during the same period. Often these filmic standards reflect an even wider range of cultural practices, such as trends in literature or television (for example, the rise of MTV-style editing in the 1980s) and even social shifts (the effects of the feminist movement on the characterization of women in the 1970s). At the same time, an individual film works to differentiate itself within these period standards. Even a masterpiece like *Citizen Kane* can be viewed as sharing period standards employed by other films of the early 1940s, such as comic interludes and ominous lighting techniques. However, its radical reworking of those standards through its kaleidoscopic narrative, dramatic editing, and rich pictorial compositions clearly sets it off as exceptional within this period.

For each of the following periods in our survey—early cinema, classical cinema, postwar cinema, and contemporary cinema—we will signal telling social and industrial events that define the historical era inside and outside of Hollywood. Within that context, we will highlight key formal shifts that provide the stylistic standards of that time, standards against which particular films might differentiate themselves. As will become clear, a history of cinematic periods also has its risks as a historical model. It tends to draw historical boundaries that can appear too rigid. It also tends to homogenize a great variety of films as part of one period. Nonetheless, periodization offers a more equitable cross-section of a period in film history than other historical frameworks, suggesting more clearly a typical movie of that period rather than the revolutionary or exceptional film found in other approaches (such as in an evolutionary or masterpiece history). Finally, although historians frequently employ different dates and nomenclature for film periods (referring to early cinema as preclassical or primitive cinema or to contemporary cinema as modern or postclassical, for example), we use the four terms *early, classical, postwar,* and *contemporary* to refer to the historical periods of Hollywood cinema.

Early Cinema

The **early cinema** period, stretching roughly from 1895 to 1913, was characterized by rapid development and experimentation in filmmaking before Hollywood settled into the more defined patterns of its classical period. In the United States, massive industrialization attracted large numbers of immigrants and rural Americans to urban centers where the movie industry

Figure 9.36 Mary Pickford: a new commercial personality.

found many of its subjects and audiences. Traditional class, race, and gender lines began to shift, and these new openings in the social fabric of the country combined with expanding economic prosperity. The women's suffrage movement succeeded at the state level by 1890, the automobile arrived around 1900, and the first airplane left the ground in 1903. Besides encouraging new energies and visions throughout society, industrialization fostered the growth of leisure time and commercialized leisure activities. In the realm of this expanding free time, popular culture competed as never before with the traditions of high culture.

Although moving pictures themselves were the defining cinematic event of this early period in film history, we can identify several other significant industrial events:

- The public exhibition of movies became part of the entertainment industry as early as 1895.
- The rise of the star (or celebrity) system began around 1910.
- The international dominance of Hollywood began in 1907–1913.

Beginning with the showing of *Workers Leaving the Lumière Factory* on March 22, 1895, the first movies attracted and fascinated the public with their various subject matters. Soon commercial and theatrical venues for showing movies to the general public arrived in the form of nickelodeon theaters. Actualities (early newsreels of everyday scenes), theatrical spectacles, and images of famous people constituted these first film programs, and subject matter and themes reflected a multitude of topics and interests as the movies experimented with undefined possibilities. The characters in these short films were originally anonymous actors and actresses, but by 1911 the Biograph Girl became the celebrity Florence Lawrence, Little Mary became the star Mary Pickford **[Figure 9.36]**, and such commercial personalities added to the growing cultural power of film. Finally, as American movies advanced in length and complexity, Hollywood quickly extended its reach around the world, producing half the films made worldwide in 1914.

Stylistically, the most important characteristics of early cinema are:

- the shift from scenes to shots
- the beginnings of continuity editing (as an early elaboration of narrative form)

Whereas the first movies relied on the impact of a single shot of a specific scene or event (such as a man sneezing), movies quickly moved to multiple shots of dramatic events and then to the dramatization of real or fictional events as a story told with many shots, logically connected in space and time. Released in 1903, *Uncle Tom's Cabin* presents a series of shots that isolate highlights of the famous story on which it is based. By 1911, however, Griffith's *The Lonedale Operator*, a short film about burglars threatening a telegraph operator, edited together numerous shots to re-create the points of view of characters, to establish different spatial relations between an office interior and its exterior, and to build narrative suspense through parallel editing.

Classical Cinema

Classical cinema is divided into two parts: silent and sound films. The first part encompasses Hollywood's classical silent period, from roughly 1913 to 1927, when the basic structures of classical narrative were put in place. With the devastation and resolution of World War I (1914–1918) at the start of this period, films often seemed a peculiar combination of energetic optimism and trembling fear. Many of the arts tested out new forms and visions—such as F. Scott Fitzgerald's modernist novel *The Great Gatsby* (1925) and Edward Hopper's painting *Manhattan Bridge* (1927)—and the "roaring twenties" became shorthand for a decade of material and social liberality often slipping into decadence. With New York City becoming the new cultural center of the world, the United States began, moreover, to assert itself as both a powerful global force and the embodiment of the progressive promise of the twentieth century—climactically symbolized in the first nonstop flight from New York to Paris by Charles Lindbergh in 1927.

Hollywood itself came of age during this period with three major historical developments:

1. the standardization of film production
2. the establishment of the feature film
3. the cultural and economic expansion of movies throughout the society

As the Hollywood industry grew in size and proficiency, standardized formulas for film production took root, creating efficient teams of scriptwriters, producers, directors, camera operators, actors, and editors. One long-term product of this standardization process was the establishment of a normalized running time: approximately one hundred minutes for a narrative movie. This model for the feature film became the dominant commercial practice of the twentieth century. Finally, along with their technological and economic growth, movies found more sophisticated subject matter and more elegant theaters for distribution, reflecting their rising cultural status and ability to attract audiences from all corners of society. Internationally, Hollywood continued to extend its reach: with World War I wreaking havoc on European economics, Hollywood would increase its exports fivefold and its overseas income by 35 percent.

The most pronounced and important aesthetic changes during this period included

- the full development of narrative verisimilitude as the center of film form
- the integration of the viewer's perspective into the editing and narrative action

Narrative realism came to the forefront of movie culture during this time, as the movies worked to legitimate themselves by adapting literary works and traditions. From Griffith's *The Birth of a Nation* and *Intolerance* **[Figure 9.37]** through King Vidor's *The Big Parade* (1925) and Buster Keaton's *The General*, narrative films learned to explore simultaneous actions, complex spatial geographies, and the psychological interaction of characters through narrative. As a very significant part of this new formal com-

Figure 9.37 *Intolerance* (1916). A landmark in narrative film form.

plexity, movies developed point-of-view shots through camera movement and editing in order to situate viewers *within* the narrative action rather than at the theatrical distance (as in the view from a seat before a stage) found in early or preclassical films.

The second part of the classical cinema period, from about 1927 to 1945, brought sound to film and represents the golden age of Hollywood. The Great Depression, triggered in part by the stock market collapse of 1929, defined the American cultural experience at the beginning of the 1930s. In the midst of economic unrest and other strains, the shadows of fascist and Marxist ideologies began to move across the U.S. landscape, demanding major changes in the traditional way of life. Franklin Roosevelt's New Deal program became the political antidote for much of the 1930s, pumping a determined spirit of optimism into society. The devastating conflict of World War II then defined the last four years of this period, in which the country fully asserted its global leadership and control.

The film industry followed these turbulent historical events with dramatic changes of its own, including

■ the coming of sound in 1927
■ the empowerment of the Hays Office and the founding of the Production Code Administration in 1934
■ the full definition and operation of an efficient studio system

Most importantly, the sensational arrival of sound technology opened a whole new dimension to film form that allowed movies to expand their dramatic capacity: after *The Jazz Singer* **[Figure 9.38]**, the "100 percent all-talkie" *Lights of New York* (1928) began a period of rapidly more complex soundtracks. With social issues more debated and the movies gaining more influence than ever, the messages of films came increasingly under scrutiny. By 1934, the Hays Office and the Motion Picture Production Code, first established in 1927 as a set of guidelines had evolved into the Production Code Administration, headed by Joseph I. Breen. The code strictly enforced a conservative list of "Don'ts and Be Carefuls" (primarily governing the depiction of crime and sex) that kept censorship efforts within the industry. During this time, the increasingly efficient movie studios produced more and better films out of generic molds that drew ever-larger audiences.

Figure 9.38 *The Jazz Singer* (1927). Sound comes to the cinema.

At this time, Hollywood films followed these industrial shifts with two important stylistic changes:

■ the elaboration of movie dialogue and the concomitant growth of characterization in films
■ the prominence of generic formulas in constructing film narratives

With sound technology came more music and, in particular, more dialogue. Accomplished writers flocked to Hollywood, literary adaptations flourished, and outspoken characters became more verbally, psychologically, and socially complex. The rapid-fire witticisms of the Marx brothers in *Duck Soup* (1933) **[Figure 9.39]** and the musically and verbally elaborate adaptation of Shakespeare's *A Midsummer Night's Dream* (1935) both reflected the new

Figure 9.39 *Duck Soup* (1933). Dialogue ushered in the comic talents of the Marx Brothers.

Figure 9.40 *The Little Foxes* (1941). A cinematic style with a literary source.

sound standards. Meanwhile, genres, always an important organizational dimension of the movies, were enlisted and explored as never before. Whether the movie was the melodramatic *Magnificent Obsession* (1935) or the literary *The Little Foxes* (1941), generic formulas became the primary production and distribution standard—sometimes superceding subject matter and stars in defining a film and expectations about it **[Figure 9.40]**.

Postwar Cinema

The period of **postwar cinema** extended roughly from 1946 to 1965. Despite the large breadth of years, several overriding historical events and motifs defined this period. In the wake of World War II, the inhuman nightmare of the Nazi concentration camps, and the atomic bombing of Hiroshima and Nagasaki in 1945, doubts about humanity and social progress shadowed the economic prosperity that became the optimistic surface of this period in U.S. history. Unease permeated traditional institutions, especially the family and the sexual and social relationships associated with it (such as the status of women and African Americans). In addition, the cold war with the Soviet Union and the communist bloc began an extended period of tension and anxiety about national identity and security.

Within Hollywood, the key events defining this period include

- the dissolution of the traditional power of the studios after the 1948 Paramount decision
- the arrival and rapid spread of television in the 1950s
- the gradual relaxation of the Production Code and the introduction of a ratings system

With the Paramount decision of 1948, which limited how studios could control the marketplace, the power of the studios began to erode. Widescreen movies, drive-in theaters, and other new cinematic strategies appeared to combat the allure of television, which threatened to undercut the cultural centrality of the movies. As society turned more to television, restrictions and censorship began to fade, and film practices began to test, often in radical ways, new themes, genres, and variations on the models of classical cinema.

Figure 9.41 *The Best Years of Our Lives* (1946). A dark and difficult postwar realism.

Figure 9.42 *Touch of Evil* (1958). Twisting traditional visual styles and narratives.

The movies themselves grew more daring and darker as they loosened or challenged the formulas of classical Hollywood, most notably by:

- exploring more controversial themes and issues as part of a new standard of realism
- developing a more self-conscious and exaggerated sense of image composition and narrative structure

By the end of the war, a new, darker realism pervaded even Hollywood as the events of World War II settled into the national consciousness. Beginning with *The Best Years of Our Lives* and its layered tale of postwar trauma in small-town America, films opened doors into such subjects as family betrayal, alcoholism and drug abuse, sexuality, racial injustice, and psychological breakdowns **[Figure 9.41]**. These topics lead naturally to more unstable and unpredictable characters and narratives as well as sometimes subversive and violent visual styles, as in *Touch of Evil* **[Figure 9.42]** and *Psycho*. Although many examples of traditional epic, glamorous, and comedic entertainment arose during this era, such as *White Christmas* (1954), even in these more upbeat entertainments, there appears a self-consciousness about film form, entertainment and its relation to society, or about the dangers of violence underlying and containing the story.

Contemporary Cinema

The most recent period in Hollywood history, beginning around 1965 and continuing through the present, can be designated **contemporary cinema.** While the social anger and confusion of the Vietnam War colored the early part of this period, new pressures emerged when that war ended in 1975. Just as the United States seemed to fragment and split its national identity over this war, the sexual and drug revolutions extended the familial and gender anxieties of the 1950s well into the 1980s and beyond. Racial and gender politics, which had informed the strains and shifts of the 1950s, became a more demanding part of the American landscape. The relaxing of some global tensions (most visibly with the fall of the Berlin Wall in 1989 and the dissolution of the Soviet bloc in the 1990s) seemed to bring attention to domestic tensions around issues such as multiculturalism, gender inequities, and sexual orientation.

The movie industry shifted noticeably in response to three forces:

1. the expansion of a youth audience as the dominant group of moviegoers
2. the increasing influence of European art films and the full globalization of Hollywood
3. the arrival of conglomerates, blockbusters, cable, and home video

In keeping with the times, Hollywood turned some of its power over to young filmmakers, who began to address the teenage audiences that made up larger and larger portions of the moviegoing public. *The Godfather* **[Fig-**

Figure 9.43 *The Godfather* (1972). The New Hollywood.

Figure 9.44 *Who Framed Roger Rabbit* (1988). Cartoon characters and modern spectacles.

ure 9.43] and *Taxi Driver* are part of a remarkable series of films from the so-called New Hollywood, which was influenced by European art cinemas and took new imaginative risks in form and narrative. This courtship of youth with experimentation changed significantly, however, when conglomerate enterprises began to assimilate and shape Hollywood. Corporate Hollywood would redirect that youthful energy toward more commercial blockbusters. Finally, VCRs, cable, and later domestic technologies such as DVDs disseminated movies in ways that offered viewers arguably more variety and certainly more control.

Amidst so many cataclysmic changes in film culture, there are two trends that suggest the stylistic dominants of the contemporary period:

1. the elevation of image spectacles and special effects
2. the fragmentation and reflexivity of narrative constructions

On the one hand, movies from this period frequently drift away from the traditional focus on narrative and instead balance or override that dimension of film with sensational mise-en-scènes or dramatic manipulations of the film image. In this context, conventional realism gives way in modern films to intentionally artificial, spectacular, or even cartoonish representations of characters, places, and actions. Playful films like *Who Framed Roger Rabbit* (1988) **[Figure 9.44]** allow cartoon characters and actions to interact with realistic ones, whereas more serious dramas like *The King of Comedy* (1983) show an obsessive fan replacing the real world with strange fantasies. On the other hand, modern movies that do fully engage narrative traditions often intentionally fragment, reframe, or distort the narrative in ways that denaturalize its coherence. *Mystery Train* (1989) portrays several interlocking tales that meet in a Memphis hotel haunted by the spirit of Elvis Presley. *Memento* (2000) reconstructs narrative through its continually changing retrospective perspectives, all subject to the narrator/protagonist's lack of short-term memory; the result is a series of overlapping episodes that leads eventually back to the murder that started the film. *Adaptation* (2002) describes the crisis of a screenwriter, Charlie Kaufman, hailed for his earlier film *Being John Malkovich* (1999), as he struggles to adapt a script from Susan Orlean's nonfiction book *The Orchid Thief*; the film folds Kaufman into a tale of drugs and murder that becomes the film *Adaptation*, whose actual screenwriter is Charlie Kaufman **[Figure 9.45]**.

Figure 9.45 *Adaptation* (2002). Turning characters and narratives inside out.

Periodization and *Taxi Driver* (1976)

One reason Martin Scorsese's *Taxi Driver* remains such a powerful and rich film today is its keen self-consciousness about its place in film history and the complex historical references it puts into play. *Taxi Driver* is suffused with the historical events that colored and shaped U.S. society in the 1970s and shares many characteristics with other contemporary films. At the same time, it echoes and recalls Hollywood's classical and postwar periods, suggesting that one of the defining features of contemporary film is its awareness of its cinematic traditions and the legacy of past eras. For instance, Scorsese commissioned the film's haunting score from composer Bernard Herrmann, best known for his collaborations with Orson Welles on *Citizen Kane* and Alfred Hitchcock on *Vertigo*, *Psycho*, and other films. The darkness lurking in these classical and postwar films is fully embraced in *Taxi Driver* and resonates in its music.

The story focuses on a New York cab driver, Travis Bickle (played by Robert DeNiro), and his increasing alienation from the city in which he lives and works. As he cruises New York locked in the isolated compartment of his cab, his voiceover narration rambles and meditates on his alienation from and entrapment in a world that has lost its innocence and seems to be progressing only toward its own destruction. Travis decries the filth and decadence of the city and considers violent and apocalyptic solutions like assassinating a politician. Attempting to break out of the bitter routines of his existence, he imagines himself the savior of Iris, a young prostitute, and attracts the ire of her pimp. The film ends with a ghastly bloodbath and the unsettling announcement that Travis has become a media hero.

The issues and atmosphere of 1970s U.S. society pervade *Taxi Driver*. Flagged by Travis's war veteran's jacket and the traumatized personality associated with young soldiers returning from that war, the specter of the Vietnam War haunts the film. Travis's violent personality echoes a whole decade of U.S. violence: the assassinations of John F. Kennedy and Martin Luther King Jr., and, as an explicit source for the film, Arthur Bremer's attempted assassination of Alabama Governor George Wallace. The violence in *Taxi Driver* associates it with many other films of the contemporary period, from *A Clockwork Orange* to *Natural Born Killers* (1994), in which modern life and identity are tied to the psychological and social prevalence of violence, and graphic and often unmotivated violence becomes a desperate means of expression for lost souls in a modern world. Five years after its release, *Taxi Driver* remained a barometer of modern America. When John Hinckley Jr. tried to assassinate President Ronald Reagan in 1981, he claimed to have been inspired by *Taxi Driver* and had hoped, in killing a president, to "effect a mystical union with Jodie Foster," the star who played Iris.

As a part of its modern consciousness about the burdens of the past, the film's plot explicitly recalls John Ford's 1956 *The Searchers* and implicitly other classical westerns, such as Ford's *Stagecoach* (suggested perhaps by the Mohawk haircut that Travis acquires midway through the film and the Native American look and name of Sport, the pimp whom Travis kills). Like Ford's Ethan (John Wayne) in *The Searchers*, Travis becomes alienated from most social interaction, yet he yearns, through his determination to "save" Iris, to restore some lost form of family and community. He wants to be a hero in an age when there is little possibility for heroic action. The recollection of earlier periods of Hollywood history and the plots and characters they produced only highlight the historical differences of this film: this Travis is a fully modern antihero, one with no frontier to explore and only imaginary heroics to motivate him. New York is not the wild West, and Travis clearly lacks the proud, clear vision and the noble purpose of a western hero like the Ringo Kid in the classical *Stagecoach*. That a younger, more cynical audience became the primary target and the vehicle for the success of *Taxi Driver* indicates that the social tastes and attitudes of audiences play a large part in determining the differences in historical periods and the films of those periods.

Stylistically, *Taxi Driver* is unmistakably a contemporary movie, consistently suggesting a high degree of self-consciousness about its narrative organization and images. In this regard, two formal patterns stand out as typical of modern cinematic strategies: an exaggerated or hyper-realistic cinematography and a self-conscious, often interiorized, narrative perspective, both suggesting the influence of French new wave directors on Scorsese and on such other films of this period as *Apocalypse Now* (1979) and *Goodfellas*. As a version of that modern imagistic style, *Taxi Driver* paints New York City through hyper-realistic images that seem to be the product of either a strained mind or a strained society. Shots of New York at night gleam and swirl with flashing colors, creating a carnivalesque atmosphere of neon and glass. Frames (like those of the cab window and its rearview mirror) constantly call attention to how what is seen is always the product of a certain point of view or subjective vision **[Figure 9.46]**. This attention to the frames through which we see and understand the world as a product of our isolated vision then crystallizes in one of the most renowned shots of the movie. Midway through the film, Travis equips himself with various guns, and while he poses himself before a mirror, he repeatedly addresses himself with the famous line, "You talkin' to me?" As he watches himself in the mirror, this image and this line become almost an anthem of contemporary movies, for in it we witness a kind of modern schizophrenia through which identity appears to split into different images of self, one violently confronting the other **[Figure 9.47]**.

Figure 9.46 *Taxi Driver* (1976). The windshield as frame.

Figure 9.47 *Taxi Driver* (1976). The divided and shifting identities of contemporary film characters.

Similarly, the first-person narration of *Taxi Driver* transforms the realism of the film into an almost psychotic staging of Travis's personal desires and anxieties: "One day, indistinguishable from the next, a long continuous chain," Travis rambles on through the private voiceover. This drifting interior narrative proceeds from one psychological jump and illogical action to others: Travis tries, for instance, to court a woman with a date at a pornographic movie and later plans to assassinate her employer, a politician running for office, for no apparent reason. When Travis initiates his final bloody attack on Iris's pimp, the narrative suddenly takes its most unpredictable turn: despite the bizarre motivation for this event (to rescue a young woman who does not wish to be rescued) and the shockingly graphic slaughter that leaves a trail of shredded bodies, Travis becomes a community hero, celebrated in newspapers for his anticipated rescue of Iris. At this moment of anticipated narrative closure, narrative logic becomes fully strained to the point of fracturing. A "happy ending" to a narrative motivated and shaped by the quirky, narcissistic, and unbalanced mind of this narrator seems to subvert the possibility of a traditional narrative logic in this movie—and possibly in this modern world.

Like many other contemporary films, *Taxi Driver* acts out the signs of its times, socially and artistically. More so than many others, however, this film demonstrates that recent cinema also bears the conscious burden of its historical past. Being true to its historical present in this case requires unusual awareness of the dramatic changes and fissures that distinguish it from its historical heritage.

 VIEWING CUES: Periodization

- Place the film you are studying in class in a particular historical period. What are some of the major social and historical events that contribute to the atmosphere of this era? What are the chief cinematic events of this period? Do these contexts elucidate the film in any way?

- Examine the content and style of the film within the context of this period. How does its content identify this movie as a part of a particular period? Which formal characteristics of this film seem common to this era?

- What about this film distinguishes it from the standards of this period? How do these differences help you understand the film better?

- If this movie seems to fit oddly into this period, how do you explain that incongruence? Does this uncomfortable fit suggest problems with the notion of periodization? Or does it suggest particular problems or accomplishments in the film?

CRITICAL VOICES: THOMAS SCHATZ ON "THE NEW HOLLYWOOD"

From the essay collection *Film Theory Goes to the Movies* (1992), this excerpt from contemporary film scholar Thomas Schatz's "The New Hollywood" indicates how the history of Hollywood masters can move in fascinating new directions in the contemporary period. Writing in the early 1990s, Schatz describes a then-recent shift in Hollywood film history: superagents began to appear as new "masters" whose creative talent lies in the packaging of new "masterpieces" through superstars.

With the shifting market patterns and changing conception of youth cul-   1
ture, the mid-1970s also saw the rapid decline of the art cinema movement as a significant industry force. A number of films in 1974–1975
marked both the peak and, as it turned out, the waning of the Hollywood
renaissance—Altman's *Nashville*, Penn's *Night Moves*, Polanski's *Chinatown*,
and most notably perhaps, Coppola's *The Conversation*. The consummate
American auteur and "godfather" to a generation of filmmakers, Coppola's
own artistic bent and maverick filmmaking left him oddly out of step with
the times. While Coppola was in the Philippines filming *Apocalypse Now*, a
brilliant though self-indulgent, self-destructive venture of Wellesian proportions, his protégés Lucas and Spielberg were busy refining the New Hollywood's . . . aesthetic (via *Star Wars* and *Close Encounters*), while replacing
the director as auteur with the director-as-superstar ethos.

The emergence of star directors like Lucas and Spielberg evinced not   2
only the growing salaries and leverage of top talent, but also the increasing
influence of Hollywood's top agents and talent agencies. The kind of packaging done by ICM [International Creative Management] on *Jaws* was fast
becoming the rule on high-stakes projects, with ICM and another powerful
agency, Creative Artists Associates (CAA), relying on aggressive packaging
to compete with the venerable William Morris Agency. Interestingly
enough, both ICM and CAA were created in 1974—ICM via merger and
CAA by five young agents who bolted William Morris and, led by Michael
Ovitz, set out to revamp the industry and upgrade the power and status of
the agent packager. For the most part they succeeded, and consequently top
agents, most often CAA or ICM, became even more important than studio
executives in putting together movie projects. And not surprisingly, given
this shift in the power structure, an increasing number of top studio executives after the mid-1970s came from the agency ranks. . . .

Ovitz's rise to power in the New Hollywood has been due to various fac-   3
tors: CAA's steadily expanding client list, its packaging of top talent in highly
desirable movie packages, and its capacity to secure favorable terms for its
clients when cutting movie deals. In perhaps no other industry is the "art of
the deal" so important, and in that regard Ovitz is Hollywood's consummate
artist. He is also a master at managing relationships—whether interpersonal, institutional, or corporate. . . . And more than any other single factor,
Ovitz's and CAA's success has hinged on the increasingly hit-driven nature
of the entertainment industry, and in turn on the star-driven nature of top
industry products.

The "star system" is as old as the movie industry itself, of course. "Marquee   4
value," "bankable" talent, and "star vehicles" have always been vital to Hollywood's market strategy, just as the "star persona" has keyed both the narrative and production economies of moviemaking. In the classical era, in fact,
studios built their entire production and marketing operations around a
few prime star-genre formulas. In the New Hollywood, however, where fewer
films carry much wider commercial and cultural impact, and where per-
sonas are prone to multimedia reincarnation, the star's commercial value,
cultural cachet, and creative clout have increased enormously. The most
obvious indication of this is the rampant escalation of star salaries during
the 1980s—a phenomenon often traced to Sylvester Stallone's $15 million
paycheck in 1983 for *Rocky IV*. . . .

Not surprisingly, the studios bemoan their dwindling profit margins   5
due to increased talent costs while top talent demand—and often get—
"participation" deals on potential blockbusters. CAA's package of *Hook* [1991]
gave Dustin Hoffman, Robin Williams, and Steven Spielberg a reported 40

per cent of the box-office take, and Jack Nicholson's escalating 15 to 20 per cent of the gross on *Batman* [1989] paid him upwards of $50 million. While studio laments about narrowing margins are understandable, so too are agency efforts to secure a piece of the box-office take for their clients, particularly in light of the limited payoff for stars and other talent in ancillary markets and in licensing and merchandising deals. And given the long-term payoff of a franchise-scale blockbuster, the stars' demands are as inevitable as the studios' grudging willingness to accommodate them.

THE NEXT LEVEL: ADDITIONAL SOURCES

Allen, Robert C., and Douglas Gomery. *Film History: Theory and Practice.* New York: Knopf, 1985. A successful combination of theoretical savvy and pragmatics, this study is a rare look at the different ways film histories can be constructed and used to illuminate individual films.

Bordwell, David, Janet Staiger, and Kristin Thompson. *The Classical Hollywood Cinema: Film Style and Mode to 1960.* New York: Columbia University Press, 1985. An extensively researched and detailed exploration of U.S. film history based on industrial standards that, according to the authors, have altered little in sixty years.

Cook, David A. *A History of Narrative Film.* 3d ed. New York: Norton, 1996. Large and exact, this excellent history of world cinema moves from the original to recent movie cultures. A superb source of information and dates that is punctuated by analysis of film masterpieces.

Harpole, Charles, general ed. *History of American Cinema.* 10 vols. New York: Scribner's, 1990–2002. With each volume edited by a different scholar, this monumental history provides a decade-by-decade compendium of details and facts that map the industrial, social, and stylistic development of American movies.

Sklar, Robert, and Charles Musser, eds. *Resisting Images: Essays on Cinema and History.* Philadelphia: Temple University Press, 1990. A collection of essays by contemporary film scholars and critics that examines the relationship between cinema history and social history through such topics as "Soviet worker clubs of the 1920s" and the "politics of Israeli cinema."

<table>
<tr>
<td>

Global and Local: Inclusive Histories of the Movies

</td>
<td>

CHAPTER
10

</td>
</tr>
</table>

There is no inevitability in cinema's history; it is the result of needs, priorities, social and economic pressures.

—Malcolm Le Grice, experimental filmmaker, whose works include *After Lumière* (1974) and *Blackbird Descending* (1977)

KEY OBJECTIVES

This chapter, complementing Chapter 9, introduces ways of using history to explore questions typically excluded from the study of Hollywood films. The models of movie history discussed in the preceding chapter inevitably omit important traditions, films, filmmakers, and cultural debates. Other ways of looking at film history can illuminate these omissions while also offering more inclusive, alternative accounts. We will examine three historical models that differ from classical Hollywood histories:

■ global history, emphasizing the distinctive shape of different national cinemas as well as transnational influences

■ history as a recovery of film practices, filmmakers, and audiences marginalized by traditional Hollywood history

■ history as an examination of the various political, social, and cultural contexts that surround the movies

Despite its dominance, Hollywood is far from the only film culture and its history is by no means the complete story of the medium. It would be a limited history indeed that ignored the rich traditions of filmmaking outside the United States, including those that have been influential since the earliest days of the movies and those that are just emerging. Even within the United States, many film cultures exist beyond commercial cinema. There are also ways to envision movie history other than as the result of evolutionary forces, as a museum of great artists and works, or as a timeline of different stylistic periods, which are the dominant approaches explored in Chapter 9. Here, we will look beyond Hollywood and suggest alternative methods for thinking about film history.

Any attempt to write a more inclusive history requires us to:

■ recognize multiple origins of film history
■ realize that particular developments were not inevitable paths
■ question whether criteria of excellence are timeless and impartial
■ look at individual contributions in the context of institutions, collaborations, and other factors

- look for omissions and marginalizations that reflect social disparities in race, gender, and national status
- consider "period style" as embedded in concrete and sometimes conflicting cultural contexts beyond the movie industry
- understand history itself as a story rather than as a series of self-evident facts

Alternative ways of looking at film history not only uncover and highlight films and issues from less visible historical periods and cultures, but also describe more subtle and complex historical pressures within the dominant film culture of the United States. For example, an examination of the historical contexts that surrounded the American classic *King Kong* (1933) might indicate that, besides its accomplishments in form and style, it is the product of social forces not immediately visible on the screen, such as unease about such factors of modern life as technology, the rapid growth and racial mix of urban centers, and the economic upheaval of the Depression. To take another example, the characteristic style and dark social vision of film noir in the 1940s can be understood as influenced in part by the many refugees of Nazi Germany who brought their experience in expressionist cinema to Hollywood **[Figure 10.1]**. In short, the alternative historical models introduced in this chapter offer us ways of opening up our experience of familiar films as well as expanding our historical sense.

Figure 10.1 *The Killers* (1946). German Jewish émigré Robert Siodmak made Hollywood films that "were more Germanic than his German ones," according to film critic Andrew Sarris.

The first two sections of this chapter will fill in gaps in the historical picture sketched in Chapter 9, looking first outside the United States to gain perspective on world cinema. Besides vastly increasing the number of films we can reference, global history challenges an evolutionary narrative of film history by locating simultaneous origins and including parallel and competing histories that cannot be mapped on a single timeline with an ultimate destination. In the second section, we will look at films excluded from the dominant narrative of Hollywood history, thus challenging a canonical history of great artists and works and the impartial criteria of selection. In the third and final section, we will look at particular cultural contexts in which film history is embedded, rather than grouping films of a particular period to detect stylistic commonalities that reflect a mythical or superimposed "spirit of the age." This alternative approach may pull individual films into a kaleidoscope of differing perspectives or fill in histories that link filmmaking to other cultural forces. The three models are offered as ways of generating more inclusive film histories. Finally, however, an all-inclusive film history is impossible to produce, not least because our ideas of history change with our changing experience of the present.

Film History beyond Hollywood

Film history begins well before the purchase of cheap California real estate started a colony called Hollywood. Moreover, early film developments—in areas such as patents, equipment, the standard length of films, and exhibition protocols—as well as stylistic innovations—in staging, camera, lighting, and cutting styles—were distinctly international. While much early activity was concentrated in Europe, vigorous film cultures sprang up during the silent film era in Brazil, Egypt, India, China, and Japan. It is not surprising that the movies had a multinational beginning. The emergence of cinema depended on technological innovations and corresponding social changes wrought by rapid industrialization at the end of the nineteenth century. Countries became tied together in many new ways, and these global transformations provoked the emergence of new forms of international mass culture.

Thinking globally—rejecting the simplistic model of "the West and the rest"—has transformed the pursuit of history as well as other disciplines. The defining events of the twentieth century, from two world wars to the Cold War, from decolonization to the rise of multinational capitalism, are international processes. Films, produced for domestic audiences as well as for export, are extremely important to the exploration of interrelationships among cultures in a global framework. Born with the twentieth century, cinema has registered these events in dynamic ways. Films circulate from their countries of origin, bringing with them diverse visions of a common, though unequal, world. At the same time, the Hollywood influence has taken root in soil worldwide along with the economic and political power of the United States. The beginning of the twenty-first century is experiencing new forms of globalization and, again, movies and other media are participating in these transformations.

Before World War II

Despite the dominance of Hollywood, movie history is a world affair involving many countries and films. Although film movements in other countries often interact with and parallel the evolution of a powerful Hollywood cinema, they have likewise created significant detours from the linear progression signified by Hollywood. These directions within film history have sometimes had significant impact on mainstream Hollywood cinema, although sometimes their historical traces are less visible. Here, we will highlight some of the most important national cinemas that have challenged a narrative centered on Hollywood. These are merely capsules, part of larger and more intricate histories.

One of the earliest public projection of films was the Lumière brothers' 1895 exhibition in France, and the first decades of motion-picture history involved competing and overlapping developments in equipment, style, and storytelling in France, England, and the United States. Without language barriers, movies produced in Italy and Denmark circulated internationally in the 1910s. American audiences watched imported films, and immigrants were able to see images of their homelands. Very early films were not necessarily fiction films, but films that delighted in the new medium's capacity simply to show things— "actualities" of real events, scenic views, and brief skits **[Figure 10.2]**. The theater environment, including boisterous audience behavior, was as central to the experience as what was shown on the screen. This era, known as the **"cinema of attractions,"** in historian Tom Gunning's phrase, was not a false start on the way to a more sophisticated storytelling form but a flourishing of equally important spectacular aspects of the cinema, surviving today in special effects and other astonishing aspects of the movies.

Figure 10.2 *Panorama of the Eiffel Tower* (1900). Exciting locales, such as this view of the Eiffel Tower and the Paris Exposition, characterize the early "cinema of attractions."

The early internationalism of the cinema allowed stylistic innovations in one country to have an impact elsewhere. From about 1917 to 1931, **Soviet silent films** provided a major break with the entertainment history of the movies. That this movement developed directly out of the Russian Revolution of 1917 suggests the distance from the assumptions and aims of the capitalist economics of Hollywood, resulting in particular aesthetic consequences:

- an emphasis on documentary and historical subjects
- a politics of the cinema aimed at audience response

Dziga Vertov, a seminal theoretician and practitioner in this movement, established a collective workshop to investigate precisely how cinema communicates both directly and subliminally. He and his colleagues were deeply committed to presenting everyday truths rather than distracting fictions. Yet Soviet filmmakers recognized that cinema is not a transparent image of the world but one that elicits different ideas and responses according to how images are structured and edited. They developed a **montage** aesthetic suited to the modern world into which the Soviet people were being catapulted. In the spirit of these theories, Vertov's creative documentary *The Man with the Movie Camera* (1929) records not only the activity of the modern city but also how its energy is transformed by the camera recording it. Moving rapidly from one subject to another; using split screens, superimpositions, and variable film speeds; and continually placing the camera within the action, this movie does more than describe or narrate the city. It introduces the viewer to the movement and power of a dynamic community.

Although Soviet cinema at this time produced many exceptional films, Sergei Eisenstein's *The Battleship Potemkin* (1925) quickly became the most renowned. In one sense his film is a document about the uprising of oppressed sailors on the ship that heralded the coming revolution, but its elevated place in film history derives from its brilliant demonstration of how conflicting or unrelated images can be linked together, as a **dialectical montage,** to generate an emotional, intellectual, and political understanding of the real events. In the powerful Odessa steps sequence analyzed in Chapter 4, images alternate tensely between the descending soldiers and the ascending protesters; the action itself describes a horrible massacre, but the construction and editing of the images also work to provoke outrage in the viewer. The film's extraordinary international and critical success enabled Eisenstein to travel throughout Europe; in 1930, he arrived in Hollywood—with a contract from Paramount Studios that was quickly terminated. Invited by painter Diego Rivera, he began shooting an ambitious project in Mexico. When his sponsors cut off his funds, Eisenstein returned to the Soviet Union, where under Joseph Stalin socialist realist filmmaking had become the official program. Consequently, the careers of Eisenstein and the other major experimental filmmakers of the revolutionary period suffered.

During these early decades of film history, **German expressionist cinema** (1918–1929) also detoured the movies from their realist drive, aiming to

- concentrate on the dark fringes of human experience
- represent irrational forces through lighting and set and costume design

Like the film d'art movement in France (1908–1912), German cinema first distinguished itself through imaginative interpretations of literature, such as theater director Max Reinhardt's adaptation of Hugo von Hofmannsthal's *The Strange Girl* (1913). After a national film industry was centralized toward the end of World War I, German films made under the postwar Weimar Republic began to compete successfully with Hollywood cinema. The most prominent achievements of the giant UFA studios exemplified the expressionist art movements of Europe. Expressionism (in film, theater, painting, and the other arts) turned away from realist representation and toward the unconscious and irrational sides of human experience. Weimar-era cinema differed from Hollywood models in successfully integrating a commitment to artistic expression into a nationalized industry. The most famous achievement of the expressionist trend in film history is Robert Wiene's *The Cabinet of Dr. Caligari* (1919), a dreamlike story of a somnambulist who, in the service of a mad tyrant, stalks innocent victims **[Figure 10.3]**. Along with its story of obsessed and troubled individuals, the film's shadowy atmosphere and strangely distorted artificial sets became trademarks of this movement. The two most important filmmakers of this period are Fritz Lang, director of *Dr. Mabuse: The Gambler* (1922), *Metropolis* (1926–27), and *M* (1931), and F. W. Murnau, director of *Nosferatu: A Symphony of Horror* (1922) and *The Last Laugh* (1924). In *Nosferatu*, Murnau re-creates the vampire legend within a naturalistic setting, one that lighting, camera angles, and other expressive techniques infuse with a supernatural anxiety; in his much more realistic *The Last Laugh*, Murnau nonetheless uses a dramatically subjective camera to disturb that realism. Camera pans, tilts, and other innovative movements express the subjective horror of an aging

Figure 10.3 *The Cabinet of Dr. Caligari* (1919). Expressionist sets make this one of the most visually striking films in history.

doorman who loses his job and sees a hostile world collapsing around him. Other notable **street films**—so called for their exterior urban settings—are G. W. Pabst's *The Joyless Street* (1925) and Josef von Sternberg's *The Blue Angel* (1930). In both, the grim realities of the streets become excessively morbid and emotionally twisted. In *The Blue Angel*, simultaneously filmed in German, French, and English, Marlene Dietrich plays her breakthrough role as a cabaret singer who seduces an aging professor, and his decadent decline under her erotic spell shifts the grim and seedy brilliance of German expressionism to a drama of bodies and actors. Much of the Weimar cinema's creative personnel emigrated to the United States during the rise of nazism, where they introduced expressionist formal elements and moral ambiguities to such Hollywood films as Lang's *The Woman in the Window* (1944).

Among the many remarkable periods and films in French cinema history, the line from **French impressionist cinema** through **French poetic realism** (1920–1939) is among the richest. The beginning portion of this period is marked by radical experiments with film form. As in contemporaneous visual arts like cubism, French cinema impressionist aimed to

■ destabilize familiar or objective ways of seeing
■ revitalize the dynamics of human perception

Representative of the early impressionist filmmakers and films are Germaine Dulac's *The Seashell and the Clergyman* (1928), Jean Epstein's *The Fall of the House of Usher* (1928), Marcel L'Herbier's *L'Argent* (1929), and Abel Gance's three daring narrative films, *I Accuse* (1919), *The Wheel* (1923), and *Napoléon* (1927). Dulac's surreal film is indicative of the daring play between matter and form that these films deploy in very singular ways. Scripted by avant-garde artist Antonin Artaud, *The Seashell and the Clergyman* barely has a story—a priest pursues a beautiful woman. Instead, it concentrates

Figure 10.4 *The Seashell and the Clergyman* (1928). In a surreal image from Germaine Dulac's film, the main character sees his own head in the seashell.

Figure 10.5 *The Rules of the Game* (1939). Jean Renoir's masterwork of French cinema is known for its fluid style and social critique.

on the consciousness of the central character, who remembers, hallucinates, and fantasizes within a dream logic of split screens and other strange imagistic effects **[Figure 10.4]**. Spanish-born director Luis Buñuel's famous avant-garde collaboration with Salvador Dali, *Un chien andalou (An Andalusian Dog)* (1928), and the films of Jean Cocteau, such as *The Blood of a Poet* (1930), are also linked to this movement.

Developing out of these avant-garde films at the other end of this time period are examples of poetic realism, more narrative or commercial variants by such directors as René Clair, Jean Vigo, Marcel Carné, and Jean Renoir. Poetic innovations are integrated into traditional movie realism to unsettle perceptions in a way that is more directly socially conscious. These filmmakers and films brought the perceptual freedoms of the avant-garde to a realistic narrative field, in which the aesthetics of seeing informed the politics of living. One film, Renoir's *The Rules of the Game* (1939) **[Figure 10.5]**, deserves special mention as one of the most applauded films in history. Like Renoir's *The Grand Illusion* (1937), discussed in Chapter 3, *The Rules of the Game* appears to be a realistic account of social conflict and disintegration. A tale of aristocrats and their servants gathered for a holiday in the country, the film is a biting and often satirical critique of the social hypocrisy and brutality of this decadent microcosm of society. Its disturbing insight and wit come from lighting, long takes, and framing that draw out dark ironies not visible on the surface of the relationships. One of the film's most noted sequences features a hunting expedition in which the editing searingly equates the slaughter of birds and rabbits with the social behavior of the hunters toward each other.

To see such films in terms of their specific cultural and national context will mean to view them somewhat differently than we see Hollywood films. For instance, Jean Vigo's *Zero for Conduct* (1933) takes up the themes of rebellion and social critique by depicting tyranny at a boy's boarding school. When the boys revolt, the spirit of rebellion is conveyed in a combination of realistic narrative and lyrical, sometimes fantastic, images that dramatize the wild and anarchistic vision of the young boys: at one point a pillow fight erupts in the dormitory and the subsequent whirlwind of pillow feathers transforms the room into a paradise of disorder.

In the first decades of the twentieth century, film flourished around the globe, keeping pace with the accelerated sense of time and the contracted feeling of space particular to modernity. Recent inquiries have begun to fill in film histories centered in countries whose cinematic influence later declined. For example, Scandinavian cinema played an important role in advancing the international language of cinema before World War I, and the golden age of Chinese cinema occurred in 1930s Shanghai **[Figure 10.6]**. Both of these cinemas flourished in favorable economic situations;

they declined because of such geopolitical events as war and revolution. In the 1930s, national cinemas became further defined, and sometimes isolated, by the coming of sound, in that shared languages are an important vehicle of the sense of national identity and of national borders. Although versions of films in multiple languages were produced for a short while, economic factors limited such ventures as well as the export of films from many smaller countries. Hollywood's dominance became firmly established.

Figure 10.6 *The Goddess* (1934). One of China's most popular actors, Ruan Lingyu stars in this affecting melodrama.

After World War II

Choosing World War II to divide our global film history makes historical sense. The war marks the virtual midpoint of the century, and it reshaped world geography and politics. It also makes cultural sense, because filmmaking changed dramatically in the wake of the conflict.

The relatively short history of **Italian neorealism** (1942–1952), does not adequately suggest its profound historical impact. At this critical juncture of world history, Italian cinema revitalized film culture by

- depicting postwar social crises
- using a stark, realistic style clearly different from Hollywood's glossy entertainment formulas

Earlier in the century, Italian film spectacles such as *Quo Vadis?* (1912) and *Cabiria* (1914) had created a taste for lavish epics, and the films produced at the Cinecittà (literally, "Cinema City") studios under fascism were glossy, decorative entertainments. In 1942, screenwriter Cesare Zavattini called for a new cinema that would forsake entertainment formulas and promote instead social realism. Luchino Visconti responded with *Ossessione* (1943), and Vittorio De Sica directed Zavattini's screenplays in such classics as *The Bicycle Thief* (1948). Perhaps the best example of the accomplishments and contradictions of this movement is Roberto Rossellini's *Rome, Open City* (1945), shot under adverse conditions at the end of the war [Figure 10.7]. Set during the Nazi occupation of Rome (1943–1944), the film intentionally approximates newsreel images of the strained and desperate street life of the war-torn city. The plot likewise utilizes the harsh reality of life in the city, as it tells of a community trying to protect a resistance fighter being hunted by the German S.S. and of the tragic deaths of those caught in between. One of its most shocking scenes shows the torture of one of these individuals. Despite the melodrama of its plot about lovers and families, the grim realism of *Rome, Open City* sounded a note that reverberated through postwar movie cultures, from the later work of Italian director Pier Paolo Pasolini through realist movements of the 1950s and 1960s, including the films of Senegalese director Ousmane Sembène (discussed later in this chapter). Subsequent Italian cinema—

Figure 10.7 *Rome, Open City* (1945). Roberto Rossellini's film exemplifies Italian neorealism in its use of war-ravaged locations.

including the work of directors Michelangelo Antonioni, Vitorio and Paolo Taviani, Marco Bellochio, Bernardo Bertolucci, and even Federico Fellini—follows from this immediate neorealist history even when it introduces new forms and subjects.

A particularly rich period of cinema history occurs from the 1950s through the 1970s, when numerous daring film movements, often designated as "new-wave cinemas," appeared around the globe. Despite their exceptional variety, these different new waves share two common postwar interests that counterpoint their often nationalistic flavor:

1. a break with past filmmaking institutions and genres
2. the use of film to express a personal vision

New-wave cinemas appeared in such countries as Brazil, Czechoslovakia, England, and Japan, among others.

However, the first and most influential of these was the **French new wave,** whose filmmakers came to prominence between 1945 and 1960 and were inspired by Italian neorealism. Following the momentum created in the 1950s with an exceptionally rich variety of films from such diverse French filmmakers as Robert Bresson and Jacques Tati, the year 1959 brought three French new-wave films: Jean-Luc Godard's *Breathless,* François Truffaut's *The 400 Blows,* and Alain Resnais's *Hiroshima Mon Amour.* Although the style and subject matter of these films are extremely different, they each describe

- the struggle for personal expression
- the investigation of film form as a communication system

The vitality of these films made a break with the past and an immediate impact on international audiences. It was expressed in memorable stylistic innovations, such as the famous freeze frame on the boy protagonist's face that ends *The 400 Blows,* the jump cuts that register the restlessness of the antihero of *Breathless,* and the time-traveling editing of *Hiroshima.*

Much of the inspiration for these filmmakers sprang from the work of film critic and theoretician André Bazin, who in 1951 helped established the journal *Cahiers du cinéma,* a forum from which emerged some of the most renowned directors of the movement, including Eric Rohmer and Claude Chabrol as well as Truffaut and Godard. (See "Cultural Spotlight: Film Journals," p. 428). The renovation of film language occurred in conjunction with the journal's policy of **auteurism,** which emphasized the role of the director as an expressive author. Writing and directing their own films, paying tribute to the important figures emerging in other national cinemas—from Michelangelo Antonioni to Ingmar Bergman to Akira Kurosawa—and rediscovering the work of Hollywood directors newly dubbed "authors," the young French filmmaker-critics helped shape the perspective and culture from which film is regarded as an art form today.

New German Cinema

Of comparable international reputation to the French new wave, **new German cinema** was launched in 1962, when a group of young filmmakers declared a new agenda for German film in a film festival document called the Oberhausen Manifesto. By 1982, when the movement's most celebrated and prolific director Rainer Werner Fassbinder died of a drug overdose, the movement's momentum was dispersing. In the interim, a unique mix of government subsidies and international critical acclaim, together with domestic television and worldwide film festival exposure, established new German cinema as an integral product of West Germany's national culture.

This extraordinarily vital and stylistically diverse cinema can nevertheless be characterized by

- a confrontation with Germany's Nazi and postwar past, approached directly or through an examination of the current political and cultural climate
- an emphasis on the distinctive, often maverick, visions of individual directors

Alexander Kluge, one of the political founders of the movement, uses modernist film practices to question the interpretation of history in *Yesterday Girl* (*Abschied von Gestern*, 1966). Fassbinder's varied body of work includes a trilogy of films about postwar Germany. In the first, *The Marriage of Maria Braun* (1979), he adapts the Hollywood melodrama to tell of a soldier's widow who builds a fortune in the aftermath of the war. Helma Sanders-Brahms takes an autobiographical approach to the World War II period in *Germany, Pale Mother* (1979). By 1984, Edgar Reitz's sixteen-hour television series *Heimat*, in part a response to the American television miniseries *Holocaust*, demonstrated that cultural silence about the Nazi era had definitively been broken.

In the collective project *Germany in Autumn* (1978), nine filmmakers, including Kluge, Reitz, and Fassbinder, responded to the divisive events of their own historical moment, notably the deaths in prison of members of the leftist terrorist group Baader-Meinhof, which had become a symbol of political unrest. The story of one of its leaders, Ulrike Meinhof, was fictionalized in *Marianne and Juliane* (*Die Bleierne Zeit*, 1981) **[Figure 10.8]**. The film's director, Margarethe von Trotta, was one of many women active in new German cinema. These women received less attention than their male counterparts.

Other filmmakers responded to the social movements of the period. Helke Sander's feminist film *Redupers: The All-Around Reduced Personality* (1978) deals with the challenges in the life of a single mother and socially committed photographer, a woman like the filmmaker, in the context of a divided Berlin. Radical gay filmmaker Rosa von Praunheim's prolific output includes the early activist documentary *It Is Not the Homosexual Who Is Perverse, but the Society in Which He Lives* (1970). While Fassbinder's several gay-themed films might share this social diagnosis, their stories are much more pessimistic. Internationally, German gay cinema made a mark when Frank Ripploh's *Taxi Zum Klo* (1981) became an unexpected hit.

On the international stage, however, the hallmark of new German cinema was less its depiction of historical, political, and social questions than the distinctive personae and filmic visions of its most celebrated participants. Wim Wenders's films, including *Alice in the Cities* (1974) and *Wings of Desire* (1987), are philosophical reflections on the nature of the cinematic image and the encounter between Europe and the United States. Werner Herzog's *Aguirre: The Wrath of God* (1973) and *Fitzcarraldo* (1982) are bold depictions of extreme cultural encounters set in the Latin American jungle. Hans-Jürgen Syberberg produced

Figure 10.8 *Marianne and Juliane* (1981). Margarethe von Trotta fictionalizes the personal story of a leftist woman terrorist whose death in prison made her a political icon.

extravagantly antinaturalist historical epics such as *Ludwig: Requiem for a Virgin King* (1972) and the six-hour *Hitler: A Film from Germany* (1977). Literary adaptations like Volker Schlöndorff's *The Tin Drum* (1979) helped elevate the cultural status of film, as did the concept of **Autorenfilm,** or "author's cinema," that was used to market these filmmakers' work as artistically significant. The visionary Wenders, the driven Herzog (whose monomania is presented in the 1982 documentary *Burden of Dreams*), and the enormously productive, despotic, and hard-living Fassbinder were easily packaged as "auteurs" with outsized personalities. Several of the most successful directors began to work abroad; with wider social shifts and changes in cultural policy in Germany, the heyday of new German cinema came to an end. In reunified Germany, where many of these filmmakers continue to work, interesting new directions are indicated by such filmmakers of Turkish descent as Fatih Akin as well as by Tom Tykwer's international hit, *Run, Lola, Run* (1998).

Postwar Cinemas outside Europe

In the 1950s, a new consciousness of film's role in national and cultural life, along with great changes and challenges wrought by the war itself, breathed vitality into cinemas globally. Long-established non-Western cinemas came to the forefront at European festivals. A long and varied tradition, characterized by a greater output of feature films than that of most Western countries, **Japanese cinema** has utilized distinct perceptual and narrative forms. Although after World War II, Hollywood forms and styles were increasingly incorporated, many Japanese films tend to

- allow character rather than action to center a narrative
- emphasize the contemplative aspect of images

Kenji Mizoguchi, Yasujiro Ozu, Akira Kurosawa, Nagisa Oshima, and Juzo Itami are among the most celebrated names associated with Japanese cinema. Ozu's distinguished career began even before the coming of sound. By the time he made his mid-career masterpiece, *Tokyo Story* (1953), his exquisite sense of the rhythms of everyday life—conveyed through carefully composed frames, long takes, and a low camera—was a trademark. The energies of postwar cinema are especially evident in Kurosawa's *Rashomon* (1950), with its famous structure using multiple, contradictory narrations of the same event. The film won the top prize at the Venice Film Festival, the oldest international festival, thereby marking Kurosawa and Japanese cinema in general as part of the emerging international postwar art cinema. Oshima helped define Japan's new wave with the violence and sexuality of his controversial *In the Realm of the Senses* (1976) **[Figure 10.9]**. More recently, Itami's *Tampopo* (1985) cannily bridges the culturally specific and the culturally shared with its depiction of the pleasures of noodle-eating.

Indian cinema provides a good case study in film historiography because it can be recorded in at least two very different ways. A perspective that looks mainly at critically prized films with a presence on the world stage would focus of the work of the most acclaimed Indian director, Satyajit Ray. His

Figure 10.9 *In the Realm of the Senses* (1976). Nagisa Oshima's film was censored in the United States and Japan and widely regarded as an erotic masterpiece.

Figure 10.10 *Lagaan: Once Upon a Time in India* (2001). This epic centering on a cricket match between Indian villagers and their colonizers was a crossover success with non-Asian audiences.

modest, black-and-white film *Pather Panchali* (1955) has been heralded internationally as a masterpiece of realist style. This film, together with the two subsequent features known as the "Apu trilogy" after their main character, is rooted in Indian landscape and culture. Yet the strong stamp of the individual artist's vision urges that Ray, like Bergman or Kurosawa, be viewed as unique, rather than as a representative of Indian national cinema. This is an example of how the conventional historical model of masterpieces and unique individuals can be used to talk about film histories outside of Hollywood, as can the evolutionary and periodization models.

Indian cinema approached as a national popular cinema is the most prolific film industry in the world. Since the 1960s, Bombay studios have produced hundreds of Hindi-language melodramas annually. **Bollywood films,** as they are often referred to, are notable for

- elaborate musical numbers erupting in almost any genre
- the presence of gods and goddesses from Hindu mythology

The stars of Hindi films are massively popular in India as well as in Africa and among the large South Asian audiences in the United Kingdom, Canada, the United States, and other parts of the world. Indian popular cinema is now as influential as the films of Satyajit Ray. Inclusive accounts of film history attempt to synthesize the multiple dimensions of a country's film cultures in a global framework, paying attention to how different aspects may be valued or overlooked by different historical approaches. For example, the film *Lagaan: Once Upon a Time in India* (2001) **[Figure 10.10]** has capitalized on the huge international popular base of Indian cinema to bid for attention from more mainstream art-house critics and audiences.

Third Cinema

If the growing influence of film festivals in the decades after World War II helped foster film art and commerce internationally, a different aspect of global film culture emerged in the politicized atmosphere of Third World decolonization in the 1960s. Manifestos such as "Towards a Third Cinema," written by Argentinian filmmakers Fernando Solanas and Otavio Getino in 1969, championed revolutionary films in opposition to Hollywood and to state-dominated film cultures elsewhere (which they dubbed "First Cinema") and in response to the sterile aesthetics of auteurist art cinema (which they called "Second Cinema"). A term coined to echo the phrase and concept "Third World," **Third Cinema** united under one rubric films from many countries, including some made by Europeans, such as *The Battle of Algiers* (1966), directed by Italian Marxist Gillo Pontecorvo in cooperation with the victorious Algerian revolutionary government. In Latin America, Solanas and Getino's *The Hour of the Furnaces* (1968) incited political opposition and cultural renewal in Argentina, and *Black God, White Devil* (1964), by prominent Brazilian cinema novo director Glauber Rocha, embraced cultural diversity and violence. Third Cinema's agenda aimed to

- reject technical perfection in opposition to commercial traditions
- embrace film as the voice of the people

These goals often entailed bringing together modernist techniques drawn from Soviet montage and filmmakers like Jean-Luc Godard—such as fragmented formal structures and analytical voiceovers—with populist documentary subject matter and traditions. The creation of the film institute ICAIC (Cuban Institute of Cinematographic Art and Industry) in postrevolutionary Cuba provided the ideal testing ground for integrating film with an emerging nation's cultural identity. Tomás Gutiérrez Alea's *Memories of Underdevelopment* (1968) is one of the best-known examples of Third Cinema. Its story of a middle-class intellectual contemplating the changes in postrevolutionary society is innovatively filmed and politically direct **[Figure 10.11]**.

Figure 10.11 *Memories of Underdevelopment* (1968). This Cuban film is linked with films from such countries as Argentina and Africa in the political concept of Third Cinema.

As we have emphasized, World War II changed political, economic, and cultural history, and the cinema played an important role in the geopolitics of the Cold War and beyond. Many nations set up state-run or subsidized film industries to foster domestic production in the face of U.S. imports, thereby promoting serious film art or promulgating state ideology. Communist countries produced and exchanged sanctioned films, while hybrids such as **spaghetti westerns,** 1960s Italian films that breathed new life into a genre that had been exclusively American, testified to the cultural collisions in free-market nations.

Contemporary Global Cinema

The contemporary post–Cold War context of **globalization,** which describes the movement of finance, information, commodities, and people across international lines, is characterized by an interdependent world film culture and the aesthetic and economic emergence of a range of new national and regional cinemas. We will highlight three such cinemas that have recently attracted particular attention: African cinema, Chinese cinema and Iranian cinema.

African cinema encompasses an entire continent and, hence, many nations, languages, styles of government, and levels of economic development. An initial distinction can be made between the Arabic-language cinema of North Africa and the sub-Saharan African cinema. The former cinema has a long history, beginning with the Lumières' Cinématographe, which premiered in Egypt in 1896. After the introduction of sound, a commercial industry developed that still dominates the movie screens of Arab countries today. Egyptian filmmaker Youssef Chahine, working both in popular genres and on more political and personal projects (in which he sometimes appears), has been a cosmopolitan presence in Egyptian cinema from the 1950s to the present. His filmed autobiographical trilogy, beginning with *Alexandria . . .Why?* (1978), is notable for its humor, its frank approach to sexuality, and its inventive structure. In Tunisian production, art films predominate. Moufida Tlatli's *The Silences of the Palace* (1994) is the woman director's portrait of the period of the country's liberation from the perspective of a young girl raised in a harem.

Taking shape in the 1960s after decolonization, often as part of the Third Cinema movement, **sub-Saharan African cinema** encompasses the relatively well-financed **francophone** or French-language cinema of West Africa, films from a range of **anglophone** or English-speaking countries, as well as films in African languages such as Wolof and Swahili. Although generalization is difficult in this rapidly expanding film culture, some of the most influential features and shorts have been united by

- a focus on social and political themes rather than commercial interests
- an exploration of the conflicts between tradition and modernity

At the forefront of this vital development is the most respected proponent of African cinema, Senegalese filmmaker Ousmane Sembène, who in 1966 directed sub-Saharan Africa's first feature film, *Black Girl* (*La noire de. . . .*), with extremely limited technical and financial resources. Already recognized as a novelist, Sembène realized that he could reach more of Senegal's predominantly illiterate population though the medium of cinema. Although he has made only seven features in thirty years of filmmaking, each film is remarkable for its moral vision, accessible storytelling, and range of characters who represent aspects of traditional and modern African life without becoming two-dimensional symbols. *Black Girl* follows a young woman who travels from Dakar, Senegal, to Monte Carlo to work with a white family as a nanny, but she soon becomes disillusioned and feels trapped in the home cooking and cleaning. Her French voiceover records her increasing despair. Visually, simply composed long shots depict her as trapped by her surroundings. Likewise, her alienation is illustrated by the traditional African mask hanging on the wall. A brief newspaper item recording the suicide of just such an immigrant woman was Sembène's impetus to make the film. Decades later, Sembène featured another female protagonist in the more affirmative *Faat Kiné* (2000) **[Figure 10.12]**. The film's heroine is a vibrant, outspoken businesswoman with children on the verge of adulthood. Her perspectives on sex, economics, family, and male inadequacy are practical and funny. The service station she runs becomes a metaphor of cultural resilience and connectedness in a film whose leisurely pace establishes an alternative to plot-driven narratives.

Sembène remains the best-known African filmmaker, in part because his work and filmmaking in Senegal have found financial support from France, the country's former colonizer. Production in the francophone countries by such internationally known filmmakers as Souleymane Cissé from Mali (*Yeelen*, 1987; *Finye*, 1982) and Idrissa Ouedraogo from Burkina Faso (*Tilai*, 1990) is responsible for the great majority of sub-Saharan filmmaking. Yet filmmakers are emerging all over the continent—in Ghana, Nigeria, Congo, Zimbabwe, and South Africa.

Figure 10.12 *Faat Kiné* (2000). The liveliness and resourcefulness of the affluent heroine are metaphors for cultural resilience.

Currently, Uganda is experiencing a boom of quickly made films shot on digital video, driven by the hunger of audiences for images of themselves and their lives.

A number of filmmakers outside of Africa bring African motifs and themes to their work, creating a distinctive cinema of the **diaspora,** a term referring to people scattered outside their homeland. Ethiopian-born filmmaker Haile Gerima's U.S.-made *Sankofa* (1993) deals with the legacy of chattel slavery through the story of a contemporary African American woman whose visit to Africa prompts a travel back in time. With *Lumumba* (2001), Haitian filmmaker Raoul Peck has produced a searing biographical film about assassinated Congo leader Patrice Lumumba. One of the biggest hurdles to the development of cinema in Africa is the lack not only of financial and technical resources for film production but also of the distribution and exhibition infrastructure that would enable African audiences to see African-made films. The Pan-African Film and Television Festival of Ouagadougou (also known as FESPACO) in Burkina Faso is vital in this context. Filmmakers from all over the continent meet at the festival, view each other's work, and strategize about how to extend the cinema's popular influence.

Chinese cinema poses its own challenge to models of national cinema because it includes films from the "three Chinas"—mainland China, Hong Kong, and Taiwan—each of which developed under a different social and political regime and differs greatly in terms of its commercial structure, the role of government oversight, audience expectations, and even language. Yet they are all culturally united and increasingly economically interdependent. In mainland China after the 1949 Communist Revolution, cinema production was strictly limited to propaganda purposes and was further disrupted under the Cultural Revolution in the 1960s, when leader Mao Tsetung referred to American films as "sugar-coated bullets." It was not until the 1980s that a group of filmmakers interested both in the formal potential of the medium and in critical social content emerged. The renaissance was led by the so-called Fifth Generation filmmakers, who entered the recently reopened Beijing Film Academy in the same class. The enthusiastic reception given *Yellow Earth* (*Huang tu di,* 1984) at international film festivals made director Chen Kaige and cinematographer Zhang Yimou (who soon after turned to directing) the most acclaimed filmmakers of the movement. *Yellow Earth* and other Fifth Generation films are notable for their

- austere rural settings observed with an almost ethnographic eye
- metaphorical stories critical of current society

The strong aesthetic vision of these films, stemming from the filmmakers' experiences growing up as marginalized artists during the Cultural Revolution, made a critical statement in its own right. Essentially art films, this body of work was ultimately deemed too obscure for China's vast popular audiences. But with Zhang Yimou's turn to directing came a series of lush, sensuous films featuring Gong Li, an unknown actress who later became an international film star. Zhang's films *Ju dou* (1990) and *Raise the Red Lantern* (1991) **[Figure 10.13]** were the targets of censorship at home and the recipients of prizes and the basis of cofinancing offers abroad.

After the phenomenal international success of low-budget Hong Kong kung-fu films in the 1970s, the **Hong Kong new wave** led by producer-director Tsui Hark introduced sophisticated style, lucrative production methods, and a canny use of Western elements to the genre. Director John Woo became internationally known for the technical expertise and visceral editing of violent action films such as *The Killer* (1998). Along with legendary stunt star Jackie Chan, featured in the *Rush Hour* series (1998, 2001), Woo brought the Hong Kong style to Hollywood in such films as *Face/Off* (1997). The more avant-garde work of Wong Kar-wai made an impact with its quirky stories of marginal figures moving through a post-modern, urban world, photographed and edited in an utterly distinctive style that finds beauty in the accidental and the momentary. *Happy Together* (1997) is the ironic title of a tale of two men drifting in and out of a relationship, set in a Buenos Aires that is not so different, in its urban anomie, from the men's home of Hong Kong. Wong's *In the Mood for Love* (2000) is set in the 1960s among cosmopolitan former residents of Shanghai, who are trying to establish a pattern of life in Hong Kong **[Figure 10.14]**. Contemplative family sagas by acclaimed auteurs, such as Hou Hsiao-hsien's *City of Sadness* (1989) and Edward Yang's *Yi yi* (2000), reflect on the identity of contemporary Taiwan, positioned between mainland China (where much of its population comes from) and the West.

Iranian cinema confronts world film culture with

- spare pictorial beauty, often of landscapes or scenes of everyday life on the margins
- an elliptical storytelling mode developed in response to state regulation

Interestingly, this influential national cinema grew up in a country in which, immediately after the 1978 Islamic Revolution, the cinema was attacked as a corrupt Western influence and movie theaters were closed. But by the 1990s, under a more moderate regime, a distinctive artistic film culture developed and came to be seen as a way of enhancing Iran's international reputation. Films by such directors as Abbas Kiarostami and Mohsen Makhmalbaf became the most admired and accessible expressions of contemporary Iranian culture as well as some of the most highly praised examples of global cinema. In Kiarostami's *A Taste of Cherry* (1997), beautiful, barren landscapes are the settings for wandering characters' existential conversations. Jafar Panahi's popular *The White Balloon* (1995) depicts a little girl's search for a goldfish. Rural settings and child protagonists helped filmmakers avoid the censorship from religious leaders that contemporary social themes would attract. These strategies also evaded strictures forbidding adult male and female characters from touching—a compromise that at least avoided offering a distorted picture of domestic and romantic life. More recently, however, filmmakers have used the international approval accorded Iranian films to tackle volatile social issues such as drugs and prostitution in portrayals of contemporary urban life, and they have tested the limits of the government's tolerance. Panahi's *The Circle* (2000), banned in Iran, focuses on the plight of women, some of whom find prison a refuge; Makhmalbaf's *Kandahar* (2000) depicts the situation of neighboring Afghanistan just before that country became the focus of international attention

Figure 10.13 *Raise the Red Lantern* (1991). Gong Li became an international art film star in the films of Fifth Generation Chinese director Zhang Yimou.

Figure 10.14 *In the Mood for Love* (2000). In the films of Wong Kar-wai, stylish characters make chance connections amidst the urban alienation of Hong Kong.

IN FOCUS

Global Cinema: *The Apple* (1998)

Modest films from emerging national cinemas can strike outside viewers with their freshness and at the same time reveal their affinity with filmmaking traditions from other periods and countries. The promise of global cinema is exemplified in such discoveries, which reward close attention to their production and reception contexts as well as to their form and subject matter. Samira Makhmalbaf's *The Apple* is among the films that have made recent Iranian cinema such an exciting contribution to world film culture. *The Apple* speaks volumes about the society from which it emerges while telling its specific story simply and directly. It builds a fictional scenario on a real-life situation, recalling the innovations of Italian neorealist cinema in the mid-twentieth century.

The film's protagonists, played by their real-life counterparts, are the twelve-year-old twin girls Zahra and Massoumeh **[Figure 10.15]**, who had been confined by their father and blind mother in their home in Tehran since birth. After neighbors reported the situation, the girls were briefly removed by social services then returned to their parents. When she saw the report on the situation on the news, eighteen-year-old first-time director Makhmalbaf persuaded her father, one of Iran's most prominent filmmakers, to collaborate with her by scripting a film about the girls. *The Apple* opens with the neighbors' letter to the authorities and with videotape footage taken just before the girls were returned to their home. The remainder of the film is scripted, structured around such simple scenes as a visit from the social worker or the boy who sells ice cream. But it is shot on location with the actual family, social worker, and neighbors, within days of the girls' return from the social services offices. The result is an extraordinary account of their emergence into the world and a striking use of documentary techniques within a fictional frame. In the course of the filming, the girls acquire communication skills, delight in running down neighborhood streets (which are themselves walled in), and learn to shop and play. They have their first taste of ice cream. The curious gazes that greet these discoveries include those from the film's audience.

This unique film does share significant characteristics with other Iranian films. It avoids direct political critique by focusing on everyday life and on children. After the girls are returned to their family, their father again locks them up. We see them behind bars from their courtyard. Little boys climb the high walls to peer down at them. The imagery of incarceration is powerful, with the camera confined to the small spaces in front of or behind the gate or in the narrow streets. Finally, the female social worker resorts to locking the father in the home to

Figure 10.15 *The Apple* (1998). Eighteen-year-old Iranian director Samira Makhmalbaf's debut film tells the story of two young girls, portraying themselves, who survive abuse.

prevent the girls' confinement. She borrows a saw from a woman in the neighborhood and instructs him to use it if he needs to get out before her return [Figure 10.16]. The film ultimately emerges as a strong indictment of both poverty and the fate of girls and women under Islamic law. Like other Iranian films, *The Apple* employs simple, poetic imagery. The girls are given handheld mirrors, and their play with these objects generates metaphors of seeing and discovery as well as interesting camera compositions. Although it is illuminating to discuss *The Apple* in relation to other examples within this artistically coherent national cinema, the film contributes something that has never been seen before in its characters and situation.

Figure 10.16 *The Apple* (1998).

Without didactic commentary, *The Apple* strongly argues for women's freedom. The women of the neighborhood speak out about the girls' fate; yet even as they do so, they are more or less restricted to their homes, dooryards, and chadors (the garments that cover most of their heads and bodies). The social worker is a figure of strength, repeatedly confronting the girls' father directly. We see Zahra and Massoumeh, physically impaired and almost mute when the film begins, quickly grow more communicative and animated. Their progress is a metaphor for women commanding language and physical space. At the same time, the film's treatment of the parents is extraordinary. The father's cooperation with the project makes it impossible to completely dismiss him for his cruelty. Their home is opened up to the camera, the young female director, and her crew. The portrayal of the mother is the film's most chilling: she keeps to the dark recesses of the home, always wrapped in her chador, often softly muttering and swearing. Without forcing the mother's participation in the film, the director achieves a potent symbol of the distortions that a patriarchal society has inflicted on the lives of this woman and her children.

A neighbor boy dangles an apple on a string to tempt the girls with a taste of life outside. In the film's final images, the blind mother, covered head to toe in her chador, is taunted with the dangling apple [Figure 10.17]. Her hand extended toward it is frozen in time, an ambiguous gesture between ridding herself of an annoying obstacle in her path and reaching toward an image of freedom. As a contribution to Iranian national cinema, the film may seem minor. It operates not on an explicitly political level but as a personal and social tragedy, ultimately imbued with humor and hopefulness. Yet the film's ambiguous status on the borderline between fiction and "real life" is one way in which it suggests the function of cinema as political catalyst. The camera's presence in these girls' lives is not directly acknowledged, but it is decisive. The filmmaker's access to image-making comes through her father; although her films represent her confident voice, in a way her situation mirrors the twins'. Makhmalbaf was asked by a critic after screening her film at the Cannes film festival, "What kind of country is Iran? Is it a place where twelve-year-old girls are incarcerated or where eighteen-year-old girls make movies?" Her film shows that this contradiction itself is a part of what makes contemporary Iranian film such a rich contribution to global cinema.

Figure 10.17 *The Apple* (1998). The film's haunting final image.

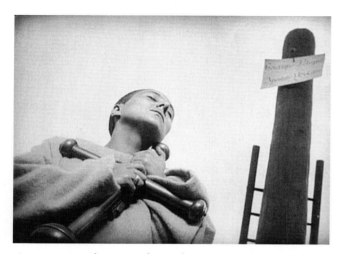

Figure 10.18 *The Passion of Joan of Arc* (1928). Carl Theodor Dreyer's striking depiction of the trial of Saint Joan was an early international art film success.

and the target of a U.S.-led military campaign. One of the most interesting contradictions in Iranian cinema is the prominence of women filmmakers. Although strict religious decrees require female characters to keep their heads covered and forbid a range of onscreen behaviors, including singing, behind the camera many Iranian women filmmakers—such as Tahmineh Milani, who was arrested for her film *The Hidden Half* (2001), and Samira Makhmalbaf (daughter of Mohsen Makhmalbaf), whose first feature film *The Apple* (1998) was made when she was only eighteen—have achieved more than their contemporaries in many Western countries.

In each of these emergent cinemas, definitions of national identity are in the process of being established in relation to postcolonial and postrevolutionary realities. Cinema serves an important role in shaping such definitions because of the strong appeal of its images and narratives. Thinking in terms of a global film history can be more than just an additive process or another application of the evolutionary, masters and masterpieces, and periodization models discussed in Chapter 9. It can look at films in multiple and overlapping political and cultural histories, while at the same time emphasizing their role in constructing identity both within and outside a culture.

It has been impossible to be fully inclusive in this survey of global film history. We have selected examples of unique contributions and important trends, but many others are worthy of attention. By focusing on national or regional cinemas, we have also overlooked individuals who do not easily fit

 VIEWING CUES: Film History beyond Hollywood

■ Scan newspaper and television film listings, noting how many different countries are represented among the offerings. If the range is limited, why do you think this is so? If you have located foreign films, what kinds of venues or channels show them?

■ Locate a film festival program on the Web and characterize its range of programming. What titles or programs interest or intrigue you? If you are familiar with films from some of the countries represented, what does this knowledge lead you to expect?

■ Research and then view an important film from a national cinema that you know little about. Is knowing the cultural context important to understanding the film? Does the film speak to members of that culture, to outsiders, or to both?

■ Compare a Western and a non-Western film. What recognizable differences exist in the narrative or visual elements? Do you think the resources that went into each film were comparable?

■ Compare at least two films from the same country and film movement (such as Italian neorealism or Hong Kong new wave) to determine whether the characteristics discussed in this chapter apply.

within certain national cinemas, who work in exile, or who may work in a country whose cinema lacks a distinctive global presence. This is the case from early in film history, when Danish director Carl Theodor Dreyer made his extraordinary *The Passion of Joan of Arc* (1928) in France **[Figure 10.18]**, to the postwar art cinema, which featured such unique auteurs as Ingmar Bergman (Sweden) and Luis Buñuel (Spain). More recently, directors like Pedro Amoldovar (Spain), Theo Angelopoulis (Greece), Chantal Akerman (Belgium), Kristof Kieslowski (Poland), Manoel de Oliveira (Portugal), Raoul Ruiz (Chile), and Lars von Trier and the Dogme 95 directors (Denmark) have helped define a truly global film culture.

The Lost and Found of American Film History

Film history comprises a great deal more than powerful individuals creating masterworks and the output of large institutions such as the Hollywood studios. One important alternative model for studying movie history excavates histories outside the mainstream. This effort can be particularly difficult in the United States given the dominance of the commercial film industry. Tim Burton's movie *Ed Wood* (1994), itself a studio film, is a clever and insightful excavation of the story of a filmmaker whose work many would consider rightfully excluded from mainstream history. The film's subject, eccentric director Edward D. Wood Jr., made bad movies with great enthusiasm. In a parodic barroom conversation, Burton's film depicts the completely marginal Wood arguing comparable status with acknowledged genius Orson Welles. Yet Wood's importance can be reassessed if we change our framework. In what are now considered cult classics, such as *Glen or Glenda* (1953) and *Plan 9 From Outer Space* (1959), his deliberate, sincere imitation of movie genres exposes how preposterous Hollywood conventions can be and illuminates the alternative economics of the exploitation film industry.

Decisions about what should be considered great and what traditions are important to know about—questions of value—are also questions of value*s*. Every inclusion is accompanied by many exclusions. In other words, standards of quality are not timeless or universally shared, and divergences may be more than a matter of difference of opinion. Often what is deemed culturally valuable is determined by those who are empowered by a culture.

Is it possible to write histories that remove the element of biased selection? One approach to an inclusive history is to try to be as thorough as possible, to strive for objectivity by letting the historical record speak for itself. A random sampling of Hollywood's yearly output will yield a very different chronology than a history of masterpieces will; the former will also tell us something different about the norms of filmmaking. Yet another approach is to excavate the cinematic past in order to uncover devalued contributions and traditions and perhaps discover the unacknowledged antecedents of some of today's diverse film practices. Such **corrective film history** does not argue that rediscovered films should replace or even be put on a par with previously lauded masterpieces. Rather, a corrective history tries to

- consider different questions about the past and its artifacts
- uncover whose version of the past has been accepted and supplement this version with missing perspectives

Debates about criteria of inclusion and exclusion are familiar in literary studies, where the accepted list of essential great works is called the **canon.** Strictly used, the term designates irrefutable church law or scripture. To refer to a film canon is to give cultural weight to the movies, which, as a form of popular entertainment, they rarely attain. Yet it is also to set up individual films and filmmakers as authoritative, obscuring the overall experience of cinema—from production to reception. Inclusive histories aim to acknowledge the benefits and drawbacks of evaluative criteria. Excavating film history might mean introducing new films to the canon and thus transforming the values of selection, or it might mean giving up on the idea of selectivity in favor of making strategic arguments. It is true that forgotten works have not had the same influence as those that have never been lost from view, but they may be worth studying precisely for the alternative vision they afford of history. This process of looking at the past from a disadvantaged point of view, called **history from below,** yields insights about how things could have been different.

In the shadow of Hollywood histories of canonized filmmakers and films, many others have been denied major historical status in spite of their significant historical contributions. Of the many important omissions, we will sketch three traditions that are central to a full historical understanding of U.S. movies: a history of women filmmakers, a history of African American cinema, and an introduction to what are known as "orphan films," ephemeral or noncommercial films that, despite their lack of traditional cultural value, have survived to yield fascinating glimpses of the past.

The Women Who Made the Movies

The movie industry remains male dominated, with women directing only 4 percent of the one hundred top-grossing films in the United States, according to a 2001 study. In independent and experimental filmmaking, access for women is less prohibitive, but their participation is still unequal. The situation is exacerbated because history so frequently overlooks the significant contribution of women, cutting contemporary women filmmakers off from an important past. Especially in the early years of a wide-open industry, women entered film history in great numbers as assistants, writers, editors, and actresses and soon turned to directing or producing. Alice Guy Blaché, who made what some consider the very first fiction film, *The Cabbage Fairy* (*La Fée aux chous*) for Gaumont studios in 1896 in France, set up her own U.S. company and turned out hundreds of films from a New Jersey studio **[Figure 10.19]**. Actress-turned-writer, -director, and -producer Lois Weber was one of the most important and highly paid American filmmakers in the 1910s, when she was almost as well known as fellow directors Cecil B. de Mille and D. W. Griffith. She directed scores of movies, often on social issues. *Where Are My Children?* (1916), for example, opposed abortion but advocated birth control. Both Guy Blaché and Weber are excluded from most mainstream histories of the cinema. Screenwriter Frances Marion got her start with Weber and went on to write screenplays for more than 150 films in a celebrated career. She is best known for her partnership with silent movie star Mary Pickford, who, like another great star of the period, Lillian Gish,

Figure 10.19 Alice Guy Blaché in 1915. The earliest and most prolific woman director in history has barely been acknowledged in mainstream film histories.

also tried directing herself. By the 1920s, most women who were active in the early U.S. industry encountered difficulties as the movies became established in Hollywood as big business. Only writers and editors continued to work in any notable numbers.

The most prominent and, for a considerable period, the only active female director in sound-era Hollywood was Dorothy Arzner [Figure 10.20], whose films *Christopher Strong* (1933) and *Dance, Girl, Dance* (1940) feature strong heroines played by top stars and significant bonds between women. The next woman to achieve director credit in Hollywood, Ida Lupino, used her prominence as a movie star to help her get started as an independent filmmaker in the 1940s. She directed hard-hitting, low-budget films such as *Hard, Fast and Beautiful* (1951), about a mother who pushes her daughter to succeed in a tennis career, and *The Bigamist* (1953), in which Lupino appears as one of the wives. She later had a successful directing career in television, which was easier to break into at the time [Figure 10.21]. Since their rediscovery by feminists in the 1970s, Arzner and Lupino have been the focus of rewarding scholarship on what it meant to be a woman director in the male-dominant power structure of the studio system.

Because of their position outside the Hollywood mainstream and because their films require less money and equipment to achieve, the experimental and avant-garde movements have been more accessible to women filmmakers than feature filmmaking. Probably the best known of all American avant-garde filmmakers is Maya Deren. A Russian immigrant, Deren began making poetic, formally inventive films that incorporated dance and music in the early 1940s. She not only appeared *in* her classic films *Meshes of the Afternoon* (1943) and *At Land* (1944) but also often appeared *with* them, traveling around the country, organizing networks, and publishing articles to promote the experimental cinema of which she is rightly considered a founder. Deren paved the way for other avant-garde filmmakers, some of them women. Shirley Clarke made both abstract films and the remarkable interview film *Portrait of Jason* in 1967. Yoko Ono pursued filmmaking in addition to music and other areas of artistic expression, producing the humorous *Film No. 4 (Bottoms)* (1966) and the harrowing *Rape* (1969).

In the late 1960s and early 1970s, an explicitly feminist avant-garde movement emerged with such filmmakers as Carolee Schneeman, who filmed herself and her husband making love in *Fuses* (1966), and Yvonne Rainer, who incorporated her work as a dancer in the experimental *Film about a Woman Who . . .* (1974). Rainer continues to make socially engaged films using collages of images and language, as in *MURDER and murder* (1996), which confronts breast cancer. Barbara Hammer uses experimental film language to explore lesbian identity and eroticism, as well as other questions of representation in more than eighty short films produced since the early 1970s. Lizzie Borden's *Born in Flames* (1983), scripted with an ensemble (mostly nonprofessional) cast, imagines a not-too-distant future in which women are still unequal citizens despite a progressive government. In this film, which uses an

Figure 10.20 Dorothy Arzner. Arzner was the only woman to direct films in the 1930s, the heyday of the Hollywood studio.

Figure 10.21 Ida Lupino. A well-known film star, Lupino retained her glamour behind the camera, presenting a persona somewhat at odds with her low-budget dramas about contemporary social problems.

Figure 10.22 *Born in Flames* (1983). A multiracial group of New York women rebel in the not-too-distant future in this widely regarded independent film.

innovative structure while presenting a more accessible narrative than is typical of experimental films, coalitions of women fight together across lines of race, class, age, and sexual orientation **[Figure 10.22]**. Bette Gordon's *Variety* (1983) is notable for exploring themes of sexuality and voyeurism that parallel feminist concerns of the period. Trinh T. Minh-ha's films, such as *Reassemblage* (1982) and *Surname Viet Given Name Nam* (1989), critique the traditions of representation that render women from non-Western cultures as silent objects. Much of this work, as well as that of experimental feminist filmmakers outside of the United States, such as Belgium's Chantal Akerman, England's Sally Potter, and France's Marguerite Duras, was analyzed and fostered in the then-burgeoning critical work by feminist film theorists, who looked both at the representation of women in mainstream film and the specific challenges to traditional film form advanced by these experimental filmmakers.

Women frequently work in noncommercial traditions, such as documentary and short filmmaking, where the influence of feminism and other social movements is often felt. Prominent among documentarians is Barbara Kopple, whose cinéma vérité account of a strike in *Harlan County, U.S.A.* (1976) earned an Academy Award, as did her later documentary on a strike among meat packers, *American Dream* (1990). Christine Choy has produced many documentaries on social issues, including *Who Killed Vincent Chin?* made with Renee Tajima (1988). African American filmmaker Ayoka Chenzira uses an animated format for *Hairpiece: A Film for Nappyheaded People* (1984). Julie Dash's influential short film *Illusions* (1982), the story of a black woman who "passes" as white in order to enter the motion-picture business during World War II, was followed by her feature *Daughters of the Dust* (1991). These and many other women filmmakers' works circulate outside of theatrical exhibition structures and still have a considerable influence on audiences and scholars.

Independent features by women writers, directors, and producers are appearing in ever-greater numbers. Allison Anders makes films based on her own experiences, such as *Gas Food Lodging* (1992), and those of other girls and women, such as *Mi vida loca* (1993), about Chicana members. As an independent feature film producer, Christine Vachon has been responsible for bringing to the screen daring and acclaimed works by a number of female directors, including Rose Troche and Guinevere Turner's lesbian romance *Go Fish* (1994); Mary Harron's portrait of Valerie Solanas, *I Shot Andy Warhol* (1996); and Kimberly Peirce's drama based on the murder of Brandon Teena, *Boys Don't Cry* (1999) **[Figure 10.23]**.

Women entered contemporary Hollywood production slowly, with some of the first inroads to the prestigious position of director made by actresses who already had industry clout: Elaine May, Barbra Streisand, Penny Marshall, and Jodie Foster, for example. Few contemporary women are associated with cinematic masterpieces and, therefore, most are excluded from histories that focus on prestige films. However, this situation suggests some of the questionable assumptions of the masterpiece tradition, particularly the suspicion and devaluation of popular genres, whose lack of elitisim perhaps makes them more welcoming of women's participation. Hence, women have often more readily been hired as directors in such genres as youth films and romantic and family comedies. Notable Hollywood women filmmakers who have made interesting statements in these genres include Amy Heckerling with *Fast Times at Ridgemont High* (1982), *Look Who's Talking* (1989), and *Clueless* (1995); Penny Marshall with *Big* (1988), *A League of Their Own* (1992), and *Riding in Cars with Boys* (2001); and Penelope Spheeris with *The Decline of Western Civilization* (1981) and *Wayne's World* (1992). Women who moved into Hollywood from independent production during the 1980s used such assignments as a springboard to more personal feature films and currently fill out their directing careers with television assignments. Martha Coolidge's *Valley Girl* (1983), a successful youth film, was followed by *Rambling Rose* (1991), a sensitive portrait of a young woman's sexuality, and *Introducing Dorothy Dandridge* (1999), a made-for-television biopic of a key figure in women's film history. Susan Seidelman wrote and directed the New York–based comedy *Desperately Seeking Susan* (1985), giving Madonna her first film role, and directed the pilot episode of the television comedy *Sex and the City*. Mira Nair's *Mississippi Masala* (1991) explores patterns of immigration through the romance between an African American man and a South Asian woman, and her *Monsoon Wedding* (2001) follows a family drama centering on a lavish marriage celebration in India **[Figure 10.24]**. Another emerging voice among the still small number of nonwhite women making feature films is Kasi Lemmons, who with *Eve's Bayou* (1997) brought a black women's regional tale to the screen.

Figure 10.23 *Boys Don't Cry* (1999). First-time writer-director Kimberly Peirce's film about the tragic death of the transgendered Brandon Teena reached unexpectedly wide audiences.

Figure 10.24 *Monsoon Wedding* (2001). Mira Nair shot this comic family drama in India.

On a bigger scale, writer-turned-director Nora Ephron is associated with a more formulaic attention to women in romantic comedies such as *Sleepless in Seattle* (1993). A director specializing in traditionally male genres, Kathryn Bigelow's body of work includes *Near Dark* (1987), a bizarre vampire film; *Blue Steel* (1990), a police drama; and *Strange Days* (1995), a futuristic thriller. Mimi Leder's feature debut with *Deep Impact* (1998) is also significant for not typecasting the director in a woman's genre.

The rediscovery of forgotten women filmmakers and the advocacy for increased participation of women in all levels of film production has been undertaken by scholars, activists, programmers, and audiences in conjunction with the women's movement since the early 1970s. However, thinking about women's role in film history goes beyond the recovery of forgotten names and films. It also involves the following issues: What is the significance of a film's having been directed by a woman? Are women employed in other technical capacities? Whose story is told? How is the female image used in this work? Are women viewers specifically addressed by the film's characters, story, sounds, and images? If so, are some women included while others are not? Adjusting the historical record involves assessing the present and shaping the future. The more that is known about how women's talents have been eclipsed, the more effective the challenge to remaining inequities can be. Our perspective toward contemporary efforts and future possibilities is enriched by evaluating historical continuities and discontinuities, exceptions and omissions.

African American Cinema

The dominant American cinema has afforded only a very limited range of representation for African, Asian, Hispanic and Native Americans. When not absent from the screen altogether, these groups have been present in a small repertoire of often demeaning stereotypes. The role of people of color behind the screen has historically been even more restricted. Still, because film is a popular medium, it registers the diversity of U.S. culture even while distorting it. In particular, the portrayal of African Americans has been crucial to evolving representations of American identity. Historian Michael Rogin points to the prominence in American cinema of films that deal centrally with race, although in a biased way. In this perspective, *The Birth of a Nation* (1915), *The Jazz Singer* (1927), and *Gone with the Wind* (1939) give evidence that the legacy of slavery and the symbolic meanings of blackness and whiteness are of crucial, though under-acknowledged, importance to America's understanding of itself. Such mainstream representations have been challenged by the alternative perspectives put forward in films by African American filmmakers. To evaluate the movies' historical role in perpetuating and shifting racial inequities, we will look briefly at depictions of African Americans in Hollywood cinema before surveying the long history of cinema produced by African Americans.

Some of the earliest U.S. films featured racial themes, usually drawn from the egregious stereotypes already circulating in such other forms of popular culture as minstrel shows. Later, African American performers such as Lena Horne were highlighted in specialty numbers in Hollywood musicals but were denied starring roles except in films with all-black casts.

Figure 10.25 *Bamboozled* (2000). Spike Lee's aggressive and historically informed film confronts the legacy of racist stereotyping in American entertainment.

An important critical perspective on mainstream representations is provided by scholar Donald Bogle in his 1973 book *Toms, Coons, Mullatoes, Mammies and Bucks* (revised in 2001). Bogle analyzes these common stereotypes and shows how the African American performers who interpreted them often transcended the limitations of their supporting roles. Spike Lee's *Bamboozled* (2000) revisits this terrain: in order to expose his white boss's hypocritical appropriation of African American culture, a contemporary black television producer proposes a modern-day television minstrel show, replete with stock nineteenth-century stereotypes of subservient, caricatured African Americans **[Figure 10.25]**. The protagonist is stunned by the enormous success of the show, which even starts a fad for blackface. Besides the historical legacy that spawns such racist representations, the film implies that the success of the show is due to the enormous talent the performers channel into the songs and dance forms. Featuring the brilliant dancer Savion Glover, Lee's film acknowledges the genius of historical performers, such as African American blackface artist Bert Williams and dancer Bill Robinson, the latter known for his pairings with Shirley Temple.

Lee's own body of work, which extends well beyond mounting a critique of mainstream films, is perhaps the most decisive recent example of the importance of the intervention and participation of people of color in making films. In the past few decades, alternative representations by Asian American, Native American, Latino, and African American filmmakers have emerged in conjunction with **identity politics,** the practice of putting social (racial, ethnic, gender, or sexual) identity at the center of political and cultural activity. Such work is often by, about, and for members of the American film audience who have never before seen their lives and images reflected on the screen. African American cinema provides an important case study because of its historical scope and contemporary breadth as well as its economic impact. In addition, African American identity bears a symbolic weight in a nation that is increasingly willing to acknowledge its historical conflicts in terms of black and white (while still marginalizing the images and voices of other people of color).

African American film production extends back to segregation and the silent film era, intensifying in the last few decades of the twentieth century as its significance began to match that of black urban cultural styles in music and fashion. Early African American film culture represents a distinguished and even heroic alternative to Hollywood history. An independent cinema arose in response to various phenomena—from the "race consciousness" of African American audiences cultivated by the burgeoning literature of the Harlem Renaissance and recordings by black musicians, to the realities of racism and segregation in the South. Opposition to the inflammatory depictions of blacks in *The Birth of a Nation* was a significant impetus for claiming film as a medium for self-representation. So-called "race movies" featured African American casts and were circulated to urban African American audiences in the North and shown in special segregated screenings in the South (including late-night screenings known as "midnight rambles"). These films often billed their stars by capitalizing on mainstream Hollywood personalities: Lorenzo Tucker was "the black Valentino." Many race movies were produced by white entrepreneurs, but several prominent production companies were owned by African Americans. As early as 1910, for example, Bill Foster founded the Foster Photoplay Company in Chicago, while in 1916, actor Noble Johnson formed the all-black Lincoln Motion Picture Company in Los Angeles with his brother and other partners.

The most important figure in early independent African American cinema is the novelist, writer, producer-director, and impresario Oscar Micheaux, who directed the first African American feature film [**Figure 10.26**]. Micheaux owned and operated his production company from 1918 to 1948, producing nearly forty feature films on extremely limited budgets. Micheaux's inventiveness in fund-raising and in filmmaking was legendary. He fashioned a distinctly non-Hollywood style whose "errors" have been interpreted as an alternative aesthetic. His most controversial film, *Within Our Gates* (1920), realistically treated the spread of lynching and was threatened with censorship in Chicago, which had just seen its worst wave of race riots. Later in *Body and Soul* (1925), Micheaux teamed up with actor, singer, and activist Paul Robeson in a powerful portrait of a corrupt preacher.

Another important writer-director-actor, Spencer Williams contributed considerably to African American film history and aesthetics with his religious films. The pictorial beauty of his *The Blood of Jesus* (1941) is echoed in scenes from Julie Dash's *Daughters of the Dust*. Although Williams contributed to sound-era cinema, and Micheaux continued to make films through the 1940s, the era of race movies peaked before the introduction of sound. By World War II, the participation of African Americans in the war effort led to increased

Figure 10.26 Oscar Micheaux. One of film's most resourceful figures, Micheaux wrote, produced, and directed feature films for African American exhibition networks from 1918 to the 1940s.

Figure 10.27 *Sweet Sweetback's Baad Asssss Song* (1971). Melvin Van Peebles's militant blaxploitation hit.

expectations of equality in other sectors, including the Hollywood film industry. The studios themselves were eager to improve relations with audiences and journalists by updating the stereotyped images of the 1930s. Paradoxically, an agreement between the studios and the NAACP to enhance the portrayal of blacks contributed to the waning of the vibrant alternative culture of films about, for, and often by African Americans. Hollywood typically showcased black actors rather than creative personnel, though sometimes it made room for the voices of African American cultural producers, as with the major studio adaptation of Lorraine Hansberry's nuanced portrait of a black family, *A Raisin in the Sun* (1961). Actor Sidney Poitier, who appeared in the film, defined the era with his charismatic and dignified onscreen presence, too often restricted to overly idealized characters.

After the studio system waned in the 1960s, new audiences for specialized films were sought by Hollywood and the genre known as **blaxploitation** emerged. Although the term cynically suggests the economic exploitation of black film audiences (particularly the identification of an urban market likely to attend films about streetwise African American protagonists), the genre was also made possible in part by the black power movement. Many blaxploitation films were made by white producers, but some African American filmmakers turned the genre to their own purposes with significant impact. The immensely successful *Shaft* (1971) was directed by noted photographer Gordon Parks. Melvin Van Peebles wrote, directed, scored, and starred in *Sweet Sweetback's Baad Asssss Song* (1971), which incorporates revolutionary rhetoric in a kinetic tale of a black man pursued by racist cops **[Figure 10.27]**.

In the final two decades of the twentieth century, the commercial and artistic leader of the resurgence of African American cinema production was Spike Lee. With his debut feature *She's Gotta Have It* (1986), Lee's sophisticated use of cinematic language and engaging storytelling helped revive independent cinema aesthetically and financially. Working through his production company, 40 Acres and a Mule, Lee addresses important topics in African American history in the biopic *Malcolm X* (1992) **[Figure 10.28]**, and explores personal issues in *Mo' Better Blues* (1990). He has also directed documentaries, such as *4 Little Girls* (1997), and produced the work of many other young filmmakers of color, including Gina Pricewood's debut film *Love and Basketball* (2000). Lee's success spurred an African American film boom in the early 1990s, centered on a wave of "gangsta" films about young men in urban settings—including, for example, John Singleton's *Boyz N the Hood* (1991), Mario Van Peebles's *New Jack City* (1991), and the Hughes brothers' *Menace II Society* (1993). Yet these youth-marketed films often obscure less commercially viable works by independent African American filmmakers, such as *Daughters of the Dust* and Charles Burnett's *To Sleep with Anger* (1990). Dash's film consciously takes on African storytelling traditions in the narration of a multigenerational family saga, while Burnett's film makes interesting use of a trickster figure.

Figure 10.28 *Malcolm X* (1992). Spike Lee argued that a big-budget biographical film about the slain leader should be directed by an African American.

Although African American cinema has historically achieved greater visibility due to the economic viability of an early independent film network and the emergence of a large "crossover" audience later on, films by and for other racial and ethnic groups have been made throughout U.S. film history and have increased in number along with greater access by people of color to the means of film production. Each of these histories is fascinating, but we are able to cite only several important films and movements here. Yiddish-language cinema, much of it produced in Eastern Europe and enjoyed by Jewish immigrants in the United States, flourished in the years between the two world wars. With the fostering of independent feature filmmaking in general and more emphasis on the multicultural nature of U.S. society, Chinese American Wayne Wang launched his significant filmmaking career with *Chan Is Missing* (1982), and playwright and director Luis Valdez brought important stories from Chicano history to the screen with *Zoot Suit* (1981) and *La Bamba* (1987). It was not until 1998 that a feature by and about Native Americans was produced: director Chris Eyre and writer Sherman Alexie's breakthrough film *Smoke Signals* (1998) received wide critical and popular acclaim.

Often these works emerge from strong critiques of mainstream representations of people of color and of underrepresentation in the industry. In addition to these feature films and journalistic and scholarly work on race and representation, other kinds of community and art world–based media have appeared. Film festivals dedicated to Asian-Pacific American and Latin American cinema showcase hundreds of short films, videos, documentaries, as well as feature-length films from Asian and Latin American countries each year. All of these traditions expand the concept of American cinema beyond the genres, personalities, and stories that Hollywood has promoted.

Orphan Films

As we consider the many different ways that film history can be regarded, it is important to remember that the very idea of reflecting on our film heritage is a relatively recent one. Precisely because film and photography capture the fleeting moment, they have been regarded as ephemeral and of little long-term value. In relation to more durable arts, such as architecture, painting, and sculpture, film is also materially ephemeral. Because the earliest nitrate-based film stock was extremely flammable, negatives and prints of countless titles are now destroyed. Film prints that were once in circulation have been altered by censors, damaged in transit and projection, and improperly stored. Approximately 85 percent of our silent film heritage is literally lost. The later format of video, which deteriorates over time, has suffered a similar fate, with television stations routinely recording over the only records of live programming. Even some films that were celebrated and successful in their day no longer exist and cannot be consulted by contemporary historians or shared with new audiences.

The historical record looks as it does because of lucky accidents—informed and not-so-informed decisions about what to keep and what to throw away—and rare acts of foresight. The Library of Congress requested copies of all film materials submitted for copyright consideration and thus has records of the very first movies. The Museum of Modern Art, under the leadership of the first curator of film, Iris Barry, made the decision to treat film as a modern art and collected prints and stills beginning in 1935. Most Hollywood films that survive today were stored in vaults by the film studios that produced them; later owners of these companies discovered a new

Figure 10.29 *What You Should Know about Biological Warfare* (1952). The U.S. government instructs citizens in Cold War protocol.

source of revenue in the preservation and re-release of old movies on television, video, or DVD. Films that have survived but have no commercial interests to pay the costs of their preservation are called **orphan films,** and it is no accident that these films tend to be rare or marginal for other reasons. Dorothy Arzner's *Working Girls* (1931), for example, was an orphan until its recent restoration through the UCLA Film and Television Archive; almost all surviving race movies are also orphans.

Orphan films is a recent category devised by those interested in film preservation—including scholars, archivists, filmmakers, and collectors—to help draw attention to an eclectic range of films and their plight. Today, it is up to those who discover orphan films to evaluate what they have to tell us about the past: they function like time capsules of cinematic history and of history more generally. For example, a 1952 informational film about biological warfare conveys the anxieties of the government and citizens of the United States during the Cold War **[Figure 10.29]**. Looking carefully at the variety of forms, styles, and uses of orphan films helps us understand how central film was to the twentieth century, and how taken for granted. Although orphans are a worldwide phenomenon, rescuing such films is a particular challenge in the United States because of the volume and commercial concentration of film.

We are accustomed to thinking of certain films as twentieth-century classics on a par with great paintings or novels—*Gone with the Wind, Schindler's List* (1993), and *Lawrence of Arabia* (1962) as well as the non-Hollywood films *The Battleship Potemkin, The Rules of the Game, 8½* (1963) and *Tokyo Story* (1953). Interestingly, many of these historically significant works are about history themselves. However, most films that grace **best films lists**—annual or regular polls of critics' and/or filmmakers' opinions—survive because they have been profitable (see Cultural Spotlight: Best Films Lists, p. 396). Copyrights have been renewed, new prints struck, high-quality digital transfers made, soundtracks remastered, DVD extras added, and "making of" movies produced, all driven by the potential to make more money from the property in an **ancillary market,** such as foreign sales, pay television, cable, or home video. Nearly all the other films—those with little or no box-office clout and that may not even be intended or able to be shown in theaters—are orphans.

What else is out there? Among others, a variety of amateur movies, avant-garde films and performance materials, censored materials, commercials, educational films, ethnographic footage, found footage, independent documentaries and features, industrials, home movies, medical imaging, newsreels, outtakes, shorts, stock footage, student films, surveillance footage, trailers, and training films exist as orphans. The term *orphan films* is a deliberate catch-all, defined by what is normally excluded and by what is interesting to varied groups of people. This diversity is important in its own right because of what it tells us about the criteria used to construct historical narratives. When we consider the reach of this definition, we get a glimpse of how daunting, and costly, the task of saving all the orphans might be.

Let us consider the case of **newsreels,** which we can easily imagine being of more interest to conventional historians, then say, old student films. In the early decades of film, audiences expected newsreels to appear before the feature film at every showing. Although at the time newsreels were considered immediately dated, think of the treasure trove of information they would offer historians—glimpses of past events just as the people of that era saw them presented. Such images would often be actual records of events, a priceless view of a bustling city street or other such fleeting moments in history that only film can record. However, because of the sheer volume of footage, preserving newsreels presents problems in cost and storage.

Another important category of orphans includes films of the silent era. Much of the surviving worldwide output of these three decades in film history is orphaned. Because film industries were not yet centralized, materials were scattered in random archives, prints were modified by exhibitors and review panels in individual states and countries, and print conditions have deteriorated irreversibly. Because copyright has expired on many silent films, there is little economic interest in their preservation, leaving this art form seriously endangered.

Other films become orphaned because they are made outside the commercial mainstream and may even threaten its norms. Avant-garde and experimental works are rarely commercially viable; in addition, they may use unusual gauges or substances that require extraordinary preservation methods, such as Stan Brakhage's *Mothlight* (1963), which used moth wings instead of celluloid. Political documentaries and features that never find commercial distributors or that are shelved by studios are also orphaned.

Some orphans—from ethnographic footage to medical films and screen tests—have special needs that raise interesting questions about the goals of preservation. Do we even want to keep all of these films? With the vast storage capacities computers have for digital media, it may not seem like we have to make such choices. Indeed, given today's technology, it can seem absurd that so many orphan films are inaccessible. But it is also important to preserve the materials in their original format. Objects created and used in the past are part of **material culture** that deserve our attention. Numerous reasons exist for saving as much as possible, and various constituencies have different roles to play in the preservation effort:

- Archivists can research, catalog, store, and make available to researchers original negatives, prints, soundtracks, documentation, and so on.
- Preservation experts can begin to restore prints to as close to their original condition as possible.
- Film historians and curators can have access to as wide a range of images as possible.
- Social and cultural historians can have access to images from particular times, places, and institutions.
- Filmmakers can ensure that their work survives and even attracts new viewers.
- Other filmmakers may use orphan films as sources for their work, such as compilation films or historical documentaries.
- Specialists in computer technology can devise new restoration and access methods.
- Specialists in information technology can organize a wide range of materials.
- Audiences can have new educational, eye-opening, and outrageous film experiences.

As we have seen, orphan film is a productive category that addresses a number of different reasons films disappear: because what they are made of can be ephemeral; because who made them might be unknown or lacking in means or influence; because what they were made for has served its purpose; because what they were about is now out of favor, disapproved of, or extremely specialized; because where they were made or ended up was not in Hollywood.

Lost and Found:
Within Our Gates (1920)

Oscar Micheaux's *Within Our Gates* is a crucial film in the counter-history of American cinema for its content, its circumstances of production and reception, and its fate **[Figure 10.30]**. Produced independently in 1919 and released in 1920, it is the earliest surviving feature film by an African American filmmaker. Despite its historical significance, the film was lost for decades. Greeted with controversy upon its initial release, it came back into circulation in the 1990s after the Library of Congress identified a print titled *La Negra* in a film archive in Spain as Micheaux's lost film and then restored it. The film's recovery was part of the efforts of film historians and black cultural critics to reinvestigate the vibrant world of early twentieth-century "race movies" and the remarkable role Micheaux played in this culture. The picture of African American life and politics in the North and South offered by Micheaux's film is completely missing from Hollywood films of the same era, as is any concept of the audience that Micheaux addressed. The film's long absence from the historical record deprived generations of viewers and cultural producers of a countertradition upon which to build.

Within Our Gates is important to an alternative film history because it offers a corrective view of a devastating historical phenomenon, the lynching of African Americans, which had reached epidemic proportions in the first decades of the twentieth century. When in the 1990s the film was returned to circulation, viewers immediately discussed it as a countervision to Griffith's *The Birth of a Nation*, which boldly uses cinematic techniques like parallel editing to tell the inflammatory story of a black man pursuing a white virgin, who commits suicide rather than succumb to rape. The Klan is formed to avenge her death, and the would-be rapist is captured and punished in what the film depicts as justified vigilante justice. Micheaux offers an equally visceral story that counters the myth of lynching as a justified reaction to black male violence with a testament to white racist mob violence against African Americans. In his film, after an African American tenant farmer, Jasper Landry, is unjustly accused of shooting the wealthy landowner Girdlestone (the guilty party is actually an angry white tenant), a lynching party attacks Landry's family. *Within Our Gates* poignantly depicts the lynching of the mother and father and the last-

Figure 10.30 Poster for *Within Our Gates* (1920). Oscar Micheaux's rediscovered film about the lives and philanthropic work of African American middle-class characters includes dramatic scenes of lynching.

minute escape of their small son as a public spectacle attended by the townspeople, including women and children, a historically accurate depiction of lynching. If race movies are often considered to have been spurred by the misrepresentations of *The Birth of a Nation*, this powerful sequence stands as perhaps the strongest cinematic rebuttal to that celebrated film's distortion of history. It uses the power of the visual to make history just as Griffith's film does. Finally, as a director, Micheaux offers an important contrast to Griffith. Whereas Griffith has been consistently heralded as a "father" of American cinema, Micheaux's diverse talents, his unique approach to film language, his business savvy, and his modernity have waited decades for full recognition.

The structure of the film also rewards historical inquiry because it requires viewers to look with fresh eyes and think about how certain modes of storytelling become naturalized. Although *Within Our Gates*'s treatment of lynching is its most noted feature, this controversial material, which threatened to prevent the film's exhibition in Chicago where racial tensions had recently erupted in rioting, is buried in an extensive flashback. The flashback fills in the past of Sylvia Landry, described by a title card as someone "who could think of nothing but the eternal struggle of her race and how she could uplift it." The language of racial uplift directly addresses the racially conscious, middle-class black audiences for Micheaux's film. Sylvia's quest to raise funds for a black school in the South, her romance with the politically active Dr. Vivian **[Figure 10.31]**, as well as several side plots featuring less noble characters, make the lynching story at the film's heart feel even closer to the historical record. The story serves a didactic purpose in the film: the demonstration of the racial injustice that propels Sylvia's struggle. But the film does not spare melodramatic detail. We learn that Sylvia, the Landrys' adopted daughter, escapes the lynch mob only to be threatened with rape by Girdlestone's brother **[Figure 10.32]**. The attack is diverted when the would-be rapist notices a scar that reveals she is actually his daughter. The film's inclusion of white male violence against black women is another rebuttal of the distortions in *The Birth of a Nation*. The unlikeliness of the rescue scenario can be understood as the use of melodramatic coincidence to right wrongs that cannot easily receive redress in other ways. In other words, Micheaux uses the form of the movies to imagine social reality differently.

Micheaux's films were made with extreme ingenuity on low budgets. Their sometimes random-seeming narrative structures and their lack of conformity with the rules of continuity editing mark the historical existence of film practices unassimilated to the classical tradition. When Micheaux's affecting melodrama of African American hardship and striving, and his contribution more generally, disappeared from film history, a great deal was lost. The film's subject matter was not undertaken in mainstream cinema. The perspective of African American filmmakers was absent in Hollywood and black audiences were not addressed by its films. The title *Within Our Gates* speaks to the film's own status—a powerful presence within American film history too long unacknowledged.

Figure 10.31 *Within Our Gates* (1920). In the framing story of Oscar Micheaux's film, the heroine speaks with Dr. Vivian.

Figure 10.32 *Within Our Gates* (1920). A last minute coincidence saves the heroine.

Best Films Lists

Many of us ritually consult our favorite critics' lists of the year's ten best films. Although there tends to be consensus among mainstream critics, across the spectrum of publications that comment on film there is often wide disagreement. Still, publications from the *Village Voice* to the *Chicago Sun Times* use the same numerical scale. What is our fascination with lists and rankings? Perhaps we enjoy the illusion of order provided by strict hierarchy and the "on or off" status. Our obsession with the quantitative encourages the promotion of films based on how many lists they are named on. Yet our interest in critics' opinions concedes that there are no objective criteria for judging what is "best."

Critics' associations such as the New York Film Critics Circle and the National Board of Review also confer value with end-of-year film awards, which are receiving more and more publicity along with increased attention to the annual Oscar race. Prestige is granted by such recognition, but the process is about more than excellence. The public is likely to be aware of complaints that the Academy Awards competition has been overrun by campaigning and advertising blitzes, and it certainly knows that Oscars do not necessarily go to the best film. For example, the Academy's best foreign language film category—one of the major platforms foreign language films have for gaining wider audiences in the United States—is always controversial because nations submit particular films for inclusion and may overlook more adventurous possibilities. Moreover, voting members of the Academy may not even have seen these contenders. Other controversies involve the criteria for the documentary awards; feature-length documentaries that received wide public exposure and acclaim—including *The Thin Blue Line* (1988), *Roger and Me* (1989), *Paris Is Burning* (1990), and *Hoop Dreams* (1994)—were not even nominated. Such objections indicate our love-hate relationship with such awards, which are generally recognized, at least in part, as popularity contests. But widely fluctuating criteria of excellence also characterize some of the most influential best films lists.

In 1998, the American Film Institute (AFI) released a highly publicized list of the "100 Greatest American Movies of all Time" to commemorate the first hundred years of cinema (and to raise the AFI's profile in the face of funding cuts to nonprofit arts organizations). This "definitive selection of the greatest American movies of all time" was voted on by celebrities such as Bill Clinton and Sharon Stone as well as by film critics. At the top of the AFI list is a film routinely invoked as the best American film, *Citizen Kane* (1941). Welles's film is by now best known for being voted the best.

The AFI 100 has been greeted with controversy by critics objecting to its poor representation of silent films (only four were included, *The Birth of a Nation* and three Charlie Chaplin films) among other glaring omissions, such as films starring Fred Astaire **[Figure 10.33]**. Billed as "timeless," the list includes more films from the 1980s than from any other decade. Some exclusions seem to matter most to scholars: no documentaries, avant-garde films, or films by women (though nonvoter Meryl Streep did get the press to point out that only four of the movies had female protagonists, and that was counting *Snow White* [1936]). Other absences rankle viewers as well: *Do the Right Thing* (1989) is missing and with it representation of African American directors. Any such list merits scrutiny of how the survey was designed and who was polled. Looking over the selections, one notices a preponderance of beloved entertainment films (with *Casablanca* and *Gone with the Wind* in second and fourth place respectively), making the list more populist than one a critics' poll would be likely to generate. Not surprisingly, Steven Spielberg is the best-represented director, with five films on the list, beating Hitchcock's three. The top-100 list recognizes what people like as "classics." But confounding popular taste with merit may be preferable to confounding elite taste with merit, as many canons do. This list of greats includes *Raiders of the Lost Ark* (which came in at 95, just before *The Searchers*), a film that one might call a "great movie" in the everyday sense of the term.

The AFI venture's veneer of objectivity and democracy made it exemplary of movie history's current bid for cultural legitimacy (and sales; one can own the AFI Century set of all one hundred movies, which are also sold separately). Such marketing keeps the films on the list in circulation (and many objected that this is a questionable goal for *The Birth of a Nation*)—but what about the films that are missing? Will they be lost from our cultural memory and our shelves? The AFI project used its considerable cultural resources—a star-studded CBS special announcing the results, several series on Turner Classic Movies, prominent kiosks in video stores, press coverage of the announcement and the controversy—to get people talking about film history. If viewers ask the right questions—and learn, for example, that AFI voters were offered only four hundred nominees of the thousands of American films to choose from—they might be led to further historical riches.

Another prestigious American institution, the Library of Congress, offers an alternative way of listing milestones in the nation's film past. The National Film Registry, founded in 1988 under the National Film Preservation Act, adds twenty-five films annually to an unranked list, and the public can nominate titles for consideration. The registry designates what in the nation's historical film output is deemed imperative to preserve, encompassing all varieties of films that are "culturally, historically or aesthetically significant," including many orphans. The list runs from *Abbott and Costello Meet Frankenstein* (1948) to Abraham Zapruder's footage of JFK's assassination, with films such as Oscar Micheaux's *Within Our Gates* (1920) and Stan Brakhage's *Dog Star Man* (1962) in between. None of these appear on the AFI's list, but familiar "greats" such as *Citizen Kane* do merit places on the registry. Whereas the AFI's list of the nation's cinematic classics is a useful myth of film's past constructed with present-day sentiments such as nostalgia and patriotism, the Library of Congress's registry aims to earn for film a claim to what makes the United States distinctive, as national parks or monuments might do.

A contrast to these institutions' uses of film history to define American national identity is the prestigious British film publication *Sight and Sound*'s critics' poll, conducted every decade since 1952 with an aspiration to define the best of world film culture. This top-ten list is instructive for many reasons, including the changing reputation of particular films and filmmakers. Climbing regard for Hitchcock's *Vertigo* (1958) is evidenced by the fact that the film did not even appear on the list until 1982. In 2002, it was only six votes away from toppling

Figure 10.33 *Top Hat* (1935). This classic musical did not make the American Film Institute's top-100 films list.

the five-time winner since 1972—*Citizen Kane*. These two Hollywood films are joined by five others in the top ten, with the top non-U.S. film, Jean Renoir's *The Rules of the Game* (1939), at number three. The best showing for a British film is Carol Reed's *The Third Man* (1949), down at number thirty-five. Commenting on the lack of surprises, British film scholar Ian Christie hopes that polling has not become an occasion for critics to "parade their knowledge and to worry about how they will appear to their peers," resulting in "a monster trivia quiz rather than the global stock-taking [the list] promises" (*Sight and Sound* 12.9, pp. 25, 27).

The fact that the composition of different lists varies and changes over time indicates that standards of quality and value are not timeless and abstract but embedded in our cultural situation and interactions. This does not mean that lists are worthless, however. Besides being fun, they are ways of participating in definitions of value and of communicating about film. They can tell us how "taste" is made for particular groups at a particular juncture—for example, a wartime list will include more patriotic films than one made during times of peace. Best films lists have practical impact as well, determining what works are preserved, shown on television, and passed on as examples in books such as this one. By creating film heritage, lists shape film's future.

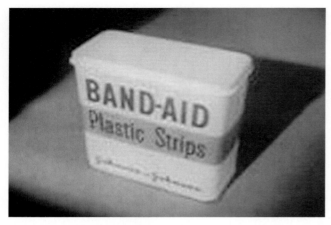

Figure 10.34 Band-Aid Commercial (1948). Early television commercials are orphan films that may no longer be useful to their original producers.

Undoubtedly, we have made a good deal of progress in considering films as not only documents of history but as having a history in their own right as well, one that is worth preserving. Orphan films remind us that conventional notions of film history also preselect what is worth saving. The fact that a research and preservation category can be based largely on the criteria of commercially untenable movies shows us how pervasive economic interests are in the very construction of film history. Many of these films were not made for commercial purposes, while others, such as sponsored films, have outlived those purposes [Figure 10.34]. Although preservation is so costly as to rarely be motivated by the desire to generate revenue, it is nevertheless likely that the orphans receiving the most attention will be those that have some commercial potential.

 VIEWING CUES: The Lost and Found of American Film History

- Research a "lost and found" tradition in American cinema. Examples include Latino film, Asian American film, documentary, and exploitation films. What are the central figures and titles in this tradition? In what ways does this particular tradition challenge mainstream film history? Would films in this tradition qualify as orphan films? Why or why not?

- Look at a film directed by a woman, such as Dorothy Arzner, Ida Lupino, or Kathryn Bigelow. By what criteria might you distinguish a woman's perspective behind the camera?

- View a "race movie" that has been rediscovered and released on video. Does the film make a creative response to limited resources? Do some of its references or actions indicate that the filmmakers had an African American audience in mind?

- Find out more about a short film or video that you have seen in class, at a festival, or on television. Who distributes the work? Is the filmmaker someone who has gone on to make theatrical films?

Film, History, and Cultural Context

A film such as *Saving Private Ryan* (1998) depicts a topic that is recognized as historical—in this case, the invasion of Normandy, which marked the beginning of the end of World War II in Europe. Much of the film's promotion and reception centered around its historical fidelity—its investment in realism made its depictions seem accurate to veterans of the campaign as well as to younger audiences who had no reference point beyond other movies depicting World War II. Seeing *Saving Private Ryan* in a cultural context, however, requires embedding it in the late 1990s. The circumstances of its production, release, and reception include the enormous cultural and economic clout of filmmaker Steven Spielberg; the business practices that made it possible to produce, advertise, and distribute a big-budget film worldwide; the aesthetic standards that value realism; technological innovations, such as CGI (computer-generated imagery) that served those aesthetic standards; and reviewing protocols in the press that elevated the film to a cultural reference point. The historian might seek to understand how the film's version of events in the 1940s was shaped by U.S. sentiment at the end of the century, including nostalgia for the "good war" and a new role as the world's only superpower. In this example, we speak of the context for the telling of history as well as the context for the events of history.

In addition to the contextual history of a particular film, there are virtually limitless ways of thinking contextually about film history. We will focus on three particular case studies. First, in the social and political turmoil of postwar America, the film industry was targeted for its capacity for ideological influence. The congressional investigation of Communist infiltration of the motion-picture business in the late 1940s and 1950s represents a specific historical context in which film played an unusually significant role. We then turn to how lesbian and gay subcultures have shaped and been shaped by film throughout the twentieth century. Finally, we look at how film plays a mediating role in cultural encounters. Ethnographic filmmaking is an attempt to record particular cultures for others to study. Recently, indigenous groups have appropriated video and film technology to tell their own stories. These diverse examples show film histories within larger social and cultural dynamics. Negotiating a multiplicity of factors, contextual histories resist teleological continuities and cultural unities. Moreover, analyses of individual films explore cultural context by highlighting contradictions and inconsistencies rather than by determining in advance how films will be used as evidence in an orderly historical narrative.

Ideology and Film: Celluloid Communism

Movies have an ideological function. The most overt example is a propaganda film, which sets out to persuade the audience that a particular view or way of life is correct or desirable. Leni Riefenstahl's documentary of the Nazi party congress, *Triumph of the Will* (1934), is one of the best-known and most effective examples of film propaganda. From camera angles to editing, the film uses aesthetic means to characterize and glorify fascism [**Figure 10.35**]. A close connection between the media and the government, such as obtained in Riefenstahl's case (despite her equivocation about her affiliation with the Nazi party), assures that ideological messages are relatively clear. Still, even in the United States, where movies are autonomous from the state, government interests can be expressed in films. *Mrs. Miniver* (1942), a Hollywood drama about one woman's courage during the bombing of London in World War II, helped clinch the support of the U.S. public for entering the war. *Song of Russia* (1943), an effort similarly made in cooperation with the Roosevelt administration in support of the Russian allies, was later attacked by cold warriors as subversive.

Ideological effects may be less intentional. The stereotypes perpetuated in Hollywood westerns have indelibly shaped ideas about Native Americans and distorted their culture and political grievances. *Mississippi Burning* (1988) is a

Figure 10.35 *Triumph of the Will* (1934). Leni Riefenstahl's documentary is ideological in form and content.

mainstream film about the civil rights era, but by showing the perspective and story of white activists in the South, it risks sending the ideological message that these characters' struggles are more easily identified with than those of the African American civil rights leaders, as well as the people whose lives the movement sought to better.

Film theorists also use the concept of ideology to discuss a film's critical, compliant, or contradictory attitude toward the status quo, or **dominant ideology,** an attitude that may come through even in the absence of overt political content. For example, in *Bigger Than Life* (1956), a melodrama about a postwar suburban father's addiction to prescription drugs, director Nicholas Ray makes use of formal elements (such as framing, camera angles, and mise-en-scène) to depict the social confinement and rigid role expectations that lead to his protagonist's dreams of grandeur. The film thus critiques the period's dominant ideology of conformism by showing the cracks in the facade.

The American cinema of the postwar period arose from and spoke to a country whose surface calm and prosperity belied insecurity and enormous change-in-the-making. The participation of African American men in the military and of women, both black and white, in the wartime workforce helped sow the seeds of the civil rights and women's movements soon afterward. In 1956, the year *Bigger Than Life* was made, Martin Luther King Jr. led the Montgomery bus boycott. At the same time, anxiety about national security and internal stability was fed by fear of atomic weapons, the arms race with the Soviet Union, and decolonization of Third World countries in the wake of wartime upheaval.

In 1946, Congress held its first hearings on Communist influence in Hollywood, the Taft-Hartley Act (1946) restricted organized labor's power to strike, and crackdowns on Communists in the unions included motion-picture industry workers. Hollywood was undergoing many changes at this time and, as a result, would never again function as the stable studio system it had been for several decades. Antitrust laws, new technologies and new tastes, and the arrival of foreign art films led to an increase in independent productions that bypassed the studios. During this period, movies interacted with political ideology in various ways—ranging from the discontent and anxiety expressed in *Bigger Than Life* and the paranoia about the atomic bomb that fueled the imagination of low-budget science fiction films made for the new drive-ins to the overt anti-Communist messages of such films as *My Son John* (1952). Most notably, the film industry itself came under more direct political scrutiny than ever before.

In the years after World War II, the government investigation into Communist infiltration in the motion-picture business was part of the postwar "red scare" associated with Senator Joseph McCarthy. It was also evidence of the unique role Hollywood played in depicting America to itself. The film industry served as a high-profile target in the sensationalist hearings conducted by the House Committee to Investigate Un-American Activities (known as HUAC), an episode that deserves to be recounted in some detail. Amidst the Cold War hysteria, accusations of present or past Communist party affiliation devastated Hollywood's creative pool and led to the blacklisting of more than three hundred screenwriters, directors, actors, and technical personnel, among them significant numbers of politically progressive Jews and African Americans. Only a few actual films, such as the U.S. government-supported wartime film *Mission to Moscow* (1943), were scrutinized in the congressional hearings. Nevertheless, their dynamics of power, intimidation, and resistance involved many other dimensions of film history, including labor relations, the self-regulation of the industry, the status of writers, and constitutional claims to freedom of expression. A conventional film history that looks at the period in terms of common style or content cannot fully illuminate the unfolding of what became a witch-hunt. It was not until much later that this event in U.S. political history was fully documented and condemned.

During Franklin D. Roosevelt's administration in the 1930s, facing the Great Depression and opposing fascism in the Spanish Civil War, many Hollywood screenwriters, actors, and others embraced leftist politics. But the postwar mushrooming of anti-Soviet sentiment that would culminate in the Cold War cast suspicion on the left. In 1944, a group of right-wing Hollywood personalities, including Walt Disney, Gary Cooper, John Wayne, and Barbara Stanwyck, established the Motion Picture Alliance for the Preservation of American Ideals. With a mission "to fight . . . any effort . . . to divert the loyalty of the screen from the free America that gave it birth," the group became a key ally in the congressional intimidation effort. In 1947, under the leadership of anti-New-Deal Republican J. Parnell Thomas, HUAC invited the alliance to testify about its efforts to purge the industry. Other "friendly" witnesses, such as eventual Screen Actors Guild president and later U.S. president Ronald Reagan and studio head Jack Warner, testified before the committee, naming names of Communists and "fellow travelers," names the committee already seemed to have on its lists. Eric Johnston, president of the Motion Picture Association of America, who was also called to Washington to testify, asserted that the political views of Communists employed in the industry did not have any influence on the films that were produced.

During the second week of these hearings, nineteen suspected Communists were called as "unfriendly" witnesses. A group of liberal industry luminaries calling themselves the Committee for the First Amendment formed in their support. Headed by director John Huston and including director William Wyler, producer Walter Wanger, and stars such as Katharine Hepburn, Humphrey Bogart, Lauren Bacall, and Groucho Marx, the committee organized a highly publicized contingent to fly to Washington, carrying five hundred signatures in support of First Amendment rights.

The testimony of the "unfriendly witnesses" was more eventful than the Hollywood supporters had anticipated, however. Thomas abruptly suspended the hearings after only eleven of the nineteen witnesses had taken the stand. Among them was Bertolt Brecht, who having fled Nazi Germany, now fled the United States after denying any Communist affiliation. The remaining ten "unfriendly witnesses" refused to answer the committee's question, "Are you now or have you ever been a member of the Communist Party?" The week began with John Howard Lawson, Screenwriters Guild founder and president. When he was denied permission to read a prepared statement, he protested vociferously and was removed from the chamber and cited for contempt of Congress. A similar pattern was repeated with the remaining witnesses: Alvah Bessie, Herbert Biberman, Lester Cole, Edward Dmytryk, Ring Lardner Jr., Sam Ornitz, Adrian Scott, and Dalton Trumbo. These writers and directors, known as the "Hollywood Ten," were eventually convicted for contempt and served short prison terms [Figure 10.36].

Figure 10.36 The Hollywood Ten. Refusing to answer the HUAC's questions, these ten directors, screenwriters, and producers were jailed for contempt of Congress.

Although HUAC's charges remained unconfirmed, its intimidation tactics were influential: industry leaders, privately convened by Johnston at the Waldorf-Astoria Hotel, attempted to control the repercussions of the hearings by issuing the so-called Waldorf Statement, condemning the actions of the Hollywood Ten and declaring that the industry would not "knowingly employ" Communists or subversives. Three hundred names were included: the blacklist era thus began. While some redress was achieved when Trumbo, one of the Hollywood Ten, received screenwriting credit for *Exodus* and *Spartacus* in 1960, the careers of many others were irreversibly affected. Although the industry had initially dismissed and resisted the tactics of HUAC, a fearful ideological climate, epitomized by the rise to prominence of the red-baiting Senator McCarthy, prevailed.

In 1951, with the blacklist in place, a second round of HUAC hearings into Hollywood Communists was dominated by the ritual of naming names. Former and suspected Communist Party members cooperated in an attempt to save their own careers. One of the most notable of these witnesses was director Elia Kazan, whose groundbreaking films *Gentleman's Agreement* (1947) and *Pinky* (1949) had brought issues of anti-Semitism and racism to the screen. Kazan provided the committee with the names of eleven Communist Party members, an action that his Academy Award–winning *On the Waterfront* (1954), about an informer, is often construed as vindicating. Another noteworthy cooperative witness was director Edward Dmytryk. One of the Hollywood Ten, Dmytryk was able to resume his career after naming fellow Communists before HUAC.

Today, it may appear that it was the committee rather than its witnesses that engaged in "un-American" activities, punishing political beliefs and violating constitutional rights. But why did the cultural context of the early Cold War encourage such efforts at direct ideological control? And why did the movies become the battleground for a fear of political difference that pervaded many other sectors of American life? A partial answer is that industry depends on stars' names to sell its products. In some sense, HUAC, in emphasizing an almost ritualistic practice of naming names, was using celebrities to publicize its own efforts. Throughout the hearings, the movies were invoked as an unparalleled medium for influencing public opinion, and the government claimed to be justified in regulating them to prevent any hints of what were considered unspeakable political views from circulating. Because fiction films are not political platforms, however, it is illuminating to consider how postwar movies depict this anxious cultural context through what *is* specific to them—genre conventions, storytelling, and visual and aural means of expression.

Fear of the unknown—encompassing fear of annihilation as well as of "others," from immigrants to children to Third World countries—was expressed in films of the postwar period in surprisingly creative and ambiguous ways. The newly energized science fiction genre provided adaptable metaphors for a familiar world now out of control. In *Invasion of the Body Snatchers* (1956), inhabitants of a small California town become convinced that their nearest and dearest are, literally, not themselves. In fact, the residents of the town are being taken over, one by one, by emotionless replicas that arrive in giant seedpods. Among the most stylish of the genre, this film can be read as an anti-red scare movie. In this nightmare world, the hero, who refuses to conform, is persecuted by irrational mobs. His girlfriend turns into a pod and blows his cover, a truly chilling moment that suggests a condemnation of the betrayals of McCarthyism. She also becomes more sensual when she changes, an anxious conflation of the unfamiliar with a sexual threat **[Figure 10.37]**.

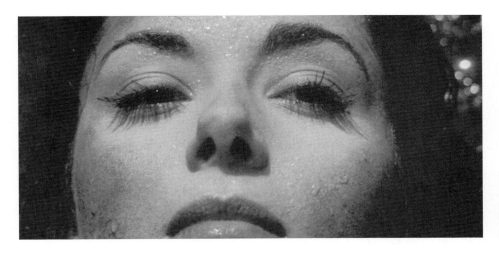

At the same time, *Invasion of the Body Snatchers*'s vivid nightmare can be read as participating in the paranoia of the red scare—you can't tell who is a Communist or recognize your nearest and dearest by looks alone. The metaphor is consistent with fears of Communist infiltration (as is the collective agriculture the pods undertake). As a story with great visual impact, the film works less as a decipherable political allegory than as a symptom of the many fears and aspirations of its cultural context. *Invasion of the Body Snatchers* (1978), a remake, presents Cold War issues differently. This film's metaphors of lack of recognition and threats from nearby resonate with the 1970s, a historical juncture that includes the cultural context of feminism and the disillusionment and alienation felt in the aftermath of the Vietnam War.

More overtly anti-Communist films of the 1950s—in *My Son John,* for example, the hero played by Robert Walker is suspected by his mother of Communist party membership—appear less effective today precisely because they lack the ambiguity of *Invasion of the Body Snatchers*. The producers' assumptions that viewers will be homogenous and share a particular response to films underestimate how ideology works in fictional representations in specific media. In film, messages come as much from genre, character, mise-en-scène, and filming and editing styles as from didactic content. With its sensual immediacy and offers of identification and closure, cinema can be a powerful tool for consensus.

However, film can also speak in an oppositional voice. Under the conditions mentioned earlier for the emergence of independent production in the late 1940s and 1950s, *Salt of the Earth* (1954)—sometimes characterized as the only U.S.-produced Communist film because it was made by blacklisted personnel, including director Herbert Biberman, one of the Hollywood Ten—integrates politics with narrative and formal choices. The film's production and its reception over the years show the importance of cultural context in film history (see "In Focus" on pp. 411–12).

Lesbian and Gay Film History

A second way to consider film history through cultural context is to look not at a specific moment but at a specific culture or subculture across a longer span of time. This is a useful response to gay and lesbian film history. Such an inclusive history provokes reflection on the relationship between representation and sexuality in general. Images help us define our desires and sexual identities. The history of sexuality in the twentieth cen-

Figure 10.38 *The Son of the Sheik* (1926). Cult star Rudoph Valentino's final film before his tragic early death, which prompted hysteria and even suicides among his fans.

tury was shaped by the mass production and circulation of images. Examples include the largely but by no means exclusively female fan cult enjoyed by film star Rudolph Valentino in the 1920s **[Figure 10.38]**, such television shows as the *Newlywed Game,* and the boom in pornography fostered by the availability of home video in the 1980s. Looking at gay and lesbian film history can tell us not only about changing representations of same-sex desire, but also about continuity and discontinuity in definitions of any form of sexual identity and community as well as about the social regulation of sexuality and its representations. This history has become more accessible since the 1990s, when mainstream images of lesbians and gay men became much more common and less stigmatized, provoking interest in the images of the past.

Because its very definition is negotiable, lesbian and gay film history presents fascinating questions for historiography. Three approaches to the topic will be mentioned here:

- films by gay men and lesbians
- films that include explicit or encoded representations of same-sex desire or lesbian/gay/bisexual identification
- films that are made for self-identified lesbian and gay communities or that such audiences have embraced (these films may have no explicit lesbian or gay content)

Our "by, for, and about" model can be used to discuss the cinema in relation to most underrepresented groups. Unique to lesbian and gay film history is the fluidity of lesbian and gay identity or content, a factor that affects all three categories. Rather than taking this looseness of definition as a liability, it can be made into a source of strength.

Looking for films made *by* lesbians and gay men is a model of **historical recovery,** an effort to locate a past that has been denied. The contributions of lesbians and gay men as filmmakers, technicians, and actors to film production are especially easy to erase or overlook because of the closet mentality that non-normative sexual orientation should be kept secret or that most people are presumptively straight. In intolerant or untested contexts, filmmakers and especially actors often pass as straight—that is, they do not correct such assumptions or they actively cultivate a heterosexual public persona. It is important to recognize that, like any identity, the sexual orientation of a filmmaker does not necessarily have any specific impact on his or her work. However, knowing whether a filmmaker identified him- or herself as lesbian, gay, bisexual, or transgendered, or whether there is significant biographical evidence of same-sex erotic attachments or activities, does make a difference in two contexts:

1. when his or her sexual identity arguably affects the filmmaker's subject matter or aesthetic approach
2. when withholding information about a filmmaker's sexual identity erases a specific historical legacy

In the first context, filmmakers may be explicit about their identity and affiliation with the gay and lesbian community or movement in order to make films for a social cause or for a specific audience or because they consider sexuality an integral part of their experience and vision as artists. The first lesbian and gay activist movie was made in 1919. *Different from the Others* (*Anders als der Anderin*) was produced in Germany amidst the social tolerance and cultural ferment of the period between the two world wars. Dramatizing the risk of blackmail to a prominent citizen because of his sexual preference, the film advocates the decriminalization of male homosexuality (no statute specifically prohibited lesbianism) and features a lecture by Magnus Hirschfeld. The writings of this pioneering doctor, a leader of this early movement for lesbian and gay rights, were burned by the Nazis when they came to power, and the film he appeared in was butchered. Another famous Weimar-era film, *Mädchen in Uniform* (1931), was written by lesbian author Christa Winsloe and based on her own play **[Figure 10.39]**. Featuring an all-women cast and directed by a woman, Leontine Sagan, the film depicts a young woman's boarding school crush on a sympathetic teacher. It achieved international success despite its consorship in the United States.

The rise of the gay rights movement during the 1970s was documented in *Word is Out* (1978). Director Rob Epstein went on to make the award-winning *The Times of Harvey Milk* (1984) and, with Jeffrey Friedman, a series of acclaimed documentaries on lesbian and gay issues, including *The Celluloid Closet* (1995), based on Vito Russo's book about the depiction of lesbians and gay men in film. The 1980s saw an explosion of activist video advocating for money for AIDS research. At the same time, British director Derek Jarman produced a significant oeuvre, including such lyrical and subversive interpretations of historical and literary subjects as *Caravaggio* (1986) and *Edward II* (1991). Probably the most internationally celebrated gay filmmaker, Jarman became one of many talented artists lost to the AIDS epidemic.

By the early 1990s, such works had prepared critics and audiences for a crop of commercially successful, aesthetically innovative films by an impressive group of young gay and lesbian filmmakers. The trend, dubbed "New Queer Cinema," arose from a cultural moment when the lesbian and gay movement had become more militant in response to the AIDS epidemic, embracing the formerly pejorative term *queer* for its connotations of going against the norm; the best of these films were "queer" in relation to cinematic as well as gender and sexual norms. Jennie Livingston's documentary *Paris Is Burning* (1990) and fiction films such as Todd Haynes's *Poison* (1991) and *Safe* (1995), Rose Troche and Guinevere Turner's *Go Fish*, and Gregg Araki's *The Living End* (1992) won awards and critical acclaim. The industry took notice and big-budget dramas like *Philadelphia* (1993) and comedies like *In and Out* (1997) addressed gay issues more openly than ever before. Because the access of lesbians and gay men to filmmaking has mirrored the gender and race imbalances of the industry as a whole, the critical and commercial success of the harrowing drama *Boys Don't Cry,* is notable. Preceding and accompanying these feature films' recognition is the burgeoning of independent lesbian and gay film and video produced for **non-theatrical exhibition,** notable examples of which include Pratibha Parmar's *Khush* (1991), about South Asian lesbians and gays, and Marlon Riggs's acclaimed video *Tongues United* (1990), about African American gay men.

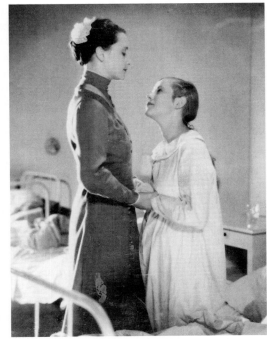

Figure 10.39 *Mädchen in Uniform* (1931). This Weimar-era film about a student's crush on her teacher features an all-female cast and was written and directed by women.

Withholding information about a filmmaker's sexual identity can sometimes erase a specific historical legacy. We recognize that gay men and lesbians worked in almost all periods and styles of film and had a particularly significant presence in avant-garde and experimental filmmaking, drawing creativity from an otherwise marginal status. But even in Hollywood, gay presence was a significant story that has until recently been excluded from dominant film histories. Knowing that Dorothy Arzner shared her life with a female partner and maintained a personal style as a director that did not conform to expectations of feminine behavior gives a deeper picture of the only woman who had a successful career as a director in Hollywood's heyday.

Asserting that it makes a difference to a given film that its director was gay or lesbian is an auteurist argument (see Chapter 11)—that is, a critic's construction of a director's distinctive style (rather than something objectively measurable in the work). Take as a test case George Cukor, the MGM studio director whose classic films include *The Women* (1939) and *A Star Is Born* (1954), among many others. Cukor was often called a "women's director" because of the excellent performances given by such female stars as Greta Garbo, Judy Garland, Katharine Hepburn, and Judy Holliday under his direction. The term was also intended as a euphemism, often pejorative, for gay—Cukor was even replaced as director of *Gone with the Wind* at the behest of macho star Clark Gable. But this characterization of Cukor can be the basis of a more nuanced auteurist reading, taking into account the professions and means of expression that were open and attractive to gay men in the first half of the twentieth century. Such an exploration might also highlight how specific codes arose in the worlds of theater, cinema, fashion, and design to communicate a shared subcultural aesthetic sensibility when overt gay content was prohibited.

Another important example of how a historiography sensitive to gay presence can illuminate film's past can be found in the underground films of the 1960s. Chroniclers of the films of Jack Smith, Andy Warhol, and Kenneth Anger sought to have them taken seriously as art, describing their outrageous transvestite actors and transgressive sexual content but failing to mention that the directors themselves were gay. Both social history and film interpretation are enhanced by correcting this omission.

An inclusive historiography began to be attempted during a period when nearly two hundred film festivals showing lesbian and gay work sprang up worldwide. The festivals reflected the growing social and cultural presence of lesbians and gay men and featured documentaries, new short works on both film and video, and mainstream and independent films. They also made history, with retrospectives of such gay film giants as Visconti, Fassbinder, and Pasolini and reinterpretations of the distorted and sometimes fascinating ways gay men and lesbians were objectified in films made for general audiences in the past.

If we try to reconstruct a history of lesbian and gay images onscreen, we face different obstacles and challenges, most notably censorship. In 1934, the U.S. motion-picture industry began strictly to enforce self-imposed restrictions on film content. The document known as the Production Code stated that: "homosexuality and any inference to it are prohibited." In this instance, cultural context matters greatly, because it is virtually impossible to eliminate "inferences" for contemporary audiences. Lillian Hellman's play *The Children's Hour* dealt with the consequences of a malicious child's gossip about the lesbian relationship between the two headmistresses of her school. The play was a hit on Broadway in 1936, but the 1937 movie version, *These Three,* implied that the child's gossip was about one teacher's heterosexual affair with the other's fiancé, a change that was transparent to the many members of the audience who were familiar with the play or the publicity surrounding it. Strictures on the theme of homosexuality finally relaxed in the 1960s, in part due to a Supreme Court decision declaring that the movies were entitled to constitutional protections of freedom of speech. One of the first films to capitalize on this shift was William Wyler's remake of *The Children's Hour* (1961). However, nearly a quarter of a century later, and with the feminist and gay rights movements just around the corner, its depiction of one teacher's suicide (when the child's accusations provoke her recognition of her own desire for her friend) had a negative impact. The trend of dead or murderous gay characters continued in mainstream treatments for a considerable period, including the notorious examples *Cruising* (1980) and *Basic Instinct* (1992). The vocal protests surrounding both films' perpetuation of stereotypes were probably more instrumental in achieving lesbian and gay visibility than the films themselves. Also during the 1980s, mainstream heterosexual stars began to appear in films offering so-called positive or complex images of gay men and sometimes lesbians, such as William Hurt's award-winning performance in *Kiss of the Spider Woman* (1985); by the 1990s, many such films were in circulation. Gay actors Harvey Fierstein, Rupert Everett, and Nathan Lane gained considerable fame, while gay director Gus Van Sant was able to make *My Own Private Idaho* (1991), banking on the stature of his mainstream stars River Phoenix and Keanu Reeves **[Figure 10.40]**.

Figure 10.40 *My Own Private Idaho* (1991). Gus Van Sant is one of the most successful gay directors of feature films.

These Hollywood films addressed themselves to broad audiences, while also hoping that the lesbian and gay **niche market**—a term referring to a segment of the audience with specialized tastes—that Hollywood had come to recognize as lucrative would also attend. This brings us to the third component in the definition of lesbian and gay film: audience. In a legacy of absence and distortion, many of the films that are most cherished by gay and lesbian subcultures have no gay and lesbian content or characters at all, a phenomenon that deserves attention. Films featuring cross-dressing and mistaken identity may eventually resolve themselves with heterosexual coupling while offering many opportunities to play with the possibilities of same-sex pairs along the way. *Peking Opera Blues* (1986), a Hong Kong martial arts movie, and *Yidl mitn Fidl*, a Yiddish-language musical from the 1930s, show the worldwide reach of such story conventions. Musicals have historically been popular in some gay subcultures (as well as among many other audiences), not only for their unabashed pleasure in color, song, and dance, but also for their lack of realism. Musicals offer a vision of a more harmonious world that can appeal to gay men who have been marginalized from the privileges and promises of the world as it is. (Such lyrics as "Somewhere over the rainbow" or "There's a place for us—somewhere" make this a theme.) Identification with Hollywood heroines, who carry such films' emotional weight, and with the stars who pull off such convincing impersonations, is historically a hallmark of gay male subculture. Vulnerable, plucky divas such as Judy Garland, perfectionists such as Barbra Streisand, and unapologetically excessive personalities such as Joan Crawford and Diana Ross have had enormous followings. An overall recognition of artifice has shaped the sensibility of **camp,** a humor found in the exaggeration or outdatedness of conventions or in failed attempts at serious art. Horror films such as *Frankenstein* (1931) often side with misunderstood monsters, another way that gay stories have been **coded,** or told indirectly, when direct depiction is prohibited. *The Rocky Horror Picture Show* (1975) successfully exploited camp for an audience that was gay and straight, appealing to another "outsider" group—young people. It is important to stress that there is nothing about gay people that predisposes them to particular tastes in movies; subcultural codes are learned, and they vary among communities and across time.

Censorship itself often leaves traces in the movies it affects. Greta Garbo's 1933 film *Queen Christina* shows the Swedish monarch kissing affectionately on the lips a lady-in-waiting, a character based on a woman at the real queen's court with whom her biographers have romantically linked her. The film's main storyline, however, concerns the monarch's romance with a male ambassador, a story with no basis in history. "Reading against the grain," a tactic advocated in modern literary studies that acknowledges both the reader's participation in making meaning and that any text has its own omissions and contradictions, has been fine-tuned by lesbian and gay audiences. In 1993, women applauded *Thelma & Louise* for hitting the road together, rerouting the road movie genre, while lesbians saw an erotic commitment even though the script includes just one good-bye kiss before the women choose death rather than a return to (male) civilization.

Inevitably such interpretations will be debunked by viewers who object to "reading things into" films, but just as the historical archive will never be without a gap, so also are our experiences of the movies never complete—or identical. There is always something that each viewer fills in for him- or herself, and a little piece of the present in the past that we encounter in film history. Periodization as a model of film history offers a tidy categorization of movies and ignores those that do not fit. In contrast, looking at the cultural contexts of film history means looking beyond lists of films and dates for artifacts and memories, beyond moviemakers to movie viewers, beyond the initial period of a film's release to its ongoing cultural life, and even beyond the borders of the frame. Reading against the grain is something all viewers do, and the movies tap into the variety of our fantasies and the fluidity of our identifications. They allow a temporary escape from socially imposed labels, whether of sexuality or nationality, gender, race, or age, and at the same time they spark recognitions from us based in our experiences and identities. Lesbian and gay film history is thus illuminating for film historiography in general because it shows that what is invisible is just as important as what is visible.

Representing Culture: Indigenous Media

A third way to understand film history in terms of cultural context is to acknowledge the role that film plays in defining and transmitting a particular culture and in shaping encounters between cultures. In this example, we emphasize the anthropological sense of the term *culture*. By this we mean culture as the ensemble of customs, relationships, and practices that comprise the way of life of a group of people. Although it is now understood expansively, anthropology arose as the study of the cultures of so-called "primitive" people. The medium of film and the history of the discipline have had an important connection. Throughout this book we discuss the film experience as an aspect of cultural life, almost a ritual for many of us.

Some of the earliest uses of film were to record the ways of life of other cultures to be exhibited to audiences in the West. Thomas Edison's early films included some whose purpose was, at least in part, to observe other cultures. In the first decades of film history, little distinction was made between science and sensation: Ernest B. Shoedsack and Merian C. Cooper, the team that made *Grass* (1925), a record of an Iranian migration, went on to make *King Kong* (1933), whose premise, it is sometimes forgotten, is a moviemaking expedition to Sumatra. But with the increased specialization of anthropology, a distinct practice of **ethnographic film,** the use of film to document cultures, emerged as an indispensable tool.

Film can record rituals in a way that written ethnographies cannot. Videotaping daily life or festivities can help bypass the traditional ethnographer's preselection of what to document. Filming interviews minimizes the mediation of an interpreter by capturing the subject's own words and gestures through the lens. (The value of objectivity associated with the camera is implied in the French word for lens: *objectif.*) However, the camera can never grant complete access to a cultural context. In a culture that does not use cameras, the equipment can hardly be invisible or neutral. Filming a ritual is necessarily intrusive; moreover, some rituals are not meant to be witnessed by nonparticipants. An on-camera interview is still a performance. The editing of an ethnographic film provides many ways of shaping its message. Because it can capture conversations and gestures, sounds and settings, time and space, film can give a strong impression of documenting a culture despite such mediations.

Nowhere do claims of film as an impartial record become more loaded than in the filming of indigenous people by Western observers. Deploying a technology like the movies in such a cultural encounter means claiming the power to represent others and their history. The camera conveys a profound feeling of presence that puts the viewer in the place of the observer or "expert." Widely considered the first feature-length documentary film and certainly one of the most influential movies ever made, Robert Flaherty's *Nanook of the North* (1922) is a record of the lives and customs of the Inuit people of the Canadian Arctic. The isolation of the people in a harsh environment, and the duration of Flaherty's stay among them, required that the film be produced in close collaboration with its subjects. In the film, Nanook (played by the uncredited Allakariallak), his family, and others engage in traditional behavior, including an exciting seal hunt and the construction of an igloo. These activities were performed and modified for the purposes of the film—the igloo was missing a wall to accommodate the camera, and the struggle of a harpooned seal was represented by men pulling at Nanook's line off camera—but they were "real" records of Inuit people carrying out Inuit hunting and building techniques **[Figure 10.41]**. Part of *Nanook of the North*'s impact at the time lay in the use of a still relatively new technology to deliver an image of a technology-free universe, so that its viewer marveled at both.

Flaherty's claims to giving an accurate representation of Inuit life are compromised by the case of reenactments and by his having paid his subjects. But it is important to factor into ethical judgments the realization that Flaherty's supposed blurring of the line between documentary and fiction occurred before such a line had been drawn—that is, before the definition of documentary truth had been accepted. The film is also often **primitivist,** using contemporary stereotypes of non-Western people as simple, childlike, and outside the process of history. For example, Nanook is shown trying to eat a gramophone record, yet he and other native collaborators were familiar with modern technology and worked as

Figure 10.41 *Nanook of the North* (1922). Robert Flaherty re-created traditional activities for the camera, but his images are nevertheless striking records of the Inuit.

Figure 10.42 *The Spirit of TV* (1990). Amazon Indians, such as the Waiāpai, have used video to record their culture and express their rights.

Flaherty's (uncredited) crew, operating the film cameras and developing the footage. The complex legacy of this film is explored in the video *Nanook Revisited* (1988), which returns to the village where Flaherty's classic was made to take on the myths and realities surrounding his great film among the people whose ancestors participated in its making.

Nanook Revisited gives a glimpse of another side to the story of the conjunction of "camera" and "primitive," one that characterizes the end of the twentieth century. The introduction of video technology to indigenous people, such as the Kayapo and Waiāpai Indians in the Amazon Basin of Brazil, has resulted in considerable output that has several empowering uses: the preservation of traditional culture for future generations; video activism for rights and the environment; and a new form of visual expression in a culture that has always relied on pictorial communication.

In 1985, a Brazilian filmmaker and several anthropologists gave the Kayapo several video cameras to use for documenting aspects of traditional culture [**Figure 10.42**]. As Kremoro, a Kayapo chief testifies, "in the past, many photographers came here and took our pictures, but they never gave us anything in return. They never attempted to teach anything. Now we, the Kayapo, we are recording our rituals for our children." Soon the Kayapo were also using their cameras to communicate among their villages and to carry on their political struggles with the Brazilian state for land rights. Kayapo videomakers received considerable publicity, including a *Time* magazine cover story. While the Kayapo are entering a new historical moment by employing this technology, the video work's primary purpose is preservation of the past.

Communication strategies were also important in the broadcasting initiatives of indigenous people in Canada, leaving the legacy of being the objects of ethnographic film behind in a campaign for self-representation. Organized activism resulted in the licensing of the Inuit Broadcasting Network in 1982, featuring programming by, for, and about native Canadians. In 1999, cable companies were ordered by the Canadian government to carry the Aboriginal Peoples Television Network, bringing this culture and its video productions to the whole country. A new phase of indigenous media-making was marked by the historic release of *Atanarjuat: The Fast Runner* (2001). Shot in digital video, this extraordinary film, directed by experienced Inuit filmmaker Zacharias Kunuk, appropriately enough deploys the genre of epic to explore a people's past [**Figure 10.43**]. But it portrays a cultural legend, not a factual past. Although at first it resembles an ethnographic film, *Atanarjuat* is set a millennium ago. By setting its depiction of the traditional way of life in the mythic past, the film represents an Inuit claim to self-representation on several levels. The film's use of amateur actors lends an "authenticity" to the scripted scenes and its script represents the longest text ever written in the Inuit language. Its images also respond to the beauty as well as the ideological dimensions of a film like *Nanook of the North*.

Figure 10.43 *Atanarjuat: The Fast Runner* (2001). Shot on digital video in the Canadian Arctic, this epic is the first feature shot in the Inuktitut language by Inuit filmmakers.

Historical Context and *Salt of the Earth* (1954)

A film about a successful mineworkers' strike, *Salt of the Earth* impresses us today as a modest and straightforward picture of the lives of working people, surprising perhaps for its compelling performances and rare focus on Chicano and especially Chicana voices. At the time it was made, however, the film was at the center of violence and controversy. Whether because of its subject matter, its marginal status vis-à-vis the film industry, or its limited initial release, it has been ignored in many histories of American cinema. Nonetheless, *Salt of the Earth* provides an excellent case for the study of the cultural contexts of film because political circumstances of its era profoundly shaped its form, its subject matter, and its reception.

Salt of the Earth is one of very few films of its time to focus on the lives of people of color. The story of an actual 1951–1952 miners' strike, the film was shot on location in Silver City, New Mexico, and features Chicano union members playing themselves. As the film acknowledges, the land they now mine for an East Coast company was originally part of Mexico. Adding even more depth to this attention to race and ethnicity is the fact that the film is told from the perspective of a woman. Esperanza Quintero (played by Mexican actress Rosaura Revueltas), the wife of the union local's president, opens the film with her voiceover. *Salt of the Earth* thus chronicles not only the strike, but also Esperanza's emerging consciousness of her own political voice **[Figure 10.44]**. This consciousness is shown to be rooted in her experience as a woman, a mother, and a working-class resident of the community called Zinc Town in the film. In the beginning of the film, the pregnant Esperanza, a name that means "hope" in Spanish, is reluctant to join the other women, who argue that proper sanitation is just as important as safety in the miners' demands. Then, at a crucial juncture in the film, she speaks for the women at a union meeting, to the shock and displeasure of her husband, Ramon (Juan Chacón). Ramon's ultimate acknowledgment of her right to speak out and of the equal status of her concerns parallels the successful resolution of the strike, bringing the film to a hopeful conclusion on both personal and political levels.

Esperanza's story is interwoven with the events of the strike throughout the film, setting up a relationship between the women's and men's struggles that can be described as dialectical, because taken together the two seemingly opposed perspectives create something much stronger. For example, Esperanza is disappointed when she realizes Ramon has forgotten her birthday, but after her son reminds him, the neighbors come by to celebrate in a scene of community life that anticipates the solidarity the families will show during the strike. Later, the silent

Figure 10.44 *Salt of the Earth* (1954). Rosaura Revueltas as Esperanza, the film's central consciousness.

presence of the neighbors outside her home prevents her family's threatened eviction. During the strike, women start out by bringing coffee to the picketers and end up taking over the lines when the men are barred by a court order. When the women are jailed, the men must take their turn at household chores. In another dialectical sequence that is very cinematically effective, images of Esperanza giving birth are crosscut with shots of Ramon being brutally beaten by strike breakers. Their parallel pains show triumph through struggle and link them as partners in their eventual victory.

Salt of the Earth stands in an interesting relationship to Hollywood films of its era that take on social issues, such as Elia Kazan's *Gentleman's Agreement*. Like them, it translates public conflicts into personal terms. Unlike them, it translates these concerns back out to a broader context so that we are left with more than regrets for the injurious effects of prejudice on individuals. Esperanza's personal journey results in her finding a public voice that is echoed in the cinematic device of the voiceover.

Salt of the Earth's producers had been blacklisted for Communist sympathies after the HUAC hearings. Director Herbert Biberman was one of the Hollywood Ten jailed for contempt of Congress. Producer Paul Jarrico had written the script for *Song of Russia* (1943), one of the HUAC's targets. Oscar-winning screenwriter Michael Wilson (*A Place in the Sun*, 1951) would later defy the blacklist by writing the pacifist drama *Friendly Persuasion* (1956). For *Salt of the Earth*, Wilson visited the miners and wrote his script in consultation with the film's participants, who read or attended readings of the work in progress, giving their input. Juan Chacón, the union president, was cast in that role in the film, giving an unforgettable performance. Nearly all the cast members were actual participants in the strike. The exceptions were Mexican actress Revueltas and several white actors in secondary roles, including blacklisted actor Will Geer as the sinister sheriff. Later, the film was used as a labor-organizing tool, bringing its involvement with working people full circle.

The production was fraught with difficulties. Members of the Hollywood union of technical workers, SMPTE (Society of Motion Picture and Television Engineers), were forbidden from working on the film, and blacklisted personnel were employed instead, including a number of African American crew members. The publicity surrounding the film was inflammatory. Shooting was sabotaged. Juan Chacón was physically attacked. When Revueltas was detained at the Mexican border and later deported, several scenes had to be shot around her. The film's exhibition history was also eventful. The projectionists' union forbade its members from showing the film. Opening briefly in New York and Toronto, *Salt of the Earth* was attacked in the press: respected critic Pauline Kael condemned it as "extremely shrewd propaganda for the urgent business of the USSR." The film was pulled from U.S. distribution and subsequently screened mainly by film societies and at union events. (It has, however, been seen by more people

Atanarjuat reflects many dimensions of its cultural context. It incorporates traditional Inuit narrative modes, myths, and customs as well as contemporary Inuit activism, which led to the establishment of a native state in the Canadian north. Canada's official policy of multiculturalism allocates funds for artists of color, including media artists, which enabled the filmmakers to receive training and cultivate their ideas in the field. The technological development of digital video made the production possible. Historical cinematic influences, including neorealism and the rich tradition than most Hollywood films because official sanction meant decades of screenings to the vast population of the People's Republic of China.)

Aesthetically, *Salt of the Earth* draws on the traditions of Italian neorealism, as it was shot on location with a mostly amateur cast. Dramatically, it conforms to the style of socialist realism, in which an individuated hero stands in for the problems of a class of people. His or her growing consciousness is meant to be echoed by that of the viewers, who are thereby convinced of the justness of a political cause—in this case, that of the striking miners. One particular sequence, in which union members across the country send their dollars to ensure that the workers' families can hold out until the union's demands are met, is intended to solicit our identification and participation. *Salt of the Earth* is unique—many of its filmmakers were Communist Party members who turned to independent production when they were blacklisted. Its treatment of class, race, and gender is unprecedented in American film history, and few narrative films made since can be said to address their intersection more sensitively.

The film did not come out of nowhere, however. Indeed, its message, in both form and content, is about how a specific context demands particular responses. A very brief review of events of the year of the film's release, a time of conflict and contradiction, provides a backdrop for its concerns as well as for the resistance with which it was met. In 1953, the Korean War ended in compromise, with the country divided into Communist and capitalist nations. Protests in the United States failed to avert the execution of Ethel and Julius Rosenberg, accused of spying for the Soviets. Gender roles were hotly contested, as evidenced by two publication events that year: the first issue of *Playboy* and the English translation of Simone de Beauvoir's *The Second Sex*. Puerto Rican nationalist Lolita Lebron, along with three others, opened fire in the U.S. House of Representatives, to draw attention to their cause. But hopefulness about racial cooperation was encouraged when the Supreme Court ended school segregation in the landmark case *Brown v. Board of Education*.

Salt of the Earth's concern with gender and with the United States' relationship with other nations in the Americas, and the virulence with which its pro-labor message was met, were unique responses to this cultural moment. At the opposite end of the spectrum of production and exhibition, Hollywood released its first films in CinemaScope and 3-D the same year. These entertainments were also consistent with their times, relying as they did on technological innovation for a sense of well-being, as did home appliances and the arms race. As an independently produced film, *Salt of the Earth* nevertheless drew on the expertise of personnel who had worked within Hollywood. Biberman, Jarrico, Wilson, and Geer had been forced out of the industry by the red scare, an event that is unthinkable today. However, one wonders whether the ideological convictions that their film represents would be compatible in the entertainment cinema of our current cultural context.

of Canadian documentary, and patterns of distribution and reception, ranging from community screenings to a prize at the Cannes International Film Festival, mark the film's journey. If Steven Spielberg offered us a historical myth in *Saving Private Ryan*, Kunuk and his collaborators offer us a mythical history, both in the content of their film and as the first feature-length film made by an Inuit filmmaker and crew.

In this chapter, we have explored inclusive and disjunctive accounts of film history. Alternatives to traditional, selective methods that strive for order and completion, these methods interrupt the certainty of a continuous history. Looking at global histories, we attempt to move beyond a single evolutionary progression to multiple sites on the map and beyond stylistic periods to a more dynamic sense of the interaction of national history and film. By introducing films and filmmakers that have been hidden from history, we may have prompted some new additions to readers' top-ten lists, even as we scrutinized the project of constructing such lists. Finally, our look at film and cultural contexts has attempted to show how interdependent representation and reality may be, cautioning us to remember both meanings of the phrase *making history*.

 VIEWING CUES: Film, History, and Cultural Context

■ What was happening in the world or the nation when the film screened in class was released? What characterized popular culture at the time—such as fashions or hit songs? Was the film successful? Research or speculate about who the audiences were for the film. What did the contemporary press say about it? Have more recent releases or reassessments of the film introduced different cultural contexts? How might different audiences receive the film through different contexts?

■ Research an event in the history of cinema—such as the introduction of the drive-in theater or the DVD format—and consider the cultural influences that resulted in this development.

■ View a film that depicts another culture. What questions would you like to have answered about what you are seeing? How might you put the film in context?

CRITICAL VOICES: VIVIAN SOBCHACK ON THE WRITING OF FILM HISTORY

In her essay "What Is Film History?" (2000), Vivian Sobchack reflects on the activity of writing film history, inspired by the recent uncovering of traces of the vast set of Cecil B. DeMille's silent epic *The Ten Commandments* in the California desert. What kind of historical evidence is provided by a movie set, which is already a tribute to artifice and reconstruction? In this introductory excerpt from her essay, Sobchack looks at how the discipline of history has changed over time.

What is film history? At the end of the twentieth century and in the 1
pervasive context of mass-mediated and high-technology culture, the responses to this question are much more complex than they once were. Some 50 years or so ago, the general response would have been that film history, as both practice and product, is the excavation, accumulation, and dissemination of knowledge about the cinema's progressive temporal evolution as an art form, an industry, a technology, and a cultural artifact. Hardly anyone would have noticed—let alone argued with—the choice and connotations of such words as "progressive" (with its linear and teleological implications of change in time as a gradual, continuous, and homogeneous process). Nor was it likely that anyone would have immediately interrogated the discrete categories or hierarchical order into which the cinema and film history were usually divided: that is, aesthetic history kept relatively distinct from (and untainted by) economical or technological history, or cinema as an art form privileged above movies as a cultural artifact.

Today, however, the question of film history is much more vexed than it was 2
mid-century when the infant discipline of film studies was first attempting to
legitimate both itself as an academic enterprise and the cinema as an aesthetic
(and secondarily historical) form worthy of serious scholarly attention. . . .
The primary task of the film historian was to uncover previously unknown
historical facts and to interpret and represent them as objectively as possible
so as to add to the cumulative storehouse of film historical knowledge.

Today, however, our interests in the field (let alone our circumscription 3
of it) have complicated our notions of both "film" and "history." In the first
instance, influenced by the transformations of cinema brought about by television, video cassette recorders (VCRs), and computers, the definition of "film"
as an object of study has not only broadened considerably but has also been
increasingly destabilized as an object and form. In the second instance, influenced by feminism, cultural studies, and a variety of "post" theories (particularly postmodernism and post-colonialism), the definition of "history"
has also undergone a significant broadening and destabilization of its objects
and forms. Indeed, both the idea of history as an "objective science" and the
totalizing coherence of "grand narratives" have been criticized and decon-
structed—as has the discipline's primary focus on political and military
events and the individual power and achievements of "great"—and white—men.

Today, both as practitioners and as writers, historians in all fields (includ- 4
ing film and media studies) question not only whether historical objectivity
is possible but also whether it is desirable. Grand, coherent, and evolution
narratives have given way to local and micro-histories—and the gaps and
ruptures in our knowledge of the past are foregrounded rather than smoothed
over. . . . [A]s historians have become increasingly self-conscious of history's
always-constructed and representational nature and its always-motivated
and selective focus, history has lost its stability as the grounded site upon
which knowledge of the past is accumulated, coherently ordered, and legiti-
mated; rather, it has become an unstable site in which fragments of past
representations do not necessarily "add up" or cohere but, instead, are subject to "undisciplined" (and often "undisciplining") contestation and use.

THE NEXT LEVEL: ADDITIONAL SOURCES

Bruno, Giuliana. *Streetwalking on a Ruined Map: Cultural Theory and the City Films of
    Elvira Notari*. Princeton: Princeton University Press, 1993. Focusing on the fas-
    cinating career of a woman producer of early films in Italy, Bruno makes an ar-
    gument about gender, cities, and the new experiences of space and time offered
    by the film medium and the institution of cinema in the context of modernity.

Cripps, Thomas. *Slow Fade to Black: The Negro in American Film, 1900–1942*. New
    York: Oxford University Press, 1977. A richly detailed social history of the repre-
    sentation of African Americans in U.S. films until World War II that continues
    in the author's *Making Movies Black* (1993).

Elsaesser, Thomas. *New German Cinema*. New Brunswick: Rutgers University Press,
    1989. This definitive study maps the historical and cultural contexts of this in-
    fluential film movement.

Hansen, Miriam. *Babel and Babylon*. Cambridge: Harvard University Press, 1991.
    Looking at the specific contexts of U.S. silent film reception as well as at such
    examples as the popularity of Rudolf Valentino, this book argues that audiences
    found a new public experience of the modern world at the movies.

Nowell-Smith, Geoffrey, ed. *The Oxford History of World Cinema*. New York: Oxford
    University Press, 1996. A comprehensive volume featuring contributions from
    experts on periods, topics, and regions of world cinema.

Reactions: Reading and Writing about Film

Our experiences of a movie begin even before we see a film. These reactions intensify while we watch it, and, as we will see in the next two chapters, often continue well after we leave the theater or turn off the DVD player. Sometimes, for instance, we respond to a film or group of films by puzzling over what they mean or why they moved us so deeply. As a consequence, we may seek out reviews, essays, or books about the film, its director, or perhaps the country where it was made. One viewer watched *Underground* (1995) and realized she needed to know more about the political history of the Balkans depicted in the film, as well as the role of the controversial director, Emir Kusturica. The more she read, the more interested she became in broader topics in film criticism and analysis, such as postcolonial theory and auteur theory. Reading film theory such as this, she realized, offers some of the most complex, challenging, and rewarding experiences of the movies, but it is also an experience that often requires clear intellectual preparation and particular reading skills.

Sometimes, our reactions to a film develop further, leading perhaps to our writing a critical essay about that film. Whether this writing project springs from a personal desire or from an assignment given in class, writing about film also can become a rich extension of the film experience, allowing us to develop, articulate, and organize our feelings and perceptions about a movie. After two friends had debated the merits of Philipe Noyce's 2002 adaptation of Graham Greene's *The Quiet American*, a story about Vietnam in the 1950s, one chose to write a research paper for his film class, focusing on the female character Phuong [Figure IV.1]. After carefully working out a thesis, then researching the novel and this period in Vietnam's history, and finally rigorously revising his first draft, this viewer discovered he had a much more complex and subtle appreciation of both the character and the film.

In the next two chapters, we will explore and explain how reading and writing about film always deepens and enriches our experiences of the movies. We will examine different critical methods that have evolved over the years and that invariably shape and color how we think about a movie, and we will map the steps and procedures for turning our initial perceptions about a movie into a sophisticated essay. Here as elsewhere, the film experience grows and develops in as many directions as we are willing to take it.

◀ Figure IV.1 *The Quiet American* (2002). A single character becomes the focus for a complex research essay on race and gender in a recent movie adaptation.

CHAPTER 11

Reading about Film: Critical Methods and Theories

The film, on the one hand, extends our comprehension of the necessities which rule our lives; on the other hand, it manages to assure us of an immense and unexpected field of action.

Walter Benjamin, "The Work of Art in the Age of Mechanical Reproduction"

KEY OBJECTIVES

This chapter explores major methods, concepts, and thinkers in film theory—from the first decades of the medium to the electronic age. It includes introductions to

- how theories work

- models of cinematic specificity, such as the ontology of film and formalist analysis

- comparative models of film, such as authorship and genre and how they help us think about the movies

- some of the major thinkers and problems in classical film theory, including montage and realism

- schools and debates within contemporary film theory, including Marxism, semiotics, and structuralism; poststructuralism and feminism; and such new directions as cultural studies, race and representation, film and philosophy, and postmodernism and new media

At the dawn of a new millennium, audiovisual technologies are more prevalent and more integrated with our experience than ever before. When television was introduced in the mid-twentieth century, and later when home video and computer games became popular, predictions that moviegoing would be eclipsed by the new leisure forms abounded. However, these pronouncements on the death of cinema were premature. In 2002, more movie tickets were sold in the United States than in any previous year. Certainly, the movies are being marketed more vigorously, with tie-ins that penetrate further and further into daily life: we watch music videos composed of scenes from an upcoming movie, take home action figures with fast food, and wear clothing emblazoned with film franchise logos. Why such strategies take hold is worth considering. What is it about the film experience that is so resonant with modern life? This question emerged with the first projected moving images and continues to reward consideration today. Reflection on the nature and uses of the medium is the province of film theory.

Precisely because cinema is so accessible and familiar, for many of us skepticism accompanies the idea of theorizing about it. This familiarity is what German pre–World War II thinker Walter Benjamin refers to in the chapter-opening quotation, but he links cinema with a fantastical and utopian potential as well. Like any specialized language, film theory requires an introduction. Yet it can be demystified at the outset by realizing that with avid moviegoing comes knowledge about the movies. Fan magazine readers throughout the twentieth century were experts about certain aspects of the medium, although the facts they took in were carefully limited by publicists and editors. Such expertise can be the foundation of a theoretical position. Every time we go to the movies, we are reflective about the experience. We evaluate elements about the film before we go: genre is invoked when we choose drama or comedy from pay-per-view menus that list films by type. If we choose to see a film because it is made by Steven Soderbergh, we have used some element of **auteurism,** the idea that movies are the creative responsibility of a single individual, in making our decision. The often dismissive term *chick flick* nevertheless invokes some understanding of **reception theory,** which focuses on how different kinds of audiences regard different kinds of films, by recognizing that female audiences have related similar types of films to their own experiences in the past. When we speak of the fictional world of *The Godfather* (1972) **[Figure 11.1]** as if it were real, we invoke the concept of **verisimilitude,** the sense of "having the quality of truth" that movies confer perhaps more than any other artistic medium. When we carefully select a seat at the movie theater, implicit in our choice is an ideal vantage point from which the film illusion will be most complete.

Figure 11.1 *The Godfather* (1972). Audiences accept the verisimilitude of the Corleone crime family's world.

Although these everyday experiences are not carrying out a project identical to that of film theory, they touch on its realm. Throughout this book we introduce questions that are more explicitly and systematically taken up in the realm of film theory, and theoretical perspectives that have their origins with the very first films underpin our discussions of film form, narrative, and genre. Film theory can be defined as a sustained interrogation of propositions about the nature of the medium, the features of individual films, or the interaction between viewers and films. In this chapter, we will make explicit the connections between the questions explored in previous chapters and theoretical issues, and we will put this discussion in the context of more specific histories of film theory.

Concepts and Methods in Film Theory

A theory is an explanatory model. *Merriam Webster's Collegiate Dictionary* (10th edition) defines *theory* as "the analysis of a set of facts in their relation to one another." In the natural sciences, a theory is verified by experimental work. In a humanistic inquiry like the study of cinema, a theory cannot be verified in the same manner; rather, it is used to relate and illuminate observed and repeatable phenomena. The very word *theory* has an interesting resonance in the context of cinema studies. It is derived from the Greek word *theoria,* meaning "a looking at, a contemplation." If theory is "a looking at," as film viewers we know that our eyes can sometimes be deceived.

Theories may not be absolute truths, but they do generate understanding. In this section, we will consider what a theory is and what it does by looking at several common approaches to film and the theoretical positions that inform them.

A theory begins as a hypothesis, a proposition about a phenomenon that awaits verification. Next, as concrete evidence is gathered, the theory may undergo modification in light of the evidence. Certain criteria will be enlisted by some theories that would not be considered by others. For example, if we were to postulate that watching a movie resembles dreaming, we would consider such factors as the darkened room, the relative immobility of the viewer, and the way that edited images flow one after the other as evidence to be used in confirmation of our hypothesis. We might also conclude from this resemblance that movies affect us at a deep, unconscious level. This theory would relegate to the background the more social aspects of attending the movies—eating popcorn, chatting with friends, emulating movie-star fashions. Our "film viewing is like dreaming" theory would also gloss over the fact that movies are produced by many individuals and represent complicated mediations—that is, they do not spring from our individual mental functioning as dreams do. In turn, the alternative theory that films have a particularly strong capacity for realism would exclude evidence supporting the films-resemble-dreams hypothesis. It might instead garner evidence from statements by technicians about how they attempt to approximate reality and from the coherence conveyed by continuity editing. In short, every theoretical approach to cinema foregrounds some elements and relegates others to the background.

Consequently, a single theory cannot account for everything about its subject. Several competing theories can be valid. They may engage in direct debate or be derived from such different traditions that they are not in dialogue with each other at all. The theory that the cinema inherently strives toward realism may not be exhaustive, but it may still be a useful way to approach a particular film or technological development. It is helpful to think of theories as a part of the tool kit of the cultural critic. Sometimes a wrench is required; at other times, a hammer. This metaphor also implies that theoretical inquiry is about not only taking something apart but also building models and connections.

Besides looking at different aspects of the experience, film theories vary in their level of analysis, selecting different features to address. Some theories regard the cinema as a mass phenomenon that needs to be approached on the basic level of the significance and organization of the institution of cinema—from the industry to the broad-based reception of films. (We will discuss this cultural approach later in the chapter.) Before we present an overview of the history and debates of film theory in subsequent sections, it will be helpful to situate some important concepts and methods in relation to two general types of theoretical inquiry and the methods that correspond to them:

- **Concepts of specificity** address the characteristics of the medium as such or the inner workings of a specific film.
- **Comparative methods** study films in relation to other films in set categories such as auteur films and genre films.

As we have implied, film theory encompasses many different kinds of writing addressed to different problems and readers. Because cinema is a relatively new phenomenon, it has not attracted the internally consistent body of commentary that we see in art or literary criticism. Therefore, the field of film theory is wide open and attempts to give it continuity can be misleading. Another drawback of an introductory survey like this one is that the reader will not experience theories and theorists in their own words. A paraphrase does not perform the same function as the theoretical work itself, in whose actual language, rhetoric, and context much of the argument resides. Reading this chapter in tandem with the theoretical texts themselves will give a more complete picture of the range and depth of film theory.

Concepts of Specificity: The Cinematic Medium and Film Form

Theories of an artistic medium often begin by trying to define their object. "What is cinema?" asks French film theorist André Bazin in his classic book of the same title. In philosophy, this is called the question of **ontology** or being. Ontology is a logical starting point, for many other questions can be derived from the "what is . . . ?" question. One way theorists debate the definition of the cinematic medium is by characterizing its relationship to the world: does the cinema represent or copy reality, or is it fundamentally artistic? Another possibility—that cinema is "just entertainment"—is a prevalent opinion but not an elaborated theory.

Sometimes theorists approach film ontologically to attempt to isolate the **specificity** of the medium in relation to the other arts. What does cinema manifest that is not found in painting, for example? Both use pictorial imagery. But film differs from painting and drawing because it is composed of photographic images captured with a camera (even if the images are of drawings, as with traditional animation). Film differs from photography in that its images are displayed to give the illusion of motion, a property that film shares with television. Unlike television, but like architecture, cinema involves an experience of spatial immersion. Like performed music, film unfolds in a specific period of time. Yet most musical performances are live, whereas film is recorded. As a storytelling medium, cinema borrows from the novel; yet associations of images resemble poetry. Each of these comparisons can and has been extended considerably and productively. The assumption is that from ever more precise statements of its properties, we will arrive at the genuine specificity of cinema.

Probably the most persistent and generative comparison in film theory is that between cinema and theater. Both present a perceptual phenomenon, foregrounding sound and vision above the other senses, to an assembly of spectators. However, at the movies, what spectators see and hear is in some sense not really there. There are no actors or, in the case of sound film, musicians present during the performance, which in this sense is more ghostly than lively. Film takes place, in the words of theorist Christian Metz, in an "elsewhere" and an "elsewhen." Theorists contemplating the nature of this absence postulate that viewers overcompensate for it. They invest in the characters and their fates, respond to the rush of colors and sounds, really *believe* in the film, or at least engage in the **suspension of disbelief.** Some theorists regard this attitude on the part of spectators as a characteristic of cinematic specificity, one that distinguishes film from theater and even from television, which is viewed in a more distracted manner and does not provoke such a strong sense of illusion.

Other theories of cinematic specificity isolate the two-dimensionality, "framed-ness," rectangular shape, and enhanced size of the moving image as defining characteristics. Still others focus on what the film is made of,

Figure 11.2 *Final Fantasy: The Spirit Within* (2000). The nature of the film image—its ontological status—is challenged by computer-generated imagery (CGI), as in this first film to feature human "actors" produced entirely through CGI.

light projected through celluloid, its **material specificity.** Recent technological developments—from videotape playback and virtual reality to computer-generated imagery (CGI), digital cameras, and digital projection—raise profound ontological questions about cinema. Altering the properties of the image itself by making it smaller or rendering it electronically, rather than capturing or generating it optically, undoubtedly changes the materiality of the image. Other practices challenge film's established relationship to space, time, or the real or **phenomenal** world, which is what we can perceive. A photographic image refers to another space, another time, and an actual object whose image is captured by rays of light striking the film emulsion and causing a chemical reaction. A computer-generated image does not have a real-world reference; the image *is* the thing **[Figure 11.2]**.

Indeed, the theoretical questions that swirl around new media today recall the period of cinema's inception, when it attracted similar—and almost instantaneous—speculation. Although the question "What is cinema?" was posed by Bazin in the singular, hundreds of answers have been proposed. Film "is" all of these things in part because film theory has been drawn from many different disciplines—philosophy, psychology, art history, literary theory, history, and sociology—as well as from the many different practices of cinema itself. We will encounter this diversity later in the chapter when we reconsider these ontological questions in the context of the development of film theory and the work of individual theorists.

One advantage of honing a definition of cinema to its specifics is that theorists who accept that definition can share terms of analysis and point to concrete elements as the basis for interpretations. Although some theorists might postulate that cinema is defined by some ineffable essence, most would characterize it by its **form,** the configuration of its specific parts. **Formalism** is a method of analysis that considers a film's form or structure to be primary. The theoretical precept behind formalism is that meaning is to be found in the work itself. We do not need to know anything else in order to interpret it—not the identity of the filmmaker, not what setup was used for a particular shot, not the fact that a film's landscape provided the backdrop for other westerns—although such factors might provide context. Of course, most critical approaches include some focus on the work itself, but formalists isolate form as the primary level of interpretation. Like the formalist art historian, the film analyst examines how elements such as light, color, and composition are utilized in a particular film. Likewise, elements unique to cinema, such as camera movement and distance, shot duration and rhythm, will provide further insights into the film's effectiveness.

Formalist approaches to specific film texts are often called **close readings.** As the term implies, this technique is derived from literary studies. Close readers analyze texts by isolating, naming, and considering the effects of individual elements and of their interrelationships. In the 1920s, formalist critics in the Soviet Union sought to define criteria for the "literariness" of works of literature. Close reading was also central to the practice of new criticism, which developed in the United States in the 1930s. New critics isolated diction, rhyme scheme, punctuation, repetition, and metaphors to speak of *how* a poem means as a crucial component of *what* it means, setting aside speculation about an author's intentions and historical and biographical information about the work. This formalist approach, very influential in the humanities in the United States, has been carried over to university film studies based in English and modern language departments. The theoretical orientation of formalism is toward the autonomy of the work of art, a relatively familiar way to discuss works considered part of high culture, such as symphonies and oil paintings. However, applying formal criteria to commercial cinema requires theorists to make an argument for film's specificity.

Although formalism looks at the work in and of itself, it also varies in context. The Russian formalists codified criticism through an elaborate nomenclature, striving for a scientific standard of objectivity that was political in aim. If interpretations of artworks could be accomplished through the application of specific techniques, they would no longer be the province of a privileged few who based their "appreciations" on ultimately impressionistic criteria. But formalism is just as often apolitical. Attempting to sever the connection between literature and social context was an expressed purpose of new criticism. Applied loosely, formalism accompanies almost any serious treatment of works of art in terms of their media, and it is a pervasive element in contemporary film studies.

However, in adapting literary techniques to film studies, several problems arise. First, the vocabulary of literary analysis is well established, whereas film studies must introduce terms and make them widely accepted. The terminology of filmmaking—jump cut, three-point lighting, over-the-shoulder shot—is available to help critics identify the properties of a shot or sequence, but sometimes new terms must be invented. Literary interpretation uses words to talk about words. In the case of film analysis, words must be used to describe images and sounds. Formalist approaches to film can borrow language from traditional art and music criticism to discuss color and composition, melody and rhythm. But film has an added temporal dimension, and its moving images are difficult to pin down without distorting the viewer's perception. Theater criticism can help in the discussion of performance and mise-en-scène. But the very act of referring to these elements in a particular film presents its own unique problems. Historically, it has been impossible to "quote" the cinematic "passage" one is analyzing, precisely because it literally passes by in an instant. One can say a great deal about a single image, but during the viewing of a film, there are twenty-four discrete images per second. Stopping the film to look closely means that the *cinematic* experience disappears—cinema means movement. New technologies can facilitate critics' references to moving images, allowing analysts to "capture" clips or still frames. Here, a problem of methodology—how to refer—has theoretical implications.

One method of close reading is to look at a segment of film shot by shot. This technique of **textual analysis** is exemplified in Raymond Bellour's detailed studies of Hitchcock's films. Bellour facilitates his analyses by setting up a chart listing all of the shots in the sequence to be analyzed and picking some variables to track. From such a chart, the analyst notes and interprets the interrelations among different formal elements and their patterns of development. For example, how do variations in camera distance correlate with camera movements in a given sequence and to what effect? Borrowing from semiotics and communications studies, analysts such as Bellour refer to elements such as shot duration, camera movement, and lighting as **codes.** A code is essentially a rule, and it structures a particular act of communication,

Figure 11.3 *The Big Heat* (1953). Low-key lighting, a code that gives us the message that this a film noir.

a **message.** The code must be shared by the sender and the receiver for the message to be understood. For example, viewers understand that the shadows in a shot from *The Big Heat* (1953) signify a threat because they recognize the code of film noir lighting **[Figure 11.3]**. Familiarity with the codes of film music allows us to understand such connotations as the time and place the movie is set as well as the concept "this is the introductory sequence." The textual analyst draws conclusions from the interactions of these codes over a series of shots. Dark shadows and threatening music reinforce each other to connote danger, for instance. Some codes used in cinema, such as lighting and dialogue, are shared with theater. Other codes, such as framing, camera movement, and shot duration, are examples of **cinematic specificity.** One of the striking features of textual analyses is that they have no apparent stopping point: there is always something more to interpret. Book-length studies have been produced that analyze a single feature film. Textual analyses are an especially effective way to train oneself to look—and listen—to the movies more closely.

Comparative Methods: Authorship and Genre Theories

In order to develop theoretical precepts about how films work, critics and theorists have found ways to classify films. Two of the primary categories for exploring groups of films in order to generate hypotheses about their commonalities and divergences are authors and genres. These two groupings of films are also commonsense ways of looking at the movies. Today, names of famous directors are even used as adjectives, as in a "Lynchean universe" and a "Spike Lee shot" **[Figure 11.4]**. We refer to genres when we discuss what kind of film we are interested in seeing on a night out. Because these are such widespread classificatory schemas, we do not always realize that they are based in part on *theories* about film. We will look at authorship and genre in some detail because they are so central to our ways of seeing cinema.

Figure 11.4 *Do the Right Thing* (1989). Recognizing the head-on close-up as a "Spike Lee shot" shows our everyday understanding of auteurist theory.

Authorship

The theory of **film authorship** means that we understand a film as bearing the creative imprint of one individual, usually the director, whether or not it is considered a great work of art. A so-called **auteur film,** from the French word for author, is taken to reveal the personality of its director. The film *Citizen Kane* (1941) is rarely invoked without mention of the film's co-writer, director, and star Orson Welles. However, many, if not most, films generate no such immediate association with a creator. Viewers often remain oblivious to the director's name or simply consider other aspects of a film to be more immediate. *Hannibal* (2001) is likely to be first identified as the sequel to *The Silence of the Lambs* (1991), and fans

Figure 11.5 *Gladiator* (2000). Director Ridley Scott crowds his frame with details, using mise-en-scène to reflect his characters' plights in a costume drama.

Figure 11.6 *Blade Runner* (1982) . . . and in a science fiction film.

of the novelist Thomas Harris will think of it as part of a series of films adapted from his work that feature the character Dr. Hannibal Lecter. However, this film can be interestingly contextualized in terms of director Ridley Scott's authorship. One might detect in the film's emphasis on an enveloping mise-en-scène visual similarities to Scott's otherwise very different *Gladiator* (2000) and *Blade Runner* (1982) **[Figures 11.5 and 11.6]**. One might find interesting parallels in the director's depiction of violence in this horror film and in his war film *Black Hawk Down* (2001), which was made in the same year. Another argument about authorship would emphasize the thematic link between the strong female character played by Julianne Moore in *Hannibal* and the heroines of Scott's *G.I. Jane* (1997), *Thelma & Louise* (1991), and *Alien* (1979). These examples show that authorship is not only a matter of crediting an individual with a film's artistry but also one of meaningfully relating works within a filmmaker's corpus. Films grouped by author reveal something about the personal style and preoccupations of that filmmaker. For example, John Ford's westerns, produced over several decades, often show an individual in conflict with a community's ethos.

Chapter 9 looks at film history in terms of a theory of authorship; notions of "masters and masterpieces" employ judgments of value. In this framework, great films and great individuals make history. Authorship is a concept obviously drawn from literary studies and with come canons and rankings. Because great literature is considered "culture," in the sense of appealing to cultivated taste, borrowing the literary concept of authorship helps lend prestige to the medium of cinema, rendering it indisputably worthy of study. (Somewhat paradoxically, the "author" role is usually reserved for directors rather than screenwriters of films—although directors who write their own scripts are especially revered.) However, the concept of value itself is relative. Alfred Hitchcock made his name known to audiences through devices such as cameo appearances **[Figure 11.7]** when most directors remained anonymous. But because he worked in the thriller genre he was critically dismissed as an entertainer who only later became considered a prestigious author. Elia Kazan, a theater director whose films, including *Gentleman's Agreement* (1947), deal with social issues, was accorded greater respect in his day. Yet among film enthusiasts today, Hitchcock is granted higher status, which is evidence of changing values.

Figure 11.7 *Strangers on a Train* (1951). Alfred Hitchcock's cameos assisted popular recognition of his authorship.

Hitchcock's self-promotion is not without precedent. In the first few decades of film, directors like D. W. Griffith made their creative role a selling point for their films. The intertitles of Griffith's films bore his initials, and he banked on his name recognition when he joined stars Mary Pickford, Douglas Fairbanks, and Charlie Chaplin (also a director) in the founding of United Artists. Griffith's contemporary Lois Weber was also known to her audiences by name, although her reputation was eclipsed until recent interest in women directors led to her rediscovery. Woody Allen is one of the most recognizable of American auteurs because he writes, directs, and appears in his films, which use recurrent actors and contain recurrent themes. Today, we increasingly identify films by their directors. The fact that a film is directed by Quentin Tarantino or made by the Coen brothers is often considered its most salient feature. Tarantino's name has been used to "present" other directors' work, such as Wong Kar-wai's *Chungking Express* (1994), and international names such as Ken Loach, Zhang Yimou, Claire Denis, and Aki Kaurismäki attract art-house and festival audiences. These filmmakers draw on the tradition of postwar art cinema, which made the filmgoing public aware of film directors, names. Such filmmakers' idiosyncracies are an important marker of this type of authorship; in contrast, the name recognition of directors such as Chris Columbus is more akin to that of a commercial novelist. Certainly there are many films whose directors we could not name. *The Brady Bunch Movie* (1995) was marketed on the name recognition of the 1970s television show. Nevertheless, the use of authorship as a critical approach brings to light the fact that this film was directed by a woman, Betty Thomas, at a time when female directors in Hollywood were still a small minority. It should be clear from these examples that a theory of authorship, or auteurism, is not an inevitable way to see films. Authorship as a critical construct has a history; it is often invoked strategically; and it is not free from the economics of filmmaking and film promotion.

This history became very visible when specific directors were vocally championed by French critics in the 1950s. The retention of the French terms *auteur* and *auteurism* marks this origin. Not only do the French words refer to a critical tradition, but simply by being French they carry connotations of cultural value for English speakers. In the 1950s, writers for the new film magazine *Cahiers du cinéma* promoted what they called *"la politique des auteurs,"* a "policy" or doctrine of singling out for praise certain filmmakers, such as Orson Welles, Fritz Lang, Sam Fuller, and Robert Bresson, whose distinct personalities made their films immediately identifiable. The criticism written by young filmmakers like François Truffaut was a rebellious gesture against commercial French filmmaking of that time, which they felt lacked vitality and currency. The journal and its polemics—impassioned paeans to the greats and denigration of those who lacked vision—attracted a great deal of attention and debate in the United States and Britain.

As noted in Chapter 10 on film history, in the post–World War II period, film culture was energized by Italian neorealism, whose immediacy allowed for the expression of filmmakers' personal visions. Italian filmmaker Roberto Rossellini and Swedish art film director Ingmar Bergman stood out as true "authors" who wrote and directed their films. The *Cahiers* critics themselves aspired to be and soon emerged as significant auteurs, defining the nouvelle vague, or French new wave. Besides Truffaut, among their number were Jean-Luc Godard [**Figure 11.8**], Eric Rohmer, Jacques Rivette, and Claude Chabrol, all of whom have made films in the past few years. These *cineastes*, film afficionados, wrote fervent appreciations of such European directors as Rossellini, whose works clearly reflected his individual vision in this case of postwar renewal. Yet *Cahiers du cinéma*'s concept of authorship was also applied to a group of filmmakers for whom the idea of such conscious and consistent creative artistry seemed less appropriate—directors working in the heyday of the Hollywood studio system. In the critics' minds, the efforts of such filmmakers were extraordinary because each left his (they were all men) unmistakable mark on even routine assignments. Despite the constraints on their artistic autonomy and the primacy of market considerations, Hollywood auteurs such as Raoul Walsh and Howard Hawks emerged as artists who left their signature on their films in the form of characteristic motifs or striking compositions. The elevation of these directors' reputations glorified the task of the critics as well. Their writings in praise of B-filmmakers like Budd Boetticher, known for his films about bullfighting, were impassioned polemics. Debates arose over whether a particular director should be classified a true auteur or a mere **metteur-en-scène** (the French term for director, derived from theatrical usage), a label that conveyed technical competence without a strong individual vision. When the *Cahiers* group began writing and directing their own films at the end of the 1950s, they combined the influences of their European and Hollywood idols into distinct auteurist styles of their own (see p. 372).

The *La politique des auteurs* was imported to the American context and popularized by critic Andrew Sarris of *Film Culture* and the *Village Voice*. In his 1968 collection *The American Cinema: Directors and Directions, 1929–1968,* Sarris lists his pantheon of directors, such as Howard Hawks, whose films often center around strong male bonds, and deflates the reputations of Academy Award winners such as William Wyler. In Sarris's hierarchy of Hollywood talent, the judgment of the critic prevails in assigning relative status to a wide array of directors based on their personal signature. Like that of the French critics, Sarris's work depends on a deep **cinephilia,** or a love of cinema, an almost exhaustive knowledge of the films—major and minor—released throughout the previous several decades. Sarris's rendering of the *la politique des auteurs* as auteur theory is somewhat misleading, both because it is less a fully worked out theory than a method and because the political connotation is lost in translation. Defining the approach, Sarris isolates as criteria of value the director's "technical competence" and "distinguishable personality" as well as the quality of "interior meaning" that

Figure 11.8 Jean-Luc Godard, auteur.

Film Journals

For many *cineastes* or film buffs, the distinctive yellow cover of *Cahiers du cinéma* in the 1950s is as iconic an image of film history as that of Fay Wray in King Kong's hairy palm. Most of us read about film in a variety of publications, from checking in on celebrity journalism in line at the supermarket to comparing reviews of films that interest us in the daily paper and in weekly publications such as the consumer-oriented *Entertainment Weekly,* the highbrow *The New Yorker,* the newsmagazine *Time,* and local alternative papers such as *L.A. Weekly* or *Chicago Reader.* Film afficionados are also likely to consult specialized publications: academic journals such as *Cinema Journal,* the publication of the Society for Cinema and Media Studies, whose membership consists of professors, graduate students, and independent scholars; trade papers such as *Variety* and *Hollywood Reporter* that report on the business end of the industry; and publications aimed at subsets of cinema fans, such as *Cinefantastique* or *Classic Images.* The Internet and cable television have widely expanded our resources for keeping up with film culture, which extends beyond new film releases to reports on the film business, profiles of movie figures such as directors, and coverage of film festivals, technology updates, DVD releases, and opinion pieces. Publications that specialize in film theory, rather than criticism or entertainment news, are relatively few, but all of these sources, carefully differentiated in terms of the interests and audiences they represent, can be used in researching and reflecting on the medium.

Film journals have played an indispensable role in the history of film culture, publishing early works of film theory, contributing to the emergence of film studies as an academic discipline, and, at times, influencing the kinds of films that were made. Journals were particularly central to avant-garde film movements. Sergei Eisenstein published in such Soviet cultural journals as *Novy Lef* ("New Left") before his essays were gathered into books of film theory. Interest in film in France during the 1910s was heightened by the circulation of publications, such as *Le Film,* edited by the film club organizer Louis Delluc. Emulating the French, from the late 1920s to the early 1930s, the British *Close Up* published opinion and analysis pieces as well as English translations of Eisenstein's writings. Eclectic and partisan, *Close Up* discussed such topics as psychoanalysis, the representation of race, and the negative effects of censorship, which would become current in film theory decades later. Starting in the 1950s, the avant-garde and underground film movements in the United States were chronicled in the pages of curator and experimental filmmaker Jonas Mekas's *Film Culture* [**Figure 11.9**].

Cahiers du cinéma, co-edited in the 1950s by André Bazin, who at the time was already known for his views on film realism, profoundly shaped film culture and film studies from its inception with its

makes his or her films art. Challenged at the time but exerting a wide influence on film education, Sarris's work stands as a humanist appreciation of cinema that helped to elevate film to significant cultural status. Certainly, the popularization of auteur theory saved many Hollywood studio productions from historical obscurity and critical neglect.

A cluster of contradictions lies at the heart of the auteurist approach: cinema is a collaborative, commercial, and highly technologically mediated form. Making a film is not as personal as the process of authoring a poem. It might make sense to call U.S. independent filmmaker Su Friedrich an author, since she writes, directs, produces, shoots, and edits most of her films. But because usually so many individuals contribute to a film, it can be hard to assign credit to a single authorial vision, especially in studio-produced controversial positions on American genres and auteurs and the prominence of the new-wave directors who published in it. After the cultural upheaval provoked by general strikes in France in May 1968, the journal became more political and theoretical. In its pages, films from *Hiroshima mon amour* (1959) to *Young Mr. Lincoln* (1939) were analyzed, Godard praised Nicholas Ray, and Jean-Pierre Oudart developed the concept of "suture" (explained later in this chapter). Rival journals in France, *Positif* and *Cinethique,* also flourished, and the polemics energized film enthusiasts.

The same goes for English-language publications. In the 1970s, writers for the British journal *Screen* introduced the Marxist, semiotic, and psychoanalytic language and ideas that would permeate Anglo-American cinema studies for more than a decade, in part by translating French material. Meanwhile, *Sight and Sound,* the British Film Institute's venerable magazine, reviewed every film released in Britain. Refurbished in the 1980s, it targeted a film-literate readership by publishing pieces by scholars, including Thomas Elsaesser, Peter Wollen, and Ginette Vincendeau. U.S. scholarly journals, such as the feminist *Camera Obscura* and *The Velvet Light Trap,* have roots in the politicized film culture of the late 1960s and early 1970s. *Projections,* edited by filmmaker John Boorman, includes writings by and about contemporary filmmakers.

Journals are just one of the social institutions that shape and contextualize film theory. Everyone interested in film—from moviegoers to students doing course work and filmmakers planning new works—avails her- or himself of the rudiments of film theory through reading about film. A "wide-angle" perspective brings journals into focus as a crucial part of a film culture that sustains both intellectual inquiry and viewing pleasure.

Figure 11.9 *Film Culture*. The first issue of the influential U.S. film magazine.

work. Critic Pauline Kael counters Sarris's position, in one famous instance asserting that writer Herman Mankiewicz rather than Orson Welles should be credited for coming up with *Citizen Kane*'s original structure and that cinematographer Gregg Toland's work is what distinguishes the film's look. Often it makes sense to speak of a body of work in terms of creative personnel other than the director. The film *42nd Street* (1933) is meaningfully grouped with the work of choreographer Busby Berkeley, even though it was directed by Lloyd Bacon. In commercial cinema, a producer, studio, or franchise may be more important than a director. Today, a credit such as "a Tom Cruise film" or even "an Oliver Stone film" is more a matter of contractual obligations and financial arrangements than of authorship. Finally, the technology involved in film production intervenes between the author/

visionary and the final product in a way that can again be contrasted with the example of poetry. Indeed, the equally strong mystique that the camera simply captures what is put before it detracts from crediting an author's vision. Yet the theory of film authorship remains strong, identifying one person as having primary responsibility for the artistic merits of a film.

Another contradiction of auteur theory is that it extended to filmmakers some of the cultural prestige of the literary "genius" just at the time when literary critics were calling this traditional notion into question. In an essay written in 1970, French literary critic Roland Barthes declared "the death of the author." The artist's conscious intention and biography were downplayed in evaluations of artworks in favor of the formal qualities and indeterminacies of the work itself and of the inventiveness of the activity of interpretation. Giving authors too much authority also perpetuated traditional associations of greatness and intellect with those already accorded status and privilege in the West—namely, white males. The new perspectives on authorship had their roots in **structuralism,** an approach to linguistics and anthropology that, when extended to literary and filmic narratives, looks for common structures rather than originality. In the case of films, these common structures might be plots or characters that recur across works. Because the cinema depends so heavily and so obviously on standard formulae, the structuralist method was very productive when applied to film. The attribution of authorship to filmmakers began to be reevaluated in light of this new work.

In his influential 1972 book, *Signs and Meaning in the Cinema,* Peter Wollen advocates a structural approach to authorship: "the *auteur* theory does not limit itself to acclaiming the director as the main author of a film. It implies an operation of decipherment; it reveals authors where none had been seen before." "Decipherment" puts the activity on the side of the critic. Wollen places the film author's name in quotation marks to designate a critical construct rather than a biographical individual. For example, John Ford's films return again and again to the **antinomy,** or opposition, between garden and wilderness. One can see this common "Ford" structure developed differently from *My Darling Clementine* (1946) to *The Man Who Shot Liberty Valance* (1962). Through his approach, Wollen attempts to reconcile the contradiction between the heralding of artistry that always informs criticism and the skepticism toward individual creative intention that is characteristic of structuralism.

Today, although informed writing about film for a general readership relies heavily on references to directors, most theorists would not admit to being auteurists, whose main business is to recognize and applaud intentional artistry. Crediting directors as the source of meanings in their films can seem too naive or biased, too much like a fan's approach to film. Yet no matter how pure one's theoretical approach, one cannot deny that individual creativity plays a role in filmmaking. Theorists concede this when they choose to write about films by directors they particularly admire.

Moreover, directions in criticism that came after structuralism and poststructuralism offer new reasons to retain the concept of authorship. Although the biography of a filmmaker may not be directly reflected in his or her films, such theories argue, aspects of social identity do have an important impact on a filmmaker's vision. In criticism using authorship, the stakes have shifted from debating where a particular film should be ranked in John Ford's œuvre to exploring, for example, writer-director Jane Campion's conceptualization of restrictions on female identity in such films as *The Piano* (1993) and *The Portrait of a Lady* (1996) **[Figure 11.10]**. Spike Lee asserted that as

Figure 11.10 *The Portrait of a Lady* (1996). Auteurist approaches to Jane Campion's work take her films' representations of female social identity into account.

an African American filmmaker he was more qualified to film the biography *Malcolm X* (1992) than a white director would have been. Filmmakers whose group identities have been marginalized or deemed irrelevant throughout the history of cinema may now find their work being admitted to the canon. The criteria for evaluation is changing to consider racial, ethnic, and gender identity alongside the elusive qualities of "distinguishable personality."

Identity categories can certainly receive too much emphasis. Filmmakers can be slotted by studios into a particular subject matter or their achievements can be diminished by such phrases as "woman filmmaker." But identity categories are not irrelevant even when they are invisible. Generally more readily thought of as "individuals" than as representatives of a group, white male filmmakers are entrusted with large-budget films with universal themes and stories—the sinking of the *Titanic* told as a love story, for example. In a different way, director Steven Spielberg claimed his Jewish heritage with his film about the Holocaust, *Schindler's List* (1993), and used his prominence and that of the film to fund a videotape archive called the Survivors of the Shoah Visual History Project.

Still, social identity does not necessarily leave an imprint on the work. Even when it does, it is often difficult to determine exactly what that imprint is. Whether or not it is important that Jane Campion is a woman filmmaker emerges in the criteria critics select for the kind of argument they want to make. More conventional auteurist arguments may or may not touch on aspects of social identity—Hitchcock's Britishness, for example. Feminist and antiracist literary critics have pointed out that "the death of the author" implied that authorial identity was irrelevant just when more women and people of color were receiving recognition as authors. If one can be excluded from making films because of one's identity, then critical accounts of the work of those who do succeed are justified in taking the social identity and struggles of the author into account.

As we have argued, authorship is a methodology that finds elements of commonality in films by the same individual. One can surely find unifying elements among the films of a particular composer, producer, or costume designer, but because a director oversees all creative elements, this figure is usually touted as the author. Although various theories of authorship exist, they all attribute elements in the film to the filmmaker, whether they argue these are intentional features, unconscious preoccupations, or traces of social experience. Some theories avow that simply grouping films by the same director is a convenient way of identifying recurrent patterns. In any case, it is important to realize that because the set of common traits is advanced by the critic, authorship itself is a critical construct.

Genre

Thinking of films in terms of **genre** is a fundamental way of classifying and theorizing about them. As noted in Chapter 8 on film genres, the word *genre* means "kind" or classification. Characters, story, iconography, a happy or sad ending—these are elements that films in a particular genre have in common. Yet the concept of genre is not a simple one. As we have suggested, what constitutes a specific genre is open for interpretation, as is the function genres serve for filmmakers, audiences, and critics. Whereas Chapter 8 emphasized the formal and cultural shapes of different film genres, here we will concentrate on theoretical approaches to the concept.

As a comparative method, the employment of genre in film theory is influenced by literary approaches dating back to Aristotle. However, the contemporary use of the term *genre* refers less to the category of the aesthetic than to mass-produced cultural artifacts as distinguished from works of art. Artworks are thought to exhibit the artistic originality of their creators; they are anything but "generic." This is a similar tension to one we uncovered in our earlier discussion of authorship. Because films are products of an industry, associating them with authors tends to raise them above genre. The term **genre film** designates a type of movie that is quickly recognizable, but the term may carry pejorative connotations of lacking originality. Because it is the unique work of art that has traditionally been invested with cultural value, genre films have less prestige. For example, it was a surprise when *The Silence of the Lambs* won an Academy Award for Best Picture because it is a thriller, a devalued popular genre.

In some ways it makes even more sense for an expensive, entertainment-oriented product like film to rely on the category of genre than it does for literature to do so. Genre distinctions are used within the film industry to differentiate its products while keeping enough commonalities to promote new films in relation to a known quantity. Genres ebb and flow according to audience response: musicals and westerns have been prominent in some periods and "box-office poison" in others. Specific film types, such as killer-couple-on-a-rampage films, might become a genre when audiences respond well to one such film. Kung-fu or surfer films are marketed in specifically generic terms.

Critics of mass culture contend that audiences are given films that follow formulae so that the market will remain predictable. This position does not acknowledge any real need or preference on the part of the audience to which a genre responds. Other commentators feel that the cycle of definition and demand is more reciprocal. For the genre contract to work, it must be honored at the points of production and reception—that is, producers and audiences must agree on what to expect from a certain kind of film. Spoofs such as *Airplane!* (1980), *Scary Movie* (2000), and their sequels acknowledge just how practiced film audiences are at recognizing genre conventions. Far from playing to the lowest common denominator, genre films actually depend on and often reward audience sophistication. *Scream 2* (1997) calls attention to the conventions of its genre—for example, that someone who leaves the room in a horror film is unlikely to return—and still satisfyingly fulfills them. Is it with the conventions or the variations that our pleasure lies? Most commentators agree that it is both. The viewing of a genre film resembles a ritual in that the participants already know the rules, but the particular enactment is a strategic use of those rules.

One explanation for the appeal of genres is that they function like **myths**—in anthropologist Claude Levi-Strauss's terms, stories that mediate or manage contradictions in social life and that cultures use to explain the inexplicable, justify the inevitable, or reconcile the irreconcilable. Many studies have focused on varieties of U.S. studio-produced films in the heyday of the Hollywood system not only as products being sold to audiences as consumers but also as modern myths.

Westerns are popular examples for genre theory. The stark outlines of the western's opposition between good and evil and the outcome that favors the cowboys and settlers' victory over indigenous Americans are ways of justifying as inevitable the course of a history now decided. The western appeared in turn-of-the-century American culture in dime novels and Wild West shows just at the time when there was no more land to settle. The genre serves as a way to keep the closed frontier open imaginatively. When we go to see a western, we know what we are getting—horses, open horizons, good guys in white, bad guys in black. Or do we? Critics have noted that genres evolve and cultural myths shift. During the Cold War in the 1950s, the need for identifiable bad guys can be associated with the U.S. attitude toward the Soviet Union. From such an easy identification of good guys and bad guys we end up with more complicated moral scenarios in existential westerns: *The Searchers* (1956), in which John Wayne's character's racism is evident, and *Unforgiven* (1992), in which violence seems pointless [**Figure 11.11**]. We see westerns featuring independent women in *The Quick and the Dead* (1995) and African American cowboys in *Posse* (1993). These films may redefine our notions of history and heroism. The fact that

Figure 11.11 *Unforgiven* (1992). Clint Eastwood's reflective western revived the genre in the 1990s.

an epic western can be transposed to an outer-space setting in *Star Wars* (1977) suggests that the geography of the western United States that the genre usually features may itself be an imaginary space. Different genres work out different cultural questions or problems; hence, their emergence and decline in particular periods. Thomas Schatz, for example, sees musicals as celebrating cultural integration, often symbolized by the couple coming together, whereas westerns require the establishment of a home, one that the wandering hero cannot himself enjoy.

As we can see from these examples of the western, a genre is both a cultural form that works as if through shorthand and a pervasive, diverse phenomenon. The common structures that genres use allow a conflict to be posed in an immediately recognizable form. The variety among films in a genre allows the conflict to be revisited with some complexity, perhaps to challenge the inevitability of a social "fact" such as Native American genocide. Genre is conservative because it uses fixed structures, but it can also register social change or dissent. The repetition so basic to genre testifies that a society needs to "solve" the same problems and open the same contradictions again and again, which evidences a measure of critique of the status quo. For example, the horror film allows for the eruption of repressed, antisocial impulses. Genre thus serves an important social function, and audiences' immediate and enthusiastic response supports this claim.

Like auteur criticism, genre criticism was invigorated by the film culture of post–World War II France. American films that had not been released during that country's occupation by Germany were finally exhibited all at once, making commonalities easy to identify. Also, like auteur criticism, genre criticism depends on cinephilia because making generalizations based on only a few films would be imprudent. Sometimes genre criticism is considered at odds with auteurism. A genius could not make a run-of-the-mill film—or if he did, it was an exception in his œuvre (the male pronoun is historically appropriate). But keeping the history of criticism in mind, we can see that auteurist approaches actually developed in tandem with genre perspectives. It was often the mark of the auteur on a genre that distinguished him. This is certainly the case with John Ford and the western. The critic would consider how the artist's intentions intersected with the set rules of genre. Auteur criticism also praised the handling of different genres by a particularly gifted auteur. Robin Wood looks at the elaboration of Hawksian themes in both Howard Hawks's male adventure films and his screwball comedies and finds them to be related to the same concerns **[Figure 11.12]**. A contemporary auteur such as Quentin Tarantino is known for his self-conscious use of the blaxploitation and crime film genres. Ridley Scott made an utterly original film in *Blade Runner* while respecting science fiction conventions. Steven Soderbergh set out to make a genre film with *Out of Sight* (1998) as well as to "tweak" crime film conventions. The critical rehabilitation of the popular cinema, especially that of Hollywood, that auteurism began to bring about in the 1950s was carried on through genre criticism more directly and without auteur theory's dependence on the literary analogy.

Figure 11.12 *His Girl Friday* (1940). Howard Hawks made classics in disparate genres, including westerns, musicals, adventure films, and comedies such as this one.

As we have intimated, genre is a category that must be analyzed across texts. While we might be able to designate a single film as a western, it is only because we have seen westerns before. This repetition of formulae leads to a complicated **intertextuality,** which means simply that one text depends on other texts for its full meaning. For example, the intertexts of the second film in the *Batman* franchise include the other movies in the series; the comic book from which the characters are derived; the 1960s television series; the toys, games, and Halloween costumes featuring the characters; and similar feature films based on other superheroes. The audience is the place where all of the intersecting intertextual meanings come together. Bringing their prior experiences with them to the movie theater, audiences have agency or control in determining meaning.

Figuring out what defines a genre is a key question for theorists. The extremely useful categories of film noir and melodrama pose interesting problems for genre criticism. The term *film noir* was coined by French critics for 1940s and 1950s American films that shared a dark sensibility and a dark lighting style, such as *Double Indemnity* (1944) and *The Big Heat*. In this case the Hollywood studios did not set out to produce a distinct genre to sell its products; rather, critical comparison brought out similarities. Some theorists related common aesthetic elements to a postwar society characterized by insecurity about gender roles, the economy, changing definitions of race, and nuclear technology. Others were concerned with whether film noir actually qualified as a genre. Many film noirs belong to the existing genre of crime films, and film noir–type lighting also appeared in occasional westerns or even musicals in the 1940s and 1950s. Some critics designated film noir a cycle, a term intended to demonstrate a closer tie to a specific historical moment than did the more adaptable and ahistorical notion of genre. Similar films made in the 1970s and after, from *Body Heat* (1981) to *Bound* (1996) **[Figure 11.13]**, were referred to as **neo-noirs.** At its simplest, film noir was a category used by critics to make sense of a group of films by comparison with each other. But debates about its parameters indicate that the ambiguity and confusion at the heart of film noir are precisely what has generated theoretical interest in the category.

Melodrama is a theatrical term with many uses predating the cinema, and film theory has introduced further meanings. Historically, film reviewers and studios referred to many kinds of films as melodramas that we would not necessarily include in the category today. Melodramatic feeling infuses a range of genres from thrillers to historical dramas such as *Gone with the Wind* (1939). Critics sometimes refer to melodrama as a mode rather than a genre because it is so pervasive, informing film history from most silent-era dramas through to films like *Eyes Wide Shut* (1999). Family melodramas of the 1950s by such directors as Douglas Sirk (*Written on the Wind*, 1956), Nicholas Ray (*Rebel without a Cause*, 1955), and Vincente Minnelli (*Home from the Hill*, 1960) were championed by film scholars for their stylistic critiques of the social and familial norms that constrained their protagonists. Such interpretations identified a critical function in apparently mainstream Hollywood films. Again, the critical definition of a category of films allowed a specific theoretical position to emerge. This position, which saw social critique in apparently escapist films, influenced contemporary independent filmmaker Todd Haynes's film *Far From Heaven* (2002) **[Figure 11.14]**, which emulates the subject matter and style of such 1950s melodramas as Sirk's *All that Heaven Allows*.

Figure 11.13 *Bound* (1996). Film noir conventions are updated with a wink to the audience.

Westerns and gangster films attracted attention from the first practitioners of genre criticism. Genres concerned with the role of violence and the status of the outsider, they also have historically appealed primarily to men and have foregrounded male characters and issues. One of the cultural problems genre attempts to address is a gender question—in this case, the viable forms of male identity. So-called female genres such as the musical and the **woman's picture,** which was marketed directly to women, received attention somewhat later in the development of film studies when feminist issues came to the fore. A type of melodrama branded by the film industry for its appeal to female audiences, the woman's picture or "weepie" has been understood by theorists as a cultural refuge, a forum for dealing with problems of female social identity. This does not mean that romance and motherhood, the concerns of these films, are the only dimensions of female experience, or that the sacrifices these films so often depict are to be applauded or emulated. Rather, the genre addresses the contradictions of the status quo, and women's pictures and their soap-opera offshoots are

Figure 11.14 *Far from Heaven* (2002). Todd Haynes's tribute to the domestic melodrama of the 1950s.

Figure 11.15 *Stella Dallas* (1937). This classic "weepie" makes maternal sacrifice seem subversive.

centered in some of the most restrictive aspects of women's lives **[Figure 11.15]**. Identifying the specific gendered or national dimensions of narratives challenges the idea of their mythic function as timeless and unchanging. Such theoretical insights are in fact behind some of the most successful revisionist genre films: *Thelma & Louise*, for instance, a road movie that makes a powerful equation between freedom and driving, is geared toward women.

In sum, genre is a powerful way to organize our experience of the cinema. We respond to the ritual of genre in unconscious ways, while also consciously recognizing its conventions and appreciating its stylistic and ideological variations. Film theory that focuses on genre enables us to appreciate both aesthetic features and audience experience. Genre criticism is a way to relate individual films to a flexible set of shared rules.

Approaches looking abstractly at the nature or ontology of the film medium, close readings, or genre and auteur criticism all operate on different levels of inquiry but are often combined in practice. For example, film theorist Stephen Heath's elaborate and influential close reading of *Touch of Evil* (1958) looks at how each segment of the film engages and elaborates specific formal and narrative codes. According to Heath, the

 VIEWING CUES: Authorship and Genre Theories

- Compare a scene from a film you have viewed in class with a passage from the book or screenplay it was adapted from. What elements are found specifically in the film?

- Do a close analysis of the film's first scene. First decide what demarcates the ending; then enumerate the shots. Decide what categories or codes will yield the most interesting results when applied to each shot or the transitions between them: for example, the codes of camera distance, mise-en-scène, presence and volume of music or speech, camera movement, shot duration, and type of shot transition are all powerfully at work in the first scene of *Citizen Kane*. Devise a way to record your observations of the variations in these codes for each shot, such as by using the abbreviations for camera distance (LS, MS, MCU) or a plus or minus sign to indicate the presence or absence of a particular element. Then make note of the patterns you detect, the interrelationships of the codes, and the interpretations you derive from these observations. Such a close analysis forms a strong basis for an essay.

- Look at a second film by the director of a film you have seen. Do you see any common themes or similar characters? Which stylistic features are used in both films? Do the films have other technical personnel or cast in common? Does your comparison reveal aspects of auteur theory?

- Now look at another film of the same genre and draw up a list of common features in setting, characters, story, and style. What differences can you identify? What is their significance? Does your comparison reveal aspects of genre theory?

prominence of the code "light" references the film's status as a representative of the crime film genre with its shadowy mise-en-scène, while the code "author" is especially meaningful because writer-director Orson Welles appears as one of the film's protagonists. In fact, Welles's imposing figure casts its shadow on most accounts of this film, even those that use it to illustrate the category of film noir. (See "In Focus" on p. 438.)

Film Theory and Historical Context

The concepts and methods that we have reviewed so far were formulated over time in the work of major film theorists and are still interrogated and practiced by contemporary scholars. An overview of film theory will allow us to contextualize and historicize important thinkers and understand how key principles and terms have been defined and debated. There are no clear boundaries to the field, however. Film theory, and the emerging theories that address new and related audiovisual media, will undoubtedly take on new questions in the future. These concerns will be shaped by an intellectual history of considerable longevity and complexity.

Early Film Theory

"Last night I was in the Kingdom of Shadows. If you only knew how strange it is to be there," wrote the Russian novelist Maxim Gorky after attending an 1896 film screening. When movies were new, observers searched for metaphors for their experience of them. They were struck by movies' magical properties and attempted to pinpoint what was distinctive about the medium. Reflection on the nature of cinema has continued throughout the more than one hundred years of its existence. Some early critics commented on moviegoing as a social phenomenon, a new form of urban entertainment characteristic of the dawning twentieth century. Others viewed the cinema in aesthetic terms, heralding the "seventh art," in reference to classical theories.

While today we consider film theory as part of an academic discipline, earlier writers on the topic came from many contexts and traditions, making any overview of the history of film theory a disjunctive one. Book-length studies represent systematic reflection on the medium and are helpful in reconstructing this history, yet equally important theoretical contributions have been made in journal articles and other forms. Writers on film might be critics of other art forms or scholars in other disciplines. Or they might be filmmakers themselves who share their ideas and excitement about the developing medium with each other in special publications.

Some of the questions taken up historically in theoretical reflection on film include the following:

- What is the specific nature of the medium?
- Is the cinema an art form?
- How does it relate to photography, painting, theater, music, and other art forms?
- What is the resemblance of film to language?
- Is film's primary responsibility to tell a story?
- How does film relate to the phenomenal world (the world perceptible to the senses)?

Authorship and Genre in *Touch of Evil* (1958)

As we have indicated, genre and authorship are critical methods that have several points of contact, especially in the analysis of Hollywood films of the studio era. Let us illustrate how a particular theoretical orientation informs a critic's work by focusing on *Touch of Evil* through each perspective in turn, bearing in mind that important aspects will be missed if either genre or authorship is considered exclusively in an analysis.

Touch of Evil is a police thriller based on the novel *Badge of Evil* by Whit Masterson, who specialized in books in this genre. Set in an unnamed, unsavory town on the U.S.-Mexico border, the film follows the power struggle between the Mexican official Vargas (played by Charlton Heston), recently married to an American woman named Susie (played by Janet Leigh), and the corrupt American detective Quinlan, played by Orson Welles. In the very first shot, a wealthy American and his girlfriend are killed, and the film leads us from the crime investigation into an investigation by Vargas of Quinlan's long history of witness intimidation and evidence tampering. Meanwhile, Susie is assaulted and then framed for drug use and homicide by the Grandi family, the border town's small-time criminal mob. It turns out that Quinlan is behind the attack on Susie, and in the end he is shot and killed by his formerly loyal sidekick and Vargas and Susie are happily reunited.

Elements of story, setting, and character quickly establish the film as a crime thriller that can be rewardingly discussed in comparison to other films of the genre and period shot in a film noir style. The plot follows the investigation. Generic characteristics include "criminal" locations such as nightclubs and bars, cheap motels, and deserted streets and alleyways. Most of the important scenes take place at night. The personae include a range of recurrent generic figures: a taciturn streetwise hero, Vargas, and a physically and morally monstrous villain, Quinlan. The two principal female characters suggest, even as they complicate, the common division between good girl and bad in the film noir. Susie is an all-American blond bride and Tanya, a woman from Quinlan's past, is a dark-haired, ethnically indeterminate fortune-teller who runs a suspect establishment on the Mexican side of the border. Yet Susie spends most of the film, however inadvertently, in sleazy motels that associate her with the femme fatale stereotype. Meanwhile, Marlene Dietrich's Tanya almost caricatures the inscrutability of the femme fatale. An eccentric denizen of the night, she has seen everything but reveals very little. Secondary characters, such as Quinlan's sidekick Menzies, the upright U.S. attorney who helps Vargas, and the corrupt Grandis, are familiar types. The plot is convoluted and characters' motives are often cynical. Beyond these narrative characteristics there are unmistakable stylistic marks of the film's genre.

Stylistically, *Touch of Evil* displays and exaggerates the conventions we have come to associate with film noir. It follows the genre's most common requirement of being shot in black and white. The extremely effective low-key lighting produces sharp contrasts that emphasize the sinister quality of people and places and the mysteriousness of unfolding events. Unbalanced compo-

Figure 11.16 *Touch of Evil* (1958). Low-key lighting and unbalanced composition characterize the film noir mise-en-scène.

Figure 11.17 *Touch of Evil* (1958). The drugged Susie wakes up to this shocking point-of-shot. Wide-angle lenses increase distortion in the images.

sition and figures lit from below produce distortions in everyday perceptions that frighten or unsettle **[Figure 11.16]**. The film's score by Henry Mancini reflects the incorporation of jazz in film noir's urban night world.

These factors fit *Touch of Evil* into the categories crime film and film noir. One cannot make sense of certain aspects of the film—like the mysterious Tanya—without reference to film noir's world of ambiguity. By the time the film was made at the end of the 1950s, the film noir cycle had nearly run its course. *Touch of Evil* supports genre theorist Thomas Schatz's contention that the end of a genre's life span is characterized by "self-conscious formalism" (Cohen and Braudy, p. 609). The film's style is so baroque that it overtakes the story. Take, for example, the grotesque low-angle shot of Grandi after he has been strangled taken from Susie's point of view **[Figure 11.17]**. The film stretches conventions in other ways. Its cynicism takes the pessimistic values of film noir to the extreme. In the exaggerated rottenness of Quinlan, the law itself is shown to be corrupt. Although the film's good characters, Vargas and his wife, experience a happy ending, at the end of the film they are pictured in a convertible, a sinister echo of the couple who had been blown up by a car bomb in the first shot.

In fact, the strangeness of *Touch of Evil* made it difficult to market. Unlike the one-of-a-kind superproductions that were beginning to be produced in Hollywood at the time, *Touch of Evil* was intended as the kind of low-budget film that uses genre to let audiences know what to expect. Welles seems to have gone beyond such expectations; the industry publication *Variety* called it a "confusing, somewhat 'artsy' film" with "so-so prospects." Interestingly, however, it is precisely as a genre film that *Touch of Evil* supports an assessment of Orson Welles's greatness as an auteur, for he certainly made the most of his "routine" assignment. In sharp contrast to his unprecedented (and never to be repeated) autonomy when he first arrived in Hollywood to make *Citizen Kane* in 1941, *Touch of Evil* was not designed as "an Orson Welles film." It was offered to Welles to direct at the behest of the film's star, Charlton Heston.

Welles's almost accidental participation on the film mitigates against assigning too much original intention to him as an author. Universal agreed to allow him to adapt the screenplay and to direct because they thought he would make an interesting Quinlan. Welles's appearance in the film enforces his authorship, drawing our attention to his character and away from his foil, the ostensible "good guy" protagonist Vargas. Welles's flamboyant presence and willingness to play a remarkably unappealing character reference his performances in films he directed, most notably *Citizen Kane*, whose hero is also larger than life and flawed. (This observation points

Figure 11.18 *Touch of Evil* (1958). Orson Welles's presence in the film is emphasized by unflattering low-angle shots.

to a reading of the film in terms of star personae. Certainly playing a Mexican character adds a dimension to Heston's image, constructed by heroic roles in biblical epics and his current-day public profile as National Rifle Association president. In a disturbing intertext, Janet Leigh would again be subject to misogynistic violence in a motel room a few years later in *Psycho* [1960]). One could almost read authorship in *Touch of Evil* allegorically, as Welles's commentary on the corruption and eventual sorry fate of a maverick coming into conflict with the system.

Auteurism, of course, goes beyond the visual presence or "signature" of the author. It is a way of connecting stylistic and thematic similarities across a group of an individual's films into a coherent body of work. Welles has been known for stylistic excess since the brilliant innovations in camera, sound, lighting, acting, and composition used in *Citizen Kane*. Many of these techniques are used in *Touch of Evil*. For example, low-angle shots, which can make a figure appear strong and powerful, provide ironic commentary on Quinlan's status by emphasizing his unsightly corpulence [Figure 11.18]. In *Citizen Kane*, Welles uses low-angle shots ironically, showing Kane just as he lost the gubernatorial election [Figure 11.19]. The use of deep-focus cinematography, so characteristic of *Citizen Kane* and *The Magnificent Ambersons* (1942), results in menacing and distorted images as the edges of the frames stretch. Wide-angle lenses include more in the frame, allowing a shot to run longer without cutting, for naturalistic or virtuosic effects. An example of the latter is *Touch of Evil*'s famous opening shot, which lasts approximately 2.5 minutes and covers a great deal of territory and ultimately explosive action. French critics were particularly admiring of this "sequence shot," so named because a whole sequence unfolds in one continuous camera take, and they helped canonize Welles as Hollywood's greatest auteur after they saw the film. Truffaut wrote, "You could remove Orson Welles's name from the credits and it wouldn't make any difference, because from the first shot, beginning with the credits themselves, it's obvious that Citizen Kane is behind the camera." American audiences were expected to respond to Welles as a familiar character actor.

Because of Welles's fame, today it is almost impossible to consider the film outside of an auteurist framework. Although *Touch of Evil* is revived in series surveying films noirs, its reputation as a classic is owed to its being a sleazy police film directed by a genius. The 2000 release of the restored "director's cut" of *Touch of Evil* demonstrates the importance of the auteurist perspective on the film. This version is not a recovered copy of the film Welles originally submitted. Rather, the restoration team construed his intentions by referring to an extensive memo that Welles wrote upon viewing Universal's cut of the original release. The story of the artist's vision being sacrificed to the studio's wishes helps construct Welles's authorial persona compellingly as a misunderstood artist.

These readings of *Touch of Evil* demonstrate that film theory is not all abstraction. Rather, it is a way of using concrete evidence to test the usefulness of propositions about how films work.

Figure 11.19 *Citizen Kane* (1941). Orson Welles uses low-angle shots ironically to depict Kane's election defeat in his earlier film.

- What is the place of film in the modern world that fostered its development?
- What is the nature of the viewer's encounter with film?

Film theorists have posed and attempted to answer these questions in many different ways.

Intellectuals began to comment on cinema from the first public exhibitions of films by Thomas Edison and the Lumière brothers. Two noteworthy book-length studies on movies appeared in the United States in the 1910s. Although they did not strongly determine the course of film theory, the questions they raised have persisted and their claims have begun to pique the interest of contemporary theorists. Poet Vachel Lindsay's *The Art of the Motion Picture* (1915) responded enthusiastically to the novelty and the democratizing potential of the medium. "I am the one poet who has a right to claim for his muses Blanche Sweet, Mary Pickford, and Mae Marsh," he gushed, invoking the popular movie stars of the day. In his idiosyncratic but suggestive book, Lindsay likened film language to hieroglyphics. The metaphor of picture writing suggests cinema's promise of universality that excited many early observers. A more systematic elaboration of ideas about cinema was contributed by Harvard psychologist Hugo Münsterberg in *The Art of the Photoplay* (1916). For Münsterberg, viewing films was linked to the subjective process of thinking. The properties characteristic of the medium that distinguished it from the physical reality to which its images referred were what made the medium of interest aesthetically and psychologically. Unlike our experience at the theater, watching movies requires specific mental activities to make sense of cues of movement and depth. "The photoplay tells us the human story by overcoming the forms of the outer world, namely, space, time, and causality, and by adjusting the events to the forms of the inner world, namely, attention, memory, imagination, and emotion," wrote Münsterberg. His ideas thus put an emphasis on the viewer's interaction with the medium. Decades later, theories of spectatorship would do the same. "Many a controversy must come before a method of criticism is fully established," wrote Lindsay, and his words aptly characterized the course of film theory. Lindsay's work praised specific films, whereas Münsterburg referred to the photoplay in general. In a sense their works mark the division between criticism, which reflects on a given aesthetic object, and theory, which is more abstract.

Outside of the United States, much early writing about cinema came from filmmakers themselves. Although movies immediately became commercial, it is important to remember they emerged in the context of modernist experimentation in the arts—music, writing, theater, painting, architecture, and photography—especially in Europe. Because film was based on new technology, many considered it an exemplary art for the machine age. Film exercised an influence on new approaches to established media, such as cubism in painting and the "automatic writing" of the surrealists. In turn, filmmakers adopted avant-garde practices, and painters like Hans Richter took up filmmaking, exploring graphic and rhythmic possibilities **[Figure 11.20]**. Modernist intellectuals debated cinema's aesthetic status and its relationship to the other arts.

In the 1910s and 1920s in France, the first avant-garde film movement (impressionism) was fostered by groups known as cine-clubs and journals dedicated to the new medium. In one of these publications, *Cinéma*, Louis Delluc coined the term *photogenie* to refer to a particular quality that distinguishes the filmed object from its everyday reality. Jean Epstein elaborated

Figure 11.20 *Film Study* (1926). Hans Richter's early abstract film.

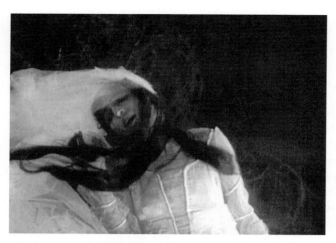

Figure 11.21 *The Fall of the House of Usher* (1928). An impressionist film by Jean Epstein.

Figure 11.22 *Borderline* (1930). Editors of the British film journal *CloseUp* collaborated with American actor, singer, and activist Paul Robeson on this experimental film.

on this elusive concept in poetic writings, such as "Bonjour Cinéma," and his film adaptation of Poe's story, *The Fall of the House of Usher* (1928) **[Figure 11.21]**. Germaine Dulac compared film to music in her extensive writings and lectures. In England, imagist poet H. D., her companion Bryher, and the latter's husband, Kenneth MacPherson, founded their own modernist film journal, *Close Up*, and collaborated on the experimental film *Borderline* (1930) **[Figure 11.22]** starring African American singer, actor, and activist Paul Robeson (see "Cultural Spotlight: Film Journals," p. 428). Film theory and practice continued to develop in tandem in the period between the world wars.

Soviet Film Theory: Montage

Perhaps most systematic in its relationship with artistic modernism and certainly most influential in world film history was the school of filmmakers working in the Soviet Union during the 1920s. After the 1919 revolution, these artist-intellectuals set about defining an artistic practice that could participate in revolutionary change. Like the avant-garde graphic and set designers, painters, and composers who were their comrades, they were eager to incorporate the materials of industrial modernity in their art. The cinema, with its industrial base and its populist reach, provided a perfect medium. Lev Kuleshov's teaching at the state film school put the theory of montage at the center of Soviet filmmaking, and as our discussion in Chapter 4 indicates, his ideas went well beyond the world of film theory to influence filmmaking worldwide. **Montage** involves directing spectators' experience through the organization of fragments, inviting them to make meaning from a juxtaposition or chain of shots. Editing experiments showed that audiences formed interpretations based on montage alone, a phenomenon known as the Kuleshov effect. The same neutral shot of an actor's face, could signify "hunger" or "joy" when juxtaposed with shots of a bowl of soup or a baby, respectively. Vsevolod Pudovkin and Sergei Eisenstein, Kuleshov's students, elaborated the theory of montage in their own writings and films. In Pudovkin's *Mother* (1926) **[Figure 11.23]** and other films, montage is a way of breaking down a scene to direct the spectator's look and understanding (see "Critical Voices" in Chapter 4). Eisenstein's theories put much more emphasis on the effects of collision between shots. He correlated the exponential increase of meaning to be gained by the juxtaposition of shots to the dialectic, a philosophical concept that Karl Marx adopted and incorporated in his theory of historical materialism. Simply defined, a **dialectic** consists of a thesis that is countered by an antithesis or opposing element, which results in a synthesis of both that is much more forceful and truthful than either element on its own. Eisenstein's extensive but unsystematic body of writing, amply illustrated with examples from his celebrated films, spans several decades and constitutes the most significant contribution to film theory by a filmmaker.

Filmmaker Dziga Vertov also wrote film theory in the form of manifestos signed by the "Kinoki," or Kino-Eye group **[Figure 11.24]**. Resisting systematicity in his poetic, avant-garde writings, Vertov rejected the fiction film and emphasized the role of sound. Eisenstein denounced Vertov's trick shots as "formalist jackstraws"; Vertov scorned Eisenstein's "filmed theater." The polemics and practices of these two great filmmakers were later championed by the 1960s generation of critic-filmmakers in France.

In 1919, revolutionary leader Vladimir Lenin had pronounced film "the most important of the arts." Film was seen as a vital force within the revolutionary culture of the early Soviet Union, one that could bring the masses, many of them illiterate, into modernity. The intensity of discussion about the properties and potential of the medium contributed as much to this importance as did the films themselves; at this time and place, theory was an indispensable part of film culture. Above all, the concept of montage survived as one of the central theoretical and practical concerns of cinema, as significant to film analysts as it has been to filmmakers from Hitchcock to Soviet editor Slavko Vorkapich, who lent his name to the "montage sequences" he supervised for classical Hollywood films.

Classical Film Theories: Realism and Formalism

Integral to the specific historical context in which they emerged and were debated, Eisenstein's writings were also taken up by thinkers and academics outside the Soviet Union as film history progressed. They form part of a corpus referred to as **classical film theory.** Europeans Béla Balázs, Rudolf Arnheim, André Bazin, and Siegfried Kracauer are central figures in classical film theory, which spanned the shift from silent to sound filmmaking (and the periods before and after World War II). This momentous technical development was accompanied

Figure 11.23 *Mother* (1926). Like other Soviet filmmakers, Vsevolod Pudovkin emphasized montage.

Figure 11.24 Poster for *The Man with the Movie Camera* (1929) by the Stenberg brothers showing the close relationship between the graphic arts and cinema of the period.

by ontological speculation: does sound finally allow film to fulfill a mission to reproduce the world as it is, or does sound hinder cinema's visual expression?

One of the organizing debates of classical film theory centers around the appeal to **realism** made first by photography and then by film. Realism is not a simple or unitary term, but in general it relates to **mimesis,** or imitation of reality, in the arts. The mimetic quality has been valued in the Western artistic tradition since ancient Greece. However, the term *realism* itself only came into use in the nineteenth century to designate a style—developed in the most important genre of the era, the novel—that embraced subject matter drawn from the experience of everyday life. Realist style was highly descriptive, a function that the photographic basis of cinema fulfills by its very nature. For theorists such as Bazin and Kracauer, the capacity of film to refer to the world through images that resemble and record the presence of objects and sources of sounds sets it apart as a realist medium. In contrast, theorists such as Arnheim and Balázs emphasize film form as fundamental; for them, realism is only a style that uses form in a particular way.

Viewers and commentators addressed the question of cinematic realism from the beginning, and digital media observers pose it anew today. Stories of the presentation of the Lumière brothers' first films at the Grand Café in Paris invariably relate how audiences shrank from the arriving train or feared they would be splashed by the waves of the sea. Whether or not these stories are true, they characterize cinema as lacking the aesthetic distance of the other arts. For many, film seems too "natural" to be a vehicle for making meaning or an object to which traditional aesthetic criteria apply. The French and Soviet modernists were concerned primarily with cinema's status as an art, distancing themselves from the impression it gives of reproducing the world, perhaps because the artist's role is downplayed by such a notion.

Before laying out the thinking of individual theorists, a brief overview of **semiotics**—the study of signs—will give us some useful vocabulary for our discussion of the divergent opinions about realism within film theory. Although this vocabulary was introduced later in the history of film theory, it illuminates what is at stake for classical theorists. Semiotics considers words and images as different kinds of signs or ways of making meaning. Words designate the things that they refer to, which are known as their **referents,** according to conventions that are arbitrary (one easy way to think about this is to note that different languages designate the same referent completely differently). In the terminology of the late nineteenth-century American philosopher C. S. Peirce, who helped develop semiotics, a word is a **symbolic sign.** Photography and film, in contrast, use **iconic signs,** which look like their referents; this resemblance often gives the impression of a natural connection. Finally, since photographic images are a product of a process in which light, reflected from an object, produces an image that is fixed by the chemical emulsion on film, these images are also **indexical signs,** Peirce's third type of sign. In other words, a direct relationship exists between the sign and the object depicted, a relationship that can be likened to pointing (indicating), implied by the word *index*. A footprint indicates that a person has walked in a particular path, a weathervane points in the direction the wind blows. Both are indexical signs. In most cases, an impression is left on film because a real object has been photographed. Marks can even be made directly on the filmstrip; Stan Brakhage's *Mothlight* (1963), for example, challenged the usual practice by pasting moths' wings on celluloid. The referential relationship strengthens cinema's claim to represent the world as it really is. Considering cinema as a reflection of the natural world is almost automatic, yet cinematic images and sounds are constructed signs. Computer-generated film imagery, which does not have a direct referent (it is iconic but not indexical), is changing our assumptions about cinematic realism.

Whether their positions argued for or against realism, classical film theorists held the nature of filmic reference of common concern. In addition to Eisenstein, two key authors associated with modernism, Béla Balázs and Rudolf Arnheim, were centrally concerned with how the medium of film became an art precisely by transcending its referential qualities. They elaborated formalist theories of film.

Béla Balázs, a Hungarian screenwriter and film critic, published his first book on film *Der Sichtbare Mensch (Visible Man)* in 1924, making him one of the earliest important film theorists. Later, his writings were published in the influential volume *Theory of Film*. Balázs was passionate about the new ways of observing the world cinema made possible, and he defended the medium against highbrow critics who simply dismissed it as entertainment. For Balázs, film was a new "form-language" that broke with the language of theater. In particular, Balázs wrote eloquently on the power of the close-up, an element of film art impossible to approximate on stage: "by means of the close-up the camera in the days of the silent film revealed also the hidden mainsprings of a life which we had thought we already knew so well" **[Figure 11.25]**. Balázs also explored the crucial phenomenon of identification in cinema as an aspect of film language, describing how in watching a movie, "we look up to Juliet's balcony with Romeo's eyes and look down on Romeo with Juliet's." Thus for Balázs, film was able to reveal aspects of reality that could not otherwise be seen. He also championed the pursuit of film theory itself, arguing that the new form-language required systematic elaboration.

Figure 11.25 Asta Nielsen as *Hamlet* (1921). Theorist Béla Balázs felt that the close-up could reveal the soul onscreen.

German art historian Rudolf Arnheim argued even more strongly for a formalist position in his 1933 study *Film*, which was later revised for English publication as *Film as Art*. For Arnheim, the quest for film realism was misguided, a betrayal of the unique aesthetic properties of the medium that equipped it to transcend the imitation of nature. He set out to "refute the assertion that film is nothing but the feeble mechanical reproduction of real life." For example, in his view, the two-dimensionality of the screen image was not a limitation but an aesthetic parameter that should be exploited by filmmakers and emphasized by theorists. The perception of lighting effects and various other artistic manipulations were what allowed film to go beyond mere duplication. Arnheim's position recalls aspects of Münsterberg's arguments about the distinctive properties and processes of film. Indeed, the two theorists shared an interest in the psychology of perception and did not value the perception of resemblance above other responses.

André Bazin, in contrast, saw film as quintessentially realist, a medium "in which the image is evaluated not according to what it adds to reality but what it reveals of it." One of the most prominent film theorists of the 1950s and 1960s, Bazin responded directly to the formalists who preceded him and serves as an important predecessor of contemporary film studies in turn. An instructive polarity in classical film theory pits Eisenstein, for whom montage was the quintessential tool of the medium, against Bazin, who, in "The Evolution of the Language of Cinema," expressed the view that cinema's

Figure 11.26 *Footlight Parade* (1933). Siegfried Kracauer cited the almost abstract patterns of chorus girls in performance as examples of "mass ornament."

ability to capture a space and event in real time is its essence. Montage interfered with this vocation, Bazin argued, by altering spatial and temporal relationships. He advocated instead the use of composition in depth, made possible by deep-focus cinematography, which kept all planes of the image in view so that cutting between parts of the image was unnecessary. A filmmaker like Jean Renoir, who staged scenes in depth using long takes, conveyed "respect for the continuity of dramatic space and, of course, of its duration." Why was this so important to Bazin? He saw the image as not only a reference to reality but also as a record of it—and ultimately as a means of transcending time. Preserving duration and the integrity of space paid tribute to the reality of the object filmed, stressing the indexical properties of the medium.

Another influential and formidable thinker on film, Siegfried Kracauer, is, like Bazin, best known for his strong advocacy of realism. Kracauer's position evolved over time. In the 1920s, he began writing newspaper essays in Weimar Germany amidst modernist experimentation with film form. In "The Mass Ornament," Kracauer explored the aesthetics of mass culture and the new rhythms of life it inspired **[Figure 11.26]**. After fleeing Nazi Germany, Kracauer settled in the United States. In *From Caligari to Hitler,* he wrote about how hypnosis and other themes of German expressionist cinema reflected the nation's growing acceptance of Nazi ideology. It was not until 1960 that he published his major work, *Theory of Film: The Redemption of Physical Reality,* in which he elaborated his views on film's capacity for realism. The cinematic medium "is uniquely equipped to record and reveal physical reality," Kracauer argued. It was not only that film provided a window on the phenomenal world. For Kracauer, it was crucial that film was able to preserve what would otherwise meet with destruction: the momentary, the everyday, the random.

Walter Benjamin, Kracauer's Weimar-era contemporary, was particularly interested in how cinema participated in the transformation of perception in the modern world. Benjamin wrote about cinema as well as photography in a famous, though difficult, essay whose title has been translated as "The Work of Art in the Age of Mechanical Reproduction." For Benjamin, the comparison of photography and film with painting did not hinge on their relative artistic value or even their technique. Rather, they differed because these new art forms did not produce unique objects with the "aura" of an original artwork. Instead, film captured the sense of accelerated time and effortlessly traversed space typical of contemporary urban life. Benjamin regarded the distracted state of the film viewer as the characteristic mode of perception of the medium and of the historical moment. Written in 1935 as the Nazis rose to power, Benjamin's essay closed with an epilogue critiquing fascism's manipulation of the masses through traditional aesthetics. Benjamin did not survive the war, and his writings on cinema remained too sparse to put him at the center of classical debates in film theory. His influence on contemporary theorists, however—particularly his description of the transformation of the senses by twentieth-century modernity—has been great.

In many ways World War II divides film culture—both filmmaking and film theory—into two periods. The theoretical issues we have outlined, and in particular the defense of realism, can be illuminated by a historical perspective. Kracauer's experience as a German Jewish refugee certainly influenced his views on the value of realism as a kind of historical evidence. Bazin, a Catholic and French Resistance activist, invested cinema with similar "healing" or redemptive properties in his post–World War II writings. The trauma and destruction of the war seemed to add urgency to the argument for film's ability to preserve the natural world. Bazin had a high regard for the postwar Italian neorealist movement. With its amateur actors and location shooting, the movement demonstrated what Bazin called "faith in reality," which he valued above films by directors who put their "faith in the image" **[Figure 11.27]**. The postmodernist postulate that our only access to the world is through representations might make the defense of realism seem outmoded. However, such positions were far from naive and responded to their historical context. Bazin and Kracauer well understood the artistry involved in creating a film, as well as the fact that a technical process intervened between the world and the image.

Figure 11.27 *Germany Year Zero* (1947). For André Bazin, Roberto Rossellini's film puts its "faith in reality."

Bazin's interest in cinema's ontology or being was explored in a posthumously published two-volume work appropriately titled *What Is Cinema?* A transitional figure between classical and contemporary film theory, Bazin co-founded *Cahiers du cinéma* in 1951. Under Bazin's mentorship, the magazine published the criticism of the young cineastes who would shape the French new wave. The journal and its writers' films, widely cine-literate and iconoclastic, energized world film culture and influenced the emergence of the discipline of film studies in universities. Eventually, *Cahiers du cinéma* also catalyzed the resurgence of theory in film culture in the early 1970s.

VIEWING CUES: Approaching Theoretical and Scholarly Articles about Film

As we have seen, film theory draws from a variety of disciplines and employs specialized, even esoteric, vocabulary. Students of moving images will encounter many different kinds of theoretical and critical articles. Approaching such disparate materials can be made easier by asking basic questions:

- What is the film theorist's principal thesis or argument? Identify and underline a specific passage for reference.

- Locate a passage that is exemplary of the author's writing style; then think about how style and rhetoric contribute to the impact of the article.

- What kinds of evidence or argumentation strategies does the author employ? Locate an example.

- Identify one point in the article that you have never thought about before.

- Which passages or references simply baffle you? Attempting to figure out what explanatory framework is missing from an essay can be very productive.

- If there are passages in the article with which you disagree, why is this so?

- Relate the reading to the films or issues presented in class.

Coding Time in *Timecode* (2000)

In its heyday—from roughly the 1920s to 1960—classical film theory sought to describe our experience of a medium distinguished by specific characteristics: the use of photographic means to capture images, generally those depicting "live action," on film; the recording of images in rapid sequence so that when passed at equivalent speed before a beam of light, they produce the illusion of movement; the accompaniment of the moving images with sound, whether "live" or recorded synchronously; the presentation of the image on a large, flat, rectangular screen in a darkened room to a collective audience that normally pays money to attend.

Many of these basic definitional requirements are no longer met by the phenomenon we call the movies. Contemporary film theory raises new questions in part because of these shifts. Yet issues debated in classical film theory are still urgently raised by a contemporary film like Mike Figgis's *Timecode*, which did not use photographic means to record its images; it was shot on digital video. Like virtually all recent theatrical films, *Timecode* is just as likely to be viewed individually—at home, on a small screen, or in an electronic format such as video or DVD—as it is to be seen projected on 35mm film onto the big screen in the company of a paying audience. These differences raise ontological questions. In addition, *Timecode* can be used to illustrate one of the most critical dichotomies in classical film theory—the dichotomy between Eisenstein's championing of montage as the most specific attribute of cinema and Bazin's advocacy of the long take. This dichotomy hinges on how much priority is given to film's referential capacity and thus to the pursuit of an aesthetic of realism.

Is *Timecode* a realist film? It is organized as four continuous ninety-three-minute takes running simultaneously onscreen in four quadrants of uniform size and shape, accompanied by a soundtrack that is edited to highlight each of four interrelated stories at different moments. The continuous takes extend Bazin's "sequence shot" to the full capacity of video technology to result in a "sequence film." (Film, in contrast, is limited in the duration of individual takes by the size of the magazine and camera.) Bazin championed qualities of democracy and ambiguity—no one tells us where to look or what to think or feel about what we see in long takes featuring composition-in-depth. Do those qualities apply here? Certainly, it is the viewer who chooses where to look, and this decision making is multiplied by having to choose among the four images onscreen. Yet the handheld camera can emulate editing strategies that direct our gaze through close-ups and eyeline matches, and the soundtrack foregrounds one of the four images at any given time. What about film's propensity to reference the reality before the camera (the profilmic event) that Bazin prized? The film's actors are almost all stars, rather than the amateurs who appeared in neorealist films. They are, however, *really* acting for a full ninety minutes, mainly improvising their lines, which upholds a certain value of referentiality. It is unlikely Bazin would see anything particularly laudatory in *Timecode*'s respect for the unfolding of real time, however, because the activities of the cast are characterized by pettiness and *self*-referentiality. The story interweaves threads about aspiring starlets, callous film producers, jaded directors, and exploitative story ideas.

Given the film's embrace of facades, is *Timecode* more illustrative of Eisenstein's advocacy of montage as constructing meaning? Certainly, the four quadrants illustrate his concept of each frame of film as a montage cell. Eisenstein advocated the contrapuntal, or contrastive, use of sound. The film's editing of dialogue is always in sync with one of the four stories, while its continuous score arguably provides parallelism with all four. The dialogue is technically in counterpoint with the three stories we are not following on the audio track at any given moment, but this technique is also an example of image-sound parallelism because it encourages us to look at the story we also hear. Moreover, sound generally reinforces the narrative. We hear one character talking about her husband and see him simultaneously cheating on her. Rather than contrasting images and ideas whose juxtaposition raises us to a new level of critical insight and potential decisive action, *Timecode* paralyzes the viewer in a hall of mirrors. One character pitches to the team of producers a movie whose premise is that of the one we are watching. He is peremptorily dismissed: "that is the most pretentious crap I've ever heard." This is far from the state of moral reflection that Bazin would have us glean from open-ended films.

Timecode's title is a reference to the numerical counter that runs continuously in the corner of the image on uncut video footage. Time code is used to log footage so that a particular shot or fragment of a shot can be located when one wants to edit out the boring sections, the accumulation of which video's inexpensive stock and extreme mobility tend to encourage. While a rapid montage style that can ultimately be traced back to Eisenstein would seem to be the most prevalent editing code of our video-transformed era, the unblinking eye of surveillance footage is probably equally characteristic. Indeed, this is what *Timecode*'s quadrants reference, as it becomes apparent that all four stories converge at the same time in the same building. The film's continuous takes ultimately capture a contemporary reality that is always potentially exposed to the camera. "Faith in reality" and "faith in the image" are no longer clearly distinct.

By emphasizing its contexts, we have shown that film theory has always been more of a public conversation than a realm of solitary reflection. Contemporary film theory is more elaborated and diverse than classical film theory, although there are many important continuities. As film culture has expanded, ways of contemplating the medium have become more numerous.

Critical Questions in Contemporary Film Theory

Our sense that film theory can be spoken about as a unified or distinct body of knowledge comes from a position within the academic discipline of film studies. The study of film in higher education began as early as 1926, with a course taught by Terry Ramsaye at the New School in New York. Although resistance from curricular traditionalists accompanied the process, by the 1970s, film studies had become an established discipline in the United States and some other countries, with strong footholds in English and art history programs as well as in its own academic departments, societies, and journals. Film studies has been fostered in the context of a wider culture of film enthusiasts who read about American, European, and some non-Western films, festivals, and directors in such publications as *Film Comment* and *Film Quarterly*. In the United States, film culture also has been characterized by the growth of art houses and film societies showing foreign films as well as by the emergence of exciting new American filmmakers—from independents like John Cassavettes to the first generation of Hollywood directors who had been educated in film schools, including George Lucas, Paul Shrader, Francis Ford Coppola, and Martin Scorsese.

Most of the writing published in film magazines has been **criticism,** which aims to illuminate a particular work or body of work to a general or more expert readership. U.S. **film theory,** which takes the more general properties of the medium as its object, has become the domain of academics. In countries such as France, film theory has also been pursued by **public intellectuals,** well-known individuals whose writings and lectures are aimed at a public beyond students and scholars. In the 1970s, the vocabulary of film theory became very specialized as the discipline gained a foothold in the academy. Theorists were interested in a more systematic approach to cinema than was offered by the often subjective and impressionistic legacy of film criticism. The following partial overview of contemporary film theory is organized according to the major critical schools within the discipline. There are important interrelationships among these schools: often one set of questions grows out of another; feminism overlaps with psychoanalytic theory on the one hand, and with cultural studies on the other. However, it is important to trace the terms and evolution of broad issues before pointing to more specific areas of connection.

Marxism, Structuralism, and Semiotics

Like film culture, which renewed itself by looking outside the United States at the wane of the Hollywood studio era, the academic discipline of film studies has been heavily influenced by European thought, especially by several currents converging in France, including semiology, structuralism, and Marxism. At first glance, these ideas would seem to have little to do with film, but in fact such iconoclastic systems of thought are well suited to interrogate a medium of comparable freshness and vitality.

A word on the encounter with such theory may be appropriate here. Beginning film students often find the work of French theorists, and the English-speaking theorists influenced by them, quite baffling until they grasp both the questions that these thinkers are trying to illuminate and something of the context in which they have worked. When theories are understood as part of intellectual history, they yield new perspectives on contemporary problems. We will be frustrated if we look to theoretical writings for universally valid truths. Rather, it is helpful to think of them as stories, as more or less compelling versions of the way things work. Sometimes what is most compelling about film theory is the language in which it is elaborated, which can be speculative, poetic, even contradictory. To preface a discussion of contemporary theory this way is not to authorize its dismissal. Rather, we hope to encourage the curiosity that accompanies intellectual inquiry even when there are no set answers.

In order to introduce semiology and structuralism, we must understand that a **language model,** one that compares a given object or system to the structure of language, is central to 1970s film theory. This might at first seem curious. After all, films consist predominantly of pictures. But the influence of linguistics was pervasive in French thought of the 1960s, and it can be traced back to the work of Ferdinand de Saussure in the early part of the century. Saussure used linguistics as the most exemplary case of a new science of signs he called **semiology,** which could include pictures, gestures, and a wide range of other systems of communication or perception. A **sign,** for Saussure, is composed of a **signifier,** the spoken or written word, picture, or gesture, and a **signified,** the mental concept it evokes. Together, the signifier *c-a-t* and the signified *mental image of domesticated feline* form a sign, and the two parts cannot be imagined without each other. In a particular instance of discourse, the sign *cat* might refer to a specific tabby, which would be its referent. The importance of Saussure's distinctions cannot be overestimated. Any system of communication substitutes signs for objects, and there is nothing natural about such naming. Language, whose use distinguishes humankind, is a purely social convention (its signs are symbolic ones, as we defined the term above).

As noted earlier, pictures, especially photographs and film or video images, give a much stronger impression of identity with their referents than do words, whose connection to what they designate is purely arbitrary. In René Magritte's painting *Ceci n'est pas une pipe,* the words *This is not a pipe* seem absurd because we take them to refer to what is unmistakably a picture of a pipe **[Figure 11.28]**. But a picture of a pipe is not a pipe. There is no essential nature of an object that is captured in a sign of whatever nature. Semiology is **anti-essentialist,** stressing human invention and social convention rather than essential, pre-given qualities of objects. The scientific methodology devised by linguistics to describe these conventions has been useful to theorists attempting to approach cinema systematically, rather than relying on subjective evaluations such as beauty and truth.

However, some film theorists question the use of the linguistic sign as a starting point

Figure 11.28 René Magritte's painting *Ceci n'est pas une pipe* (1926) contrasts verbal and visual signs.

for cinematic analysis. For example, philosopher Gilles Deleuze returns to the contributions of C. S. Peirce, who defined the sign as that which "stands for something to someone in some respect or capacity," a conceptualization that emphasizes the mental process of association. Earlier in the chapter, we introduced Peirce's three varieties of signs: *icons* refer through resemblance, *indices* refer through a trace of the object, and *symbolic signs* such as words are purely arbitrary. Although Saussure's linguistics-based semiology is the more dominant influence in film as well as literary and narrative theory, today his term is more or less interchangeable with semiotics.

The comparison of film and language is by no means new. Throughout film history, filmmakers and theorists touted film's universality, its ability to transcend linguistic barriers. Classical film theorists—from Lindsay to Eisenstein and Balázs—have used linguistic metaphors of hieroglyphics, rhetoric, and grammar in their writings, and filmmakers sought a visual esperanto. But contemporary theorists, most notably French theorist Christian Metz in *Film Language,* used the analogy even more systematically. Eisenstein had concluded that a shot was more like a sentence than it was like a word, in that a shot could be subdivided again and again and its components would still "make sense." Yet is there a cinematic grammar? Metz wanted to know. One can combine shots in an infinite number of ways, so on that level no film grammar exists. But in narrative filmmaking, there are many similarities among types and sequences of narrative units. As in Chapter 4, Metz gives names to the limited number of units in use, such as "scene," "sequence," and "alternating syntagma" (which designates a crosscutting sequence), to build something like a narrative grammar of film.

The legacy of linguistics has been felt in theories of film narrative more generally. French anthropologist Claude Lévi-Strauss titled his important 1957 work *Structural Anthropology,* building on Saussure's structural linguistics. Lévi-Strauss studied thousands of myths and discovered that they share a limited number of basic structures that profoundly shape cultural life. In a number of disciplines, **structuralism** arose as an approach to empirical data, abstracting from the individual and rejecting essences to identify structures. Russian folklorist Vladimir Propp noticed a similar unity in his study of folktales. There are a limited number of what he called character functions (eight), a limited number of plot elements, and certain kinds of plot events always occurred in the same order, leaving only thirty-two basic plots from a corpus of hundreds of tales. **Narratology,** the study of narrative forms, is a branch of structuralism that encompassed stories of all kinds, including films. Are there a limited number of basic plots available to filmmakers? Are genres like myths? Because movies are so formulaic and so strikingly similar to myths and folktales even when they are not explicitly based on them, narratological studies had fruitful results. The characters in the *Star Wars* series, for example, closely match the heroes, antiheroes, magical helpers, princesses, and witches of the folktales Propp studied.

Linguists known as the Russian formalists, contemporaries of Eisenstein and Propp, have contributed the important distinction between **syuzhet (plot)** and **fabula (story)** to the study of narrative. These terms refer to the way events are arranged in the actual tale or film (plot) versus the chronologically ordered sequence of events as we rationally reconstruct it (story). The distinction gives us a very helpful tool for discussing an individual text. A detective story's *plot* follows the detective's progress through the investigation. Its *story* commences with the circumstances leading up to the committing of the crime. The story of *The Lord of the Rings: The Fellowship of the Ring* (2001) resembles that of the first volume of J. R. R. Tolkien's novel.

But the plot is different. Not only are incidents omitted from the film version, but also the means of the story's telling is language in one version and moving pictures and sounds in the other. Here the question of **adaptation** of films from literary works arises as a theoretical issue. In response to the common plaint "the book was better," theorists point to distinctions between these two means of expression.

Structuralist theorists reduce narrative to its most basic form: a beginning situation is disrupted, a hero takes action as a result, and a new equilibrium is reached at the end. The novel, the distinctive middle-class cultural form of the nineteenth century, gave that hero psychological depth and a realist field of action. The novel's basic narrative form is adopted by motion pictures just as many famous novels were adapted for the screen. Film theory and film practice have challenged whether this **classical narrative cinema** is necessarily the norm. According to its critics, classical narrative form affirms values of middle-class culture, such as the agency of the individual, the transparency of realism, and the inevitability of the status quo, through processes of identification, verisimilitude, catharsis, and closure. **Modernism** favors a more fragmented human subjectivity, a foregrounding of style, and an open-ended narrative. **Postmodernism** mixes and matches different kinds of narratives and formal approaches. The disjunctive incidents of surrealist films, Vertov's kaleidoscopic urban documentary *The Man with the Movie Camera* (1929), abstract films by avant-garde filmmakers such as Maya Deren and Michael Snow, and murky postmodern tales such as *Blade Runner* and *Fight Club* (1999) intentionally reject classical narrative characteristics adopted from the realist novel: cause-and-effect linearity, rounded or even identifiable protagonists, and neat happy endings. Non-narrative films reference film's **materiality** when celluloid, movement, sprocket holes, or light becomes their subject matter as well as their means. In such work, film language is no longer based on an analogy with the verbal, and narrative, such as it is, is stripped to its structural stability.

In many of these examples, the rejection of narrative is based on an ideological argument against the naturalization of conventions and the mystification of how things work. **Marxism** is most immediately understood as a political and economic discourse, one that looks at history and society in terms of unequal class relations. In contemporary U.S. political discourse, Marxism may even be considered marginal or dated. But it can still be used to approach wider social questions through the lenses of economic realities and class hierarchies and to interrogate the cultural structures that underpin exploitation. Varieties of Marxism have been very prominent among international intellectuals historically, with Marxist approaches to film and mass culture exerting a profound influence long before the 1970s. In the Soviet Union, the work of Eisenstein, Vertov, Pudovkin, and other practitioner-theorists was made possible by a Marxist state. Walter Benjamin also theorized film in a Marxist frame when he welcomed the democratization of culture made possible by "the age of mechanical reproduction." At the same time, the group of Frankfurt, Germany–based thinkers with whom Benjamin was associated, known as the Frankfurt School, critiqued film and other forms of mass culture for reinforcing the capitalist social structure. Theodor Adorno and Max Horkheimer's essay "The Culture Industry," written in America in 1944 but not widely read until republication in 1969, greatly influenced postwar academic and popular perceptions that mass culture duped its viewers, churning out movies in the same manner as it did new cars or brands of toothpaste, with only superficial differences among the products.

While the approach to mass communications in the United States in the 1960s and '70s tended to follow the thesis of "The Culture Industry," a different strain of Marxist thinking became prominent in French film theory, which, as we have noted, was catalyzed by the radical social disruptions, political protests, and intellectual currents of that decade. One of the most important theorists to influence contemporary film studies, French Marxist Louis Althusser approaches the traditional Marxist question of the nature of **ideology**—a systematic set of beliefs that is not necessarily conscious—with a new understanding of the structures of representation. He wants to explain how people come to accept ideas and conditions contrary to their interests. Althusser defines *ideology* as "the imaginary representation of the real relations in which we live." Real relations, such as paid work that contributes to the profits of others, disempower working people in the interests of the ruling class, and our imaginary representations (that this is the way it is supposed to be, according to the evening news and the fashion magazines) make this powerlessness seem inevitable and tolerable.

For the critics at *Cahiers du cinéma,* film is an important test of Althusser's theories about ideology. Jean-Luc Comolli and Jean Narboni open their 1969 editorial "Cinema/Criticism/Ideology" by acknowledging that their own work as critics is "situated fairly and squarely inside the economic system of capitalist publishing." They then looked at varieties of film practice and classified them according to their relationship with the "dominant ideology." The most highly valued films are those that broke with this ideology, not only on the level of content (portraying decolonization and the conflict over U.S. involvement in Vietnam) but also on the level of form—experimental films that disturb easy viewing processes. Jean-Luc Godard's obscure political film *Le Vent d'est* (credited to the Dziga Vertov Group, 1969) was heralded by leftist critics of the period.

But Comolli and Narboni's essay sets an even more lasting agenda for film theory with one of their other categories. In an alphabetical list of types of films to study, category "e" designates those films that seem to uphold the status quo but register, in their formal excesses or internal contradictions, the stresses and strains of trying to make ideology work, thus exposing it to close viewers as a representation rather than an unchangeable reality. Soon critics followed their lead to read *Imitation of Life* (1959) and other films by Douglas Sirk, as well as films by many other studio-era auteurs, in this way. Sirk's 1950s melodramas were considered too color-coordinated, and his characters too hysterical and their environments too artificial to be taken at face value **[Figure 11.29]**. These glossy surfaces were cracking under the brittle hypocrisies characterizing the capitalist prosperity of Eisenhower America, including anticommunist hysteria, repression of civil rights movements, and enforcing of gender roles that had been challenged during the war. Sirk's films are **progressive texts;** the uneasy feeling they leave us with critiques dominant ideology. This subtle, and sometimes wishful, approach is known as **symptomatic reading,** a fruitful legacy of Althusser's Marxist influence on contemporary film theory.

Figure 11.29 *All That Heaven Allows* (1955). Ideology critics regarded Douglas Sirk's melodramas as "progressive texts" whose formal excesses and improbable situations showed the cracks beneath Eisenhower America's facade of prosperity and social consensus.

Poststructuralism: Psychoanalysis, Apparatus Theory, and Spectatorship

As the term implies, *poststructuralism* is the intellectual development that came after structuralism and in some sense supplanted it, calling into question the rational methodology and fixed definitions that structuralists bring to their various objects of study. Because the term is not descriptive but relational, it is versatile enough to include many areas of thought, from psychoanalysis to postcolonial and feminist theory. In some sense it is unfortunate that the term *poststructuralism* has stuck because it builds obscurity into its very name. If you don't know what structuralism is, how can you understand poststructuralism? Regrettable as the elitism of this situation is, the question is part of the point. Poststructuralism is a position of critique, asking us to reconsider everything we take for granted, including attitudes that we might hold without recognizing the names others have given them. For example, our implicit standard that a satisfying film ties up all its loose ends is a structuralist position that posits closure as a basic narrative element. Poststructuralism stresses the open-endedness of stories: what if we daydream about the characters we have been introduced to or pick up on the relationship between a film and topical events? Closure is a relative quality.

Structuralism attempts to be more rigorous than common forms of humanist criticism by introducing scientific protocols into the study of literature. It tried to be systematic with empirical observation by looking for transhistorical patterns into which specific data would fit (for example, anthropologists compared dozens of creation myths; film critics compared westerns). Poststructuralism, in turn, questions the assumption of objectivity and the disregard for cultural and historical context. Hence, it is a whole lot messier as an intellectual movement. A shorthand definition might be: structuralism + subjectivity = poststructuralism. Most of contemporary film theory is poststructuralist in orientation, although some schools refer to the thinkers and tenets identified with structuralism and poststructuralism more explicitly than others. Key movements in poststructuralist film theory include psychoanalysis, apparatus theory, and spectatorship.

Althusser's work has been central to poststructuralist currents in film theory. His elaboration of how an individual comes to believe in ideology as "imaginary representation" refers to **psychoanalysis** and in particular to the French psychoanalyst Jacques Lacan's definition of the **imaginary.** In his teachings from the 1950s through his death in 1981, Lacan spoke of three domains of psychic experience: the imaginary, the symbolic, and the real. The Lacanian imaginary is not simply opposed to "reality"—in fact, "the real" in Lacan's thought is a domain akin to trauma that cannot even be represented. Rather, the imaginary realm deals in images, and the symbolic realm is the domain of language. The human subject relates to pictures in a particularly powerful way, rooted in one of the earliest images to leave an impression on us, our own reflection in the mirror. In the **mirror stage,** the infant comes to recognize him- or herself as a human individual. But this recognition is also a "misrecognition," for the image is really just that, an illusion. Lacanian film theorists liken this early sense of self that is both powerful and illusory to the experience of viewing a film and "believing" in its world. We are immobile and surrounded in darkness when we watch, and a grandiose image appears lit up on the wall. Moreover, films are peopled with stars and characters with physical powers superior to ours and with whom we identify [**Figure 11.30**]. In Plato's ancient parable of the

Figure 11.30 *Mission: Impossible II* (2000). Star Tom Cruise and his character's physical prowess represent idealized objects of identification.

cave, people chained underground watching shadows on the wall had no way of knowing that what they saw was not real.

Film theorists followed Althusser in understanding the cinema as an **apparatus,** an ideological mechanism based in a physical set of technologies, with the power to convince us that an illusion is real and true. If the everyday world we live in is a collection of images imbued with capitalist ideology, how much more saturated with dominant ways of thinking are movies, whose images are selected and combined by filmmakers working for huge entertainment companies? The essays of Jean-Louis Baudry use the term *apparatus* to argue that the actual arrangement of equipment, such as the invisible projector and the illuminated screen, influences our unconscious receptivity to the image and to ideology—as if we too were trapped in Plato's cave. **Apparatus theory** explores the values built into film technology through the particular context of its historical development. The camera's monocular (single-eyed) view and use of **perspective** incorporate the values of human-scaled Renaissance art. Such art posits a viewer standing at the point where perspective lines converge. This viewer-addressee is in the same position as the camera and can thus imagine him- or herself as the originator or possessor of the illusion on the canvas or the screen. Anthropocentrism (human-centeredness), individualism, possession, and the primacy of the visual are all particular cultural values. It goes without saying, we may think, that a camera depends on perspective. But what "goes without saying" is one way to define ideology. A culture that did not put the possessive individual at the center of representation—a culture that valued empty space, inanimate objects, and animals as well as people; multiple subjects or scrolls instead of frames in pictorial depictions; or senses other than sight in the arts—might never have developed the technology of photography.

Poststructuralist theory goes on to claim that the position constructed by the representation actually preexists the human **subject** that will later assume it and thus constructs that subject as a subject of vision. In other words, an individual who stands in front of a Renaissance painting or who watches a classical Hollywood movie is "subjected" to the apparatus's positioning and understands his or her "subjectivity" in terms that are pre-given by the culture. Theorists argue that subjects are constituted through language or through other acts of signification (meaning-making) such as film. For example, the word *I* has no definite meaning until it is used by someone in a sentence. It will then designate the person saying "I," and its meaning will shift as a conversation progresses and each speaker uses *I* to refer to him- or herself in turn. Although viewers cannot "talk back" when they watch a film (as they can in other forms of audiovisual representation such as video games, Web sites, and interactive films), they can be said to be constituted as the object of the film's address—they are meant to laugh, cry, or put clues together as the film unfolds.

The topic of how subjects interact with films and with the cinematic apparatus is known as the theory of **spectatorship.** As suggested earlier, spectatorship has been a concern in film theory since Münsterberg, who used psychology to explain the mind's role in making sense of movies. Theorists such as Eisenstein were also very interested in the viewer's interaction with images and sounds. In the poststructuralist theory of the 1970s, however, spectatorship stood at the convergence of theories of language and subjectivity, psychoanalysis, and Marxism. Metz, one of the most prolific and influential contemporary theorists, has also been at the center of spectatorship theory. He refers to linguistic and psychoanalytic terminology in the title of his influential (1977) book *The Imaginary Signifier*, which argues that film's strong perceptual presence makes it an almost hallucinatory experience, gratifying to our voyeurism (our love of looking without being seen ourselves) and to our unconscious self-image of potency. The work of Metz and other French theorists began to appear in translation in the English journal *Screen* in the early 1970s; the theory of spectatorship refined there by English and American contributors is sometimes known as screen theory or gaze theory.

Theories of Gender and Sexuality

The poststructuralist concern with spectatorship and subjectivity remains abstract if spectatorship is generalized and the nature of subjectivity is not questioned. Psychoanalytic theory revolves around the issues of desire and identification. Gender and sexuality soon became key to film theory's exploration of how subjectivity is engaged by and constructed in cinema.

Feminist Film Theory   Feminism also began to have wide social and intellectual currency during the 1970s. Commentators point out that the female image is treated differently in film—as well as in advertising, pornography, and painting—from the male image **[Figure 11.31]**. While the protagonists of many more films and genres are male, the objectification of the female image seems to solicit a possessive male gaze (or, in the case of fashion photography and advertising, a woman's desire to emulate the look of the female model in order to solicit a male gaze). In film theory, feminist critics note, the spectator is envisioned in a similarly gendered way. The association of

vision with ownership and power is a male privilege in our culture, and previous theorists had ignored this assumption. "Is the Gaze Male?" asks E. Ann Kaplan in an essay of that title.

British theorist and filmmaker Laura Mulvey's "Visual Pleasure and Narrative Cinema," published in *Screen* in 1975, is one of the most important essays in contemporary film theory. Arguing that psychoanalysis offers a compelling account of how the difference between the sexes is culturally internalized and valued, Mulvey observes that the glamorous and desirable female image in film is also a potentially threatening vision of difference, or otherness, for male viewers. Hollywood films repeat a pattern

Figure 11.31 *And God Created Woman* (1968). Brigette Bardot exemplifies what Laura Mulvey calls women's "to-be-looked-at-ness."

Figure 11.32 *The Devil Is a Woman* (1935). Marlene Dietrich's image offers an example of fetishism for feminist theorist Laura Mulvey.

of visual mastery of the woman as "Other" by attributing the onscreen gaze to a male character who can cover for the camera's voyeurism—its capacity for looking without being seen—and stand in for the male viewer. Film narratives also tend to domesticate or otherwise tame the woman, Mulvey shows, offering analyses of Alfred Hitchcock's *Vertigo* and *Rear Window* (1954), whose stories are driven by voyeurism and female make-overs. In another primary example, Mulvey uses the psychosexual concept of fetishism to explain the effect of the elaborately controlled presentation of Marlene Dietrich's image in the films of Josef von Sternberg as fetishism **[Figure 11.32]**. In Freudian theory, fetishism is a denial of, by way of overcompensation for, female lack, a lack defined as difference from masculinity, or castration.

Although generations of students have resisted Mulvey's emphasis on such questionable psychoanalytic concepts as castration, most have also granted the accuracy of her formulation of the standard dichotomy in Hollywood film: "woman as image/man as bearer of the look." Mulvey's essay is polemical: she champions "a political use of psychoanalysis" and a new kind of filmmaking that would "free the look of the camera into its materiality in time and space" so that it could not be ignored through assimilation to the viewer's or characters' perspective. In their film *Riddles of the Sphinx* (1977) **[Figure 11.33]**, Mulvey and Peter Wollen use 360-degree pans, with the camera positioned around waist level, to emulate the circularity of a young mother's rhythms of work and to avoid objectifying the woman's body in a centered, still image. The film deliberately sets out to destroy conventional visual pleasure and narrative satisfaction. Like many theorists of this period, Mulvey and Wollen believed that making spectators think about what they were seeing was the first step toward a critical perspective.

Building on Mulvey's provocative argument, other feminist critics raise the question of female spectatorship. If narrative cinema so successfully positions the viewer to take up a male gaze, why are women historically often the most enthusiastic film viewers? One way to approach this question is to consider films produced with a female audience in mind. During Hollywood's heyday, women's pictures featured female stars that had a strong appeal to women, such as Bette Davis and Joan Crawford. At first glance, women's pleasure in these films seems self-defeating in that what these heroines do best is suffer. However, feminists argue that a film like *Now, Voyager* (1942), which shows Davis as a dowdy spinster taking control of her life (through psychoanalytic treatment and new clothes!), enables female spectators to explore their own dissatisfaction with their lives by fantasizing a more fulfilling version of that existence. In this way, the contradictions of women's situations are revealed, while no satisfactory solutions are posited. Perhaps no easy solutions exist, the films imply. Today's films aimed at women are not that different from those of the 1940s.

Figure 11.33 *Riddles of the Sphinx* (1977). Laura Mulvey puts her own theories into practice in a film made with Peter Wollen.

Divine Secrets of the Ya-Ya Sisterhood (2002) reveals similar contradictions to *Now, Voyager*: mother-daughter bonds are both destructive and primary. Many feminist critics argue that women's pleasure in these complicated, mixed-message movies should be taken seriously. Because film is a mass medium, it will never radically challenge existing power relations, but if it speaks to women's dilemmas, it is doing more than much official culture does.

Still other feminist scholars turn to the work of past women filmmakers. The political and aesthetic options and strategies of contemporary feminist filmmakers—from Kathryn Bigelow to Julie Dash in the United States, Ann Hui in Hong Kong, and Marta Meszaros in Hungary—are very different from those of Matilde Landeta, a Mexican woman director working in the 1940s, or Larissa Shepiko, a Soviet filmmaker of the 1950s. (See our discussion of American women filmmakers in Chapter 10.) Nevertheless, there are important continuities and common questions to ask about the conditions under which these women work, the sources that inspire them, and the cinematic languages they draw on and develop. Overall, feminism has had more of an impact on the relatively young discipline of film theory than on many more established ones. Arguably, gender in film cannot be ignored. As Mulvey's work suggests, cinema—certainly entertainment film but also the avant-garde—depends on the stylized image of woman for its appeal. Moreover, the cinema, because it is part of the fabric of daily life, necessarily comments on the everyday, private sphere. In the private sphere, women's role is pervasive (if undervalued). Feminism's significant inroads in film theory have laid the groundwork for related, though not always parallel, critiques of cinema's deployment of sexuality, race, and national identity.

Lesbian and Gay Film Studies   Feminist and psychoanalytic theory stress that unconscious processes of desire and identification are at play when we go to the movies. Our everyday ways of talking about stars and films acknowledge how strong the element of fantasy is in our viewing. Despite the sexist historical legacy of psychoanalysis, many feminists find its focus on subjectivity, gender, and sexuality very useful. Like cinema itself, however, psychoanalysis historically concentrates on heterosexual scenarios (such as the Oedipus complex) and pathologizes gays and lesbians (as cases of "arrested development," for example). **Lesbian and gay film theory** critiques and supplements feminist approaches by pointing out that films allow for more flexible ways of seeing and experiencing visual pleasure than the binary opposites of male versus female, seeing versus seen, and being versus desiring that are the basis of Mulvey's influential model of spectatorship. The gender of a member of the audience need not correspond with that of the character he or she finds most absorbing or most alluring. Marlene Dietrich, Mulvey's example of a "fetish" or mask for male desire, cross-dressed for songs in many films and even kissed a woman on the lips in her first American movie, *Morocco* (1930) **[Figure 11.34]**. Dietrich's gender bending is more than theoretical. Her onscreen style borrows directly from the fashions of the lesbian and gay subculture of Weimar-era Germany, where her career began. Dietrich thus appealed to lesbian and gay

Figure 11.34 *Morocco* (1930). Lesbian and gay theorists interpret Marlene Dietrich—here kissing a woman—in a different way than Mulvey does.

viewers of the past, as well as to heterosexual women and men, on many different levels. In fact, this very multiplicity could be seen more generally as a key to cinema's mass appeal. Although movies do conform to the dominant values of a society—in this case, to heterosexuality as the norm—they also make unconscious appeals to our fantasies, which may not be as conformist (anyone may identify with or desire a character of either gender in a particular movie). Moreover, films leave room for viewers' own interpretations and appropriations, such as when fan writers continue the adventures of particular mainstream characters or celebrities and share them on the Internet. Spectators positioned at the margins, such as gay men and lesbians, often "read against the grain" for cues of performance or mise-en-scène that suggest a different story than the one onscreen, one with more relevance to their lives. An interest in stars (such as Dietrich and Jodie Foster, whose strong images have appealed to lesbian viewers) that goes beyond any particular film they may be cast in is one way to circumvent the mandate of heterosexual resolution required by narrative closure. Lesbian and gay portrayals and responses to the cinema constitute one of many areas that have demanded fresh concepts in film theory.

New Directions in Film Studies

We will broadly consider three new directions in film studies in this section. Cultural studies scrutinizes aspects of the cinema that are embedded in the everyday life of individuals or groups at particular historical junctures and in particular social contexts, rather than analyzing individual texts or theorizing about spectatorship in the abstract. The phenomena it addresses can range from the reception of film stars to the transformations of postcolonial societies; it is thus impossible to encompass all applications of its methods in a brief discussion such as this one. Another new direction in the field of film studies, one that critiques poststructuralist film theory explicitly, comes from scholars rigorously exploring the philosophical dimensions of film as well as the cognitive processes involved in viewing and comprehending them. Finally, characteristics of contemporary society designated by the term *postmodernism*, and the potential and uses of new media technologies that are altering the place of cinema in the twenty-first century, have also emerged as important concerns in recent film theory. These three new directions in film study address questions left open by poststructuralist models, bringing theory in touch with present-day viewers' diverse experiences.

Cultural Studies

A useful way of understanding the fresh approach that cultural studies employs toward cinema lies in the shift from the definition of "culture" as great works produced by transcendent artists and appreciated by knowledgeable patrons to a definition derived from anthropology: culture as a way of life, including social structures and habits. In other words, it is how movies are encountered, understood, and "used" in daily experience that interests cultural studies scholars. **Cultural studies** is a loosely defined set of approaches drawn from the humanities and social sciences and united by the refusal to isolate an artistic text from the processes of production and consumption. Social critics at the influential Birmingham Center for the Study of Contemporary Culture in England were among the first to use the term, in studies of youth culture and of television audiences conducted in the 1970s. The way social background and education influence taste, legal decisions on monopoly practices or censorship in film, how films were exhibited in the first decade of cinema, the reception of particular films by particular groups at particular times, and the activities of movie fans are all topics that have been pursued under the rubric of cultural studies. We shall look at a few key examples of cultural studies: reception, stars, and race and representation.

Reception Theory   One of the most important approaches used by cultural studies of film is termed **reception theory** because it focuses not on who made a film or on its formal features or thematic content but on how it is received by audiences. As we have suggested throughout this book, audiences are at the center of the film experience. The global reach of contemporary films should persuade us that any theory that does not take audiences into account would give a limited picture of film culture. Composed of actual individuals whose habits and preferences may be researched through surveys and testimonies, audiences provide a concrete basis for theorizing. Collecting information about audience composition or preferences is not itself film theory—the film industry is as interested in audience demographics as is the sociologist, and the studios themselves have initiated some of the best viewer surveys. Cultural studies goes further, theorizing that a work's meaning is only achieved in its reception **[Figure 11.35]**. This implies a theory of audiences as active rather than passive. Obvious examples are participatory viewing practices such as the costumes and call and response of *The Rocky Horror Picture Show* (1975) fans and the imaginative play inspired by kids' viewing. In addition, films from the past may be received by today's audiences in entirely new ways. We might have a response that goes "against the grain" of the text—rooting for the Native Americans rather than the cowboys; enjoying a supporting character's subversive wit rather than investing in the romance of a pair of bland leads. Studying reception details the complexity of viewer-text interactions.

Figure 11.35 *Gone with the Wind* (1939). The reception of this film classic reveals contradictory attitudes.

Beyond the idiosyncrasies of personal history and circumstances, aspects of our **cultural identity**—age, immigration status, and educational background—can predispose us toward particular kinds of reception. The gay subtext of *Rebel without a Cause* is likely to be more salient to an audience knowledgeable about the subculture. Such an audience is referred to as an **interpretive community** because its members share particular knowledge, or **cultural competence,** through which a film is experienced and interpreted. The panoply of West African–derived hairstyles in *Daughters of the Dust* (1991) is more likely to be enjoyed and understood by black women than other audience members; indeed, filmmaker Julie Dash intended this special gratification as part of the movie's **address,** or vision of its ideal audience. Those who have read the book on which a movie is based have different cultural competences from those who have read only reviews of the film.

The responses of particular viewers to cultural phenomena are considered **situated responses,** readings that are influenced, though not predetermined, by geography, age, gender, wealth, and a host of other contingent factors. *Shrek* (2001) is appreciated by children for its simple fairy-tale story and for the expected pleasures encountered through repeat viewings, whereas Eddie Murphy's fans appreciate his performance of the donkey's voice and those interested in technology scrutinize the advances in animation. Theorists see these multiple ways of interacting with a text as confirmation that individuals actively make meaning even in response to otherwise homogenous mass media.

The methodologies associated with reception studies include comparing and contrasting the protocols of reviews drawn from different periodicals, countries, or decades; conducting detailed interviews with viewers; and tracking **commodity tie-ins,** the goods that are marketed with the "brand name" of a particular film or characters. Here, we focus on two kinds of reception studies: ethnographic and historical.

The word **ethnography,** literally meaning "people" and "writing," is adopted from anthropology. As noted in setting up our discussion of indigenous media in Chapter 10, ethnographic film is a way of documenting a culture's daily life. Ethnographic reception studies focus on film users and are often based on surveys or interviews. They may look at a cross-section of an audience, but they are often designed to illuminate the behavior and situation of a particular group (an "ethnos") that is socially nondominant and lacking cultural power. Advocating for social change that extends rights and recognition to such a group is part of identity politics. Reception is an important dimension of identity-based critiques of mainstream cinema.

Because social out-groups are often denied access to the creation of representations that reflect their lives, members of such groups may find meaning and creativity in their own kind of consumption of popular forms. To give an example, African American audiences might enjoy Paul Robeson's performance in *Show Boat* (1936) while critiquing aspects of the film's racial politics. Reception differs from spectatorship in that it deals with actual audiences rather than a hypothetical subject constructed by the text. Reception studies thus address actual responses to movies and the behavior of groups; spectatorship is concerned with the unconscious patterns evoked by a particular text or by the process of film viewing in the abstract. British cultural studies scholar Stuart Hall has argued that groups respond to mass culture from their different positions of social empowerment. They may react from the position the text slots them into, a **dominant** reading, offer a **negotiated** reading that accommodates different realities, or reject the framework in which a dominant message is conveyed through an **oppositional** reading. Ethnographic studies can map these three positions. Social identity considerably complicates the picture of subjectivity offered in poststructuralist film theory, including that of feminism.

In **historical reception studies,** critics remind us that our understandings of films from the past are very partial if they do not take into account the meanings those texts carry with them from the contexts in which they were produced and consumed. Control of film production is much more entwined with economic incentives than other forms of art-making, but popular media are not devoid of the spirit of the people, a spirit that resides in reception. Scandalous films, exhibition contexts in different communities, scrapbooks and other artifacts, mentions of films in works by contemporary writers—these all help fill in the texture of historical experience. The huge impact of the countercultural film *Easy Rider* (1969) changed the kinds of films Hollywood produced. *The Birth of a Nation* (1915) is fascinating to study textually; it used more shots, more close-ups, more editing, and more scoring innovations than had ever been seen in films. But its reception is also a defining event of both film history and of the politics of race in America. The NAACP gathered prominence as an organization through opposition to the film's racism. The African American independent cinema, discussed in Chapter 10, was catalyzed by Griffith's film. At the same time, *The Birth of a Nation* was screened at a Ku Klux Klan rally in 1978—though not without protesters. Concretely, the historian could look at ad campaigns **[Figure 11.36]** as well as contemporary reviews and commentaries in newspapers and publications of different orientations. The historian might also research the film's reception by interviewing moviegoers who saw it during one of its many re-releases. The film is embedded in personal and cultural memories, including those of the students who study it in contemporary film studies classes.

Topics ranging from the impact of protests against *Year of the Dragon* (1985) on Asian American political organizing to the patent wars that shaped the early film landscape yield insights into film's reception history. Methodologically, historicizing means looking at non-film or **extratextual sources** in one's research: laws governing where films could or could not be shown, the design of buildings that exhibited films, studies of immigrant populations, import tariffs, equipment patents, records of censorship boards, and the like. Historians of reception regard films as social events whose meaning can only be determined by understanding and decoding the many forces that intersect with them.

Figure 11.36 The poster for *The Birth of a Nation* (1915) used Ku Klux Klan imagery.

Stars An important component of reception is our response to **stars,** performers who become recognizable through their films or who bring celebrity to their roles. In addition to analyzing how a star's image is composed from various elements—not only film appearances but also promotion, publicity, and critical commentary—theorists are interested in how audience reception helps define a star's cultural meaning. Although one of the most pervasive aspects of cinema, stars are among the least likely topics to be considered in a theoretical approach. After all, stars are the province of entertainment and newsmagazines, tabloid journalism, and on-line chats. Textual critics, in particular, can have difficulty dealing with stardom, which is fundamentally an intertextual phenomenon. In contrast, familiar and ephemeral sources such as fan magazines have an important place in cultural studies, as do the responses of fans themselves. One understands a film in relationship to what one knows of its stars outside the world of the film's fiction. *Eyes Wide Shut* is a film about a marriage. The fact that the marriage of co-stars Tom Cruise and Nicole Kidman failed shortly after the much-anticipated film's release adds another dimension to viewers' interpretation of its tale of jealousy (see Chapter 1).

Beyond the range of roles that a star becomes familiar for playing, other discourses about stars, including promotion (studio-arranged exposure such as Web sites and television show appearances), publicity (romances, scandals, and political involvement), and commentary (critical evaluations and awards), help construct their images. Star images become texts to be read in their own right. Sean Penn's promise as a teen star was associated with "acting" rather than cosmetic appeal. His brief marriage to Madonna and his arrest for assaulting a photographer, his portrayals of a condemned

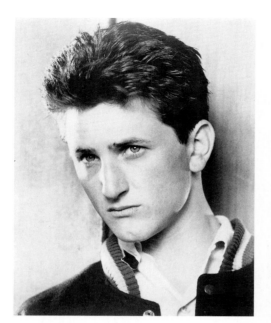

Figure 11.37 Sean Penn. Star images are approached seriously in cultural studies of film.

man in *Dead Man Walking* (1995) and of a mentally disabled father in *I Am Sam* (2001), and his work as an independent director in films like *The Pledge* (2001) construct him as an individualist, even an "outlaw," a persona that carries connotations of "authenticity" **[Figure 11.37]**. Even when a particular star is billed as "just an ordinary guy" like Tom Hanks, or "the girl next door" like 1950s star Doris Day, this image is carefully orchestrated—hence, the fascination of so many paperback star biographies that purport to look behind the facade. We will never have access to the star as a real person. Instead, we experience his or her constructed image in relation to cultural codes (including age, race, class, gender, region, fashion, and more) and according to filmic codes (genre, acting, and even lighting). For example, the silent film star Lillian Gish was sometimes lit from above as she stood on a white sheet. The reflected light enhanced her pallor and the radiance of her blond hair, connoting a virginal whiteness that was a very important component of her star image in her films with D. W. Griffith. We use aspects of star images as a kind of cultural shorthand—Sidney Poitier stands in for a particular aspect of 1950s and 1960s American race relations. A wishful image of overachieving middle-class black men disguised aspects of everyday and structural racism and encoded some of the gains of the contemporary civil rights movement. We also construct our own identities and communities through stars whom we will never know, and this is not necessarily a negative aspect of the phenomenon. Young girls who patterned themselves after plucky singing star Deanna Durbin in the 1940s or Madonna in the 1980s incorporated the quality of independence they embodied and identified themselves in solidarity, rather than in competition, with other girls who shared their appreciation.

Stars are often considered the embodiment of types. For example, John Wayne connotes rugged individualism; Meg Ryan, perky romanticism; Morgan Freeman, quiet dignity; Robin Williams, manic mayhem. Different film roles, such as Robin Williams's creepy stalker in *One Hour Photo* (2002), add new inflections to these personae. In recent years, critics have made efforts to theorize the phenomenon of stardom and to illuminate not just the sociological significance of particular types but also how stars' images contribute to a film's meaning. Judy Garland became a teenage star when she appeared in *The Wizard of Oz* (1939). Her later troubles with drugs, a direct result of her "grooming" by the studio, lend irony to the image of girlish innocence she projects in the film classic. According to critic Richard Dyer, who urges us to consider stars' images in general in terms of contradiction, Marilyn Monroe's phenomenally successful image reconciled innocence and sexiness. At the root of the star phenomenon is a basic conflict between the ordinary and the extraordinary. Stars are not better people than the rest of us, which facilitates our identification with them. And yet they are a breed apart. One kind of research we might undertake to account for star images' contributions to films involves looking at fan magazines, a type of publication that emerged very early in the twentieth century, to see how films were promoted and received as star vehicles. Star discourse is a particularly revealing and useful critical approach to cinema because it is based in our everyday experience as fans. We have many immediate and unexamined responses to stars—from crushes to antipathies. But we also appreciate stars in very nuanced ways that yield considerable critical understanding. Cultural studies of stars often begin with viewer testimonials—taking them not at face value but using them as a starting point for a more sociological analysis.

What ethnic groups are represented in a nation's most popular stars? Do popular female stars transgress the boundaries of what is considered proper female behavior? Are people of color limited to supporting roles? Stars are powerful forces for gathering up what is important to a culture at any given moment. They represent conflicts that are not necessarily worked out.

Race and Representation   The concept of race—for race is a socially constructed category based on historical experiences and valuations of perceived difference, not an objective fact—intersects with the film experience on many different levels, raising important questions about the possibilities for cross-racial identification and other aspects of spectatorship. Cultural studies of film offer ways to address these questions. The psychoanalytic models for understanding gender in film have provided inadequate explanations of race. What might be called the fetishism of whiteness in Hollywood movies, a dominance and idealization of representations of one race, has for decades left people of color out of the picture and squirming in their seats at the cinema. It is helpful to distinguish in this area two senses of the term **representation:** (1) the aesthetic sense whereby we may speak of representations of African Americans in the films of Spike Lee versus those of *Gone with the Wind,* for example, and (2) the political sense of standing for a group of people, as an elected representative does. Both senses are at play in the cinematic representation of race. Cultural studies models are flexible enough to address racialized images, such as stereotypes and their reception by diverse audiences, as well as how discourses of imperialism, colonialism, and nationalism, often related to racial representations, are embedded in film stories, genres, and star images. Recent theories of exile and home, cultural hybridity and diaspora, and the global and the intercultural have added to the store of explanatory frames we have for looking at race and representation in cinema. Here we can only introduce issues that will reward further exploration.

If gender and sexual identifications are more mobile in cinema than they might at first appear, identification across race is a fraught and often obligatory process for nonwhite viewers because of the lack of racial diversity onscreen. Cinematic history reinforces the assumption of a white, western, "unmarked" spectator-subject. In classical Hollywood films, nonwhite characters are relegated to the periphery of the action as villainous or comic or sometimes noble—but always secondary—characters. Colonialism, the assumed primacy of Western values, peoples, and power over people from other parts of the globe, pervades such genres as the western and the adventure film and even appears in the musical *The King and I* (1956), in which one white woman proves to be a match for a king and his entire court **[Figure 11.38]**. In their 1994 book *Unthinking Eurocentrism,* theorists Robert Stam

Figure 11.38 *The King and I* (1956). Colonialism as a charming musical story.

Figure 11.39 *West Side Story* (1961). The film's Puerto Rican heroine is played by white actress Natalie Wood.

and Ella Shohat show how a Western gaze and voice are reproduced in such popular films as the *Indiana Jones* series, in which an ancient Eastern culture provides colorful background for the exploits of Western heroes. They also discuss how nondominant cultures are marginalized by casting, when white actors play other races, and even by sound, when everyone speaks English in films set in another country or when jazz scores are used in films in which all the characters are white **[Figure 11.39]**. But Stam and Shohat's examples show that American cinema often reflects a multicultural society in other ways. The importance of the western as a genre, or of the plantation as a motif, gives evidence of a cultural preoccupation with racial difference and conflicts. Although stereotyped in such film representations, people of color stand at the center of the nation's definition of itself.

The increasing success of filmmakers of color in the United States has paralleled theoretical explorations of alternative aesthetics, which are closely linked to literary and other artistic movements. The trickster figure of West African tradition appears in *To Sleep with Anger* (1990) by Charles Burnett and *Zajota and the Boogie Spirit* (1989) by Ayoka Chenzira as an expression of the identification of these African American filmmakers with the **diaspora,** a scattered community of people who share an original homeland. Aesthetic expressions of politics are a major concern in postcolonial cinemas that have emerged around the world. **Third Cinema,** discussed in Chapter 10, is one theorization of this conjuncture. The term, derived from Third World, names film practices that are politicized in relation to the dominant cinemas of the West (First Cinema) and the artistic films that still remain disengaged from social contexts and popular audiences (Second Cinema). These works often use narrative forms more in keeping with specific cultural traditions or political ideas than the linear cause-and-effect structures of Hollywood films. Humberto Solás's *Lucía* (1969), for instance, uses a three-part structure to link the fates of three Cuban women in different historical moments **[Figure 11.40]**.

By arguing that there is room for agency and divergence in our spectatorial and reception experiences, and in opening up the kinds of films and related cinematic phenomena that are deemed worthy of theoretical attention, critics associated with cultural studies take apart the unity and inevitability that characterized poststructuralist film theory in the

Figure 11.40 *Lucía* (1969). Humberto Solás's film uses formal innovation to reflect on Cuban history.

1970s. Cultural studies is less concerned with the specific film text or with the generalized film apparatus than with concrete dimensions of cinematic experience. For example, the advertising practices that surround films, the costumes designed for them and related retail schemes, censorship campaigns, and fan clubs all might be considered in a cultural studies approach. With roots in sociology, cultural studies takes a broader approach to contemporary media than film studies based in the humanities often do, shifting scholars' attention to the even more pervasive media form of television. Concepts of "the gaze" and the spectator do not translate directly to the case of television, with its much more interactive and everyday mode of consumption. Comparison of these media has opened up space to address the distinctiveness of new media, such as computer-based art, as well as the many social and economic transactions that surround cinema today, from the viewing of works on cable, tape, or disc to the incorporation of movie franchises into our daily lives. While cultural studies critics reject the overt formalism as well as the abstractions of 1970s film theory, film philosophers critique the same dominant school for its lack of empirical support and theoretical rigor.

Film and Philosophy

As we have described, the film theory of the 1970s draws on a closely linked body of works from Marxist, psychoanalytic, and linguistic traditions to produce an account of the film experience in which an abstractly conceived spectator is "subjected" (in the double sense of "ruled by" and "given subjectivity") to a visual system that conforms with the principles of a philosophical tradition equating vision with truth and possession. Although the set of ideas codified in film theory did expand to include certain challenges to its model, particularly from feminism, other key concerns of film studies, including questions of aesthetics and history, are given short shrift. The paradigm is being challenged by eminent American film scholars, some of them philosophers, who attack its evidence and arguments (and especially the lack thereof). The dominant school has been dubbed "grand theory" because of its sweeping claims and failure to distinguish among the effects of specific films. To some extent all film theory is related to philosophy and characterized by

- a search for underlying principles
- a logical argument

Noel Carroll carefully and gleefully debunks such proposals as an analogy of film to dream; other scholars point out the flawed reasoning in using linguistic models to describe sounds and images. David Bordwell, one of the most prolific and well-respected film scholars, advocates a **cognitivist** approach to the medium. Cognition is the overall process of knowing, including perception, memory, and judgment. Cognitivist film theory understands our response to film in terms of rational evaluation of visual and narrative cues. Based in psychological research, it advocates verifiable scientific approaches. Rejecting analysis that invokes unconscious fantasy or employs idiosyncratic interpretation, cognitivism claims that we respond to the visual stimuli of the moving image with the same perceptual processes we use to respond to visual stimuli in the world—adjusting film images for lack of depth, perceiving the identity of objects that are moving and changing in time. Not simply a backlash against the obscure terminology and French-influenced syntax of poststructuralist theory, cognitive film theory argues for a less metaphorical, more scientific, and historically verifiable definition and practice of theory. American philosopher Stanley Cavell, in *The World Viewed* (1971) and subsequent works, discusses the aesthetic experience of watching films as a philosophical encounter in its own right, one related to the rhetorical tradition of philosophy.

Phenomenology, which stresses that any act of perception involves a mutuality of viewer and viewed, has also had a profound effect on film theory. Lacan and Metz drew their emphasis on the gaze from phenomenologists, but the psychoanalytic concept of the unconscious drew away from the more embodied consciousness that phenomenology described. More recently, Vivian Sobchack returns to the phenomenology of perception in accounting for the film experience as intersubjective.

Finally, French philosopher Gilles Deleuze has made a unique contribution to recent film theory, building on the semiotics of Peirce and the work of other philosophers. More than the writings of almost any other film theorist, Deleuze's work must be studied on its own terms because he develops ideas through specific interrelated terminology. But the investment is rewarding. In his books on cinema, Deleuze's basic distinction is between two types of cinema that correspond roughly to two historical periods. The "movement image," prevalent in the cinema of the early twentieth century, reflects what might be called a cause-and-effect view of the world. The physical comedy of Buster Keaton and the collision at the heart of Eisenstein's montage represent action and a linear or dialectical forward movement that provoke a response in the viewer. The "time image" is displayed in films by such masters as the neorealist Roberto Rossellini and the more metaphorical Michelangelo Antonioni in the wake of the disillusionment and uncertainty of postwar Italy. In such movies, images and sounds do not give clear signals of spatial connection or logical sequence; instead, they represent the open-endedness

Figure 11.41 *L'Avventura* (1960). According to philosopher Gilles Deleuze, this classic art film presents "a direct image of time," in part through its unpredictable editing patterns.

of time and the potentiality of thought **[Figure 11.41]**. Deleuze's philosophy of film goes beyond the specific films and directors he uses as examples to suggest new ways of imagining the relationship between images and the world. **Referentiality,** the idea that filmic images refer to actual objects, events, or phenomena, which had remained something like a first principle (an undisputed, though often implicit, given) throughout the history of film theory, was now being rethought. For Deleuze, the film image is not a representation of the world; it is an experience of movement or time itself. For other thinkers, referentiality is no longer a tenet of film theory because both film and the world are not what they used to be.

Postmodernism and New Media

Obviously, film is no longer the only medium that organizes our audiovisual experience. At least since the 1940s, when television became rapidly adopted into U.S. homes, other moving-image media have challenged cinema's dominance. Francis Ford Coppola predicts that digital media will soon replace film stock. However, such developments also suggest that this book's title is more apt than ever before: film has so thoroughly transformed our overall experience that we are prepared for the integration of digital media and other image technologies in our lives. Rather than defining film more narrowly, we can think of it more broadly.

Referentiality is no longer primary in this conception because since the late-twentieth century, we can be understood as living in the era of **postmodernism.** The term *modernism* refers both to the group of artistic movements—from atonal music to cubist painting to montage filmmaking—and to the period in which those movements emerged and to which they responded—generally, the first half of the twentieth century. Similarly, *postmodernism* has two primary definitions:

1. Stylistically, in architecture, art, music, and film, postmodernism is a style that incorporates many other styles through fragments or references in a practice known as **pastiche.** That is, it is a triumph of style itself.
2. Historically, postmodernism is the cultural period in which political, cultural, and economic shifts engendered challenges to the tenets of modernism, including its belief in the possibility of critiquing the world through art, the division of high and low culture, and the genius and independent identity of the artist.

The most important thinkers on postmodernism have addressed both aspects of this definition. Fredric Jameson defines postmodernism historically as "the cultural logic of late capitalism," referring to the period in postwar economic history when advertising and consumerism, multinational conglomerates, and globalization of financing and services took over from industrial production and circulation of goods. Stylistically, postmodern cinema represents history as nostalgia, as if the past were nothing more than a movie that could be quoted.

For Jean Baudrillard, the triumph of the image in our cultural age is so complete that we live in a **simulacrum,** a copy without an original, of which Disneyland is one of his most illuminating examples. In *The Matrix* (1999) and its sequels, the characters' belief that they live in the "real world" is mistaken: the city, food, intimate relationships, and physical struggles are all computer-generated **[Figure 11.42]**. This lack of referentiality is frightening in that it represents the absence of any overarching certainty to ground postmodern fragmentation. But on the hopeful side, the "real" is now open to change. When *The Matrix* shows a (fake) book written by Baudrillard, the film is both making an in-joke and illustrating postmodernism's feeling that there is nothing new in the world.

It is no accident that the postmodern world is most vividly presented in a movie because movies themselves are simulations. Film theorist Anne Friedberg notes that the way we consume film images can be generalized to a society characterized by image consumption and mobility. But the variety

Figure 11.42 *The Matrix* (1999). "What is the matrix?" the film's ad campaign asked. Postmodern theorist Jean Baudrillard is quoted in the film.

Clueless about Contemporary Film Theory?

et us start with the assumption that the issues debated within an academic discourse such as film theory are important issues of the times. This is not to say that the term "referent" will turn up on the evening news. But the fact is that when the Supreme Court rules that virtual pornography must be considered constitutionally protected speech because it does not involve actual photographs of subjects posing, the problem of referentiality is of critical social importance.

Theoretical questions will be present in all the sites that a culture uses for debate and conversation, including popular films. Although the title of the 1995 film *Clueless* would seem to disclaim any form of knowledge whatsoever, many theoretical issues are raised by the film. *Clueless* helps "clue us in" to the concerns of postmodern cinema and is also of particular interest to feminist and cultural studies critics.

Clueless takes place in Los Angeles, a city whose freeways (the view through the windshield resembles that of a movie screen), location, cultural diversity, entertainment industry, commercial and artistic gems of pastiche architecture, and rampant consumerism have made it exemplary for theorists of postmodernism. The film's main character is a high school student, whose age and gender give her marginal social power. But as a blonde, white, rich girl, she is the perfect representative of consumerism. A "remake" or update of Jane Austen's novel *Emma*, the film is a nostalgic but inauthentic citation of the culture of another era. The main character's name, Cher, is another citation, this one of the inauthentic culture of the recent past (pop star Cher is known for her costumes and transformations). The multiculturalism of postmodern Los Angeles is signaled by Cher's group of school friends. Yet this is a tongue-in-cheek depiction because Cher's African American best friend, Dionne, is as fabulously wealthy as she is: the girls are worlds apart in socioeconomic terms from Cher's Latina housekeeper, for example.

The film opens with a montage of fresh-faced teenagers, and with postmodern irony Cher's voiceover compares it to the montage of an acne-product commercial. The fact that identity is a matter of surface is underscored in the next set of images—Cher "tries on" different outfits using a computer program

of "looks" one finds by window-shopping or identifying with other characters at the movies has a positive side. The postmodern breakdown of singular identity has as its corollary a recognition of identities—of African Americans, women, immigrants, and other "others"—formerly relegated to the margins of society.

In the context of today's postmodern society, film theory must meet the challenge of new technologies such as computer-generated imagery, which literally does not have a referent. Extinct species can be brought to life containing simulations of the ample contents of her closet **[Figure 11.43]**. After the character transformation she undergoes in the course of the film, Cher nevertheless still understands social problems in commodity-culture terms: she donates her skis to the homeless. Appropriately, while window shopping Cher finally realizes what she truly wants as bits of the film replay in her mind, a thorough confusion of "real" and cinematic perception that perfectly illustrates what Anne Friedberg calls postmodernism's "mobilized virtual gaze."

Figure 11.43 *Clueless* (1995). Postmodern style and attitude in a film that found a welcome reception among young women.

Admittedly, the description thus far makes the film seem as if it is concerned only with the trivial. But feminist theorists point out that women's consignment to the domestic sphere with its "trivial" concerns of shopping and romance has direct effect on the public sphere, which was as true in Jane Austen's day as it is in our own. Cher's ostensibly minor concerns have important consequences in her world. Moreover, the film portrays her subjectivity by her voiceover and her optical point of view, which gives her perspective validity. The film was directed by a woman, Amy Heckerling, who has specialized in youth genre films that pay special attention to young women's perspectives; Austen, too, was consigned to a circumscribed genre within which she made enduring works of art. Viewers might find *Clueless*'s romantic ending disappointing in that it undermines what has so far been the film's most important relationship—the one between Cher and Dionne and the other girls—by conflating plot closure with heterosexual coupling. But this convention is also derived from traditionally female genres, and, like earlier examples, it represents the triumph of the young woman's concerns over other, usually more culturally valued, agendas. In fact, the film winks at the "happily-ever-after" convention, ending with a wedding and suggesting for a moment it is Cher's. "As if!" her voiceover exclaims—two schoolteachers she helped fix up are getting married. She escapes the strictures of the plot with postmodern irony.

To viewers familiar with the film, an analysis of its visual system is somewhat beside the point; what is most remarkable about it is its reception. *Clueless* successfully addressed a teenage interpretive community, both in and outside the United States, which quickly adopted the film's styles in fashion and slang. Young women's "use" of the film was generally positive. *Clueless* validated and enabled (coded) communication among young girls who, far from being treated yet again as know-nothings, were now the only ones fully "clued in." Multiple viewing makes for an open-ended text; *Clueless* sums up the complexity of postmodern simulation in a succinct "as if!"

through modern science—not through biology as *Jurassic Park* (1993) imagines, but through digital technology in the form of the film itself.

Our survey of the history of contemporary film theory evokes the fortuitous institutional climate of the academic discipline of film studies in Anglo-American universities, which has consolidated and developed ideas from France and elsewhere since the late 1960s. This story of the origins of contemporary film theory can be told fairly smoothly, and that should make us suspicious. Fields of knowledge tend to advance by active questioning and dissent. As we have noted, cultural studies and cognitivism have challenged the orthodoxies that began to emerge in film theory, and their pluralism and skepticism add a welcome perspective on ideas that might otherwise become rote and ossified, simply "applied" to new cases. Scholars continue to draw on the legacies of previous inquiries in order to identify the salient questions our contemporary audiovisual experience raises and to develop tools with which to address those questions.

This chapter has aimed to demystify the field of film theory, which is not to imply that we will not have to struggle with theory or do some work to understand film on a more abstract plane. Because film theory is a notoriously impacted discourse, any breezy summary gives it much more continuity than it warrants. In reading and picking apart theorists' work, it is important to recall that referring to "theory" in the abstract is misleading. The term is a useful, shorthand way to refer to a body of knowledge and a set of questions. We study this corpus to gain historical perspective, to acquire tools for decoding our experiences of particular films, and, above all, to comprehend the hold that movies have on our imaginations, desires, and experience.

CRITICAL VOICES: CHRISTIAN METZ ON SPECTATORSHIP

In *The Imaginary Signifier* (1975), film theorist Christian Metz explores the nature of our deep involvement with the cinematic illusion. He attributes our receptiveness to the medium's images and sounds to their close resemblance to fantasy and dreams, the realm that French psychoanalyst Jacques Lacan called the imaginary. Paradoxically, the means of expression, or signifiers, that cinema uses are not really present in time and space when we watch movies. The strength of their effect on spectators is derived from our earliest perceptual impressions. The following excerpt from *The Imaginary Signifier* is taken from the section headed "Identification, Mirror."

What first strikes one then is that the cinema is *more perceptual*, if the phrase is allowable, than many other means of expression; it mobilizes a larger number of the axes of perception. (That is why the cinema has sometimes been presented as a "synthesis of all the arts"; which does not mean very much, but if we restrict ourselves to the quantitative

1

tally of the registers of perception, it is true that the cinema contains within itself the signifiers of the other arts: it can present pictures to us, make us hear music, it is made of photographs, etc.)

Nevertheless this as it were numerical "superiority" disappears if the cinema is compared with the theatre, the opera and other spectacles of the same type. The latter two involve sight and hearing simultaneously, linguistic audition and nonlinguistic audition, movement, real temporal progression. Their difference from the cinema lies elsewhere: they do not consist of *images*, the perceptions they offer to the eye and the ear are inscribed in a true space (not a photographed one), the same one as that occupied by the public during the performance; everything the audience hear and see is actively produced in their presence. . . . This is not the problem of fiction but that of the definitional characteristics of the signifier: whether or not the theatrical play mimes a fable, its *action*, if need be mimetic, is still managed by real persons evolving in real film and space, *on the same stage or "scene" as the public.* . . .

At the theatre, Sarah Bernhardt may tell me she is Phèdre or, if the play were from another period and rejected the figurative regime, or she might say, as in a type of modern theatre, that she is Sarah Bernhardt. But at any rate, I should see Sarah Bernhardt. At the cinema, she could make the same two kinds of speeches too, but it would be her shadow that would be offering them to me (or she would be offering them in her own absence). Every film is a fiction film.

THE NEXT LEVEL: ADDITIONAL SOURCES

Andrew, Dudley. *Concepts in Film Theory*. Oxford: Oxford University Press, 1984. A thoughtful introduction to issues taken up in contemporary film theory.

Braudy, Leo, and Marshall Cohen, eds. *Film Theory and Criticism*. 5th ed. New York: Oxford University Press, 1999. This anthology brings together important essays from classical and contemporary theorists from Münsterberg to Mulvey.

Lehman, Peter, ed. *Defining Cinema*. New Brunswick: Rutgers University Press, 1997. Essays and contemporary commentaries on five major theorists, from Eisenstein to Metz.

Stam, Robert. *Film Theory: An Introduction*. Malden: Blackwell, 2000. A concise, vivid account covering contemporary classical contributions and including fresh examples from global traditions.

Stam, Robert, and Ella Shohat. *Unthinking Eurocentrism: Multiculturalism and the Media*. London: Routledge, 1998. Rich with examples from many film traditions, this book is a theoretical intervention that also opens up Western thinking about the cinema.

Writing a Film Essay: Observations, Arguments, Research, and Analysis

As a critic, I thought of myself as a film-maker. Today I still think of myself as a critic, and in a sense I am, more than ever before. Instead of writing criticism, I make a film, but the critical dimension is subsumed. I think of myself as an essayist, producing essays in novel form or novels in essay form: only instead of writing, I film them. Were the cinema to disappear, I would simply accept the inevitable and turn to television; were television to disappear, I would revert to pencil and paper. For there is a clear continuity between all forms of expression. It's all one. The important thing is to approach it from the side which suits you best. . . .

—Jean-Luc Godard, writer and critic for *Cahiers du cinéma* and director of *Breathless* (1959), *Contempt* (1963), and *New Wave* (1990)

KEY OBJECTIVES

How do you write a paper about a movie? How do you conduct and then use research on a film? For students especially, writing about films is another important experience in their relationship with them. Writing extends the complex relationship we each have with films by challenging us to articulate our feelings and ideas and to communicate convincingly the validity of our response. This chapter will explain

- how to distinguish between reviews and critical essays
- how to take notes on films
- how to organize those notes
- how to choose a topic and develop it into a thesis and argument for a paper
- how to conduct and integrate research sources
- how to turn your work into a polished essay

Writers can be found everywhere in films and film history. In modern movies alone, famous and not-so-famous writers populate and drive many kinds of stories about many kinds of experience. *Mishima* (1985) describes the intense blend of radically conservative politics and restless creativity in the life of Japanese author Yukio Mishima. In Cameron Crowe's semi-autobiographical *Almost Famous* (2000), a young music reviewer, William Miller, encounters rock journalist Lester Bangs **[Figure 12.1]** from whom he receives the advice that motivates his life—to always "write honestly and mercilessly." In *Central Station* (1998), a middle-aged woman, Dora, sets up a stand in the middle of a crowded railroad station where illiterate people come to have her write letters to their friends and loved ones. Why have writers such as these been such regular and important subjects in movies? The answer is that writing is one of the most fundamental, incisive, and discriminating ways of making sense of the world and our many experiences of it.

Writing about films is, in turn, one of the most incisive and discriminating ways to respond to this cultural and personal experience that many of us consider central to our lives.

Figure 12.1 *Almost Famous* (2000). "To write honestly and mercilessly."

After being entertained or annoyed or moved by a movie, most people do not naturally respond by putting their thoughts down on paper. Professional film critics might write regular columns about why particular movies succeed or fail, but most viewers are satisfied with sharing a few casual remarks about a movie with other viewers and a quick evaluation about whether they enjoyed it or not. Few experiences, however, trigger the energies and interests that promote good writing more than going to the movies does. Even a casual experience at the movies usually leads to discussion and sometimes argument, not only about whether a movie is good or bad but about what happened in the film and why. After seeing David Fincher's *Fight Club* (1999) [Figure 12.2]—about a disaffected young man, his strange bond with an odd new friend, and their creation of male "fight clubs" in the United States—two viewers might disagree vehemently about it. One might see it as an incoherent and self-indulgent celebration of macho culture, whereas the other might see a biting satire on consumerism and male identity. As they refine, develop, and muster details to support their positions, each begins to shape an argument. This same process, moving from an opinion or interpretation to a refined argument, is behind most strong essays on films.

Writing about film has been a significant part of film culture since the beginnings of movies. Almost simultaneously with the arrival of the cinema, writers debated the function and value of this new art. Film critics such as Vachel Lindsay (in his 1915 book *The Art of the Moving Picture*) and Dorothy Richardson (in the 1920s art magazine *Close Up*) wrote passionately about movies in the first few decades of film history. Since then movie reviews, scholarly essays, and philosophical books—by writers James Agee, Pauline Kael, Trinh T. Minh-ha, and Umberto Eco, for example—have debated the achievements of individual films and the cultural importance of movies in general. As with other arts and cultural activities, movies inspire a common

Figure 12.2 *Fight Club* (1999). Provoking critical debate.

and fundamental human need to explain one's feelings about and responses to a significant encounter, to shape, clarify, and order those reactions as an understanding. In this chapter, we will see how writing about film develops from these needs and inspirations and show how it can become a rich extension of our fundamental film experiences.

Writing an Analytical Film Essay

Ways to write about film are as diverse as the individuals doing the writing. In 1915, early reviewers and critics often focused their responses to films on the dangerous or uplifting effects that movies might have on women or children. In the 1960s, film was frequently discussed in terms of its political impact or social meaning. Today's writers focus on a range of topics—from characters, stars, and stories to new film technologies or historical questions, such as how censorship influences film content.

Personal Opinion and Objectivity

The process of writing about a film usually involves a play between subject matter and meaning. The **subject matter** of a film is the material that directly or indirectly comprises the film, whereas the **meaning** is the interpretation a writer discovers within that material. In *Crouching Tiger, Hidden Dragon* (2000), for instance, the subject matter includes the five main characters and their adventures in feudal China. The warrior Li Mu Bai returns to a town where he encounters his soul mate, Yu Shu Lien, the vengeful Jade Fox and her ferocious but naive companion Jen Yu, and Jen Yu's lover, the desert fighter Lo. The interaction of these characters describes a journey through China that ends in love and death. The subject matter's meaning, however, is more complicated than any simple description; the meaning will depend on the film's style and organization, the values and traditions informing it, as well as the experience and thinking of the viewer responding to it. Other films certainly use the subject matter of martial arts combat or the trials of love and honor in ancient China, but *Crouching Tiger, Hidden Dragon* creates and elicits more specific meanings for those who have seen it. For some writers, this martial arts tale of love and honor weaves subtle and often complex points about women and their desires and about the importance of love over mastery **[Figure 12.3]**. For other writers, the film transforms its Asian subject matter into a Western take on self-knowledge and sacrifice.

Figure 12.3 *Crouching Tiger, Hidden Dragon* (2000). Discovering the meaning behind the subject matter.

Figure 12.4 *Crouching Tiger, Hidden Dragon* (2000). A matter of opinion: suicide or liberation?

The meanings a writer finds in a film are not simply personal and arbitrary. No film can mean whatever one chooses to make it mean, and useful and insightful writing always balances opinion and critical objectivity. **Opinion** or **subjectivity** indicates personal responses and evaluations. **Critical objectivity,** however, refers to a more detached response, one that offers judgments that others would or could agree with but that bases those conclusions on facts and evidence. Good writing about film is a balance of both: your personal views and opinions are where insights and evaluations usually begin, but for your essay to make sense to others, you must convince your readers that your insights have a larger, more objective truth.

An essay that hides behind personal opinion—constantly inserting "I feel" or "In my opinion"—will seem too personal to have any value for others. Writing about *Crouching Tiger, Hidden Dragon*, a writer may attempt to hide behind a lack of certainty about the meaning: "In my opinion, Jen's final leap off the mountain side is very ambiguous. I think her decision was probably a suicide, but it seemed to me to be a strangely beautiful act" [**Figure 12.4**]. Conversely, writing that relies only on flat, descriptive statements fails to interest readers in its argument and often misses the subtleties of a film: "Jen's leap off the mountain is a suicide. It is a liberating flight into mist." Balancing opinion and critical objectivity, as in the following passage, results in writing that engages and convinces your reader that your insights could be useful revelations for most viewers of the film:

> The conclusion of *Crouching Tiger, Hidden Dragon* is both shocking and uplifting, a combination that disturbs and confuses me, as it probably does for most viewers. This confusion about Jen's motives is, however, part of the strange and mysterious beauty of the film because it asks us to recognize a central theme: the possibility that love and passion can transcend any physical limitations when we have faith in that love.

Identifying Your Readers

Knowing or anticipating your readers is central to writing about film and indeed to all writing, often guiding a writer in balancing opinion and objectivity. If we think of writing about film as an extension of those conversations or arguments we may have with friends about a film, we realize that the terms and tone of our personal discussions change with different people.

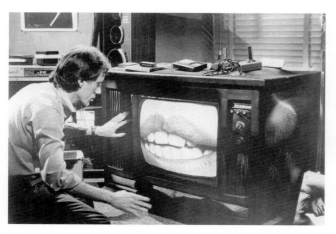

Figure 12.5 *Videodrome* (1983). The finer points of science fiction.

A conversation between two knowledgeable fans of science fiction films would likely presume that they have both seen many of the same films and know a great deal about special effects technologies; the discussion might thus get quickly to the finer points about what makes *Videodrome* (1983) and its tale of mind control through television successful—or not—within this genre **[Figure 12.5]**. In talking about Ken Loach's *Raining Stones* (1993) with an American film buff, a British viewer might have to provide some political and social background—about Manchester, England, where the film is set, about the government of then–Prime Minister Margaret Thatcher, or about the particular cultural complications of the protagonist being a Catholic in this British industrial town. Possessing an awareness of your readers is like knowing the person you are talking with: it helps determine the amount of basic information you need to provide, the level of complexity of the discussion, and the kind of language you should use.

The following four questions are useful guidelines in gearing your essay to certain readers:

- How familiar are your readers with the specific film being discussed?
- What is your readers' level of interest in the film?
- What do your readers know about the film's historical and cultural contexts?
- How familiar are your readers with the terminology of film criticism or theory?

For most critical essays, anticipating your readers' knowledge of the film means assuming they have seen the film at least once and, consequently, do not require an extensive plot summary. In these cases, their interest in the film generally means they are not primarily concerned with whether a movie is good or bad or with other general observations. Rather, they want to be enlightened about a specific dimension of the film (such as the opening shot) or about a complicated or puzzling issue in the film (why the races of different characters in the 1987 *Lethal Weapon,* for instance, are important to understanding the action of the film). A good writer works to convince readers that their interests can be deepened and enriched by following the interests of the writer. Knowledge of historical and critical contexts refers to how much your readers may know or need to know about the place and time of the film's appearance. If the film was made in the United States in the 1920s, would information about that period help your readers better understand the film? Finally, determining your reader's familiarity with the terminology of film criticism and theory means choosing language that can efficiently and clearly communicate your argument. Can you assume that a term like *continuity editing* will be easily understood or will you need to define it? In making these decisions about language, keep in mind that overly simplistic language and jargon can equally undermine your analysis.

In most college and university film courses, you will have in mind an audience that is not only your professor but also your classroom peers: intelligent individuals who have seen the film, who share information and knowledge about film criticism, but who are not necessarily experts (to whom you could tell little). This means you can concentrate on a particular theme or sequence that may have been overlooked by an intelligent viewer. It also means your writing style and choice of words should be more rigorous and academic than the typical movie review.

Elements of the Analytical Film Essay

Two common forms of film writing are film reviews and analytical essays. Aimed at a general audience who has not seen the film, a **film review** tends to be a short essay that describes the plot of a movie, provides useful background information (about the actors and the director, for example), and pronounces a clear evaluation of the film to guide its readers. In contrast, the **analytical essay,** distinguished by its intended audience and the level of its critical language, is the most common kind of writing done by film students and scholars. It typically focuses on a particular feature or theme of a film, provides an interpretation of that material, and then gives a careful analysis to prove or demonstrate that interpretation. Unlike the writer of a movie review for a magazine, the writer of an analytical essay presumes that readers know the film and do not require an extensive plot summary or background information. Although a clear and engaging style is the goal of any kind of writing about film, the writer of an analytical essay often chooses words and terms that can effectively communicate complex ideas and uses the language of intelligent readers of film criticism.

Consider this passage from a hypothetical essay about *O Brother, Where Art Thou?* (2001) **[Figure 12.6]**, written for a college film course. Whereas a newspaper review might summarize the plot, offer some background information, and employ more casual language, note how this analytical essay concentrates on a specific and subtle argument:

```
      Joel and Ethan Coen's O Brother, Where Art Thou? (2001)
is much more than a musical comedy loosely structured around
The Odyssey. Woven through the distinctive soundtrack, the
plot set in Depression-era America, and the comic exaggera-
tions of its characters, the film is a sharp ideological
critique of race and class in modern America. Regularly mis-
taken to be African Americans, the three escaped convicts,
Everett, Pete, and Delmar, learn quickly that their lower-
class white status binds them most importantly to the fate
```

Figure 12.6 *O Brother, Where Art Thou?* (2001). The focus for a precise analysis.

Figure 12.7 *O Brother, Where Art Thou?* (2001). Race, class, and the meaning of the movie.

of the black men and women they encounter, and from this predicament the film explores the economic and political power structures that then and now make poverty color blind. Two sequences in particular dramatize this less noticed but more provocative dimension of the film: the arrival of the prisoners at a church to see a movie (a direct reference to Preston Sturges's film *Sullivan's Travels,* in which the Coens found the title for their movie) and the Ku Klux Klan rally where the fugitives rescue their black comrade Tommy.

Here, the essay's focus is relatively refined and sophisticated, assuming its readers have seen and know the film and concentrating not on general information, but on a specific thesis about race and class **[Figure 12.7]**. Along with its choice of a polemical thesis (an analysis directed at two particular sequences that may not have been carefully considered by many viewers), this critical essay employs terms (such as "ideological critique") suited to academic writing.

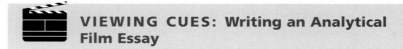

VIEWING CUES: Writing an Analytical Film Essay

■ Examine a short critical essay about a film you have seen in class. What subjective versus objective claims does the author make about the film? How does the writer argue in support of his or her opinions in order to justify their validity for readers?

■ Prepare to write an analytical essay about a film you have seen in class. First, consider your readers. What defines them? What are their interests? What do they need or want to know about the film?

■ What is objectively true in your argument? What might be considered opinion? Write a passage arguing for the validity of your opinion while also eliciting your readers' interest.

■ Examine the language of your essay (or another analytical essay). Which words and phrases best identify your intended audience? The level of your analysis? Where could your language be improved or clarified?

IN FOCUS

Analyzing *Citizen Kane* (1941)

For more than sixty years, viewers have responded to Orson Welles's *Citizen Kane* with a seemingly endless variety of opinions. Some find it fascinating; others feel it is boring or confusing. The character of Susan Alexander fascinates some viewers; the final sequence in which the camera surveys a large room full of Kane's many acquisitions intrigues others. Any of these opinions about or reactions to *Citizen Kane* could be developed into an interesting and provocative essay about the film, but only if those ideas can be substantiated or proven useful, true, and important—only if, that is, they can be shown to have objective accuracy.

One such viewer decides to write a review of *Citizen Kane* for his college newspaper in anticipation of the film's upcoming appearance at the college art house. Despite the celebrity of the film, the writer presumes that many of his potential readers have not yet seen it and need both information and balanced opinions. He proceeds with a clear sense of what his readers already know, don't know, and need to know about the film:

> *Citizen Kane* is one those movies that everyone talks about but few have ever seen. When it first appeared in 1941, the film was surrounded by enormous hype about the debut of the "boy genius" Orson Welles and his ballyhooed transition from the New York stage to the Hollywood screen. Before the film even appeared, rumors also connected *Citizen Kane* to the life of William Randolph Hearst, the U.S. newspaper mogul, and this too made the movie something of a fascinating scandal. In the six decades since its release, *Citizen Kane* has appeared at the top of almost every list of the "greatest movies ever made" and appears in practically every film course in the world.
>
> Be prepared for a bit of a disappointment. The story is simple enough: played wonderfully by Welles himself, Charles Foster Kane grows, with the help of a windfall fortune, from a boy torn from his childhood home in Colorado into a lonely man obsessed with power and possessions. For me, the story is melodramatic and overblown, and Kane never becomes a very likeable character. What redeems *Citizen Kane*, however, is the construction of the story: different parts of Kane's story are told through the eyes of his friends and acquaintances, and these shifting perspectives create a kind of visual puzzle that the movie never really solves, enlivening an otherwise dull tale.

This black-and-white film is a continuous series of stunning (and famous) shots, such as the opening sequence of dark shots that takes viewers past a "No Trespassing" sign to Kane's deathbed. In our age of computer technologies and new-wave television commercials, these images will probably seem less surprising and innovative than they did when the movie first appeared. Yet *Citizen Kane* remains a film to see—if only to judge for yourself whether it is among the "greatest movies ever made."

The same writer later chooses to write the following critical essay about *Citizen Kane* for a film history course. In this case, his readers are his professor and the other students in the class, readers who are familiar with the film and have even read other material about *Citizen Kane*.

Of the many critical essays on *Citizen Kane*, three different perspectives on its meaning dominate the analytical writing about the film: analyses that focus on the mythic character of Kane, discussions of the kaleidoscopic narrative structure that shapes the story, and detailed interpretations of the stylistic compositions (such as the use of deep-focus and dramatic editing techniques). Using the first two types of analysis as a background, I will examine a single, early scene in *Citizen Kane* to demonstrate the legendary visual power of the film. In this scene, *Citizen Kane* crystallizes a family drama of loss and division inseparable from a life lived in dense and complex spaces and perceived from many points of view.

In this tale of Charles Foster Kane's rise to a position as one of the richest and most powerful men in America, the episode in question sets the stage for the entire film. It succinctly describes the sudden wealth of Kane's mother, an unexpected windfall from a deed to a gold mine (mistakenly presumed useless), and her subsequent arrangement to send Charles to be educated on the East Coast. The film's setting is the rustic family cabin in Colorado, with glimpses of the snowy yard outside where the child, Charlie Kane, plays.

In this scene, one shot begins by showing Charles making snowballs in the field, then moves back to show his mother in the foreground watching from inside and, through an open window, the boy building a snowman in the background [**Figure 12.8**]. Here the window frame within the film frame calls attention to how a point of view controls perspective in certain ways, specifically the point of view on the child Kane.

Figure 12.8 *Citizen Kane* (1941). Analytical detail.

As the shot pulls back further, the frame then expands to include the central conversation about the boy and the money, while the original subject of the shot, Charlie, now becomes a much smaller, background figure in the action and the frame.

The shot pulls back even further, following the mother's movement away from the window, and the frame creates visible tensions and conflicts among the individuals. The stern face and upper body of the mother, Mrs. Kane, dominates the center of the image, flanked by the banker Thatcher, while Charlie's father drifts along the edges of the frame, complaining, "You seem to forget I'm the boy's father." Moments later, Thatcher and Mrs. Kane sit at a table in the foreground of the image and prepare to sign papers authorizing the child's departure, while the father protests in vain in the middle ground and Charlie remains barely visible in the far background playing outside in the snow [**Figure 3.30**]. The rectangular shape of the frame crowds these characters within a tight visual space, even including the ceiling on the top of the frame as a way of further drawing in the space. Positioned between the adult individuals but in the far background is the diminutive shape of Charlie, the subject of their quarreling and plans to remove him from the home. Visually it is fairly clear how power and control are being distributed through this frame: the mother and Thatcher visually overwhelm the father, and the tiny figure of Charles is the impotent object of exchange.

In *Citizen Kane,* Charles Foster Kane grows up to become obsessed with the power of images—paintings, newspaper pictures, images of himself [**Figure 12.9**]. This obsession perhaps acts out his semi-conscious struggle to replace the image of his lost childhood and family torn apart in this early scene in the film. Throughout the remainder of his life, Kane struggles to create, own, and control the people and things around him by imposing his perspective on them—the way the perspective of others controlled him early in his life. The film is also a narrative constructed around the multiple points of view of Kane's friends, wife, and associates, all of whom dramatize how points of view can attempt to frame a man's life as a way of understanding or interpreting that life. The irony and tragedy of Charlie Kane's life is that no one, not even Kane himself, is able to reconstruct the complete picture and harmony that were lost in that early childhood scene.

Figure 12.9 *Citizen Kane* (1941). Describing and interpreting.

Preparing to Write about a Film

Despite some common ground, an effective film essay does differ from a casual conversation or debate about a movie. Few writers can dash off a perceptive commentary on a film with little preparation or revision. Most writers gain considerably from anticipating what they will write about and later reviewing carefully what they have written. Few of us casually watch *The Sorrow and the Pity* (1970), a powerful documentary about fascism in France during World War II, and then immediately type a brilliant paper on Marcel Ophuls's use of documentary strategies to expose certain myths about French history or the French Resistance. Like all good writers, you must follow certain steps in preparing to write an essay.

Asking Questions

One of the most fundamental and useful first steps is to try to identify your own interests *before* you view the film. Ask yourself how you think the film might relate to your own background and experiences or what you have heard about the film. Are you drawn to technology or to questions about gender? To a particular filmmaker or period in movie history? To a certain national cinema? What direction of inquiry does your interest point toward? In Howard Hawks's 1938 *Bringing Up Baby*, Katharine Hepburn plays an audacious heiress, Susan, whose pet leopard Baby becomes the foil in her zany relationship with a bumbling paleontologist, David, played by Cary Grant [**Figure 12.10**]. If you are about to see this film, perhaps you've seen other films by Hawks, like *His Girl Friday* (1941), or other films with Hepburn, like *The Philadelphia Story* (1940). Might you consider comparing the two Hawks films or Hepburn's two different roles?

Figure 12.10 *Bringing Up Baby* (1938). What to write about?

This sort of preparation is not meant to preclude your being drawn to new ideas and in unexpected directions when you view the film. Surprising discoveries are certainly one of the great values in approaching films with an open mind. While watching *In the Bedroom* (2001), one viewer might become puzzled by how the film seems suddenly to change directions: after depicting the excruciating pain of two parents who have lost a son, the last part of the movie becomes a revenge tale in which the father seeks out and murders his son's killer. For this viewer, what seems at first a slow meditation on inexpressible grief becomes a tense thriller. How do the two parts work together? Does loss always require retribution? Does violence always beget violence? By asking these kinds of questions, you can intellectually interact with a film, sharpening your responses and shaping the direction of your essay.

Taking Notes

Note taking, an essential part of writing about film, stimulates critical thinking and generates precise and productive observations about a film. Whereas most students find it natural to take notes on a biology experiment or on their reading of a Shakespeare play, annotating a film is both awkward and unnatural: it is difficult to write while watching a movie in a darkened room, and most films ask that we constantly attend to them so as not to miss information that passes quickly. Note taking is, however, absolutely necessary to writing about film because a good analytical essay must produce concrete evidence for the argument—and precise notes provide that support.

The three general rules for annotating a film are as follows:

1. Take notes on the unusual—events or formal maneuvers that stand out in the film.
2. Take notes on events or techniques that recur with regularity.
3. Take notes on oppositions that appear in the film.

For instance, most viewers of *Bringing Up Baby* would note that the sequence involving David and Susan at the local jail stands out as one of the funniest and most unusual moments in the film, with Hepburn pretending to be a hardened gangster's moll. Equally important, however, are those actions or images whose repetitions suggest a recurring theme or pattern, such as David's repeatedly losing his clothes or glasses. Oppositions can be equally illuminating, such as the contrast among the rival women: the goofy Susan, and David's staid fiancée, his scientific assistant.

Each writer develops his or her own shorthand for taking notes on films. The trick is to jot down information about the story or characters that seems significant while also recording visual, audial, or other formal details. Some common abbreviations for visual compositions include the following:

es: establishing shot   **ha:** high angle   **ct:** cut
cu: close-up   **la:** low angle   **trs:** tracking shot
ls: long shot   **ds:** diegetic sound   **ps:** pan shot
mls: medium long shot   **nds:** nondiegetic sound   **vo:** voiceover

More specific camera movements and directions can often be re-created with arrows and lines that graph the actions or directions. The following drawings suggest the movements of the camera:

↗ low camera angle   ↘ high camera angle   ⌇ tracking shot

For example, part of the jailhouse sequence in *Bringing Up Baby* [**Figures 12.11 and 12.12**] might be annotated as follows to indicate cuts, camera movements, or angles.

—   mcu of constable and Susan through bars

—   ct mcu David

Figure 12.11 *Bringing Up Baby* (1938). "Swinging Door Susie."   **Figure 12.12** *Bringing Up Baby* (1938). An object of analysis.

Later, these notes would be filled in, perhaps by again reviewing the sequence for more details—such as pieces of the hilarious monologue of "Swinging Door Susie." Drawings of shots can supplement such details. Critical comments or observations might also be added—about, for instance, how the organization of the shot composition and editing provides the contrast between the officious and tongue-tied authority figure of the sheriff and the zany and loquacious Susan.

Selecting a Topic

After taking and reviewing your notes on the film, you need to choose the topic for the paper. Because a film offers so many dimensions to write about—characters, story, music, editing—selecting a manageable topic for an essay can prove daunting. Even a lengthy essay will suffer if it attempts to accomplish too much and address too many issues in a limited amount of space. Narrowing your topic in order to allow your argument to investigate the issues fully and carefully always produces better writing. In a five-or six-page essay, a topic such as "fast-talking comedy in *Bringing Up Baby*" would most likely need to rely on generalities and large claims, whereas "gender, order, and disorder in the jailhouse" is a more focused and manageable topic for a short essay.

Although good critical analysis tends to move among different features of a film, we can distinguish two sets of topics for writing about film—formal and contextual topics. **Formal topics,** which concentrate on forms and ideas within a film, include character analysis, narrative analysis, and stylistic analysis. **Contextual topics,** which relate the film to other films or to surrounding issues, include comparative analysis and historical or cultural analysis. As a formal topic, **character analysis** concentrates its argument on a single character or on the interactions between more than one character, while **narrative analysis** chooses a topic that relates to the story and its construction. **Stylistic analysis** offers a wide variety of topics that engage the formal arrangements of image and sound, such as shot composition, editing, and the use of sound.

Although character analysis appears more available and perhaps easier than other kinds of analyses, a good essay about a character requires subtlety and eloquence. Rather than write about a central character, like Susan in *Bringing Up Baby* or the schizophrenic genius John Nash in *A Beautiful Mind* (2001), a less predictable topic might concentrate on a minor character, such as Susan's aristocratic aunt or Nash's wife Alicia, respectively. Similarly, a topic that involves narrative should usually be refined so that the paper addresses, for instance, the relation of the beginning and end of the film or the way a voiceover comments on and directs the story. A paper that deals with a stylistic topic will be more controllable and incisive if, for instance, it isolates a particular group of shots or identifies a single sound motif that recurs in the film. Therefore, one student may find a topic for a paper by examining the role of the various narrators of Terrence Malick's *The Thin Red Line* (1998). Another student may choose to look more carefully at repeated editing patterns in *The Battleship Potemkin* (1925) or at the use of framing in Yasujiro Ozu's *Tokyo Story* (1953). Any one of these topics will grow more interesting and insightful if you continue to ask questions during the entire writing process: How is the character David in *Bringing Up Baby* a product of costuming or shot composition? How do the various narrators in *The Thin Red Line* reflect different attitudes about war?

A **comparative analysis** develops a contextual topic by evaluating features or elements of two or more different films or perhaps a film and its literary source. A comparative analysis might thus contrast Susan in *Bringing Up Baby* with one or more heroines in more recent films, such as Julia Roberts's character Vivian in *Pretty Woman* (1990) **[Figure 12.13]**. A comparative analysis always allows for some common ground in order to link what you are comparing and contrasting (in the above example, heroines). Conversely, **historical or cultural analysis** investigates topics that relate a film to its place in history, society, or culture. Such a topic might examine historical contexts or debates that surround the

Figure 12.13 *Pretty Woman* (1990). Vivian or Susan: comparing images of cinematic women.

film and help explain it—for example, the social status of women or the importance of class in 1938 America. With historical or cultural analysis, the pertinence of the topic to understanding the film is crucial (in our example, the role of women is obviously important; the historical status of leopards probably is not).

Once a topic has been selected (the more specific, the better), the writer should view the film again. This second viewing allows the writer to refine and build on those initial notes, precisely in terms of the topic he or she now has in mind. The writer who comes to *Bringing Up Baby* with a vague interest in how this film portrays the battle of the sexes might, after seeing the film again, find that she wishes to refocus her topic on how the leopard becomes a metaphor for that battle.

 VIEWING CUES: Preparing to Write about a Film

- In preparation for the film you will view next in class, jot down three or four specific questions you want to direct at the film. While viewing the film, ask three or four additional questions about specific shots or scenes. Then, later on, attempt to answer all of your questions as precisely as possible.

- Which events, sounds, or shots in the film stand out as unusual? As most important? As examples of a pattern of repetition? Describe clearly and concretely one or two events, sounds, or shots from the film.

- Select one key scene or sequence to annotate as precisely as possible. Where are the characters positioned? How are the camera and frame positioned? If the frame moves or cuts occur, describe that movement or the exact location of the cuts. How would you describe the sound, including the dialogue? Support your description with a rough sketch, if applicable.

- Review your notes for possible topics to write about. Look for different categories of topics: character analysis, narrative, stylistics, and historical or comparative issues, for example. Do your notes point you in one of these directions? Make a list of possible topics.

Analyzing Character and Style in Sally Potter's *Orlando* (1993)

Sally Potter's *Orlando* (1993) surprises many first-time viewers. Perhaps most unsettling, the film follows the character Orlando time-traveling through numerous periods of British history. From court life in 1610 and 1650 to the political and social drawing rooms of 1700 and 1750, Orlando, without aging, appears again in the romantic landscapes of 1850 and in the twentieth century from World War I to the 1990s. Complicating this time travel, Orlando, at first a man, unexpectedly becomes a woman. More than in other films, questions come fast and furious: How does one account for the jumps between historical periods and the sexual transformation of the main character? What is the movie saying about gender and identity?

Sketching the story might be the writer's first note-taking task for *Orlando*. After that, the film features so many unusual shots and actions that the writer would need to choose carefully which ones are most important or suggestive. Among the most powerful moments in the film, for example, is Orlando's discovery, as she sees herself in a mirror, that she has transformed from a man into a woman; she casually comments, "Same person, different sex." In addition, the brilliant red hair and alabaster face of actress Tilda Swinton as Orlando stand out as more and more significant through many repeated close-ups, creating a series of images whose radiant beauty seems to supercede the changing historical place and gender. One writer immediately notes the dramatic beginning of the film **[Figure 12.14]**:

— mls: centered tree, Orlan. reading/track back and forth/vo: "There could be no doubt about his sex . . . ."

— cu: Orlan. staring right/vo: "but when he . . . "/quick glance a camera—"That is I"

Later, the writer fills in these annotations—from memory and from another viewing—and formulates a succinct description of the scene:

The opening shot of Sally Potter's *Orlando* shows Orlando reading in a field beneath a single oak tree; as Orlando walks back and forth, the medium long shot tracks back and forth in the opposite direction. After the Elizabethan youth sits down to continue his reading, a close-up shows his profile staring off to the right, while a commentary describes his situation in life. As the female voice-over continues, "But when he . . . ," the luminously pale and red-haired Orlando suddenly turns and looks directly into the camera and corrects the commentator, "That is, I."

During this process, the writer begins to consider topics for her paper. "The meaning of history in *Orlando*" seems far too grand and would most likely need to rely on generalities and large claims. She also considers "the image of the oak tree in *Orlando*" and a comparison of the film with the Virginia Woolf novel on which it is based. Her personal interests lead her to questions about gender, politics, and history, and she is struck by how Orlando's passionate self-expression seems to complicate those issues in fascinating ways. In the end, she gathers her notes and thoughts around a sophisticated character analysis of gender and expression in *Orlando*.

Lee 1

Anna Lee
Professor Corrigan
Film 102
3 November 2003

Expression, Gender, and Character
in Sally Potter's *Orlando*

In the opening shot of Sally Potter's *Orlando*, the title character reads in a field beneath a single oak tree. As Orlando (Tilda Swinton) walks back and forth, the medium long shot tracks back and forth in the opposite direction of his movements. He sits down under the tree, and a close-up shows his profile staring off to the right, while the commentary describes his current situation in life as a privileged member of the Elizabethan aristocracy. As the female voiceover continues, "But when he . . . ," the luminously pale and red-haired Orlando suddenly turns and looks directly into the camera and corrects the commentator, "That is, I." The film then shifts to a series of shots describing a grand court ceremony: a medium long shot shows Queen Elizabeth (Quentin Crisp) arriving by torch light in a regal barge, while close-ups focus on small, expressive details, such as the queen washing her hands in a silver finger bowl [**Figure 12.15**]. In later historical eras, similar rich and dynamic shots, created through erratically tracking shots and shifting

Figure 12.14 *Orlando* (1993). Dramatic beginnings.

Figure 12.15 *Orlando* (1993). Expressive details.

angles, re-create Orlando's perspective on a British history and culture moving through rapid changes. History becomes a pageant of images, and, stylistically, both the narrative and specific shots and edits describe this pageant as an abundant and luxurious activity through which the character of Orlando becomes a carnival of changing identities. Unlike a documentary or a more conventional fiction film, the pageant of this history is the drama of a character relentlessly looking for self-expression in every moment.

Certainly the most remarkable feature of the film's plot, Orlando's character radically changes identities many times throughout the film—and even changes gender. In the beginning, Orlando lives as a male youth in Elizabethan England, but by the eighteenth century, he has become a glamorous "she." In the nineteenth century, Orlando transforms into a romantic heroine, and with the twentieth century, she flies through the horrors of World War I to survive as a single mother with a daughter of her own.

Through the course of this history, social and cultural formulas continually threaten to define and reduce the character of Orlando or to re-create him or her within the strict framework of a single time and place. After his father dies, for example, a medium shot shows Orlando from behind, looking at a large portrait of that man on the wall, an austere and traditional image of the father that displays his dignity, wealth, and aristocratic stature **[Figure 12.16]**. When Orlando turns toward the camera and assumes the same pose as his father, the figure in this painted picture becomes re-created in the stance and look of Orlando, suggesting how generational history might re-create Orlando in the social image of his father. This image is so important because the remaining film acknowledges power of heritage and history to capture and control an individual—in terms of class, gender, or other social positions—while at the same time working to liberate Orlando from those defining powers (and this original patriarchal power). The power of social and historical perspectives to frame and determine the character of Orlando is thus at the heart of this cultural drama, but in situation after situation, Orlando's identity rejects or overcomes those historical images of what he/she *should* be.

Orlando's character wrestles with those social forces of history primarily through the force of passionate self-expression. Early in the film the male Orlando falls deeply in love with the young Russian woman Sasha, despite the clear disapproval by British society

Figure 12.16 *Orlando* (1993). Against the image of the patriarch.

and despite the language barrier. As a determined poet and incurable romantic, Orlando reenacts this kind of rebellious encounter in many forms and with many people, writing poems, seeking exotic adventures, and leaping fully into different romantic trysts. Whether in eighteenth-century Turkey or nineteenth-century England, Orlando is a character who passionately loves life and who seeks passionately to express an identity through love.

In *Orlando*, character is thus a combination of historical conditions and the passionate resistance of the self to those conditions. Out of this conflict arises perhaps the most important quality of character in this film: self-consciousness or self-awareness. From the beginning of the film, Orlando continually reflects on her/his own character and its place in the cultures through which he/she passes, as he/she comments on the relation between identity and its social place and creates an ironic distance between the expression of his/her character in its historical situation. During one conversation in the eighteenth century, a medium shot pans back and forth behind Lady Orlando while a group of famous writers (Alexander Pope and Jonathan Swift, among others) demean the importance of women, so that Orlando's perspective both reveals and debunks the mean-spirited interrogation by the celebrated wits. Indeed, this kind of distance and analysis of Orlando's self and its social context occurs most clearly when Orlando, usually in close-up, turns and directly addresses the camera **[Figure 12.17]**. When Orlando examines the mirror image of herself as a man suddenly turned into a woman, she turns and wryly comments, "Same person. . . . different sex." Later, amidst her ecstatic embrace with the Byronic Shelmerdine, she self-consciously claims the romantic force of this moment by turning to the camera and saying, "I think I'm going to faint. I've never felt better in my life." Orlando's identity and character appear and evolve, consequently, through the complementary activities of both perceiving and reflecting, demonstrating how an individual's passion and love for life can and should engage self-consciously with values and choices about how to live that life.

Whether as a man or a woman, a sixteenth-century nobleman or a rebellious twentieth-century mother, Orlando champions the vibrancy of human presence, moving above and beyond all those historical and cultural differences, beyond all those defining frames. In the last sequence of the film, Orlando, now a modern

Figure 12.17 *Orlando* (1993). Close-ups brimming with expression and confrontation.

woman lounging under the aged oak that opens the film, becomes the object of her own daughter's video recorder. As the child runs toward her mother, we see Orlando now in a bouncing handheld shot that closes in on her face as a tilted out-of-focus image. As the culmination of so many images of Orlando across four centuries, the framed image now seems to deny its own ability to control and capture this character, freeing Orlando as a presence that will not be constricted even by her own daughter and even by the most technologically modern images of her or him.

Although *Orlando* is based on a novel by Virginia Woolf, Potter's stunning adaptation re-creates the essence of the novel as a drama of perception, visual and social frames, and passionate self-assertion. Like other Woolf novels, *Orlando* presents individual character and historical change embracing each other in the changing intensities of human expression. Like other Woolf characters, Orlando is defined not by his/her social or sexual status but rather by the quality of the consciousness through which Orlando perceives and lives those experiences.

Writing a Film Essay

With notes in hand and a topic clearly in mind, writing a film essay becomes a less daunting task. The next step, composing a first draft, will also be less cumbersome because the writer has prepared for the task with a topic and notes. Ideally, the writer should view the film again while working through the following stages of the writing process, in order to sharpen the analysis and confirm details from the film. When a topic leads to a clearly defined thesis, focus, and argument, another viewing of the film inevitably reveals other useful details and leads to new or better formulated ideas and interpretations.

Interpretation, Argument, and Evidence

Whether your topic is a formal analysis of a sequence or a comparison of the narrative point of view of a novel and its filmic adaptation, it needs to be honed and shaped into a precise interpretation and argument. Your **interpretation** is your explanation of what the film or a part of it means. In addition, a good essay must construct a logical **argument**—the presentation and analysis of **evidence** from the film—that convinces readers of the validity of your interpretation. Although different audiences interpret the meaning of all or part of a movie in somewhat different ways, a valid and interesting argument distinguishes itself by the extent to which the analysis of evidence supports the interpretation. Without good evidence, precise analysis, and logical argument, an essay will appear to be simply one viewer's impression or opinion.

Perhaps the single most important element in a good analytical essay is the **thesis statement,** a short statement (often a single sentence) that succinctly describes the interpretation and argument to be presented and proven, with evidence, in the pages that follow. As a significantly refined and focused version of the topic, the thesis statement identifies clearly the writer's critical perspective on the film and should indicate what is at stake in the argument and perhaps how that argument is important to an understanding of the film. Many excellent theses succinctly anticipate each stage of the argument that will follow in the paper. Usually this statement, which appears in the first paragraph of the essay, undergoes various revisions throughout the writing process. Having a **working thesis,** a rough version of a thesis, in mind as you begin your first draft, however, will help anchor your argument. In its final form, a precise and assertive thesis statement is likely to engage readers' interest in the essay.

As with most films, Steven Soderbergh's *Traffic* (2000) and Stephen Frears's *My Beautiful Laundrette* (1985) both offer a wide variety of topics that could be developed into specific arguments and thesis statements. For *Traffic*, a film about the drug trade that flows from Mexico into various U.S. communities, one student writer considers analyzing either the cinéma-vérité camera movements used in the Mexican settings or the transformation of the central character, a U.S. drug czar who sees his daughter destroyed by heroin **[Figure 12.18]**. For *My Beautiful Laundrette*, a contemporary romance between a young Pakistani man and a male friend involved with right-wing British gangs, the writer weighs the advantages of two possible topics—the developing sexual relationship of the two main characters or the mise-en-scène of the laundrette where the climactic scenes take place. After reflecting on these topics and seeing the films again, the student opts for the second film and develops a thesis statement that demonstrates clear and specific direction: "*My Beautiful Laundrette* looks at contemporary British politics from numerous angles: family politics, sexual politics, racial politics, and economic politics. In the end these various political motifs coalesce and climax in a single space that is both practical and fantastic, the mise-en-scène of the laundrette" **[Figure 12.19]**. As clear and intelligent as it is, this proposed thesis statement will no doubt be revised for the final draft of the paper, as the writing will certainly generate new insights and possibly new issues.

Figure 12.18 *Traffic* (2000). An abundance of topics.

Although some writers prefer other methods of organization, preparing an **outline** results in an indispensable blueprint of the essay, allowing the writer to see and examine the different parts and overall development of the argument as it proceeds out of a strong thesis. An outline can be a simple list of ideas to address or shots and scenes to highlight—such as "weak father figures," "house squatting as metaphor for identity," and "description of the laundrette"—or a more complete (and more useful) list that includes subheadings and perhaps full sentences, which can be used as topic sentences (see p. 494) in the essay.

Figure 12.19 *My Beautiful Laundrette* (1985). The climactic mise-en-scène of the laundrette.

Here is the detailed outline prepared by the student working on the essay about *My Beautiful Laundrette:*

```
      The Politics of Laundry in My Beautiful Laundrette

  I. Family politics: the most immediate and complicated type
     A. Fathers and authority
     B. Family traditions and repression
 II. Sexual politics: underpins family situations in way
     that exposes hypocrisy
     A. Heterosexual politics: Nasser, his wife, and his
        mistress Rachel
     B. Feminist politics: Tania, Nasser's daughter
     C. Gay politics: Johnny and Omar
III. Racial politics: nearly lost in this drama is the
     way they permeate all other relationships
     A. Johnny, race, and right-wing politics (National Front)
     B. Papa, race, and left-wing politics
 IV. Economic politics: where the other confrontations
     are—presumably and ironically—resolved
     A. Papa as businessman
     B. Salim as drug dealer
     C. Johnny and Omar as laundry entrepreneurs
  V. These political motifs coalesce and climax in a single
     space that is both practical and fantastic: the mise-
     en-scène of the laundrette
     A. Detailed description of mise-en-scène of laundrette
     B. Pragmatics meet fantasy
     C. Analysis of climactic gathering
```

As this example illustrates, a detailed outline allows the writer to review the structure of the essay and note any problems with the scope or logic of the argument or with the transitions from one section to another. At this stage the topic should be focused on a specific thesis whose parts develop as logical steps in the body of the paper.

Whether you work from an outline or not, a clear organization and structure are paramount for an effective essay, most notably coherent paragraphs introduced and linked by topic sentences. Well-developed paragraphs, which tend to be four to six sentences long, demand coherence and evidence. The most critical part of a good paragraph is the **topic sentence,** the sentence, usually the first, that announces the central idea around which all other sentences within the paragraph cohere. The remainder of the paragraph then develops the idea stated in the topic sentence and provides evidence from the film as support. In the example from the essay on *My Beautiful Laundrette,* note how the strong and lucid topic sentence that opens the paragraph is then supported by evidence:

```
        In My Beautiful Laundrette, the drama of the characters
     is invariably about space, territory, and, most importantly,
     home. In the first sequence of the film, Salim and a hench-
     man evict Johnny and another squatter from an abandoned tene-
```

CULTURAL SPOTLIGHT

From Viewing a Film to Writing a Film Essay

As you grow more confident and practiced as a writer, you will be able to write about films in a fluid motion: watching the film, taking some notes, sketching an outline, and writing the first draft and final essay. Even the most competent writers, however, pause to reflect on their work by consulting a checklist like this one:

1. Review your notes, filling in details where you can. Ideally, view the film one more time.
2. Try to summarize the most important themes or motifs in the film.
3. Formulate a working thesis and argument for the essay.
4. Outline the argument. If possible, use full sentences for headings because they can then become your topic sentences.
5. Develop the central idea of each paragraph with details from the film that support that paragraph's topic sentence.
6. Rewrite your thesis statement to reflect any changes or refinements in your thinking that occurred while writing your first draft.
7. If you are writing a research essay, be sure to use the correct documentation format for in-text citations and the Works Cited list (see pp. 504–6).
8. Revise your essay, checking for large problems such as vague or illogical organization, and proofread for surface errors in spelling and grammar.
9. Select a title that reflects the main argument of your paper.
10. Print out the essay and correct any remaining typographical errors.

---

ment building, and for the rest of the film the metaphor of "squatting" describes the characters' unstable and temporary relations to the places they live and interact. Although most of the characters are driven by the idea that, as one character puts it, "people should make up their minds where they want to live," places and homes are never more than shifting locations that always seem to be foreign territory where one lives uncomfortably. In this sense, "home" is at best a dream and usually just a temporary convenience. Nasser's daughter Tania wants to be anywhere but with her family and is willing to have either Johnny or Omar as a lover, depending on who will take her away from her home. In the end, Nasser watches from a window as a medium shot shows Tania being visually swept off the platform by a series of trains that rush off the screen, on her way to another home that she will define for herself.

Revision, Manuscript Format, and Proofreading

A completed first draft of an essay is not a completed essay. The final stage in writing about film requires at least one revision of the paper, with special attention to manuscript format and proofreading. Last-minute corrections should be kept to a minimum and should be clear and simple changes.

A good revision begins by reading the essay with fresh eyes, achieved best by allowing time away from the first draft before returning to work on the revision. In addition, carefully check **manuscript format,** including margins, title position, footnotes, and other mechanical arrangements on the pages. Typically, the manuscript format for a film essay should follow these guidelines, which are based on recommendations by the Modern Language Association (for more information, consult the *MLA Handbook for Writers of Research Papers,* Sixth Edition, 2003):

- Your name should appear in the top left-hand corner of the first page, along with your instructor's name, the course title and number, and the date of submission. Your title should be centered on the next line.
- The entire essay should be double-spaced, including any quotations running more than four lines, which are indented ten spaces at the left margin and reproduced without quotation marks.
- Leave one-inch margins at the top, bottom, and sides of each page. Indent paragraphs five character spaces or one-half inch.
- Number each page (including the first) with your last name and the page number in the upper right-hand corner.
- Be certain quotations and documentation are in the proper format.

Once your final revision is completed, **proofreading**—checking deliberately for errors or omissions that can be easily corrected on a hard copy—is essential. With any kind of writing, your presentation determines much of how your reader views your work, and an accurate, professional look to your writing can promote an accurate, professional reading of it. Typographical mistakes and other small goofs do not ruin a good essay, but they do undermine it by creating an impression of carelessness.

 VIEWING CUES: Interpretation, Argument, and Evidence in a Film Essay

- Try to formulate the specific core of your interpretation for the film you are writing about. Why is that interpretation important? What new light does it shed on the film for your readers?

- Sketch an argument for your paper. What is the logic of its development? What conclusions do you foresee making?

- Write a precise thesis statement, one that describes your interpretation and anticipates each stage of your argument. Is your thesis specific enough, or does it need refinement? Is it sufficiently interesting or polemical so to encourage readers to continue reading your essay?

- Create a detailed outline of your essay. Try to begin each section with a topic sentence that summarizes the issues you will address. Do your topic sentences relate to each other? Do they accurately describe the logic of the essay? Does your outline also include subsections that develop and support each topic sentence with details and evidence?

- After writing your first draft, revise your thesis statement to reflect changes in your thinking. How can you sharpen your thesis to better describe how your argument develops?

- In your draft, look for consistent errors and trouble spots that you need to pay special attention to during revision.

IN FOCUS

Interpretation, Argument, and Evidence in *Rashomon* (1950)

After a reviewing his notes on Akira Kurosawa's *Rashomon,* a student writer considers some possible topics. He begins by thinking about the film's unusual narrative structure: as three men, including a priest, seek shelter from a rainstorm under an ancient city gate, they hear the tale of a murder and rape through four different points of view—those of the bandit, the woman, the ghost of the dead man, and the woodcutter. The narrative tension in the film, the writer realizes, develops around the discrepancies in these competing narrative points of view, the result of which is a dark ambiguity about the truth of this violent and tragic event. After seeing the film again and trying to refine his thinking about it, the writer develops a thesis, a clear interpretation of the film:

> In Akira Kurosawa's *Rashomon,* four different perspectives contrast four different versions of the truth about a violent attack. At the conclusion of the film, after we have been presented with these various narrative perspectives and the evidence in them, the opening confusion of the three men is even more pervasive, setting the stage for the only possible response to a world defined by egotism and uncertainty: compassion.

The student's next step is to sketch an outline, one in which he uses topic sentences to mark the development of the argument and the places where key evidence will appear:

Rashomon: Beyond Understanding and Evidence

Thesis statement
  I. Central to this film is the drama of interpretation and evidence.
     A. Four accounts of same horrifying event
     B. The opening focus on evidence
 II. Although more evidence appears through the perspective of the different witnesses, that evidence does not always agree and seems to befuddle a clear interpretation.
     A. Overlaps and inconsistencies in describing the facts
     B. The dagger as key piece of evidence
III. The heart of the fragmented narratives of *Rashomon* is the egotism that fashions those various perspectives.
     A. The bandit's violent sexual desire and the crime
     B. His story of conquest and surrender

IV. Both the wife's and the husband's perspectives are
    likewise mostly about themselves
    A. The wife's tale of a helpless woman
    B. The husband's tale of honor and self-sacrifice
 V. The woodcutter's narrative is more problematic, but
    equally locked into its own needs for self-justification
    and protection.
    A. His revised vision: a base and cowardly world
    B. His acknowledging stealing the evidence of the dagger
VI. That each of these perspectives is distorted by dif-
    ferent degrees of ethical failures of the individuals
    telling them indicates both the horrifying indeterminacy
    of a world determined by isolated egos and the corrup-
    tion of these perspectives by human egotism.
    A. Natural disaster and moral depravity
    B. Editing and shot compositions add considerably to
       this sense of confusion, disorientation, and failure
       to see facts and events clearly.
VII. Although the humane conclusion of the film seems unex-
    pected (and somewhat sentimental), its unexpectedness
    is what makes the film so engaged with modern times.

After writing his first draft, the writer sets the paper aside for three days
before undertaking a careful revision. He proofreads a printed version of
the essay and then submits this final copy:

Fred Stillman
Professor White
Film 101
10 October 2003

                    Beyond Understanding and Evidence:
                    The Surprise of Compassion in *Rashomon*

        The setting that opens and closes Akira Kurosawa's
Rashomon is the collapsed Rashomon gate in the ancient city
of Kyoto. Amidst a torrential rainstorm, a woodcutter, a
commoner and a priest huddle together, and the first recounts
a horrifying tale of rape, murder, and possibly suicide told
through four different perspectives that structure the narrative of the film. Seen respectively through the eyes of a
criminal, the female victim, the dead husband, and the woodcutter, each of these four perspectives offers a contrasting
version of events and the truth of what happened, and each
introduces pieces of evidence to support that particular
version. Despite having heard these witnesses, however, the
priest can only murmur, "I don't understand." At the film's

conclusion, moreover, that opening confusion of the men is more pervasive than ever, setting the stage for the only possible response to a world defined by egotism and uncertainty: compassion.

    Rashomon is a drama of evidence and interpretation. As the priest and woodcutter explain to the commoner, the original staging of the different testimonies was a police court trying to gather evidence to determine the truth behind a horrible crime in which a noble woman and her husband were attacked in the wilderness—she was raped and he was killed. Appropriately, the first point of view presented is that of the woodcutter, who follows a trail of evidence through the woods—a woman's hat, a man's hat, a belt, and an amulet case—to the sudden discovery of the dead body of the samurai nobleman, his stiffened arms and hands stretched grotesquely toward the horrified woodcutter in a low-angle shot **[Figure 12.20]**. Shortly thereafter, a man describes how he captured the bandit Tajomaru, emphasizing the discovered evidence of the samurai's horse as well as "17 arrows" and a "Korean sword" found on the criminal. Yet even the seemingly incontestable claim and evidence immediately become subject to doubt when the bandit suddenly denounces and denies the man's interpretation of certain details.

    Although more evidence appears through the perspective of the other witnesses, that evidence does not always agree and seems to befuddle a clear interpretation. Most importantly, the significance of a pearl-handled dagger, the weapon that supposedly killed the husband, changes dramatically in the different narratives, acting as an evidential marker to distinguish the interpretations of events.

    Focused on the shifting place of this dagger, the heart of the fragmented narratives of *Rashomon* becomes the egotism that informs each perspective. Or, more exactly, each version becomes more about the personal desire and greed of the person explaining what happened than about the factual events and evidence. Appropriately, what initiates the horrendous crime is the violent sexual desire of the bandit, who happens to witness, in a sharp shot/reverse-shot exchange beginning with his awakening eyes, the exposed face and feet of the wife. After that, his entire account emphasizes greed and desire: he deceives and entraps the nobleman by suggesting he will sell him riches

Figure 12.20 *Rashomon* (1950). The mystery of a horrifying death.

from an old tomb, and his leering gaze at the young woman turns quickly to a brutal sexual attack. Not surprisingly, in his version, his desires and demands fulfill the woman, she becoming the mirror image of his greed and lust when she ecstatically surrenders to his sexual assault. At this moment, the critical object, the dagger, drops passively from her hand, according to the bandit, who claims to then kill the husband "honestly."

Both the wife's and the husband's perspectives are likewise mostly about themselves. From the beginning, she appears discreet and demure, partly hidden by veils and white make-up and barely moving as she rides her horse through the forest. In her account, she becomes a "poor helpless woman" whose husband turns viciously on her after the assault. Unable to bear his hateful stare, she claims to have fainted—only to later discover her dagger in her husband's chest. The husband's narrative, in contrast, paints a picture of his suffering devotion and lost honor, weeping from the grave as he recounts killing himself with the controversial dagger. Light and shadow fill the images of this account, suggesting an ambiguity and lack of certainty even in this testimony by a dead man.

Finally, the woodcutter's narrative is more problematic, but equally locked into its own needs for self-justification and protection. After introducing the story at the beginning of the film, he returns to offer a final version that reveals deceptions and lies in his first account. Now, he admits to having witnessed the entire scene, and his subsequent description of the part-clownish, part-terrified fighting of the two men shows a world that is fundamentally base and cowardly, a reflection of his own base and cowardly position in failing to intervene or fully disclose the truth of what he saw. Most disturbing perhaps, he tacitly acknowledges stealing the crucial piece of evidence, the dagger, in order to sell it for personal gain.

That each of these perspectives is distorted by different degrees of ethical failures on the part of the individual behind it indicates the source of the horrifying indeterminacy and chaos of this world [Figure 12.21]. This is a world described by the priest in the opening as full of "war, earthquake, wind, fire, famine, plague . . . each

Figure 12.21 *Rashomon* (1950). Trying to make meaning in a chaotic world.

year full of disaster . . . hundreds of men dying like animals." Stylistically, the stunning editing and shot compositions of *Rashomon* dramatize this world of confusion and disorientation, in which seeing and understanding seem constantly to combat each other. Witnesses are introduced with a wipe that crosses the screen in one direction or the other, almost violently wiping out the perspective of the preceding account. Within the different accounts, rapid tracks and flash pans re-create the desperately unsettled struggle to discover facts through perspectives that dart across surfaces blocked by branches and leaves.

Within all this moral darkness and despair, however, the conclusion of *Rashomon* suggests a possible way out of the terror and blindness that results from so much visual and narrative ambiguity. In this final sequence, the three-some who tell and hear that tale of violence discover an abandoned baby in the ruins of the gate. The commoner urges them to steal the baby's blankets and clothing because "you can't live unless you're what you call selfish." At this point, a dramatic turn occurs when, in a head-to-head con-frontation in the rain, the commoner accuses the woodcutter of hiding his theft of that crucial piece of evidence, the dagger. In dazed silence, the priest and woodcutter stand against a wall. As the rain stops, the commoner suddenly insists on taking the child home with him to his already crowded family. Despite his shame about his selfishness and despite the missing evidence of the stolen dagger, a glimmer of human value returns to the world. Compassion overcomes the evidence of mistakes, and as they all depart, the sun gleams through the clouds and the saved child becomes the emblem of a new future. During this sequence, the priest shouts the fundamental truth so often lost in this violent courtroom, "if men don't trust each other, then the world becomes a hell."

Although this conclusion seems unexpected (and some-what sentimental), its unexpectedness is what makes the film so engaged with modern times. Danish philosopher and theologian Søren Kierkegaard uses the term "leap of faith" to describe the only possibility for a spiritual faith in mod-ern times. What his term implies is that both spiritual and human faith—the grounds for ethical behavior—often occur *despite* the evidence before our eyes and *despite* the failure of human reason to understand it. As in *Rashomon,* truth and morality may need to leap over the confusion of facts and logic in order simply to do what is right.

While not all writers about film precisely follow all of these guidelines for outlining, formulating a thesis statement, revising, proofreading, and so on, experienced writers almost always do so unconsciously or in abbreviated ways. Keeping a checklist of these mechanics in mind can alleviate much of the anxiety about writing, providing working frameworks that lead to stronger and more interesting essays.

Researching the Movies

While in some critical film essays the writer aims simply to convey a personal response to a film based on critical distance and careful reflection, in other essays the writer wants or needs to use research in order to sharpen and develop his or her interpretation of a film. Research enables the writer to identify significant issues surrounding a film and to contribute his or her opinions and ideas to the ongoing critical dialogue about it. A student intending to write about Jean Cocteau's *Orpheus* (1950), for example, may be intrigued by the film but uncertain about her specific argument. With some reading and research about Cocteau, his relation to the surrealist movement, and his work as a poet and painter, she discovers a more specific argument about the complicated role of poetry in the film and the relevance of the Orpheus myth to Cocteau's vision of the modern artist **[Figure 12.22]**. Whether limited or extensive, research helps determine why your essay is important and what critical questions are at stake in writing the essay.

Distinguishing Research Materials

Primary and Secondary Sources   There are various kinds of materials that qualify as research sources for a film essay. **Primary research sources**—such as films on videotape or DVD and film scripts—have a direct and close relationship with the original film. **Secondary research sources**—including books, critical articles, Internet sites, supplementary DVD materials, and newspaper reviews—contain ideas or information from outside sources such as film critics or scholars. A student planning to write a research essay on Don Siegel's *Invasion of the Body Snatchers* (1956) might first view a 16mm projection of that film and then access other primary sources, such as a videotape and script, as follow-ups to the first screening **[Figure 12.23]**. Later research via secondary sources might include film reviews published at the time of release, scholarly essays on Siegel's work, and perhaps a book on 1950s American cinema.

Various primary sources are an indispensable asset because they allow the writer to review specific scenes on a videotape or DVD or to check the exact dialogue in a published script. With primary sources, however, it is important to keep in mind that they may approximate, but not duplicate exactly, the look of a film when seen in a theater (see pp. 30–33). Videotapes may format images differently from the format used in theatrical screenings, while scripts may represent a simple blueprint from which the actual film dialogue deviates.

Figure 12.22 *Orpheus* (1950). Researching the complexities of a film.

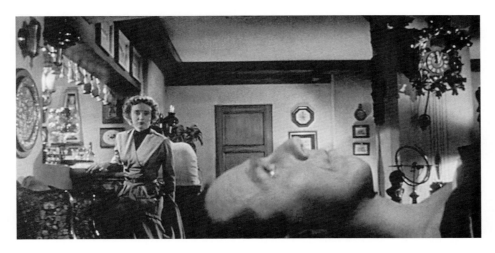

Figure 12.23 *Invasion of the Body Snatchers* (1956). Following a film from 16mm to videotape to scholarly essays.

Even in our electronic age, libraries and their databases remain the most reliable places to find solid secondary materials. Check such databases as the *Humanities Index, Lexis/Nexis,* and *Comindex* for essays and books on your subject, and don't underestimate the more conventional approach of exploring the library's shelves. Annual bibliographic indexes, for example, identify journal articles and books that may support and broaden your thinking, including especially *The Readers' Guide to Periodical Literature,* the *MLA International Bibliography,* and the *Film/Literature Index.* Once you have a topic and a working thesis, you can search for sources relevant to your topic and argument. After checking general categories like "film," "cinema," and "movies," a more precise topic, such as "contemporary Australian cinema" or "sound technology and the movies" will lead you more quickly to pertinent research materials.

In addition to databases and bibliographic indexes, specialized encyclopedias, which identify important topics and figures in film studies, are useful resources for initiating research on a film. Examples include Ephraim Katz's *The Film Encyclopedia,* Pam Cook's *The Cinema Book,* Leonard Maltin's *The Whole Film Sourcebook,* Ginette Vincendeau's *Encyclopedia of European Cinema,* and Amy Unterburger's *The St. James Women Filmmakers Encyclopedia.* Film guides such as these provide factual information about and short introductions to a subject. The entries typically do not offer the sort of detailed analysis or arguments required for a good research paper, but they can suggest pertinent information and issues that can lead to more research and a refined argument.

Internet Sources   For students with Internet access, the Web offers useful discussion groups, access to various library and media catalogs, and numerous other information sites. However, with so many Web sites available, the writer must be careful to distinguish among the three kinds of reputable **Internet sources** for film studies:

- sites and databases that provide basic facts about a film and the individuals involved with that film—such as biographical facts about the director, the different running times of a film, and the like
- sites that offer reviews or essays from academic film journals—such as *Film Comment, Jump Cut,* and *Sight and Sound*
- film-specific sites (almost every major film released in recent years has its own Web site, as do the studios and distributors) that provide information ranging from production facts to gossip as well as reviews and interviews

While the Internet is fast becoming an important source for accessing information of all kinds, film researchers and writers must be cautious about the quality of the material found there. One obvious reason for this caution is the difficulty in determining the authenticity and authority of Internet-based information. Unlike material published in academic journals or books, Internet essays and articles may not have been through a review process to determine their value. Virtually anyone can post on a Web site any opinion or any set of facts—often without substantial evidence. When using the Internet for research, therefore, writers need to differentiate substantial and useful material from chat and frivolous commentary. Especially with Internet sources, there are three important rules to follow:

- Determine the quality of the Internet source: Does it provide reliable information and a carefully evaluated argument supported by research? Is the source a refereed publication (one whose material is evaluated by experts) or a reputable institution? Is its information supported by references to other research? What are the credentials of the authors?
- Define your search as precisely as possible. Beyond just the title of a film, focus your search on, for example, "lighting in *Double Indemnity*" or "politics and Iranian cinema." Pursue your topic through the advanced-search option.
- Explore links to other sites. Does your research link you to sites on other films by the same director or to such related issues as the film genre or the country in which the film was made?

Here is a list of Web sites useful for film research:

- *Internet Movie Database* (<www.IMDb.com>): provides detailed information on films
- *ScreenSite* (<www.tcf.ua.edu/ScreenSite/contents.htm>): provides data on films, film conferences, archives, and useful links to other academic cinema sites
- *History on/and/in Film* (<www.mcc.murdoch.edu.au/Reading Room/ hfilm/contenth.html>): contains conference papers and scholarly essays on a range of film history topics
- *American Film Institute* (<www.afi.com>): offers recent industry news, events, educational seminars, and reviews
- *Library of Congress Motion Picture & Television Reading Room* (<lcweb .loc.gov/rr/mopic/>): provides access to the library's catalogue, the national Film Registry preservation list, and the American Memory Collection of online early films.

Using and Documenting Sources

Writers gather research material in a wide variety of ways: some record paragraphs and phrases on handwritten note cards, while others prefer to type that material directly into their computers, allowing them to sort, move, and insert it easily. In either case, the bibliographic information for quotations should be double-checked for accuracy and should include all of the publication data required for the Works Cited list (and sometimes the Works Consulted section) of your research paper. Just as sloppy technical errors in making a movie (such as a boom microphone appearing in a frame) can undermine the look and effect of that film, inaccurate or careless source documentation will make the research paper look amateurish.

Integrating research material into the text of your paper requires both logic and rhetoric. Sometimes research can be used to locate and describe how your argument differs from prevailing positions on a film or issue. In this case, the writer frequently identifies one or more opposing positions as a way of highlighting how the essay will distinguish itself: "While Annette Michelson has claimed that Kuleshov's films are best understood as part of a debate with Eisenstein, this paper argues that the French films of Jean Epstein are equally important to Kuleshov's development." Conversely, research can be used to support and validate a point or a part of the overall argument: "Both Patrice Petro and Judith Mayne have produced complex feminist readings of silent-era German films that support my interpretation of *Mädchen in Uniform* (1931)." Yet another possibility is to use research sources to back up the validity of facts or critical frameworks necessary for introducing an argument: "In *The Zero Hour: Glasnost and Soviet Cinema in Transition*, Andrew Horton and Michael Brashinsky convincingly show that Russian cinema after 1985 returned to the center of the world stage, an argument that will provide the background for my claims about the importance of *Little Vera* (1988) in Europe and America."

Once research material has been gathered, selected, and integrated into an essay, all of the research sources used must be properly documented. There are two kinds of research material that require documentation: **direct quotation** from a secondary source and **paraphrasing** in which the writer puts the idea or observation from another source in his or her own words. When the information is considered common knowledge and is well known to most people, there is no need to document where you found that information. If, however, there is any doubt about whether the observation is common knowledge, always document the source so as to avoid any potential suspicion of plagiarism. For example, a critic's remark that Ousmane Sembène is one of Africa's premier filmmakers and that his films work in a realist tradition would be considered common knowledge by many seasoned filmgoers. But a writer new to Sembène's work may feel more comfortable documenting the source of that information, and, like all writers, should *never risk the charge of plagiarism*. Quotations of dialogue from a film usually does not require documentation.

There are various **documentation formats** for listing authors, titles, and publication data. Here, we will describe the format that is advocated by the Modern Language Association (MLA) and widely used in the humanities. (See the *MLA Handbook for Writers of Research Papers*, Sixth Edition, 2003.) The primary components of the MLA format are in-text citations and the Works Cited list. An **in-text citation** is required wherever the writer refers to or quotes from a research source within the essay's text. The in-text citation includes the author's name and the page number. When the author's name appears in the discussion that introduces the quotation, only the page numbers are enclosed in parentheses. Note that p. and pp. are not used:

> As Patricia Zimmerman has noted, filmmakers such as Stan Brakhage and Jonas Mekas "appropriated home-movie style as a formal manifestation of a spontaneous, untampered form of filmmaking" (146).

However, when the author is not named in the introductory text, enclose both the author's last name and the page number, without any intervening punctuation, within the parentheses:

> Filmmakers such as Stan Brakhage and Jonas Mekas "appropriated home-movie style as a formal manifestation of a spontaneous, untampered form of filmmaking" (Zimmerman 146).

The same citation formats are used whether the material is quoted directly or paraphrased:

> Much of the American avant-garde movement experimented not so much with the techniques of modern art but with the spontaneous actions associated with home movies (Zimmerman 146).

When you use two or more sources by the same author in your essay, you must distinguish among them by also including an abbreviated version of the title in either the introductory text or the parenthetical citation: as in "Zimmerman writes in *Reel Families* . . ." or "(Zimmerman, *Reel Families* 146)", respectively. Each source cited in the text must also appear in the Works Cited section with full bibliographic detail.

Another type of annotation is the **content,** or **explanatory, note** which may or may not include secondary sources. These notes offer background information on the topic being discussed or on related issues, suggest related readings, or offer an aside. They should be placed on a separate page after the text (but before the Works Cited list) or as footnotes at the bottom of the page. Thus a writer discussing horror films and Brian De Palma's *Carrie* (1976) might include this text and content note:

> Although *Carrie* focuses on female anxiety and violence, it is difficult to pinpoint a specific audience for this film.[1]

> [1]Especially since *Psycho,* horror films seem fixated on violence against women, but there is good reason to consider how both female and male audiences identify with these films. An important discussion of this issue is Carol Clover's *Men, Women, and Chain-Saws* (3-21).

Full documentation for every source cited in your essay should be included in the **Works Cited** section, positioned on a separate page immediately after the last page of the essay text. Sources that have been consulted but not cited in the text or notes of the essay can be included in an optional **Works Consulted** section, which appears on a separate page after the Works Cited list. (Note, however, that for reasons of space, we do *not* show the Works Cited and Works Consulted sections as separate pages in the essay on p. 513 in this chapter.) Punctuation and other mechanics of the different entries must be absolutely correct. Titles should be typed either in italics or underlined, according to your instructor's preference. Some of the most common types of Works Cited entries include the following:

Book by One Author
Zimmerman, Patricia. *Reel Families: A Social History of Amateur Film.* Bloomington: Indiana UP, 1995.

Book by More Than One Author
Bordwell, David, Janet Staiger, and Kristin Thompson. *The Classical Hollywood Cinema: Film Style and Mode of Production to 1960.* New York: Columbia UP, 1985.

Edited Book
Cook, Pam, and Mieke Bernink, eds. *The Cinema Book.* 2nd ed. London: British Film Institute, 1999.

IN FOCUS

From Research to Writing about
The Cabinet of Dr. Caligari (1919)

A writer researching an essay on *The Cabinet of Dr. Caligari* has probably more sources and materials than can ever be read in a short period of time. Responding to the strange look and feel of this silent film from Germany and looking for some basic information, one student writer, for instance, starts his research by examining the introductory material in David Cook's *History of Narrative Film* (2003) and in two film guides, Richard Roud's *Cinema: A Critical Dictionary* (1982), and Ginette Vincendeau's *Encyclopedia of European Cinema* (1995). In the indexes of these books, he checks various headings, such as "German cinema" and "Weimar cinema," as well as the title of the film and the name of its director, Robert Wiene. Next, he searches the Internet by entering the title of the film in a search engine, which results in dozens of different Web sites containing reviews, plot summaries, stills, and even early posters: *Carafax Abbey: The Horror Film Database*, *Internet Source for Early German Cinema*, and *"Das Kabinett des Doktor Caligari"* by Damin Canon are a few of the many possible sites he investigates. Although much of this Internet information is too general, he keeps a list of these sources and their bibliographic details, noting one particular site that provides early reviews of the film. Even this preliminary research starts to shape his thinking about a topic involving the period known as the Weimar era.

Following this preliminary work, the writer then checks the databases at his college library for more substantial critical books and essays on the Weimar period in German history. This initial search leads him to dozens of books and critical articles, but he selects *The Weimar Republic Sourcebook* (1994) because it is a relatively recent publication and seems quite comprehensive. He continues his work by refining his research to concentrate on books that deal with films made during this period; here, he discovers numerous scholarly studies devoted to this particular film culture and even whole books devoted only to this film. He reads and takes notes on appropriate sections of well-known books, such as Siegfried Kracauer's *From Caligari to Hitler* (1947) and Lotte Eisner's *The Haunted Screen* (1973, a work he has seen mentioned frequently by other writers), as well as two recent scholarly books, Michael Budd's The Cabinet of Dr. Caligari: *Texts, Contexts, Histories* (1990) and Thomas Elsaesser's *Weimar Cinema and After* (2000).

Armed with information about how this period in German history became the prelude to fascism and the rise of Hitler, the writer realizes he needs to refine his topic as a more focused thesis. He reviews the film on videotape and begins to concentrate on the social violence that seethes beneath the surface of *The Cabinet of Dr. Caligari*. This is not a simple horror film, he realizes, but one in which the violence and horror seem connected to the social context of a prefascist Germany. As his thesis about social violence begins to take shape, he returns to the library, where he finds a good recent study of film violence, Stephen Prince's edited collection *Screening Violence* (2000).

With each step, the writer makes notes, doublechecks quotations for accuracy, and makes certain to record accurate bibliographic information on all the sources he consults. As he formulates his thesis statement and constructs an outline, he tries to indicate where the different parts of his research would be most effective in directing and supporting his argument. His final essay, reproduced here, clearly demonstrates the important contribution that careful research makes to writing about film.

Thompson 1

Steven Thompson
Film Criticism 101
Professor Corrigan
10 Dec. 2003

History, Violence, and
The Cabinet of Dr. Caligari

Background research clearly sets up the writer's argument.

In his detailed study of *The Cabinet of Dr. Caligari* (1919), Michael Budd identifies the complex cultural history of the film's arrival in the United States, an arrival that intentionally obscured the origins of one of Germany's most famous movies. When the film premiered in New York on April 3, 1921, it followed a well-crafted promotion and distribution campaign that stressed *Dr. Caligari*'s novelty, global appeal, and generic formulas. One 1921 poster identifies the film as "a mystery story that holds the public in suspense every minute," while another describes it as "thrilling, fantastic, bizarre, gripping." However accurate these descriptions may be, these promotions, as Budd notes, intentionally present the film "out of context, [with] its origins both cultural and national deliberately obscured" (56-58). That obfuscation has continued to dog *The Cabinet of Dr. Caligari* in the many decades since its initial release, so that American and other viewers have remained less attuned to the specific historical and social realities dramatized in the film than to the psychological mysteries played out in its thrills, fantasies, and horror.[1] Exploring the social drama of *Dr. Caligari* reconnects the film more concretely to its original German context and makes clear that this film is about national unrest and violence, both of which are far more historically tangible than the usually acknowledged fantasy of the film's madmen and monsters.

The thesis statement announces the argument.

[1] A fascinating and rich source of information about the reception of *The Cabinet of Dr. Caligari* is the Web site at <www.filmgeschichte.de/film/caligari.htm>. Besides numerous early reviews of the film (in German) this site offers information about the many films, plays, and books that describe or are based on the original film.

The film's story tells of the hypnotist Dr. Caligari who comes to a town with a carnival [**Figure 12.24**]. In his sideshow act, Caligari presents Cesare, a somnambulist who can supposedly see the future. At the same time, a series of murders occurs in the town. Francis, a student who discovers that Caligari and Cesare are behind the killings, pursues Caligari to an insane asylum. The final twist occurs when the narrative shifts its perspective and we discover the truth: that Francis has been the narrator of the tale, that he is in fact the mad patient in the asylum, and that Caligari is the kind director of the hospital allowing Francis to tell his delusional tale.[2]

While watching this film, many (if not most) viewers understandably fixate on the exaggerated sets and backdrop paintings. These factors, together with the twisted narrative that turns the story into the vision of a madman, place this film squarely in the cultural and aesthetic tradition of expressionism, a movement in which unconscious or unseen forces create a world distorted by personal fears, desires, and anxieties. According to this position, Cesare acts out the evil unconscious of Caligari, while the violence and chaos associated with that unconscious spread through the entire community.

Figure 12.24 *The Cabinet of Dr. Caligari* (1919). The malevolent or benevolent Caligari.

Many critics have, in fact, made intelligent connections between the psychological underpinnings of expressionism and the German society that, bereft of so many fathers after the devastation of World War I, gravitated toward malevolent authority figures. Most famously, Siegfried Kracauer's *From Caligari to Hitler* offers the most direct statement of Dr. Caligari as the unconscious of a social history predicting the imminent arrival of fascism [**Figure 12.25**]. He writes that Caligari becomes "a premonition of Hitler" (72):

> Whether intentionally or not, *Caligari* exposes the soul wavering between tyranny and chaos, and facing a desperate situation: any escape from tyranny

[2] In *A History of Narrative Film,* David Cook notes that it was the great German director Fritz Lang who urged this frame tale: "Lang correctly thought that the reality frame would heighten the expressionistic elements of the mise-en-scène" (110).

This summary paragraph assumes readers know the film, but refreshes their memory of its story and plot.

A content note provides additional information about a point raised in the text.

This overview of a major scholarly position establishes the writer's authority and prepares readers for what will distinguish his argument.

A succinct quotation sums up a complex critical viewpoint. Because it is more than four lines in length, the quotation is presented without quotation marks in the block (indented) format.

seems to throw it into a state of utter confusion. Quite logically, the film spreads an all-pervading atmosphere of horror. Like the Nazi world, that of *Caligari* overflows with sinister portents, acts of terror and outbursts of panic. (74)

Although *Dr. Caligari* certainly responds to readings like this, which see the film as part of an expressionist aesthetic or a projection of the unconscious of the German masses around 1920, the more concrete social realities informing the film frequently get overlooked. In *The Weimar Republic Sourcebook,* Anton Kaes, Martin Jay, and Edward Dimendberg have assembled a compendium of documents on this period in German history, and many of the topics for this cultural history of Germany from 1918 to 1930 could act as social blueprint for the thematic history that permeates *Dr. Caligari.* Three topics stand out as especially pertinent: the traumatic legacy of war (creating a fatherless generation), economic upheaval and social instabilities (that rattled almost every social institution at the time), and the rise of fascism (through repressive authority figures). With traces of each of these three motifs throughout the film, *Dr. Caligari* becomes, from one angle, a study of social violence within the interpersonal relationships and the cultural institutions of Weimar Germany.

At the heart of *Dr. Caligari* is a social melodrama concentrated on conscious sexual activities that quickly turn violent. According to Thomas Elsaesser, "It is essentially the tale of a suitor who is ignored or turned down" (qtd. in Budd 184). The threesome at the center of the story, Francis, Alan, and Jane, suggests both male bonds and a heterosexual romance that moves toward the conventional outcome of marriage, but, like Jane's anxious worry over "her father's long absence," each member of this standard social group seems physically and emotionally handicapped by a missing parental or patriarchal figure. Essential to the plot is the rivalry that creates a tension among the three characters, with Alan and Francis competing for the affections of Jane. That seemingly normal and playful tension, however, turns dark when Cesare becomes a stand-in for the simmering violence implicit in this group, murdering Francis's rival Alan and sexually seducing and abducting Jane. In the midst of these events, the dazed Jane can only

Against the backdrop of these other critical positions, the writer reasserts and develops his thesis.

The writer refines and focuses his thesis as three motifs in the film.

A strong topic sentence presents the first motif, supported by a secondary source.

An exact quotation from the film's dialogue provides supporting evidence for the writer's claim.

Figure 12.25 *The Cabinet of Dr. Caligari* (1919). A premonition of Hitler?

mutter that "we queens may never choose as our hearts dictate," and Francis goes mad [**Figure 12.26**]. If heterosexual melodramas take many forms through history and in different cultures, here a common love triangle suddenly and inexplicitly erupts with unusual violence, suggesting that the problem may be less about Caligari and Cesare than about the enormous social stress and strain within this fundamental social grouping.

The violent stress and strain of this heterosexual drama spreads and appears through every social institution in *Dr. Caligari*. If the home is where the melodrama explodes, the film identifies this violence with three other social spaces: the city government, the carnival, and the mental hospital. With the first, an officious town clerk is murdered on a whim for enforcing restrictions that annoy Dr. Caligari. With the second, entertainment turns ominously threatening when a sideshow amusement tells Alan, "You die at dawn." With the third, a traditional institution for healing becomes a prison to subjugate or control human beings who have lost all ability to interact socially. In each case— and most notably in the hospital where the narrative pretends to return to a normal world—the visual disturbances of the graphically twisted walls and out-of-kilter windows become a measure of not merely an unbalanced expressionistic mind but, more importantly, of the social violence that surrounds all individuals as part of the institutions in which they must live.

A smooth transition from the previous paragraph to the second motif about "social institutions," analyzed here as three different "social spaces."

Visual details strengthen the argument.

The third motif builds on a more general secondary source on "screen violence."

If violence has always been an ingredient and attraction of films, the brand of social violence in *Dr. Caligari* is clearly linked to a specific time and place, a Weimar Germany from which the Nazi regime would soon spring. In "Graphic Violence in the Cinema" from *Screening Violence*, Stephen Prince correctly argues that "screen violence is deeply embedded in the history and functioning of cinema" and the "appeal of violence in the cinema—for filmmakers and viewers—is tied to the medium's inherently visceral properties" (2). Although Prince claims that "screen violence in earlier periods was generally more genteel and indirect" (2), there is nothing genteel about the social violence of *Dr. Caligari,* even if it lacks the physical excess of contemporary movies. With the crucial insights of historical

Figure 12.26 *The Cabinet of Dr. Caligari* (1919). Horror, or a romance gone awry?

hindsight, this violence should not be relegated merely to the unconscious and the psychological distortions of dark fantasies, but should be recognized as the shadow of a historical and social reality. In its original historical context, the melodramatic violence in the relationship of Alan, Francis, and Jane maps a frustrating and often desperate problem with heterosexual romance in a fatherless Germany, while the troubled, anxious, and repressive interactions at town halls, carnivals, and hospitals refer to a real political and structural crisis in the social arenas of post–World War I Germany. If the social violence of *Dr. Caligari* seems tame (to modern eyes accustomed to Technicolor blood baths), there is no doubt that such violence reverberates with more extensive, if less intensive, implications for the state of German society in 1920.

Many viewers without a precise sense of German history and *Caligari*'s original cultural context can still appreciate its dark tale, striking visual effects, and unsettling frame tale. The psychological dimension that permeates this murder mystery is, moreover, an undeniable and critical component to its disturbing plot and expressionistic mise-en-scène. Yet, in the wake of World War I, the nightmarish violence of the film resonates with particular historical and social meaning that cannot be explained as fantasy. *The Cabinet of Dr. Caligari* will always be a specific cultural space whose violence remains historically tangible.

The assertive conclusion restates the central thesis.

[According to MLA, begin new page here]

Article in an Anthology of Film Criticism
Gaines, Jane. "Dream/Factory." *Reinventing Film Studies*. Ed. Christine Gledhill and Linda Williams. London: Arnold, 2000. 100–13.

Journal Article
Spivak, Gayatri. "In Praise of *Sammy and Rosie Get Laid*." *Critical Quarterly* 31.2 (Summer 1989): 80–88.

Articles in Daily or Weekly Periodical
Corliss, Richard. "Suddenly Shakespeare." *Time* 4 Nov. 1996: 88–90.

Interview (Published)
Seberg, Jean. Interview with Mark Rappaport. "I, Jean Seberg." *Film Quarterly* 55.1 (Fall 2001): 2–13.

Works Cited

The Works Cited list starts on a new page at the end of the research essay.

Budd, Michael. The Cabinet of Dr. Caligari: *Texts, Contexts, Histories*. New Brunswick: Rutgers UP, 1990.

Cook, David A. *A History of Narrative Film*. 4th ed. New York: Norton, 2003.

Elsaesser, Thomas. "Social Mobility and the Fantastic: German Silent Cinema." The Cabinet of Dr. Caligari: *Texts, Contexts, Histories*. Ed. Mike Budd. New Brunswick: Rutgers UP, 1990. 171–90.

Kaes, Anton, Martin Jay, and Edward Dimendberg. *The Weimar Republic Sourcebook*. Berkeley: U of California P, 1994.

Kracauer, Siegfried. *From Caligari to Hitler: A Psychological Study of German Film*. Princeton: Princeton UP, 1947.

Prince, Stephen. "Graphic Violence in the Cinema: Origins, Aesthetic Design, and Social Effects." *Screening Violence*. Ed. Stephen Prince. New Brunswick: Rutgers UP, 2000. 1–46. 7 Dec. 2001 <www.filmgeschichte.de>.

[According to MLA, begin new page here]

Works Consulted

The optional Works Consulted list when included starts on a new page following Works Cited.

Eisner, Lotte. *The Haunted Screen: Expressionism in the German Cinema and the Influence of Max Reinhardt*. Berkeley: U of California P, 1973.

Elsaesser, Thomas. *Weimar Cinema and After: Germany's Historical Imaginary*. London: Routledge, 2000.

Carroll, Noel. "The Cabinet of Dr. Kracauer." *Millienium Film Journal* 1.2 (Spring/Summer 1978): 77–85.

Article in an Online Journal (Including Access Date)

Firshing, Robert. "Italian Horror in the Seventies." *Images Journal* 8 Nov. 2001. 23 July 2003 <www.imagesjournal.com>.

Information from an Online Site (Including Access Date)

Magnolia: The Official Movie Page. 1999. New Line Productions. 23 March 2003. Accessed 14 Nov. 2003 <www.magnoliamovie.com>.

For information on the formats for other types of sources, consult the *MLA Handbook for Writers of Research Papers.* Always keep in mind that plagiarism—using sources without giving proper credit to them—is one of the most serious offenses in writing and research.

CRITICAL VOICES: PHILLIP LOPATE ON PAULINE KAEL

Contemporary film essayist Phillip Lopate writes widely about various film experiences. In this excerpt from *Totally, Tenderly, Tragically* (1998), he offers an evaluation of the writings of film reviewer Pauline Kael, historically one of the most important critics of the cinema. Although sometimes Lopate disagrees with Kael's strong opinions and judgments, he clearly admires the passion of her engagement with films as well as her ability to bring them to life as a skillful writer.

Before I ever met Pauline Kael, I thought of her as one of several film 1 critics I liked to read, each of whom balanced the others with strengths and blind spots. Vincent Canby might have a lighter touch with everyday movies, Andrew Sarris a deeper grasp of film tradition, J. Hoberman a more adventurous coverage of offbeat pictures and Manny Farber a stronger insight into film as a visual medium. But no one can *nail* a picture with Kael's passion.

Among her many virtues, she is a brilliant observer of acting styles, and 2 can capture in apt metaphor the look and bounce of a performer. "Astaire's grasshopper lightness was his limitation as an actor—confining him to perennial gosh—oh—gee adolescence . . ." she will write, or summarize Faye Dunaway's appeal with: "Perfection going slightly to seed is maybe the most alluring face a screen goddess can have." She understands the morality of narrative structure, zeroing in unerringly on the script imbalances brought about through self-approval, hypocrisy or panderings to the *Zeitgeist*. She has an eye for good editing—less so for the rigors of camera composition. Hence it comes as no surprise that she is strongest on comedies, weakest on Westerns. A dedicated fan of independent women characters and witty repartee, she is inevitably drawn to screwball comedies. Most American comedies are gender-driven: Kael delights in disentangling the most gnarly problems of relations between the sexes. She can answer the question, "What do women want?" But she does not like to watch men interacting with other men on the range. She is snortingly contemptuous of the virile claims of aging male stars like John Wayne and Kirk Douglas, "grinning with their big choppers, sucking their guts up into their chests, and hauling themselves onto horses." She has a real distaste for the male valedictory mode, which causes her to dismiss much of John Ford's late work, including a beautiful elegiac work like *The Man Who Shot Liberty Valance.* Her coolness toward the Western goes hand in hand with a lack of feeling for the spatial qualities of film—for *mise en scène.*

Her insensitivity to formalist rigor and precision is her greatest limitation as a film critic. It causes her to overpraise certain visually muddy directors, like Hal Ashby, and then express disappointment later on when their mediocrity becomes undeniable. She will write intelligently about film technique when it suits her, but the rest of the time she dismisses formalist concerns as a sterile, academic interest—a boy's game. Her real genius is sociological. She can show how and why a particular film is reaching audiences by analyzing the social currents of the moment. She is devastatingly sharp on trendy, overrated films to which the public responds for fuzzy-headed narcissistic reasons (*Blow-Up, 8½, Butch Cassidy and the Sundance Kid, Network, Rain Man*). Ironically, she can turn around and enthrone certain other underbaked, overrated films, like *Bonnie and Clyde* or *Last Tango in Paris,* because to her they touch a nerve, catch the spirit of the moment. 3

No one has written better about the appeal of "trash," or the tangible pleasures we get from movies that aren't very good (a sexy actor, a song, an outrageous scene). She tends to forgive silliness in the name of "fun," while being extra-hard on serious-minded or artistic pretensions. Her position that "vulgarity is not as destructive to an artist as snobbery" sometimes leads her into a distorting antagonism toward the art film. "The educated person who became interested in cinema as an art form through Bergman or Fellini or Resnais is alien to me (and my mind goes blank with hostility and indifference when he begins to talk)." I flinched when I read that. Fortunately, Kael's occasional anti-intellectualism is counterbalanced by her immense cultivation. When she discusses dramatic classics like *The Trojan Women, Henry V,* or *Long Day's Journey into Night,* one realizes she could have been as gifted a literary critic as a movie reviewer. She seems also well versed in painting, music, dance. Would that her imitators had an equal measure of erudition to buttress their indulgence of pop culture. . . . 4

Though Kael regards the criticism she did for *The New Yorker* as her most important work, in some ways I prefer her first two collections, *I Lost It at the Movies* and *Kiss Kiss Bang Bang.* Perhaps the fact that these early reviews were written largely for periodicals like *Partisan Review* and *The New Republic* enforced a more intellectually responsible tone. In 1966, in *The New Republic,* she is criticizing "American works that are out of control" and warning against the prejudices of a generation for whom "art is the domain of the irrational." By 1976 she has seemingly joined that generation, writing in *The New Yorker* that "what we all sometimes want from movies" are "sensations we can't control, an excitement that is a great high." . . . 5

The New Yorker supplied her with security and the chance to write regularly and at length. But it also encouraged her bad habits: not only prolixity and redundancy (which she acknowledges), but insiderism, excessive quoting of friends' bon mots, verbal inflation (a fondness for words like "beezie-wheezies" and "stiffs"), special pleading for favorites (Bertolucci, Louis Malle, Robert Towne, Irv Kershner, Peckinpah, Philip Kaufman), an increasing tendency to scold and an oversymbiotic merging with the readership (her "we/you" mode).

Kael's *Bonnie and Clyde* review, the first major piece she did for *The New Yorker,* was a daringly complex piece of analysis; but it also initiated a 6 steamrolling approach. If you didn't like this movie, it was because you were afraid of the truth, out of touch with your feelings. It began: "How do you make a good movie in this country without being jumped on? *Bonnie and Clyde* is the most excitingly American movie since *The Manchurian Candidate*. The audience is alive to it."

Notice the almost demagogic use of first-personal plural as a way for Kael to identify herself with the "correct" instincts of the mass audience, whose spokesperson she becomes. "The audience is alive to it"—but is that the same audience who "jumped on" it? Surely not. The jumpers must be the snobs, for whom film "art" is a learned discipline and not a birthright. Kael, in writing for *The New Yorker*'s educated albeit nonexpert audience, came to adopt a curiously jingoistic populism, flattering their ignorance of the art of film by telling them they already knew everything they needed to by national inheritance. . . .   7

[W]hether commenting on a masterpiece or clunker, Kael is always a pleasure to read. What will Pauline say about the newest film? Will she skewer your favorites or your bêtes noires? When she is on a roll, irreverently dissecting a movie you also think is not so hot, it's a consolation you wish would go on forever.   8

THE NEXT LEVEL: ADDITIONAL SOURCES

Donald, James, Anne Friedberg, and Laura Marcus, eds. *Close Up 1927–1933: Cinema and Modernism*. Princeton: Princeton University Press, 1998. Featuring some of the earliest and best writers about film—such as Dorothy Richardson, Harry Potamkin, and H.D., who still have much to tell contemporary writers about style and substance—this volume collects relatively early, passionately serious, and still-important reviews and essays on the art of film as it moved from the silent to the sound era.

Lopate, Phillip. *Totally, Tenderly, Tragically: Essays and Criticism from a Lifelong Love Affair with the Movies*. New York: Anchor, 1998. Opinionated and smart, Lopate mediates journalistic reviews and scholarly criticism across topics that range from Michelangelo Antonioni's *La Notte* (1960) to "Images of Children in Film."

Nichols, Bill. ed. *Movies and Method*. 2 vols. Berkeley: University of California Press, 1976 and 1985. This two-volume anthology, a classic collection of film criticism and film theory, includes historical and recent writings. Although the material and arguments are largely scholarly and theoretical, the wide scope of topics suggests the many avenues students might follow in writing a critical film essay.

Rich, B. Ruby. *Chick Flicks: Theories and Memories of the Feminist Film Movement*. Durham: Duke University Press, 1998. Covering a range of topics and films that engage several decades of feminist film criticism, Rich writes as both a journalist and a film scholar, with each essay demonstrating a skillful balance of personal experience and intellectual argument.

Stam, Robert, and Toby Miller, eds. *Film and Theory: An Anthology*. Oxford: Blackwell, 2000. One of the most current collections of scholarly film essays available, this volume arranges its many essays around various topics, such as "questions of realism" and "class and the culture industry"; the selections are often demanding and theoretical, representing some of the most sophisticated and important writing in film studies today.

Glossary

A picture: A feature film with a considerable budget and prestigious source material or stars or other personnel that has been historically promoted as a main attraction receiving top billing in a double feature; see **B picture.**

academy ratio: An **aspect ratio** of screen width to height of 1.33:1, or 4:3, the standard adopted by the Motion Picture Academy of Arts and Sciences in 1931 and used by most films until the 1950s; see **widescreen ratio.**

adaptation: The process of turning a novel, short story, play, or other artistic work into a film.

ADR: Automated dialogue replacement, a widely used postproduction process in which actors watch the film scene and re-record their lines to be mixed into the soundtrack; also called **looping.**

alternative film narrative: Film narratives that deviate from or challenge the linearity of **classical film narrative,** often undermining the centrality of the main character, the continuity of the plot, or the verisimilitude of the narration.

analytical editing: Continuity editing that establishes spatial and temporal clarity by breaking down a scene, often using progressively tighter framings.

anamorphic lens: A camera lens that compresses the horizontal axis of an image or a projector lens that "unsqueezes" such an image to produce a widescreen image.

ancillary market: A venue other than theatrical release in which a film can make money, such as foreign sales, airlines, pay television, cable, or home video.

animation: A process that traditionally refers to moving images drawn or painted on individual cels or to manipulated three-dimensional objects, which are then photographed onto single frames of film. Animation now encompasses digital imaging techniques.

antagonists: Characters who oppose the **protagonists** as negative forces.

apparatus theory: A critical school that explores the cinema as an ideological phenomenon based on a physical set of technologies, including the camera and the arrangement of projector and screen, that reinforces the values of individualism and the transcendence of the material basis of the cinematic illusion.

archetype: An original model or type, such as Satan as an archetype of evil.

art director (also production designer or set designer): The individual responsible for supervising the conception and construction of the physical environment in which the actors appear, including sets, locations, props, and costumes.

aspect ratio: The width-to-height ratio of the film frame as it appears on a movie screen or television monitor.

asynchronous sound: A term that describes sound that does not have a visible onscreen source; also referred to as offscreen sound.

auteur: French term for **author;** implies a director with a unique vision or style; see **auteur theory.**

auteur theory: An approach to cinema first proposed in the French film journal *Cahiers du cinéma* that emphasized the role of the director as the expressive force behind a film and saw a director's body of work as united by common themes or formal strategies; also referred to as auterism.

avant-garde films: Aesthetically challenging, noncommercial films that self-consciously reflect on how human senses and consciousness work or explore and experiment with film forms and techniques. Avant-garde cinema thrived in Europe in the 1920s and in the United States after World War II.

axis of action: An imaginary line bisecting a scene corresponding to the **180-degree rule** in **continuity editing.**

B picture: A low-budget, nonprestigious movie that usually played on the bottom half of a double bill. B pictures were often produced by the smaller studios referred to as Hollywood's Poverty Row; see **A picture.**

backlighting: A **highlighting** technique that illuminates the person or object from behind, tending to silhouette the subject; sometimes called edgelighting.

block booking: A practice in which movie theaters had to exhibit whatever a studio/distributor packaged with its more popular and desirable movies; declared an unfair business practice in 1948.

blocking: The arrangement and movement of actors in relation to each other within the mise-en-scène.

boom: A long pole used to hold a microphone above the actors to capture sound while remaining outside the frame.

camera lens: A piece of curved glass that focuses light rays in order to form an image on film.

camera movement: See **mobile frame.**

canted frame: **Framing** that is not level, creating an unbalanced appearance.

casting director: The individual responsible for identifying and selecting which actors would work best in a particular role.

character actors: Recognizable actors associated with particular character types, often humorous or sinister, and often cast in minor parts.

character development: The patterns through which characters in a particular film move from one mental, physical, or social state to another.

character types: Conventional characters (e.g., hard-boiled detective or femme fatale) typically portrayed by actors cast because of their physical features, acting style, or the history of other roles they have played.

chiaroscuro lighting: A term that describes dramatic, high-contrast lighting that emphasizes shadows and the contrast between light and dark; frequently used in German expressionist cinema and **film noir.**

chronology: The order according to which shots or scenes convey the temporal sequence of the story's events.

chronophotography: A sequence of photographs of human or animal motion such as those produced by Eadweard Muybridge and Etienne-Jules Marey and the immediate precursors of the cinema.

cinéma vérité: French term literally meaning "cinema truth"; a style of documentary filmmaking first practiced in the late 1950s and early 1960s that used unobtrusive lightweight cameras and sound equipment to capture a real-life situation; the parallel U.S. movement is called **direct cinema.**

cinematography: Motion-picture photography, literally "writing in movement."

classical film narrative: A style of narrative filmmaking centered on one or more central characters who propel the plot with a cause-and-effect logic wherein an action generates a reaction. Normally plots are developed with linear chronologies directed at definite goals, and the film employs an omniscient or a restricted third-person narration that suggests some degree of **verisimilitude.**

classical film theory: Writings on the fundamental questions of cinema produced in roughly the first half of the twentieth century. Important classical film theorists include Sergei Eisenstein, Rudolf Arnheim, André Bazin, and Siegfried Kracauer.

claymation: A process that uses **stop-motion photography** with clay figures to create the illusion of movement.

click track: Holes punched in the film corresponding to the beat of a metronome that can help actors, musicians, and the composer keep the rhythm of the action.

close-up: **Framing** that shows details of a person or object, such as a character's face.

code: A term used in linguistics and semiotics meaning a system of signs from which a message is generated. In a communication act, a code must be shared by the sender and the receiver for the message to be understood. For example, traffic signals use a color code.

Film analysts isolate the codes of camera movement, framing, lighting, acting, etc., that determine the specific form of a particular shot, scene, film, or genre.

color balance: Putting emphasis on a particular part of the color spectrum to create realistic or unrealistic palettes.

color filter: A device fitted to the camera lens to change the tones of the filmed image.

commodity tie-ins: The saleable goods that are marketed with the "brand name" of a particular film or film characters.

compilation or anthology films: Films comprised of various segments by different filmmakers.

computer-generated imagery (**CGI**): Still or animated images created through digital computer technology. First introduced in the 1970s, CGI was used to create feature-length films by the mid-1990s and is widely used for visual effects.

computer graphics: Electronically generated images used to create special effects and elaborate settings.

continuity editing: The institutionalized system of Hollywood editing that uses cuts and other transitions to establish verisimilitude, to construct a coherent time and space, and to tell stories clearly and efficiently. Continuity editing follows the basic principle that each shot or scene has a continuous relationship to the next; sometimes called **invisible editing.**

continuity script: A screenplay that presents in detail the action, scenes and dialogue, transitions, and often camera setups, in the order planned for the final film.

continuity style: The systematic approach to filmmaking associated with classical Hollywood cinema, utilizing a broad array of technical choices from continuity editing to scoring that support the principle of effacing technique in order to emphasize human agency and narrative clarity.

contrasting balance: A use of color that creates dramatic oppositions and tensions.

counterpoint: Using sound to indicate a different meaning or association than the image.

coverage: Shooting a particular scene from different angles and setups to allow options for smooth editing of the finished scene.

crane shot: A shot taken from a camera mounted on a crane that can vary distance, height, and angle.

crosscutting: An editing technique that cuts back and forth between actions in separate spaces, often implying simultaneity; also called **parallel editing.**

cue: A visual or aural signal that indicates the beginning of an action, line of dialogue, or piece of music.

cut: In the editing process, the join or splice between two pieces of film; in the finished film, an editing transition between two separate shots or scenes achieved without optical effects. A version of the edited film, as in rough cut, final cut, or director's cut.

cutaway: A **shot** that interrupts a continuous action, "cutting away" to another image or action, often to abridge time.

dailies: The developed prints of a day's shooting that are viewed and evaluated by the filmmaker and other creative personnel.

deadline structure: A narrative structure that accelerates the action and plot toward a central event or action that must be accomplished by a certain time.

deep focus: A focus in which multiple planes in the shot are all in focus simultaneously; usually achieved with a wide-angle lens.

depth of field: The range or distance before and behind the main focus of a shot within which objects remain relatively sharp and clear.

dialectical montage: A concept developed in the theories and films of Soviet silent film director Sergei Eisenstein that refers to the cutting together of conflicting or unrelated images to generate an idea or emotion in the viewer.

diegesis: A term that refers to the world of the film's story (its characters, places, and events), including not only what is shown but also what is implied to have taken place. It comes from the Greek word meaning "narration."

diegetic sound: Sound that has its source in the narrative world of the film, whose characters are presumed to be able to hear it.

digital cinematography: Shooting with a camera that records and stores visual information electronically as digital code.

direct cinema: A documentary style originating in the United States in the 1960s that aims to observe an unfolding situation as unobtrusively as possible; related to **cinéma vérité.**

direct sound: Sound captured directly from its source.

directional lighting: Lighting that may appear to emanate from a natural source and defines and shapes the object, area, or person being illuminated.

disjunctive editing: A variety of alternative editing practices that call attention to the cut through spatial tension, temporal jumps, or rhythmic or graphic pattern so as to affect viscerally, disorient, or intellectually engage the viewer.

dissolve: An **optical effect** that briefly superimposes one shot over the next. One image fades out as another image fades in and takes its place; sometimes called a lap dissolve because two images overlap in the printing process.

distribution: The means through which movies are delivered to theaters, video stores, and television and cable networks, which make them available to consumers.

documentary film: A non-fiction film that presents (presumably) real objects, people, and events.

edgelighting: See **backlighting.**

ellipsis: An abridgment in time in the narrative implied by editing.

establishing shot: Generally, an initial long shot that establishes the location and setting and that orients the viewer in space to a clear view of the action.

ethnographic documentary: An anthropological film that aims to reveal cultures and peoples in the most authentic terms possible, without imposing the filmmaker's interpretation on that experience.

exclusive release: A movie that premieres in restricted locations initially.

exhibition: The part of the film industry that shows films to a paying public, usually in movie theaters.

experimental films: Films that explore film form and subject matters in new and unconventional ways, ranging from abstract image and sound patterns to dreamlike worlds.

extratextual: Characterizes aspects of the film experience available to the scholar that exist outside of the film itself, including production, distribution, exhibition, and reception.

extreme close-up (ECU): A framing that is comparatively tighter than a **close-up,** singling out, for instance, a person's eyes, or the petal of a flower.

extreme long shot: A framing from a comparatively greater distance than a **long shot,** in which the surrounding space dominates human figures, such as in distant vistas of cities or landscapes.

eyeline match: A principle in **continuity editing** that calls for following a shot of a character looking off-screen with a shot of a subject whose screen position matches the gaze of the character in the first shot.

fade-in: An **optical effect** in which a black screen gradually brightens to a full picture; often used after a **fade-out** to create a transition between scenes.

fade-out: An **optical effect** in which an image gradually darkens to black, often ending a scene or a film; see **fade-in.**

feature film: Running typically 90 to 120 minutes in length, a narrative film that is the primary attraction for audiences.

fill lighting: A lighting technique using secondary fill lights to balance the **key lighting** by removing shadows or to emphasize other spaces and objects in the scene.

film genre: A set of conventions and formulas, repeated and developed through film history, which organize and categorize films according to repeated subjects, icons, and styles.

film noir: A term introduced by French critics (meaning literally "black film") to describe Hollywood films of the 1940s set in the criminal underworld, which were considerably darker in mood and mise-en-scène than those that had come before. Typically shot in black and white in nighttime urban settings, they featured morally ambiguous protagonists, corrupt institutions, dangerous women, and convoluted plots, and they used stylized lighting and cinematography.

film script: The text from which a movie is made, including dialogue and information about action, settings, etc.; also known as a **screenplay.**

film speed: The rate at which moving images are recorded and later projected, standardized for 35mm sound film at 24 frames per second (fps); also, a measure of film stock's sensitivity to light.

film stock: Unexposed film consisting of a flexible backing or base and a light-sensitive emulsion.

filters: Transparent sheets of glass or gels placed in front of the lens to create various effects.

final cut: The final edited version of a film.

first release: A movie's original exhibition, also referred to as its first run, often limited to specific theaters in major cities.

flare: A spot or flash of white light created by directing strong light directly at the lens.

flashback: A sequence that follows images set in the present with images set in the past; it may be introduced with a dissolve conveying a character's subjective memory or with a voiceover in which a character narrates the past.

flashforward: A sequence that connects an image set in the present with one or more future images and that leaps ahead of the normal cause-and-effect order.

focus: The point or area in the image that is most precisely outlined and defined by the lens of the camera; the point at which light rays refracted through the lens converge.

foley artist: A member of the sound crew who generates live synchronized sound effects such as footsteps, the rustle of clothing, or a key turning in a lock, while watching the projected film. Named after their inventor, Jack Foley, foley tracks are eventually mixed with other audio tracks.

following shots: A **pan, tilt,** or **tracking shot** that follows a moving individual or object.

formalism: A method of analysis and critical school that considers a work's form or structure to be primary. It posits that objective meaning is to be found in the work itself and not in an outside source, such as the author's biography.

framing: The portion of the filmed subject that appears within the borders of the frame; it correlates with camera distance, e.g., **long shot** or **medium close-up.**

frontal lighting: Techniques used to illuminate the subject from the front. Related terms are side lighting, under lighting, and top lighting.

gauge: The width of the film stock; e.g., 8mm, 16mm, 35mm, and 70mm.

graphic editing: A style of editing creating formal patterns of shapes, masses, colors, lines, and lighting patterns through links between shots.

graphic match: An edit in which a dominant shape or line in one shot provides a visual transition to a similar shape or line in the next shot.

handheld cameras: Smaller, lightweight cameras (such as the Arriflex) that can be carried by the operator rather than mounted on a tripod. Such cameras, widely used during World War II, allowed cinematography to become more mobile and fostered the advent of on-location shooting.

handheld shot: A film image produced by an individual carrying the camera, creating an unsteady shot that may suggest the point of view of an individual moving through space.

hard lighting: A high-contrast lighting style that creates hard edges, distinctive shadows, and a harsh effect, especially when filming people.

high angle: A **shot** directed at a downward angle on individuals or a scene.

high concept: A short phrase that attempts to sell a movie by identifying its main marketing features, such as its stars, genre, or some other easily identifiable connection.

highlighting: Using lighting to brighten or emphasize specific characters or objects.

historiography: The writing of history; the study of the methods and principles through which the past becomes organized according to certain perspectives and priorities.

horror film: A film genre with origins in gothic literature that seeks to frighten the viewer though supernatural or predator characters; narratives built on suspense, dread, and surprise; and visual compositions that anticipate and manipulate shocking sights.

hybrid genres: Mixed forms produced by the interaction of different genres, such as musical horror films.

iconography: Images or image patterns with specific connotations or meanings.

ideology: A systematic set of beliefs, not necessarily conscious or acknowledged.

IMAX: A large format film system that is projected horizontally rather than vertically to produce an image approximately ten times larger than the standard 35mm frame.

independent film: Films that are produced without initial studio financing, typically with much lower budgets; they include feature-length narratives, documentaries, and shorts.

insert: A brief shot, often a **close-up,** filmed separately from a scene and inserted during editing, that points out details significant to the action.

intercutting: Interposing shots of two or more actions, locations, or contents.

internal diegetic sound: See **semidiegetic sound.**

intertitle: Printed text inserted between film images, typically used in silent films to indicate dialogue and exposition and in contemporary films to indicate time and place or other transitions.

invisible editing: See **continuity editing.**

iris-in: An optical effect used as an editing transition that gradually opens from a small, usually circular, portion of the frame to reveal the entire image. It is infrequently used in modern cinema.

iris-out: An optical effect used as an editing transition that begins by masking the corners of the frame in black and gradually reduces the image to a small circle. It is infrequently used in modern cinema.

iris shot: A shot in which the frame is masked so that only a small circular piece of the image is seen.

jump cut: A disjunctive edit that interrupts a particular action and intentionally or unintentionally creates discontinuities in the spatial or temporal development of shots.

key lighting: The main source of non-natural lighting in a scene. High-key light is even (the ratio between key and fill light is high); low-key light shows strong contrast (the ratio between key and fill light is low).

lighting: Sources of illumination—both natural light and electrical lamps—used to present, shade, and accentuate figures, objects, and spaces, or **mise-en-scène.** Lighting is primarily the responsibility of the director of photography and the lighting crew; see **key lighting, fill lighting,** and **highlighting.**

limited release: The practice of initially distributing a film only to major cities and expanding distribution according to its success or failure.

location scouting: Determining and securing suitable places besides studio sets to use for shooting particular movie scenes.

long shot: A framing that places considerable distance between the camera and the scene or person so that the object or person is recognizable but defined by the large space and background; see **establishing shot.**

long take: A **shot** of relatively long duration.

looping: An image or sound recorded on a loop of film to be replayed and layered.

low angle: A **shot** from a position lower than its subject.

masks: Attachments to the camera or devices added optically that cut off portions of the frame so that part of the image is black.

master shot: A continuous shot of a scene's entire action that is usually intercut with other shots (such as close-ups) to form a completed scene; see **coverage.**

match on action: A cut between two shots featuring a similar visual action, such as when a shot in which a character opening a door cuts to a shot depicting the continuation of that action, or when a shot of a train moving left to right cuts to a character running in the same direction.

matte shot: A shot that joins two pieces of film, one with the central action or object and the other with additional background, figures, or action (sometimes painted or digitally produced) that would be difficult to create physically for the shot.

medium close-up: A framing that shows a comparatively larger area than a close-up, such as a person shown from the shoulders up; typically used during conversation sequences.

medium long shot: A framing that increases the distance between the camera and the subject compared with a **medium shot;** it shows most of an individual's body.

medium shot: A middle-ground framing in which we see the body of a person from approximately the waist up.

metteur-en-scène: Derived from the French term for director (particularly a theater director); in **auteur theory** this term refers to a director who conveys technical competence without possessing a strong streak of individual vision, in contrast to an **auteur.**

mickey-mousing: Overillustrating the action through the musical score, drawn from the conventions of composing for cartoons. An example of mickey-mousing is accompanying a character walking on tip-toe with music played by plucked strings.

miniature model: A small-scale model constructed for use during the filming process to stage special effects sequences and complex backgrounds.

mise-en-scène: A French theatrical term meaning literally "put on stage"; used in film studies to refer to all the elements of a movie scene that are organized, often by the director, to be filmed and that are later visible on-screen. They include the scenic elements of a movie, such as actors, lighting, sets, costumes, make-up, and other features of the image that exist independently of the camera and the processes of filming and editing.

mix: The combination by the sound mixer of separate soundtracks into a single master track that will be transferred onto the film print together with the image track to which it is synchronized.

mobile frame: A property of a **shot** in which the camera itself moves or the borders of the image are altered by a change in the focal length of the camera lens.

montage: The French word for "editing." It can be used to signify any joining of images, but it has come to signify a style that emphasizes the breaks and contrasts between images joined by a cut, such as in Soviet silent-era filmmaking or in certain rapid sequences in Hollywood films used for descriptive purposes or to show the rapid passage of time. See **disjunctive editing.**

movement editing: An editing technique through which the direction and pace of actions, gestures, and other movements are linked with corresponding or contrasting movements in one or more other shots.

narration: The telling of a story or description of a situation; the emotional, physical, or intellectual perspective through which the characters, events, and action of the plot are conveyed. In film, narration is most explicit when provided as asynchronous verbal commentary on the action or images, but it can also designate the storytelling function of the camera, the editing, and verbal and other soundtracks.

narrative: A **story** told by a narrator or conveyed by a narrational **point of view; see plot.**

narrative frame: A context or person positioned outside the principal narrative of a film, such as bracketing scenes in which a character in the story's present begins to relate events of the past and later concludes her/his tale.

narratology: The study of narrative forms, encompassing stories of all kinds, including films.

narrator: A character or other person whose voice and perspective describe the action of a film, either in voice-over or through strict limitation of what is shown to a particular point of view.

natural lighting: Light derived from a natural source in a scene or setting, such as the illumination of the daylight sun or firelight.

naturalistic acting: An actor's effort to embody the character that he or she is playing in order to communicate the essential self of the character.

negative cutter: The individual who conforms the negative of the film to the final cut. Release prints are then struck from the negative.

niche market: A term referring to a segment of the audience with specialized tastes, which Hollywood increasingly has come to recognize as lucrative.

nickelodeons: Early movie theaters, typically converted storefront or arcade spaces, where short films were shown continuously for a five-cent admission price to audiences passing in and out. They were prominent until the rise of the feature film in the 1910s demanded more comfortable settings.

nitrate: The highly flammable chemical base of 35mm film stock used until 1951.

nondiegetic insert: An **insert** that depicts an action, object, or title originating outside of the space and time of the narrative world.

nondiegetic sound: Sound that does not have an identifiable source in the characters' world and that consequently the characters cannot hear; see **diegetic sound** and **semidiegetic sound.**

nonfiction films: Films presenting (presumed) factual descriptions of actual events, persons, or places, rather than their fictional, or invented, re-creation.

non-narrative films: Films organized in a variety of ways besides storytelling; they employ organizational forms such as associations, lists, repetitions, or contrasts.

nontheatrical formats: Formats such as video and narrow gauge film (8mm, Super 8, and 16mm) and documentary, short, and experimental genres in which films intended for community, artistic, or educational use rather than theatrical exhibition are produced.

objective point of view: A point of view that does not associate the perspective of the camera with that of a specific character.

offscreen space: The implied space outside the boundaries of the film frame.

omniscient narration: Narration that presents all elements of the plot, exceeding the perspective of any one character; see also **third-person narration.**

180-degree rule: A central convention of **continuity editing** that restricts possible camera setups to the 180-degree area on one side of an imaginary line (the **axis of action**) drawn between the characters or figures of a scene. If the camera were to cross the line to film from within the 180-degree field on the other side, onscreen figure positions would be reversed.

onscreen space: Space visible within the frame of the image.

optical effect: Special effects produced with the use of an optical printer, including visual transitions between shots such as **dissolves, fade-outs,** and **wipes,** or process shots that combine figures and backgrounds through the use of **mattes.**

optical printer: The photographic equipment used by technicians to create **optical effects** in films by duplicating the already exposed image onto new film stock and altering the lighting or adding additional components.

optical sound recording: A sound recording process that converts sound waves into electrical impulses that then control how a light beam is projected onto film. The process enables a soundtrack to be recorded alongside the image for simultaneous projection.

orthochromatic: A property of black-and-white film stock used in the 1920s, sensitive to greens and blues but registering red light as black.

overhead shot: A **shot** that depicts the action from above, generally looking directly down on the subject; the camera may be mounted on a **crane.**

overlapping dialogue: Mixing two or more characters' speech to imitate the rhythm of speech; the term may also refer to dialogue that overlaps two scenes to effect a transition between them.

overlapping editing: An edited sequence that presents two shots of the same action; because this technique violates continuity, it is rarely used.

pace: The tempo at which the film seems to move. It is determined by the duration of individual shots and the style of editing, as well as by other elements of cinematography and mise-en-scène and the overall rhythm and flow of the film's action.

pan: A left or right rotation of the camera, whose tripod or mount remains in a fixed position that produces a horizontal movement onscreen.

"pan-and-scan" process: The process used to transfer a widescreen-format film to the standard television aspect ratio. A computer-controlled scanner determines the most important action in the image, and then crops peripheral action and space or presents the original frame as two separate images.

panchromatic: A property of a black-and-white film stock introduced in the 1920s that responds to a full spectrum of colors, rendering them as shades of gray, for a more nuanced and realistic image.

parallel editing: An editing technique that alternates between two or more strands of action in separate locations, often presented as occurring simultaneously; see **crosscutting.**

parallel plot: The implied simultaneity of or connection between two different **plot** lines, usually intersecting.

parallelism: An instance in which the soundtrack reinforces the image, such as synchronized dialogue or sound effects or a voiceover that is consistent with what is displayed onscreen; see **counterpoint.**

performative development: Changes in a character described through an actor's performance.

persistence of vision: The eye's retention of a visual imprint for approximately one-fifth to one-twentieth of a second after the object has disappeared; as a result, the continuous projection of a series of still images at a rate of sixteen or more frames per second will give the illusion of movement; see **phi phenomenon.**

perspective: The manner in which the distance and spatial relationships among objects are represented on a two-dimensional surface. In painting, parallel and converging lines were used to give the illusion of distance and depth; in film, perspective is manipulated by changes in the focal length of camera lenses.

phi phenomenon: The psychological illusion of motion when two or more still images of an object in different positions are shown in sequence; see **persistence of vision.**

pixilation: A type of animation that employs **stop-motion photography** (or instead simply cuts out images from a continuous piece of filmed action) to transform the movement of human figures into rapid jerky gestures.

platforming: The distribution strategy of releasing a film in gradually widening markets and theaters so that it slowly builds its reputation and momentum through reviews and word-of-mouth.

plot: The narrative ordering of the events of the **story** as they appear in the actual work, selected and arranged according to particular temporal, spatial, generic, causal, or other patterns.

point of view: The position from which a person, event, or object is seen or filmed; in narrative form, the perspective through which events are narrated.

point-of-view (POV) shot: A subjective shot that reproduces a character's optical point of view, often preceded and/or followed by shots of the character looking.

postproduction: The period in the filmmaking process that occurs after principal photography has been completed and usually consisting of editing, sound, and special effects work.

postproduction sound: Sound recorded and added to a film in the **postproduction** phase.

postsynchronous sound: Sound recorded after the actual filming and then synchronized with onscreen sources.

process shot: A special effect that combines two or more images as a single shot, such as filming an actor in front of a projected background.

producer: The person or persons responsible for steering and monitoring each step of a film project, especially the financial aspects, from development to postproduction and a distribution deal.

production: The industrial stages that contribute to the making of a finished movie, from the financing and scripting of a film to its final edit; more specifically, the actual shooting of a film after preproduction and before **postproduction.**

production mixer: The sound engineer on the production set; also called sound recordist.

promotion: The aspect of the movie industry through which audiences are exposed to and encouraged to see a particular film; promotion includes advertisements, trailers, publicity appearances, and product-tie-ins.

protagonists: Individuals identified as the positive forces in a film; see **antagonists.**

rack focus (or **pulled focus**)**:** A dramatic change in focus from one object to another.

reaction shot: A **shot** that depicts a character's response to something shown in a previous shot.

reception theory: A theoretical approach to the ways different kinds of audiences regard different kinds of films.

reestablishing shot: A **shot** during an edited sequence that returns to an **establishing shot** to restore a seemingly "objective" view to the spectator.

reflected sound: Recorded sound that is captured as it bounces from the walls and sets. It is usually used to give a sense of space; opposed to **direct sound.**

reflexive narration: A mode of narration that calls attention to the narrative point of view of the story in order to complicate or subvert its own narrative authority as an objective perspective on the world.

reframing: The process of moving the frame from one position to another within a single continuous shot.

restricted narration: A **narrative** in which our knowledge is limited to that of a particular character.

rhythmic editing: The organization of editing according to different paces or tempos determined by how quickly cuts are made.

room tone: The aural properties of a location that are recorded and then mixed in with dialogue and other tracks to achieve a more realistic sound.

rough cut: The initial edited version of a movie in which an editor approximates the finished film.

saturation booking: Releasing a film simultaneously in as many locations in the United States—and sometimes the world—as possible.

scene: One or more shots that depict a continuous space and time.

screenplay: See **film script.**

segmentation: The process of dividing a film into large narrative units for the purposes of analysis.

semidiegetic sound: Sound that is neither strictly **diegetic** nor **nondiegetic,** such as certain voiceovers that can be construed as the thoughts of a character and thus as arising from the story world; also known as **internal diegetic sound.**

sequence: Any number of **shots** or **scenes** that are unified as a coherent action or an identifiable motif, regardless of changes in space and time.

sequence shot: A **shot** in which an entire **scene** is played out in one continuous take.

set lighting: The distribution of an evenly diffused illumination through a scene as a kind of lighting base.

shallow focus: A **shot** in which only a narrow range of the field is in focus.

shock cut: A cut that juxtaposes two images whose dramatic difference aims to create a jarring visual effect.

shooting ratio: The relationship between the overall amount or length of film shot and the amount used in the finished project.

shot: A continuous point of view (or continuously exposed piece of film) that may move forward or backward, up or down, but not change, break, or cut to another point of view or image.

shot/reverse shot: An editing pattern that begins with a shot of one character taken from an angle at one end of the **axis of action,** follows with a shot of the second character from the "reverse" angle at the other end of the line, and continues back and forth through the sequence; often used in conversations.

slow motion or fast motion: A cinematic special effect that makes the action move at unrealistic speeds (achieved by filming the action faster or slower than normal and then projecting it at standard speeds).

soft lighting: A diffused, low contrast lighting that reduces or eliminates hard edges and shadows and can be more flattering when filming people.

sound bridge: The term for sound carried over a picture transition, or a sound belonging to the coming scene playing before the image changes.

sound continuity: The range of scoring, sound recording, mixing, and playback processes that strive for the unification of film meaning and experience by subordinating sound to the aims of the narrative.

sound designer: The individual responsible for planning and directing the overall sound of a film through to the final mix.

sound editing: Combining music, dialogue, and effects tracks to interact with the image track in order to create rhythmic relationships, establish connections between sound and onscreen source, and smooth or mark transitions.

sound mixing: An important stage in the **postproduction** of a film that takes place after the image track, including the credits, is complete; the process by which all the elements of the soundtrack, including music, effects, and dialogue, are combined and adjusted; also called re-recording.

sound perspective: The apparent location and distance of a sound source.

sound recording: The recording of dialogue and other sound that takes place simultaneously with the filming of a scene.

sound reproduction: Sound playback during a film's exhibition.

soundstage: A large soundproofed building designed to construct and move sets and props and effectively capture sound and dialogue during filming.

source music: Diegetic music; music whose source is visible onscreen.

special effects cinematography: A variety of technical processes that alter the filmed image to achieve a visual effect, such as **slow motion, color filters, process shots,** and **matte shots.**

spectatorship: The process of film viewing; the conscious and unconscious interaction of viewers and films as a topic of interest to film theorists.

splice: The physical join between two pieces of film.

spotting: The process of determining where music and effects will be added to a film.

Steadicam: A camera stabilization system introduced in 1976 that allows a camera operator to film a continuous and steady shot without losing the freedom of movement afforded by the handheld camera.

stinger: Sound that forces the audience to notice the significance of something onscreen, such as the ominous chord struck when the villain's presence is made known.

stop-motion photography: A process that records inanimate objects or actual human figures in separate frames that are then synthesized on film to create the illusion of motion and action.

story: The subject matter or raw material of a **narrative,** or our reconstruction of the events of a narrative based on what is explicitly shown and ordered in the **plot.**

studio system: The industrial practices of the large production (and, until 1948, distribution) companies responsible for the kinds and quality of movies made in Hollywood. The five major studios are MGM, Paramount, RKO, Twentieth-Century Fox, and Warner Bros.

subgenres: A specialized **genre** that defines a specific, more limited version of a more general genre, often by refining it with an adjective, such as the spaghetti western or slapstick comedy.

subjective point of view: A point of view that recreates the perspective of a character.

supporting actors: Actors who play secondary characters in a film, serving as foils or companions to the central characters.

surrealist cinema: One of the most influential of the **avant-garde** movements, surrealist films confronted middle-class assumptions about normality using the powers of film to manipulate time, space, and material objects according to a dreamlike logic.

suture: A term that refers to our sense of being inserted in a specific place in the film, from which to look at its fictional world through editing and point of view.

synchronous sound: Sound that is recorded during a scene or that is synchronized with the filmed images; as used by scholar Siegfried Kracauer, a term that describes sound that has a visible onscreen source, such as moving lips; also referred to as onscreen sound.

syntagma: A term derived from linguistics for sequential units of meaning and used by Christian Metz to refer to the smallest combinable narrative units of film—sequences, scenes, and autonomous shots.

take: A single filmed version of a shot during production or a single shot on screen.

talking heads: An on-camera interview that typically shows the speaker from the shoulders up, hence "talking head."

Technicolor: Color processing that uses three strips of film to transfer colors directly onto a single image; developed between 1926 and 1932.

telephoto lenses: A lens with a focal length of at least 75mm, capable of magnifying and flattening distant objects; also **zoom lens.**

theatrical trailer: A promotional preview of an upcoming release presented before the main feature or as a television commercial.

third-person narration: A narration that assumes an objective and detached stance vis-à-vis the plot and characters, describing events from outside the story.

30-degree rule: A cinematography and editing rule that specifies that a shot should only be followed by another shot taken from a position greater than 30 degrees from that of the first.

three-point lighting: A lighting technique common in Hollywood that combines **key lighting, fill lighting,** and **backlighting** to blend the distribution of light in a scene.

tilt shot: An upward or downward rotation of the camera, whose tripod or mount remains in a fixed position, producing a vertical movement onscreen.

tone: The shading, intensification, or saturation of colors (such as metallic blues, soft greens, or deep reds) in order to sharpen, mute, or balance them for certain effects.

tracking shot: A **shot** that changes the position of the point of view by moving forward, backward, or around the subject, usually on tracks that have been constructed in advance (a dolly shot is mounted on a dolly that follows a determined course); also called a traveling shot.

treatment: A succinct description of the content of a film written before the **film script.**

two-shot: A shot depicting two characters.

underscoring: A film's background music; contrasts with **source music.**

unreliable narration: A type of **narration** that raises questions about the truth of the story being told.

verisimilitude: The quality of fictional representation that allows readers or viewers to accept a constructed world, its events, its characters and their actions as plausible; literally "having the appearance of truth."

voice-off: A voice that originates from a speaker who can be inferred to be present in the scene but who is not visible on screen.

voiceover: A voice whose source is neither visible in the frame nor implied to be offscreen; it typically narrates the film's images, such as in a flashback or the commentary in a documentary film.

walla: A nonsense word spoken by extras in a film to approximate the sound of a crowd during sound dubbing.

wide-angle lens: A lens with a short focal length (typically less than 35mm) that allows cinematographers to explore a depth of field that can simultaneously show foreground and background objects or events in focus.

wide release: The premiere of a movie at many locations simultaneously, sometimes on as many as 1500 to 2000 screens.

widescreen processes: Any of a number of systems introduced in the 1950s that widened the aspect ratio and the dimensions of the movie screen.

widescreen ratio: The wider, rectangular **aspect ratio** of typically 1.85:1 or 2.35:1; see **academy ratio.**

wipe: A transition used to join two shots by moving a vertical, horizontal, or sometimes diagonal line across one image to replace it with a second image that follows that line across the frame.

work print: The processed film that is cut during the editing process; after the editing process release prints are made to show in cinemas.

zoom-in: The act of changing the lens's focal length to narrow the field of view of a distant object, bringing it into clear view and reframing it, often in close-up, while the camera remains stationary; see **zoom-out.**

zoom-out: Reversing the action of a **zoom-in,** so that objects that appear close initially are distanced from the camera and reframed as small figures.

Acknowledgments

Text credits

Béla Balázs: Excerpt from pages 283–287 in *Theory of the Film: Character and Growth of a New Art*, translated by Edith Bone. Copyright © 1952 by Dennis Dobson, Ltd. Reprinted by permission of the publisher. **John Belton:** Excerpt from pages 85 and 87–89 in *Widescreen Cinema* by John Belton. Copyright © 1992 by the President and Fellows of Harvard College. Reprinted by permission of the publisher, Harvard University Press. **Carol Clover:** Excerpts from pages 21, 42–46, and 61–62 in *Men, Women and Chain Saws: Gender in the Modern Horror Film* by Carol Clover. Copyright © British Film Institute, 1992. Reprinted by permission of Princeton University Press. **Maya Deren:** Excerpt from "Cinematography: The Creative Use of Reality." Published in *Daedalus,* Journal of the American Academy of Arts and Sciences, Winter 1960, Volume 89, Number 1. Copyright © 1960. Reprinted by permission of *Daedalus,* American Academy of Arts and Sciences. **Manthia Diawara:** Excerpt from pages 211–220 in *Black American Cinema* by Manthia Diawara. Copyright © 1993 by Manthia Diawara. Reproduced by permission of Routledge/Taylor & Francis Books, Inc. **Mary Ann Doane:** "Ideology and the Practice of Sound Editing and Mixing." Excerpt from pages 54–62 in *Film Sound,* edited by John Belton and Elizabeth Weis. Copyright © 1985 by Columbia University Press. Reprinted with the permission of the publisher. **Douglas Gomery:** Excerpt from pages 18–19 and 31 in *Shared Pleasures: A History of Movie Presentation in the United States* by Douglas Gomery. Copyright © 1992. Reprinted by permission of The University of Wisconsin Press. **Phillip Lopate:** Excerpts from page 220–222, 224–225, and 227 in "The Passion of Pauline Kael." *Totally, Tenderly, Tragically* by Phillip Lopate. Copyright © 1998 by Phillip Lopate. Used by permission of Doubleday, a division of Random House, Inc. **Vsevolod Pudovkin:** Excerpt from pages 10–11 in "On Editing." Originally published in *Film Technique and Film Acting* translated by Ivor Montague. Copyright © 1958 by Vision Press, Ltd. Reprinted by permission of Harper-Collins UK. **Thomas Schatz:** Excerpts from page 20 and 31–33 in "The New Hollywood." Published in *Film Theory Goes to the Movies: Cultural Analysis of Contemporary Film,* edited by Ava Preacher Collins. Copyright © 1992. Reproduced by permission of Routledge/Taylor & Francis Books, Inc. **Vivian Sobchack:** Excerpt from pages 300–301 in "What Is Film History? Or The Riddle of the Sphinxes." Published in *Reinventing Film Studies,* edited by Christine Gledhill and Linda Williams. Copyright © 2000. Reprinted by permission of the author and Edward Arnold Publishers.

Illustration Credits

Color Plate 27, Photofest; **Figure 1.1, 1.13,** Photofest; **1.14,** John Coletti/Stock, Boston; **1.26,** Photofest; **1.44,** J. R. Eyerman/TIMEPIX/Getty Images; **I.1,** Photofest; **3.6,** Bettmann/CORBIS; **3.12, 3.15,** Photofest; **3.43,** courtesy, British Film Institute; **4.6,** Photofest; **4.13,** Anthology Film Archives; **4.14,** Private collection (Berlin), Giraudon/Art Resource; **4.59, 4.63, 4.64, 4.97,** Anthology Film Archives; **4.98,** courtesy, Women Make Movies; **5.7,** courtesy, Joseph Yranski; **5.8,** courtesy, Edison Historic Site, NPS; **5.9, 5.10, 5.13, 5.16,** Photofest; **5.17,** courtesy, Killer Films and Focus Features; **5.26,** Zeitgeist Films; **5.27,** courtesy, British Film Institute; **5.28, 5.30,** Photofest; **5.33,** Culver Pictures; **5.44,** courtesy, Women Make Movies; **5.46,** courtesy, Ulrike Ottinger; **5.47, 5.48, II.1, 6.3, 6.20, 6.26, 6.27, 6.31,** Photofest; **6.49,** Everett Collection; **6.53,** Photofest; **7.8,** Anthology Film Archives; **7.9, 7.12,** Photofest; **7.13,** courtesy, British Film Institute; **7.15, 7.17, 7.19, 7.20,** Photofest; **7.21,** Anthology Film Archives; **7.22,** Photofest; **7.23,** Zipporah Films; **7.29, 7.39,** Photofest; **8.6,** Anthology Film Archives; **8.10,** Photo; Felix Nadar, "Mme. DeBureau as Pierrot: The Surprise" (1854), Musée d'Orsay/Réunion des Musées Nationaux/Art Resource; **8.18, 8.28, 8.38,** Photofest; **9.5,** from "L. J. M. Daguerre: The History of the Diorama and the Daguerreotype" by Helmut and Alison Gernsheim (Dover, 1968); **9.14, 9.21, 9.23, 9.38,** Photofest; **10.4,** courtesy, British Film Institute; **10.5,** Everett Collection; **10.6,** courtesy, Kristine Harris; **10.8, 10.11, 10.12,** Photofest; **10.15, 10.16, 10.17,** New Yorker Films; **10.19,** Ft. Lee Public Library, Silent Film Collection, Ft. Lee, NJ; **10.20,** Photofest; **10.21,** Collection of Patricia White; **10.22, 10.26,** Photofest; **10.29,** courtesy, Prelinger Archives; **10.30, 10.31, 10.32,** courtesy, Oscar Micheaux Society, Duke University, with thanks to Jane Gaines; **10.33,** Photofest; **10.34,** courtesy, Prelinger Archives; **10.36,** AP/Wide World Photos; **10.39,** Photofest; **10.42,** courtesy, the Video Data Bank; **10.44,** Photofest; **11.8, 11.9,** Anthology Film Archive; **11.14,** courtesy Focus Features and Killer Films; 11.20, Anthology Film Archive; **11.22,** courtesy, Beinecke Library, Yale University; **11.23,** Photofest; **11.24,** Hershenson-Allen Archive; **11.27,** Everett Collection; **11.28,** René Magritte, *Ceci n'est pas une pipe* (1929), © 2004, C. Herscovici, Brussels, Artists Rights Society/Art Resource; **11.31,** courtesy, Women Make Movies; **11.32,** Everett Collection; **11.33,** courtesy, Women Make Movies; **11.40,** Everett Collection.

Index